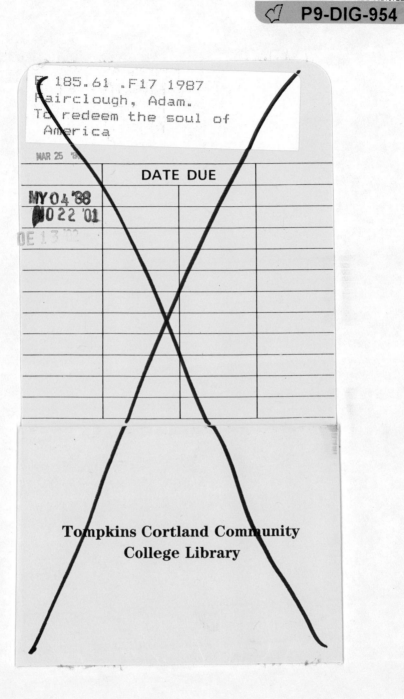

To Redeem the Soul of America

Adam Fairclough

To Redeem the Soul of America

The Southern Christian Leadership Conference

and Martin Luther King, Jr.

The University of Georgia Press

Athens and London

© 1987 by the University of Georgia Press

Athens, Georgia 30602

All rights reserved

Designed by Barbara Werden

Set in Linotron Trump Medieval

Typeset by the Composing Room of Michigan

Printed and bound by McNaughton & Gunn Lithographers

The paper in this book meets the guidelines for
permanence and durability of the Committee on
Production Guidelines for Book Longevity of the
Council on Library Resources.

Printed in the United States of America

91 90 89 88 87   5 4 3 2 1

Library of Congress Cataloging in Publication Data

Fairclough, Adam.

  To redeem the soul of America.

  Includes index.

  1. Southern Christian Leadership Conference—History.
2. Afro-Americans—Civil rights—Southern States.
3. Afro-Americans—Politics and government.   4. Southern
States—Race relations.   I. Title.

E185.61.F17   1987   323.1′196073′075   86–11352

ISBN 0–8203–0898–6 (alk. paper)

ISBN 0–8203–0938–9 (pbk.: alk. paper)

British Library Cataloging in Publication Data available.

To the Memory of
Alan Fairclough
(1923–1973)

Contents

Abbreviations

ACLU	American Civil Liberties Union
ACMHR	Alabama Christian Movement for Human Rights (Birmingham)
ADS	Americans for a Democratic Society
AFON	American Foundation on Nonviolence (SCLC)
AFSC	American Friends Service Committee
AFSCME	American Federation of State, County and Municipal Employees
CCCO	Coordinating Council of Community Organizations (Chicago)
CCCV	Chatham County Crusade for Voters (Savannah)
CCHR	Chicago Commission on Human Relations
CCRR	Chicago Conference on Religion and Race
CEP	Citizenship Education Program (SCLC)
CFM	Chicago Freedom Movement
CHA	Chicago Housing Authority
COFO	Council of Federated Organizations (Mississippi)
COINTELPRO	Counterintelligence Program (FBI)
COME	Community on the Move for Equality (Memphis)
CORE	Congress of Racial Equality
CREB	Chicago Real Estate Board
DCPA	Danville Christian Progressive Association
DCVL	Dallas County Voters League (Selma)
FOR	Fellowship of Reconciliation
FRCC	Freedom Rides Coordinating Committee

HEW	Department of Health, Education, and Welfare (U.S.)
ICC	Inter-Civic Council (Tallahassee)
Inc. Fund	NAACP Legal Defense and Educational Fund, Inc.
LCCR	Leadership Conference on Civil Rights
LCFO	Lowndes County Freedom Organization
MFDP	Mississippi Freedom Democratic Party
MIA	Montgomery Improvement Association
MLTP	Ministerial Leadership Training Program (SCLC)
MPD	Memphis Police Department
NAACP	National Association for the Advancement of Colored People
NCLC	Nashville Christian Leadership Council
SANE	Committee for a Sane Nuclear Policy
SCLC	Southern Christian Leadership Conference
SCEF	Southern Conference Educational Fund
SCOPE	Summer Community Organizing and Political Education (SCLC)
SDS	Students for a Democratic Society
SLC	Summit Leadership Conference (Atlanta)
SNCC	Student Nonviolent Coordinating Committee
TWO	The Woodlawn Organization (Chicago)
UAW	United Auto Workers
VCLC	Virginia Christian Leadership Conference
VEP	Voter Education Project

To Redeem the Soul of America

Introduction

To Charles Morgan, a white lawyer from Alabama who served

for a time on its board of directors, the Southern Christian Lead-

ership Conference (SCLC) all but defied rational analysis. It could

not be judged as other organizations, he believed, because the

normal rules of bureaucratic behavior simply did not apply.

"SCLC is not an organization," he told a reporter from the *New

York Times;* "it's a church." It seemed an apt description. SCLC

was led by black ministers and firmly rooted in the black church.

It patterned its meetings after Sunday services and clothed its

statements and actions in biblical phraseology. Ralph Abernathy,

its vice-president, called SCLC a "faith operation" which de-

pended on Christian inspiration. "When you are called upon to

witness," he explained, "you . . . can't always analyze what

might happen. You just have to go."[1]

Outsiders often found SCLC totally baffling. It was a "wondrous machine," marvelled the journalist Paul Good. "No one could be certain precisely how it worked." It was confusing even to its own members, one of whom, Andrew Young, regularly suggested hiring a management consultant to straighten out its tangled organizational structure. But the consultants came and went; SCLC remained, to all appearances, a study in confusion. It stubbornly resisted bureaucratic routine, preferring to operate according to the "movement spirit."[2]

Movement, organization, or church, SCLC was *effective.* Its accounts may have been slipshod and its internal structure chaotic, but SCLC excelled in the area that mattered most in the early 1960s: the theory and practice of nonviolent direct action. Its campaigns in Birmingham and Selma sent shock waves through the South which reverberated across the nation and administered a decisive and salutary jolt to the federal government. The achievements of other civil rights organizations cannot be gainsaid. The National Association for the Advancement of Colored People (NAACP), founded in 1910, won the critical legal victories that culminated in the Supreme Court's overturning of the "separate but equal" doctrine—the legal bulwark of racial segregation—in the 1954 case *Brown* v. *Board of Education.* The Congress of Racial Equality (CORE), founded in 1942, originated the 1961 "Freedom Rides" which resulted in the ending of segregation in interstate transportation. The Student Nonviolent Coordinating Committee (SNCC), organized in 1960, spearheaded the voter registration drives in the rural Black Belt of the Deep South. But the most significant gains of the civil rights movement were embodied in the 1964 Civil Rights Act and the 1965 Voting Rights Act, and these owed their existence, in large part, to SCLC's protests in Birmingham and Selma. In the constellation of forces that comprised the civil rights movement, SCLC became, in the words of veteran black activist Bayard Rustin, the "sustaining mechanism" and "dynamic center."[3]

Yet SCLC has received scant attention from historians. The reason for this neglect lies partly in the towering stature of its leader, who has inspired numerous biographies. But although it is entirely fitting that Martin Luther King, Jr., should provide an important focus for historians of the civil rights movement, biography has certain limitations as an interpretive form. Often, especially in the case of strong, dynamic leaders, individuals are abstracted from their social and political context and afforded a freedom of thought and action which did not, in reality, exist. As the historian Herbert Butterfield once wrote, "We constantly imagine that the range of options open to a statesman at a given moment is greater than . . . turns out to be the case." Even the best biographers are liable to this error, exaggerating the role of the individual actor. By placing its subject at the center of events, biography can illuminate the individual psyche. But this perspective is not the best one for understanding a social movement or social process.[4]

King biography, moreover, has its own limitations. Balanced and objective assessments of King have always been difficult to find: like that other controversial figure, Franklin D. Roosevelt, he evoked extremes of hero worship and hatred during his lifetime. The manner of his death made the task of sober judgement more difficult still. The bullet fired by James Earl Ray clothed King in martyrdom: critics fell silent; even enemies hid their venom. Revered by blacks, saluted by whites, King has become a national icon. With the exception of David L. Lewis, King biographers have ill-served their subject. The hagiographic memoir of King's widow, Coretta, did nothing to encourage a more critical and realistic appraisal. Even the best biographies offer little insight into SCLC, giving only a superficial glance at King's organizational base.

There are other reasons for SCLC's neglect. One is technical: the paucity, until quite recently, of documentary sources. In the absence of evidence that might directly illustrate SCLC's internal workings, historians naturally focused on King. The fact that newspaper reports, one of the mainstays of the historian, also singled out King increased this disposition. However, the news media do not simply reflect reality; they also, willy-nilly, help to structure reality. As the political scientist David J. Garrow has stressed, SCLC not only manipulated the media in order to further its goals; such manipulation was also central to its strategy of protest. And it suited SCLC's purposes to frame its public image around its leader, King. SCLC's oft-noted "cult of personality" was, to some extent, a deliberate strategem; one staff member called it a "careful, methodical process of image-building."[5]

SCLC has also been slighted on account of its alleged inefficiency as an organization. Even sympathetic journalists found SCLC frustrating to report. It changed its plans with exasperating rapidity: mass meetings waited hours for the appearance or nonappearance of speakers; marches, demonstrations, and even whole campaigns were announced and then abruptly cancelled. Reporters waited impatiently as King arrived at a press conference two, three, four hours late. A journalist who followed it for five years called SCLC "an exercise in organized chaos," adding, by way of explanation, that "the delivery of telephone messages is a sometime thing and if anyone has ever been dismissed for incompetence, no one can remember who." The abiding image of SCLC presented by the press was that of a bungling organization that hindered, rather than helped, its leader's best intentions.[6]

In his study of how the news media select and present their stories, Herbert Gans suggested that Northern-based reporters, "accustomed to the relatively tidy bureaucracies of their beats," were far more critical of SCLC than those who had covered the civil rights movement regularly; the latter soon became inured to "the chaos in which the movement, like all underfunded and understaffed groups, operated." There is much truth in this observation, yet it misses a more important point. In the turbulent, fast-moving, and unpredictable world of the civil rights movement, organizational hardness was a liability rather than an asset. Thus the NAACP, the most bureaucratic of the civil rights organizations, found it difficult to adapt and respond to the rapidly changing circumstances of the early 1960s, when crisis followed crisis and the situation changed from day to day. SCLC, by contrast, had the capacity to make quick decisions, to think on its feet. Too great a concern with bureaucratic routine would have undermined this ability. King himself was keenly aware of this, consciously neglecting internal structure so that SCLC's staff could move quickly as the circumstances changed and opportunities presented themselves. What appeared to outsiders as chaos and inefficiency was often the inevitable consequence of flexibility, spontaneity, and a capability for swift decision making and mobilization. As Eugene D. Genovese was one of the first to suggest, SCLC's loose, informal structure was probably the best way—perhaps the only way—of effectively mobilizing Southern blacks.[7]

Although King loomed large in its history, SCLC was not, as has frequently been asserted, a mere extension of his personality. Neither in Montgomery at the time of the bus boycott, nor in subsequent years, did King build his own organizational base. SCLC was created *for* him but not *by* him. Moreover, the men (rarely women) who comprised SCLC were not ciphers or sycophants who paid blind obeisance to a "charismatic" leader. SCLC had its share of timeservers and flatterers, but most of the people who worked with King were forceful individuals who did not hesitate to assert their own points of view. Randolph Blackwell, one of the few laymen to serve on SCLC's executive staff, described King's colleagues as stubborn, egotistical, and arrogant. But they were also highly talented. Men like Wyatt Walker, Andrew Young, James Bevel, and Hosea Williams contributed to SCLC in distinctive and important ways.[8]

A study of SCLC, however, must not only go beyond King, it must also go beyond the Baptist ministers who made up the bulk of its executive staff and governing board. Far greater than the sum of its parts, SCLC embraced groups and individuals whose formal connections with the organization were tenuous or nonexistent. The most important of these consisted of a small group of New York intellectuals who worked quietly in the background providing King with assistance and advice. Members of this group not only founded SCLC but also helped to give it organizational cohesion, financial stability, and political direction. The significance of SCLC's informal links with these veterans of the "Old Left" has only recently been grasped. Although at the fringe of SCLC organizationally, Northern activists like Bayard Rustin and Stanley Levison were often at the heart of its affairs.

In a different world altogether, but more basic to its success, were the local black leaders who headed SCLC's "affiliates" or sat on its board of directors, or both. Not all, by any means, represented popularly rooted local organizations; some represented little more than themselves. Many, on the other hand, were the genuine products of local black insurgency—enough to impart to SCLC the underlying dynamism of the southern civil rights movement. Without this grassroots thrust, this push from below, King would have remained a little-known clergyman and SCLC would not have come into existence. There is much truth in the statement of Ella Baker, who helped to organize SCLC, that "the Movement made Martin," not vice versa. SCLC's history must be related to the origins and evolution of black protest in Baton Rouge, Montgomery, Tallahassee, Birmingham, and elsewhere.

Yet King was not merely a local leader writ large. SCLC's great strength, its capacity to mediate between high political strategy and popular grassroots activism, owed much to the fact that King was the product of two cultures: the fundamentalist culture of the Southern black church and the intellectual culture of the Northern white university. His upbringing gave him emotional health, religious conviction, and cultural identity; his student days in Boston and Chester exposed him to Hegel, Marx, and Reinhold Niebuhr. King could move with ease from South to North, from church to lecture hall, from black audiences to white ones. He spoke to the humblest and poorest, but also dealt with the wealthy and powerful. He exhorted the downtrodden blacks of Georgia and Alabama, but also cultivated the "limousine liberals" of New York and Chicago. He helped to build a political bridge, however fragile, between the black proletariat and the white power elite. As one movement activist sagely observed, King had one foot firmly planted in the cotton field, the other in the White House. He was a man of rare abilities.

A history of SCLC, therefore, must give due weight to King's role; it will, to a large extent, be "about" King. An organizational study, however, requires a wider focus than the individual leader. As the sociologist Robert Merton has suggested, it should ask questions about the organization's size, membership, hierarchy, structure, goals, values, autonomy, cohesion, stability, power, and relationship to other groups. How was SCLC organized, administered, and financed? How did it recruit, deploy, and discipline its staff? What were its aims and ethos? How did it make decisions? What were its relations with the NAACP, SNCC, and other organizations within the civil rights movement? Some of these questions involve King to a large degree, others only marginally. As SCLC grew as an organization—by 1965 it had a million-dollar budget and a staff of about two hundred—its operations became far too intricate and diverse to be directed, or even closely monitored, by one person. Many of its programs, notably its far-flung voter registration work, involved King only tangentially. Even its direct action campaigns were often partly or wholly led by subordinates. A rounded view of SCLC must look at the role of second-level leaders, rank-and-file staff members, and local activists. Such a view, however, does nothing to detract from King's stature. Rather, by placing his work within its institutional, social, and political context, it reveals his stature in its true dimensions.[9]

But the details of SCLC's day-to-day operations are far less significant than the way in which it planned and executed its major campaigns of nonviolent direct action. Purposive action takes place within, and is therefore influenced by, institutional structures. Those structures are nevertheless man-made: they can be altered; they do not have to determine goals and outcomes. The historian's task is to analyze institutions and social structures without denying "the individually human . . . in terms of actors, reasons, and purposes." This study attempts to expose SCLC's inner dynamics without becoming enmeshed in the kind of organizational minutiae that obscures the aims and actions of identifiable human agents. It investigates how, given the limitations of their organizational base, SCLC's leaders evolved and executed their strategic plans. The sophistication of its strategy in terms of premeditation and rational calculation enabled SCLC to transcend its organizational confines.[10]

Contemporaries often failed to comprehend the logic and purpose of

SCLC's strategy. It was hardly surprising, then, that its tactics attracted strong criticism: they broke the law; they provoked white violence; they exploited local black communities; they created a "white backlash"; they were ineffective. Such criticisms, moreover, came from blacks as well as whites, radicals as well as conservatives, friends and foes of the civil rights movement. It would be wrong simply to dismiss them out of hand, for they all contained some element of truth. Nevertheless, SCLC's critics usually failed to appreciate how tactics that appeared objectionable or ineffective, or both, often furthered the higher aim of promoting federal action against white supremacy. SCLC's tactics were invariably geared toward this larger strategic goal. Whatever limited concessions blacks might secure through the pressure of nonviolent protest, SCLC knew full well that whites clearly held the upper hand in terms of political and economic power. If blacks were to find a solution to their age-old conundrum—how to secure equal treatment under the law from a racist white majority—they would have to bypass the South's white-controlled political and judicial institutions, making a direct appeal to the centers of federal power. Only federal intervention could resurrect the Fourteenth and Fifteenth amendments, for these had also been undermined by the resistance of Southern whites. Only a Second Reconstruction could revive the promise of the first.

This is not to say that SCLC regarded local protests solely as "media events" designed to induce federal involvement. Nor did it cold-bloodedly "sacrifice" local black communities on the altar of some grand strategic design. Its local contests were not sham battles but serious, often successful, campaigns of pressure against dominant white elites. Because of that pressure, white supremacy was already fraying at the edges before the decisive federal action of 1963–65. But the logic of the political situation, not to mention the poverty of the civil rights movement, made it sensible to concentrate on the most promising local confrontations. If a campaign failed to progress as planned, far better to cut one's losses and try somewhere else than become bogged down in a frustrating and debilitating stalemate (as happened with SNCC in Mississippi). It was its very *lack* of staying power, its strategy of "hit-and-run," that helped to make SCLC so effective. SCLC's task, King insisted, was not to "marry" a particular local community but to generate action and protest in one community after another.

The fact that SCLC sought to turn white violence to its advantage is undeniable: in Birmingham, St. Augustine, and Selma it clearly anticipated and invited a violent white response. Yet SCLC's campaigns elicited relatively *little* white violence, a fact which casts doubt on the argument that its primary intention was to "provoke" southern racists into committing violent acts. In much of the South, of course, it took very little "provocation" on the part of blacks to prompt a white show of force: the mildest expression of public protest often sufficed. By carefully selecting its targets, SCLC merely publicized white repression to the best possible effect. It contrived to do this, moreover, while keeping white violence to a minimum: SCLC's very presence, accompanied as it was by a phalanx of reporters and cameramen, inhibited white officials and restrained them in their use of violence. SCLC thus performed a delicate balancing act, inviting extreme racists to come out of the woodwork but framing its confrontations in such a way as to minimize the suffering of the demonstrators. The term "provocation" is inaccurate and inadequate as a description of its tactics.

SCLC had its share of failures; indeed, after 1965 it lost much of its effectiveness as a pressure group. In many ways, however, its defeats are as deserving of study as its successes—not only for what they reveal about King and his organization, but also for the truths they disclose about the civil rights movement, the black community, and the structure of American society. Were SCLC's failures evidence of basic weaknesses in its approach, or were they merely the by-products of a successful strategy? Was SCLC's "King-centeredness" an asset or a liability? Did SCLC fail to adapt to the Northern ghetto, or were its efforts there doomed by the changing political climate? Was the so-called white backlash an expression of deeply entrenched racism or a superficial reaction to specific circumstances? Although the answers to such questions are seldom clearcut, an analysis of SCLC's decline is essential to understanding and delimiting the Second Reconstruction of 1954–68.

It might be objected that I have neglected the role of religious inspiration in the history of SCLC and the civil rights movement. King himself constantly referred to the "supranatural" and the *Zietgeist*, as if some divine hand were guiding the movement and himself. He often described how, over a cup of coffee in his Montgomery home one dark morning in January 1956, "I experienced the presence of the Divine as I had never experienced Him before." His colleagues later spoke with reverence of their leader's "faith act" of April 12, 1963, when King went to jail on Good Friday. After his death, Coretta King likened her husband to Christ, depicting him as "an instrument of a Divine plan and purpose." One of his white Northern advisers, Harry Wachtel, spoke somewhat less reverently of King "hearing voices." In the opin-

ion of Charles Morgan, the civil rights movement "wasn't that
rational."[11]

I do not deny the importance of religious inspiration. I plead guilty,
however, to the charge that this study focuses on the rational calculation behind SCLC's actions, on logic rather than emotion. The civil
rights movement might not have been entirely rational, but, compared
to its segregationist opposition, it was a paragon of reason. Under
SCLC's leadership, Southern blacks not only out-sang, out-marched,
and out-prayed their oppressors, but they also out-thought them.

This book has been long in the making, and many people have
helped me along the way. Dr. John Harper made trenchant and constructive comments on an early draft; Professor August Meier also
offered useful suggestions. The assistance of American librarians has
also been invaluable. Without the help of Dr. Elinor D. Sinette (Ralph
J. Bunche Oral History Collection, Howard University) and Louise
Cook (Library and Archive, Martin Luther King, Jr., Center for Nonviolent Social Change, Atlanta), my work would have been impossible.
These two collections are indispensable to any serious study of the
civil rights movement, and their directors were unfailingly sympathetic to my requests. It is also a pleasure to thank the staff of the
Mississippi Valley Collection at Memphis State University for sending
me important material relating to the Memphis sanitation strike of
1968. The assistance and cooperation of their respective staffs made it
rewarding and enjoyable to work at the City Archives, Birmingham
Public Library; the Florida State Archives, Tallahassee; the Manu-
scripts Division of the Library of Congress; the Mugar Library, Boston
University; the Peace Collection, Swarthmore College; the John F. Kennedy Presidential Library; and the Schlesinger Library, Radcliffe College. The British Academy provided a generous research award which
enabled me to visit many of these collections; I could not have completed this work without it. Saint David's University College also gave
financial assistance to my research. For encouragement over the years,
I wish to thank Dr. John Prest of Balliol College, Dr. Mary Ellison of
Keele University, Professor Charles Crowe of the University of Georgia, and Professor William Wallace of Glasgow University. Finally, I am
grateful to Professor David J. Garrow of City College, New York, for
sharing with me his extensive knowledge of the sources on SCLC.

One

The Preachers and the
People: The Origins of SCLC

The most wonderful thing has happened right here in Montgomery, Alabama," wrote Virginia Durr, one of that city's handful of white radicals, on December 7, 1955. For the second day, blacks had boycotted local buses as a protest against their unfair treatment under the segregation laws. "It is almost 100 per cent effective," Durr told a friend, "and they are carrying it on in the most orderly and disciplined way and with the utmost determination."[1]

The Montgomery bus boycott was not the first of its kind. Two years earlier, in Baton Rouge, Louisiana, blacks had also boycotted city buses, and by means of economic pressure, assisted by a willingness to compromise by both white and black, succeeded in establishing the principle of "first come, first served" segregated seating. Under this arrangement white passengers took seats from the front of the bus towards the rear, while blacks seated themselves from the back towards the front. It eliminated the more objectionable features of bus segregation: the need for blacks' having to surrender their places to whites, or being compelled to stand while reserved "white" seats remained empty. While the boycott lasted, the blacks, led by the Reverend T. J. Jemison, utilized 150 cars and taxis to provide free lifts. Virtually no blacks rode the buses.[2]

Blacks in Montgomery did not expect their own boycott to last long; after all, they were not seeking the abolition of segregation, merely equality of treatment within the existing system. They were not aware of the events in Baton Rouge, but they did know that other cities in the Deep South, notably Mobile and Atlanta, had already conceded the "first come, first served" principle. They would need only to stay off the buses for a week or two to achieve this eminently reasonable demand. In Baton Rouge, it had taken precisely seven days.[3]

If white officials in Montgomery had shown the same degree of flexibility as those in Baton Rouge, they could have both ended the boycott within days and preserved segregated seating. Their intransigence, however, prolonged the boycott and persuaded blacks that there could be no just solution within the framework of segregation. When negotiations with the city and the bus company broke down, the organizers of the boycott confronted the stark choice of pressing on with their protest or backing down. If popular support had ebbed or crumbled, the latter would have been the only realistic alternative. As it was, the degree of black optimism and solidarity made an admission of defeat unthinkable. "The people are just as enthusiastic now as they were in the beginning of the protest," wrote the leader of the boycott, Martin Luther King, Jr., in September 1956. "They are determined never to return to jim crow buses. The mass meetings are still jammed and packed and above all else the buses are still empty."[4]

By then, another bus boycott was underway, in Tallahassee, Florida. When this protest began, whites of influence instinctively turned to the black leaders they knew best, the teachers, who had traditionally deferred to white sensibilities and pandered to white paternalism with the tact and finesse of seasoned diplomats. In an attempt to mediate, the editor of the *Tallahassee Democrat*, Malcolm Johnson, asked a respected high school principal to select five or six "responsible" Negroes with whom the city and the bus company could do business—with the understanding, of course, that the principle of segregation was not negotiable. To his shock and discomfiture, however,

Johnson found himself confronted by a roomful of angry blacks who resisted the usual evasive courtesies and insisted upon pressing their demands. The figures with whom white officialdom preferred to deal could not stop the boycott: blacks were not only rejecting the status quo, they were also following new leaders. And the latter refused to observe the old rules: they were not interested in paternalism, they regarded deference as demeaning, and, above all, they were uncompromising in their opposition to segregation. The relationship between black and white had been transformed, Johnson recalled some two decades later. "The preachers took over from the teachers."[5]

The bus boycotts in Baton Rouge, Montgomery, and Tallahassee were led by ministers and organized through the black church. The Tallahassee boycott movement, the Inter-Civic Council, numbered six clergymen among its nine officers and was led by the Reverend C. K. Steele. The boycott organization in Montgomery, the Montgomery Improvement Association, was similarly top-heavy with men of the cloth, with two dozen ministers helping Martin Luther King keep the protest in motion. When the state of Alabama outlawed the National Association for the Advancement of Colored People, a clergyman, Fred Shuttlesworth, organized an alternative organization in Birmingham. Preachers were indeed moving into the vanguard of black protest in the South.

White leaders, dumbfounded by the sudden emergence of hitherto obscure clerics, refused to acknowledge their legitimacy. These new men, they reasoned, must be radicals, Communists, outsiders—self-seeking parvenus whose hold over their followers rested on a clever combination of duress, demagogy, and deceit. But however much whites ignored, denigrated, or persecuted them, the new leaders won respect and support from ordinary blacks and became forces to be reckoned with. And out of these church-led protest movements came a new civil rights organization, the Southern Christian Leadership Conference, founded in 1957. SCLC was an unusual, unorthodox, and in some ways even bizarre outfit. After a faltering start, however, SCLC became a dynamic force within the civil rights movement and one of the most effective political pressure groups in American history. It has left an indelible mark on the South.

The formation and importance of SCLC mirrored a basic fact about leadership in the Southern black movement of the 1950s and 1960s: ministers wielded influence out of all proportion to their numbers. Such prominence reflected the economic facts of life in the South. Most blacks, educated or not, middle-class or working-class, depended on a white landlord or employer; they could ill afford to be identified as "troublemakers." To oppose segregation was to invite eviction, loss of livelihood, loss of credit. Teachers were particularly vulnerable to economic retaliation: in some Southern states they could be fired merely for advocating integration or belonging to the NAACP. College teachers were more difficult to get rid of, but they, too, might be squeezed out of their posts for challenging the status quo.[6] On the other hand, churches were owned and controlled by blacks themselves; ministers could be fired by their congregations alone. With a high degree of economic independence, preachers enjoyed a freedom of speech and action denied to the majority of blacks. This vital connection between economic safety and black leadership is also evident in the occupations of laymen who became prominent in the civil rights movement: many, if not most, were self-employed businessmen and professionals whose clientele was wholly or mainly blacks—doctors, dentists, lawyers, undertakers, store owners. Like ministers, they enjoyed economic security which gave them the latitude to defy white opinion. It was ironic that segregation, by helping to create a self-sufficient black middle class, inadvertently nurtured its leading adversaries. The most effective opponents of segregation were often its principal black beneficiaries.[7]

The appearance of church leadership in movements against segregation reflected a shift in black attitudes rather than a bold initiative by preachers; the relationship between clergy and community was one of symbiosis rather than leaders and led. Churchmen had always functioned as leaders and spokesmen, but they had usually accommodated to the racial mores of the time; indeed, generations of black activists and intellectuals had excoriated the church for its conservatism and lack of social and political awareness. It would be unrealistic, however, to suppose that ministers were completely out of step with their parishioners. In Myrdal's blunt words, "If the preachers have been timid and pussyfooting, it is because Negroes in general have condoned such a policy and would have feared more radical leaders." There had always been exceptions, of course, but in the 1930s segregation seemed unassailable and few black ministers saw much sense in hitting their heads against this particular brick wall. It was a period in which preachers reached the nadir of their prestige; black businessmen and professionals were far more active in supporting trade unions and civil rights organizations.[8]

The Second World War engendered a fundamental reorientation of black expectations and attitudes. Servicemen returned home with broader mental horizons, increased confidence, and greater self-esteem. They had fought and defeated the racist tyranny of the Axis; they were in no mood to readapt passively to the South's humiliating caste system. The injustices of segregation rankled more than ever, and clashes over the "color line," especially in buses and streetcars, became increasingly common during and after the war. Fewer blacks now accepted the system without question or regarded it as inevitable; why should they when the federal government itself was beginning to openly oppose it? Roosevelt's Fair Employment Practices Committee, the Democrats' civil rights plank in 1948, Truman's decision to integrate the armed forces, and Eisenhower's support for desegregation in the District of Columbia—all these pointed to the conclusion that white supremacy, in its formal-legal expression at least, was doomed.[9]

Political involvement fostered rising expectations. In 1944 the Supreme Court outlawed the "white primary," the complex of rules which had excluded blacks from the Democratic party and barred them from voting in the all-important Democratic primary elections. This epochal decision marked the reentry of Southern blacks into political life (although it took another quarter of a century to complete that process).[10] Throughout most of the rural South, as well as in cities like Birmingham and New Orleans, the vast majority of the black population was still disfranchised. But in many cities some, if not all, of the obstacles to black voting came down. Taking the South as a whole, the proportion of black adults who were registered voters increased from 5 percent in 1944 to 20 percent in 1952. By the early 1950s blacks were beginning to exert a palpable political influence in parts of the South. Blacks were elected to city councils in the North Carolina cities of Winston-Salem (1947) and Greensboro (1951); in 1952 a black candidate won a public election in Georgia. However circumscribed, political leverage encouraged blacks to agitate for pay parity with white teachers, the appointment of black policemen, a more equitable share of municipal services, and "first come, first served" segregated bus seating. Such campaigns were often successful, and a growing number of black Southerners confidently looked forward to fairer treatment, better conditions, and improved opportunities.[11]

Thus the impulse which led to the civil rights movement came from outside the church and was nurtured by politics. In Montgomery, in the period before the bus boycott, the leading black activists were E. D. Nixon, a railroad porter and trade union official; Rufus Lewis, a businessman; and Jo Ann Robinson, a college teacher. All three headed political clubs which, in the early 1950s, became increasingly vociferous in articulating black grievances and demands. One issue which they repeatedly raised was that of segregation on the city buses: between 1953 and 1955 they met city and bus company officials on at least four occasions to complain about abusive drivers and about company policies which made blacks stand over empty seats or surrender their places to whites. Mrs. Robinson's group, the Women's Political Council, took the lead in these meetings, and the conviction that a united black vote had helped to elect one of the city commissioners encouraged it to adopt an increasingly forthright stand. The bus boycott was no bolt from the blue.[12]

The inception of the boycott underlined the fact that the original dynamic came from without the black church, not from ministers but from lay people. The contribution of Rosa Parks should not be underestimated. Her decision to choose arrest rather than humiliation when driver J. F. Blake ordered her to give up her seat on December 1, 1955, was more than the impulsive gesture of a seamstress with sore feet. Although shy and unassuming, Rosa Parks held strong and well-developed views about the iniquities of segregation. Long active in the NAACP, she had served as secretary of the local branch. In the summer of 1953 she spent two weeks at Highlander Folk School in Monteagle, Tennessee, an institution which assiduously encouraged interracial amity. Founded and run by Myles Horton, Highlander flouted the local segregation laws and gave black and white Southerners a virtually unique opportunity to meet and mingle on equal terms.[13] Rosa Parks's protest on the Cleveland Avenue bus was the purposeful act of a politically aware person. It was also part of a groundswell of discontent among Montgomery's black population. The arrest of fifteen-year-old Claudette Colvin earlier in 1955 had had the makings of a cause célèbre, but when the girl became pregnant the case was dropped. But as Virginia Durr explained, Rosa Parks was known throughout the community as a woman of unblemished character: "So as the Negroes said, 'when they messed with her they messed with the WRONG ONE,' and the whole Negro community united overnight."[14]

Plans for a mass protest were well advanced by the time the church entered the picture, with the Women's Political Council again taking the initiative. Upon learning of the Parks arrest, Jo Ann Robinson immediately suggested a boycott and spread word of the plan through the women's club; she also ran off forty thousand handbills from a mimeograph machine at Alabama State College. The black ministers who met on the evening of December 2 to discuss the boycott were

confronted with a fait accompli. And it was not until December 5 that
Martin Luther King became president of the boycott organization; by
the time he made his first speech as leader, blacks had been off the
buses for a day. The ministers took over the leadership of the boycott
with obvious reluctance: the protest would never have got off the
ground but for E. D. Nixon, lawyer Fred Gray, and the Women's Political Council.[15] The fact that they selected King, a newcomer to
Montgomery, to be their spokesman is perhaps the most revealing
comment on the timidity of the local clergy. As one of the woman
activists put it, "The ministers who didn't want the presidency of the
MIA . . . were just chicken, passing the buck to Dr. King." Nevertheless, the formation of the Montgomery Improvement Association
brought the preachers into the forefront of the protest, and they remained there for the duration.[16]

Why did the leadership of the boycott pass so swiftly to clergymen?
Their economic independence was obviously important: as Professor
Lawrence D. Reddick of Alabama State put it, the more vulnerable
teachers like himself and Jo Ann Robinson were obliged to remain
"discreetly in the background." Equally important, ministers were
pushed to the forefront because the principal activists, Robinson, Nixon, and Lewis, realized that blacks could be far more effectively mobilized for mass action through the church than through secular
organizations. The existing political clubs were small and dispropor-
tionately middle-class. They were also, quite often, at loggerheads. As
Rufus Lewis put it, "It was a small group working over here for this
reason and another small group working over there for that reason. . . .
They were not thinking of bringing in the mass of the folks." E. D.
Nixon agreed with this assessment: the established leadership had
been fragmented, cliquish, and quarrelsome.[17] The church, by contrast, extended throughout the community, bridging political factions
and spanning political classes. As an organizational tool it was second
to none. In a city with neither a black radio station nor a widely read
black newspaper, the church provided the information network. It also
provided the meeting places, the fundraising machinery, and the means
of organizing an alternative transportation system.[18]

The church also possessed unique prestige. It was the oldest and
most respected institution in the black South. Central to their culture,
the symbol of their historical experience, the expression of their subli-
mated hopes and aspirations, the church gave blacks solidarity, self-
identity, and self-respect. When it came to arousing and manipulating
an audience, the black preacher knew few rivals. "I had never truly

understood the term 'collective experience,' " wrote sociologist John Dollard in 1937, "until participating in a well-planned Negro revival service." Through the church, the boycott harnessed the emotionalism and theatricality of black religion. The morale-boosting mass meetings, with their hymns, sermons, and "pep talks," provided entertainment and a sense of involvement. "With the help of those preachers who could preach and those other folks who could pray," remembered the Reverend S. S. Seay, "we kept the churches filled." Its links with the church gave the boycott coherence, respectability, and religious fervor.[19]

It might still be wondered why the black ministers of Montgomery, with their record of political passivity, accepted the leadership that was thrust upon them in this way. They did so, in part, because they did not anticipate the herculean task that lay before them. Most, King included, were skeptical about the boycott's chances of success. Had the first day proved a flop, they doubtless would have quietly but quickly disengaged themselves.[20] But with the buses practically empty and support for the protest solid, they had little choice but to continue. The obstinacy of the white officials and the enthusiasm of the black population trapped the ministers in their leadership role: if they dropped out now they would be branded as cowards and traitors.

As the boycott went from strength to strength, the ministers began to enjoy their new role. By early 1956 the protest was attracting national and international publicity. Although many of the news stories focused on King—a fact which caused some jealousy and resentment— the other leaders shared in the limelight; initially cagey about revealing their identities, they now enjoyed the prestige conferred by media coverage. As the authorities resorted to repression, the MIA's leaders won the respect and affection of the black population: when the city indicted them under Alabama's rusty antiboycott law, they did not wait to be arrested but gave themselves up. They were "laughing and slapping each other" as they turned themselves in, wrote Virginia Durr, "and saying, 'Man, man, where you bin, must have slept late,' and then all dying laughing." Arresting the leaders had been precisely the thing needed to make the protest more united and determined. At a packed church meeting after the arrests, about two thousand blacks vowed "by thundering stamping applause" to continue the boycott. Each repressive act by white officialdom tightened the bonds of pride and trust between the preachers and the people.[21]

In Tallahassee, as well, the bus boycott was initiated by lay people but organized through the church. In this case, the arrest of two black

students, Wilhelmina Jakes and Carrie Patterson, created the precipitating event. Their offense was to sit beside a white passenger on
the last empty seats, for which they were charged with behavior liable
to "incite a riot." The next day, in a crowded auditorium, three thousand students of Florida A&M University voted to stay off the buses.[22]

Dr. James Hudson, chairman of Florida A&M's philosophy department and an ordained minister, provided the link between the college
and the black church. Acting under his other hat, president of the
Interdenominational Ministerial Alliance, Hudson called a meeting of
the city's black clergymen to consider a response to the students' initiative. Meeting on May 29, the ministers appointed a committee to
treat with city and bus company officials. C. K. Steele, pastor of Bethel
Baptist Church and president of the local NAACP, proposed that a
mass meeting be held in his church that evening. "The atmosphere
was just that intense," Hudson related years later; "Reverend Steele's
motion carried without any trouble, no debate." The meeting with the
white officials proved fruitless, so an organization to continue the
boycott, the Inter-Civic Council (ICC), came into being later that day
when about 450 blacks turned out for the meeting at Steele's church.
The people elected to serve as officers included a dentist, a store
owner, a funeral director, and half a dozen ministers. Despite pressure
from the president of Florida A&M, Dr. George Gore, Hudson and
several other faculty members played prominent roles in the boycott.[23]

As in Montgomery, white officials tried to undermine the protest by
circumventing and isolating the leaders. In Tallahassee, however, their
tactics were more subtle. The authorities displayed a greater willingness to make concessions, accepting the ICC's demands for courteous
treatment and the employment of black drivers. They also assented to
the "first come, first served" principle, with the proviso that "members of different races may not occupy the same seat." Since the ICC's
principal demand was "first come, first served," this response satisfied
some blacks. On June 4, however, the ICC shifted its ground, now
insisting that "passengers shall have the right to sit wherever they
choose." The change created confusion and dissension within the
ICC's ranks, and a faction led by the Reverend David H. Brooks pressed
for acceptance of the bus company's proposals. Steele, however, rejected them and the boycott continued. Suspension of the bus service
in June fuelled doubts about this stand, and Steele noticed that "as we
went on . . . over a period of months there were those who thought a
compromise should have been accepted."[24]

Years later, Steele ruefully admitted that "Tallahassee was very, very suave in dealing with us." Even more obstinate than Montgomery in clinging to segregation, the city avoided some of the tactical blunders committed by Montgomery's white officials. For this the city could thank Frank Stoutamire, the chief of police, who stubbornly resisted pressure from the commissioners and others to clap the boycott leaders in jail. He saw how the mass indictments in Montgomery had created martyrs and buttressed support for the boycott. When he did begin to make arrests, he arrested people in twos and threes rather than en masse. Stoutamire proved to be a difficult adversary. Police repression often evoked black solidarity: the civil rights movement was to win its most notable victories when it confronted unscrupulous police officials like "Bull" Connor of Birmingham and Jim Clark of Selma. But Stoutamire kept his men on a tight rein. "He kept down that beating thing," recalled one veteran of the boycott. "He didn't believe in that." Moreover, the chief of police cultivated friendly relations with the boycott leaders, who grew to like and respect him. "He was an uncannily nice person," Steele thought. Stoutamire personified a type that would, in a paradoxical fashion, create great difficulties for the civil rights movement—as King discovered to his cost when he confronted Laurie Pritchett in Albany, Georgia.[25]

It is wrong to depict the Montgomery bus boycott as the decisive, initiating event of the civil rights movement. Such a view ignores the earlier Baton Rouge boycott and exaggerates the extent to which the Tallahassee protest was a mere imitation of the Montgomery movement. It is true that blacks in Tallahassee knew about the Montgomery bus boycott, and that C. K. Steele, who had been a pastor in Montgomery before moving to Florida, was well in tune with events there. But the Tallahassee boycott had a dynamism of its own: "Montgomery was not a spark-plug for Tallahassee," claimed one leader. "Tallahassee was its own spark-plug."[26] The Montgomery protest itself was organized in ignorance of the earlier boycott in Baton Rouge—a fact which, as Meier and Rudwick argue, suggests that necessity, not precedent, explains the rise of mass nonviolent direct action.[27]

It is tempting to point to *Brown* v. *Board of Education* (1954) as the crucial impetus behind the growth of black opposition to segregation. Without doubt, *Brown* heightened black aspirations. Yet the impact of the decision in the short term was not so clear-cut. After all, the MIA did not originally demand desegregation but rather "the right, under segregation, to seat ourselves from the rear forward on a first come, first served basis." As late as April 1956, nearly three months after the MIA filed its desegregation suit in federal court, King indicated that it was still willing to settle on these terms. Even in Tallahassee, when two years had elapsed since *Brown*, blacks hesitated before openly pressing for integration.[28]

What accounted for this hesitation? In his study of the Montgomery bus boycott, J. Mills Thornton suggested that black Southerners did not yet feel confident that the courts would sustain them if they attacked segregation itself. Other explanations come to mind. Blacks generally assumed that the dismantling of segregation would be long and protracted; few foresaw that it would be swept away, in its legal forms at least, within a decade. In 1955–56 it still struck many as quixotic to demand an immediate end to segregation. Then again, many blacks harbored reservations, ranging from mild uneasiness to outright opposition, about the use of direct action to change the law. To dismiss these dissenters as "conservatives" or "Uncle Toms" is neither accurate nor enlightening. In Tallahassee, for example, many of the doubts about the efficacy of the boycott came from within the ICC. As the Reverend David Brooks put it, "I don't believe a negative boycott without legal basis [i.e., court action] is going to get us very far. We're just wasting our time charging the city commission with not granting us integration." This debate over the relative merits of legal action and direct action became a persistent theme within the civil rights movement.[29]

If it was the intransigence of the white authorities that converted the initially mild demands of the Montgomery bus boycott into an uncompromising insistence upon desegregation, then *Brown* could be judged as important for its effect upon whites as for its impact on blacks. For that decision unleashed a wave of racism that reached hysterical proportions, drowning out the voices of moderation and compromise. "This schools thing is like dynamite," Virginia Durr noted shortly before the decision. Although *Brown* applied only to schools, it fostered a political climate in which the defense of segregation in general became a sine qua non for the survival of any white politician. Adamant opposition to blacks' demands and strident denunciations of the NAACP soon dominated political debate. Shortly before the boycott, a racial moderate on Montgomery's city commission, who had been elected with substantial black support, was ousted by an arch-segregationist, Clyde Sellers, who conducted the most racist campaign since the 1920s. Sellers became the first city commissioner to join the citizens council, the spearhead of "massive resistance" to integration. Such was the council's burgeoning prestige that both other commissioners followed his example. Governor James Folsom, who tried to stem the tide of racial hysteria and attempted, without success, to mediate the bus dispute, found himself isolated and impotent. "Today

I couldn't be elected dog-catcher," he admitted. Whites ruled out compromise within segregation, not blacks. As Thornton has suggested, "The inflexibility of segregation was something which black leaders had to learn."[30]

Why did the bus boycotters create new organizations instead of working through the NAACP? In some ways an NAACP branch was ill-suited for the conduct of a mass protest like a bus boycott: it had a relatively small membership and tended to be slow-moving and bureaucratic; how much support it would receive from the national office was problematic. But political considerations were probably more important. Many blacks opposed fighting under the banner of the NAACP because they considered that organization too radical; they were still thinking in terms of equality within segregation. Indeed, the national NAACP considered the demand for "first come, first served" too weak to support. Other blacks—including NAACP members—considered it prudent from a tactical point of view to organize apart from the NAACP. In the climate of massive resistance that organization had become too vulnerable to segregationist witch-hunts. Whites regarded the NAACP as the source of all evil and, except insofar as they harassed it, refused to deal with it. Writing about the emergence of locally based "movement centers" in Montgomery and Tallahassee, Aldon D. Morris argued that the decision to organize independently was a calculated attempt to minimize the impact of persecution and repression: the protesters avoided the attacks being aimed at the NAACP, and their own spontaneous, loosely structured groups were more difficult to prosecute. They also reasoned that whites might negotiate with "local" Negroes; at least, they would not necessarily reject negotiation out of hand.[31]

It was doubly ironic, therefore, that the bus boycotts in Montgomery and Tallahassee were laid at the NAACP's door, exposing that organization to yet greater persecution. Most white Southerners simply refused to believe that local protests against segregation were exactly that. Given the racist premise that blacks were happy and content, the only rational explanation for the boycotts lay in the machinations of some external force. Whites in Montgomery, wrote Alistair Cooke, regarded King as "the cat's-paw of the NAACP." Governor LeRoy Collins of Florida blamed the Tallahassee bus boycott on the NAACP.[32] If the level of official harassment is anything to go by, white Southerners saw the NAACP as the most potent threat to their racial supremacy. In blaming it for the bus boycotts, however, they were shooting at the wrong target. And the fact that their persecution of the NAACP inadvertently strengthened local protest movements com-

pounded the irony—the Birmingham-based Alabama Christian Movement for Human Rights (ACMHR) came into being as a direct response
to the suppression of the NAACP by the state authorities.[33]

The origins of the civil rights movement must be sought in all of
these indigenous, locally based, independent mass movements: the
three bus boycotts and the Birmingham movement. The origins of
SCLC, however, are to be found in the Montgomery bus boycott—
without this event, SCLC would probably not exist. The Baton Rouge
boycott had been too brief to have much national, or even regional,
impact. The Tallahassee and Birmingham movements were far less
united or skillfully led. In solidarity, duration, and quality of leadership, the Montgomery bus boycott was in a league of its own. Its
significance lay not merely in the event itself, but also in the way it
attracted national attention and—in the widest sense of the term—
political support.

It took a month for the news of the boycott to reach page 71 of the
New York Times, and thereafter it stayed in the headlines for a year.
During February 1956, after King's home had been bombed and in the
third month of the boycott, Northern-based pacifist organizations began to marvel at this example of nonviolent direct action: could it
become the basis for a wider Southern movement? If so, they reasoned,
it needed guidance and training. Two professional pacifists, one white,
the other black, travelled to Montgomery during the last week of February. Both became convinced that Montgomery's example of mass
action represented the wave of the future. Both assessed Martin Luther
King, Jr., as a leader of imposing character, impressive intellect, and
immense potential. One, Glenn Smiley, probably did most to win King
to the philosophy of nonviolence. The other, Bayard Rustin, helped to
place King at the head of a new organization of black Southerners.

Rustin is the more important figure in the history of SCLC: he
influenced the organization from its inception in 1957 until King's
death eleven years later. Born in Chester, Pennsylvania, in 1910, Rustin
was an illegitimate child, brought up by a Quaker grandmother. By his
late twenties, after a flirtation with the Young Communist League, he
switched his political allegiance to the Socialist party and became an
employee of the Fellowship of Reconciliation, an international pacifist
organization whose American arm had its headquarters in New York.
In 1942 Rustin helped James Farmer to set up the Congress of Racial
Equality, an offshoot of the FOR which pioneered the use of Gandhian
tactics of passive resistance—CORE coined the term "nonviolent direct action"—against racial discrimination. Rustin also assisted A.
Philip Randolph, the black trade union leader, in his "March on Wash-

ington Movement" for fair employment practices, a collaboration which marked the beginning of a long and close friendship between the two men. The draft put a temporary halt to Rustin's activities when, like most FOR staff members, he served time in jail as a conscientious objector. In 1948 he was working with Randolph again in a campaign against segregation in the armed services. In 1949 he ended up on a North Carolina chain gang after taking part in a bus trip organized by CORE and the FOR, the "Journey of Reconciliation," which highlighted the fact that segregation in interstate travel was still being practiced in the South in defiance of the Supreme Court. At the time of the Montgomery bus boycott Rustin was an official of the War Resisters League, and one of the leading lights of American pacifism.[34]

With the blessing of Randolph and with a leave of absence from his job, Rustin flew to Montgomery with a journalist and friend, William Worthy, to offer his services to King. As well as being an experienced organizer, Rustin was an excellent singer with a talent for leading mass meetings in folk songs and spirituals. Finding his help welcome, he also discovered that King was "very simpatico to discussing the whole question of nonviolence." Arriving during the critical week that saw the indictment of the entire MIA leadership, Rustin suggested the emphasis on "passive resistance" that was evident in King's speech to the packed mass meeting of February 23.[35]

After barely a week in Montgomery, however, Rustin found it politic to leave. His former employer, the FOR, had objected to his going in the first place, lest his presence in Montgomery attract damaging publicity. For Rustin was doubly "tainted": not only had he once belonged to the Young Communist League but he was also a homosexual, and both facts had become a matter of public record. Rustin's key supporter, Randolph, had second thoughts about having him in Montgomery when it became evident that the local press, and most likely the police as well, had been alerted to Rustin's identity. The fact that Rustin's companion, William Worthy, had written a series of controversial articles from the Soviet Union added to the potential embarrassment. After receiving some worried phone calls from local blacks, Randolph discussed the situation with a group of Socialist, pacifist, and civil rights colleagues. All agreed that Rustin ought to leave Montgomery forthwith.[36]

Glenn Smiley of the FOR arrived in Montgomery on February 27, shortly before Rustin left. After interviewing King the next day, he could scarcely suppress his excitement. "I believe that God has called Martin Luther King to lead a great movement," he wrote immediately after the meeting. "King can be a Negro Gandhi, or he can be made into an unfortunate demagogue destined to swing from a lynch mob's tree." Later, still excited, Smiley elaborated on his initial impression of King in a report to the FOR:

> He had Gandhi in mind when this thing started, he says. Is aware of the dangers to him inwardly, wants to do it right, but is too young and some of his close help is violent. King accepts, as an example, a body guard, and asked for a permit for them to carry guns. This was denied by the police, but nevertheless, the place is an arsenal. King sees the inconsistency, but not enough. He believes and yet he doesn't believe. The whole movement is armed in a sense, and this is what I must convince him to see as the greatest evil. At first King was asked to merely be the spokesman of the movement, but as sometimes happens, he has really become the real leader and symbol of growing magnitude. If he can *really* be won to a faith in non-violence there is no end to what he can do. Soon he will be able to direct the movement by the sheer force of being the symbol of resistance.

Smiley impressed upon King the absolute necessity to abjure weapons—before they gave the authorities a ready-made excuse to employ violent repression.[37] He also helped to clarify for King the character and philosophy of nonviolence. When blacks in the South had so little political, financial, and physical power, Smiley argued, the aggressive legalism of the NAACP was proving to be counterproductive. Neither court cases nor appeals to the white elite matched the profound effect of a direct and open confrontation with the powers that be on the part of the Negro masses. When conducted on the elevated plane of love, nonviolent resistance generated unity, dynamism, and power.[38]

King was receptive to these ideas. He encouraged Smiley to speak at the mass meetings, and his own speeches constantly stressed the need for "love" and "nonviolence." In his first published article, in April 1956, he insisted that "the only way to press on is by adopting the philosophy and practice of non-violent resistance." In September, when it appeared increasingly likely that the Supreme Court would affirm the illegality of Montgomery's bus segregation laws, King placed a new emphasis on reconciliation, setting up a special committee "to consider ways of creating the most wholesome attitude possible among the mass of the whites." Blacks had to learn not to react in kind, King stressed during the pre-integration workshops, if white passengers subjected them to verbal or physical abuse. Yet King did not accept nonviolence uncritically, Smiley remembered: they argued and debated for months before King finally resolved his doubts about the philosophy. After describing his "pilgrimage to nonviolence" in his first book,

Stride Toward Freedom (U.S. edition, 1958), King asserted that blacks could convert their white oppressors into friends if they accompanied their protests with redemptive love: "We will wear you down by our capacity to suffer. And in winning our freedom we will so appeal to your heart and conscience that we will win you in the process." Thus the lion, he argued, might be persuaded to lie down with the lamb.[39]

Blacks in Montgomery were confused by the Gandhian philosophy. To some extent, it is true, the idea of loving the enemy accorded with their Christian faith. They might also appreciate the practical wisdom of refraining from violence. But the majority of blacks were not pacifists, and many considered the notion of converting the oppressor through love and self-sacrifice faintly ridiculous. Smiley himself admitted that "there is and always has been a deep resentment toward the white man on the part of the Negro people." Meier and Rudwick are probably correct, therefore, in arguing that the growing appeal of nonviolent direct action had little to do with the Gandhian doctrines which King and others read into it.[40]

Nevertheless, there could be no doubting the intense loyalty and affection that King came to command from the blacks of Montgomery. Certainly, the press, with its propensity to highlight personalities rather than issues, singled out and magnified King's role in the boycott. Even so, the preeminence of his leadership was no creation of the media, as Virginia Durr—who had many reservations about King—reluctantly admitted: "King has captured the imagination and the devotion of the masses of the Negroes here and has united them and done a wonderful job—no doubt about it. They adore him and my wash lady tells me every week about how she hears the angel's wings when he speaks, and God speaks directly through him and how he speaks directly to God. There is a great deal of mysticism in him and the Negroes absolutely believe in his 'vision' and his 'sainthood.' "[41] King was the undisputed hero of the mass meetings.

How did he acquire such extraordinary influence? It has often been noted that King was an "accidental" leader: he neither precipitated the Montgomery bus boycott, nor organized it, nor sought its leadership. As he confessed in 1956, "If anybody had asked me a year ago to lead this movement, I tell you very honestly, I would have run a mile to get away from it."[42] Academic study, not political activism, had dominated his adult life; when he moved to Montgomery in 1954 to take up his first pastorate, he was still a student at Boston University and had yet to finish his doctoral thesis. One of his contemporaries remembered him as "a thoroughgoing intellectual, born wealthy. . . . I simply did not expect to see him leading a movement."[43] King did not shirk civic responsibility, for his family background, educational attainments, and position as pastor of the old and distinguished Dexter Avenue Baptist Church automatically thrust him into the upper echelons of Montgomery's black society. But he declined the presidency of the NAACP to concentrate on his pastoral duties. When Rufus Lewis, one of his parishioners, nominated him as the MIA's spokesman, King was taken by surprise. It was apparent to everyone at the meeting that Lewis proposed King because the Reverend L. Roy Bennett, president of the Interdenominational Ministerial Alliance, had chaired the first meeting so poorly. Lewis knew that King could do better, but "I certainly didn't know that [he] was the type of man of rare courage and rare abilities that he had—nobody knew that."[44] The fortuitous manner of his selection, however, merely highlighted the qualities that King displayed as leader of the MIA: courage, intelligence, self-possession, and a superb ability to communicate.

As the journalist Paul Good once noted, words on paper can only suggest the cadences and inflections that King employed to such telling effect in his sermons and speeches. Other preachers used more spectacular verbal pyrotechnics. But the tub-thumpers, or "whoopers," too often sacrificed substance for style and preached only to the converted. King eschewed rhetorical excess but nonetheless aroused the emotions of his audience. His rich, deep voice suggested intimacy and warmth; it was calming and reassuring. He began his speeches slowly, pronouncing each word clearly and carefully, in an effort to capture and hold the attention of his listeners. Almost imperceptibly, as he neared his peroration, the words came more quickly, the pitch and volume rose, and through repetition of a single phrase or question he built up to a powerful climax.[45]

More important was what he said. King did not talk down to his audience; nor did he allow the demands of rhetoric to obscure his message. "His greatest contribution," Rufus Lewis believed, "was interpreting the situation to the mass of the people. He could speak better than any man I've ever heard in expressing to the people their problem and making them see clearly what the situation was and inspiring them to work at it." King also appealed to the not-so-pious. Young blacks, often cynical about preachers, warmed to his message. King did not simply quote the Bible, recalled Yancey Martin, then a student at Alabama State: "He was talking about what we ought to have, and what we ought to be, and what the situation ought to be in the South."[46] Above all, perhaps, King helped to sustain morale by imparting to blacks a sense of mission and destiny. In his first speech to the MIA, he struck the moral tone that came to dominate the protest: "We are going to walk together. Right here in Montgomery, when the history books are written in the future, somebody will have to say that there lived a race of people—a black people—a people who had the moral courage to stand up for their rights, and thereby injected new meaning and dignity into the veins of history and of civiliza-tion."[47] The rapport King developed with his audience brings to mind the observation made by John Dollard nearly twenty years earlier: "No more exhilarating form of leadership . . . exists than that possible be-tween the Negro preacher and his congregation."[48]

When negotiations with the city and the bus company broke down and the boycott continued into 1956, King had his willpower and cour-age severely tested. Deluged by threatening letters and telephone calls, harassed by the police, his house damaged by a bomb, he almost broke under the strain, but did not. His father pleaded with him to give up the leadership—on one memorable occasion assembling a group of Atlanta notables, including Professor Benjamin Mays, president of Morehouse College, to bolster his entreaties. But King insisted on returning to Montgomery.[49] "It would be the height of cowardice for me to stay away. I would rather be in jail than desert my people now. I have begun the struggle, and I can't turn back. I have reached the point of no return."[50] References to death crept into his speeches, betraying his own fears. But in dwelling upon the dangers he faced, King affirmed his own resolve and stiffened the backs of his followers.

He led the boycott with skill and intelligence. Aware of his own inexperience, he was receptive to advice. When it came to organizing an alternative transportation system, for example, he sought the help of T. J. Jemison, who provided details of the car pool he had set up during the Baton Rouge boycott. King had the administrative ability to handle the huge volume of mail that flowed into the MIA's office, replying to well-wishers and critics in the appropriate way. He became the MIA's ambassador, representing its cause throughout the nation before white and black audiences, and, in doing so, he acted as the MIA's chief fundraiser. He had the education and self-assurance to cope with the press, and he developed a keen sense of public relations. Calm and articulate, he handled reporters well, presenting the boycot-ters' case reasonably and persuasively. He was careful to make sure that all the MIA's public statements were cleared by him personally. He also displayed cool intelligence in moments of crisis. When his home was bombed he acted decisively to avert a riot. When the MIA's recording secretary, the Reverend U. J. Fields, charged his colleagues with misuse of funds, King not only disproved the charge but also persuaded Fields to recant in public. He was not above threatening to resign in order to enforce unity. Astute and quick to learn, he displayed admirable tactical finesse. Virginia Durr thought he had "a genius for the right act at the right time." By any objective appraisal, King made a massive contribution to the success of the boycott.[51]

Through Smiley and Charles Lawrence, its national chairman, the FOR brought King into contact with other black leaders with a view to fashioning a Southern nonviolent movement. At a conference on May 12 at King's alma mater, Morehouse College, they debated the possibility of duplicating the example of Montgomery elsewhere. Could groups like the FOR help to initiate protests, or should they wait until they developed spontaneously? Summarizing the discussion, Smiley wrote, "There is a need to call together men from each of the 11 states, allowing them to go back and teach others the methods of nonviolence." The FOR organized another conference in July, and held a regional conference in Atlanta on January 8–10, 1957, to which it invited about 150 Southern activists. The FOR's intention was to create a formal organization to promote nonviolent action in the South, either an affiliate of the FOR or an independent offshoot like CORE. This proposed organization never got off the ground, however, because immediately after this conference another conference took place, also in Atlanta. And it was from this second conference, organized by Bayard Rustin, that SCLC emerged.[52]

Why did King opt for Rustin's organizational plan rather than Smiley's? The reasons are complex and significant. Although Smiley's idealism impressed King, Rustin could offer much more in terms of practical assistance than the FOR. Rustin, after leaving Montgomery in February, had stayed in contact with King by letter and telephone. They also met occasionally when King visited New York and other Northeastern cities. Working behind the scenes, visiting Montgomery rarely, Rustin gave invaluable help to King and the MIA. He ghosted King's first article, which appeared in the pacifist magazine *Liberation*. He raised funds for the boycott. Most important of all, he functioned as a link between the MIA and the Northern Left—not merely the pacifist fringe, but also the Socialist-liberal-labor forces represented by such figures as Norman Thomas and A. Philip Randolph. It was Rustin's ability to mobilize these forces behind the boycott that helped persuade King to adopt the organizational concept that became SCLC.[53]

Rustin developed the idea for SCLC with two other left-wing activists, Stanley Levison and Ella Baker, who had also come of age politically in the radical ferment of 1930s New York. Five years older than Rustin, Ella Baker grew up in North Carolina, graduating from Shaw

University, but moved to New York in 1927. After working for the Young Negro Cooperative League and the Works Progress Administration, she joined the national office of the NAACP shortly before the war. As a national field secretary, and later as director of branches, she acquired an extensive knowledge of the South and its black activists. She had worked to build up the NAACP branch in Montgomery, for example, and was well acquainted with E. D. Nixon. During these years she also became friendly, in her words, "with people who were in the Communist Party, and all the rest of the Left forces."[54]

Stanley Levison came from a different background in terms of class and race, although he shared the same political milieu. Born in 1912 of Jewish parents, Levison trained as a lawyer and qualified for the New York Bar. Over the years, however, various business interests occupied most of his time, and he acquired a substantial income. A staunch Roosevelt Democrat, he also involved himself in liberal groups like the American Jewish Congress and the NAACP. His activities in the latter introduced him to Baker, who was president of the New York branch, and the two soon discovered that they shared a similar political outlook. Levison, too, moved in left-wing circles, and he worked with Baker in the unsuccessful fight against the McCarran-Walter Act, which provided for the deportation of immigrants—even naturalized immigrants—for "Communist and Communist-front" affiliations. According to David Garrow's study, Levison was a Communist sympathizer during the early 1950s, and may even have been "closely involved in CP financial activities between 1952 and 1955."[55] Later, when questioned about the allegations of communism, Levison shrugged off his past associations with the observation that "in the 1930s and 1940s you could scarcely have been an intellectual in New York without knowing some [Communists]."[56]

By 1955 the American Left was at its nadir. Since 1945 it had suffered a series of shocks and disasters: the death of Roosevelt, the ideological chill of the Cold War, the failure of the CIO's Southern organizing drive, the debacle of the 1948 Henry Wallace campaign, and the trauma of McCarthyism. With liberals clambering aboard the anti-Communist bandwagon, and with the Democratic party divided and ineffective, the outlook for progressive reform looked bleak. To radicals like Rustin, Baker, and Levison, therefore, the Montgomery bus boycott appeared like an oasis in the desert. And as the protest unfolded, they began to discuss the possibility of using the Montgomery movement as the springboard for a new organization. As Baker put it, "We began to talk about the need for developing in the South a mass force that would . . . become a counterbalance, let's call it, to the NAACP."

SCLC was thus conceived as a means of capitalizing on what had developed in Montgomery in terms of mass action. Its object, Levison recalled, was "to reproduce that pattern of mass action, underscore mass, in other cities and communities."[57]

They also believed that to be effective, any organization that grew out of Montgomery had to be composed of and led by Southern blacks. Rustin's experience of CORE had convinced him that blacks could not be attracted to this kind of pacifist-oriented, interracial organization. Such groups tended to be dominated by white middle-class intellectuals whose earnestness and sincerity often disguised a paternalistic attitude to blacks. While passionately devoted to nonviolent direct action, CORE had failed utterly to win a mass following. Indeed, by 1955 it seemed moribund. Rustin therefore opposed the FOR's attempt to set up an interracial organization in the South. The great strength of the Montgomery bus boycott was that blacks organized it themselves: as Virginia Durr noted in May 1956, "The Negroes are so proud of the fact that this is an all-Negro movement, led, financed to a large degree and activated by Negroes." It was obvious to Rustin and his colleagues that mass action in the South could best be promoted by an indigenous, independent, church-based organization of Southern blacks.[58]

In creating such an organization they regarded the backing of A. Philip Randolph as crucial. Randolph's union, the Brotherhood of Sleeping Car Porters, was not one of the more powerful forces in the labor movement. Yet Randolph, by virtue of his age, integrity, and personality, commanded enormous respect and influence. To Rustin, Baker, and Levison, Randolph was the key to securing financial and political support from organized labor. Randolph's backing would also be essential if the NAACP were to acquiesce in a new organization. Through Randolph, King might even gain access to the White House. Finally, Randolph's imprimatur brought respectability; a staunch anti-Communist, his signature on an appeal letter told liberals that a cause was free of subversive taint and politically "safe."

Levison and Baker had already persuaded Randolph to chair a group called In Friendship, which they and Rustin organized early in 1956. Its original purpose was to provide financial help for "victims of racial terror"—blacks in the South who found themselves without homes or jobs as a consequence of their civil rights activities, particularly with regard to school integration. No sooner had it been organized, however, than it shifted its efforts toward raising money for the Montgomery bus boycott. In May, In Friendship staged a rally in Madison Square Garden that marked one of the first occasions on which prominent entertainers like Pearl Bailey and Sammy Davis, Jr., lent their talents to the cause of civil rights. The event netted over $7,000, half of which went to the MIA. In Friendship was designed to be a nonradical, non-political group that could appeal to trade unions, civic organizations, and religious bodies. It also sought and won the support of the NAACP, to which it presented no obvious threat of competition.[59]

Securing Randolph's backing for a new civil rights organization was not easy. He had been reluctant to chair In Friendship, fearing that his name was becoming devalued by appearing over too many appeal let-ters. More important, he opposed the idea of Northern activists seek-ing to exploit, control, or manipulate the emerging Southern movement. The Montgomery leaders had managed quite well on their own, he noted, without the help of Northern-trained "experts" on non-violence—in fact, they could probably teach these "experts" some important lessons. Randolph would support a national or regional pas-sive resistance conference, "but only if it is called by Reverend King or . . . the Montgomery church leadership."[60]

It was vital, therefore, that the initiative for a new organization came from the South, and that it appeared to be spontaneous. Rustin tried to put the organizational ball in motion by asking C. K. Steele to call publicly for a conference of Southern Negro leaders. Steele de-clined to go out on a limb, but he agreed to support such a call if it came from King himself. Finally, on New Year's Day, 1957, King, Steele, and Shuttlesworth sent out about one hundred invitations to a conference in Atlanta on January 10 and 11. About sixty people re-sponded. Furnished with working papers by Rustin and Baker, the par-ticipants agreed to establish a "Southern Leadership Conference on Transportation and Nonviolent Integration." Rustin scheduled another meeting for February 14 in New Orleans. Here, in the Baptist church of A. L. Davis, about one hundred people voted to establish a permanent organization. In August, at its first annual convention, in Montgomery, it adopted the name by which it is still known: the Southern Christian Leadership Conference. The theme of the first convention became SCLC's motto: "To Redeem the Soul of America."[61]

It would be misleading to imply that SCLC was the creation of a small group of Northern activists. Rustin, Baker, and Levison may have facilitated the birth, but the conception took place in the South. Noth-ing was more natural than the formation of a new, Southern organiza-tion, especially when the NAACP had been suppressed throughout Alabama and was being severely harassed elsewhere. The Montgomery bus boycott stimulated black organizations to send money to the MIA, and with the inception of the Tallahassee boycott and the Birmingham movement, Steele and Shuttlesworth began to meet King, usually in

Montgomery, to exchange information and ideas. The Reverend Joseph Lowery from Mobile joined this informal group. It was a short and obvious step to forming an organization to assist, coordinate, and widen their activities. SCLC "arose out of a great deal of collective discussion," Levison wrote more than twenty years later, "and if there was one individual who clarified and organized the discussion it was unquestionably Dr. King."[62]

The decision to include the word "Christian" in the new organization's name was not taken lightly. Most of SCLC's founders were ministers, and their original manifesto, drafted by Rustin, laid great stress on the fact that the new organization would be guided by Christian principles. Most of the ministers, therefore, felt that this religious orientation ought to be apparent in the organization's title. Some objected that the term "Christian" was too narrow and might deter potential supporters. The Reverend Roland Smith of Little Rock, however, provided a clinching argument: by calling itself "Christian," the organization might be less vulnerable to charges of radicalism and communism—charges which the NAACP continually attracted.[63]

SCLC was a very different animal from the NAACP. For one thing, it confined itself to the South; for another, it did not offer individual memberships. As designed by Rustin, Levison, and Baker, SCLC was an umbrella organization which joined local groups, or "affiliates," in a loose alliance. Each affiliate paid $25 to SCLC and received in return a certificate of affiliation bearing King's signature and the right to send five delegates to the annual convention. The affiliates could also seek advice and assistance from SCLC's staff. This amorphous structure had a clear purpose: to minimize direct competition with the NAACP. Most of SCLC's founders were NAACP members; many, like Steele, were branch presidents. The affiliate structure enabled blacks to support SCLC without feeling any disloyalty to the older organization. It also preempted the charge that SCLC intended to supplant the NAACP. But SCLC's structure had obvious weaknesses. The fact that it had a regional rather than a national base meant that when SCLC shifted its operations to the North after 1965, it floundered badly. The lack of a membership program meant that SCLC did not enjoy a steady income from individual subscriptions.[64]

The affiliates came in all shapes and sizes, but there were two basic types. Most of them comprised a group of ministers and their churches; they were often of recent origin and modelled themselves on the MIA. These included the Alabama Christian Movement for Human Rights, in Birmingham; the Baton Rouge Christian Movement; and the Nashville Christian Leadership Council. The second, more disparate, category consisted of voter registration organizations and miscellaneous civic groups—although these affiliates were also in many cases led by ministers. A handful of affiliates were founded and led by laymen. For example, a dentist, Dr. C. O. Simpkins, created the United Christian Movement in Shreveport, Louisiana. The only non-Southern affiliate, the Los Angeles–based Western Christian Leadership Conference, served exclusively as a fundraising outpost.[65]

The constitution and bylaws adopted in 1958 gave SCLC a governing board of thirty-three people. Of the original members, all but two lived in the eleven ex-Confederate states. A breakdown of the board members by state is not especially illuminating except in one respect: Alabama contributed the largest number—eight, with five from the MIA—and became SCLC's strongest base and main area of operations.

What kind of people sat on SCLC's board? They were all black, and at least two-thirds were ministers. The lay minority included a dentist, a pharmacist, a professor of history, several businessmen, and an official of the International Longshoreman's Association. Only one woman sat on the board. All but a handful of the ministers were Baptists, a fact partially explained by the numerical preponderance of black Baptists in the South. Baptists made up perhaps two-thirds of the churchgoing population: "The Baptists had the masses of the people and what we needed at that time were the masses," admitted S. S. Seay, one of the few Methodists on the board. Even so, Methodists were clearly underrepresented, accounting for only one in five of the ministers. The journalist Louis Lomax attributed the disproportionate influence of Baptists to denominational bigotry. Clannishness, however, would be a more apt term: Baptists knew each other and tended to stick together. Graduates and professors of Morehouse College (Atlanta) and Alabama State College (Montgomery) accounted for eight of SCLC's nine original officers.[66]

Three other characteristics of SCLC's founders are worthy of mention. First, they all came from the urban South: none resided in a town smaller than Valdosta, Georgia, or Clarksdale, Mississippi, and most lived in the dozen biggest cities. With a few exceptions, the civil rights movement originated in the cities and only later, in the early 1960s, penetrated the rural Black Belt. Second, the ministers in SCLC were representative in some ways but unrepresentative in others. Social activists everywhere tend to be a self-selecting minority and are in that sense atypical. The black clergymen who took part in the civil rights movement were certainly atypical of the black clergy as a whole, the vast majority of whom, in the words of one authority, were "primarily interested in their pastoral role . . . [and] have little apparent interest in . . . the general citizenship status of their own parishioners, to say nothing about that of the Negro masses."[67] During the Birmingham protests of 1963—one of the most highly organized and effective of all the civil rights campaigns—only about 20 of the city's 250 black ministers actively supported SCLC.[68]

In a larger sense, however, the socially conscious minority was far more representative of the black population at large than was the uninvolved majority. As the bus boycott movements illustrated so dramatically, blacks would respond en masse, and with enthusiasm and determination, to vigorous antisegregationist leadership. Activists like King and Steele reflected the opinions of black Southerners far more accurately than did the much larger group which abstained from the struggle. Finally, as defined in terms of education, occupation, wealth, and social standing, most of SCLC's founders came from the relatively small upper middle class. Few had failed to graduate from college; many had higher degrees and seminary training. They were among the best educated and the most dedicated of the black clergy.

That the black church had immense potential as a force for political change had long been accepted. "It has the Negro masses organized," Myrdal asserted, "and . . . could line up the Negroes behind a program." The Montgomery bus boycott seemed to provide concrete evidence that this latent strength was at last being utilized. SCLC's attempt to politicize the church, however, was sharply limited by the absence of organizational and ideological cohesion that characterized the black religious tradition. Timidity, venality, sectarianism, and otherworldliness continued to inhibit the capacity of the church for large-scale collective action. It was one thing to assemble a relatively small group of clergymen-activists under the auspices of SCLC; it was quite another to build a South-wide mass movement. SCLC's early efforts to mobilize and coordinate the black church en masse, therefore, achieved little. Only when it acquired a cadre of full-time agitators and initiated specific, planned actions did SCLC become effective. Until then, it was up to King to keep the fledgling organization alive, and he shouldered this burden with a fatalistic sense of duty. After Montgomery, he explained, there could be no turning back. "As I became involved, and as people began to derive inspiration from their involvement, I realized that the choice leaves your own hands. . . . [Y]ou can't decide whether to stay in it or get out of it—you must stay in it."[69]

Two

The Fallow Years: 1957–1959

There is no mystery about King's selection as president of SCLC: he stood head and shoulders above his fellow clergymen in terms of influence and prestige. He had led the Montgomery bus boycott to a triumphant conclusion on December 21, 1956, when, after receiving a mandate from the Supreme Court, the bus company and the city at last allowed black passengers to sit wherever they pleased. During the course of the struggle King had become the symbol of the protest, a figure of national and international significance. Men like Steele and Shuttlesworth, by comparison, were virtual unknowns, and they could certainly not rival King in terms of intellect and ability.

But if his role in Montgomery explained King's elevation to SCLC's presidency, something else is needed to account for the fact that SCLC, the organization, never managed to establish a separate identity from King, the individual. SCLC was not only dominated by King: its very structure appeared to be built around him. On paper, the board of directors acted as SCLC's governing body. In practice, as far as policy was concerned, it functioned as a rubber stamp. Consisting for the most part of King's own nominees, it rarely questioned, and even more rarely opposed, the policies and statements that King placed before it. As C. K. Steele put it, "Dr. King was the last word on every-thing."[1] Equally striking was the extent to which SCLC framed its public image and appeal around the King persona: King was unique and indispensable, a black leader—*the* black leader—of heroic propor-tions. Others in SCLC received little public exposure. SCLC became an autocratic organization which revolved around King, and this absence of internal democracy, plus the failure to project other personalities, eventually contributed to its decay. But these problems lay in the fu-ture. When SCLC came into being, Rustin and Levison deliberately structured it so as to capitalize on King's enormous prestige.

It is difficult to overestimate the contribution of Rustin, Levison, and Baker to SCLC's early development. Baker went to Atlanta to set up SCLC's office and attempted to weld the affiliates together through an organized regional program. Meanwhile, Rustin and Levison labored behind the scenes, in New York, to furnish King with assistance and advice. The documents to be found among King's papers at Boston University testify to the scope of their help: Rustin and Levison briefed him for meetings; they arranged speaking engagements; they advised him about handling journalists and publishers; they drafted speeches and press releases; they ghosted articles and arranged for their publication; they helped King with *Stride Toward Freedom;* they told him how to approach groups and individuals. Most important of all, perhaps, their astute political advice provided a broad framework within which SCLC could develop its strategy and tactics.

King badly needed this kind of help. Barely twenty-eight at the time of SCLC's inception, he had little experience of secular organizations and no great knowledge of politics. Rustin and Levison, both about twenty years older, could tell him that Walter Reuther, with his com-mitment to anticolonialism, would be worth approaching for funds. They could advise him that Chester Bowles had a longstanding in-terest in Gandhi and nonviolence—a politician worth cultivating. They could suggest that when speaking to an audience of black trade unionists he employ a "less cultured" style of language. They could tell him that a $1,000 contribution from Corliss and Margaret Lamont required an immediate letter of thanks. They could also tell him which appeal letters not to sign, which invitations not to accept, and which organizations not to bother with. Levison, in particular, wished to protect King from being exploited or manipulated by the publishing and news media. "I am not advocating the development of a cynical frame of mind," he wrote, but King ought to be on his guard against the "tricky practices" of "fast-moving and fast-talking" media personalities.[2]

Rustin later argued that he and Levison "created the direction" for King during SCLC's early years. Harris Wofford, a white lawyer who got to know King at this time, noted that "Rustin seemed ever-present with advice, and sometimes acted as if King were a precious puppet whose symbolic actions were to be planned by a Gandhian high command." But King was no puppet. In a conversation after King's death, which the FBI recorded, Rustin told Levison that "I can name five or six instances I said, 'Martin, if you do that you are finished,' and he did it and got more prestige." King was always independent, Levison agreed. "Basically . . . we were analyzing Martin and saying: 'How did he view these kinds of problems? What would be the way for him to tackle them?' It was not we directing him so much as we working with him and giving expression to ideals we knew he had or would quickly accept."[3]

Soon after SCLC's formation, King received valuable national exposure when he addressed an outdoor rally, the Prayer Pilgrimage, in Washington, D. C. The idea for this event originated at SCLC's New Orleans meeting on February 14, 1957. A. Philip Randolph had repeatedly asked President Eisenhower to discuss the school integration crisis with a group of black leaders. SCLC now promised a "mighty Prayer Pilgrimage to Washington" if the President continued to turn down this request.[4]

To Rustin and Levison, the Prayer Pilgrimage was a golden opportunity to project King as a national figure. For the event to succeed, however, SCLC needed the cooperation of the NAACP. The NAACP had the machinery to ensure a respectable turnout. Moreover, the appearance of King alongside Roy Wilkins, the NAACP's executive secretary, would imply an equality of status between the two leaders. Once again, Randolph was the key to securing the NAACP's cooperation. In a memo to Randolph delineating the strategy of the pilgrimage, Rustin and Levison stressed the need "to protest against the harassment, curtailment and outlawry of the NAACP in the south"; in this way, the NAACP would be given an organizational stake in the success of the event. They also argued that the protest should be aimed at Congress rather than the president: the focus of national attention had shifted from the South to the struggle over the civil rights bill; it might not be wise, moreover, to criticize "a singularly popular president" too strongly. Randolph considered the plan sound and helped persuade Wilkins to support it. The three leaders sealed their alliance at a meeting in New York on March 25, setting up a national coordinating office.[5]

Both Rustin and Levison advised King on what to say at the rally. Rustin thought Levison's draft lacking in spiritual content. "I hope you will consider using this occasion," he wrote King, "to call upon Negroes north and south to adhere to non-violence in word, thought, and deed." In expounding the theme of nonviolence, he added, King ought to use the rhetorical form of "Yes-No-Yes." Rustin also urged him to mention the need for economic uplift through participation in the labor movement: "The Negro cannot be free so long as there are poor and underprivileged white people." It was a theme Rustin continually reiterated in the years to come.[6]

The Prayer Pilgrimage, held on May 17, the third anniversary of *Brown* v. *Board of Education*, attracted a disappointing crowd of about twenty-five thousand; the fact that it took place on a Friday could not have helped. The event generated little national publicity. Nevertheless, King had appeared on the same platform as Randolph and Wilkins. Through his reputation and oratory, moreover, King demonstrated that he could dominate this kind of gathering. "Give us the ballot," he repeated, over and over again. His style of delivery was identical to that of "I Have a Dream," noted David Lewis in his 1969 biography of King.[7]

King's reputation received another fillip on June 13, when he visited Vice-President Nixon at the White House for a two-hour discussion of the civil rights question. Nixon had extended the invitation to King when the two men met in Lagos, during the Ghanaian independence celebrations in March. Rustin and Levison impressed upon King the significance of the meeting: "[It] is already regarded among Negro forces and the Negro press as . . . a 'summit conference.' Hence, every word expressed to Nixon and the press, every concept, requires careful weighing." As well as arming King with a prepared statement, a list of anticipated press questions, and a list of suggested answers, they gave him some broad political advice. He had to remain nonpartisan, they insisted. To become identified with one party would expose the movement to grave danger and King himself to political attack. "The central issue of race relations would become confused and compromised by allowing it to become tied to the many political issues a party deals with simultaneously." Lawrence Reddick later poked fun at the speed with which Rustin, who acted as King's press representative, whisked King from the steps of Nixon's office "toward a waiting automobile for a quick getaway."[8]

A nonpartisan strategy clearly made sense in the late 1950s. In terms of support for civil rights, there seemed little to choose between the two parties. The Democrats had adopted a sweeping civil rights plank in 1948, but had subsequently failed to implement it. During the 1956 campaign, moreover, Adlai Stevenson had played down the civil rights issue, the party having rejected "all proposals for the use of force" in carrying out decisions of the Supreme Court. "Fundamentally," Senator Paul Douglas remembered, "the Stevenson policy was not to do anything to offend the South seriously."[9] The Republicans, although woefully delinquent in enforcing *Brown* v. *Board of Education*, did not seem notably bad by comparison; indeed, their 1956 platform contained a stronger civil rights plank than the Democrats'. Consequently, Eisenhower attracted significant black support in the South; according to Virginia Durr, King himself cast a ballot for "Ike." Now, in 1957, the Republican administration had introduced a civil rights bill—a weak measure, to be sure, but the first of its kind since Reconstruction. There was little to be gained and much to be lost by aligning with one particular party. To the Republicans, King seemed eminently worth befriending. Both Randolph and Wilkins were regarded as hostile; King, on the other hand, had no political record, and might well help the Republicans to attract more black votes.[10]

To such stalwarts of the Old Left as Virginia Durr and Aubrey Williams, who witnessed King's rise firsthand, SCLC's emphasis on nonviolence and nonpartisanship seemed bafflingly naive: blacks needed to work with the trade unions and with the Democrats, they argued, in order to fashion an interracial radical movement in the South. But this was precisely the strategy, Rustin and Levison believed, that had failed during the 1930s and 1940s. Black Southerners had to face the reality that white support would come from the North, not the South. They also had to adapt their tactics to the Cold War climate which had made radicalism a synonym for subversion.[11]

Like In Friendship, SCLC was designed to be a "nonpolitical" organization that could win support from across the political spectrum. By emphasizing Christian principles and nonviolence it projected a noncontroversial image of peace and moderation. The concept of nonviolence was ideologically neutral; it gave a patina of respectability to the politically suspect weapon of mass direct action—a crucial consideration in the conservative 1950s. Thus the right-of-center organ of Republican publisher Henry R. Luce, *Time* magazine, could put King on its front cover in January 1957 with an approving inside feature. *Time* found reassurance in King's views on clothes—"I don't want to look like an undertaker, but I do believe in conservative dress"—and pronounced its subject free from "the excesses of radicalism."[12]

Further confirmation of King's status as a "national" leader came in June 1958, when he met President Eisenhower as part of a black delegation that included Wilkins, Randolph, and Lester Granger, the head of the National Urban League. The meeting provided additional evidence of friendly Republican interest in King, for the White House invitation came in response to a request from SCLC. Rustin and Levison drafted a memorandum to be presented to the president, which the four leaders discussed at a seven-hour meeting at the NAACP's Washington office the night before the appointment. King's advisers also "labored long into the night" to provide King with a statement on Adam Clayton Powell, the black congressman from Harlem, who had invited himself to the White House conference and was decidedly unwelcome. The conference itself yielded nothing of substance and evoked a palpable lack of enthusiasm in the black press. Randolph suggested that the four leaders hold a public forum to combat this "pessimism and cynicism," but only King supported the idea and it fell through. Nevertheless, King had come a long way in two years. Although it was far from clear who or what he represented, he was being honored by universities, indulged by foreign heads of state, and consulted by the president.[13]

Despite King's soaring personal prestige, however, SCLC still confronted grave difficulties in establishing itself as an organization. Some of its problems were the usual kind of teething troubles that afflict new organizations. It took time to form a stable group of officers, for some of the board members soon lost interest or, for various other reasons, ceased to participate. T. J. Jemison of Baton Rouge decided that his activities with the National Baptist Convention (which he would eventually head) left him no time for his duties as SCLC's secretary. Fred Shuttlesworth of Birmingham took over the post. A. L. Davis of New Orleans, SCLC's second vice-president, also dropped out, to be replaced by Joseph E. Lowery of Mobile. These changes underscored the fact that Alabama was SCLC's center of gravity.

A more serious problem was the absence of a clear strategy. SCLC's

initial goal had been to spread the example of Montgomery by supporting bus boycotts in other cities. But with the exceptions of Tallahassee
(where the boycott failed to achieve a clear victory) and Rock Hill,
South Carolina, (where a six-month boycott put the bus company out
of business) no other sustained bus boycotts took place. In cities like
New Orleans, Atlanta, and Mobile, compliance with court-ordered desegregation made long boycotts unnecessary. "What happened,"
Levison recalled, "was that in some of the cities victory came very
fast. The city power structure . . . decided that they didn't want to go
through a Montgomery. So they quietly desegregated buses. And, therefore, a great wave of boycotts didn't develop."[14]

Thus many of the "boycotts" often bracketed with Montgomery and
Tallahassee were little more than one-day protests designed to provoke
the necessary arrests on which to base a legal challenge after the precedent of *Browder* v. *Gayle*, the MIA-backed suit which brought about
integration in Montgomery. Such, for example, was the Atlanta boycott, a decorous affair in which a group of black ministers had themselves arrested and then filed suit in federal court. Their action had the
tacit support of Mayor William B. Hartsfield and of the Atlanta Transit
Co., which agreed to mount a token legal fight and then accede to
court-ordered integration. Blacks made no attempt to boycott the segregated buses during the two years that it took the case to wind its way
through the courts. Similar tactics prevailed in Memphis, Baton Rouge,
New Orleans, and Savannah.[15]

Even when, as in the case of Tallahassee, cities ignored *Browder* v.
Gayle or tried to circumvent court orders, blacks did not always resort
to boycotts. In cities like Miami they were too few, proportionately, to
make a boycott succeed. Elsewhere, the repressive climate, combined
with timid or erratic leadership, made the boycott weapon ineffective.
In Birmingham, for example, police intimidation, poor planning, black
disunity, and the problem of devising alternative transportation in
such a large city all militated against a successful bus boycott. When
Fred Shuttlesworth tried to launch one in October 1958, it fizzled out
after a few weeks. "We tried . . . to take Montgomery to Birmingham,
and fell flat on our faces," Glenn Smiley recalled, "because Montgomery was not exportable."[16]

When the bus boycott movement failed to develop, therefore, SCLC
decided to shift its efforts toward voter registration. A focus on voting
had a number of putative advantages. The civil rights bill currently
before Congress dealt with voting rights, and it included a proposal for
a federal Civil Rights Commission to investigate complaints of dis-

crimination. Second, SCLC calculated that Southern whites were far less united in their opposition to black voting than they were in their opposition to integration. "In almost all other spheres," King reasoned, "confused people can argue the separate but equal doctrine. Here they cannot. . . . The right to vote does not raise the issue of social mixing." The benefits of an expanded black electorate seemed self-evident. Finally, through a voter registration drive, SCLC could involve its local affiliates in a coordinated regional program.[17]

Rustin and Levison drew up plans for the program in July 1957, after discussing the idea with King and Ralph Abernathy, SCLC's treasurer and King's close friend. Their plans called for a budget of $200,000 to finance a central office in Atlanta, with a full-time executive director to administer the program and a paid staff of field-workers to implement it. The program itself involved the setting up of city and county voter registration committees, to be formed from churches, civic groups, and other local organizations. These committees would hold voting "clinics," encourage people to register, and collect evidence of deliberate disfranchisement. By establishing this network of local committees, SCLC could build a "strong mass organization indigenous to the South," especially in areas like Alabama where the NAACP had been suppressed.[18]

SCLC's relationship to the NAACP was an issue of extreme sensitivity, to which Rustin, Levison, and King devoted considerable thought. They took great pains to avoid any impression that SCLC sought to challenge or supplant the NAACP. They decided not to institute an individual membership program. They took care not to publicly criticize the NAACP. Above all, they sought the active cooperation of the NAACP in SCLC's voter registration efforts. King invited an NAACP representative to serve on SCLC's national advisory board. He also met Roy Wilkins in November 1957 to discuss how best to coordinate their voter registration work. "I am certain that the efforts of the Southern Christian Leadership Conference and those of the NAACP . . . will be mutually helpful," Wilkins wrote King afterwards.[19]

Behind these assurances of cooperation, however, the two organizations eyed each other warily. The NAACP's national officials immediately perceived SCLC as an unwelcome competitor and a threat to its Southern base. According to James Farmer, who joined the NAACP's New York headquarters in 1959, fundraising lay at the heart of their concern: "King's mass meetings in churches across the South were drawing away dollars that otherwise would have come to the association." In addition, a large proportion of the NAACP's Southern branch presidents were ministers; if they switched their allegiance to SCLC they would take the fundraising potential of their churches with them. Even if they remained in the NAACP, ministers might involve themselves in SCLC fundraising to the detriment of the older organization. The NAACP also suspected SCLC's leaders of making a deliberate attempt "to use our staff, our branch officers and our members to build their organization." When Medgar Evers, the NAACP's Mississippi field secretary, volunteered to serve as SCLC's assistant secretary, Roy Wilkins told him to "quietly ease out" of the new organization.[20]

In a confidential report to Wilkins, John M. Brooks, the NAACP's voter registration director, noted that although SCLC's leaders "were too shrewd to make outright criticisms of the NAACP," they "constantly played up the fact" that SCLC represented "the only salvation for the Negroes in the South." In Brooks's view, however, SCLC was still a one-man band, and, as such, quite ineffectual. "There is no discipline among the Baptist ministers," he observed; many of them gave only lip service to the organization. Some, he contended, saw SCLC as a threat to their status. "Take Rev. King, Jr. away and the Conference would die a natural death."[21]

The NAACP's fears and suspicions were not entirely groundless. The claims of SCLC's founders that the new organization intended merely to "supplement" the NAACP were disingenuous: despite its attempts to minimize direct competition, SCLC inevitably competed with the NAACP for money, support, and influence. The very fact of SCLC's existence, moreover, was an implied criticism of the NAACP's effectiveness. Rustin, Levison, and Baker had the NAACP's inadequacies very much in mind when they encouraged SCLC's formation, and King evidently shared many of their reservations. In the early days of the Montgomery bus boycott he reportedly complained about the supercilious attitude of the NAACP national office towards local protests, noting that the association had not seen fit to make even "a small contribution" to the MIA. Later, when he asked the NAACP to help defray the MIA's legal costs, he complained to Wilkins that people were giving money at NAACP mass meetings with the erroneous impression that it was going to help the bus boycott. The NAACP eventually provided lawyers for the MIA's crucial cases and paid the bulk of the boycotters' legal expenses.[22]

What made SCLC's growth all the more galling to the NAACP was the fact that SCLC inadvertently benefitted from the South's harassment of the association. Clearly, when the state of Alabama put the

NAACP out of action completely, there was an obvious need for an alternative, locally based organization. Elsewhere in the South, however, where the NAACP was being persecuted but had not been suppressed, SCLC may have further weakened the NAACP's support by offering an apparently "safer," less radical alternative. The evidence on this point is sketchy, and there is none to suggest that SCLC set out to deliberately undermine the NAACP. In many cases, people would participate in an SCLC event when fear kept them away from the NAACP. Nevertheless, the existence of SCLC probably persuaded some to curtail their involvement in the more vulnerable NAACP. It could even be argued that SCLC's leaders were deserting the NAACP at its hour of maximum need, failing to stand up for it when it most needed defending. According to the editor of *Jet,* Robert E. Johnson, who visited Montgomery in the first week of the boycott, King argued that organizing the protest through the NAACP would necessitate "a two-front battle," which the boycotters could ill afford. "What we really need is a new organization, still with the NAACP's everything, and make it homegrown."[23]

King sometimes displayed a certain naivete over matters of organizational self-interest. According to some colleagues, he was a pure idealist whose commitment to the cause of social justice far outweighed any concern for organizational empire building. He had little patience with the NAACP's fear of competition, and regarded organizational rivalry as a petty distraction. He did not understand why the NAACP failed to welcome SCLC's appearance, and grew resentful of the "seeds of dissension being sown by persons in the top echelons in the NAACP."[24]

Too much emphasis on King's idealism, however, obscures another crucial facet of his leadership: an astute pragmatism. It is scarcely credible that King had no interest in building up his organization. Quite the contrary: he provided the driving force for SCLC's inception and growth. He was also notably shrewd in protecting SCLC from potential threats. In particular, as Aldon Morris points out, he marshalled "a complex array of arguments to decrease NAACP animosity." At King's initiative, for example, SCLC had several conferences with Wilkins and his colleagues in an effort to minimize organizational conflict. At a meeting in late 1959, according to James Farmer, King suggested a quid pro quo over fundraising: if the NAACP allowed it to concentrate on church rallies, SCLC would refrain from adopting a membership scheme. But Gloster Current, the NAACP's director of branches (whom Joseph Lowery dubbed Roy Wilkins's "hatchet-man"), rejected King's offer as a one-sided bargain: the NAACP would be giving, he argued, while receiving nothing in return. King might have pointed out that he himself continually raised money for the association by speaking at its meetings. To the NAACP, however, SCLC's very existence represented a threat.[25]

The mutual dislike of SCLC and the NAACP stemmed from organizational rivalry rather than from any deep-seated ideological differences. To be sure, King became the leading exponent of nonviolent direct action, a strategy about which the NAACP had profound reservations. Yet King repeatedly emphasized that direct action was no substitute for litigation and political pressure: it merely added drive and momentum to those methods. It was in SCLC's interests, of course, to make such disclaimers, but they also represented King's actual assessment of the situation. He recognized quite clearly that the example of Montgomery could not and should not be reproduced in a mechanical fashion; as he told the Atlanta conference of May 1956, "Collective resistance must be used with care in a controlled situation."[26]

For all the NAACP's worries, SCLC had little impact on that organization's fundraising because between 1957 and 1960 SCLC raised little money itself. The funds that Rustin and Levison anticipated from foundations and trade unions failed to materialize, although SCLC did receive a donation of $11,000 from the United Packinghouse Workers. This windfall was exceptional, however, and it represented a collection among the members, organized by Russell Lasley, rather than a contribution from the union's funds. Some money arrived from sympathetic whites, including such well-known figures as Gov. Averell Harriman of New York and former Sen. Frank Graham of South Carolina. A trickle of money came from abroad; Canon John Collins, dean of St. Paul's Cathedral, was an early contributor. But without any dues-paying members or a systematic fundraising program, SCLC depended upon the black church for the bulk of its income. Some of this came from the South, via the affiliates, but according to Morris the major share derived from "black church-oriented mass meetings outside the South." Its income from all sources, however, barely kept SCLC afloat: in 1960 its annual budget amounted to about $60,000, and its staff consisted of Ella Baker, the acting executive director, and two clerical workers.[27]

By then, Baker had spent more than two years trying to get SCLC off the ground, although she had gone to Atlanta in January 1958 with the intention of staying just long enough to set up an office and launch

SCLC's voter registration program, the "Crusade for Citizenship." She had to start from scratch. "I worked out of my vest pocket and whatever access I could have to a telephone at Ebenezer Baptist Church," she recalled. "Frequently, I had to make use of pay coin telephones." With the help of Sam Williams, King's old philosophy teacher at Morehouse College and an SCLC board member, she managed to find office space. She then set in motion the Crusade for Citizenship, which kicked off on February 12, 1958, when SCLC affiliates staged rallies in twenty cities. Meanwhile a committee of board members cast about for a permanent executive director, preferably a man and a minister. The Reverend John L. Tilley, a Baltimore pastor who had achieved notable success in the field of voter registration, took up the post in May.[28]

The achievements of the Crusade for Citizenship were not impressive. Voter registration work required extensive local organization, something that SCLC simply did not possess, and the plan to establish a network of local committees never went beyond the drawing board. SCLC had budgeted $200,000 for the project, but it raised only about a quarter of that sum. "It is now imperative that we assemble and work out a clearly defined program . . . and a method for future financial expansion," King wrote Abernathy in June. The situation had improved little by the end of the year, however. "The organization is now burning the furniture to keep the house warm," Levison warned. "To run down 'out of gas' would be extremely demoralizing for the group and discrediting in the public eye." SCLC could only generate significant financial support, he added, if it did something. Plans to establish a "national advisory board" to assist SCLC's fundraising appeals had to be shelved because not enough "big names" could be induced to support the effort.[29] Nine months after it began its voter registration program, SCLC had still not submitted any evidence of discrimination to the new Civil Rights Commission. Unfairly perhaps, SCLC blamed Tilley for its poor showing, and in April 1959 King asked for his resignation. Ella Baker agreed to fill the gap again. She even accepted a cut in her salary.[30]

Thus for most of 1958 and 1959 Baker had to work virtually single-handed: "There was no machinery, no staff, except me." And in addition to coordinating the Crusade for Citizenship, she also had to make frequent field trips, prepare SCLC's newsletter, arrange the conventions and board meetings, and make reports to both King and SCLC's administrative committee. Given this burden, she did well to encourage SCLC affiliates to compile sworn complaints of discrimination.

With Baker's help, the MIA presented a list of such complaints at the first public hearings held by the Civil Rights Commission, in Montgomery in December 1958. Baker then went to Shreveport to work with Dr. C. O. Simpkins and the United Christian Movement. After a daylong "stand-in" outside the Caddo Parish voter registration office, some sixty-eight people agreed to file complaints with the Civil Rights Commission. Because of a legal challenge by the state authorities, however, the commission had to delay its Louisiana hearings until December 1960.[31]

Baker received little assistance from King, who was absorbed in writing, fundraising, and travelling, or from the other ministers on SCLC's administrative committee. In fact, she became increasingly disenchanted with SCLC's leadership and structure. Accustomed to the disciplined bureaucracies of organizations like the NAACP and the YWCA, she found the haphazard informality of the Southern black church exasperating. She also resented the arrogance and egocentricity of many black ministers. They contributed little to SCLC's administration, she later complained, and showed scant consideration for SCLC's staff. The ministers used to begin the day late and then expect the secretaries and typists to work on into the evening. Baker was the first in a long line of administrators whose attempts to instill discipline and efficiency into SCLC were as often as not baffled.[32]

Baker also found it difficult to get along with King. "He wasn't the kind of person you could engage in dialogue with," she later stated, "if the dialogue questioned the almost exclusive rightness of his position." She came to regard King as a rather pompous preacher, with little political awareness but with an inflated sense of self-importance and a condescending attitude to women. King's most recent biographer has dismissed these criticisms on the grounds that Baker is an embittered and unreliable witness. Yet hostile witnesses are sometimes more reliable than friendly ones. The assertion that King was intolerant of criticism is wide of the mark, but it is plain that he liked to be treated with a certain amount of deference, especially from people he perceived as subordinates. Baker, a veteran activist old enough to be his mother, was the last person to treat King deferentially. The fact that she was a woman, moreover, certainly affected the way King responded to her criticisms: like most of the other preachers in SCLC, he found it difficult to treat women as intellectual equals. The two women who served on SCLC's executive staff during the 1960s both testified to the male attitudes which restricted their influence. "It's a man's organization," noted Septima Clark, "and I don't think women's words had any weight whatsoever. . . . I kind of had the feeling that [Dr. King] didn't feel as if they should do things." Dorothy Cotton was less sweeping; "I did have a decision-making role," she claimed, "but I'm also very conscious of the male chauvinism that existed. . . . [Black preachers] are some of the most chauvinistic of them all." King himself possessed a decidedly conservative view of sexual roles. "The primary obligation of the woman is motherhood," he once wrote.[33]

Baker also became increasingly skeptical about the "cult of personality" that King seemed to tolerate and even encourage. At the first anniversary celebration of the Montgomery bus boycott she complained that the printed literature said little about what the movement stood for, focusing almost entirely on the leaders. In Baker's view, mass movements ought to be organized democratically, from the bottom up. SCLC should be trying to develop indigenous local leadership, she believed, instead of encouraging blacks to await a Moses figure to deliver them out of their bondage. She regarded the latter approach as unhealthy, unrealistic, and ideologically backward. SCLC's dependence on King, she felt, retarded the emergence of a democratic mass movement.[34]

Other people, too, criticized King's apparent willingness to exalt his own role. Perusing the manuscript of *Stride Toward Freedom*, Stanley Levison cautioned King against implying that "everything depended on you"; as it stood, his account of the bus boycott conveyed an impression of egocentricity. From her vantage point in Montgomery, Virginia Durr catalogued the grumblings and complaints of local activists who felt that the MIA had become a one-man band, with everything revolving round King. "He cannot stand criticism," she observed, "and has to be a LEADER of the sheep, not a real democratic worker along with the others." Lawrence Reddick, the historian from Alabama State College who sat on SCLC's board, referred to these criticisms in his 1959 biography of King, *Crusader Without Violence*. There was a growing feeling, he wrote, that King was "taking too many bows and enjoying them, . . . forgetting that Montgomery had been the result of collective thought and collective action." This, plus his obvious liking for fine clothes, expensive restaurants, and first-class hotels, placed a question mark over his sincerity; even some of his MIA colleagues "felt that he was bent on making a fortune." King was also "too much in motion," Reddick thought, "flying about the country, speaking almost everywhere."[35]

Dissatisfaction with SCLC's progress came to a head in October 1959, when King and the board of directors, prodded by Baker, took a long, hard look at the organization's direction. SCLC had received virtually no publicity, they lamented. It had barely scratched the surface in the field of voter registration. It had failed to concert action among the local affiliates. It had been holding too many speech-filled conferences, too close together, leaving no time for analysis and long-term planning. It had not yet developed a "positive, dynamic and dramatic program." Finally, it was the board's view that King had yet to give "the maximum of his time and energies to the work of SCLC."[36]

This reappraisal led to several positive steps. The number of board meetings was cut from three a year to two, the number of conventions from two to one. Recognizing that SCLC's thirteen-member administrative committee was too large and cumbersome to function effectively, the board appointed a subcommittee of five to assist Baker in working out a program for 1960. This small inner group consisted of four clergymen (Sam Williams, Ralph Abernathy, Fred Shuttlesworth, and Joseph Lowery) and one layman, Lawrence Reddick. King agreed to resign his pastorate at Dexter Avenue Baptist Church so that he could move to Atlanta and devote more time to SCLC. Henceforth he would share the pastorate of Ebenezer Baptist Church with his father, an arrangement that freed him of the obligation to preach every Sunday. It also had the advantage of enabling SCLC to utilize Ebenezer's spacious education building.[37]

King submitted his own recommendations to the "committee on future program" on October 27. SCLC had to continue its work on voter registration, he argued, but it should also consider moving into "other areas." Two suggestions of Ella Baker merited study: setting up literacy classes in cooperation with the Highlander Folk School; and having James Lawson, the FOR's Southern field secretary, train "action teams" in the techniques of nonviolent protest. King's strongest recommendation was that SCLC hire Bayard Rustin as its public relations director. He conceded that such an appointment entailed "possible perils." Nevertheless, King felt that "Mr. Rustin's unique organizational ability, his technical competence, and his distinctive ability to stick with a job until it is thoroughly completed" justified the risk. He promised that Rustin "would quietly resign" in the event of any embarrassing publicity about his past. King asked Levison to let him know the moment Rustin returned from Africa: "We are in desperate need of his services."[38]

In assessing SCLC's early failures, contemporary observers and later commentators sometimes pointed to a certain naivete in King's conception of nonviolence. According to the political scientist David J. Garrow, for example, King initially viewed direct action as a means of persuasion, a way of convincing Southern whites of the moral injustice of segregation and discrimination. After the failure of SCLC's protests in Albany, Georgia, in 1961–62, however, King abandoned this view as unrealistic, adopting a strategy of "nonviolent coercion." Thereafter, Garrow argues, instead of trying to persuade their adversaries of the rightness of their goals, King and SCLC sought to put pressure on the federal government by staging dramatic confrontations that publicized segregationist violence. Elliott M. Zashin, another political scientist, pointed out that their experiences in the Deep South convinced most black activists, including King, that nonviolent protest had virtually no effect on the thinking of white racists: its only value lay in its utility as a form of pressure.[39]

Without doubt, King became more hardheaded and politically astute as a result of age and experience. There is little evidence, however, that he ever believed that nonviolent protest functioned solely, or even mainly, as a form of moral persuasion. Quite the contrary: in his earliest public writings King equated nonviolence with struggle and resistance organized through a militant mass movement. Philosophically and in practice, he explicitly rejected the notion that blacks—or any other oppressed group—could overcome their subjection through ethical appeals and rational argument: they also needed an effective means of pressure. The assertion that King failed to appreciate the necessity for power is simply erroneous. "A mass movement exercising nonviolence," he wrote in 1957, "is an object lesson in power under discipline." Having led a successful yearlong economic boycott supported by fifty thousand black people, he surely knew what he was talking about. A *New York Times* profile published in March 1956 noted that King stressed the Hegelian concept of "struggle as a law of growth," and that he regarded the bus boycott "as just one aspect of a world-wide revolt of oppressed peoples."[40]

To emphasize King's political realism is not to deny his underlying idealism. For King, nonviolence was an ethical imperative, a total way of life, and his commitment to it was absolute and consistent. Moreover, he did sometimes imply that nonviolent protest worked partly through persuasion, by awakening "a sense of moral shame in the opponent." The nonviolent resister, he explained, touched the heart and conscience of his adversary, converting an oppressor into a friend.[41] But the significance of such statements should not be exaggerated. King never made an unqualified assertion that nonviolent protest succeeded through moral persuasion. He admitted that "when the underprivileged demand freedom, the privileged first react with bitterness and resistance"; nonviolence could not change the "heart" of the oppressor until the social structures that perpetuated injustice and false ideology had been destroyed. King's belief that some adversaries might still be touched by the suffering and goodwill of the nonviolent resister was quite genuine, but it was marginal, not central, to his strategy of protest. When King spoke of "converting" the oppressor, therefore, he was thinking of a long-term historical process rather than an immediate personal response. King was not as naive as his religious rhetoric sometimes implied.[42]

SCLC's difficulties stemmed less from King's political un-worldliness or his administrative inexperience, both of which have been greatly exaggerated, than from the limitations of SCLC's structure, the conservatism and quiescence of many blacks, and SCLC's own failure to experiment with new forms of direct action.

The weaknesses of SCLC's structure soon became apparent. The local affiliates were independent bodies subject to no organizational discipline. Moreover, like churches of the same denomination everywhere, each Negro Baptist congregation was a sovereign body, impervious to outside interference. Requesting the affiliates' cooperation was one thing, getting it quite another. In practice it proved extremely difficult to mobilize them behind a common program. When it came to taking initiatives, King had to be very careful not to tread on the toes of local leaders. Men like Steele and Shuttlesworth were proud, sensitive, egotistical individuals who, to quote one commentator, "saw themselves as potential Martin Luther Kings, and . . . did not want his organization moving into their parishes to capture the power and the glory."[43] They might seek SCLC's help, and they might invite King to address a mass meeting, but they would not defer to him. "Having worked with many of our Negro leaders," King told Glenn Smiley, "I am aware of the various problems that arise if one is not very discreet in dealing with them."[44]

SCLC's lack of impact before 1960 also stemmed from the reluctance of Southern blacks to embrace direct action. Although the Montgomery bus boycott, in the words of Meier and Rudwick, "made an extraordinary impression on Afro-Americans across the country," blacks did not rush to emulate it. Proposals to use mass direct action against segregated theaters, motels, restaurants, and other businesses aroused even less enthusiasm. Few blacks doubted that they had a clear right to deny patronage to a business or public service—they could spend their money as they pleased. But it was one thing to boycott segregated buses, quite another to "sit in," or otherwise physically intrude, at the premises of a private business. Such tactics involved breaking the law, courting arrest, and risking fines and incarceration. True, all state and local segregation laws were of dubious standing in

light of *Brown* v. *Board of Education* and *Browder* v. *Gayle.* There
seemed to be a distinction, however, between public services and private businesses. The right of private individuals to practice racial discrimination was a legal gray area which involved the sensitive and—
especially in the South—emotional issue of property rights. And this
was ground upon which many blacks preferred not to tread.[45]

The postboycott histories of the Montgomery Improvement Association and the Inter-Civic Council both underlined this reluctance to
embrace the tactics of civil disobedience and physical confrontation. In
Montgomery, the MIA evinced little enthusiasm for directly challenging other aspects of segregation; further progress in desegregation had
to wait until the 1964 Civil Rights Act. King's influence waned, and,
according to one study, "reversion to accommodation as the leadership
form . . . was an accomplished fact within eighteen months after the
boycott."[46] It was a similar story in Tallahassee, where C. K. Steele
proved unable to persuade the board of the ICC to endorse civil disobedience or the "jail without bail" tactic. Ministers like Steele, it should
be added, often came under pressure from their congregations to limit
or tone down their civil rights activities.[47]

The difficulties involved in mobilizing blacks behind more radical
tactics cannot be attributed to conservative attitudes alone. No matter
how they felt about direct action, the economic facts of life constrained most blacks. Economic reprisals had been relatively uncom-
mon during the Montgomery and Tallahassee bus boycotts—it was
difficult to visit retribution upon an entire community. Arrest on a sit-
in, a picket line, or a demonstration, on the other hand, invited economic disaster. Apart from the cost of bail (usually exorbitant), legal
fees (often considerable), and fines (frequently heavy), there was the
real possibility of a spell in jail. Either way, fine or jail, arrestees faced
the likelihood, often amounting to a near certainty, of losing their jobs.
Again and again during the course of the civil rights movement, SCLC
was confounded by the fact that relatively few blacks would take part
in its protests if the action entailed a high risk of arrest.

Only in 1960, when black students entered the fray in large numbers, did a broad assault on segregation become possible. In the late
1950s the campuses seemed quiet. A sociologist who taught at a black
college in Augusta, Georgia, noted that "apathy and indifference" prevailed among the students, an observation that could be applied to the
great majority of such institutions. Yet black youth were already beginning to stir. The students at Florida A&M had initiated and sustained
the Tallahassee bus boycott. Another portent was the boycott of

classes conducted by students at State Teachers College in Orangeburg, South Carolina, in April 1956—a protest against harassment by the white citizens council and the persecution of the NAACP. In 1958, in Nashville, a group of students began to hold workshops on non-violence. The year 1958 also saw the first "Youth March for Integrated Schools," a rally in Washington, D.C., prompted by the Little Rock crisis. Like the Prayer Pilgrimage, it was organized by Rustin and Levison under the auspices of A. Philip Randolph. "It definitely triggered a student movement for civil rights on major campuses," Levison wrote King. "Our efforts have long been hampered by the relative apathy of youth and labor."[48]

The student sit-in movement of 1960 solved none of SCLC's organizational problems. But it did infuse SCLC with new blood, new dynamism, new sources of financial support, and new tactical concepts. The difficulty of mobilizing black adults remained, but the demonstration in 1960 that black parents would rally behind their children pointed towards an answer. During the heyday of the civil rights movement, young people—teenagers and children—furnished the most numerous and eager volunteers for jail. "They are your militants," C. K. Steele observed. "They are your soldiers." The tactics of nonviolent protest still needed refining, but SCLC soon learned that the surest way to mobilize the adults was first to involve their children. Young people made up the initial phalanx, the entering wedge.[49]

From the standpoint of 1970, Stanley Levison interpreted the late 1950s as a time when "a little-observed internal struggle between two tendencies" took place. One tendency, articulated by King and SCLC, stressed mass action and direct action; the other, most effectively represented by the NAACP, was firmly wedded to the established legal and political processes. By the end of the decade the second viewpoint was still in the ascendant, and the NAACP regarded direct action with great suspicion. Levison vividly remembered a discussion of direct action between John Morsell of the NAACP and Socialist leader Norman Thomas: "John Morsell said he and Roy Wilkins had been talking about mass action, and they came to the conclusion that mass action had been discredited by Hitler. That Hitler had shown that he could pull hundreds of thousands of people out in public squares and, as a consequence, the average person looked with contempt and little sympathy on mass gatherings. . . . They concluded that the day of mass action was over. Norman Thomas exploded and said, 'You're exactly wrong. The day of mass action has just begun.'" The Socialist leader had been right, Levison added, "because then the '60s followed."[50]

Three

Sit-ins and Freedom Rides

Although it had been founded to promote direct action in the South, SCLC was itself caught unawares by the mushrooming of nonviolent protests in 1960–61. It found itself a marginal participant in events initiated by other people and other organizations. When black students launched a sit-in movement to protest against segregated lunch counters, they did so spontaneously. The daring and imaginative Freedom Rides, launched by the Congress of Racial Equality in 1961, pushed SCLC yet further from the limelight.

The sit-ins and the Freedom Rides not only exposed SCLC's organizational weaknesses, they also cast doubt upon King's own qualities of leadership. While others were pioneering innovative methods of nonviolent direct action, King seemed strangely ambivalent about embracing the new tactics by personal example. Although fulsome in his praise of the lunch counter protests, for example, he showed little eagerness to lead a sit-in himself. His vacillations over the Freedom Rides were even more acute, and his failure to go to jail brought his tactical judgement—and even his personal integrity—into question.

King's failure to lead was not mere irresolution. He lacked a strong local base, and was understandably reluctant to join movements not of his own making. He and his advisers were also keenly aware that King's symbolic coin would rapidly become devalued if he went to jail too often, or at the wrong time at the wrong place. It is often forgotten, moreover, that SCLC's principal thrust before 1963 was in the field of voter registration, not direct action. Whatever the reason, however, King's leadership seemed less than inspiring and betrayed an impression of timidity and indecisiveness. SCLC's dynamism was not being generated by King but by locally based leaders like Steele in Tallahassee, Abernathy in Montgomery, Shuttlesworth in Birmingham, and, especially, James Lawson in Nashville. SCLC's response to the upsurge of direct action in 1960–61 consisted less of a planned, central thrust than of a series of uncoordinated local initiatives. There was still no coherent strategy.

The period saw SCLC in a state of transition. In 1960 it was still a blueprint for an organization; two years later it had acquired a professional fundraising apparatus, recruited a cadre of full-time organizers, and received a life-giving injection of administrative talent. It was also a time when SCLC cast about for a strategy, for a means of applying the tactical innovations of 1960–61 in a manner calculated to produce the maximum amount of social change. In Birmingham, in 1963, SCLC finally pulled the right levers and became an initiator of events rather than a follower of events. The protests in Albany, Georgia, in 1961–62 marked SCLC's first, fumbling, unsuccessful attempt to make this crucial transition.

The sit-ins caught SCLC by surprise; nobody anticipated that the solitary protest of four black students from North Carolina A&T would, within a matter of weeks, be emulated throughout the South. The action of Joseph McNeil, Ezell Blair, Jr., Franklin McCain, and David Richmond was simplicity itself: they sat down at the lunch counter of the Woolworth's store in downtown Greensboro and—having made sure to carry receipts showing that they had purchased goods elsewhere in the store—asked for four cups of coffee. When the waitress, acting according to the time-hallowed custom, declined to serve the Negroes they, in turn, refused to vacate their stools, leaving only when the store closed. The following morning they returned with more students, the day after with even more. By Friday, February 5, the fifth day of the protests, hundreds of black students crowded the lunch counters at Woolworth's and Kress. On Saturday both stores closed their doors to the public. As a stone dropped in still water sets off expanding, concentric, circular ripples, the example of the Greensboro sit-in spread first to nearby cities in North Carolina and then to sur-rounding states. *Time* called it "a non-violent protest the likes of which the U.S. had never seen." By the end of 1960 about seventy thousand black students had "sat in" at a lunch counter, marched in a demonstration, or walked on a picket line. Some thirty-six hundred had been arrested.[1]

King flew hither and thither to exhort the protesters. But with little money and no field staff, SCLC's role in the sit-ins depended for the most part upon initiatives from its local affiliates. Indeed, SCLC ex-erted its greatest influence not through King, but through a student of theology at Vanderbilt University, James M. Lawson, Jr. Preaching a similar mixture of Christian pacifism and Gandhian civil disobe-dience, Lawson became the protagonist of the Nashville student move-ment and an important figure in both SCLC and SNCC, the new organization that emerged from the sit-ins.

The same age as King, thirty-one, Lawson had embraced philosoph-ical nonviolence much earlier than his more famous contemporary. Raised in Ohio, and educated in the progressive atmosphere of Bald-win-Wallace College in Berea, Lawson became a pacifist while still in his teens. He demonstrated the courage of his convictions during the Korean War when, rather than register as a conscientious objector, he spent thirteen months in prison for refusing to cooperate with the draft. Paroled in 1952, and ordained in the mainly white United Meth-odist church, he lived in India during the next three years, working as a teacher and campus minister at Hislop College in Nagpur. Returning to the United States in 1956, he enrolled at Oberlin College to study for a degree in theology.[2]

Lawson and King first met in 1957; with their shared interest in philosophy and theology, and their common commitment to non-violence, the two men became friends. Dropping out of Oberlin, Law-son took on the post of Southern field secretary for the FOR and opened a regional office in Nashville. In 1958 he enrolled in Vander-bilt's divinity school, taking over the weekly discussions on non-violence that Glenn Smiley had started. These Tuesday evening sessions (or "workshops") attracted students from Vanderbilt and, more particularly, from Fisk University, a black institution, and from the American Baptist Theological Seminary. About a dozen young blacks became regular attenders, and they soaked up Lawson's idealism. "Jim was really the thinker in this group," recalled John Lewis, a future leader of SNCC. "In his own right, he was a great moral force. We regarded him as our real teacher in nonviolence."[3]

In November 1959, Lewis and a number of others formed the Nashville Student Movement and began laying plans for a campaign of direct action against segregation in the city's department stores. While the Greensboro four were first off the mark, the Nashville students were close behind, justly meriting King's praise as "the best organized and most disciplined in the Southland."[4] Lawson was among the first to be arrested, and the press, not entirely accurately, cast him in the role of ringleader. Mayor Ben West charged him with fomenting anarchy. On March 3, in a move that prompted the dean of the divinity school and eleven other faculty members to resign in protest, Vanderbilt University expelled him.[5]

Lawson also provided an important link between the Nashville Student Movement and SCLC, both through his friendship with King and his connection with the Nashville Christian Leadership Council, SCLC's local affiliate. The NCLC, headed by the Reverend Kelly Miller Smith, rendered crucial assistance to the students. It not only proffered moral support but also, more to the point, raised bail money and organized an economic boycott of the downtown merchants. Smith himself served as the chief black spokesman on the biracial committee appointed by Mayor West to work out a settlement.[6] It was Lawson's personal influence with the student leaders, however, that proved the more important link. The Lawson workshops served as a training ground for the leaders of the Nashville sit-ins. More than that: they brought together an extraordinary group of people who went on to make outstanding contributions to the civil rights movement. Lawson's disciples helped to found SNCC in 1960; they kept the Freedom Rides going in 1961; they took the civil rights movement to Mississippi in the same year. Three of them—James Bevel, C. T. Vivian, and Lawson himself—became close associates of King in SCLC.

The support given the sit-ins by SCLC's affiliates depended on the energy, courage, and resourcefulness of the local leadership. In Tallahassee, Birmingham, Montgomery, and elsewhere, ministers connected with SCLC backed the students with great determination. In Montgomery, Ralph Abernathy tried to rally the MIA behind the pro-

test. When nine students were expelled from Alabama State College at
the behest of Governor John Patterson—an action which aroused black
support far more effectively than the sit-ins themselves—Abernathy
and another minister, Robert DuBose, led eight hundred blacks to a
"prayer meeting" on the steps of the state capitol. Upon leaving the
church, however, a crowd of several thousand whites barred their way,
forcing them to retreat. The police eventually restrained the whites
but did nothing to facilitate the march, and the Montgomery sit-in
movement petered out as the authorities outlawed demonstrations and
clamped down on the college. Among those forced out was Lawrence
D. Reddick, who found another teaching position in Maryland. Despite
the activism of Abernathy and one or two other ministers, the MIA
failed to mobilize the adult community with anything like the solidarity of the Montgomery bus boycott. As S. S. Seay put it, "A lot of
our people don't seem to understand what the young people are
doing—they say they don't agree with them."[7]

The results of the sit-ins in Nashville and Montgomery typified
what became a larger pattern. The student protests split the South. In
the upper South, and in areas like Texas and southern Florida, segregation began to crumble under the twin pressure of the sit-in and the
boycott. On March 19, stores in San Antonio peacefully integrated
their lunch counters. In May, Nashville followed suit. By 1961 more
than eighty other towns and cities had undergone some desegregation.
Moreover, the sit-ins exposed the moral weakness of the South's defense of segregation. The concept of "separate but equal" at least had a
theoretical semblance of fairness. The total exclusion of blacks from
eating facilities was far more difficult to justify. Increasingly, segregationists resorted to the narrow doctrine of property rights to explain
and justify such practices; in doing so, they tacitly evacuated the moral
high ground. The sit-ins even led one Southern governor, LeRoy Collins of Florida, to criticize segregation in a statewide radio and television broadcast: while it might be legally enforceable, he argued,
segregation was both bad for business and morally wrong. The South's
ideological barricade had been breached.[8]

Throughout most of the Deep South, on the other hand, whites
resisted the sit-ins unrelentingly and effectively. "The white people are
not planning to give an inch," wrote Virginia Durr from Montgomery.
"You never saw such unanimity in your life." In city after city, the
police suppressed public protests and allowed Klan elements to
threaten, manhandle, and even assault black demonstrators. When
Fred Shuttlesworth and two other ministers staged a sit-in in Bir-

mingham, they were arrested for vagrancy and held for three days before being allowed bail. Their action failed utterly to spark a larger movement. Even in Florida, segregationist sentiment remained strong. The reaction to Collins's Jacksonville speech was largely hostile, the governor recalled: "Many just said I had sold out to the blacks—only they didn't call them 'blacks.' " In Tallahassee, despite strong support for the sit-ins from the large student population and despite an effective boycott of downtown stores, repression soon gained the upper hand. In Louisiana, Mississippi, Alabama, Georgia, and South Carolina, the first wave of sit-ins collapsed in almost total defeat. Thousands of students were expelled from state-supported colleges.[9]

The sit-ins represented both a revolt against segregation and a departure from the cautious legalism of the NAACP. Yet the students, for the most part, also refused to accept King's leadership or that of SCLC. It could hardly be otherwise given SCLC's limited and secondary role in the sit-in movement. However supportive and sympathetic, SCLC's local affiliates found themselves playing second fiddle to the students. In Tallahassee, for example, the focus of black protest passed from the church-based Inter-Civic Council to the college-based CORE chapters; in Nashville, from the NCLC to the student movement at Fisk. However much SCLC claimed indirect authorship of the sit-ins via the Montgomery bus boycott and the teachings of King, the fact remained that black students, acting independently, had seized the initiative and given the civil rights movement a decisive push forward. As Ella Baker noted with some acerbity, "None of the great leadership had anything to do with the sit-ins starting. . . . [They] spread, to a large extent, because of . . . the young enthusiasm and the need for action."[10]

Proud of their accomplishment, the students had not the least intention of surrendering control of their movement to others, as became abundantly clear at the Southwide Youth Leadership Conference, held at Shaw University on April 15–17, 1960. Organized by Baker with $800 from SCLC, this meeting assembled about 140 students from fifty Southern colleges. King, the keynote speaker, urged the youths to set up a permanent organization in order to sustain the momentum of the sit-ins and "take the freedom struggle into every community in the South." He advised them to use the boycott, as well as "jail without bail"—the tactic of refusing to post bond in order to fill the prisons and tax the resources of the state. Accepting King's advice, but also following their own inclinations, the students established a "Temporary Student Nonviolent Coordinating Committee." The "Temporary" was soon dropped, and the Student Nonviolent Coordinating Committee (whose acronym, SNCC, was pronounced "snick") came into being as an independent organization having fraternal relations with, but no formal ties to, SCLC.[11]

Legend has it that Ella Baker played a decisive role in frustrating an SCLC plan to "take over" the student movement. According to Baker herself, others in SCLC—probably Wyatt Walker, the incoming executive director, and Bernard Lee, a student leader from Montgomery—made a definite attempt "to get the students to become an arm of SCLC." The fact that Baker positively encouraged the students to move away from SCLC, urging them to create a "group-centered leadership" rather than a "leader-centered group," may well have influenced the students. But as Stephen Oates has rightly emphasized, there is no evidence that King himself ever put any pressure on the students to affiliate with SCLC. He certainly hoped that they would align with SCLC, but only if they did so of their own volition. According to Lawson and others, King possessed the influence to sway the decision, yet he deliberately refused to do so. As James Bevel put it, "The emphasis was on how do you make a nonviolent movement . . . rather than on organizations." The assertion that King attempted to co-opt the student movement is, according to Lawson, "nonsense"—a backward projection of later SCLC-SNCC rivalry.[12]

Lawson himself exerted as much, if not more, influence as King. His role in the Nashville sit-ins and his expulsion from Vanderbilt had made him something of a hero in the eyes of the students. He had around him, moreover, "a small group of out-and-out believers in the philosophy of nonviolence who were quite coherent." Due largely to Lawson and the Nashville students, SNCC adopted a "statement of purpose" which affirmed nonviolence as the aim, the philosophy, and the technique of the new organization. It was his blunt and radical language, not merely his Gandhianism, that made him so popular. His speech to the conference was "dynamite," Julian Bond recalled; "it really stirred people up." His biting criticisms of the NAACP struck an especially responsive chord. "This movement is not only against segregation," Lawson insisted. "It's against Uncle Tom Negroes, against the NAACP's over-reliance on the courts, and against the futile middle-class technique of sending letters to the centers of power." Ridiculing "half-way efforts to deal with radical social evil," he issued a clarion call for "nonviolent revolution."[13]

An articulate and persuasive intellectual, Lawson possessed a much deeper grasp of the philosophical and historical basis of nonviolence than did King. His conception of nonviolence was also more far-reaching. Instead of viewing segregation as a "peripheral custom," he argued, blacks should recognize it as a "basic pattern" and ask searching questions about the political and economic foundations of their society. Belittling piecemeal reform, he envisaged a "nonviolent revolution" that would "transform the system." How the system was to be transformed, and into what, remained unclear, and Lawson struck some as an impractical visionary. But his concept of a Gandhian "nonviolent army" that would challenge state power held a tremendous fascination for many young blacks. Although he never held any position in SNCC beyond that of informal adviser (and that for only a brief period), his ideas gained widespread currency through John Lewis, Diane Nash, James Bevel, and other members of the Nashville group. They also influenced SCLC, which Lawson served for many years as teacher and adviser.14

If the formation of SNCC foreshadowed organizational rivalry and ideological dissension between SNCC and SCLC, a more serious division was already opening up between these two organizations and the NAACP. The students' readiness to denigrate the NAACP as conservative and ineffectual infuriated the association's leaders. To make matters worse, King seemed to be tacitly endorsing these negative views. They were especially incensed by Lawson's Raleigh speech, which prompted an angry letter to King from Roy Wilkins. He was appalled, Wilkins wrote, that open criticism of the NAACP "should come out of a meeting called by you, and that it should be made there by one widely regarded as voicing your opinions"; King's failure to repudiate Lawson, plus his own comments about "moving away from tactics which are suitable merely for gradual and long-term change," seemed tantamount to an endorsement of Lawson's attack. A few days later, King received a briefer, but equally forthright, protest from Jackie Robinson about "individuals who are knocking the NAACP in promoting the SCLC."15

King had made a serious effort since 1957 to achieve a correct and cooperative relationship with the NAACP. He had met Wilkins as recently as December in order to coordinate their respective voter registration programs. He could not escape the impression, however, that the NAACP had consistently failed to reciprocate his conciliatory attitude, and in a long and candid reply to Robinson he gave vent to his frustration and annoyance. "I have no Messiah complex, and I know that we need many leaders to do the job," he averred.

> I have refused to fight back or even answer some of the unkind statements that I have been informed that NAACP officials said about me and

the Southern Christian Leadership Conference. Frankly, I hear these
statements every day, and I have seen efforts on the part of NAACP
officials to sabotage our humble efforts. . . . I am sure that if criticisms
were weighed it would turn out that persons associated with the NAACP
have made much more damaging statements about SCLC than persons
associated with SCLC have made concerning the NAACP. . . . The job
ahead is too great . . . to be bickering in the darkness of jealousy, deadening competition, and internal ego struggles.

Disturbed by the wrangling, Benjamin Mays sternly instructed King
and Wilkins to "definitely discourage anyone in your organization
from taking a crack at either the NAACP or the SCLC." Both leaders
tried to eliminate the sniping, and after some fence-mending meetings
the row blew over.[16]

The ill feeling over Lawson's speech, of course, involved more than
orgazational rivalry: it was also symptomatic of the growing cleavage
between the advocates and opponents of mass direct action. Wilkins's
letter to King was revealing in this respect. Direct action was old hat,
he told King: the NAACP had marched, boycotted, and picketed since
1917. None of the examples Wilkins cited, however, involved the kind
of deliberate law breaking that the sit-in movement was utilizing on
such a large scale. The gulf was also revealed when Ella Baker took two
student leaders to see Thurgood Marshall, head of the NAACP Legal
Defense Fund. The tactic of "jail without bail" made no sense to him,
Marshall told them; the job of any lawyer was to get people out of jail,
not get them in.[17]

To Rustin and Levison, these disputes over tactics held a wider
historical and ideological significance. As older political activists, who
recalled the mass movements of the 1930s, they immediately recognized that the sit-ins had taken mass action to a higher stage. Far from
deploring the quarrel between the students and the NAACP, they applauded it. In a letter, Levison tried to impress upon King the import of
the new movement. The sit-ins had picked up the struggle where the
Montgomery bus boycott had left off. They were demonstrating the
futility of relying upon the courts, Levison argued, and had exposed the
"feebleness and the foolishness in Congress." The NAACP was rapidly
using up the good will it had accumulated from its past legal victories,
he added; if its leaders failed to change their policy of gradualism,
"their influence will sharply diminish and the true forces of struggle
will move into effective leadership."[18]

The success of the Committee to Defend Martin Luther King provided further evidence that an opportune moment had arrived to chart

SCLC's organizational expansion. Rustin and Levison formed the committee in March 1960, after a Montgomery grand jury indicted King for allegedly falsifying his Alabama tax returns. Although its primary purpose was to pay for King's legal defense, the committee also channeled money to SCLC and to Southern students. By the end of July it had raised $85,000. Ironically, the indictment actually helped SCLC, demonstrating the increasing willingness of Northern liberals to support the civil rights movement. The success of Harry Belafonte in involving prominent actors and singers in the work of the committee seemed especially significant: entertainers had generally withdrawn from left-of-center politics during the McCarthy period. Their readiness to back King not only pointed to a freer political atmosphere but also testified to the failure of segregationist attempts to portray the civil rights movement as Communist-inspired. During the 1960s Belafonte and his Hollywood connections provided SCLC with an important source of funds.[19]

In May, to nearly universal surprise, an all-white Alabama jury acquitted King of the tax charges. But although the Committee to Defend Martin Luther King lost its raison d'être and soon disbanded, it laid the groundwork for a permanent and professional fundraising apparatus, supervised by Levison and based in New York. Levison hired Jack O'Dell, a young Negro who had worked for the committee, as his full-time assistant. The basis of SCLC's fundraising program comprised a list of past contributors to whom direct appeals could be made through the mail. Organizations with common interests frequently exchanged their mailing lists, but SCLC found it impossible to obtain any lists when it had nothing to offer in return. Levison and O'Dell had to start from scratch, therefore, compiling a list of twelve thousand people who had given money to SCLC. This list yielded $53,000 in 1960–61. Levison and O'Dell also organized an outstandingly successful benefit concert at Carnegie Hall, starring Frank Sinatra, Dean Martin, and Sammy Davis, Jr. All told, the New York office raised $91,000, of which $80,000 represented clear profit. King had every reason to be satisfied with Levison and O'Dell. He had no inkling as yet that both men were under FBI surveillance as supposed "Communist agents."[20]

With a small but burgeoning income, SCLC could begin to put flesh on its organizational bones. In May 1960, King held a two-day meeting in New York with Rustin, Levison, and Wyatt Walker in order to redefine SCLC's structure and map out a new program. The principal outcome was that Walker replaced Ella Baker as executive director in

July, putting two of his colleagues from Petersburg, James Wood and
Dorothy Cotton, on the SCLC staff. Walker also hired SCLC's first
voter registration worker, the Reverend Harry Blake, whom he assigned
to Shreveport to work with C. O. Simpkins and the United Christian
Movement.[21]

Voluble, ambitious, and energetic, Walker brimmed with ideas for
putting SCLC on the map. The tenth of eleven children, several of
whom died in childhood, Walker grew up in Merchantville, New
Jersey. The same age as King, he was also, like King, the son of a
Baptist clergyman who followed in his father's footsteps. Whereas King
sought an education in the North, however, Walker went south, earn-
ing degrees in science and divinity at Virginia Union University in
Richmond. He became pastor of one of the oldest black churches in
the country, Gillfield Baptist Church in Petersburg, Virginia, in 1952.
In addition to his pastoral duties, Walker served as chairman of the
local NAACP and as Virginia director of CORE, under whose auspices
he organized a two-thousand-strong "Pilgrimage for Integrated Education" to the state capitol on New Year's Day, 1959. He also helped to
organize the Virginia Christian Leadership Conference, SCLC's first
state unit, and the Petersburg Improvement Association. After mounting a sit-in at the public library, the PIA filed a successful suit in
federal court to have segregation outlawed. Walker was among those
arrested.[22]

Walker had met King while a student, and King, with his impressive
memory for names and faces, asked him to serve on SCLC's board.
Before long he was engrossed in the board's committee work, and the
offer of SCLC's executive directorship soon followed. Outwardly,
Walker and King presented a sharp contrast. King strove towards modesty and humility; Walker openly extolled his own virtues. King wrote
awkwardly, with little attempt at humor; Walker's letters were fluent
and witty. King was patient, easygoing, and tolerant of mistakes;
Walker was short-tempered and could not abide inefficiency or slipshod work. Anything but pompous, he did not possess King's impertur-
bability or diplomatic finesse. "Some of that crap Martin puts up
with—you know, rubbing folks' fur the right way—I couldn't." During
the heat of a campaign he barked orders and dispensed with the social
niceties. "I've got to get the job done," he confessed. "If you get in the
way, I'll run smack dab over you." Like Lawson, he was contemptuous
of the NAACP, which he regarded as a hidebound bureaucracy. Unlike
Lawson, he knew better than to publicly attack the association when
he was so closely associated with King.[23]

Walker's first task was to give SCLC a viable program, and the Citizenship Education Program (CEP) bore the impress of his efforts. The program was taken, literally, from the Highlander Folk School, which had been holding classes in citizenship education since 1953, teaching a range of skills from basic literacy to voter registration and the techniques of union organizing. Highlander, however, had been assailed by segregationists as a "Communist training school": it was investigated, raided, and eventually, in 1960, closed down by the Tennessee authorities. While the case was under appeal the school's director, Myles Horton, arranged with Walker to have the citizenship classes transferred to SCLC—the latter agreed to take over this program lock, stock, and barrel. The Marshall Field Foundation undertook to finance the program, and the American Missionary Association, which disbursed the $40,000 grant, furnished a disused college building in McIntosh, Georgia, an hour's drive south of Savannah. The site of the new school made it ideal for the purposes of citizenship education: McIntosh County was one of the very few majority-black counties in the South where Negroes voted. SCLC hired Andrew J. Young, a young black minister in the mainly white Congregational church, the AMA's parent body, to supervise the program.[24]

SCLC's association with Highlander entailed a certain amount of political risk, for the school was widely suspected—and not only by conservative segregationists—of having Communist connections. Highlander had incurred the enmity of Cold War liberals by failing to adopt a "totalitarian disclaimer" and refusing to denounce the allegedly Communist-controlled Mine, Mill, and Smelter Workers Union. In 1949 the CIO, which had used Highlander as a conference facility, severed all connections with the school. Highlander also maintained close links with the Southern Conference Education Fund (SCEF), another supposedly "subversive" organization. SCEF had been attacked not only by reactionary bodies like the House Un-American Activities Committee, but also by such beacons of liberalism as Americans for Democratic Action. Indeed, the ADA had kept up a dogged campaign to isolate and destroy SCEF ever since the latter's inception in 1946, its principal target being SCEF's executive director, Dr. James Dombrowski.[25]

Both King and Walker regarded the issue of communism as a distracting and destructive irrelevancy. Temperamentally and politically, they abhorred the still-current obsession with seeking "Reds under the bed," and deplored the activities of HUAC and their ilk. Nevertheless, SCLC's connection with Highlander provided grist for the segregationists' mill—a photograph of King at the "Communist training school," taken in 1957, was plastered on billboards across the Deep South. However, the charges against Highlander were so patently spurious—not even the FBI gave them credence—that SCLC gave barely a second thought to cooperating with the school. SCEF, on the other hand, presented a more serious problem, and some in SCLC, notably Andrew Young, thought it politic to keep that organization at arm's length, as the NAACP did.[26]

Cooperation with "tainted" groups and individuals proved a constant headache for SCLC. King and Walker refused to be drawn into the sterile politics of the Cold War: SCLC was not actively "anti-Communist" like the ADA; its constitution contained no "totalitarian disclaimer"; it declined to take communism seriously as an internal—or even external—threat to the United States. Yet King knew he had to tread carefully in order to protect SCLC from political attack. He was extremely cautious about his relationship with Rustin, placing him on SCLC's staff only on condition that he step down if he became a political liability. King's own public abjurations of communism caused Virginia Durr to privately criticize him for "Red-baiting."[27]

In July 1961 SCLC's citizenship school, the Dorchester Center, held its first classes. What exactly did the Citizenship Education Program do? Walker described it as community mobilization: "teaching people the techniques to organize themselves for action." The ballot provided the unifying theme. The week-long courses gave poorly educated rural blacks a crash course in the American political system, including such down-to-earth advice as how to overcome the myriad obstacles which tripped up would-be black voters. Much of the course covered the "basics" of voter registration: how to locate the registrars, how to fill in the form, how to prepare for the literacy and "understanding" tests. "Graduates" of the course could, SCLC hoped, return to their localities equipped not only to tackle the registrars but also to start up classes of their own. If SCLC could pick out, to quote Andrew Young, "those Ph.D. minds that have been wasted in the cotton patch," it could develop local leadership and accelerate the momentum of the civil rights movement.[28]

A woman, Septima P. Clark, did most of the teaching. Mrs. Clark had a long career behind her. She began teaching in 1916, when eighteen years old, and spent forty years in South Carolina public schools. In 1956 she was fired by the Charleston Board of Education for refusing to relinquish her NAACP membership, whereupon Myles Horton offered her a job at Highlander. Clark became Highlander's director of education, and when the program changed hands in 1961 she became a full-time member of SCLC's staff. Her vast experience of teaching—especially her years on Johns Island, one of the poorest and most illiterate Negro communities in the South—made her the ideal person to carry out this type of instruction. Walker described her as "one of the great spirits of the movement [and] one of the most unpublicized."[29]

Walker's second task was to help boost SCLC's income. He realized that SCLC's biggest asset was King himself, and, in contrast to Ella Baker, he recognized that part of his job was to exploit King's public image as fully as possible. Speeches and public appearances by King represented an obvious source of income for SCLC which had so far barely been tapped. "I began to do it on what I called a business-like basis," he recalled, "looking at the size of the town, how many Negroes were there, getting the right auditorium, going in eight weeks ahead of time, getting the ministers behind it, then getting community leaders, the head of the Urban League and, you know, giving it the hoopla. That way, where we used to get $2,000, we'd get $10,000." King's ability to command large fees reflected his ability to draw large audiences, and this, in turn, depended on the public perceiving him as a figure of weight and influence. The fact that he led a tiny organization was neither here nor there: if he acted like an important national leader he would be treated like one. Walker therefore encouraged the development of a system of protocol in order to bring about parity of status between King and the heads of other organizations. King should deal only with the top men, Walker insisted, not with deputies or middle-ranking officials. If, for example, the United Auto Workers wished to contact King, it would have to go through Walker first; only Walter Reuther, the union's president, would be allowed direct access to King. By encouraging people to treat King with deference, Walker also made it easier to attract support from wealthy whites, who, he noted, required "careful cultivation" in small, intimate meetings with SCLC's president.[30]

Thanks largely to the increasing professionalism of its fundraising efforts, SCLC's income climbed to almost $200,000 during the twelve months following August 1960. Part of this increase, admittedly, can be attributed to the changed climate brought about by the sit-ins and the Freedom Rides. This surge of direct action engaged the sympathies of Northern whites in growing numbers, and many expressed their feelings in dollars-and-cents terms. As one authority on the civil rights movement has stressed, rising white financial support was a consequence of black insurgency rather than a cause of it.[31]

At SCLC's 1960 convention, held in Shreveport in October, King proposed a number of steps to strengthen the organization's baffling structure. One suggestion was to tighten the links between the Atlanta office and the local affiliates by grouping the latter into state conferences; another was to seek new affiliates outside the South. In practice, however, neither innovation proved very successful. The first, by attempting to subordinate the affiliates to an SCLC "general program," merely created confusion and friction. In January 1961, for example, a demonstration planned by the Virginia Christian Leadership Conference had to be postponed because King and Walker objected to one of SCLC's local units directly approaching other national organizations for sponsorship and support. The president of the VCLC, Milton Reid, duly apologized, but felt constrained to add that the new rules seemed "unnecessary and burdensome." In August, Reid was still complaining that "we have never gotten down to a definite policy of working relations between the State Conference and the National Office." Indeed, it seemed difficult to understand just what purpose state units like the VCLC served.[32] The plan to turn SCLC into a national organization also failed to bear fruit. King hankered after a national base but, unlike Walker, was loathe to make a direct bid for the position occupied by the NAACP. Making SCLC a membership organization would involve a head-on collision, fragmenting the fragile unity of the movement. It would give rise to accusations of ruthless ambition, and entail a bruising power struggle. Year after year, board members raised the questions of extending SCLC into the North, or accepting individual members, only to have their suggestions shunted into a committee and forgotten until the following year.[33]

As black colleges ended their summer term, with the students going home and the sit-ins subsiding, the forthcoming presidential election became a central concern of the various civil rights organizations. Common to their thinking was a conviction that Negro voters were peculiarly well placed to extract concessions from both the parties. First, the election promised to be a close one; neither party could afford to neglect such a sizeable segment of the electorate. Second, although the Negro vote had been overwhelmingly Democratic since the Roosevelt landslide of 1936, a significant swing to the Republicans had occurred in 1952 and 1956, especially in the South. This trend appeared to indicate that black voters were no longer safely and solidly Democratic: it would be folly for either the Democrats to take them for granted or the Republicans to write them off. Both parties, it seemed, had everything to play for. King himself had little enthusiasm for John F. Kennedy at first, as he explained during a dinner attended by the Durrs. "We were all horrified," Virginia Durr wrote afterwards, "when King said that Negroes more and more are turning to Dick Nixon, and he is evidently strongly tempted. Nixon calls him over long distance for his advice . . . and he says that while he has some doubts about Nixon, still he is the ONLY candidate that does these things. . . . As far as Lyndon is concerned he is simply out as far as Negroes are concerned." It is not inconceivable that King was deliberately trying to shock these old New Dealers and Republican-haters.[34]

The most important channel through which blacks sought to influence the political parties was the Leadership Conference on Civil Rights (LCCR). This had been set up in 1949 to work out a common position among groups sympathetic to the Negroes' cause. A broad coalition, its efforts were coordinated by a small inner group: in practice, a handful of men—Joseph Rauh of the ADA, Andrew Biemiller of the AFL-CIO, Clarence Mitchell and Roy Wilkins of the NAACP—formulated the LCCR's strategy and tactics. SCLC played a distinctly minor role in the LCCR. Wedded to grandiose rhetoric and dramatic, symbolic gestures, it was not good at drawing up legislative proposals, preparing expert testimony, or lobbying congressmen—skills of the lawyer rather than the preacher. Not until 1964 did SCLC open an office in Washington.

SCLC's efforts to influence the party conventions, therefore, should be viewed as a minor variation on the LCCR's larger theme. Bayard Rustin acted as King's main political adviser, preparing his public statements and platform testimony. He also laid plans for picketing the convention halls. At this juncture, however, Rustin fell foul of Adam Clayton Powell, who, on June 19, denounced Rustin and threatened to rake over his past, both personal and political. Both King and Rustin agreed that a Red-baiting attack by Powell might be extremely damaging to SCLC, and so Rustin resigned. There is no doubt that King feared to alienate Powell, who enjoyed immense popularity among Northern blacks. "I have terrible agonies of conscience," he once admitted, about indulging Powell's vanity and political opportunism. Levison thought King naive: "It takes Martin an awful long time," he noted, "to wake up to the fact that certain people are scoundrels. He hates to believe it."[35]

Despite Rustin's departure, the planned demonstrations went ahead with the blessing of the LCCR. The latter felt considerable satisfaction with the outcome of the conventions. The civil rights plank adopted by the Democrats was more far-reaching than anyone had thought possible. The Republican one was not as strong, but, as Joseph Rauh noted, it went "further than any past plank and had enough in it to support vitally-needed legislation."[36]

After the conventions, civil rights organizations made strenuous efforts to extract further promises from the candidates. At a private meeting in June, King urged Kennedy to "do something dramatic" to demonstrate his commitment to civil rights, but the senator was far too canny to tie himself down. Although Kennedy made a favorable impression on him, King maintained a nonpartisan stance so as to maximize the political leverage of the much-mooted Negro vote. "We must make it crystal clear," he reminded a black audience in Louisville, "that neither party can boast of having the Negro vote in its pocket." In September, SCLC began negotiating with Harris Wofford, Kennedy's adviser on civil rights, for a public meeting between Kennedy and King. SCLC stipulated that for symbolic reasons the rendezvous should be in the Deep South—Miami or Atlanta—a condition which proved unacceptable to the Kennedy camp. As election day approached, and with the candidates running neck and neck, it seemed increasingly likely that the black vote would determine the outcome.[37]

The story of King's imprisonment during the election campaign, and of how Kennedy's response purportedly swayed black voters, has often been told. The irony of the whole affair is that King, round whom the events revolved, went to jail reluctantly and with little expectation that his act would have such weighty political repercussions. In September, when a group of Atlanta University students asked him to lead a sit-in at Rich's department store, King begged off. The students were at odds with some of Atlanta's older, established black leaders, including Martin Luther King, Sr., and his son did not want to take sides. Preferring to delay plans for direct action until after the election, he scheduled an SCLC board meeting on the day the sit-ins were due to begin. This meeting was cancelled, however, when Kennedy decided against addressing it. King now had no excuse for not joining the Atlanta protest, and the students pressed him relentlessly. They were disappointed by his failure to take part in a sit-in and frankly told him so. At a meeting at King's home, the student leaders complained that he had been standing on the sidelines, leaving Sam Williams to carry the SCLC flag in Atlanta. Finally, King agreed to take part; as Andrew Young put it, "They literally shamed him into getting involved." Walker, who thought the students' plan sound, arranged for King to be on the picket line with Sam Williams on the morning of

October 19. Both Walker and the students intended to solicit comments from Nixon and Kennedy when King was arrested.[38]

When they demanded to be served at Rich's cafeteria, King wound up in jail with fifty-one others. Harold Middlebrook, a Morehouse student who soon joined SCLC, remembered that the philosophy of nonviolence dominated the prisoners' discussions: "Dr. King meant letting nonviolence control even your inner being. . . . [He] talked constantly of Thoreau and of Bondurant and of Gandhi and Christ." SCLC took advantage of King's incarceration to mail an appeal letter under King's signature ostensibly "dictated . . . to you from the Fulton County jail."[39]

On October 24, concerned that they were still being detained, Harris Wofford contacted Morris Abram, a prominent Atlanta attorney and friend of Mayor Hartsfield, to complain about the situation. Two hours later, the mayor told a meeting of blacks that he was about to release the sit-in prisoners in response to a direct request from Senator Kennedy. "I'm giving him the election on a silver platter," he explained to an astonished Wofford, "so don't pull the rug from under me." Kennedy, ignorant of Wofford's call to Abram, was livid. Torn between wooing Negro voters and placating Southern whites, he wanted all the maneuvering room he could get; Hartsfield's statement threatened to upset this balancing act. In a desperate effort to play down the incident, Kennedy issued a brief press release stating that he had merely asked for "all the facts on the situation." Griffin Bell, the Democrats' campaign chief in Georgia, tried to reassure white voters that "Senator Kennedy would never interfere in the affairs of a sovereign state."[40]

Thanks to Judge Oscar Mitchell of the DeKalb County court, however, the pot continued to boil. Two months earlier, Mitchell had given King a year's suspended sentence for driving without a Georgia license. He now ordered the Atlanta authorities to hand over their prisoner and, on October 25, sentenced King to four months' hard labor for violating his probation. Early on the morning of Wednesday, October 26, he was transferred to the Reidsville state prison. Once again, King's sympathizers were up in arms. Walker sent identical telegrams to the presidential candidates demanding a response. John Calhoun, Atlanta's leading black Republican, instantly sensed the political implications and contacted the Republican National Committee. Nixon ought to say something, he urged; the incident would have tremendous repercussions. But Nixon decided to sit tight. "He said he would lose some black votes," Calhoun recalled, "but he'd gain white ones."[41]

On Wednesday afternoon, King wrote a poignant letter to Coretta from his cell at Reidsville. He hoped that she and the children could find some way to visit him on Sunday; he missed them badly. He asked her to bring a radio, a Bible, a dictionary, a thesaurus, a biography of Gandhi, some theology texts, and a number of his sermons.

> I know this whole experience is very difficult for you to adjust to, especially in your condition of pregnancy, but as I said to you yesterday this is the cross that we must bear for the freedom of our people. So I urge you to be strong in the faith, and this will in turn strengthen me. I can assure you that it is extremely difficult for me to think of being away from you and my Yoki and Marty for four months, but I am asking God hourly to give me the power of endurance. I have the faith to believe that this excessive suffering that is now coming to our family will in some little way serve to make Atlanta a better city, Georgia a better state, and America a better country. Just how I do not yet know, but I have faith to believe it will. If I am correct then our suffering is not in vain.[42]

When she learned of her husband's move to Reidsville, Coretta King phoned Wofford for help. After doing his best to reassure her, Wofford drafted a statement for Kennedy which condemned, in forthright terms, Mitchell's refusal to grant bail. Governor Ernest Vandiver of Georgia urged Kennedy not to release it, promising to "get the son of a bitch out" himself. This, however, he proved unable to do. Wofford then suggested that Kennedy himself phone Coretta to express his sympathy and concern. Kennedy approved the idea and talked to her on October 26. The next day, acting on the suggestion of Vandiver but without his brother's knowledge, Robert Kennedy phoned "that bastard Mitchell" to ask him, politely, that King be allowed bail. On October 28 the judge set King free on a $2,000 bond. Under Wofford's direction, the Democratic machine distributed a million pamphlets outside black churches across the country: the campaign tract contrasted Kennedy, "the candidate with a heart," with "no-comment Nixon."[43]

In the days before the election, Wofford and the other Democratic strategists sensed that "a tide was running for the Senator in practically every Negro community, North and South." Ironically, Nixon carried Atlanta itself, but overall blacks voted Democratic three to one, enabling Kennedy—with a little help from the Cook County Democratic machine—to squeak past Nixon. Reflecting on the affair several years later, Walker felt that Kennedy's gesture, taken at some political risk, was admirable: "I think he deserved everything he got." King himself emerged from the affair with his prestige considerably enhanced.[44]

Although pleased by Kennedy's victory, black leaders found little to celebrate in the new administration's civil rights policy. Kennedy, worried about the narrowness of his victory and the weakness of his political base, told them that he intended to combat discrimination through executive action rather than legislation. It would be futile to press for legislation, he argued: Congress would not pass it; worse, it would jeopardize all his other legislative proposals. To Roy Wilkins of the NAACP, this "executive action" strategy seemed to be little more than a mask for inaction. Writing to Wofford, Kennedy's civil rights assistant, Wilkins accused the administration of being all style and no substance. He also poured scorn on the idea that Kennedy could win Southern support by going slow on civil rights: "The Southerners and their Northern satellites . . . function whether civil rights legislation is proposed or withheld. An Administration gets as much from whacking them as by wooing them."[45]

King shared Wilkins's disappointment over the administration's self-denying ordinance in respect of civil rights legislation. He was more sympathetic, however, to the underlying logic of the "executive action" strategy. Levison, now King's main political adviser, had little confidence in Congress; without a change in the political climate or in the composition of Congress itself, blacks were more likely to extract concessions from the president. When he met Kennedy early in 1961, therefore, King stressed the scope of the president's inherent power and set out a number of proposals which he had previously outlined in *Nation*. Although he should still press for legislation, especially in voting rights, Kennedy could also exercise moral persuasion by speaking out, often and vigorously, against segregation. The core of King's argument was that the president could virtually wipe out segregation and discrimination "through a stroke of the pen." Kennedy listened attentively, and assured King that the executive branch was already moving forward.[46]

SCLC still lacked a clear strategy for influencing the federal government; it also lacked an effective method for promoting desegregation on a local level within the South. When the administrative committee met in March 1961, no consensus emerged as to which direction SCLC ought to take. Shuttlesworth wanted SCLC's leaders to tour various cities in order to mobilize the black clergy. King himself suggested that SCLC concentrate on voter registration, a proposal influenced by the fact that there was money to be had from some of the foundations for this kind of work. King and Walker had already met Stephen Currier, the president of the Taconic Foundation who, with encouragement from the administration, planned to set up a central fund whereby money for voter registration could be channeled to the civil rights movement. The money eventually came on tap in 1962, under the auspices of the Voter Education Project (VEP). Contributions to the VEP were to be tax-exempt.[47]

SCLC's cautious approach meant that in 1961, as in 1960, other groups extended the frontiers of direct action and dominated the headlines. This time it was CORE's turn. The Freedom Rides, launched by CORE in May, were a spectacular demonstration against Jim Crow practices in interstate travel. The concept was simple: have an interracial group take a bus journey across the South, demanding service at all the terminal facilities along the way. If arrested, as seemed probable, the volunteers intended to refuse bail for at least forty days. Thirteen people, led by James Farmer, CORE's national director, set out from Washington on May 4. They travelled in two buses, a Trailways and a Greyhound. In Atlanta they had dinner with King; Walker arranged for Shuttlesworth to be on hand when the riders arrived in Birmingham. They were entering dangerous territory now, the SCLC leaders warned.[48]

Only one of the buses reached Birmingham: six miles from Anniston, Alabama, a crowd of whites forced the Greyhound to stop, then slit the tires and smashed all the windows. With the bus in flames, the passengers stumbled into the open air, with a plainclothes policeman keeping the crowd at bay with his pistol. Coughing and vomiting from smoke inhalation, the riders were taken to the hospital in Anniston, but the staff there refused to treat them. The Trailways bus managed to reach Birmingham, but as it pulled into the bus station the police were nowhere to be seen. A crowd organized by the Klan had ten minutes to beat up the riders as they descended from the bus.

As the Freedom Rides ground to a violent halt, Shuttlesworth, acting on his own initiative, led a fifteen-car convoy to Anniston to collect the stranded riders. They had no police escort, one of the CORE volunteers remembered, "but every one of those cars had a shotgun in it." Speaking to Robert Kennedy by phone, Shuttlesworth stated that the riders intended to press on with their journey, travelling to New Orleans by way of Mississippi. Kennedy was appalled, but had little choice but to support their right to travel. When he called the manager of Greyhound's Birmingham terminal, however, he was told that the drivers refused to a man to transport the Freedom Riders to Montgomery. An exasperated Kennedy suggested that he "get in touch with Mr. Greyhound" if necessary—"surely somebody in the damn bus company can drive a bus can't they?" But no driver could be found, and the battered riders decided to disband, proceeding to their destination by plane.[49]

The violence in Alabama placed SCLC in an awkward dilemma. On the one hand, King and others had strong misgivings about CORE's tactics, regarding them as brave but also reckless and provocative. They also worried that the Freedom Rides might antagonize potential supporters among that large group of uncommitted whites who stood between the ardent segregationists and the active liberals. The picture of "irresponsible" Yankees "invading" the South in order to spark violence was hardly conducive to SCLC's desired image of reasonableness and moderation. On the other hand, CORE had successfully dramatized both the continuing injustice of segregation and the unrestrained brutality of the segregationists. Tactical quibbles apart, the Freedom Riders had the law—in the form of Supreme Court decisions—on their side.[50] To bow to racist violence by abandoning the Freedom Rides would represent a supine admission of defeat, an intolerable sacrifice of principle, and a major reverse for the civil rights movement. As happened so often in such situations, white violence created a spirit of unity among blacks which submerged their tactical differences.

The sheer pace of events, moreover, compelled SCLC to rally behind the CORE-inspired protests, for a group of students in Nashville decided to continue the Freedom Rides whatever the cost. Led by Diane Nash, James Bevel, and John Lewis, the students asked the Nashville Christian Leadership Conference to give them money for tickets. The ministers were horrified. "You cannot go," Lewis remembered them saying. "We cannot give you this money to go. You're just asking for death; this is suicide." But the students had two key supporters among the ministers: one was C. T. Vivian, a Nashville-based official of the (Negro) National Baptist Convention; the other was James Lawson, now the pastor of Scott Chapel Methodist Church in Shelbyville, a town about sixty miles from Nashville. With money and reluctant blessings from the NCLC, a party of ten, which included Lawson and Vivian, boarded a Greyhound bus to Birmingham. Upon arriving in the city they were arrested, held overnight and all of the next day, and then driven to the Tennessee state line where they were unceremoniously dumped. Back in Birmingham by the afternoon, with reinforcements from Nashville, the students ate a hasty repast at Shuttlesworth's house and then returned to the bus station. None of the drivers would take them to Montgomery.[51]

Robert Kennedy considered the Freedom Rides senseless and dan-

gerous. With an apparently limitless supply of volunteers from
Nashville, however, the protests were gathering an unstoppable momentum—in spite of the fact that they were at a literal standstill. After
stifling his initial anger, Kennedy eventually persuaded the bus companies to transport the Freedom Riders to Montgomery; he had secured a personal assurance from John Patterson, the governor of
Alabama, that the state had the situation well under control and that
federal marshals would not be needed. As the buses pulled out of
Birmingham on May 20, accompanied by sixteen cars of the highway
patrol, Shuttlesworth professed astonishment at the need for "an
armed guard to take a bunch of niggers to a bus station so that they
can break these silly old laws."[52]

SCLC was being sucked into the protests by Shuttlesworth, Lawson,
and the Nashville students. The riders' reception in Montgomery,
moreover, compelled SCLC's leadership to become more closely involved. Patterson's assurances turned out to be worthless: when the
buses approached Montgomery the highway patrolmen disappeared,
and the local police, as in Birmingham, gave the waiting crowd ten
minutes to wreak its fury on the integrationists. Six of the riders were
beaten, three sustaining serious injuries. The attitude of the white
onlookers, Virginia Durr lamented, "was one of general satisfaction
that they 'were getting what was coming to them. . . .' Only two of the
white people of Montgomery of all the hundreds that were there came
to the defence of the riders . . . and they were later convicted of 'disorderly conduct' and fined $300." John Doar, an assistant attorney
general, watched the entire episode from the roof of the federal building, and he relayed a blow-by-blow account to the Justice Department.
Disgusted by Patterson's duplicity, Robert Kennedy decided to send a
force of U.S. marshals to Montgomery.[53]

The next day, a Sunday, Ralph Abernathy arranged a service in
honor of the riders at the First Baptist Church. King cancelled an
appearance in Chicago to be there, and Walker flew in from Atlanta. By
the time James Farmer arrived from Washington, about a thousand
whites had encircled the church. Shuttlesworth, who collected Farmer
from the airport, was not one to be intimidated. "[He] was either
insane or the most courageous man I have ever met," Farmer relates.
"Shuttlesworth just walked through them, cool as a cucumber. I think
they were intimidated by his boldness." As the crowd swelled and
became more menacing, the people inside the church realized that
they were trapped. "I really thought we'd had it," Walker recalled.
"Ralph Abernathy suggested we go out and give ourselves up to the

mob." Just as some of the whites burst into the church, however, the federal marshals arrived and pushed the whites back. Around midnight, Governor Patterson finally agreed to call out the National Guard, but their arrival merely alarmed the people in the church. A frightened and angry King phoned Robert Kennedy to protest that the Alabama guardsmen would be no protection. Kennedy tried to reassure him, but King still feared for their safety. Finally, Kennedy blurted out, "Now Reverend, don't tell me that. You know just as well as I do that if it hadn't been for the United States marshals you'd be as dead as Kelsey's nuts right now!" The protection of the guardsmen proved adequate, although the siege continued for most of the night.[54]

Should the rides go on? SNCC people from Nashville insisted that they continue, thus forcing the hands of SCLC and CORE by challenging King and Farmer to support them. Despite their fear that rides into Mississippi would result in certain mayhem and possible murder, the two leaders agreed to back the students. However, when a party of twenty-seven riders set off from Montgomery on May 24, King was not among them. Farmer, who decided to go himself only at the last moment, recalled the scene at the bus station: "The SNCC kids expected Martin to go with them, but he refused. As he put it, he had to choose the 'when and where of his own Golgotha.' He also said he was on probation, and the ride would be a violation. The SNCC people wouldn't accept that. They said, 'Look, I'm on probation, too. . . .' They were furious with him, and accused him of being yellow." King reacted angrily to these aspersions on his integrity, but to the students who were risking their lives his reasons seemed flimsy. For Diane Nash, to whom King had been a hero, his refusal came as a shock, and she never looked upon him in the same uncritical light again. Some of the students began referring to King as "De Lawd."[55]

In fact, there was no violence when the riders, having travelled under heavy National Guard escort, arrived in Jackson. Instead, the police simply arrested them. This established the pattern for the rest of the summer: there was to be no repetition of the appalling scenes in Alabama, but any integrationists entering Mississippi could expect to be arrested as soon as they reached the Jackson bus station. Kennedy, primarily concerned with keeping the lid on an explosive situation, assured Mississippi's Senator Eastland that he would not challenge the arrests as long as the riders were not physically abused. Eastland gave his word and, unlike Patterson of Alabama, he kept it.[56]

Because of its local connections in Montgomery, SCLC now became instrumental in keeping the Freedom Rides in motion. As volunteers

descended on the city, Abernathy assumed the responsibility for collecting them, housing them, and taking them to the bus station.
Among the first to arrive was the chaplain of Yale University, William
Sloane Coffin, accompanied by three professors and three students. As
they gathered in Abernathy's house to debate whether to go on to
Jackson, Robert Kennedy tried to persuade King to cancel the protests.
The fact that the riders arrested in Jackson were refusing bail would
not have the slightest effect on him, Kennedy told King. And when the
latter warned that hundreds, nay thousands, might join the rides, Kennedy frostily told him not to make veiled threats—"That's not the way
to deal with us." King changed his tone: "It's difficult to understand
the position of oppressed people. Ours is a way out—creative, moral
and nonviolent. It is not tied to black supremacy or Communism but
to the plight of the oppressed. It can save the soul of America. You
must understand that we've made no gains without pressure, and I
hope that pressure will always be moral, legal and peaceful. . . . I'm
deeply appreciative of what the Administration is doing. I see a ray of
hope. But I am different from my father—I feel the need of being free
now!" The attorney general seemed unmoved by this sermonette. King
would have to make up his own mind, Kennedy said, but he should
know that the government was ready to help get the prisoners in
Mississippi out of jail. "They'll stay," King insisted. Coffin and the
other Northerners decided to go to Jackson, and the next morning
Walker, Shuttlesworth, and Abernathy took them to the Trailways terminal. But they never saw the inside of a bus—they were arrested at
the cafeteria lunch counter.[57]

Rejecting Kennedy's request for a "cooling-off" period, the civil
rights forces met in Atlanta to map their strategy. They agreed to step
up the protests and attempt to fill the jails of Montgomery and Jackson. To orchestrate their efforts they set up a "Freedom Rides Coordinating Committee," (FRCC) with King, Walker, Diane Nash, and
CORE's Gordon Carey serving as permanent members. The committee
also decided to seek an interview with the president or attorney general, and to make discreet efforts to meet Patterson and Ross Barnett,
the governor of Mississippi. SCLC and CORE undertook to jointly
finance the rides. When the existence of the committee was made
public, King explained that the NAACP had not been included because
it was primarily "a legalistic body."[58]

Throughout the summer of 1961 the FRCC routed Freedom Riders
through Atlanta, Birmingham, and Montgomery, and by the time it
wound up its operations 328 people had been arrested in Jackson.

Walker, the committee's treasurer, played an important role in coordinating the rides: "We bought a garb [*sic*] of tickets and made a hell of a lot of arrangements." He also dealt with the civil rights lawyers in Alabama and Mississippi, who, the committee complained, charged exorbitant fees. In June, Walker himself boarded a bus, accompanied by his wife and seven others. After returning to Atlanta he sent an account of their trip to Robert Kennedy, drawing his attention to the discourtesy of the bus company, the "insulting behavior" of the concessionaires at the stations, and the bus driver's "evident collusion with police forces to make our trip uncomfortable." He added a harrowing description of the Hinds County jail, which "resembles something out of the Middle Ages." In August Walker testified before the Interstate Commerce Commission which, two months later, issued a ban on racial segregation and discrimination in interstate travel. The order became effective on December 1, 1961.[59]

SCLC could claim some share of the credit for this victory. Any feeling of achievement, however, was mitigated by the knowledge that the victory belonged primarily to CORE, which had initiated the Freedom Rides, and to the SNCC students from Nashville, who had ensured their continuation. CORE also shouldered most of the financial burden. The most relevant, and unpalatable, fact was that SCLC had once more found itself climbing aboard a bandwagon which had been set in motion by others. King's own response to the Freedom Rides, moreover, had not been particularly inspiring. SCLC still seemed to be weak and ineffective. "Frankly," L. D. Reddick complained, "many thoughtful persons are wondering why it is taking us so long to build a mass movement in the South."[60]

The Freedom Rides marked the end of the honeymoon between SCLC and SNCC. Relations between the two organizations were further strained in August, when King became caught up in a sharp policy dispute within SNCC. The issue was straightforward: should SNCC shift from direct action to voter registration? Such a move was urged by Timothy Jenkins, an officer of the National Student Association, and Charles Jones, a SNCC staff member. Others in SNCC, notably Ella Baker and Bob Moses, also backed the idea of a switch to political action. At a conference at the Highlander Folk School, however, a faction dominated by the Nashville group vigorously opposed this suggestion. By that time, plans for a two-year "Voter Education Project" (VEP), to be financed by the Field and Taconic foundations, were well advanced; SNCC itself stood to receive a substantial sum. But the enthusiasm of the Justice Department for the project aroused suspicion: Diane Nash and other devotees of the "nonviolent army" idea attacked the VEP as an administration-inspired strategem to deradicalize the civil rights movement. King, who attended the conference as an observer, denied that the VEP had any sinister overtones and defended voter registration as necessary and legitimate. A compromise put forward by Ella Baker finally settled the dispute: henceforth SNCC should have two wings, one under Nash devoted to direct action, the other headed by Jones to carry out voter registration. The opposition within SNCC to voter registration soon diminished: when SNCC members moved into the rural Black Belt they discovered that the distinction between voter registration and direct action was academic.[61]

A more persistent cause of bad feeling between SNCC and SCLC concerned the latter's habit of telling the press that SNCC operated as an adjunct of their own organization. This not only offended SNCC's pride but also impeded its fundraising efforts. To Walker, on the other hand, the students wanted to have it both ways: they expected money from SCLC but did not wish to give SCLC any say in SNCC's decisions. This issue arose soon after the Highlander conference when a group of Freedom Riders, including James Forman, SNCC's new executive director, arrived in Monroe, North Carolina. "This was a rabid, racist town," Walker recalled, a notorious Klan stronghold. Most of the group were soon in jail, and SNCC asked for SCLC's help. When he visited the imprisoned students, Walker made it clear that SCLC agreed to foot the lawyers' bills on condition that "you do what we say." He then negotiated a truce with the help of an emissary from the governor. For his pains, Walker was attacked on the steps of the courthouse while waiting to see the sheriff. After seeing Walker beaten almost senseless, the police took the offender away. "His name was Vann Vickery," Walker related. "He didn't want no niggers standing on the steps of the court house." Three months later, in the town of Albany, Georgia, SNCC's simmering resentment against SCLC—especially Walker—boiled over in public. The consequences were disastrous.[62]

Four

First Battle: The Albany Campaign

The year between the end of the Freedom Rides and the preparations for the Birmingham campaign (September 1961 to September 1962) saw SCLC's modest but steady growth. It was a time, as Wyatt Walker described it, "of laying permanent foundations, re-structuring the organization, building a team and charting the course we should travel."[1] The most significant aspect of that year, however, was SCLC's first real taste of mass nonviolent protest. True, SCLC had participated in the Freedom Rides, when hundreds of dedicated activists from across the nation had sought out arrest and jail. But in Albany, Georgia, direct action involved ordinary men and women acting, as in Montgomery, as a community. Albany taught SCLC how to mobilize black Southerners. Although it made grievous errors and finally had to withdraw in defeat, SCLC learned vital lessons and matured as an organization.

The chain of events which led SCLC to Albany was set in motion by SNCC workers Charles Sherrod and Cordell Reagon. Following SNCC's new orientation towards voter registration, they moved to Terrell County, in the heart of the southwest Georgia Black Belt, in the summer of 1961. Finding "Terrible Terrell" too dangerous for comfort, however, they moved their base to Albany, in Dougherty County, in October.[2]

Sherrod and Reagon initially planned a voter registration drive, but then shifted to the idea of a broadly based direct action movement that would mobilize Albany's blacks—adults as well as students—against segregation. They met a frosty response from the president of the NAACP, but members of the recently formed NAACP Youth Council showed a strong interest, as did a number of students at Albany State College. Despite their youth, they also won the confidence of many adults, including several local ministers. Joined by a third SNCC worker, Charles Jones, they persuaded six black organizations to form a coalition, the Albany Movement. The new group represented, on paper at least, a formidable combination. As well as including several women, its leadership comprised half a dozen preachers and numerous businessmen and professionals—a doctor, a dentist, a realtor, a newspaper editor, and the only black lawyer in southwest Georgia.[3]

Compared to cities like Shreveport or Birmingham, Albany enjoyed good race relations. Blacks could register and vote; the police were better disciplined and less brutal; the Klan was weak. Contacts between the races were, on the surface, cordial and easygoing. Behind the superficial civilities, however, the relationship between white and black was one of domination. Blacks voted but did not hold office. There were no black policemen. Public accommodations and municipal facilities were rigidly segregated. White officials listened to black complaints but rarely acted upon them; they displayed a certain paternalism, but it was the kind of paternalism which the powerful accord the powerless. When the city commission appointed a twenty-six-member Citizens' Advisory Committee on Urban Renewal, its two black members were translated into a "special subcommittee on minority group housing." The population of Albany was 40 percent Negro.[4]

Blacks had never been entirely quiescent. A branch of the NAACP had existed since 1919; at its peak, in 1946, it claimed one thousand members. Although it declined sharply during the 1950s in terms of both membership and activity, its postwar voter registration drives had brought into being a small but significant black electorate.[5] With the

NAACP in decline, some blacks preferred to work outside the organization. In 1960, for example, four members of the Criterion Club, a men's organization, petitioned the city commission to eliminate segregated polling stations. Rebuffed, they filed a successful suit in federal court. In 1961 the same men formed the Lincoln Heights Improvement Association, which pressed the commission to better street conditions in one of Albany's black districts.[6] Another sign of reviving activism was the formation in May 1961 of an NAACP Youth Council. Despite the torpor of the adult branch, the Youth Council thrived: in October the NAACP's Georgia field secretary, Vernon Jordan, reported that it was "ready to move and act" with or without the blessing of the adults.[7]

The NAACP regarded the coming of SNCC with horror. With the arrival of Sherrod and his co-workers, Jordan made a desperate effort to stymie their plans for a new organization; failing that, he wanted to make sure that the Albany Movement came under the NAACP's control. But his attempts to revive the local NAACP branch failed to bear fruit: its meetings were cold and unenthusiastic, Jordan complained, and its leaders were doing nothing. They had done nothing, in fact, for ten years. As was so often the case, it took members of SNCC— "outside agitators"—to impart dynamism and urgency to black protest. When it became clear that the Albany Movement could not be controlled, however, Jordan and Ruby Hurley, the NAACP's regional director, ensured that it received no help from their own organization. The NAACP wanted nothing to do with SNCC or with "anything initiated by SNCC." Slater King, one of the local black leaders now cooperating with SNCC, was appalled by the venom which the NAACP officials displayed towards Sherrod, Reagon, and Jones. Organizational rivalry would wreak havoc during the coming months.[8]

Born at a meeting on November 17, 1961, the Albany Movement adopted the goals of fair employment, an end to police brutality, and the desegregation of the bus station, the train station, and all municipal facilities. It appointed a committee to negotiate with the city commission, but it also prepared for street demonstrations and mass arrests. Later, it became evident that these initial demands had probably been too ambitious, leading to a diffusion of energy and lack of impact. It might also be argued that the Albany Movement committed a grave mistake in launching demonstrations when talks with the city had only just begun.[9]

The insurgent blacks made one other error, perhaps their most serious: they underestimated their opponent. In the person of Chief of

Police Laurie Pritchett, the city commission had an able and resourceful defender of white supremacy. Through an informant and by means
of police surveillance, Pritchett learned of the Albany Movement's
plans. On October 30 he alerted the commissioners to the impending
demonstrations and placed his men on double shifts, "with no days off
during the period of expected tension." The wily chief of police decided to emulate the tactics employed by Captain A. L. Ray of Jackson
in his dealings with the Freedom Riders: instead of charging demonstrators with breaking the segregation laws, he planned to arrest them
on other, ostensibly nonracial, grounds.[10]

On November 22, five young blacks were arrested by Pritchett in
the Trailways bus terminal. Their trial five days later prompted the
first of many demonstrations, with Charles Jones leading six hundred
people to city hall on a "prayer pilgrimage." On this occasion there
were no arrests. On December 10, however, Pritchett gave SNCC the
dramatic incident it needed in order to spark a campaign of direct
action. That day, to quote the chief's report, "the first freedom riders
composed of a mixed group of the Student Non-Violent Coordinating
Committee arrived in Albany from Atlanta, Georgia. This trip was
made by train in order to desegregate train facilities and to desegregate
the waiting room at the terminal station. These arrests of the freedom
riders were made in violation of City Ordinances concerning disorderly conduct, blocking the streets, and failure to obey a lawful command of an officer." On December 12, when the Freedom Riders stood
trial, 265 people were arrested for marching to city hall in protest.
More than 200 others went to jail the following day.[11]

Enter King and SCLC. The president of the Albany Movement, Dr.
William G. Anderson, knew Ralph Abernathy from their student days
at Alabama State College; on December 14, after phoning his friend,
he sent a telegram to King inviting him to address a mass meeting.
King arrived in Albany the next day with Abernathy and Walker. That
night he made an emotional speech to a rapturous audience of about
one thousand people at Shiloh Baptist Church; moved by the spirit of
the occasion, he promised to lead a march the very next day. On the
afternoon of December 16, King, Abernathy, and Anderson headed a
procession of 250 people to city hall. When they refused to disperse,
Pritchett had them arrested. King declined to post bond, vowing to
spend Christmas in jail. SCLC intended to throw its "total resources"
into this fight, Walker told the press; he began contacting board members and supporters for a massive demonstration.[12]

But SCLC's plans went awry. Soon after King's arrest, Ella Baker arrived in Albany. Now an adviser to SNCC and a bitter critic of SCLC, she hastily devised a plan with Charles Jones, who had come out of jail on bond, to wrest the leadership of the movement away from King. On December 17, when Walker was visiting King in jail, the Albany Movement held a press conference at which it denied that Walker was in charge of the demonstrations. "We welcome any help from outside," stated Marion Page, Anderson's deputy, "but as of now we need no help." The following day, amid newspaper reports of an "open break" between SNCC and SCLC, the Albany Movement concluded a truce with the city, after negotiations had been restarted through the mediation of the Southern Regional Council and the Anti-Defamation League. The agreement provided for the release of jailed demonstrators on bond, compliance by the city with the Interstate Commerce Commission's directive on bus and train facilities, and the formation of a "committee of representative white and colored citizens" after a thirty-day cessation of demonstrations. King, Abernathy, and Anderson came out of jail on bond.[13]

Why did the Albany Movement thus embarrass SCLC, hastily accepting a "cooling-off" period in return for a vague promise of future negotiations? David Lewis has suggested that SNCC and the local leaders swallowed this one-sided compromise in order to get rid of King and SCLC. But this is only part of the story. When King arrived on the scene the Albany Movement was on the verge of a settlement with the city. A black delegation had met Mayor Asa Kelley for two hours on December 10, and negotiations continued over the next few days. At this point, however, the Albany Movement committed a major tactical blunder: anticipating that King's presence would frighten the city commissioners, it not only stiffened its demands—bypassing the negotiating committee and sending them directly to the city commission—but also issued an ultimatum. The commissioners did not dismiss these new demands out of hand; indeed, they had already prepared a counteroffer when King arrived. But they then received a telephone call from Solomon Walker, chairman of the black negotiating committee, stating that more demonstrations would take place if the city failed to accept the new demands. They later received a telegram from Anderson which demanded a response by 10:00 A.M. on December 16. Incensed by this ultimatum, Mayor Kelley fired off a curt rejoinder in which he accused Anderson of bad faith and broke off the negotiations. A few hours later, King and Anderson were in jail.[14]

At this juncture, however, the other local leaders began to get cold feet. Instead of making the commissioners more pliable, King's intervention had made them intransigent. Disputes about who was in charge further muddied the waters and vitiated the strategy of putting increased pressure on the city. Before going to jail, Anderson agreed that Walker should coordinate the protests, an arrangement accepted by Marion Page, the Albany Movement's executive secretary. But Page's resolve to carry on with the demonstrations rapidly weakened as he became a vortex of doubts and pressures: doubts about Anderson's judgement; pressure from SNCC to cut loose from SCLC; fear that King's presence might ruin the possibility of a pact with the city. On December 18, therefore, Page accepted the terms of an agreement worked out between Kelley, Pritchett, and Donald Hollowell, the black lawyer from Atlanta being retained by SCLC. The question of how to get the arrested demonstrators out of jail was crucial. The city adamantly refused to drop charges against any of them, but it did agree to no longer insist upon cash bonds. The other terms represented no real improvement on those already offered before King's arrival. Page, however, felt a pressing responsibility to secure the release of those in prison. Alarming reports were circulating about the terrible conditions in the crowded and filthy jails. Moreover, as Page explained several years later, "We were dealing with adults who had a lot of responsibility and could not stand the pressure of being in jail indefinitely." As David Lewis put it, "Until the truce, it had been a question of whose nerves were sounder, the Movement's or the city's." The commissioners, well aware of the disarray within the opposing leadership, proved to have the sounder nerves. This convoluted story had a final, bizarre twist. King and Abernathy endorsed the agreement and posted bond because they had to get Anderson, who was on the edge of a mental breakdown, out of the Albany jail.[15]

It is unlikely that King had been properly briefed on the delicate state of the negotiations before going to jail. If he was, then he made a tactical error in escalating the protests when a settlement had been worked out. Either way, SCLC had ample justification for feeling ill-used by SNCC and the Albany Movement. As Lewis concluded, "The sins imputed to Martin, Ralph, and Wyatt were certainly venial and probably hugely exaggerated. . . . [S]urely [they] were offences whose denunciation could be delayed for the sake of organizational unity." Characteristically, King refused to engage in recriminations. But Walker, in a 1967 interview, accused SNCC of exploiting King's publicity value, taking SCLC's money, and then attempting to exclude SCLC from the decision making. "We should have won Albany and we could have won Albany but for the anxiety and the ambition of a

Charlie Jones and the bitterness of an Ella Baker." SNCC manipulated
the local leaders, he believed, "and the internal fighting, the tribal
jealousies, got the best of them."[16]

In early January, putting the Albany fiasco behind him, King held an
informal meeting of key staff and board members in Atlanta. "For two
days," Walker reported, "we brainstormed the major areas of our concern." All agreed that SCLC urgently needed a field staff in order to
establish a solid presence in the South. With the promise of foundation
money from the newly formed Voter Education Project, they decided to
employ five full-time field secretaries to work on voter registration.
With Harry Blake, this gave SCLC a field staff of six, to be deployed in
Louisiana, Mississippi, Alabama, and Georgia. After an orientation session in February, they departed to their assigned areas. Jack O'Dell,
based in New York but making frequent visits to Atlanta, supervised
the program.[17]

How effective was SCLC's voter registration effort, and what kind of
men implemented it? Few new voters were registered in Mississippi,
but that fact reflected the state's harsh racism, not the abilities of
James L. Bevel, SCLC's field secretary. Born in Itta Bena, Mississippi, a
small town in Leflore County, Bevel belonged to that remarkable group
of students who had been indoctrinated into nonviolence by James
Lawson. Like John Lewis and Bernard Lafayette, he was studying for
the ministry at the American Baptist Theological Seminary in
Nashville when the sit-ins began. All three became leading figures in
the Nashville sit-in movement, as did Bevel's future wife, Diane Nash,
then a student at Fisk University. In 1961 this group travelled with
Lawson on the first Nashville-to-Birmingham Freedom Ride, their ultimate destination a Mississippi jail.[18]

When he left Parchman prison after serving four weeks, Bevel decided to stay in Mississippi, and with Nash, Lafayette, and three other
students tried to instigate sit-ins in Jackson. They had little success.
For the rest of the summer of 1961, Bevel and Nash travelled back and
forth between Jackson, Nashville, and Atlanta, helping the Freedom
Rides Coordinating Committee. In February 1962 they attempted,
again with scant success, to start a sit-in movement in Laurel. Joining
the staff of SNCC, which had reoriented its efforts in Mississippi from
direct action to voter registration, Bevel became one of its first full-
time civil rights workers in the South. When he moved to SCLC he
continued to work closely with SNCC, which by that time had twenty
field-workers in Mississippi, and spearheaded the civil rights coalition
known as COFO (Council of Federated Organizations).[19]

What exactly did Bevel and other field-workers do? Much of their time was spent canvassing: going from shack to shack, driving from one hamlet to another, trying to persuade blacks to go to the mass meetings, attend the voter registration workshops, and ultimately to go through the unnerving, often terrifying ordeal of going to the registrar's office and applying for the vote. Few ever passed. Finding churches in which to hold meetings, printing and distributing leaflets, recruiting canvassers, locating people who could provide accommodations—all this was grist to the civil rights workers' mill. They were continually harassed by local whites, frequently shunned by local blacks, and occasionally thrown into jail by the local sheriff. The work required stamina, persistence, and nerves of steel. Bevel excelled in it. He stayed in Mississippi for most of 1962 and early 1963, acquiring a reputation as a fearless "rabble-rouser." When SCLC assigned him to Albany in August 1962, Dr. Aaron Henry, COFO's president, begged Walker to send him back. "Bevel had a great hand in setting up this project," he wrote. "It has bogged down since he left."[20]

In Louisiana there was no equivalent of COFO, and Harry Blake, the SCLC field secretary based in Shreveport, found himself working in depressing isolation. Conditions in northern Louisiana resembled the worst parts of Mississippi. "This entire area is plagued by fear," Andrew Young reported to the Southern Regional Council. "Negroes are so well controlled . . . that the registrar can afford to be nice and rely on the 'Uncle Tom' mentality." Blake's only real support came from Dr. C. O. Simpkins, an SCLC vice-president and head of the United Christian Movement. Both men became targets for violence. Blake narrowly escaped an attempt on his life; Simpkins was repeatedly arrested and had his two houses dynamited. Walker gained a firsthand insight into local conditions when he visited Shreveport in June 1962 to launch a voter registration drive. Arrested for "loitering," he and Blake spent two days in the Caddo Parish prison before being allowed to post bond. Blake received little help from the local clergy. By the end of 1962 Simpkins had moved to New York, and Blake, in the words of Young, was "pretty much at the end of his rope."[21]

SCLC recruited the Reverend Bernard Lee as a general factotum and "troubleshooter." Lee had met King and Abernathy at the time of the bus boycott, when he was stationed at Maxwell Air Force Base in Montgomery. After completing his national service, Lee stayed in Montgomery and enrolled at Alabama State College. In 1960 the college expelled him for leading a sit-in. He completed his studies in Atlanta, where he helped prod King into joining the fateful sit-in at

Rich's department store. Lee became part of SNCC and travelled on the first Freedom Ride to Albany in December 1961. He idolized King and jumped at the chance of joining SCLC. Lacking a field secretary in Alabama, Walker assigned him to Etowah County.[22]

Neither Gadsden, Lee's base, nor the surrounding county, Etowah, qualified as an area of "hard-core" racism by the standards of north Louisiana, Mississippi, or such Alabama counties as Lowndes, Wilcox, and Dallas. Even so, barely a third of the county's nine thousand adult blacks were registered voters. With half of the remainder "functional illiterates," the complex registration procedures acted as a major barrier. Lee sent five people to the Dorchester Center for training as "citizenship class" teachers. He then divided Gadsden into six districts and tried to build precinct organizations in each one. In what had become a standard technique for voter registration workers, Lee first launched sit-ins at downtown lunch counters in order to dramatize his arrival. His drive made little headway during 1962: black applicants still had to face literacy tests, "interpretation" tests, and biased registrars who did business only two days a month.[23]

SCLC's efforts in Virginia were concentrated in the Fourth Congressional District, which comprised eighteen counties and three independent cities in the tidewater, the southeastern portion of the state. This was the northernmost tip of the South's Black Belt, and generally considered, according to new staff member Herbert V. Coulton, "the untouchable area of Virginia." True, black voters could be found in every county, but they rarely made up more than a quarter of the adult black population. The proportion was often much lower, especially in counties with black majorities. In Dinwiddie, for example, only about 400 of the county's 8,000 black adults were registered voters; in Prince George County, a mere 175 out of more than 3,000. Coulton found that most blacks were apathetic or indifferent about voting. Many were disfranchised through failure to pay the poll tax. "They felt this was a blessing," he reported, "because here was a tax they didn't have to pay." Outwardly at least, most seemed resigned to an inferior status: "Their trust in 'Mr. Charlie' overpowered the truth." A paucity of middle-class leadership handicapped Coulton's efforts. In Powhatan County, for example, there were no black doctors, no dentists, and only two resident ministers. Teachers, vulnerable to dismissal at the best of times, felt especially insecure in Virginia owing to the situation in Prince Edward County, where the public schools had been closed altogether in order to avoid integration.[24]

By early 1963 Coulton sensed that he was finally "breaking through the wall" of apathy and fear. Ministers, he wrote, were leavening their sermons with the social gospel, telling their congregations about "God's kingdom right here on earth." Beauticians were talking about the ballot in the seclusion of their parlors. Even the teachers, Coulton found, "are not as fearful." The pall of indifference seemed to be lifting. "The little man doesn't feel as small anymore"; he was beginning to realize that the vote might help him. For the next several years Coulton continued his labors, one of SCLC's most dedicated and effective voter registration workers.[25]

SCLC assigned two field secretaries to Georgia: John H. Calhoun and the Reverend Fred L. Bennette. Bennette had made a name for himself during the Atlanta sit-ins of 1960–61. As a student at Morris Brown College, he had organized the "logistics" of the protest—designating post offices to act as "field stations," inducing taxi companies to donate free rides, and recruiting women to provide demonstrators with soup and coffee. His military bearing—he had attained the rank of sergeant in the army—earned him the nickname "the Commandant." Calhoun, an older man, was an experienced political activist. A longtime NAACP official, having served as president of the Atlanta branch during the 1950s, he also chaired the Statewide Registration Committee. One of Atlanta's leading black Republicans, Calhoun was the first black candidate to run for Congress, although without success, in Georgia's Fifth Congressional District, the seat eventually captured by Andrew Young in 1972. Putting him on the staff gave SCLC the considerable advantage of being able to work through the Statewide Registration Committee. Calhoun and Bennette held voter registration "clinics" in eight towns and cities, working with local black organizations like the Bibb County (Macon) Coordinating Committee. Later in the year, Calhoun went to Albany and helped the Reverend Samuel B. Wells set up the Dougherty County Voters League. By October they had added fifteen hundred new voters, increasing black registration by a third.[26]

The most impressive results in the state were achieved by the Southeastern Georgia Crusade for Voters. This was an extension of the Chatham County Crusade for Voters, a Savannah-based organization which had been founded in 1960 by local NAACP officials. Hosea Williams, vice-president of the Savannah NAACP, headed both organizations, and much of their success stemmed from his driving leadership. A rousing speaker, Williams possessed a combative temperament, a boundless ego, and marked organizational talent. He molded the Chatham County Crusade into a disciplined political machine whose influence extended throughout the black community. An up-to-date card index of registered and unregistered blacks furnished the raw political intelligence. Ministers, teachers, parents, and teenagers provided the manpower. Williams himself supplied the energy and discipline. An ambitious man, frustrated by his failure to receive promotion within the NAACP, he turned the crusade into his own, autonomous, power base. He secured financial support from the Highlander Folk School which enabled the crusade to extend its work—despite objections from the NAACP—to the eighteen counties of the First Congressional District. Thus the Chatham County Crusade fathered the Southeastern Georgia Crusade. Williams's organization soon severed its links with the NAACP. When SCLC took over Highlander's citizenship program, the crusade became an SCLC affiliate. In August 1962 it received a grant of four thousand dollars from the VEP, whereupon the NAACP withdrew its financial support. In the opinion of John Calhoun, Williams ran "the most effective political action group in the state." Andrew Young agreed: "We ought to be identified with it," he advised SCLC. "It is the best in the South."[27]

As Young's comment implied, SCLC's voter registration work was largely dependent upon the vigor of local organizations. Sometimes, as with the Southeastern Georgia Crusade, those organizations saw an advantage in nurturing a link with SCLC. Often, however, local groups found their relationship with SCLC highly unsatisfactory. The Bibb County Coordinating Committee complained that SCLC had supplied only one-quarter of the funds it had promised for the Macon area. "SCLC had exploited the . . . area for its own benefit," a local activist told the VEP; monies raised in Macon, instead of being spent in Macon, had been appropriated by SCLC.[28]

Such complaints did not sit well with the VEP. In February 1963 Wiley Branton, the project's director, received a trenchant critique of SCLC's voter registration efforts from Jack Minnis, his research officer. Apart from praising Herbert Coulton's work in Virginia, the evaluation was entirely negative. It criticized SCLC for slipshod accounting procedures; for failing to provide regular reports; and for using VEP funds, contrary to the rules, to pay staff salaries. Minnis judged SCLC's operations in Georgia to be ineffective and cast doubt on the soundness of its voter registration work as a whole.[29]

SCLC's voter registration program was undoubtedly in a mess. It had not been helped when the FBI, in October 1962, leaked to the press that Jack O'Dell—described as a secret Communist party official—held an important post in King's organization. Bowing to pressure,

King asked for O'Dell's temporary resignation pending an internal inquiry. Although O'Dell continued, in fact, to work on SCLC's fundraising program, he relinquished his role as coordinator of voter registration. This job now fell to Andrew Young, who had numerous other duties as SCLC's program director. The transition inevitably caused problems, and Young made some mistakes. "There is really no excuse for the reporting of the finances," he confessed to Minnis. "This is strictly my inadequacy." In December, Young summoned SCLC's field secretaries to a three-day meeting in Atlanta to straighten out the program, and on February 28 King met Branton to respond to the VEP's criticisms. Nevertheless, Branton cancelled SCLC's next grant and withheld further funding until November. In its first annual report the VEP complained—clearly referring to SCLC—that "organizational structure has been a problem in the case of at least one of the major agencies. . . . VEP has frequently been in the position of not knowing what the organization was doing . . . until we read a news release." Nevertheless, SCLC claimed to have added forty-two thousand people to the voter rolls by September 1962.[30]

While it sank roots in the South, SCLC also strengthened its Northern supporting apparatus. By creating a network of "regional representatives" SCLC laid the basis for a coordinated Northern response to its Southern campaigns. The representatives, all unpaid volunteers, could organize sympathy demonstrations, deal with offers of help, and act as official spokesmen for SCLC. Equally important, they could help to raise funds in the North by arranging speaking venues for King. By 1963 Walker had recruited half a dozen Northern "contact men," including George Lawrence in New York City and Walter Fauntroy in Washington, D.C. Fauntroy also had the task of acting as SCLC's liaison with Capitol Hill. All the regional representatives were black clergymen. A plan to encourage Northern affiliates, however, was quietly dropped after Roy Wilkins, at a meeting of civil rights leaders in March 1962, accused SCLC and SNCC of attempting to supplant the NAACP.[31]

SCLC also strengthened its legal representation. Like the other civil rights organizations, it was continually entangled in expensive litigation, the demands of which had long since swamped its part-time general counsel, I. M. Augustine of New Orleans. Defending King against the Alabama tax indictment cost over $50,000 and required the services of half a dozen lawyers. No sooner had SCLC parried that attack than it became the target of a second legal onslaught from Alabama: the city commissioners of Montgomery filed a $3 million libel suit against Abernathy, Shuttlesworth, Lowery, and S. S. Seay over an SCLC appeal which had been published over their signatures in the *New York Times*. The libel case dragged on for years—it had to be fought all the way to the Supreme Court—and involved no fewer than eighteen lawyers on SCLC's side. On top of these particular cases, SCLC faced burgeoning litigation arising out of the sit-ins, the Freedom Rides, the Albany protests, and other instances of direct action.[32]

Stanley Levison, the guiding hand behind SCLC's direct-mail fundraising program, was also instrumental in the formation of the Gandhi Society, SCLC's legal arm. Impressed by the success of the Committee to Defend Martin Luther King, Levison nurtured the idea of a permanent body that would not only furnish legal defense when needed but also act as a fundraising device. SCLC itself paid no tax, but contributions to SCLC were taxable. SCLC therefore needed a charitable foundation which could receive tax-exempt donations, the money being channeled to SCLC. Levison pursued this idea indirectly by encouraging attorneys Clarence Jones, Theodore Kheel, and Harry Wachtel to become interested and involved in SCLC's work. Jones, a young Negro, had worked on the King tax case, and Levison engaged him on a regular basis. Kheel, one of the most eminent members of the New York Bar, headed a lawyers' advisory committee which worked on the libel cases. It was through Jones and Kheel that Wachtel gained an introduction to King and offered his help.[33]

Then in his midforties, Wachtel was a wealthy corporation lawyer, the general counsel and executive vice-president of the McCrory Corporation, the well-known chain store. Troubled by the persistence of segregation in his own company's stores, he sought King's advice: should he stay with the company or make a dramatic protest against segregation by resigning? King proffered the same counsel he gave to white Southern ministers when confronted with a similar dilemma: if he quit, his replacement might be less morally sensitive—he should stay in his post and use his influence as best he could. Wachtel discussed making a sizeable contribution to SCLC and asked King if he could send the money to a tax-exempt foundation. Surprised to learn the contrary, he offered to investigate the possibility of forming one himself on SCLC's behalf.[34]

When he apprised himself of Wachtel's background, Levison realized that this stocky lawyer-businessman was definitely worth cultivating. Apart from his expertise in the arcane world of tax law, Wachtel's religion and his business connections brought him into contact with some of the wealthiest Jews in New York. Wachtel also knew Abe

Fortas, head of one of the most prestigious law firms in the country and an intimate of Vice-President Lyndon B. Johnson. Through Clarence Jones, Levison arranged for Wachtel and his wife, Lucy, to spend two days with King in Atlanta. In a conversation picked up by the FBI's newly installed wiretap on his telephone, Levison urged King to invite the couple to his home: they would be impressed by the modesty of his dwelling. Wachtel and King got on well, and a friendship developed that lasted until King's death six years later.[35]

With King's blessing and Levison's behind-the-scenes encouragement, Wachtel went ahead and formed the Gandhi Society, with help from Jones, Kheel, and William Kunstler, a New York lawyer attached to the American Civil Liberties Union who had become involved in SCLC's legal work after the Freedom Rides. With a board of glittering public figures to lend it prestige, the Gandhi Society was actually managed by Jones and Wachtel. Launched in May 1962, it took another three years, however, to gain the coveted status of charitable foundation. By that time, moreover, the original conception of the society had altered, after a conflict of opinion between Kunstler and the others. Whereas Kunstler viewed the society as SCLC's equivalent of the NAACP's Legal Defense Fund, providing SCLC with "front line emergency legal assistance," Levison, Wachtel, and Jones saw it mainly as a fundraising device. Their view prevailed, and early in 1964 SCLC handed over all its important legal work to the NAACP. When it finally won tax-exempt status in 1965, through the assistance of Abe Fortas's law firm, it was renamed the American Foundation on Nonviolence.[36]

The Levison wiretap reflected the growing concern of the FBI and the administration over Levison's obvious importance in SCLC's affairs. In January 1962, the bureau advised Robert Kennedy that "a member of the Communist Party, USA," had become one of King's close advisers. Kennedy took the allegation seriously, and he asked two of his subordinates, John Siegenthaler and Burke Marshall, to warn King against associating with this man. The warnings were delivered, but King apparently found it impossible to believe the charges against Levison, especially without any specific proof. After more reports detailing the King-Levison connection, Kennedy had authorized a tap on Levison's telephone.[37]

In April, Levison had to appear before the Senate Security Subcommittee, chaired by James Eastland of Mississippi, a confidante of FBI director J. Edgar Hoover. "Isn't it true that you have gotten funds from the Soviet Union and given them to the Communist Party, USA?" the senator asked. On the advice of William Kunstler, however, Levison took the Fifth Amendment after stating that "I am not now and have never been a member of the Communist Party." McClellan of Arkansas called him the worst witness ever to appear before a congressional committee, prompting Levison to joke, in a conversation with O'Dell the next day: Did that mean he was worse than Jimmy Hoffa? In May, a week before the Gandhi Society was inaugurated, the FBI placed King's own name on "section A" of the Security Index—people to be interned in the event of a national emergency.[38]

The matter did not rest there. In June the FBI learned that Levison, who was becoming disenchanted with Wyatt Walker, had suggested to King that Jack O'Dell become his administrative assistant. In another intercepted conversation, moreover, Levison disclosed that O'Dell's past involvement with the Communist party did not trouble King, who said that "no matter what a man was, if he can stand up now and say he is not connected, as far as I am concerned he is eligible to work for me." On July 20, Hoover directed the bureau's New York and Atlanta offices to "determine whether the CP is exerting any influence on the SCLC through Levison and O'Dell or others and/or whether the party is making any attempts to infiltrate this organization." Three months later, the FBI's Internal Security Section began a "COMINFIL" (Communist infiltration) investigation of SCLC.[39]

If Hoover's view of SCLC was becoming increasingly hostile, King's opinion of the FBI plummeted after his return to Albany in the summer of 1962. Since his departure in December, the Albany Movement had run into serious trouble and appeared at times to be in danger of disintegrating. Whereas interorganizational bickering continued to plague the movement, the city commission became increasingly united in its defense of segregation. The new commission, installed in January 1962, was distinctly more conservative than the old, and Mayor Asa Kelley, the main proponent of negotiation and compromise, found that his appeals for moderation evoked little sympathy or support. On January 23 Anderson and Page appeared before the commissioners to present the Albany Movement's case. Their petition was hardly a model of strident militancy; it contained no list of demands but, in conciliatory language, sought a reaffirmation of the December 18 agreement and the creation of a "bi-racial planning committee." Having established a basis for communication, the black leaders reasoned, they could then present a bill of particulars. But the commission was in no mood to negotiate with "outside agitators," some of whom belong to "subversive" organizations. On January 30 it repudiated the pact of December 18 and, for good measure, chided Negroes for their high crime rate, complaining that blacks received far more from the city in services than they paid to it in taxes and advising the Albany Movement's leaders "to help earn acceptance of their people . . . by encouraging the improvement of their moral and ethical standards."[40]

The city showed the depth of its intransigence over the bus question. Blacks began a boycott of the buses on January 12, when one of the drivers had a black passenger arrested. The privately owned company soon agreed to desegregate its seating and take steps to employ black drivers. Unwisely, perhaps, the Albany Movement refused to call off the boycott until the city gave a written assurance that it would not interfere with these policies. Tottering on the edge of bankruptcy, the company begged the commission to issue such a statement: "If it is not written and the boycott is not stopped, we must cease operations as of January 31." Among the commissioners only Kelley thought this request acceptable, arguing that "it is more important to save the buses and avoid continued turmoil and strife than to refuse to allow the Company to operate the way they desire." The majority, however, preferred to let the company go to the wall. The commission ruled out a subsidy. Kelley now found himself in a majority of one, with C. B. Pritchett, brother of the police chief, leading the rest in a policy of no compromise. And in the future, the commission decided, it would avoid all direct communication with the Albany Movement—if blacks had any requests, let them address them in writing to Chief Pritchett.[41] The chief, despite his jovial manner, gave away nothing. According to black lawyer C. B. King, Pritchett once joked to a black delegation, "It's a question of mind over matter. I don't mind and you don't matter." King recalled that A. C. Searles, the editor-publisher of the local black weekly, "got quite apoplectic and turned red—and if you have ever seen Mr. Searles, you know that that is an impossibility."[42]

Over the next few months the city's position hardened. In April the Albany Movement began picketing and sitting in at the Carnegie library and other municipal facilities, but these protests caused the police only minor inconvenience. The long delay in bringing the December cases to trial, together with Pritchett's refusal to let those awaiting trial redeem their cash bonds, dampened any enthusiasm for further mass demonstrations. The movement's only real success was its boycott of white-owned stores. This hurt the city's merchants, as their letters to Pritchett attest. "At least 90 to 95% of all the negro business I have enjoyed in past years has been lacking," the owner of a fabric store reported. Whites, he added, were also staying away for fear of being caught up in demonstrations and violence. "Our business is at present suffering an approximate 50% decrease. . . . It is an intolerable situation." The merchants were not, however, clamoring for negotiations. Instead, like the manager of J. C. Penney, they expected Pritchett "to curb all of the demonstrations." In June the Albany Movement dropped its demand for a biracial committee, but this had no effect on the city's attitude other than to encourage the belief that it had the "agitators" on the run.[43]

Pritchett anticipated that SCLC might once more inject itself into the situation when King and Abernathy returned to Albany to be sentenced in July. Indeed, the burly chief looked forward to this, regarding King as a challenge to his professional skills. He therefore prepared for the probable contest well in advance: "I researched Dr. King. I read about his early days in Montgomery, his methods there. I read that he was a great follower of Gandhi's. . . . We had planned for mass arrests. We had known that their plan was . . . to overcrowd our jail conditions, thus making us have to give in. . . . [I] made preparations that at no time would any be housed in Albany or Dougherty County. I had made arrangements, and we had it on a map—Lee County, which was ten miles away, and then we'd go out twenty-five miles, go out fifty miles, a hundred miles—and all those places had agreed to take prisoners." Pritchett had another ace up his sleeve: he trained his men to arrest demonstrators courteously and without violence. As he reported to the city commission, "For a period of four to five months members of the Albany Police Department was indoctrinated to this plan of non-violence. . . . At each roll call [they] were lectured and shown films on how to conduct themselves in this non-violent operation."[44]

Pritchett's assessment of King's intentions proved accurate. King, dismayed to see the December agreement unravel, decided to make his return to Albany the occasion of a dramatic gesture of defiance: he would refuse to pay any fine and go to jail instead. His impending arrival generated enormous excitement in the black community. "Mass meeting at Shiloh. Huge throng," wrote SNCC staff member Bill Hansen on July 9. "The anticipation of tomorrow gives it a circus-type atmosphere." The following day, King and Abernathy chose to serve forty-five days rather than pay $178 fines. The effect upon the protest movement was dramatic. "As much as we may disagree with MLK about the way he and SCLC do things," Hansen noted, "one has to admit that he can cause more hell to be raised by being in jail one night than anyone else could if they bombed city hall." Newspaper reporters swarmed into town; the mass meetings filled two churches to capacity. Another SNCC worker, Peggy Dammond, described the meeting in Mount Zion Baptist Church on July 11 and the events which preceded it: "We began to see the Albany we had heard of so much. The people marching up and down the streets with black arm-bands signifying the death of justice! . . . The songs which swelled the churches; the t.v. cameras and sweating white newsmen—elbowing their way through the crowd of people in the doorways and on the steps as they craned to see the pulpit and hear talk of Freedom, Courage and Dignity." C. K. Steele arrived from Tallahassee to lead a demonstration; thirty-three people went to jail with him.[45]

The protests might have snowballed, but on July 12 the unexpected happened. "Doom!" wrote Hansen. "MLK is out of jail." After serving a mere two days, an anonymous and unwanted benefactor, described by Pritchett as "an unknown well dressed negro man," paid the fines of King and Abernathy. This embarrassing anticlimax punctured the bubble of enthusiasm. "The people are confused," Hansen lamented. "Now that MLK is out of jail they don't have anything to rally around." The SNCC workers implored King to immediately invite arrest and return to jail, but King demurred: SCLC's fundraising needs, he explained, required him to stay in circulation; the shortage of bail money, moreover, made it advisable to put a temporary stop to the demonstrations. Acting on the theory that "MLK can't let a SNCC person be more willing to go to jail than himself," SNCC selected Hansen to lead a protest to city hall. "The fact that I'm white," Hansen wrote, "may be an added incentive calling him back to jail. We hope." But SNCC's ploy failed to move King and infuriated Walker, who viewed it as an appalling exhibition of bad faith and poor planning.[46]

Nevertheless, King's refusal to lead a renewed offensive generated widespread disappointment, even in SCLC's own camp. In a sermon dated July 17, Andrew Young described the pressure upon King to march, and King's personal reaction to that pressure a few days earlier:

> The people were somewhat outraged because Dr. King would not lead them in a mass demonstration that night. And the talk going through all the Negro community was that Martin Luther King was going "chicken. . . ." [A]nd when Dr. King was not quite so sure, and when he avoided every question from us about why not and seemed to resent our pressing him, we began to wonder about him ourselves. . . . [W]hen he finally came around to talking in religious terms he said, "You know, you can't

just irresponsibly send a thousand people off to fill up the jails . . . until you do feel as though there is some spiritual urging in this direction."

Thus far, SCLC's return to Albany had backfired.[47]

King hoped that further demonstrations might not be necessary: a settlement, based on the December agreement, appeared to be imminent. Mayor Kelley was known to favor negotiations. Moreover, the Albany Movement no longer insisted on a biracial committee: informal contacts would suffice. But the hard-line stance maintained by a majority of the commissioners—typified by the refusal to drop charges against the seven hundred people arrested in December—soon deflated this optimism. King decided to go to jail again in another attempt to rally local blacks. If the protests were carried far enough, SCLC calculated, public pressure would compel the federal government to intervene in some way. SCLC and SNCC ordered most of their staff members to Albany for the new round of demonstrations.[48]

On July 20, however, federal judge Robert Elliott granted the city an injunction banning further marches. To SNCC's dismay, King decided to abide by the order and cancel the impending marches. Of all the branches of government, he argued, only the federal judiciary had given blacks strong support; some of the greatest victories of the civil rights movement had come from the federal courts. They could not pick and choose which court orders to obey and which to defy: the correct strategy was to obey Elliott's injunction, however unjust, until they had successfully appealed it.[49]

King's position infuriated SNCC. On July 22 four SNCC workers argued over strategy with King at the home of a local black leader. With Charles Jones taking the lead, they took King to task for his erratic and autocratic conduct of the protests. He made decisions in the most undemocratic manner, they complained, rarely consulting SNCC or the Albany Movement. As for the injunction, why should blacks obey the likes of Elliott, a well-known segregationist? King's faith in the federal judiciary was misplaced, they contended—the courts had helped blacks slowly, grudgingly, and not very much. The movement was now running aground through lack of decisive action. C. B. King marvelled at his namesake's ability to quietly absorb criticism: "Martin was about the most imperturbable person I have ever known." His brother, Slater, was similarly impressed: "Here was King, a man internationally known, and yet for about two or three hours he was there sitting with them attempting to justify SCLC's role in saying that, 'Well, Ralph and I have families, and you know that we are bound to be a little more conservative than you guys who have no responsibilities. We would like to think that you are the creative antagonists who make this sort of situation, and that we could come in and help you work in them.'" King did not convert his critics, but simply by listening he succeeded in mollifying them.[50]

He also had to pacify the NAACP, which steadfastly opposed any infraction of the court order. On July 23, after a memorably enthusiastic meeting at Shiloh Baptist Church, the Reverend Sam Wells marched out of the church toward city hall, with about 150 people from the audience behind him. King, who had entered the church to thunderous applause and chants of "freedom," studiously avoided associating with Wells's contempt by secluding himself in the pastor's study. This did not suffice, however, to prevent a long-distance call from Gloster Current of the NAACP's head office, who sternly lectured King on his duty to obey the spirit as well as the letter of the injunction. Wells and his marchers were arrested, booked, and then bused to outlying jails in Mitchell and Lee counties.[51]

Judge Elbert Tuttle's reversal of the Elliott injunction on July 24 seemed to vindicate King's tactical judgement. Once again, however, King had to postpone going to jail. That evening he went to a mass meeting at Mount Zion Baptist Church, to be met, in Pritchett's words, "with a loud observation." When a group of forty marchers set off towards city hall at the end of the rally, a crowd of black spectators, perhaps two thousand strong, followed the line of march and, according to the police report, began "chanting, harassing, and intimidating" the officers. A smaller group broke away from the main body and ran into the street, forcing cars to swerve. When Pritchett ordered his men to disperse the crowd, "police [o]fficers were met with a volley of rocks and bottles and other objects thrown from the backyard of Eureka Baptist Church." One highway patrolman was struck on the cheek by a rock, losing several teeth. King suspended the demonstrations and called for a "day of penitence." The mayor ordered the city's bars to close at 6:00 P.M. On July 25 King, Abernathy, Anderson, Sherrod, and Jones toured Harlem, the main black district, stopping at a pool hall, a shoeshine parlor, a drugstore, and a saloon. In his brief speeches, Pritchett reported, King "was abating [sic] non-violence and ask[ing] them to help prevent violence." During the course of July, the police issued a record number of thirty-eight pistol permits.[52]

King finally went to jail on July 27, along with Abernathy, Anderson, Slater King, and six others. Upon being locked up, he wrote in his prison diary, "We immediately began singing freedom songs." Determined not to be tricked out of jail again, King refused a summons to

Pritchett's office, telling the jailer to have the chief come to *him.* "Come on Doctor," Pritchett reassured him, "I am not trying to get you to leave; there is a long-distance telephone call for you from a man named Spivack." King had been booked to appear on NBC's "Meet the Press" on July 28; the show's host, Lawrence Spivack, begged him to post bond so that he could fulfill the engagement. But after consulting C. B. King and Wyatt Walker, King decided to send Anderson instead.[53]

"The big job now," Stanley Levison argued, "is to put the heat on Washington. . . . This is no time for the federal government to be weak." True, the Justice Department was in touch with both sides trying to promote negotiations, and President Kennedy himself, in a statement on August 1, called upon the city commission to "sit down with the citizens of Albany, who may be Negroes." Beyond this, however, the administration refused to go. The government had done all it could under existing law, Robert Kennedy informed an SCLC-picked delegation on August 2: "We could do a great deal more if our hands weren't tied." On August 15, William Taylor of the Civil Rights Commission outlined a plan for federal mediation to presidential assistant Lee White. Taylor proposed that Kennedy send a high-ranking officer such as the vice-president, or perhaps a distinguished private citizen like General Lucius Clay, to bring the two sides together in Albany. Crises like Albany were bound to recur, he warned; the government needed some kind of policy for dealing with them. But nothing came of his plan.[54]

With little fear of federal intervention, the city commission had no real incentive to negotiate. Nor, with the demonstrations well under control, did they see any reason to offer SCLC a face-saving exit. King became increasingly exasperated by the inaction of the Justice Department and, in particular, the FBI. The role of the federal government seemed to be entirely negative: it sought to dissuade him from breaking the injunction, dissuade him from going to jail, and dissuade him from demonstrating. "This can't go on," he told Robert Kennedy before his July 27 arrest. "I'm tired. We're sick of it." The government, he complained, had no idea what blacks in Albany were up against.[55]

By the end of July newspaper reporters agreed that the protests were running out of steam. That month had seen about five hundred arrests—an impressive number, but less than the total during a shorter period in December. In August the demonstrations had to be scaled down: picketing of city hall by small groups replaced the embarrassingly thin marches. Confident they had broken the back of the Albany Movement, city officials made light of the demonstrations.

"Chief Pritchett approached the group of pickets," the city manager reported, "announced that they had sung all the songs in their repertoire, informed them that their quality was giving out and they were prayed out, and ordered them to disperse." The incident ended, of course, with the arrest of the pickets. Starved of local volunteers, Andrew Young made arrangements for a "prayer pilgrimage" by Northern ministers and rabbis. Coretta King agreed to lead a "mother's march."[56]

There seemed little sign of an end to the city's war of attrition when, on August 10, the Albany Movement agreed to suspend the demonstrations "with the hope that good faith talks might be set." King and Abernathy were given suspended sentences and released that day, but when they left the city on August 11 to help clear the air the commissioners merely gloated. It was true that the city attorney admitted that local segregation laws were not legally enforceable, but this did not detract from the commission's determination to perpetuate segregation by other means. Indeed, when advised by Georgia's assistant attorney general that the federal courts would sooner or later require all publicly owned facilities to be desegregated, the commission closed the parks, the library, and the swimming pools. As for hotels, restaurants, and other privately owned facilities, the city repealed all its segregation laws the better to uphold segregation: far better to deny that segregation existed, and arrest black interlopers for trespass or breach of the peace.[57]

When the city turned down the latest requests of the Albany Movement, the pause in demonstrations ended. It had lasted barely a week. SCLC's "prayer pilgrimage" took place on August 28, giving Pritchett, on his own admission, "some of my most tiring times," as more than seventy ministers, priests, and rabbis picketed city hall and went to jail. At the end of the year, however, the commission was still refusing to negotiate, and in February 1963 it again rejected the idea of a "biracial planning committee." SNCC kept up its picketing and at one time had twenty field secretaries in jail. But a growing sense of defeat hung over the Albany Movement. Visiting the city two years after the heyday of the protests, one reporter described Albany as "a monument to white supremacy." Slater King, who succeeded Anderson in the summer of 1963 as the Albany Movement's president, thought the gains of the campaign "negligible and hardly worth mentioning"— desegregated waiting rooms at the bus and train stations, a desegregated library with no tables or chairs. Most blacks, he reported, "are disillusioned, frightened, and bitter."[58]

In September 1962, shortly before SCLC's annual convention, King held a three-day meeting of the executive staff in order to analyze what had gone wrong: whatever lessons they learned could be used to good effect in Birmingham, which had already been earmarked as the target of their next major campaign. That something had gone seriously awry was obvious, but, contrary to press comments, King and his colleagues decided that Albany was not an unmitigated failure. When a Southern city was forced to sell public facilities, open integrated libraries without tables and chairs, and repeal all its segregation laws, things could never be the same again. "When we came to Albany there was an inflexible position on the part of the city council," Walker argued, "but when we left with the cessation of hostilities . . . they had altered their position. We had not changed our position. We said we were against segregation."[59]

Albany also underlined what had become manifest in Montgomery during the bus boycott and apparent throughout the South during the sit-ins: blacks were ripe for revolt and, given the right leadership, were prepared to take direct action. In Albany, moreover, direct action had been taken a stage further: "That was the first instance," Walker contended, "where we had a community mobilized and organized to the point . . . they were willing to go to jail in large numbers." If the validity of segregation depended on its "normality"—the broad acceptance of white supremacy by blacks and whites as the natural order of things—then the foundations had surely been rocked in Albany.[60]

Accentuating the positive, however, could not disguise the fact that SCLC had committed major errors. It had gone off at half cock, relying on inspiration and spontaneity rather than planning and analysis. It had failed to anticipate the opponent's reactions and make contingency plans. By attempting to provide "ambulance service" to a beleaguered movement, it had tied itself to a weak and divided local leadership. The lack of a clear chain of command—the vague division of authority between SCLC, SNCC, and the Albany Movement—had been a recipe for disunity. Albany revealed the need for a reliable local base and clear control over decision making.

This much was common sense. Not so obvious, yet more important still, were two other tactical lessons. The first concerned the power of numbers; the second the role of violence.

Albany disabused King and Walker of their more romantic notions about nonviolent direct action. The concept of a "nonviolent army" that could steamroller the opposition through sheer weight of numbers turned out to be highly unrealistic. Albany demonstrated that no more than 5 percent of a given black population could be expected to volunteer for jail. SCLC had to frame its tactics accordingly. Any attempt to "fill the jails" at the outset of a campaign would backfire, as it did in Albany. People who were arrested once proved extremely reluctant to risk a second arrest, especially when they had experienced difficulty in getting out of jail the first time. By insisting on cash bonds, of course, Pritchett had delayed the release of prisoners and tied up about $400,000 in bail money. The Birmingham campaign, SCLC decided, should start with small-scale protests and gradually build up to mass demonstrations and jail-ins. It had to be a crescendo, not a diminuendo.[61]

Finally, SCLC learned that, to quote Bayard Rustin, "protest becomes an effective tactic to the degree that it elicits brutality and oppression from the power structure." The conduct of the federal government during the Freedom Rides—it had intervened in Alabama, where Klan mobs had been permitted to run amok, but adopted a "hands-off" policy towards Mississippi, where the police had kept order and carried out "peaceful" arrests—sent an unmistakable message to Southern segregationists: federal intervention could be avoided if the authorities kept violence in check. Laurie Pritchett applied this lesson with skill. Despite all his arrests, Walker noted, "not once did the Federal government raise a finger to protect the rights of Negro citizens." Captain Ray and Chief Pritchett had shown that "legal" repression foiled direct action far more effectively than violence. If emulated across the South, their tactics might destroy the civil rights movement. Indeed, direct action was already on the wane by the end of 1962; CORE-led protests in Rock Hill, Huntsville, and Baton Rouge also ended in failure.[62]

Pritchett's "nonviolence" also demonstrated the double-edged impact of press coverage. The Albany city fathers learned earlier than SCLC that violence attracted media attention—strongly adverse attention—as did no other issue. Press coverage therefore inhibited the segregationist response to direct action: as Levison pointed out in 1970, white officials were reluctant to employ violence "when the demonstrations focused public attention from all over the country because of their mass nature." Indeed, Wyatt Walker exaggerated but slightly when he called Pritchett "the darling of the press." Thus, while SCLC's lifeblood, media coverage was also a danger. Unless it concentrated on the repressive violence inherent in Southern society— state violence—it would not be much help. "Pritchett was a pretty smart boy," thought C. T. Vivian. "He wasn't just a dumb policeman. It was an interesting thing because it helped us in a certain respect." SCLC learned to choose its targets more carefully. In Birmingham, SCLC had a strong local base, a clear chain of command, a carefully planned strategy, and a "dumb policeman."[63]

Five

Breakthrough at Birmingham

There were other Southern cities equally determined to maintain white supremacy. Birmingham, however, had become the
best-known symbol of the intransigent South. In 1951 a young
black reporter, Carl Rowan, described the Alabama steel center as
"the world's most race-conscious city, . . . a city of gross tensions, a city where the color line is drawn in every conceivable
way [and where] Eugene 'Bull' Connor, white-supremacist police
commissioner, sees that no man, white or black, crosses the
line." Race relations continued to deteriorate, despite Connor's
scandal-induced retirement in 1953, under the impact of the
Brown decision and the rise of the white "massive resistance"
movement. With the demise of the Interracial Council in April
1956, dialogue between the two communities virtually ceased.

When, soon afterwards, the National Conference of Christians and Jews sent out two thousand invitations to a meeting entitled "Building Brotherhood," only twenty-two people turned up. The organizer of the event had to disconnect his telephone after receiving a barrage of threatening and abusive calls. Under the direction of Asa "Ace" Carter, the Klan-like citizens council pumped out a steady stream of racist and anti-Semitic propaganda.[1]

In 1956 Connor emerged from retirement to win back his old post, commissioner of public safety, from a now unpopular moderate. During the next few years he exercised virtually unbridled power, "arresting innocent citizens, openly monitoring and occasionally harassing civil rights activists, and stridently accusing segregation's critics of Communist sympathies."[2] Visiting the city in 1960 for the *New York Times*, Harrison Salisbury depicted Birmingham as a racist tyranny paralyzed by fear: "Every channel of communication, every medium of mutual interest, every reasoned approach, every inch of middle ground has been fragmented by the emotional dynamite of racism, enforced by the whip, the razor, the gun, the bomb, the torch, the club, the knife, the mob, the police and many branches of the state's apparatus." Telephones were tapped, mail intercepted and opened; "the eavesdropper, the informer, the spy has become a fact of life." A year later the Civil Rights Commission reported that "racial prejudices are incredibly tense . . . [and] the slightest provocation can be expected to unleash acts of violence." When rioters put the first Freedom Ride out of action, Connor ingenuously explained that the police had been slow to respond to the violence on account of Mother's Day. In fact, Connor knew—the FBI had told him—that the Klan was waiting to ambush the riders.[3]

Since founding the Alabama Christian Movement for Human Rights in 1956, Fred Shuttlesworth had doggedly fought against Birmingham's vicious system of white supremacy. Before moving to the city's Bethel Baptist Church in 1953 he pastored a church in Selma; there, he had clashed bitterly with his board of deacons. With a prickly personality and frequent want of tact, he was plagued by such conflicts over the years. But although he was often criticized for being autocratic and egocentric, Shuttlesworth's reckless courage evoked universal admiration.[4] On Christmas night, 1956, an explosion blew him out of bed; the next day he took a seat at the front of a bus and was hauled off to jail. In September 1957 he tried to desegregate the school system by taking his children to a "white" high school and demanding their admission. He was promptly set upon and beaten up. The following month he launched an unsuccessful bus boycott.[5]

Shuttlesworth then turned to the issue of police harassment and the appointment of black policemen. On June 25, 1958, four days after he had written to the city commission, a stick of dynamite blasted his church. The proximity of the two events might have been coincidence, but Shuttlesworth needed little convincing that the police, under the control of "Bull" Connor, were either actively assisting such attacks or, at the very least, doing nothing to stop them. In August, he wrote to Mayor James Morgan complaining that "some policemen assigned in certain areas are conducting virtually a reign of unholy terror against Negroes. . . . Why must it be a standard thing, almost, for the Officers to accost most Negroes they stop about knowing 'that Negro preacher,' and the like? Why must people who watch around the church be intimidated by Police? Why are your officers so prone to strike Negroes? In fairness, these things ought to be looked into."[6] His pleas merely evoked further harassment; another eight years passed before the city appointed its first Negro policemen. Although Birmingham remained a bastion of segregation, Shuttlesworth turned the ACMHR into SCLC's most vigorous affiliate. With a core of about six hundred active supporters, most of them women, its weekly meetings attracted larger and more fervent audiences than those of the postboycott MIA.[7]

In September 1962, immediately after the Albany debacle, SCLC began to make definite plans for a campaign of direct action in Birmingham. It scheduled the protests to begin in the fall, with the aim of disrupting the central business district when it was most vulnerable, during the Christmas shopping season. A boycott of downtown stores, initiated in March by students at Miles College, was already hurting the city's merchants: some establishments saw their trade cut in half.[8]

Rumors of the impending demonstrations threw Connor's white opponents into a panic. Such protests, they believed, would merely stir up racial hysteria and scuttle their efforts to install a more moderate city government. Connor's action in closing the city's parks in order to avoid integration had evoked angry protests from many whites. More important, many of Birmingham's business grandees—the so-called Big Mules—were now convinced that Connor's strident racism was damaging the local economy by deterring investors. As the president of the chamber of commerce, Sidney Smyer, complained, "These racial incidents have given us a black eye that we'll be a long time trying to forget." In late 1962 a faction led by David Vann, a young lawyer, forced a successful referendum to replace the existing commission form of government—which, in their eyes, gave Connor far too much power—with a mayor-council charter. Under this new charter, the current administration had to face reelection in 1963 rather than 1965.

The moderates hoped to cap their victory in the referendum by install-
ing Albert Boutwell as mayor. They desperately wanted to forestall
demonstrations by Shuttlesworth and King which, they believed,
would not only play into Connor's hands but also lead to a bloodbath.
"We are trying to produce a political miracle," Vann wrote Burke
Marshall. "Things which grate on the emotions of the people" had at
all costs to be avoided.[9]

The chamber of commerce attempted to dissuade Shuttlesworth
from proceeding with the protests. A subcommittee headed by Sidney
Smyer met Shuttlesworth himself—the first biracial talks of any significance for many years and the first time that white business leaders
had personally approached Shuttlesworth. For the black clergyman,
who had been reviled and persecuted for the past six years, the meeting represented a moment of sweet triumph, and he savored it. The
merchants offered to desegregate their water fountains, but Shuttlesworth insisted on the toilets as well—"We passed water a long
time ago." Reluctantly, the whites agreed to integrate the public facilities in five downtown stores. Shuttlesworth advised King to cancel the
demonstrations.[10]

This victory, however, proved short-lived. When Connor threatened
to prosecute the stores, the "white" and "colored" signs reappeared.
This episode provided SCLC with conclusive evidence of the need for
direct action. By then it was too close to Christmas to build an effective campaign, so King and Shuttlesworth agreed to reschedule the
protests to coincide with the Easter shopping season. If they waited
any longer, moreover, SCLC might have to face a new city administration; as Shuttlesworth put it, "The idea of facing 'Bull' Connor was the
thing."[11]

During the second week of January 1963, SCLC's leadership met at
the Dorchester Center where, for two days, they mapped the basic
strategy and analyzed the main difficulties. "We decided on Birmingham with the attitude that we may not win it, we may lose
everything," Walker related in 1967. "But we knew that as Birmingham
went, so would go the South. And we felt that if we could crack that
city, then we could crack any city."[12] They also weighed the attitude of
the federal government and its probable reaction to the protests. "It
was decided that there was a kind of tacit alliance between . . . the
Kennedy Administration and the civil rights movement," Levison recalled; "that if the civil rights movement could arouse the country and
create the demand, . . . this Administration would hear it and respond." At the close of the meeting, Levison warned that Connor had

fought tooth and nail against the CIO; SCLC would be taking on a rough adversary, and with far less power than the labor movement of the 1930s. King solemnly agreed, adding that in his judgement not all of them would return from Birmingham alive.[13]

Two weeks later, on January 23, SCLC's executive staff met in Atlanta to confirm the decision. They were moving into Birmingham, they noted, for three reasons: blacks there wanted action, they had the experience of Albany to build on, and victory was possible. They decided to launch the campaign on March 14, shortly after the mayoral election.[14] In order to avoid the kind of leadership conflicts which had bedevilled the Albany campaign, King and Shuttlesworth decided that all important decisions should be made by the two of them jointly, with Abernathy substituting for King if necessary. Once the protests were underway, the leaders undertook to consult an ACMHR strategy committee each day. Although the role of the committee was purely advisory, this arrangement helped to reassure the more conservative blacks in the ACMHR that Shuttlesworth's impulsive tendencies would not get completely out of hand. During the first week of February, King and Walker met the board of the ACMHR to seal the alliance. At a mass meeting afterwards W. E. Shortridge, the ACMHR's treasurer, dropped a broad hint to the audience: "In March we hope to show you something that has never been seen before in Birmingham, something you will all be proud of." This enigmatic statement puzzled the two detectives who were recording the proceedings. The police had not yet, it seems, recruited an informant on the ACMHR board.[15]

Most blacks were also kept in the dark. Walker, who made several trips to Birmingham to lay the groundwork for the campaign, operated on the "need to know" principle. "We were sort of working like the French Underground," he later stated. "We were working with the movement people, the grass roots organization that Shuttlesworth had mobilized."[16] The mayoral election provided another reason for secrecy: publicity about SCLC's plans would only assist Connor, one of the three contenders. In addition, as King explained over the phone to Levison, "a lot of the Negro middle class who would want to criticize the movement anyway, would have this as a good excuse to lash out against us."[17] As things turned out, the election eliminated one of the candidates but left neither Connor nor Boutwell with an overall majority. The campaign had to be delayed until the runoff on April 2. "Some few Negroes are not for D.A. at this time," Shuttlesworth informed King and Walker in mid-March. "Since Bull Connor is very definitely a Contender in the Run-Off, it appears advisable to lay low, with no visible signs of forthcoming action." Walker agreed to withdraw SCLC staff members from the city and cancel his and King's appointments there.[18] As the runoff approached, Shuttlesworth tried to squash the argument that a Boutwell victory would make demonstrations unnecessary. "There isn't a whole lot of difference between Mr. Bull and Mr. Boutwell," he assured a mass meeting at the Abysinnia Baptist Church. Connor was merely an "undignified Boutwell" and Boutwell a "dignified Connor." Whoever was elected, he promised, "is going to catch hell."[19]

Walker planned the campaign meticulously. Working with Lola Hendricks, the Reverend Ed Gardner, and others in the ACMHR, he collected the names and addresses of about three hundred people who promised to go to jail, and of a much larger number who pledged to help in some other way. He formed a telephone committee, a transportation committee, a food committee, and even a jail visitation committee. A. G. Gaston, a black millionaire generally regarded as a conservative, contributed a rent-free headquarters at his motel. In choosing its targets, SCLC had the benefit of hindsight. In Albany, Walker explained, "we took on all segregation. We bit off more than we could chew." In Birmingham, therefore, SCLC singled out lunch counters—the most hated symbols, now that buses were integrated, of segregation. Lunch counters also had the attraction of being vulnerable. Shuttlesworth, although not entirely happy with such a narrow scope, selected a handful of stores in the central business district, all within two blocks of each other. Walker then surveyed these targets. From the Gaston Motel, "I measured how long it would take a person walking to get down there—a youngster, an old person, a person my age. When I say young, I mean a kid. Then I surveyed and went in on the pretext of buying camera equipment or looking at some men's clothes. I would then find out exactly where the eating facility was. . . . I even plotted how many stools there were, where the places of ingress and egress were." Walker also selected secondary targets—the federal buildings and city hall—and tertiary targets in the outlying shopping malls. One way or another, "we were going to have a confrontation somewhere." By the end of March, Walker remembered, everything was set: "When Dr. King came to town and started pushing those buttons, . . . stuff started popping."[20]

King, meanwhile, stepped up his fundraising efforts and, in early March, offered his comments on the president's recent civil rights message in an article for *Nation.* Praising Kennedy for proposing legislation, King urged the government to abandon its misguided attempt to act as a neutral mediator and, instead, to "commit its immense resources squarely on the side of the quest for freedom." In a conversation with Levison, who helped him to draft the article, King noted that the administration's attempt to balance the interests of the civil rights movement against those of the segregationists had led to a kind of schizophrenia: on the one hand it appointed the NAACP lawyer Thurgood Marshall to the federal bench; on the other hand it elevated segregationists like Robert Elliott. Kennedy had often told him, he went on, that a civil rights bill stood no chance of passage, but, in King's view, "if [Kennedy] would go out and really fight—crusade for it—it would have a stronger chance of getting through."[21]

While King was writing and fundraising, SCLC's rudimentary Northern support apparatus began preparing for its first real test. Harry Belafonte contacted wealthy friends in New York and Los Angeles and solicited money for bail bonds. SCLC's regional representatives set up fundraising rallies for the same purpose. The officers of the Gandhi Society—Ted Kheel, Harry Wachtel, Clarence Jones, and William Kunstler—anticipated the inevitable legal onslaught by the Alabama courts and prepared an appropriate response in conjunction with the NAACP Legal Defense Fund (now headed by Jack Greenberg, who was much more sympathetic to direct action than his predecessor, Thurgood Marshall). Walter Fauntroy, SCLC's man in Washington, recruited a large contingent of Northern clergymen who could be ready to descend upon Birmingham at a moment's notice if the need arose for additional demonstrators.[22]

At the end of March, King and Shuttlesworth spoke to about seventy-five potential or committed supporters at a confidential meeting in Belafonte's New York apartment. Kheel outlined the legal implications of the campaign and explained that the Gandhi Society had primary responsibility for organizing the legal and financial support. King disclosed that the protests would begin three days hence, on April 3, the day after the runoff. If Boutwell were elected, he confessed, they would undoubtedly be criticized for not giving him a chance; however, the campaign had already been postponed twice, and a further delay would entail sacrificing the advantage of striking during Easter. Shuttlesworth then made an emotional appeal for support: "We hope that you will join us in the good fight. If you don't, we are prepared to go it alone"—and, if necessary, to die in the streets. In his account of the meeting, King recalled the shocked silence that followed this statement.[23]

After the meeting, King and Shuttlesworth consulted the lawyers as to how they should respond when, as was certain to happen, the Alabama courts enjoined the demonstrations. Unless challenged, they agreed, such an injunction would paralyze the campaign. They would be faced with the alternatives, therefore, of violating the order or suspending the protests while they appealed to the federal courts. Shuttlesworth and Clarence Jones favored the latter course. However, as Jones recounted to Levison the next day, King insisted that they should break the injunction without waiting for the outcome of an appeal. The federal courts, he reasoned, could hardly punish the violation of a clearly unjust state injunction—such a violation involved no challenge to federal law, no real civil disobedience, and was, in fact, entirely justified.[24]

On April 3, the day after Boutwell defeated Connor, "twenty well-dressed Negroes, their timing apparently synchronized, staged sit-in demonstrations at downtown Birmingham stores." Such was the campaign's modest opening as reported by the *Chicago Defender*. For a good week, however, it looked as if SCLC might fall flat on its face. King expected opposition from the black middle class, but its extent took him by surprise. Many blacks were appalled by SCLC's timing. Demonstrations now, they believed, jeopardized the slow but steady progress towards racial moderation of which Connor's defeat was the most significant manifestation. It seemed churlish and provocative to begin the protests before Boutwell had even taken office. Blacks also felt peeved that SCLC had kept them in the dark about its plans. "We had no opportunity to come in and meet with local groups for fear of influencing the election," explained Walker. "We had to start cold." However unavoidable, the failure to consult exacerbated old leadership divisions and evoked strong criticism of both Shuttlesworth and King. The city's black weekly, the *World*, described Shuttlesworth as a "non-responsible, non-attached, and non-program 'leader,'" and dismissed King as a "glossy personality." During the following weeks it persistently belittled SCLC's tactics.[25]

Confronted by widespread opposition and resentment, King delayed going to jail and spent his first week in Birmingham drumming up support. "Some people have told us to wait, it is not the time," he told a meeting at St. James Baptist Church. "But we have waited too long. Now is the time to get rid of the injustice. The time is always right to do right." Behind the scenes, he appealed to groups of ministers, businessmen, and professionals. Many of the arguments which he later addressed to whites in "Letter from Birmingham City Jail" he originally aimed at these blacks: the absurdity of calling him an "outsider";

the futility of trusting in Boutwell; the need for pressure; the necessity for a socially conscious ministry. At a meeting of the Baptist Ministers Conference attended by more than one hundred clergymen, King excoriated "preachers riding around in big cars, living in fine homes, but [who are] not willing to take part in the fight. . . . If you can't stand up with your people, you are not fit to be a preacher." The Reverend John H. Cross, an ACMHR activist who pastored the Sixteenth Street Baptist Church, proposed that the ministers record their support for SCLC. The president of the conference, Dr. J. L. Ware, seemed reluctant to call a vote, Cross recalled. "So we kept demanding. We said, 'Brother President, there's a motion.'" Ware and Shuttlesworth were longstanding rivals, and the *World* was trumpeting the former as the black leader most worthy of support. Although the motion passed, relatively few ministers—about 10 percent, according to Walker's estimate—actively supported the movement.[26]

William Kunstler, who watched King address a meeting of Negro businessmen and professionals, wrote a vivid description of how King handled a critical audience. He began by opening the meeting to the floor, inviting people to ask questions and state their opinions. When the audience had let off steam, he calmly and in some detail explained the purpose and tactics of the campaign. He concluded with a strong and eloquent appeal for support. Kunstler recorded that after King had spoken for about half an hour, "those who hadn't been won over were at least neutralized and the rest seemed eager to help. . . . I don't know quite when the turning point had been reached, but I was very much aware that it had." Most blacks, however, were still reserving judgement, waiting to see how the protests unfolded and whether, as in Albany, they would peter out inconclusively.[27]

SCLC also consolidated its support within the ACMHR. The nightly mass meetings presented a mixture of exhortation and entertainment, skilfully designed to generate enthusiasm and emotional involvement. The meetings followed the same pattern. First, junior SCLC workers like Andy Young, James Bevel, and Dorothy Cotton led the audience in "freedom songs." When the audience had warmed up, the leaders made their entrance: King, followed by Abernathy, Shuttlesworth, and several local ministers. Their appearance usually prompted a standing ovation. When the preachers had seated themselves on a platform at the front of the church, the meeting proper began. The Reverend Ed Gardner, vice-president of the ACMHR, introduced the speakers in order of precedence: a local name spoke first, followed by Shuttlesworth, Abernathy, or Walker, and then King. Hymns, sung gospel-fashion by the church choir, were interspersed among the speeches. At some stage during the proceedings a collection was taken. Detectives from the Birmingham Police Department, who sat in and recorded every meeting, described the procedure: "A section of the benches is asked to stand up as a body and then file down in a continuous line, rear bench first, next bench etc. Using this system each person is obligated to file down by the collection plate or become immediately conspicuous by remaining in his seat or breaking line." At the end of each meeting, Shuttlesworth or King asked for volunteers to go to jail. Those who responded walked to the front of the church, amidst cheering and applause, to shake hands with the leaders and have their names recorded. As King later described it, the scene resembled "those invitational periods that occur every Sunday morning in Negro churches, when the pastor projects the call to those present to join the church."[28]

During the first week King laid great stress on the boycott of downtown stores. "We can't all go to jail," he told a packed meeting at Thurgood Baptist Church, "but we can all keep our money in our pockets and out of the downtown merchants' pockets. The white man is trying to black out our movement by not giving news coverage. Over the next few days we want to make this movement ninety-nine per cent effective. . . . If we can do that, then the downtown businessmen will sit down and talk this thing out with us." He urged blacks to refrain from acquiring new Easter clothes: "Buy nothing but food"; any Negro walking downtown with a package in his hand "isn't fit to be free."[29] There is no doubt of the boycott's effectiveness. During the week leading up to Easter, department store sales were barely 4 percent above the weekly average for the previous year; the corresponding figures for Atlanta and New Orleans were 14 and 22 percent. After Easter, when the demonstrations grew in size and frequency, sales plummeted even further.[30] A survey by Walker indicated that only thirty Negroes entered five of the largest downtown stores on April 16–18. On April 18, four of the stores had no black customers, the fifth only one. Those who did not attend the mass meetings learned of the boycott through word of mouth or through leaflets—local volunteers distributed some fifty thousand on April 16 and 17. Fear of violence and disorder, of course, also kept many whites from shopping downtown.[31]

Recruiting people for jail, however, proved much more difficult. Only about 70 of the 250 people who had volunteered in March actually came forward on April 3. The first three days of lunch counter sit-ins produced a mere thirty-five arrests. When SCLC began staging marches, it soon became obvious that not enough blacks were coming forward. The certainty of arrest deterred many, for Connor had refused to issue a parade permit. Another difficulty concerned unease over the timing of the protests and skepticism about their chances of success. The restrained behavior of the police posed another problem: nothing generated black unity better than police brutality against unoffending people. SCLC thirsted for a dramatic confrontation, but thus far Connor had failed to oblige. According to Walker, King told him "to find some way to make Bull Connor tip his hand."[32]

Connor's first tactical lapse occurred on April 7, Palm Sunday. Saturday had witnessed SCLC's first march, which ended with Shuttlesworth and forty-two others being politely herded into paddy wagons. The next day, barely two dozen turned out for a march led by A. D. King. More than a thousand spectators, however, gathered along the route. Angry and disappointed to see the marchers arrested after walking but two blocks, they milled about and hurled abuse at the police. One youth poked at a police dog with a lead pipe. An altercation broke out which took fifteen policemen, with dogs, to quell. The incident quickly blew over, but it taught Walker two valuable lessons. First, by delaying the marches until late afternoon he ensured that a large number of onlookers congregated around the church. A confrontation was much more likely to occur between the police and the spectators than between the police and the demonstrators. Second, many of the newsmen had described the spectators as "demonstrators," implying that they were part and parcel of SCLC's protests. "We weren't marching but 12, 14, 16, 18," Walker admitted. "But the papers were reporting 1,400."[33]

At the mass meeting on April 8, Walker milked the incident for all it was worth. It was shameful, he told the audience, that the police had to "sic" dogs on nonviolent Negroes. For the time being, however, the police did not repeat their error, and active support for the marches continued to slide. On April 10 only thirty people volunteered. It was imperative for King to go to jail in order to inspire support. "Ralph Abernathy and I will make our move," he promised the meeting at St. James Baptist Church. "And I can't think of a better day than Good Friday," April 12.[34]

Connor and Hanes—still, thanks to a dispute over the new charter, in control of the city government—now played their trump card: they obtained a temporary restraining order from Judge Walter A. Jenkins of the state circuit court. It enjoined King, Shuttlesworth, and 136 others from taking part in demonstrations or other forms of public protest. When served the document in the small hours of April 11, King told reporters that "we've got an injunction from heaven." At a press conference later that day, King, Shuttlesworth, and Abernathy confirmed that they had no intention of obeying the order. At the strategy committee meeting on Friday morning, some doubts were expressed about the wisdom of defying the courts. But King was adamant. "You don't quite understand what's involved," he told his father; he had to march.[35]

But King's decision did not simply concern the wisdom or necessity of breaking the injunction: it was also a question of timing. "We had a financial crisis," Walker explained. "There were people in jail who were due to come out. . . . [S]ome of them had been in jail for nine days and we didn't have the bond money to get them out." The crisis had been triggered by the city's decision on April 11 to insist upon cash bonds. As the strategy committee pondered the situation, King later wrote, "A sense of doom began to pervade the room. . . . No one knew what to say, for no one knew what to do. Finally, someone spoke up and, as he spoke, I could see that he was giving voice to what was on everyone's mind. 'Martin,' he said, 'this means you can't go to jail. We need money. We need a lot of money. We need it now. You are the only one who has the contacts to get it.'" But King decided to make a "faith act." With Abernathy at his side, he led a procession of fifty people from the Zion Hill church towards city hall. After letting them walk seven or eight blocks, Connor had them arrested.[36]

King felt compelled to go to jail in order to stiffen the resolve of his supporters, to stimulate national publicity for the protests, and to exert pressure on the federal government to make some kind of positive intervention. The last goal was the most important. Talks between the ACMHR and the Senior Citizens Committee (representing the chamber of commerce) had resumed on April 9. But the whites were in no mood to compromise. Charles Morgan, a local white attorney who acted as a go-between, recalled that one of the whites opened the proceedings by asking, "What is it that you niggers want?" More talks took place on April 11 and 16, whereafter the whites refused to carry on until the courts ruled on the validity of the recent election.[37]

The key to breaking the deadlock lay in the hands of the federal government. If the government could bring pressure to bear on the merchants, SCLC calculated, the latter might be willing to negotiate. Neither the president nor the attorney general, however, had much sympathy for SCLC's tactics. Having pleaded with King and Shuttlesworth to postpone the campaign, they regarded the timing of the protests as a calculated attempt to force their hand. King's imprisonment elicited a noncommittal statement of concern from the president but still no hint of federal action. The Justice Department insisted that it possessed no legal authority to intervene, a declaration that prompted the *Chicago Defender* to draw pessimistic parallels with Albany.[38]

King's plight in jail provided SCLC with an obvious focus for its efforts to involve the federal government. When Abernathy and King were placed in solitary confinement, Walker sent telegrams to the White House and Justice Department to protest their being held "incommunicado." His concern was not feigned: Clarence Jones told Stanley Levison that Walker was anxious, which, they agreed, was unusual for him. Levison suggested that Connor was trying to "break" King. In Atlanta, Coretta was beside herself with worry, and at Walker's suggestion she tried to contact the president by telephone. On Monday, his jailers asked King if he wished to place a call to his wife. When Coretta picked up the receiver in Atlanta she revealed, to King's astonishment and delight, that "I just got a call from the President and he told me you were going to call me in a few minutes. I talked with Bobby last night. He called twice and told me he would call today, and it was the President himself, and he assured me of his concern. He asked me if we had any complaints and said if we did to be sure and let him know." Surmising (correctly) that their line was tapped, King spoke in guarded tones. He assured his wife that he was not being ill-treated, and then asked how the Atlanta papers were covering the protests. But his overriding concern was to make sure that Walker learned of the president's call so that the press could be told. "Do that right now," he insisted. "I'll probably come out in the next day or so. Be sure to get in touch with the Reverend. I think this gives it a new dimension."[39]

Now permitted visitors, King asked Walker to send a copy of his April 11 statement to Burke Marshall, so that the government had a clearer understanding of their reasons for breaking the injunction. On April 19 Shuttlesworth saw Marshall in Washington to put forth SCLC's case in person. "Fauntroy says Fred was tremendous," Walker wrote King, "and cleared up a lot of questions on timing, new city government, etc." Marshall told Shuttlesworth that although the government still saw no reason to intervene, it would try to be helpful. In his report on the meeting to Robert Kennedy, Marshall warned that while the police had so far acted with restraint, "the situation in Birmingham continues to be dangerous. The Negro population has no confidence at all in the local police and there is no doubt but that a good number of the Negroes carry weapons of some sort."[40]

In "Letter from Birmingham City Jail," which he completed before leaving prison on bail on April 20, King set out to systematically demolish the various objections to nonviolent direct action, and to justify his own particular decision to violate a court order. He and his colleagues had expounded the basic arguments of the "Letter" many times before in various speeches and articles.[41] But "Letter from Birmingham City Jail," with its flashes of anger, pathos, and mocking irony, contained an urgency and intensity of feeling often absent from his other writings. Wyatt Walker deciphered and roughly edited the pages of crabbed handwriting as they were conveyed by King's lawyers, bit by bit, from the jail. Published as a pamphlet by the American Friends Service Committee (although too late to influence the campaign), it soon became a classic document of the civil rights movement, its most cogent and persuasive defense of civil disobedience.[42]

King's conviction on April 26 for criminal, rather than civil, contempt represented a victory of sorts: civil contempt carried an indefinite sentence, criminal contempt a penalty of only five days. Clearly anxious to keep King out of jail, the court allowed the seven defendants twenty days to file an appeal.[43]

By the end of April, however, the demonstrations were once again running out of steam. Despite Kennedy's phone call, the situation in Birmingham remained deadlocked. Having shifted down into voter registration during King's incarceration, the campaign now had to shift into the high gear of mass jail-ins. Herein lay the difficulty. Attendance at the mass meetings was higher than ever, but the stream of volunteers for jail had dwindled to a trickle. Kunstler watched in dismay "as both King and Abernathy exhorted a packed church for almost an hour in order to persuade a dozen people to volunteer." As Walker put it, "We had run out of troops. We had scraped the bottom of the barrel of adults who could go." King had always known that SCLC needed to involve students, but Miles College, the city's largest black institution of higher education, was failing to respond. SCLC's recruiting committee—James Lawson, Dorothy Cotton, Bernard Lee, Andrew Young, and James Bevel—urged King to let schoolchildren march. King was loathe to do this: the tactic was fraught with danger and would inevitably evoke widespread censure. He had still to make up his mind when he flew to Memphis, with Shuttlesworth, Abernathy, and Walker, for a two-day meeting of SCLC's board.

The leaders absent, James Bevel took a decisive step. Enlisting the help of young volunteers like William Douthard, James Orange, and Andrew Marrissett, he decided to organize a children's march. On April 30 an FBI agent informed the police that "several hundred leaf-

lets [were] put out yesterday at Parker, Ullman and other high
schools. . . . [They] asked all the students to leave the schools at 12:00
noon on Thursday, to go to the Sixteenth Street Baptist Church for
preparation for the March Thursday afternoon." The children were told
to ignore objections from their parents or teachers. That night, at a
mass meeting in the Metropolitan AME Church, Bevel divulged that
Thursday was to be "D-Day."[44]

When SCLC's leaders returned to Birmingham on May 1, they discovered that the protest had already been set in motion. To Walker,
Bevel's action was rank insubordination, but King endorsed the use of
children and marked Bevel as a resourceful and enterprising tactician.
On May 2, black students from four schools converged on the Sixteenth Street Baptist Church. During the course of the afternoon several thousand children left the church, in groups of fifty, and headed in
the direction of city hall. The police arrested about six hundred. "I
have never seen anything like it," an amazed and jubilant King told a
rally of two thousand people that evening. "Some of us will have to
spend three or four hours tonight planning our strategy for tomorrow."
The meeting, the largest so far, ended with a song session led by Bevel.
The fervor of the singing clearly impressed the omnipresent detectives:
"The Negroes got all worked up . . . stomping their feet and waving
their arms and screaming."[45]

Mobilizing the children saved the movement from collapse. "The
parents were working," explained James Orange. "They couldn't go and
march . . . [because] if they marched, they'd lose their jobs. But there
was nothing for the kids to lose." By May 6 the classrooms were virtually empty. With at least a thousand children turning up at the
Sixteenth Street Baptist Church each day, Walker had the time of his
life outfoxing Connor. Before each demonstration, without telling
King, "I dispatched eight or ten guys to different quarters of the town
to turn in false alarms to deploy the fire[men] and the police." Then he
arranged diversionary marches—small groups which distracted the police while the real marches took place elsewhere. "That's when we
brought in the walkie-talkies," he remembered. "We were sending
them this way and that. Oh, man, it was a great time to be alive!" The
arrests mounted: 250 more on May 3; 1,000 three days later. By May 7,
the final day of demonstrations, the jails overflowed with about 2,500
protesters. The city jail, designed for 900 people, crammed in 1,300.
The authorities had to house 600 more in the state fairgrounds. "When
I *say* I'm going to fill up the jails," Bevel exulted, "I *mean* I'm going to
fill up the jails."[46]

The use of dogs and fire hoses on May 3 was a maladroit move by Connor that heartened SCLC. They inflicted no serious injuries, but gave the press dramatic images to splash across the front pages. Equally important, they aroused a strong emotional response from blacks—the dogs, in particular, with their connotations of slavery, triggered a surge of support for the protests. "The dogs just drawed a bigger crowd for our marches," Ed Gardner chuckled. Thousands of black spectators gathered outside the Sixteenth Street Baptist Church. Most took being doused by high-pressure hoses with amazing good humor, but a few retaliated by throwing bricks and bottles. SCLC found itself treading an exceedingly thin line. It had little control over these spectators, and by prolonging the confrontation risked a serious riot. On the other hand, the dogs and hoses were SCLC's best propaganda. Walker recalled how he told Bevel "to let the pep rally go on a while and let these firemen sit out there and bake in the sun until their tempers were like hair triggers." According to James Forman of SNCC, when Walker watched the ensuing scenes replayed that evening on television, he jumped up and down in elation.[47]

SCLC's new tactics sparked an acrimonious controversy. "An injured, maimed, or dead child is a price that none of us can afford to pay," lectured Robert Kennedy.[48] In the mass meetings, which now had to be held in several churches at once, King had to reassure the parents of arrested demonstrators. "We are going to see that they are treated right, don't worry about that. The Justice Department is already in here." Abernathy was at his mellifluous best trying to soothe the anxious adults. Referring to the fact that some of the children were being held in an open stockade, he promised that "if anything happens to them out on that fence, we're going to sue hell out of the City of Birmingham." If the Justice Department official failed to do anything about conditions in jail, "we'll call Bobby. And if Bobby doesn't do anything about it we'll call Jack. And Jack is *known* for getting things done."[49]

The arrival on May 4 of Burke Marshall, head of the Justice Department's Civil Rights Division, underlined the seriousness with which the administration now viewed the crisis. It still disclaimed any legal or constitutional authority to intervene. The scale and character of the demonstrations, however, threatened a rapid descent into uncontrollable violence, and, as Levison remarked to Jack O'Dell on May 14, "The one thing the Administration is afraid of is violence in the streets." Birmingham, moreover, was fast becoming an international cause célèbre. In daily reports, Donald Wilson of the U.S. Information Agency summarized the foreign reaction to the protests. "Sensational aspects of the Birmingham crisis including arrests of children and use of dogs and hoses . . . have received widespread play," Wilson noted, especially in Africa. Even in Western Europe, where the news stories were "surprisingly mild and understanding," the press expressed incomprehension as to why the administration had declined to intervene, often criticizing the president directly. It went without saying that Birmingham gave the Soviet Union a propaganda bonanza.[50]

Clearly, while the federal government could neither impose a settlement nor supersede the civil authorities, it could do a great deal to bring about negotiations if—as it so conspicuously failed to do in Albany—it exploited its inherent prestige and influence. Without Marshall's efforts, which enjoyed vigorous support from John and Robert Kennedy, negotiations might never have started, let alone succeeded. Marshall acted as the crucial intermediary. It needed an outside mediator of his authority to give the merchants, many now desperate to end the crisis, an opportunity to enter fresh talks which did not involve a direct—and to them demeaning—approach to SCLC.

The two sides commenced negotiating on the evening of May 5. Sidney Smyer, David Vann, and Erskine Smith represented the Senior Citizens Committee. The black negotiators included Shuttlesworth; A. G. Gaston; lawyer Arthur Shores; Lucius Pitts, president of Miles College; and John Drew, an insurance executive and business associate of Gaston. The whites readily accepted, albeit with conditions, SCLC's demand for the desegregation of all store facilities. However, they hedged on the demand for "immediate up-grading of employment opportunities available to Negroes"; nor would they ask the city council, as SCLC also demanded, to create a biracial committee and drop all charges against the thousands of arrested demonstrators. Nevertheless, Shuttlesworth considered that the whites were negotiating in good faith and recommended that SCLC continue talking. By May 6, with the whites' acceptance of "token" employment of Negro sales clerks, a settlement appeared within sight.[51]

But could Smyer persuade the Senior Citizens Committee, which met on May 7 in emergency session, to accept these concessions? For two hours the businessmen refused to swallow this bitter pill. As the day wore on, however, their resistance weakened. Some were persuaded to support the agreement by Robert Kennedy, whose creative use of the telephone was already legendary. A few received personal calls from the president. By midday the need for a truce had become blindingly obvious: downtown Birmingham was thronged with demonstrators,

Marshall recalled. "There were fire engines going by all the time out-side, sirens screaming; reports would come in from the police chief and the sheriff that they didn't think they could handle the situation for more than a few more hours." The alternative to an agreement, Smyer warned, was an explosion of violence. Reluctantly, sullenly, the businessmen allowed him to conclude a settlement.[52]

That evening, the two sides met at the home of John Drew and talked until the early hours of the next day. For the first time, King accompanied the black negotiators. The latter failed again to secure any promises in respect of the dropping of charges. The whites also refused to help SCLC raise bail money for the 790 demonstrators still behind bars. But the meeting made some progress towards agreeing on a biracial committee; and the presence of William C. Hamilton, an aide of Mayor-elect Boutwell, gave the blacks some assurance that the incoming city government intended to respect the agreement. King and Marshall informed Washington that a deal had been concluded. The president arranged to announce the truce at a press conference and add his endorsement.[53]

King had overlooked one crucial fact, however: Shuttlesworth had not been present during the final negotiations. On Tuesday, May 7, a fire hose bruised him so badly that he needed treatment in the hospi-tal. Upon leaving the hospital on Wednesday morning, he learned that King had accepted a truce and intended to announce an end to the demonstrations at a noon press conference. Shuttlesworth exploded. King could not cancel the demonstrations, or conclude a settlement, or hold a press conference, unless he, Fred Shuttlesworth, agreed. More important, the settlement did not satisfy him. Marshall could not be trusted, he warned King; the only concern of the federal government was to end the protests. "When you came into Birmingham," Shut-tlesworth said, according to his own recollection, "you didn't ask Pres-ident Kennedy. Burke Marshall . . . wasn't nowhere around. There were some people here who had confidence in me, because they knew I wasn't going to lie and wasn't going to let them down." He would not let King stop short of victory, as in Albany; he would sooner "die in the streets" than accept these terms.[54]

King's colleagues seemed to regard Shuttlesworth's outburst as little more than a temper tantrum, a bid for attention, or an expression of jealousy towards King. Clarence Jones told Levison at the time that "the reasons for the differences are largely ego; it's sort of an aggrava-tion of the problem that Martin has with Ralph"—Abernathy being notoriously envious of King's eminence. "Fred got carried away with an exalted sense of importance," thought Walker, speaking in an oral history interview in 1967. "But Fred was under a great deal of strain. . . . He was not well physically."[55]

But Shuttlesworth's opposition to the settlement as it then stood did not merely reflect an inflated ego. It also concerned a real difference over tactics. King had consented to stop the demonstrations in return for the vaguest of promises. With no timetable for desegregation and no specific details of how many blacks were to be hired, the agreement depended almost entirely upon the goodwill of the white merchants, in which Shuttlesworth, with good reason, had very little trust. He also had strong doubts—which, as events would show, were not entirely without foundation—about King's willingness to resume demonstrations if the merchants reneged on their promises. Finally, King's unilateral action did more than wound Shuttlesworth's pride: it also breached the important principle of joint consultation and decision making between SCLC and the ACMHR.

At Shuttlesworth's insistence, SCLC announced a twenty-four-hour pause in the demonstrations, rather than a permanent cancellation, while negotiations continued in an effort to obtain better terms. The agreement was amended to specify that each major department store should hire at least one black clerk, and that lunch counters were to begin serving blacks within ninety days. With Shuttlesworth mollified, the Kennedy administration removed another obstacle to peace by prevailing upon Walter Reuther of the United Auto Workers to raise enough bail money among the labor unions to free those still in jail. On Friday, May 10, at 2:00 P.M., Shuttlesworth finally confirmed that a settlement had been finalized. "The city of Birmingham," he began, "has reached an accord with its conscience."[56]

What had the protests achieved? The *New York Times* thought the pact "won for the Negroes at least the promise of concessions." *Time,* less charitably, described it as "a fragile truce based on pallid promises." Later assessments were generally negative. Joanne Grant, who reported the campaign for the *National Guardian,* saw the agreement as a typical and unfortunate example of SCLC's modus operandi: King "shot the Birmingham movement down with his usual technique of coming in, being the big wheel . . . and settling for a lot less than even the moderate demands." In his 1970 memoir, James Forman asserted that SCLC stopped short of victory because "people had become too militant for the government's liking and Dr. King's image." In calling the settlement a triumph, wrote biographer Jim Bishop, King lied either to the public or to himself. According to one of the most widely read texts on black history, SCLC won "token concessions that were later not carried out."[57]

It is conceivable, as these critics imply, that SCLC might have secured better terms if it had continued the demonstrations. However, the risks of such a course far outweighed any possible advantages. The clashes with the police were becoming uglier every day: by May 7 the situation was slipping out of SCLC's control. As a settlement began to emerge, it became clear to King that further demonstrations, far from helping SCLC, would play into the hands of the die-hard segregationists. These were now trying to sabotage any agreement by provoking a bloody clash between angry blacks and the bellicose state troopers who had been sent into Birmingham by Governor George Wallace. Thus on May 8 King and Abernathy were suddenly jailed when they could not produce appeal bonds amounting to five thousand dollars; on May 11 bombs exploded at the Gaston Motel and the home of A. D. King; on May 20 the board of education expelled or suspended eleven hundred black children.[58]

In each case, King refused to fall into the trap of resuming the demonstrations. More marches, he reasoned, would have no effect whatever on the diehards while making life more difficult for the moderates, who desperately needed time and calm to rally support for the agreement. Talking to Levison by phone after the school expulsions, he spelled out more reasons for caution:

> I feel that we would have made a mistake today if we had called for a mass walkout tomorrow and more demonstrations. We would have put ourselves in a position of moving before we really thought through—we still have the moral offensive, you see. And the troopers are here. They want to beat the heads of Negroes as much as possible. They are just waiting. I have never seen anything like it—those guns cocked just like we were some kind of lawless criminals. And if all of those kids are out of school, they are going to beat some, and I do not feel right now that we have the violent elements of the Negro community in hand enough to keep a riot from emerging.

SCLC's protests had achieved controlled disorder; further demonstrations invited uncontrollable chaos.[59]

King's restraint paid off. Although the bombings of May 11 sparked a night of black rioting, Kennedy's threat to send in federal forces held the state troopers in check and forestalled what could have been an ugly overreaction. On May 22 the federal courts overruled the school expulsions. The following day the Alabama Supreme Court ejected the Hanes-Connor administration from office. The May 10 pact had survived the racist backlash.

Certainly, that agreement fell short of SCLC's original demands.

Stores agreed to desegregate their facilities, but within ninety days rather than at once. Similarly, there was to be gradual, rather than immediate, "hiring of Negroes as clerks and salesmen." On the question of a biracial committee, SCLC had to make do with talks with the Senior Citizens Committee "within the next two weeks." Its fourth demand, the dropping of all charges arising out of the demonstrations, had to be abandoned altogether. No mention was made of hiring black policemen or desegregating schools, parks, theaters, and hotels.[60] Yet in all likelihood, the terms of the agreement represented the best that could be obtained. The negotiations, by their very nature, had to exclude schools, parks, and other areas that fell within the responsibility of city government. Nor could the businessmen make decisions concerning the arrested demonstrators. They could only speak for themselves; they could not commit the political leaders. This is the context in which the pact must be judged.

Many white Southerners maintained that the demonstrations had been superfluous. As Congressman Richard Sikes of Florida put it: "It is common knowledge that a moderate city government has just been elected in Birmingham . . . and that concessions would have been forthcoming with neither strife nor rioting under the new city government." Others contended that the demonstrations delayed rather than accelerated progress. The most obvious objection to such arguments is that fact that the first steps towards desegregation occurred precisely when the demonstrations reached their peak. Would Boutwell have taken similar steps, without pressure, upon taking office as mayor? Most blacks thought not. "Albert Boutwell was no liberal by a long shot," observed John Cross. A "moderate" segregationist, Boutwell had to compete for the segregationist vote—and the electorate was nine-tenths white—with crude racists such as Connor. The contention that he would have volunteered concessions smacks of wishful thinking.[61]

Acutely aware that Boutwell's hands would be tied by the exigencies of Alabama politics, SCLC deliberately picked on the merchants. Businessmen enjoyed greater freedom of action; they were also far more vulnerable to black pressure. If the merchants moved, SCLC believed, the politicians would follow: as King put it, "The political power structure always responds to the economic power structure."[62] Few blacks thought that either would have accepted desegregation but for the combined effects of the demonstrations and the boycott. By early May, retail sales had been reduced by almost one-fifth. "This was the real concern of men like Sidney Smyer," recalled the Reverend Abraham Woods. "I had never seen an old white man cry, but at one of the meetings at the Chamber of Commerce . . . he actually broke down and cried. The merchants were hurting."[63] Black conservatives like A. G. Gaston, who had initially been skeptical about direct action, rallied behind the protests when they saw the merchants bending: "The demonstrations gave us a wedge we never had before."[64] In the most thorough study of the negotiations, Robert Corley concluded that "the end of segregation was dramatically hastened because King and his demonstrators threatened chaos in a city whose leaders were now desperate for order."[65]

Was the agreement honored? No sooner had the truce been signed than the merchants attempted to backtrack. On May 15, announcing his own version of the terms, Smyer held that stores were to desegregate not ninety days hence, but ninety days after the new city government took office. He also implied that the hiring of a single black clerk would satisfy the employment agreement. Faced with apparent duplicity, King exuded goodwill. In a letter cosigned by Shuttlesworth and Abernathy, he asked Smyer to clarify this "misunderstanding." Praising him for having been "a tower of strength amid the adversity of the past week," King reassured Smyer that "[we] will not break our commitment to cease demonstrations." It remained unclear, however, to what extent the Senior Citizens Committee actually supported the pact. In June the editor of the *Birmingham News*, Ed Holland, penned a pessimistic assessment to Burke Marshall: "Nothing within the commercial community is being done to take action on the Negro-white agreements . . . [and] the atmosphere here is one of no follow-through by the whites." The deadline for the hiring of Negro sales clerks came and went. None had been employed by October.[66]

The other parts of the agreement fared better: at the end of July five department stores desegregated their lunch counters. The new city government did not interfere and indicated by its actions that it was committed to the pact. On July 16 Boutwell appointed a "community affairs committee" with two dozen blacks, including Ed Gardner and Lucius Pitts, among its two hundred members. A few days later the city council repealed its segregation laws and allowed the municipal golf courses, which had been closed by Connor, to reopen on an integrated basis. Boutwell's aides even hinted that the first Negro policeman might soon be appointed.[67]

Yet black leaders were unimpressed. The merchants had interpreted the agreement as narrowly as possible. The biracial committee did not meet until October. Negro policemen remained an unfulfilled promise. Above all, as King complained, "a bleakness of spirit militated against wholehearted progress." Typical of this bleak spirit was the reply of

James O. Haley, president of the Birmingham Bar Association, to
Jerome Cooper's application for membership. "We might be liberal in
our attitude," Haley responded, "but I do not believe that the Bir-
mingham lawyers and their wives are willing at this time to associate
socially with Negro attorneys and their wives." The admission of
Negroes, he added, would merely aggravate racial tensions. Because of
SCLC Birmingham had moved, in the words of local editor Emory O.
Jackson, "from total exclusion to tiny tokenism." Narrow as it was, the
May 10 agreement represented the city's first decisive break with its
white-supremacist past.[68]

Did the protests in Birmingham give birth to the civil rights bill,
which Congress eventually enacted in 1964? SCLC, not unnaturally,
believed so. "But for Birmingham," Shuttlesworth boasted in 1964,
"the Civil Rights Bill would not be before Congress today." Wyatt
Walker was even more emphatic: "Birmingham brought about the
1964 Civil Rights Act."[69]

The claim that Birmingham created the Civil Rights *Act* is difficult
to sustain. The bill did not reach the statute book until July 1964, and
until Lyndon Johnson became president it looked doubtful that it
would pass at all. The assertion that Birmingham prompted the civil
rights *bill*, on the other hand, is more plausible. The political scientist
David Garrow, however, has challenged it. The Birmingham protests
produced "no widespread national outcry," he argues, "no vocal reaction by the nation's clergy, and no immediate move by the administration to propose salutary legislation." Garrow suggests two reasons for
this lukewarm response: the black rioting of May 7 and May 12, which
alienated white sympathy and confused the issue; and the absence of a
single, clear goal that could be easily conveyed both to and by the
press. Birmingham, he concludes, was far less effective than SCLC's
campaign in Selma two years later, which led directly to the passage of
the Voting Rights Act.[70]

But this argument can be faulted on several grounds. Comparisons
between Birmingham and Selma must be treated with caution. It is
quite true, as Garrow notes, that Birmingham produced a relatively
muted response from Congress: Selma prompted nearly two hundred
sympathetic speeches, Birmingham a mere seventeen.[71] A simple statistical comparison, however, fails to reveal the fact that the political
context of 1963 was very different from that of 1965. Non-Southern
congressmen were far more wary about speaking out on civil rights in
1963. Most regarded it as a sure vote loser, and Northern Democrats
were anxious to avoid a damaging intraparty dispute that would re-

dound to the benefit of the Republican party. In 1965, with the Republicans routed in the previous year's elections, they felt less politically inhibited. By 1965, moreover, the nation had become more accustomed to the idea that the government ought to play a central role in combatting racial discrimination; far fewer people still maintained that the South's racial problems could be solved through local, voluntary action. Finally, by 1965 the civil rights movement had reached a higher stage of development; it enjoyed greater legitimacy and respectability.

The success of Birmingham should not, in any case, be judged according to its impact on Congress: the initiative for the civil rights bill came from the administration, not the legislature. And the evidence strongly suggests that SCLC's demonstrations played a decisive role in persuading the Kennedy administration to introduce legislation. For two years Robert Kennedy had attempted to deal with each racial crisis on an ad hoc basis. Birmingham finally convinced him that crises would recur with such frequency and magnitude that the federal government, unless it adopted a more radical policy, would be overwhelmed. Birmingham, Edwin Guthman recalled, "convinced the President and Bob that stronger federal civil rights laws were needed. When Marshall returned from Birmingham on May 17 . . . he flew with Bob to Asheville, North Carolina. . . . Aboard the plane they worked out the essential elements of the Civil Rights Bill." Five days later, the president confirmed that he was considering new legislation and that "the final decision should be made in the next few days." At the end of May, against the advice of most of his aides and cabinet officers, he decided to endorse his brother's strategy. Outlining the bill in his televised address of June 11, Kennedy noted that "the events in Birmingham and elsewhere have so increased the cries for equality that no city or state or legislative body can prudently choose to ignore them."[72]

There was a direct connection, therefore, between SCLC's demonstrations and the introduction of the civil rights bill. Of course, the Kennedy administration had sponsored civil rights legislation before, only to see it fail in Congress. The difference now lay in the broad scope of the bill and, even more important, in the administration's determination to see the measure through Congress. Contemporaries agreed that Birmingham, and the protests that immediately followed it, transformed the political climate so that civil rights legislation became feasible; before, it had been impossible. Roy Wilkins of the NAACP refused to ascribe the civil rights bill to Birmingham alone: what happened before—the Freedom Rides, the integration crisis at

the University of Mississippi, the legal battles over voter registration
and school desegregation—had paved the ground and contributed to
the political education of the Kennedys on civil rights. "I see the
Birmingham episodes as clinching the business . . . [and] convincing
the President at long last that we had to have legislation." Even allowing for such qualifications, history must regard Birmingham as the
decisive factor. As Burke Marshall noted, "The Negro and his problems
were still pretty much invisible to the country . . . until mass demonstrations of the Birmingham type."[73]

Why did Birmingham have such a profound impact on the administration's thinking? If direct action had died down after May 10, its
effects would have been transient and indecisive. But the protests in
Birmingham also sent shock waves across the South. The fact that
white leaders had made concessions in a city notorious for its racial
intransigence gave new hope to blacks in Baton Rouge, New Orleans,
and other segregationist strongholds. Widely acclaimed as "the best-
organized and most highly disciplined action ever mounted by
Negroes," Birmingham became a model for SNCC, CORE, and local
black movements. As James Farmer acknowledged, Birmingham
showed the need to involve thousands rather than hundreds. "A score
of Birminghams followed the first. Birmingham thus set the stage for a
full-scale revolt against segregation." By the end of the summer the
South had experienced about one thousand demonstrations involving
more than twenty thousand arrests. Enthusiasm for direct action swept
even the NAACP which, at its annual convention in July, called upon
its local branches to employ "picketing, mass protest actions, [and]
selective buying campaigns." As Meier and Rudwick have written,
Birmingham "both epitomized the change in mood and became a major stimulus for direct-action campaigns."[74]

To the Kennedy administration, the growth of direct action represented a dangerous and disturbing development. Throughout the summer, the president warned against "demonstrations, parades and
protests" that "create tensions and threaten violence and threaten
lives." The civil rights bill was designed, in large part, to get blacks off
the streets. It gave blacks a legal redress, thus obviating the need, in
Kennedy's view, for "demonstrations which could lead to riots, demonstrations which could lead to bloodshed." The bill also proposed a
professional, full-time federal mediation service, an idea which had
been rejected at the time of the Albany protests. The improvised,
"crisis-management" methods of the Justice Department no longer
sufficed: the crises were too many and too dangerous.[75]

Did the black rioting in Birmingham—trivial by the standard of

Watts and Detroit, but serious in the context of the early 1960s—
weaken the effectiveness of SCLC's campaign? Given the administration's deep fear of domestic violence and disorder, it may well have
actually helped. The Birmingham riots raised the specter of black retaliation, of a violent black revolt touching off a sanguinary race war.
This prospect frightened and appalled the Kennedys. Robert, in particular, feared that nonviolent protest might give way to the violent tactics
of irresponsible extremists. As he told a group of Alabama newspaper
editors on May 15, "Remember, it was King who went around the pool
halls and door to door collecting knives, telling people to go home and
to stay off the streets and to be nonviolent. . . . If King loses, worse
leaders are going to take his place. Look at the black Muslims."[76]

That was precisely the argument which King made so forcefully in
"Letter from Birmingham City Jail." If whites remained obdurate to
the reasonable demands of nonviolent leaders, he warned, "millions of
Negroes will . . . seek solace and security in black-nationalist ide-
ologies—a development that would lead to a frightening racial nightmare." True, black leaders had been saying this for years; indeed, such
warnings are a rhetorical commonplace among liberal reformers. But
the rioting of early May demonstrated that the alternative posed by
King was more than a rhetorical flourish. It forced the administration
to acknowledge the importance of rendering positive support to "responsible" black leaders.[77] Robert Kennedy had this point brought
home to him in a dramatic and personally discomfitting manner when
he met a group of black artists and intellectuals on May 24. The blacks
criticized the administration in angry and emotional terms, subjecting
the hapless Kennedy to what Clarence Jones considered "the sharpest
attack that he had seen anyone undergo." Kennedy was shocked by
their aggressiveness and, as he saw it, their irrationality. Yet these
blacks were hardly extreme on the widening spectrum of black opinion. "There is obviously a revolution within a revolution in the Negro
leadership," he reflected in 1964. "We could obviously see the direction
of Martin Luther King going away from him to some of these younger
people, who had no confidence in the system of government." It was
essential, he thought, to ensure the confidence of the black population
"in their government and in the white majority."[78]

Garrow's assertion that SCLC lacked a single, clear goal in Birmingham is surely correct. Burke Marshall formed the impression that
King had no specific objective in mind such as the intervention of
federal troops or the passage of legislation: "He wasn't thinking that
far ahead. He was reacting, like most people, to the situation." But did
this weaken the campaign's impact? King maintained to the end of his

life that it was far more important to dramatize the broader issues and generate the pressure for change than to draft precise or specific legislation. The exact manner in which the federal government responded to the problem of discrimination did not greatly concern SCLC. What mattered was that its response should be determined, vigorous, and thorough.[79]

The administration responded to pressure, King reasoned, not proposals. And in the aftermath of Birmingham he sensed that the time had come to escalate the pressure in order to achieve a decisive breakthrough. Blacks were aroused as never before, he told Levison and Jones on June 1; organized into a mass movement they could break the political logjam and convince the president to crusade for legislation. But the protests required a national focus, he added, such as a mass rally in Washington involving up to one hundred thousand people: "It would be a mass march and also a unified demonstration all over America." King's decisiveness made a deep impression upon the two advisers. The next day, discussing the conversation, they agreed that King's cautious and thoughtful nature made his sense of urgency all the more significant. The one thing he had learned about King, Levison observed, "is that Martin's assessment of how Negroes feel is a very acute one; that he doesn't go wrong on that." A week later, as SCLC began to canvass support for the idea of a March on Washington, Kennedy announced his intention to press for legislation. To King, the lesson was obvious. "When we started out in Birmingham, Alabama," he told his staff, "we didn't have one thing on paper—nothing." By creating the pressure for reform, however, "we got a Civil Rights Bill that had ten titles."[80]

Planning and premeditation gave SCLC the keys to success in Birmingham. As Joseph Rauh of the ADA noted, "The thing about Birmingham was that King knew how Connor would react." Hence SCLC's unstated reason for acting before the new city government took office: it wanted to confront Connor, not Boutwell. As SCLC predicted, Connor's resort to dogs and fire hoses put the Birmingham story on the front pages of the nation's newspapers and triggered angry condemnations in Congress. Connor's methods, Senator Wayne Morse stated on May 6, "brings to mind . . . the assault of the Nazi storm troopers against the Jews, and the unleashing of Communist soldiers in Eastern Europe." In a similar vein, Congressman John Gilbert of New York condemned "the use of police dogs and fire hoses to subdue school-children" as a "national disgrace." Northern congressmen spoke of "police brutality," "barbarism," and "government by hate and hysteria." In one sense, therefore, SCLC invited the very repression which

it denounced. As *Life* commented beneath a double-page spread showing the police dogs in action, "This extraordinary sequence . . . is the
attention-getting jackpot of the Negroes' provocation."[81]

But the argument that SCLC deliberately provoked white violence
must be treated with caution. By adhering to nonviolence, SCLC
placed the conflict on the level of symbol; as one reporter put it, the
campaign was "a scenario, a staging under rigid conditions of what
seem to be spontaneous events." The "Battle of Birmingham" produced
few casualties; the ubiquitous presence of the press restrained even
Connor. SCLC wanted vivid images, not bloodshed; it sought to evoke
drama rather than provoke violence. "You see a policeman beating
somebody and with water hoses," Shuttlesworth pointed out, "that's
news, that's spectacularism." The "shameful scenes" in Birmingham,
Kennedy thought, were "so much more eloquently reported by the
news camera than by any number of explanatory words." And a week
after its reference to "the Negroes' provocation," a *Life* editorial asserted that the "technical legal infraction" of the demonstrators in
violating the parade ordinance "was far outweighed by the broader
right of citizens in a free society to assemble peaceably to seek redress
of grievances." The contrast with Albany could not have been
sharper.[82]

If the threat of black violence so alarmed the administration, did
SCLC do anything to directly or indirectly encourage black violence?
The evidence is overwhelmingly to the contrary. In the mass meetings,
speakers repeatedly stressed that violence played into the hands of the
opposition. When violence did erupt, SCLC worked assiduously to
quell it. On May 4, for example, Bevel persuaded King to suspend the
demonstrations when bystanders started to throw rocks. Two days
later, Young admonished an audience that "we have a nonviolent
movement, but it's not nonviolent enough." In retrospect, the thing
that most surprised veterans of the campaign was that there had been
so *little* black violence. Birmingham was "probably the most violent
city in America," Young thought, "and every black family had an arsenal." Volunteers for demonstrations had to surrender their weapons—
John Cross remembered collecting "almost half a trashcan of knives"
one day—and receive two hours' indoctrination into nonviolence.
SCLC took great pains to disown the rowdy spectators, and when they
threatened to get out of control King stopped the demonstrations.[83]

How did SCLC contain this latent violence? In the mass meetings it
constantly emphasized the Christian ethic of "love thine enemy."
Speaking at New Pilgrim Baptist Church on May 6, for example, King
gave an exegesis on the three Greek words for love, and commended

agape—"an overflowing, redemptive love toward all men"—as the guiding ideal. Most blacks, it might be argued, misunderstood or rejected this philosophy. Yet they could understand well enough that violence would be futile; nothing would please Connor and Wallace more, King told them, than for blacks to engage in violence. The discipline to passively endure the police dogs and fire hoses was difficult to come by. But SCLC explained the logic of nonviolent protest in simple, practical, and convincing terms. Young asked the mass meetings, "How many people have ever been bitten by a dog before?" How many had been hit by a baseball bat as a child? How many had fought in World War II or Korea? " Well, if you ran this kind of risk to fight for somebody else's freedom, why aren't you willing to run the risk of facing dogs and possibly billy clubs, when you did that as a child . . . just for kicks?"[84]

Finally, the mass meetings themselves provided an emotional release. The speakers had the difficult task of exploiting their audience's anger while at the same time restraining it. They achieved this balance by mixing rabble-rousing with humor, abusing their adversaries for their barbarity but also mocking them for their stupidity. Connor, rather than an ogre to be feared, was depicted as a buffoon to be laughed at. At one of the mass meetings, Ed Gardner found, or pretended to find, an electronic "bug" on the pulpit. To the delight of the audience, he called it a "doohickey" and began talking to it as if Connor were on the other end, listening. Abernathy began doing the same. "He'd preach to it," Young recalled. "He'd say, 'Mr. President,' 'Mr. Hoover,' 'whoever you are,' and then he'd tell them what we were all about. It got to be a crowd-pleasing routine." But nobody excelled Shuttlesworth—whose courage and persistence over the years had made the campaign possible—in his ability to evoke mirth by combining righteous indignation with a sense of the ridiculous. He had been at city hall, he told a mass meeting, looking for a water fountain. Finding the "Negro" fountain dry, he tried the "white" one—"Let's use the best that's down there. I think white water is better than black water anyhow." But all the water in city hall had been turned off, which meant that the toilets were out of action as well. "So I left there and went on over to the bus station, to the men's room"—one of the few places in Birmingham where black and white could mingle on equal terms. "And there we were, all of us there together. But what bothered me most was . . . four or five city policemen come in, and I said, 'What y'all doin' over here? Is segregation hard on y'all too, huh?' You know what one of them said? Said, 'Yeah, Reverend, you got this damn town rocking.' "[85]

Six

Summer of Discontent, Autumn
of Tragedy

The surge of nonviolent protest which swept the South after Birmingham was largely unplanned, uncoordinated, and unforeseen. "Finally we opened our eyes," Walker exulted, "and the white man all over the South is catching hell." SCLC applauded the protests, exhorting blacks to boycott, sit in, march, and go to jail. The pressure had to be stepped up, urged King, even when "the highest officials in the land [are saying] that we ought to stop." As Young told a rally in Savannah, "The white folks don't pay any attention to us unless we're on the streets."[1]

A survey of SCLC's work in the summer of 1963 reveals involvement in half a dozen local campaigns and a mixed pattern of failure and success. But the most striking feature of these campaigns was the tenuous nature of SCLC's commitment.

King's own involvement was slight; Walker, Young, Bevel, Cotton, and a new staff member, C. T. Vivian, acted as roving plenipotentiaries, alternately troubleshooters and troublemakers, making on-the-spot decisions in each local situation. In many cases, however, SCLC was playing second fiddle to SNCC or CORE. Even in Savannah, its most successful campaign, SCLC's role was mainly supportive, the energy and drive coming from a largely independent local organization. Critics began to question SCLC's effectiveness. It seemed to specialize in "a few showy projects," leaving to others the arduous, painstaking, and unspectacular job of organizing the black community.[2]

Simple logistics, in fact, restricted SCLC's local operations. At a superficial glance SCLC appeared to be flush with funds. During the year ending August 31, 1963, its income climbed to three-quarters of a million dollars; the previous year it stood at less than two hundred thousand dollars. But although a larger budget enabled it to hire additional staff, SCLC was still far too small to mount more than one major campaign each year. Part of its income was already earmarked for its ongoing programs of voter registration and citizenship education. The bail bonds of those arrested in Birmingham still soaked up $400,000. Legal fees, the *SCLC Newsletter*, and the wages of sixty-one staff members accounted for most of the remainder.[3]

SCLC's finances, moreover, rested upon a shaky foundation. The Gandhi Society failed to attract the anticipated contributions, and by 1964 it had accumulated a string of debts. A plan to raise $50,000 a year through the sale of individual memberships, although approved by the board in May, never got off the ground. The virtual absence of proper financial controls encouraged profligacy and waste, as Jesse Blayton, SCLC's auditor, persistently complained. It was commonplace for members of the staff to take time off without permission, make unauthorized trips, run up motel and car-hire bills, and otherwise waste the organization's money. By May 1964 SCLC owed $50,000 in unpaid bills. And the task of paying those bills still fell largely on King, whose burden of fundraising, speech making, writing, and civil rights "summitry" was quite staggering.[4]

King might be faulted for paying insufficient attention to SCLC's organizational structure, thereby damaging its prospects for long-term growth and stability. Yet that neglect was more an intelligent recognition of necessity than a lack of interest in building an organization to last.[5] King realized that the qualities demanded by the hectic climate of the times—spontaneity, mobility, freedom of action—did not permit the growth of a stable bureaucracy and a tidy administrative routine. Looking back in 1967, King argued that "if we had concentrated on organizational structure during those days, we would not have created the atmosphere for the Civil Rights Bill." In the summer of 1963 administrative concerns had to take a backseat. "Moving from crisis to crisis," King remembered, "it was well nigh impossible for us to give ourselves to the job of internal structuring."[6]

After Birmingham, the cries for help rarely stopped: SCLC was wanted in Savannah, Georgia; Danville, Virginia; Williamston, North Carolina; Gadsden, Alabama; and many others besides. SCLC had to adopt a strategy of hit-and-run, striking one target at a time. It was scarcely surprising that King and his staff "gave the impression of being overworked firefighters, rushing from one crisis they had not created to another."[7] SCLC's willingness to "run" as well as "hit" evoked persistent criticism from SNCC, which organized in the same communities for years rather than months or weeks. But SCLC had sound strategic reasons for wanting to avoid becoming bogged down in scattered local campaigns. Nonviolent protest entailed a law of diminishing returns in respect of publicity and national attention. The press liked a sense of drama, but it easily lost interest if the tension relaxed. A sustained, dramatic confrontation took months to plan and months to execute; it also required a good deal of money. Above all, it required the right combination of circumstances. Not every local conflict could have the impact of a Birmingham. Rather than fritter away its resources heeding every plea for assistance, SCLC husbanded its energy for a "big push" of its own making.

The protests in Savannah provide a good illustration of SCLC's complex role in providing local direct action movements with timely support and expertise. Demonstrations in this Georgia coastal city were initiated in early June by the Chatham County Crusade for Voters (CCCV), led by Hosea Williams, after three movie theaters reneged on an agreement to desegregate. During the next six weeks, Savannah witnessed some of the largest and most assertive street protests ever seen in the South: almost daily, Williams addressed lunchtime crowds of one thousand people and led marches of three thousand in the evening. One demonstration attracted six thousand blacks. The night marches, Williams's own innovation, drew an enthusiastic response from young blacks. "Williams' flamboyant style, his provocative oratory, and his daring tactics," one historian wrote, "attracted many blacks that the NAACP had never reached." After a week, about five hundred blacks had been arrested.[8]

Williams had no shortage of demonstrators, but he did lack trained organizers. The protests constantly threatened to degenerate into violence as marchers confronted police and National Guardsmen in Savannah's downtown squares. At Williams's request, King sent Dorothy Cotton, Andrew Young, and James Bevel to instill nonviolent discipline—their recent experience in Birmingham made them adept at training young people. In July, when a local judge jailed Williams under "good behavior" warrants amounting to $100,000, Bevel and Young had to take over the campaign in order to prevent it from disintegrating into leaderless anarchy.[9] On July 11 the demonstrations reached a Birmingham-like climax, with the police and National Guard resorting to tear gas and fire hoses, and angry marchers responding by throwing stones, setting fires, and breaking windows. Bevel and Young now suspended the demonstrations. The art of nonviolent protest lay not merely in promoting direct action, but also in ending it at the appropriate time. With the demonstrations getting out of hand, with hundreds of blacks in jail, and with no more money for bail to get them out, that time had clearly come.[10]

The protests had served their purpose. White businessmen, now thoroughly alarmed, were ready to talk about desegregation. After intensive negotiations with black leaders, with Bevel speaking for the CCCV, a committee representing one hundred businessmen accepted a desegregation plan covering hotels, motels, theaters, and bowling alleys, to take effect on October 1. The blacks, in return, agreed to a sixty-day cooling-off period free of demonstrations. King cancelled a visit to the city lest his presence jeopardize the truce. Williams's release from jail was delayed until Bevel had persuaded the young militants in the CCCV to abide by the agreement. He eventually emerged from jail on August 9, after a prominent white banker paid his bond. The Justice Department, Mayor Malcolm MacLean, and Monsignor John Toomey, a white clergyman, had all lobbied hard to have the desegregation plan accepted.[11]

The campaign by SCLC's affiliate in Danville, Virginia, had no such successful outcome, and SCLC's role in it prompted a good deal of criticism. It is instructive, therefore, to compare the two movements. Despite its location in the upper South, Danville had a record of racial intransigence more characteristic of the Deep South. In 1960 the city council had closed its public libraries in order to avoid integration, and then reopened them without tables and chairs. No blacks served in the police force or in city government.[12] In Savannah, by contrast, the city had appointed blacks to all its public boards, hired the first black firemen and bus drivers, and increased the number of black policemen from seventeen to thirty. These gains directly reflected the strength of the NAACP and the CCCV. Under vigorous leadership, these mass organizations had used political action and direct action to great effect, and their rivalry, far from hampering the attack on white supremacy, had given it added momentum.[13]

In Danville, on the other hand, blacks did not enjoy a strong organizational base: the NAACP was weak and ineffectual; its newly formed rival, the Danville Christian Progressive Association, had not yet acquired mass support. The DCPA's lack of experience in the ways of direct action became evident when it launched its demonstrations. As in Albany, the protests were directed against the city council rather than the white business community. In the absence of a strong black vote, however, white politicians remained relatively invulnerable to this kind of pressure. The DCPA also committed a more basic error: it failed to ensure unity within its own ranks before embarking upon direct action. On May 31 the president of the DCPA, the Reverend Lendell Chase, assured whites that no demonstrations were in the offing. When his colleagues decided to organize a march that very evening, Chase tried in vain to stop it. The first demonstrations not only produced an open split within the DCPA, they also convinced white leaders that the blacks had broken a clear undertaking not to march.[14]

The response to the protests by the white authorities has become a case study in legal repression. On June 6, Judge Archibald M. Aiken of the municipal court issued a temporary restraining order against further demonstrations. Three days later, a local grand jury indicted three leaders of the DCPA—Julius Adams, the Reverend I. A. Campbell, and the Reverend L. G. Dunlap—for "conspiracy to incite the colored population of the State to acts of violence and war against the white population"—a statute enacted in 1859 in response to John Brown's raid on the Harper's Ferry arsenal. The police now utilized more forceful methods, and on June 10 attacked a "prayer pilgrimage" outside the city jail, using clubs and fire hoses. All but three of the fifty demonstrators received medical treatment. Three days later the police used clubs and tear gas to quash a sit-in at city hall. The council banned marches and limited pickets to six. Those arrested required bonds of $5,000 and could expect hefty prison sentences. Parents of young demonstrators were charged with "contributing to the delinquency of minors." Blacks claiming unemployment benefits found that being arrested stopped their payments. And on June 21 the grand jury indicted ten more activists, including Dr. Milton Reid and the Reverend Curtis Harris, officials of SCLC's Virginia state unit who had responded to the DCPA's request for help.[15]

Judge Aiken began trying the arrested demonstrators on June 17. An ardent proponent of "massive resistance" to desegregation, Aiken swiftly convicted the first two defendants, imposing fines and jail sentences and refusing time to appeal. He also did everything he could to discomfit the defense lawyers. As Aiken refused to tell them which cases would be brought to trial when, they had to attend court, with their clients, every day. William Kunstler, who arrived in Danville with Wyatt Walker on June 16, found himself barred from the proceedings when Aiken refused to accept his credentials. An observer from the Justice Department described the proceedings as "extraordinary." The public was excluded; "witnesses, and even attorneys, are 'frisked' for weapons. All of the city personnel, however, wear sidearms. The last two days there have been approximately 30 armed police in the courtroom. Judge Aiken has been wearing a pistol while presiding on the bench." Even the staunchly segregationist *Richmond News-Leader* criticized the trials as "gold-plated stupidity," and denounced the city's "trumped-up ordinances, unwarranted arrests . . . and autocratic decrees."16

Hopes that King might personally take command of the campaign received a boost on June 28, when Milton Reid announced plans for a "mass pilgrimage" to Danville on July 3. King promised to address a rally and be "an involved participant." On July 2, however, federal judge Thomas Michie granted the city a temporary ban on demonstrations, specifically enjoining King, Reid, and the leaders of the DCPA. Although the rally was permissible, Fred Shuttlesworth appeared in King's place. Michie dissolved the injunction on July 10 and King arrived the following day. His two-day visit sparked more demonstrations which produced about one hundred arrests. But King did not lead a march himself; nor did he commit SCLC to an all-out campaign. Speaking again in Danville on July 19, he praised the protesters and declared that "injunctions won't stop our movement."17

But continuing arrests and legal repression exacted a heavy toll on morale: Kunstler and the other attorneys failed to invalidate the picketing ordinance or set aside the Aiken injunction; Judge Michie refused to remand the prosecutions to federal courts; the money tied up in bail climbed to $200,000. SCLC's "D-Day," a mass jail-in planned for July 28, proved to be a dispiriting anticlimax: of the 311 people who signed up to march, only 77 honored their commitment by going to jail. A second march had to be cancelled because there were too few volunteers. On July 30, Milton Reid informed King that "the Danville situation is growing steadily worse. . . . The people here are tired, weary, frightened and woefully divided." Aiken delivered another blow on August 2 when he made the injunction permanent. The legal battles dragged on for a decade, but the injunction, as Kunstler acknowledged, "paralyzed the protest movement."18

As the demonstrations petered out, SCLC shifted its efforts to voter registration. Herbert Coulton, its Virginia field secretary, arrived in Danville in mid-June and spent three weeks identifying blacks who were not on the voter rolls. He then contacted them through their churches or, failing that, through leaflets, posters, and word of mouth. Coulton also ensured that applicants had paid the poll tax, including any arrears. When the registrar's office opened on July 10, it approved 177 applications within five days. Five hundred blacks became voters in the space of six weeks.[19]

SCLC's little-known work in Louisiana affords a vivid insight into the confused, fast-moving pace of black protest after Birmingham, as well as providing a good illustration of the repressive climate and demoralizing isolation in which SCLC field secretaries often operated. Major Johns, who had led the student protests in Baton Rouge in 1960, replaced Harry Blake in April 1963. He soon found out, however, why Blake's work in Shreveport had been so fruitless. George D'Artois, the city's commissioner of public safety, threatened to arrest Johns if he took anybody to the registrar's office, calling him "an outsider and a troublemaker." On June 5, when the office opened for the first time in a month, only one black passed the test. Two weeks later thirteen applied; only five were accepted. Johns quickly became discouraged. Local blacks, he complained, were "not willing to put forth any effort to register," and the United Christian Movement had become "completely apathetic" since Dr. C. O. Simpkins moved to New York in 1962. Daniel Harrell, Johns's assistant, tried to hand in a petition to D'Artois, only to be arrested for vagrancy. "Unless additional people come into this city, . . . not too much will be accomplished," Johns reported. What blacks really wanted, he added, was for King to "come in and direct a freedom movement."[20]

Johns and Harrell attempted to shock blacks out of their torpor by staging sit-ins in mid-July. After three days, thirty people had been arrested. But these protests failed to ignite a larger movement, and the SCLC workers turned their energies to organizing a conference on voter registration, which took place in Lake Charles on August 10–11. They then travelled to the town of Plaquemine, where CORE was involved in a direct action campaign in conjunction with the local black voters league. With a third SCLC worker, Lavert Taylor, Johns and Harrell picketed the jails. On August 20, after the police used tear gas to break up a march of five hundred people led by James Farmer, Taylor and others sought a conference with the mayor. The latter, according to Taylor's report, "began and ended with one word: 'NO.'" The protests reached their climax the following night when three hundred blacks tried to march to the sheriff's office. They were attacked, in Taylor's words, by "tear gas, cattle prodders, mounted police, and even a DOG (1)." Both Taylor and Johns were arrested, while James Farmer, CORE's national director, escaped from Plaquemine hidden in a hearse. As Meier and Rudwick have written, the campaign "neither received much publicity nor galvanized the White House to intervene."[21]

In September SCLC abandoned Shreveport and moved to the southern part of the state. Taylor began working in Iberia, an isolated coastal parish between Lake Charles and New Orleans which did not have a single black voter. Johns and Harrell based themselves in Lake Charles. There, in addition to white hostility, they also had to contend with strenuous opposition from the Calcasieu Parish Coordinating Committee, a local black group which barred SCLC from churches and asked them to leave. Detecting the despair in Harrell's reports, Andrew Young urged him to "bear with our brethren of the clergy, [and] remember they have been brainwashed for 300 years." It would take more than a few weeks, he added, to "unbrainwash them." The results in Calcasieu Parish, while far from spectacular, were more encouraging than in Shreveport, with 646 voters enrolled during the six-week drive. But this gain failed to make up for the black voters who had been recently "purged" from the rolls.[22]

The demonstrations in Gadsden, Alabama, failed as conclusively as those in Plaquemine. Bernard Lee had begun voter registration work there in November 1962, and he returned to the city after Birmingham. With local black leaders and several CORE workers, Lee organized the Gadsden Freedom Movement, which began demonstrations on June 10. Four days later the city obtained an injunction from a state court, and thereafter responded with mass arrests. On June 18, 450 marchers were taken into custody. The next day, 300 blacks who gathered outside the Etowah County Courthouse were driven away by state troopers wielding clubs and cattle prods—sticklike devices that gave a harmless but painful electric shock. It took John Nolan of the Justice Department two weeks to arrange a truce, based upon a suspension of demonstrations by SCLC-CORE and a commitment by the city to desegregate buses and allow further negotiations. The biracial talks soon broke down, but when demonstrations resumed at the beginning of August they were swiftly crushed. A federal judge upheld the injunction and declined to assume jurisdiction over the cases of those arrested under it. The denouement came on August 3, when the police arrested 685 demonstrators. Both King and Farmer visited Gadsden to bolster morale, but, as Meier and Rudwick noted, "This kind of repression completely exhausted the protesters. . . . The campaign was a failure and tied up the local movement in litigation for two years."[23]

The examples of Danville, Plaquemine, and Gadsden seemed to illustrate, in the words of one scholar, "the ease with which the South could maintain racial segregation absent federal intervention."[24] Throughout much of the South, demonstrations failed to elicit concessions and appeared instead to solidify white resistance. Blacks often marched into a wall of segregationist opposition, observed Howard Zinn, resulting in "pain, frustration, bewilderment." As happened so often after a period of sustained protest, the initial optimism and élan gave way to exhaustion and disappointment. In some areas, as one CORE worker reported from Louisiana, blacks were "fast losing faith in the effectiveness of the movement."[25]

King saw this kind of pessimism as premature and misguided. "Seen in perspective," he wrote, "the summer of 1963 was historic . . . because it witnessed the first offensive in history launched by Negroes along a broad front." A Danville or a Gadsden could not be viewed in isolation. Even apparent defeats contributed to this broad pattern of revolt and, as the political analyst Samuel Lubell noted at the time, helped to demonstrate "that segregation can no longer be enforced in the South except by constant police repression." To the extent that it generated national concern and federal action, nonviolent protest could not fail. "The enduring achievement of the civil rights movement," a more recent study concluded, "was less the reforms won in local confrontations . . . than the successful dramatization, before a national audience, of the injustice and inhumanity of the Jim Crow system."[26]

In the summer of 1963, however, the outcome of the Kennedy administration's initiatives on civil rights hung in the balance. In meetings with groups of businessmen, the president and the attorney general made a vigorous attempt to persuade hotels, theaters, restaurants, and chain stores to desegregate voluntarily, warning that the alternative consisted of economic pressure, racial tension, more demonstrations, and possible violence.[27] Many businessmen proved receptive to their advice: as Leon Godchaux, the New Orleans departmentstore proprietor, admitted, the example of Birmingham "is helping us to make decisions that we would otherwise be reluctant to make. . . . We've already had a good taste of what Birmingham is going through, and we don't want any more."[28]

But the keystone of the Kennedy policy was the civil rights bill;

SCLC's strategy would stand or fall according to the fate of that measure. As the bill went before Congress, SCLC sought to shift the focus of black protest from the dusty streets of the South to the marble halls of government.

King conceived the idea for the March on Washington some ten days before John Kennedy announced his firm intention to seek an omnibus civil rights bill. Strictly speaking, the genesis of the march can be traced to A. Philip Randolph, who was already planning an "Emancipation March to Washington for Jobs," to take place during two days in October. But this proposal had aroused very little interest.[29] After Birmingham, however, King borrowed, revived, and transformed Randolph's idea, turning it into the most memorable mass demonstration in American history. Despite most accounts, it was King who recruited Randolph to his concept of a March on Washington, not the other way round. King shifted the focus from jobs to civil rights and moved the date from October to August. He also supplied the drive and sense of purpose to make the event succeed.

King decided the basic shape of the march as soon as he heard that Randolph was receptive to his proposed changes. On June 10 he consulted his advisers by telephone to consider three key questions: Was the march feasible? What form should it take? And should it be aimed at the president or the Congress? Stanley Levison stressed that nothing less than a turnout of one hundred thousand could make the demonstration a success; moreover, as blacks in Washington tended to be apathetic because of their exclusion from politics, SCLC would need strong participation from the New York area in order to reach that kind of figure. Another way to achieve a large turnout, the conferees agreed, was by enlisting the support of religious leaders, especially through the National Council of Churches. As far as recruiting the other civil rights leaders, King needed to secure a firm commitment from Randolph before meeting Roy Wilkins and James Farmer on June 11—he might even consider announcing the march at a press conference beforehand "so as to force Roy to go along."[30]

When they discussed the target of the march, King confessed to uncertainty: "I've had mixed emotions about the President. I'm just not sure. I feel that he should be made to know that we aren't satisfied with him and what he's done." But on the other hand, he admitted, Kennedy was very popular among Negroes; most considered his record excellent. They eventually agreed to aim the march towards Congress, although, as Clarence Jones pointed out, it would be impossible to ensure that it coincided with the expected filibuster in view of the necessary advance organization. In a conversation with Levison on

June 12, King agreed that Kennedy's televised civil rights speech made it all the more inadvisable to target the president. "He was really great," King thought.[31]

SCLC had a particular interest in good relations with the administration. Racist and right-wing circles were trying to portray the civil rights movement as politically subversive. Rumors about Communist influence on King, put out by the FBI, were going the rounds of the Senate. The White House and the Justice Department had, moreover, received specific allegations from J. Edgar Hoover that Communists were at work in the highest echelons of SCLC. Jack O'Dell, the bureau's memoranda pointed out, was still working in SCLC's New York office, despite King's claim to the contrary. More damning, according to the FBI, was the fact that Levison—allegedly a "conscious agent of the Soviet conspiracy"—had become increasingly involved in SCLC's affairs. King's failure to break with these men, despite repeated warnings from the government, made the Kennedys treat him with a deliberate coolness and reserve. But they also realized that it was prudent to support King's leadership as an insurance against black extremism. Some kind of mutual understanding, therefore, would be in the interests of both SCLC and the administration.[32]

When King visited the White House on June 22 to discuss the march, the nature of that understanding became apparent. Stopping at the Justice Department beforehand, King received a stern injunction from Burke Marshall and Robert Kennedy to break with Levison and O'Dell. Taking King aside in the White House garden, the president himself underlined this warning. Pointing to the Profumo scandal, then unfolding in Britain, he spoke of the dangers of carrying personal loyalty too far. Prime Minister Macmillan was likely to lose his government because his trust in a friend proved misplaced: King had to be careful not to lose his own cause for the same reason. A public exposure of his relationship with O'Dell and Levison, Kennedy went on, would not only hurt King; it would also damage the administration and the civil rights bill. Levison and O'Dell were Communists; King had to get rid of them.[33]

Dismayed by this advice, King insisted on some kind of proof. A few days later, Andrew Young met Burke Marshall in New Orleans; Marshall repeated the FBI's allegations about Levison but offered no specific evidence. King asked for O'Dell's resignation and reluctantly severed his relationship with Levison. According to Levison, he had to persuade King to make the break, arguing that if the administration had doubts about him it was in the best interests of the movement if he withdrew from SCLC. Somewhat reassured, the attorney general publicly rebutted allegations of Communist influence in the civil rights movement. "We have no evidence," he informed suspicious senators, "that any of the top leaders . . . are Communists, or Communist controlled. This is true as to Dr. Martin Luther King, Jr., about whom particular accusations were made, as well as other leaders." In July, the president felt sufficiently confident to endorse the March on Washington, scheduled for August 28: "I look forward to being there."[34]

King assured Kennedy that the march would be a peaceful, disciplined event. In fact, he never seriously entertained plans for civil disobedience in Washington. SCLC knew full well that the NAACP, whose attitude to the march was still noncommittal, would never agree to take part unless it stayed firmly within the spirit and letter of the law. SCLC also recognized that if the march were perceived as a crude attempt to pressure or coerce Congress, it might well wreck the civil rights bill rather than assist it.[35] King was somewhat embarrassed, then, to hear George Lawrence, SCLC's New York representative, inform the press that demonstrators might "tie up public transportation by laying our bodies prostrate on highways . . . [and] railroad tracks and at bus depots." Levison was furious, telling Clarence Jones that King ought to repudiate people "who shoot their mouths off in his name." But King chose the more subtle method of semantics: speaking in New York the next day, he spoke merely of "presenting our bodies in a nonviolent, creative protest."[36]

The notion that the March on Washington started out as a plan for radical civil disobedience only to be turned into a tame rally is, therefore, erroneous. That this interpretation gained widespread currency was due partly to Bayard Rustin, who, appointed by Randolph to organize the event, sought to enlist action-minded groups like SNCC, CORE, and the Fellowship of Reconciliation by holding out the possibility of more dramatic kinds of protest. One suggestion called for two thousand ministers and rabbis to stage a "prayer vigil" outside Congress by forming a huge circle around the Capitol. When he discussed his plans with the District of Columbia police, however, Rustin stressed that the march involved no disruption and no lobbying of Congress. The only significant change to occur between conception and execution was the physical relocation of the march from the area facing the Capitol to the Lincoln Memorial.[37]

At a meeting of civil rights leaders on July 2, Roy Wilkins finally agreed to support the march, having been presented with what amounted to a fait accompli. At a session of the LCCR later in the day, the civil rights forces considered their strategy towards the pending legislation. They readily agreed that the Kennedy proposals needed strengthening, that their lobbying should focus on the Republicans, and that the bill stood a much better chance if representatives of the three major faiths actively campaigned for it. They also decided that the lobbying of Congress and the March on Washington should be kept separate and distinct. "What this boils down to," wrote the ADA representative, "is that King, who knows how to organize demonstrations effectively, will organize the Washington demonstrations, and others who know the ins and outs of Congress will concentrate on building support for civil rights legislation."[38]

What did the march, for all its size, spectacle, and fervor, actually achieve? Very little, some argue. It is doubtful that it swayed many congressmen. Nor did it persuade the administration to change its strategy of postponing debate on the civil rights bill lest a prolonged filibuster bottle up the rest of its legislative program. Indeed, Kennedy was increasingly inclined to delay the decisive vote until after the 1964 elections. "This is going to be an eighteen-month delivery," he told the press on November 14. Looking back, Joseph Rauh thought it "unreal to suggest that [the march] had anything to do with the passage of the Civil Rights Bill. Because three months later, when Kennedy was killed, the bill was absolutely bogged down." Had he lived, Kennedy would almost certainly have bargained part of it away—perhaps the crucial public accommodations section—in order to win Republican support. Many doubted that the bill would have passed in any shape. The impact of the march on the legislative process seems to have been minimal.[39]

Yet the March on Washington did help the civil rights movement. Never before had leading representatives of the Catholic, Protestant, and Jewish faiths identified so closely and visibly with black demands. During the next ten months the churches proved to be the most effective champions of the civil rights bill, exerting an especially notable influence on congressmen from the Midwestern and Rocky Mountain states, where trade unions were generally weak and the black population relatively small. The religious leaders, Rauh admitted, "were troops that we had never had before. . . . It made all the difference in the world." As Norman Hill, one of the organizers, later argued, by involving the white churches the march helped "to generate an ongoing lobby" for the civil rights bill.[40]

The March also presented the civil rights movement as united, responsible, and determined. Whites could not help but be impressed by the size, solemnity, and sobriety of the occasion, as the press coverage attested. The conservative *Wall Street Journal*, while deprecating the march as an "unsound precedent," paid tribute to the "discipline and

dignity of the actual event." Even Southern newspapers commented
favorably on its conduct. The *Montgomery Advertiser* thought it "a
negative achievement"; the *Birmingham News* called it "a peaceful
piece of nonsense." From such sources, this was tantamount to praise.
The government's very real fear of disorder—it had prepared contingency plans for the use of troops and National Guardsmen to quell
possible violence—turned out to be groundless. The U.S. Information
Agency distributed a film of the event, entitled simply "The March,"
throughout the world.[41]

This favorable response to the march was all the more striking in
light of how the press had covered the demonstrations of the preceding
summer and spring. It is often forgotten that this eruption of nonviolent protest evoked deep fear and anxiety in most Northern whites.
Southern blacks were constantly warned against upsetting the white
majority. The *Washington Post* had criticized SCLC's tactics in Birmingham for "keep[ing] alive old hates" and "fortifying the uncompromising racists in their ancient prejudices." The *Wall Street Journal*
equated direct action with "the madness of a mob," warning that "it
will breed a reaction, as the crowd's excesses always do, and the injury
will be not least to the Negro's own cause." People like King, it implied, "give ammunition to those who say the Negro is socially and
politically immature." The danger of a "white backlash," although the
phrase had not yet entered the political vocabulary, had been clearly
identified. As CORE and the NAACP attacked de facto segregation in
the North, white opposition to black demands became loud and clear.
Opinion polls depicted most whites as strongly hostile to all forms of
direct action and far from ready to accept genuine racial equality. Liberals began to find common ground with conservatives in agreeing that
demonstrations had reached the point of diminishing returns. Un-
checked, they seemed to portend a descent into anarchy. "These demonstrations have increasingly endangered lives and property, inflamed
emotions and unnecessarily divided communities," warned President
Kennedy. "When you get violence, . . . the cause of advancing equal
opportunities only loses."[42]

The March on Washington became a means—how successful is impossible to measure—of allaying such fears. It was not, despite Bayard
Rustin's later claim, intended to "close down the period of protest."
But King, Andrew Young, and others in SCLC did recognize the political and tactical benefits of a temporary lull in direct action. As August
28 approached they came to view the march as the splendid climax,
the grand finale, of a summer of protest. Ed Clayton, SCLC's resident
journalist, captured this feeling in his piece on the march for the *SCLC
Newsletter*: "The fires that had burned hotly across the nation . . . had

become smoldering coals, still crackling and sputtering, their intense heat too alive and dangerous to ignore or risk leaving unattended. Perhaps it could be cooled down in one giant demonstration." King's "I Have a Dream" speech perfectly expressed this calming, conciliatory approach. Although warning that the "whirlwinds of revolt" would not soon be stilled, he also admonished blacks against bitterness, violence, and hatred, holding out a vision of harmony and reconciliation.[43]

To those accustomed to King's oratory, "I Have a Dream" is unremarkable. His delivery was restrained, even mechanical. Much of the speech was unoriginal: he had used the "dream" passage in Detroit in June, and in Birmingham in April; the peroration "Let Freedom Ring" dated back to 1956, if not further. But the impact of "I Have a Dream" derived from its context rather than its content. "Through live and delayed coverage," wrote a historian of American television, "millions shared the experience." The speaking style King used in addressing a predominantly black rally bore little resemblance to the flat, bland diction which he usually reserved for white audiences. Most of the whites who heard the speech on television had never been exposed to this kind of oratory; hence its extraordinary impact. "I Have a Dream" virtually defined the March on Washington, effectively stamping it as King's personal platform. The march and the speech enhanced King's prestige beyond measure.[44]

"I Have a Dream" made a powerful impression on J. Edgar Hoover and the FBI. Hoover had watched the growth of King's influence with profound suspicion. His subordinates attempted to reassure the director that neither King nor the civil rights movement were significantly influenced by the Communist party. But Hoover would not have it. When Assistant Director William Sullivan submitted a lengthy memorandum which characterized SCLC as a "legitimate Negro organization" and described Communist attempts to infiltrate the civil rights movement as "an obvious failure," Hoover administered a stinging rebuke. This memo, he wrote, "reminds me vividly of those I received when Castro took over in Cuba. You reported then that Castro and his cohorts were not Communists and not influenced by Communists."[45]

Hoover's underlings quickly backtracked: they had misinterpreted the evidence, they explained; their definition of "Communist" had been too narrow and legalistic. "We are in complete agreement with the Director that communist influence is being exerted on Martin Luther King, Jr.," affirmed Sullivan, noting that his "powerful demagogic speech" at the March on Washington showed King to be "the most dangerous and effective Negro leader in the country." Thus prodded by Hoover, bureau researchers prepared a report on "Communism and the Negro Movement" which concluded that "as the Communist

Party goes, so goes Martin Luther King." For once, however, Hoover overreached himself: when Robert Kennedy discovered that he had distributed copies of the report to numerous officials in the government and armed forces, he ordered the document withdrawn. Nevertheless, the FBI had other cards up its sleeve. On December 23, Sullivan held a daylong conference at FBI headquarters to develop plans "aimed at neutralizing King as an effective Negro leader" by exposing him "as a [   ] opportunist who is . . . exploiting the racial situation for personal gain." The ensuing campaign to discredit King and disrupt SCLC has been lucidly analyzed by David J. Garrow. It gathered momentum during 1964 and culminated in a crude attempt at blackmail.[46]

If the March on Washington appeared to the FBI as a portent of revolution, the events of the following weeks revealed that behind the image of strength and solidarity presented on August 28, the civil rights movement was still weak and disunited when measured by the harsh realities of political power. The prosecution of nine black leaders in Albany, Georgia, seemed shockingly unfair. Indicted by a federal grand jury for obstruction of justice, Slater King and the Reverend Sam Wells received jail sentences of a year and a day; six others, charged with perjury, drew fines and suspended sentences. The fact that Robert Kennedy personally authorized the prosecutions made the case of the "Albany Nine" seem like a political ploy on the part of the administration to appease the segregationists. SCLC sponsored a national defense committee and King led a delegation to the Justice Department to protest the sentences. Five days later, in his speech to the SCLC convention, Wyatt Walker noted bitterly that "in the one single instance where the Federal government has moved [in Albany], it has been against Negroes intimately involved in the desegregation movement." In the text of his speech, these words were underlined.[47]

Events in Birmingham exposed the apparent impotence of the civil rights movement in a far more cruel manner. On September 15, barely three weeks after the optimism and idealism of the March on Washington, a bomb exploded at the Sixteenth Street Baptist Church. Four little girls were killed. Shortly afterwards, the city swarming with state troopers and National Guardsmen sent by Governor Wallace, two more children died. One, a thirteen-year-old boy, was shot while riding his bicycle. The second, a lad of sixteen, received a fatal wound from a police shotgun. Birmingham had witnessed seventeen bombings since 1956, seven of them within the past six months. The inability of the police to apprehend the perpetrators created a profound—and, as later events showed, quite justified—suspicion that the criminals were being deliberately shielded from justice.[48]

How should SCLC respond? Two days after the bombing, Diane Nash, now an SCLC field secretary and the wife of James Bevel, presented Fred Shuttlesworth with a plan for demonstrations in Montgomery. She proposed to force the resignation of George Wallace, whom many blacks, including King, held partly responsible for the resurgence of Klan terrorism. But Shuttlesworth was cool towards the kind of disruptive civil disobedience which Nash had in mind; it was a time for mourning, he told her, not lying in the streets tying up traffic. Disappointed, Nash appealed to King to initiate some form of protest. Black people in Birmingham wanted to take a stand, she wrote; without leadership they would gravitate towards violence: "You can tell people not to fight *only* if you offer them a way by which justice can be served without violence. . . . Just to tell people not to fight after children are murdered and leave it at that is wrong and you are expecting and appealing to them to be less than men." In her plan, Nash called for the recruitment of twenty-five thousand blacks into a "freedom army" that would spearhead a campaign of civil disobedience with the ultimate aim of pressuring the federal government to guarantee universal suffrage. Declaring the Wallace government "null and void," blacks throughout Alabama should disrupt transportation in and out of Montgomery, refuse to pay state and local taxes, and paralyze the city's communications by jamming the telephone switchboards.[49]

Having won SNCC's backing, Nash canvassed support for her plan at the SCLC convention in Richmond, which opened a week after the bombing. In his keynote address on September 25, Wyatt Walker excoriated the administration for its "kid glove treatment of the . . . Barnetts and the Wallaces" and called for an "all-out war" against racism: "Is the day far off that major transportation centers would be deluged with mass acts of civil disobedience; airports, train stations, bus terminals, the traffic of large cities, interstate commerce, would be halted by the bodies of witnesses nonviolently insisting on 'Freedom Now'? I suppose a nationwide work stoppage might attract enough attention to get this monkey of segregation and discrimination off our backs, once, now and forever. Will it take all or one of these? Of course, there is always the fast unto death. Why not?" Shuttlesworth, on the other hand, cautioned against "giving way to the excesses of the moment." Nonviolence, he observed, "is a precarious way."[50]

King regarded the Nash plan as impractical and unwise. However, he and Shuttlesworth both agreed that the bombing, together with the merchants' failure to hire Negro clerks, had so demoralized local blacks that the victory of May 10 was close to being negated. Nothing less than the employment of Negro policemen, they decided, could restore a sense of hope and progress. Visiting the White House four days after the bombing, they persuaded President Kennedy to support this demand and intercede with the Boutwell administration. To this end, Kennedy sent two envoys to Birmingham—Earl Blaik and Kenneth Royall. Boutwell all but promised them that the city was going to hire Negro policemen, or take definite steps in that direction, by October 8. He also, at long last, appointed a biracial "group relations subcommittee," chaired by Bishop C. J. J. Carpenter (one of the white clergymen to whom King had addressed "Letter from Birmingham City Jail"). Satisfied with this, Blaik and Royall departed.[51]

But SCLC was far from satisfied. Dismissing the Carpenter committee as a sham, Shuttlesworth and King asked for direct negotiations with the mayor and city council. Boutwell, however, ignored them, refusing to deal with "professional agitators." Shuttlesworth was incensed. Accusing the city and the merchants of betraying the May 10 agreement, he called a boycott of downtown stores from October 1. That night, he and Bevel spoke at an ACMHR meeting. "I thank God for the fool we have as governor," Bevel shouted. "This summer was just a little boot camp for Birmingham. We are going to turn Alabama upside down." Shuttlesworth, in equally combative mood, denounced A. G. Gaston and Arthur Shores for opposing more demonstrations and, according to the police report, added, "Reverend King is not going to see when we start. I am here and Bevel will be here; and I am tired as Hell of all these other people trying to butt into Negroes' business. We are going further than we went before."[52]

If Shuttlesworth's petulance soured their relationship, King disguised the fact when he returned to Birmingham on October 7 to affirm SCLC's support for the boycott. He gave the city two weeks to appoint its first Negro policemen. The presence on the platform of Young, Cotton, Bevel, Vivian, Lee, and Lowery seemed to indicate that SCLC meant business.[53]

In fact, King was playing a subtle game of bluff. When he presented his own "master plan" for Birmingham to a special SCLC strategy meeting a few days later, King stressed the difficulty of mounting another round of demonstrations and outlined a scheme for winning without them. Demonstrations could only be effective, he warned, "if they are bigger and more determined than before."

> This would be no minor undertaking. The other serious problem . . . would be securing funds for bail bonds. At present some $400,000 are tied up in cash and property bonds. This means that all available resources are pretty well exhausted.
>
> So we must realistically recognize that demonstrations must be an absolute last resort on our part. Our challenge is to be ingenious enough

to keep the threat of demonstrations alive so as to give the local and
national public a picture of our determination and continued militancy
and yet constantly find face-saving retreats in order to avoid demonstrations if possible.

King proposed to visit Birmingham every few days, with SCLC staff
members, in order to make the threat credible.[54]

Clever as it was, King's strategem failed. By giving the city a two-
week deadline, King and Shuttlesworth inadvertently painted themselves into a corner, giving Boutwell a perfect excuse for inaction. On
October 17 King extended the deadline, and five days later withdrew it
altogether, claiming to discern a "strong indication" that Negro policemen would be hired shortly. He was mistaken: Birmingham did not
recruit its first black policemen until 1967. Burke Marshall considered
SCLC's threat of demonstrations singularly unhelpful: it "obviously
made all the whites in Birmingham mad." The president himself
proved unable to make the city budge. The bombing and its humiliating aftermath left blacks, in the words of Lucius Pitts, "sick, frightened, angry, disappointed, disillusioned." For SCLC, it was a clear
defeat.[55]

During the following weeks and months, Shuttlesworth pressed
King to commit SCLC to another major campaign in Birmingham, to
take place no later than the spring of 1964. The situation now called
for more radical tactics, he wrote King on November 7: "If such is
needed, we will have to think in terms of tying up telephones, and
effectively immobilizing Birmingham and Montgomery." They might
even need to march from Birmingham to Montgomery with forty thousand people. SCLC's principal thrust, he argued, should be directed
towards "the 'One Man, One Vote' ideal in Alabama before the National Conventions." Shuttlesworth, in effect, was putting forward the
Nash-Bevel plan which six weeks earlier he had turned down. "The
masses are with us," he said by way of explanation, "but we can lose
them by inaction and indecisiveness. . . . [W]e must either keep leadership, or give it over to more active elements." People were complaining of a leadership vacuum, he added; King, as the symbol of the
movement, ought to spend less time writing and speaking in the
North and more time "stirring up people in the South."[56]

King now found his own argument in "Letter from Birmingham
City Jail"—if we fail, the radicals take over—echoing in his face. Bayard Rustin made the same point in a long paper which backed Shuttlesworth's argument for concentrating on Birmingham. Rustin's
analysis of the strategic situation was pessimistic. The March on
Washington had failed to achieve the expected breakthrough, he noted.

In every field, progress had been paltry: police brutality had not declined; opposition to integration seemed to be growing, even in the North; Congress was dawdling over the civil rights bill; the administration appeared reluctant to put its full weight behind that measure. Only a "new dimension of Direct Action," Rustin argued, could break this impasse. A renewed drive in Birmingham, with the focus on police brutality and terrorism, could take advantage of the moral revulsion which had swept the nation after the church bombing. If backed by a March-on-Washington-type coalition of civil rights, labor, and religious leaders, SCLC could achieve a significant breakthrough.[57]

Amid the clamor for more, and more disruptive, direct action, voices of caution could be heard. Speaking at the SCLC convention, Roy Wilkins reiterated that the ballot could be far more effective than boycotts and demonstrations. As a presidential election year approached, the argument for concentrating on voter registration gained potency: with the right-wing senator from Arizona, Barry Goldwater, the likely Republican contender, the fortunes of blacks were inextricably linked to Kennedy's reelection. Indeed, the Democratic National Committee, aware of the president's popularity among blacks, was already sounding out civil rights organizations about voter registration drives in the cities of the North.[58]

To Andrew Young, a political strategy made far more sense than a program of disruptive civil disobedience. Young acknowledged that the administration was trimming with regard to civil rights. "If Goldwater stays out front," he warned King, "the Kennedys will continue to pull the kind of tricks that they pulled on . . . the Albany Movement all year long in an attempt to 'balance' their image."[59] The most effective way to "counter this conservative swing," Young contended, was to kill the Goldwater threat, and the best means of achieving this lay in a concentrated voter registration drive in key Northern cities. Most of the South was probably in Goldwater's pocket already. But if the Republicans saw black registration booms in swing states like Ohio, "they will write Goldwater off in nothing flat. . . . If we can get a liberal Republican candidate, we can keep Kennedy moving." Such a strategy had the additional advantage of saving money on bail bonds and legal fees. Young firmly believed that SCLC had to expand into the North in order to supply "real nonviolent leadership."[60]

To the dismay of his colleagues, King refused to commit SCLC one way or the other. Although impressed by Young's argument, he was not prepared to abandon direct action and still harbored strong doubts about moving north. Evident black disunity, on the other hand, led him to rule out a return to Birmingham. While sympathetic to the idea of another major campaign in Alabama, centered on the right to vote, he put off a firm decision. SCLC's finances were not adequate for such a project; King had to devote more time to fundraising. He also needed to complete his new book, *Why We Can't Wait*, now considerably behind schedule.[61]

King felt duty bound, however, to make another effort in Danville. SCLC had made repeated offers of help, but its failure to follow through had engendered cynicism in the press, in SNCC, and in the local population. King therefore drew up a plan of campaign, "Operation Showdown," to remedy the current stalemate. Like his plan for Birmingham, Operation Showdown called for a series of graduated threats with the aim of avoiding, if at all possible, a resort to demonstrations. In order to convince white leaders of SCLC's serious intent, King set a November 10 deadline for the start of good-faith negotiations.[62]

Despite its earlier failure, SCLC had reason to feel optimistic about the chances of a breakthrough. The city council appeared intransigent, but it was actually split. If Mayor Henry Stinson, now in the middle of the two factions, decided to oppose John W. Carter, the popular spokesman for the far-right group, the moderates would be in a majority and negotiations could start. The city's major businesses, moreover, wanted the council to ease racial tensions. The tobacco warehouses and processing plants were suffering from a boycott by Negro tobacco growers. Danville's largest industry, Dan River Mills, wanted to forestall a possible nationwide boycott of its textile products. A boycott of white retail stores had been in effect for months.[63]

With the arrival of SCLC's "reconnaissance task force," led by C. T. Vivian, Stinson began to lean towards the moderates. On October 17, the city appointed its first Negro policeman. On November 12, five members of the council, Stinson among them, had talks with the NAACP and the Danville Christian Progressive Association (DCPA). They agreed to commit the city, in writing, to a nondiscriminatory hiring policy. As the talks continued, SCLC kept the threat of demonstrations alive. Staff were pulled out of Birmingham and Louisiana and sent to Danville, where they began recruiting students for voter registration and direct action. "Things seem to be picking up," Young reported on November 18. "Sunday's mass meeting was well attended. . . . We had good spirit too. Two old ladies even got out in the aisle to do the 'Holy Dance' while we were singing Freedom Songs. It looks like we may yet work up a Movement." On November 22, King visited Danville to emphasize that "we mean business." That day, however, the assassination of John Kennedy put a question mark over all SCLC's plans.[64]

KU KL
R
MORGAN C
HWY.
AU
WORLD KN
WHO HAS O
AND IN MANY FOR
ALSO OTHER
COUNT
FREE

Seven

Desegregation: Keeping up
the Pressure

The year following Kennedy's assassination was a time of apprehension and frustration for SCLC. After the shock of the Birmingham church bombing, the murder of the president seemed like a frightening confirmation that the body politic was being attacked, cancerlike, by a dangerous political and moral sickness. The popularity of George Wallace and Barry Goldwater also disturbed blacks and liberals. The two men worked in rival parties, spoke a different language, and represented different people, but they articulated similar political sentiments. If enough Northern working-class Democrats joined the Southern segregationists and traditional middle-class conservatives, the civil rights movement would collide with a political barrier of profound strength. People speculated about the rise of a native fascism. Lyndon Johnson's robust liberalism, therefore, shone like a beacon in a storm, and SCLC showed naked partisanship in the vehemence with which it denounced Johnson's opponents.

Colleagues and advisers urged King to start thinking in national terms: SCLC could no longer ignore the North. Journalists, economists, sociologists, and educationalists were turning their attention to the crime, poverty, and squalor of the ghettos. They offered different explanations: unemployment, mass migration, family instability, "cultural deprivation," "educational deficiency." Yet Northern academic experts, like Northern white liberals in general, found it difficult to recognize the reality and depth of Northern racism. It took black rioting to raise the issue of pervasive police brutality, and it took the revival of black separatism, exemplified in the growing popularity of Malcolm X, to reveal a mood of utter disillusionment with the path of liberal, nonviolent reform. But King was not yet overly concerned with the North: his was not a mercurial nature; and the job in the South was only half-done.

SCLC underwent important internal changes. Wyatt Walker left the staff in July, partly because his conception of SCLC, and of his own role within it, differed from King's. Walker had struggled to tighten SCLC's lax discipline. He made staff members sign in and out: "Be there at ten minutes to nine," he told the office secretaries, "and when nine o'clock comes, start hitting on that typewriter." But Walker felt that his authority over the staff was being eroded by King's reluctance to fire or even reprimand delinquent subordinates, and this, he claimed, contributed to his decision to leave. "This is not a church," he remembers telling King, "it's an organization. If I'm your executive director and I fire somebody, they're fired. You don't have nothing to talk to them about."[1]

Walker also felt undervalued. During his administration, he boasted, "SCLC went into orbit. . . . It might have gone into orbit under 'Joe Blow,' I don't know. But I was there." Only a promotion and a pay raise, he decided, could induce him to stay on. His dissatisfaction came to a head at SCLC's annual convention in September, held in Richmond. The board's administrative committee refused his request for an increase in salary. In addition, it not only declined to promote him but also redefined his position as "executive assistant" rather than "executive director." Not without reason, Walker viewed this as a demotion. Then, to Walker's disgust, King questioned his action in docking the pay of four staff members for acts of "irresponsibility and insubordination" during the convention. A few days later, on October 3, Walker submitted his resignation, effective from the end of 1963. "The conditions under which I work have become completely intolerable," he told King. In 1967, reflecting on his departure, Walker put forward the strain and exhaustion of three years' work as his principal reason for leaving. "I was always in the trenches," he recalled. "I don't know where I didn't go, by bus, train, mule, car, whatever." After Birmingham he felt physically, emotionally, and psychologically drained: "I began to feel like I'd had it. I really felt a creeping bitterness coming over me."[2]

For at least some of the SCLC staff, Walker's imminent departure came as a relief. The office staff, in particular, regarded him as an intolerant martinet who was far too ready to fire or discipline them for relatively minor lapses. People were leaving the staff, Dora McDonald complained to King, because they found Walker impossible to work for. "One certainly cannot function at best," she added, "when there is so much insecurity job-wise." Stanley Levison, who had at first been so enthusiastic about Walker, came to the conclusion that although brilliant and dedicated, his egocentricity brought him into continual conflict with others in SCLC. The reason he left, Levison told an acquaintance, "is that he was nobody's cup of tea, and the staff just rose up in revolt against him." The hypercritical Levison had a habit of souring on people who had initially impressed him. Yet Walker's undoubted ability to alienate people must have disturbed King. When Walker wished to fire James Bevel for insubordination, King overruled him; the loss of someone as talented as Bevel was too high a price for sustaining Walker's exacting discipline. King probably had mixed feelings about seeing Walker leave, but he was anxious that the parting should be amicable. He persuaded him to stay on until the summer of 1964, and suggested that he continue to serve SCLC in some other capacity.[3]

Andrew Young took over Walker's job and stayed with SCLC until 1970. Perhaps it was Young's administrative talent that persuaded King to give him the executive directorship; William Kunstler marvelled at his "amazing organizational ability." Yet Walker, for one, thought his work sometimes careless: "A lot of things he'd just forget and let go." More likely, King was impressed by Young's skills as a conciliator and diplomat. Affable, soft-spoken, and even-tempered, he lacked the bumptiousness and abrasiveness that often estranged people from Walker. He was less outspoken: less insistent on pressing his own views and less inclined to provoke rows. King certainly found him more comfortable to work with, and he became, next to Abernathy, his closest colleague. Young was also better able to settle quarrels and disputes within SCLC. "He was always more or less the reconciler," recalled C. K. Steele. But his promotion also marked a deterioration of staff discipline. Given the growth in staff numbers and the promotion of men like James Bevel and Hosea Williams, this was probably un-avoidable. But whereas Walker had insisted upon having complete authority over his subordinates—the entire SCLC staff—Young was more tolerant of King's habit of interfering. After 1964, staff members got away with breaches of discipline that would have been unthinkable in Walker's day.[4]

Less of an administrator and disciplinarian than Walker, Young was a better negotiator and committee person. When he represented SCLC in meetings with other organizations, for example, he invariably created a favorable impression; he was less prone, for example, to alienate people in SNCC or the NAACP. Young had also become adept at negotiating with whites, a talent which reflected not only a difference in temperament from Walker but also a difference in outlook. Walker had seen massive nonviolent disruption as the most potent weapon available to blacks; Young set greater store by diplomacy. He had faith in the basic decency of white Southerners, and confidence in the ability of the business elite to realize that racial turmoil lowered their profits. He sometimes talked of white "goodwill" as if it were a tangible commodity, and his colleagues on the executive staff jokingly referred to him as SCLC's resident Uncle Tom. All agreed, however, that he was a useful man to have around. "When you got through fussing and fighting," said Steele, "Andy was a good man to sit down at the table." As Randolph Blackwell put it, "Andy could always find a way to save our face without necessarily completely capitulating."[5]

Politically, Young was to the right of Walker, a difference clearly brought out in their respective attitudes towards the Southern Conference Education Fund. Walker had urged SNCC to accept SCEF's help, dismissing the notion that SCEF was a Communist "front." Young, on the other hand, was wary of SCEF—not because he believed the allegations, but because others did. SCEF had refused to adapt to the political realities of the Cold War, Young argued, thereby inviting attack from the Right; it had no "realpolitik and tactical sense." He rejected a proposal to cooperate with SCEF in Mississippi, explaining that "we have to keep free of the Communist *charge* even." SCLC could not afford to risk guilt by association; it had to ensure that it only accepted help from "institutions within the establishment."[6]

Young's promotion might appear to mark a palpable shift from "militancy" towards "moderation," especially as it coincided with a cooling of relations between King and Shuttlesworth, who played an ever-decreasing role in SCLC's affairs. But this proved not to be the case. James Bevel, C. T. Vivian, and Hosea Williams, who joined the executive staff in 1963–64, were skeptical about Young's approach and shared Walker's predilection for direct action.

The words most often applied to Bevel were "firebrand" and "rabble-rouser." In Birmingham he had been one of the most popular and effective speakers in the mass meetings, his abuse of Connor and Wallace delighting the audiences. By 1963 he was already SCLC's most experienced field secretary, having served in Mississippi for more than two years. He had a tremendous appeal to young people: his role in organizing the children's marches in Birmingham had been pivotal. Bevel was a true believer in Gandhian nonviolence. Like other disciples of James Lawson, he pushed the doctrine of nonviolence to its logical extreme—to its logical absurdity, some thought. "I can see the possibility of a worldwide nonviolent student movement," he once enthused, "uniting the students of India and Russia, and China and America. I can even see a nonviolent movement on the battlefield." Despite his provocative, even virulent, declamatory style, Bevel regarded nonviolence as an absolute commitment. Yet he was also well aware that the appeal of nonviolence was conditional for most blacks: if nonviolent tactics failed to produce results, black nationalism could make rapid headway among the young. To counter this threat, he and Diane Nash, whom he married, developed the concept of a "nonviolent army" to carry out mass civil disobedience. Arrogant, argumentative, and insubordinate, Bevel never developed the kind of friendship with King that Abernathy and Young enjoyed. But King recognized his talent and in 1964 put him in charge of direct action. What this post entailed remained to be seen.[7]

Hosea Williams shared Bevel's rabble-rousing skills as well as his arrogance. He struck one reporter as "a cocky man who does not doubt his own organizing abilities"; others thought him petulant and overbearing and considered his self-confidence misplaced.[8] Unlike most of King's lieutenants, Williams had neither trained for nor entered the ministry: the "Reverend" he sometimes prefixed to his name was an affectation. In some ways alike temperamentally, he and Bevel were poles apart politically and philosophically. Bevel looked forward to a kind of Christian socialist utopia; Williams was an unabashed capitalist who admired the American way of life. To Bevel, nonviolence was both means and end; to Williams, direct action and the ballot were

merely handy battering rams with which to force an entry into the
existing society. Bevel believed in nonviolence as a philosophy;
Williams took the philosophy with a pinch of salt. Both men, however,
distrusted white expressions of goodwill and had little faith in diplomacy. Organizing demonstrations became second nature to them,
Williams's specialty being the night march. A hard boss, who could be
abusive and bullying, Williams was described by Steele as SCLC's
"hatchet man." Impressed by his record in Savannah, King placed him
in charge of voter registration.[9]

C. T. Vivian—known to all as "C. T."—joined the executive staff as
director of affiliates. His early career in the civil rights movement
paralleled that of Bevel: both had taken part in the Lawson workshops;
both had been prominent in the Nashville sit-ins; both went on the
second Freedom Ride and spent time in jail in Mississippi. Like Bevel,
Vivian held to nonviolence as a total philosophy; less of a rabble-
rouser, he believed that the civil rights movement had to maintain a
sense of dignity and moral purity. Unlike most of King's staff, he was
not a native Southerner. Born in Missouri and raised in Illinois, he did
not train for the ministry until the age of thirty, when he entered the
American Baptist Theological Seminary and secured a job as editor of
religious publications for the National Baptist Convention. By the
time he joined SCLC he had also pastored churches in Nashville and
Chattanooga. Five years older than King, and a generation removed
from Bevel and the student activists of 1960, Vivian's outlook had a
tinge of the Old Left radicalism of the Roosevelt era. An admirer of
Bayard Rustin, he had an interest in broader social and economic issues that was unusual in SCLC until the ghetto riots forced its members to grapple with them.[10]

SCLC might be described as a benevolent autocracy: King had the
last word, but he made decisions after consulting—usually—an amor-
phous and ever-expanding circle of friends, colleagues, and advisers. Of
these, the least important was SCLC's board of directors. The board
had never functioned as a genuine policymaking body; its resolutions
might define SCLC's official position, but they had little intrinsic importance. Only rarely did the directors balk at the policies proposed by
King. Some of them—Steele, Lowery, Reddick—attended the important staff retreats and also served on the various boards and committees that came into being as SCLC generated new programs. As SCLC's
full-time staff grew, however, the board's "inner circle," the administrative committee, diminished in importance as decision making
gravitated to King and the Atlanta-based executive staff.

The executive staff met regularly, usually every other week. About half the members had specialized duties which kept them on the fringes of SCLC's protest campaigns, giving them a distinctly junior status. The two women, Dorothy Cotton and Septima Clark, were accorded a doubly junior status. In practice, about half a dozen people—the men, the ministers, the direct action specialists—dominated the discussions. As the training and experience of the black preacher was not conducive to compromise, cooperation, and consensus, decision making was rarely a smooth process. The arguments were often long and heated, and sometimes exacerbated by strong personal antagonisms. Only half-jokingly, King and Abernathy complained about the lack of nonviolence within SCLC. As Randolph Blackwell put it, "We used to have terrible staff meetings."[11]

How did King control such a fractious group? He possessed patience, self-control, a sense of humor, and a willingness to listen to other points of view. He was an effective chairman. During discussions he frequently kept silent, refusing to constrain the debate and encouraging what Young termed a "dialectical" approach: "He would push people to extremes . . . [and] he would want somebody to express as radical a view as possible and somebody to express as conservative a view as possible." When prolonged argument had produced catharsis, exhaustion, and deadlock, he summarized the discussion and concluded with a personal statement—often resembling a sermon—of his own. He could impose, without seeming dictatorial, decisions that represented a rough balance or consensus. Young suspected that King expected him "to take the conservative side, to . . . neutralize what Bevel and Hosea were trying to do, to give him an excuse to come down in the middle." The fact that Bevel and Williams seldom agreed themselves—rivalry soon ripened into strong mutual dislike—made King's task less difficult. Sometimes, admittedly, King left decisions hanging in the air, or relied on Abernathy and Young to settle a dispute.[12]

King exerted authority, too, by virtue of his unique popularity as a black leader and his unassailable position as president of SCLC. He also set his staff a superlative example of industry, integrity, and dedication. Joining the inner circle brought advancement and glory, but it also implied a limitation on personal ambition, and a commitment, in Blackwell's words, "to a broader something than any of us had been involved in."[13]

King's constant references to his own sacrifices both underscored this sense of commitment and highlighted his own sense of mission.

By his own acknowledgment, King consciously strove to avoid developing a "martyr complex," but, as one of his biographers has suggested, the ever-present threats to his life, together with what friends described as a guilt-ridden personality, made this a difficult battle. The story of the 1958 attempt on his life, accounts of the threatening telephone calls he received, and affirmations of his readiness to lay down his life for the cause recurred throughout his speeches and sermons. Such references could move a black audience to near hysteria, and it is tempting to dismiss them as the kind of oratorical ploy beloved of American demagogues—the example of Huey Long springs to mind. But King also dwelt on death in private, during staff meetings, retreats, and in personal conversation; "Martin used to talk about it all the time," Young remembered, "to make us think about it." Given the real dangers inherent in leadership in the civil rights movement, the possibility of death was bound to be a topic of discussion. But intentionally or not, King's talk of death served as a sort of manipulative device whereby he asserted a kind of moral authority over his colleagues. "I may die in this movement, but I don't mind. I settled that long ago," he often told his staff. "I don't think anybody can be free until you solve this problem." After 1965, adversity and criticism magnified what William Robert Miller called King's "sense of a literal discipleship of the cross." Others regarded his talk of death as a morbid obsession which betrayed an increasingly heavy burden of fear, anxiety, and depression.[14]

King's sermonizing cut little ice with the worldly intellectuals who made up the research committee, SCLC's second main forum of debate. The research committee came into being because Harry Wachtel and Clarence Jones considered King badly informed on current events, especially in the North, and in danger of becoming intellectually stale. In May 1964, at Wachtel's suggestion, King agreed to meet a small group of advisers every two or three weeks in New York, with a view to exposing himself to new ideas and deepening his knowledge of contemporary issues, especially in politics and economics. In addition to Jones and Wachtel, the group comprised L. D. Reddick; Bayard Rustin; Cleveland Robinson, secretary-treasurer of the Retail, Wholesale, and Department Store Workers, District 65; and Ralph Helstein, the white president of the Packinghouse Workers. King nearly always brought two or three staff members to the meetings, usually Abernathy, Young, and Walter Fauntroy, now head of SCLC's newly opened Washington bureau.[15]

The research committee met in Wachtel's Madison Avenue law office for sessions that lasted most of the day. At its first meeting, Reddick presented an analysis of Wallace and the white backlash. But the committee failed to develop its "research" function in the sense of presenting King with carefully prepared papers. Meeting at King's request, often at short notice, the committee undertook discussions that were informal, wide-ranging, and usually completely unstructured. King used the committee as a source of information and advice, a sounding board for his own ideas, and a means of contact with the Northern Left. Simply listening to the debates enriched his thinking; he found them immensely stimulating. "The committee often disagreed," said Levison, who joined the group in 1965. "But in that exchange Martin learned a lot, and it always assured him of being up to date because each of these people is an expert in different areas." Although it discussed every aspect of SCLC's work, the committee was probably most useful for helping King to formulate an informed position in respect of controversial public issues.[16]

But the research committee was no more a policymaking body than the executive staff. No votes were ever taken; they would have carried no weight. As Wachtel pointedly observed, the "democracy" of SCLC was such that King always had the last say.[17] And with an unpredictable single-mindedness that often exasperated his advisers, King frequently ignored their counsel and followed his own judgement. Equally important, the research committee played little part in the most important area of SCLC's existence: its campaigns of nonviolent direct action. In Albany, Birmingham, St. Augustine, Selma, Mississippi, and Chicago, King made the crucial decisions with little reference to Rustin, Levison, Jones, or Wachtel. Southern preachers, not Northern intellectuals, comprised SCLC's essential core.

Once or twice a year, King brought together a few senior board members, the executive staff, and his Northern advisers for a "retreat" that lasted from two days to a week. In the seclusion of rural Georgia, the North Carolina mountains, or the woods of Virginia, he could escape from the press and take a holiday from fundraising to discuss, listen, and debate, as well as relax, amid the most congenial of surroundings. At these seminal meetings, SCLC, in its most complete expression, analyzed large questions of philosophy, strategy, and politics in an atmosphere of convivial informality. Retreats for the field staff often preceded, followed, or overlapped these sessions. Here, the people on the bottom rungs of SCLC could discuss their problems, air their grievances, and enjoy some rare contact with King, who lectured to them on nonviolence, Marxism, and the problems facing them as SCLC staff members.

The FBI, apparently, discovered little of what transpired at these retreats, save what it gleaned from its wiretaps. It had a plethora of information, on the other hand, concerning King and his Northern advisers, and, utilizing this material, persistently misrepresented the research committee as a sinister and dominating influence on King. Characterizing Jones, Levison, Rustin, and Wachtel as Communists or Communist sympathizers, the bureau portrayed King as a weak personality who was constantly manipulated by subversives. Levison was considered the most insidious influence. On the strength of his contacts with King—which, after June 22, 1963, the date of Kennedy's warning to King, were very few indeed—the FBI had installed wiretaps on the telephones of Jones, Rustin, King himself, and the SCLC offices in Atlanta and New York. Millions of dollars and millions of man-hours were expended in processing and evaluating the enormous quantity of information thus yielded, as well as in the "physical surveillance"—tailing—of Levison and King. It became an article of faith in the FBI that Levison virtually controlled King. When asked by a congressional committee in 1978 whether he considered King a Communist, Hoover's chief assistant, Cartha DeLoach, simply replied—as if no further proof were needed—that Levison had written speeches for King, advised him on financial matters, and made policy decisions for him.[18] In the same year, shortly before his death, Levison himself ridiculed this argument. "No one with a modicum of sense," he insisted, could conclude that "a man with the force of intellect and fierce independence that Martin King had could have been dominated by anybody." The FBI's whole argument, he added, rested upon a "racist contempt for the intellect of the black man."[19]

The "raw" FBI transcripts of Levison's tapped telephone conversations, declassified in 1983, illustrate King's stubborn independence in a striking fashion. Time and again, King rejected the arguments of Levison and his other advisers to do, in the words of Harry Wachtel, "whatever he damn well pleased."[20] Crucial decisions affecting SCLC's future, like the decision to go to Chicago in 1966, were made in the teeth of opposition from all the key members of the research committee. King's commitment to the peace movement in 1967 is another revealing example. Far from encouraging this move, Levison tried to restrain King. King marched in the 1967 Spring Mobilization Against the War in Vietnam contrary to the unanimous opinion of the research committee.[21]

But did Levison put words into King's mouth by "ghosting" his books, articles, and speeches? King found writing difficult and welcomed help; Levison was his most dependable source of help, but

Rustin, Wachtel, Jones, and others all rendered similar assistance. As
the demands on his time grew, moreover, King became increasingly lax
about scrutinizing material that had been written for him.[22] Nevertheless, as the Levison transcripts reveal, most of what King wrote or
published came from his own pen, and he usually criticized and
amended that which did not. No passive mouthpiece, King rarely accepted either advice or written material without subjecting it to the
critical analysis of a trained and independent mind.[23]

When compared with the verbatim transcripts, the FBI's summaries
are exposed as blatant distortions and outright lies. The copious memoranda which Hoover sent to the president, the attorney general, and
other high government officials constantly stressed those occasions
when King's actions happened to coincide with the views of Levison
and other advisers. In this fashion, they depicted King as a pliant tool.
The countless instances when he asked for advice, listened, and then
did something different were rarely mentioned. That the FBI, with its
vaunted expertise in evaluating intelligence, could use these wiretapped conversations to prove King's thraldom to communism illus-
trates the power of ideology and prejudice over truth. The bureau's
archconservative, "security-state" mentality, with its hatred and suspicion of all social criticism, had a ruthless and rigid illogic which made
rational political discourse impossible.

The fact that the Kennedy administration authorized these wiretaps
has been variously interpreted. Kennedy partisans not unnaturally opt
for the most innocent explanation. The installation of the wiretaps,
they argue, as well as the pressure on King to reject O'Dell and
Levison, were part of an administration effort to protect King. As Theodore Sorenson wrote in 1965, King "was privately persuaded to reject
some Communists who had infiltrated the movement, and the President in turn rejected the claims of the Wallaces and the Barnetts that
the whole civil rights movement was Communist-inspired." In his
biography of Robert Kennedy, published more than a decade later,
Arthur Schlesinger put forward a similar view: the attorney general
approved the wiretaps in order "to protect King, to protect the civil
rights movement, to protect themselves." Testifying before the Church
committee in 1975, Nicholas Katzenbach, Kennedy's successor as attorney general, explained that "the leadership and support of Dr.
King . . . was an essential ingredient in the Kennedy administration
and its dedication to [equal rights]."[24]

In reality, the relationship between King and the Kennedy administration was more ambiguous; as David Garrow has recently stressed,

the Kennedys harbored strong reservations about King's leadership and
political judgement. With their own political fortunes uppermost in
mind, their predominant perception of King was of an irritating prob-
lem-creator. Their attitude to direct action was almost wholly negative, and they regarded some of SCLC's tactics as utterly irresponsible;
the use of children in the Birmingham demonstrations appalled them.
King's failure to completely sever his relationship with Levison further
weakened their confidence in him. In an oral history interview recorded in 1964, Robert Kennedy admitted that "we never wanted to get
very close to him just because of these contacts . . . which we felt were
damaging to the civil rights movement and because . . . it also
damaged us." John Kennedy's opinion of King remains elusive. Harris
Wofford, his first civil rights adviser, remembered that he preferred the
company of Roy Wilkins and Whitney Young: "There was always a
strain in his dealings with King, who came on with a moral tone
that . . . made him uncomfortable." According to Jim Bishop, Kennedy
regarded King as a demagogue and a hypocrite—a statement which
probably reflected Bishop's own antipathy to King as much as
Kennedy's.[25]

Less than two weeks after Kennedy's murder, King had an invitation
to visit the new president. In 1959, like most liberals, King regarded
Lyndon B. Johnson, then the majority leader in the Senate, as a Southern conservative who was completely unfitted to occupy the White
House as the head of a Democratic administration. When he met Johnson as vice-president, however, King, to his surprise, had been favorably impressed. His fifty-minute interview on December 3 confirmed
that initial impression, and in the final pages of *Why We Can't Wait*,
written shortly afterwards, he praised Johnson's "comprehensive grasp
of contemporary problems," and his "sincerity, realism and wisdom."
The new president's forthright statement on civil rights in his speech
to Congress struck King as courageous. Johnson's accession, he believed, significantly enhanced the prospects for the civil rights bill in
view of both his Southern background and, more important, his legendary reputation as a "cloak-room persuader" of congressmen.[26]

With the civil rights bill before Congress, the debate between the
advocates of legal-political action and the adherents of nonviolent direct action acquired a new intensity. Yet King dismissed the argument
that demonstrations might jeopardize the bill: more outside pressure,
not less, had to be directed towards Congress in order to break the
"unholy alliance of Dixiecrats and Northern right-wing Republicans."
And he also rejected the notion that continuing street protests under-

mined respect for the law and invited violence and rioting: as long as blacks saw tangible signs of progress, they would firmly shun violence and extremism. He made it clear to President Johnson that SCLC intended to resume direct action after the month-long period of mourning for John Kennedy.[27]

Events in the South, however, kept alive the long-standing argument over the effectiveness of direct action. After the tumultuous summer of 1963 came a lull; exhaustion, defeat, and the commencement of a new school year contributed to a sharp decline in the number of demonstrations. Where integration gains had been few or nonexistent, blacks became skeptical about protests whose only result seemed to be mass arrests, economic reprisals, and staggering legal costs. In Jackson, Danville, Plaquemines, and elsewhere, local movements turned once more to economic boycotts and voter registration drives. Charles Evers, who succeeded his murdered brother, Medgar, as the NAACP's Mississippi field secretary, urged blacks to "stay out of jail, keep your money in your pockets, and register every voter you can get your hands on."[28] SNCC, too, although critical of the NAACP's alleged conservatism, also placed a higher priority on voter registration. Now emphasizing political power rather than desegregation, SNCC began to draw up plans for a massive campaign in Mississippi to strike at the very foundation of white supremacy—the one-party state based on black disfranchisement—and realize the ideal of "One Man, One Vote."

The Atlanta demonstrations of 1963–64 represented SNCC's last major drive against segregation and the first time since Albany that SNCC and SCLC undertook a joint campaign. Pressure for direct action had been mounting since October 19, when the city's shaky civil rights coalition, the Summit Leadership Conference, submitted more than thirty demands to Mayor Ivan Allen. Shortly before its November 14 "deadline," the SLC postponed its threatened boycott of downtown stores when the chamber of commerce publicly urged an end to segregation. Upset by this delay, and unmollified by the merchants' statement, SNCC chafed at the bit during the postassassination moratorium. In December, by which time desegregation had advanced barely at all, SNCC organized a rally in Hurt Park to set the stage for direct action. "Something strange and appalling has happened to Atlanta," King told the thin crowd on December 15. "While boasting of its civic virtue, Atlanta has allowed itself to fall behind almost every major southern city in progress toward desegregation." Only one restaurant in ten served blacks; only 3 out of 150 hotels and motels. And almost a decade after *Brown*, Atlanta's elementary schools were entirely segregated, while a mere 153 black children attended "white" high schools. Two days later, SNCC began a series of demonstrations against the city's segregated eating places.[29]

In early January, Wyatt Walker presented the SLC with a "Battle Plan to Totally Desegregate the City of Atlanta." It was a blueprint for direct action designed to create a maximum of disorder and "creative tension." It would not be easy to find a "sensitive spot," Walker admitted, for "police conduct will be exemplary." Under determined pressure, however, "the presence of segregation . . . will cause it to break. Persistence must be the theme."[30] On January 6, pressed by SNCC, SCLC, and a faction within the NAACP led by Sam Williams, the SLC agreed to support a scaled-down version of the "battle plan." Five days later, Walker and John Lewis were arrested in the restaurant of the Heart of Atlanta Motel. Also arrested were John Gibson, Andrew Young's assistant, and Harry Boyte, a white North Carolinian who had joined SCLC as an aide to King.[31]

The "Open City" drive continued until the end of the month, despite the early desegregation of fifteen restaurants. After a week of small-scale sit-ins, John Lewis announced an escalation of the protests, with mass demonstrations to commence on January 25. By the fourth day of demonstrations, arrests totalled three hundred. The adoption of Walker's "battle plan," however, evoked stiff opposition within the SLC, prompting its chairman, the aged black lawyer A. T. Walden, to resign rather than see it implemented. King's father also opposed the plan; at the January 6 meeting he had stormed out after being jeered, booed, and laughed at. The conservatives were appalled by the plan's thinly veiled argument that tactics should be geared towards "provoking" police violence. The style of the SNCC-led demonstrations, moreover, particularly the tactic of "going limp" upon arrest, seemed to confirm that such was, indeed, the underlying intention (although Walker himself disapproved of such tactics). On January 30 the SLC voted to sanction "limited demonstrations" only. Walden and Allen tried to negotiate a thirty-day "cooling-off" period, but the SLC turned it down. Attempting to steer between the factions, the SLC outlined its own terms for a truce, which Allen, in turn, rejected. The demonstrations attracted little active support from Atlanta's black population and petered out inconclusively. "That's the one time that I went to jail that I felt was useless," Walker recalled. His "battle plan" could have succeeded, he thought, had the older leaders not scuttled it.[32]

King himself watched the campaign from the sidelines. He was still working on *Why We Can't Wait*, a task that stretched well into the

New Year. But he had no desire, in any case, to become closely involved. He realized that he carried little weight with the city's famous
"power structure," which had long worked through older black leaders
like Walden, C. A. Scott, William H. Borders, and Martin Luther King,
Sr. His respect for Mayor Allen, moreover, gave him little stomach for
a bruising confrontation in Atlanta; perhaps also, as Bishop speculated,
King's emotional ties with his hometown made him reluctant to see it
turned into another Birmingham.[33] For the most part, SCLC confined
its work in Atlanta to voter registration and Operation Breadbasket, an
ongoing job-creation program launched in September 1962. Modelled
on the work of the Reverend Leon H. Sullivan in Philadelphia, Operation Breadbasket used the threat of consumer boycotts, loosely organized through the local black churches, to prize jobs for blacks from
stores and industries. Fred Bennette directed the program.[34]

At about this time James Bevel wrote to King to complain that
SCLC's activities in Atlanta were a waste of time. Instead, he argued,
SCLC ought to be concentrating its resources and energy in Alabama,
where it could achieve a real breakthrough. The kind of work it was
doing in Atlanta could be done by anybody; only SCLC, on the other
hand, had an understanding of "true non-violence." Without this,
Bevel contended, direct action degenerated into aimless militancy—
demonstrations becoming almost an end in themselves—and a dangerous kind of "brinkmanship" that could all too easily spill over into
violence. SCLC should be undertaking a project "that can accomplish a
tangible change for the masses of poor people"; the alternative, he
warned, was a loss of faith in nonviolence and a growth in support for
black nationalism, whose foremost exponent, Malcolm X, was already
becoming increasingly popular. He concluded with a complaint that
there were only five SCLC staff members in Alabama: "We need the
whole non-violent staff put on the non-violent project in Alabama and
we need to stop this splinter work that is not going to restore the
confidence of the masses to the non-violent movement."[35]

King read Bevel's paper with great interest. However, SCLC was
beset by so many organizational problems that the kind of ambitious
campaign envisaged by Bevel had to wait.

The most serious problem concerned the New York office. The enforced departure from SCLC of O'Dell and Levison had left the office
in the hands of one junior staff member, Ruth Bailey, who received
virtually no supervision or support from Atlanta. SCLC's direct-mail
fundraising program, one of its most important sources of income,
became increasingly disorganized. When Ed Clayton visited the office

in November 1963 he complained about its "junky" appearance and general air of inefficiency. "Moreover," he added, "it seems to attract strange-looking 'be-bop' types with goatees who wear sweaters and no ties in the office." The situation remained much the same in January, when Clarence Jones noted the office's dingy look and the "increasingly frequent appearance of various sizes of rats." King tried, without success, to persuade either Wyatt Walker or Bayard Rustin to take over the office. The appointment of Adele Kanter in February went some way towards solving the problem, but the confusion of the preceding months meant that SCLC failed to fully exploit the impact of Birmingham. The fact that a single advertisement in the *New York Times* pulled in $66,000 gives some indication of how much money SCLC lost by neglecting its mailing list.[36]

The problems of the Gandhi Society contributed to SCLC's financial predicament and forced it to devise new arrangements for its legal representation. Far from being a reliable source of income for SCLC, the Gandhi Society had become a financial burden. Lacking a 501-C3 tax exemption, it never attracted sufficient funds to enable it to undertake more than a fraction of SCLC's legal work. Indeed, what little income it generated failed to cover the fees of William Kunstler, its principal attorney. Kunstler's conduct, moreover, produced a string of complaints. With a penchant for self-advertisement, a manner of exploiting his relationship with King, and a habit of making commitments in SCLC's name on his own initiative, Kunstler soon alienated his colleagues in the Gandhi Society. He also antagonized Jack Greenberg, head of the NAACP Legal Defense and Education, or "Inc.," Fund. The fact that SCLC had become more and more dependent on the Inc. Fund for its legal representation made Kunstler an even greater liability. When the Gandhi Society expired in June 1964, with the Inc. Fund taking over all SCLC's important litigation, Kunstler's role in SCLC ended.[37]

By then, SCLC had accumulated a sizeable deficit which grew larger by the day. When the executive staff met in Atlanta on May 4, King insisted upon an immediate and drastic austerity program with the aim of reducing monthly expenditures from $50,000 to $35,000. It might be necessary to postpone any direct action, he warned, in order to concentrate on fundraising.[38]

What alternatives for direct action offered themselves to SCLC? In January, at a two-day retreat at Black Mountain, near Asheville, North Carolina, King had assembled about two dozen colleagues and advisers to plan for the immediate future. Out of this session came a rough

strategy in respect of the civil rights bill. In the event of a prolonged
filibuster by the Southern senators, SCLC needed to stage some kind of
dramatic protest in Washington to put pressure on Congress. One suggestion—Walker's apparently—was that King should engage in a
Gandhi-like fast. Revealing this plan to SCLC's board, King added that
he had "not yet decided how far I will go—whether unto death—but
this is a decision I have [to make]."[39] If and when the bill became law,
SCLC should systematically "test" public accommodations to ensure
prompt compliance and enforcement.[40]

The second alternative was Bevel's plan for Alabama. By February,
Bevel had produced a detailed program for his proposed campaign, with
a thoughtful and thorough consideration of goals, strategy, and tactics.
King gave his tentative approval, and Bevel proceeded to lay the
groundwork. On March 4, about two hundred delegates from SCLC's
Alabama affiliates assembled in Montgomery to pledge their support
for a "statewide coordination of the masses" to achieve the right to
vote. Bevel was under no illusions, however, about the ability of the
church-based affiliates to mount effective action: experience had
taught that students provided the manpower for demonstrations.
Working from a "recruiting center" in Montgomery, therefore, he set
out to raise a "Freedom Army" from students across the state. By May
he claimed to be training volunteers in twelve cities and towns.[41]

At the May 4 executive staff meeting, Bevel argued cogently and
forcefully for his plan, as the terse minutes show: "We must address
ourselves to a political problem. Alabama is the project. The problem:
the disfranchisement of Negroes. Solution: create awareness of plight
in young to act; in the old to understand. . . . There must be two areas
of confrontation: State government; Federal government. Present 'decent voting law' to Governor Wallace. Ask President Johnson to protect
all citizens' right to vote in November election. At the moment that
Governor Wallace refuses to receive law, confrontation takes place, the
Federal government will be aroused, and the nation." Bevel envisaged
an eight-month campaign, with "large numbers of people . . . staying
in jail for at least 4 or 5 months." This, he stressed, would necessitate
the leaders remaining in jail as well.[42]

King found the audacity and ambition of Bevel's conception impressive. But he still had doubts about its feasibility and gave himself
ten days to choose between Washington, Alabama, and a third alternative, St. Augustine. During the next two weeks, King was wracked
by indecision. On "Face the Nation," on May 10, he declared quite
emphatically that "we definitely plan to have massive demonstrations

in the State of Alabama this summer." Eight days later, however, he
visited St. Augustine and promised to "return at a later date,
and . . . bring with me our nonviolent army." But SCLC possessed only
one nonviolent army; where was it to fight?[43]

Bevel's plan for Alabama had the disadvantage of being exactly that,
a plan. In reality, SCLC had no reliable base from which to launch an
Alabama campaign. Another major direct action campaign in Birmingham was out of the question. Selma, a possible target, had already
been colonized by SNCC. The Montgomery Improvement Association
had grown staid and conservative; it shied away from direct action.
The impact of the Montgomery bus boycott had been dissipated. At
the end of 1963, Virginia Durr gloomily noted that "Montgomery is
just as segregated as when we came here [in 1953] except for the buses
(on which practically no whites ride) and for the Library (which practically no Negroes use) and for the airport, and the same is true there."
In December, King told a poorly attended rally that Montgomery was
living in the past: "It is time we had the struggle here, where Governor
Wallace will understand." But the MIA looked askance at Bevel's "revolutionary" plan, declining to vote for SCLC's Alabama program. There
was no leadership in Montgomery, Andrew Young complained. "The
people are floundering in confusion." The practical objections to Bevel's scheme did not stop with the absence of a local base. Could SCLC
afford such an ambitious project? Was it realistic to dispense with bail,
as Bevel suggested, and allow arrested demonstrators to languish in jail
for months on end?[44]

St. Augustine, by contrast, looked much more inviting. With an
ultrasegregationist city government and a spirited black resistance, it
appeared to resemble a small-scale Birmingham. Blacks there wanted
SCLC's help. Above all, the Florida city was vulnerable. With a large
part of its economy geared towards servicing the tourists who came to
enjoy the Spanish-colonial charm of the "Nation's Oldest City," it
offered a tempting target. Its segregated motels and restaurants were
hardly the central concern of the local black population, most of
whom worked as domestics, service workers, and laborers, but they
were extremely susceptible to SCLC-style disruption. In addition, St.
Augustine was building up to its four hundredth anniversary, which
promised to attract visitors in record numbers during 1965. In view of
the fact that the city sought federal grants to help defray the cost of
restoring its old buildings and mounting its quadricentennial, St. Augustine was doubly—trebly—assailable. As journalist Paul Good put
it, "Why expend energies bringing Boll Weevil junction to the national

consciousness when storied St. Augustine is already there, needing
only a demonstration or two to change its Fountain of Youth into a
wellspring of bigotry?"[45]

SCLC had already discovered the city's publicity value during
Easter, when C. T. Vivian and Hosea Williams organized a week of
demonstrations involving the Massachusetts Christian Leadership
Conference, a supporting affiliate composed mainly of white ministers
and university people.[46] The Massachusetts group sent sixty volunteers to St. Augustine on March 28, each pledged to stay in jail for
three days. Alerted by SCLC well in advance, 150 reporters and cameramen were on hand to record the highlight of the protests: the arrest
of Mrs. Malcolm Peabody, the seventy-two-year-old mother of Endicott
Peabody, the governor of Massachusetts. But for this event, news of the
287 other arrests would not have constituted a major story. Mrs. Peabody, however, received front-page treatment; the *New York Times*
carried her picture three days in succession.[47] Newspaper and television coverage of the protests, especially the Peabody arrest, produced a
crop of angry letters to Gov. Farris Bryant. "How on earth can anybody
have any positive feelings towards the State of Florida when they see a
newsreel . . . showing police in St. Augustine using cattle prods on
demonstrators?" wrote a doctor from New York. "Won't you use your
good offices to prevent such medieval practices?"[48]

The Easter protest was no more than a probing action; it implied no
commitment on SCLC's part to a sustained campaign. Having sanctioned an initial foray, however, King was loathe to simply abandon St.
Augustine. Brilliant as a publicity coup, the protest had little impact
on the city fathers, and when the New Englanders posted bond and
returned to their Ivy League havens, St. Augustine resumed its "placid,
segregated way of life." Mayor Joseph Shelley brushed aside the demands of local black leader Robert Hayling and, assuring reporters that
"God segregated the races . . . when he made the skins a different
color," promised to restore the "excellent race relations that have
existed in this community for a long, long time."[49] To SCLC, these
were fighting words; at the beginning of May, King sent John Gibson to
St. Augustine to assess the prospects for further direct action.

After sounding out local black opinion, Gibson drew up a plan for
workshops to train people in nonviolence, thrice-weekly mass meetings, and a boycott of white businesses backed up by leafleting and
picketing. All this should lead up to "an all out push"—demonstrations and jail-ins—in early June. In his report, Gibson singled out St.
Augustine's vulnerability. "This is a tourist town," he stressed; "tour-

ism is the only means of survival . . . and they are banking on making a killing [out of the quadricentennial]." SCLC should also, therefore, discourage Northern tourists and persuade foreign governments to shun the 1965 celebrations. According to his own account, Gibson sent the plan directly to King when Walker seemed uninterested. King liked the idea and told Gibson to discuss it with Andrew Young. On May 23, he assigned Hosea Williams to prepare local blacks for more demonstrations.[50]

Walker was then preparing to leave SCLC to take up a post in New York, and he had no desire to become embroiled in a new campaign. Nevertheless, he agreed to make a brief visit to St. Augustine in order to evaluate the situation. Walker considered the emphasis on tourism sound and was favorably impressed by the enthusiasm of the local black community. SCLC's organizing efforts, on the other hand, struck him as "ragged," and he thought the first march far too undisciplined. Demonstrators must be clean, neat, and thoroughly trained, he told King; otherwise, the protest would "assume the character of a minstrel show," or convey the impression that SCLC was "trying to 'out-Snick' SNICK." Walker also stressed nonviolence: "I share with you very strongly that the St. Augustine movement must visually pull the non-violent thrust of the Negro back on center. The national press calls *every* activity of the Negro community, whether it be picketing or throwing rocks, 'demonstrators' [*sic*]. Somehow, we must re-capture the moral offensive so that it can not be suggested that the nonviolent revolution has become surly, irresponsible, and undisciplined. THIS IS AN ABSOLUTE MUST!" Too much publicity had been accorded such distortions of nonviolent protest as the proposed "stall-in" at the New York World's Fair by Brooklyn CORE. The nation had to be reminded of the strength and dignity of the Southern movement. Walker envisaged a brief campaign of little over three weeks. "I get the feeling St. Augustine is going to play it cagey," he cautioned King. "They may not arrest in the early stages of the campaign."[51]

But neither Gibson nor Walker anticipated the kind of reaction which SCLC's demonstrations in fact evoked. The first march, on May 27, passed without violence or arrests, although a crowd of hostile whites had gathered inside the "Old Slave Market," the symbolic focus of the protests.[52] The following night, however, white onlookers assaulted the marchers with fists, clubs, tire irons, and sundry other implements and objects. Harry Boyte was knocked down while taking photographs. Journalists at the scene charged the police with conniving in the attack. As King wired President Johnson for federal protection, the police banned marches in the downtown area. The city imposed a 9:00 P.M. curfew on minors under the age of eighteen.[53]

The following weeks exposed extensive ties between the police and the Klan. During hearings on SCLC's suit to have the march ban put aside, federal judge Bryan Simpson insistently questioned Sheriff L. O. Davis about the "Ancient City Gun Club," a seemingly innocuous organization led by Holstead "Hoss" Manucy, a local bootlegger. Their cars equipped with guns and CB radios, "Manucy's Raiders" had for months been patrolling the streets in an increasingly brazen manner. Simpson was appalled to discover that Manucy, a convicted felon, and several other members of the "club"—which the judge called "just the local name for the Klan down here"—had been deputized by Sheriff Davis. Elmer Emrich, Governor Bryant's assistant, was equally shocked by the open collusion between Klan and police. When he visited the county jail he saw "a large number of tough white individuals," including Manucy, hanging around the building. The FBI reported that three klansmen had been caught trying to scale the federal building, apparently in an attempt to attack some people on the balcony whom they mistook for photographers.[54] The attitude of the local police chief, Virgil Stuart, can be inferred from his assertion that the violence had arisen because "white males marched . . . holding hands with negro females," thus causing "resentment on the part of the local white population."[55]

It is scarcely conceivable that SCLC had been unaware of the Klan presence in and around St. Augustine. Dr. Robert Hayling, the black dentist who first brought St. Augustine to SCLC's attention, had been trying to alert the authorities to the growth of the Klan since the summer of 1963, when a series of sit-ins which he organized through the NAACP prompted a spate of telephone death threats. Then, he had contacted the FBI, only to be referred back to Sheriff Davis. Despairing of protection from the local police, Hayling organized his own armed defense unit, which posted sentries on the periphery of the black section. He also tried to procure incontrovertible evidence of the Klan's activities so that the FBI and the state authorities might take his assertions seriously. In September, he surreptitiously tape-recorded a Klan rally, at which he heard himself called "that burr-headed bastard of a dentist" who "ought to wake up tomorrow with a bullet between his eyes." But towards the end of the proceedings he had been detected and, with his three companions, beaten almost to death. Sheriff Davis, who arrived on the scene in the nick of time, naturally arrested the four Negroes for assault and battery.[56]

A month later, on October 25, a carload of armed whites entered St. Augustine's black section to be greeted by gunfire; one of the whites was killed. Hayling disclaimed any knowledge of who pulled the trigger, but he did admit having observed the car as it circled his house at least three times. Sheriff Davis was convinced that "Hayling's boys" did the deed, having been alerted by the lookouts who were stationed by telephone booths at the three points of entry into the neighborhood. The three surviving whites claimed that the fatal shot came from the house of Goldie Eubanks, Hayling's ally in the NAACP. But the police could prove nothing, and the killer of William Kinard escaped justice. Hayling and Eubanks were induced to resign from the NAACP.[57]

When Hayling approached SCLC early in 1964, he described St. Augustine as a Klan stronghold. On February 10, three days after his house was riddled with buckshot, he and SCLC vice-president C. K. Steele went to see Mal Ogden, an assistant to Governor Farris G. Bryant, to stress the need for action against the Klan. "It is Dr. Hayling's belief that the KKK is concentrated in this area," Ogden informed Bryant. "As to the local law enforcement and officials, he feels that Sheriff L. O. Davis is becoming much more aware of the seriousness of the situation, but feels that the local Police Chief is only superficially concerned." Bryant agreed to send additional units of the highway patrol into the area.[58]

It is tempting to conclude, therefore, that the Klan presence, far from deterring SCLC, actually attracted it to St. Augustine. Why else would King overlook Hayling's atheism, excuse his armed self-defense unit, and forget his widely publicized statement to the effect that blacks ought to "shoot first and ask questions later"? Is it not clear that SCLC discovered a hornet's nest and determined to stir it up? There is not a shred of direct evidence, however, to support this theory. Indeed, the absence of any mention of the Klan in Gibson's and Walker's plans, their emphasis on disrupting the tourist industry, and their proposal for a relatively short campaign all point to the conclusion that SCLC either failed to take the Klan into account or, at least, did not expect the police to accord it such license.

After the violence of May 28, however, the campaign acquired a new dimension: SCLC had no choice but to force the Klan out into the open. The night march served this purpose admirably. Adopted at the instance of Hosea Williams, who had pioneered the tactic in Savannah, the night march magnified the likelihood of a violent confrontation. In the darkness of St. Augustine, with its maze of narrow streets, the marchers would present a target of such vulnerability that the Klan would be unable to pass it up. An attack by the Klan would show the police in their true colors and expose the utter inadequacy of local law enforcement. "The night march is a tremendous thing," recalled C. T. Vivian. "They unnerve the community."[59]

SCLC found an unexpected ally in Judge Simpson. On June 9 Simpson concluded that the police could have and should have prevented the violence of May 28. He therefore granted SCLC the injunction it wanted and lifted the city's march restrictions. In a related suit, the judge condemned conditions at the county jail as "studied and cynical brutality, deliberately contrived to break men, physically and mentally." He forbade Davis to keep prisoners in open stockades or cram them into padded cells and "sweatboxes." He also reduced the bail set by Davis and the county court from $3,000 to $300.[60]

Within hours of the ruling, three hundred marchers led by Andrew Young set off for the Old Slave Market. As they approached the square, klansmen waded into the column; journalist Paul Good watched Young "get knocked down on three street corners around the square, punched, blackjacked, and kicked." The police merely watched, another eyewitness noted. Returning to St. Augustine on June 10, King sent another telegram to Johnson requesting federal marshals to quell the violence. That night, Young and Vivian led another march under a hail of rocks, bottles, and paving stones. Although a few of the marchers were struck, two hundred local and state police held the klansmen in check with the help of dogs and tear gas.[61]

The campaign now entered a critical stage. The city still refused to negotiate, and most of St. Augustine's blacks, including the student population, were staying aloof from the movement. King therefore appealed for outside help and ordered staff members in Alabama and elsewhere to bring volunteers to the city. King also decided to go to jail as a means of strengthening local support, arousing liberal concern, and putting pressure on the federal government. He was arrested on July 11, with Abernathy and sixteen others, at the Monson Motor Lodge. SCLC now pleaded with the White House and the Justice Department for FBI protection, federal marshals, or, at the very least, a team of federal mediators. There had been a complete breakdown of law and order, Walker told presidential assistant Douglass Cater, and he feared for King's safety. Harry Boyte claimed that "the Klan element has complete free run of the [St. Johns County] jail." But Johnson decided against federal intervention, even in the form of mediators. Bryant assured the president that he could handle the situation himself, and dispatched fifty more highway patrolmen to the area. On June

12, at Bryant's direction, King was transferred to the Duvall County Jail in Jacksonville for his own safety.[62]

The SCLC staff took advantage of King's symbolic act to drum up local support. "The good Lord doesn't make a Martin Luther King every day," they told the meetings. "If he can come down here and go to jail, the least you can do is go with him."[63] But as SCLC pressed on with its campaign of marches, sit-ins, and beachside "wade-ins," local blacks hung back. Reporters agreed that SCLC had failed to strike a responsive chord: the "mass meetings" were small, volunteers for the demonstrations few. Fear of the Klan inhibited support. So did doubts about Hayling, whom many regarded as a brave but foolhardy hothead. Then there was puzzlement over SCLC's tactics—where was the logic in deliberately seeking to stir up Klan violence? In addition, the factor which limited participation in all SCLC's campaigns, fear of losing one's job, was especially applicable in St. Augustine, where an un-usually high proportion of the black population worked in intimate contact with white employers in unskilled, low-paying positions. Fi-nally, the city's black population was simply too small to sustain the protests. In SCLC's experience, no more than 5 percent of a given black community could be persuaded to go to jail voluntarily. Applied to St. Augustine, this percentage produced a figure of about 250. Even had this many submitted to arrest, SCLC still would have needed outside help. With James Orange and other staff members arriving with bus-loads of demonstrators, the marches could for the moment continue. Meanwhile, the Klan leader, J. B. Stoner, began organizing white coun-termarches through the black section.[64]

King left jail on June 13 and flew to New Haven to receive an honorary degree from Yale, many of whose students and faculty mem-bers had taken part in the Easter protests. After his departure Young announced a lull in the demonstrations; "We're just over-pro-grammed," he confessed, "and everybody's tired."[65] On June 15 Judge Simpson rejected a request from the attorney general of Florida to ban demonstrations, suggesting that it was high time for the state to effect "some arrests and some real charges . . . against those hoodlums that everybody down there seems to be afraid to move against."[66] Finally waking up to the situation, Bryant declared St. Johns County a "special law enforcement area," placing Davis and Stuart under the direct com-mand of Major J. W. Jourdan of the highway patrol. Jourdan's own men were reinforced by beverage agents, game and fish officers, and various other state officials. This 135-man "special police force" began to bring the situation under control. Night marches on June 16 and 17 took place without violence.[67]

Anxious to escape from the impasse, King reduced SCLC's demands
to one: the creation of a biracial committee. He also stated that SCLC
no longer insisted upon the inclusion of Hayling in any negotiations.
There were other signs that a compromise might be in the offing. State
senator Verle Pope prevailed on twenty-six businessmen to call for a
"study of the legitimate problems of this community by responsible,
local law-abiding citizens." On the same day, June 18, the St. Johns
County grand jury promised to name a ten-member biracial committee
after SCLC's departure and after a thirty-day "cooling-off" period. Both
statements, however, contained an obvious loophole: SCLC had no
guarantee that if it left the city a biracial committee would actually
materialize. King wrote out a statement of rejection on the back of a
legal document. "We would be happy to bring about a cessation of
demonstrations," he affirmed, "if we could see a good faith move to
solve St. Augustine's racial problem." The biracial committee should
be appointed at once.[68]

SCLC now girded itself for a final push. Only too aware that the
well of local volunteers was running dry, it resorted to the tactic of
importing Northern clergymen. On June 18 King, Shuttlesworth, and
Vivian took seventeen rabbis to the Monson Motor Lodge, whose unfortunate owner, James Brock, had unwittingly registered two of
SCLC's white staff members, Allen Lingo and Arthur Funderberk.
When Brock turned the interracial party away, Lingo, Funderberk, and
several black youths jumped into the motel swimming pool. Forty-one
people were arrested, including the rabbis. According to a police report,
King watched the incident from across the street, saying, "We are going
to put Monson out of business."[69] Pictures of a police officer thrashing
about in the water trying to arrest the swimmers put St. Augustine
back on the front page of the *New York Times*. It was indicative of
SCLC's desperation, however, that it was reduced to such tactics; despite Wyatt Walker's warning, it seemed that SCLC was, indeed, trying
to "out-Snick SNICK." A march that evening attracted fewer than two
hundred people; only the arrest of Hosea Williams made it
newsworthy.[70]

SCLC also initiated a series of "wade-ins," an ingenious tactic
which, because the public beach had been desegregated, did not involve arrest and hence saved bail money. It also enabled a small
number of demonstrators to cause a large amount of disruption. The
policemen had to wade into the surf in order to ward off the whites—
sometimes several hundred strong—who lay in wait for the black
swimmers. "It was often necessary for several officers to pursue and
subdue a single attacker," Major Jourdan reported. "It was difficult to

grasp the wet, bare arms of the attackers and these people often used grease on their bodies to give them an additional advantage." On June 25 the state officers arrested ten of the segregationists and, during a melee lasting about a minute, used their billy clubs for the first time. "Extreme care had to be used in the handling of the baton," wrote Jourdan—one white youth suffered a cracked skull.[71] But the klansmen took their revenge that night, when about five hundred of them broke through the police lines and pummeled two hundred marchers. Twenty had to be taken to the hospital. Bryant, who had tried unsuccessfully to ban night marches, sent eighty more highway patrolmen to St. Augustine and flew there himself to "open up communications between the two sides."[72]

On June 22 King and the research committee wracked their collective brain to find a means of extricating SCLC from St. Augustine without having to concede failure. King asked Harold DeWolf, his old theology professor at Boston University, to act as a mediator. Andrew Young called the Justice Department to ask once again for federal protection. Predictably, Burke Marshall reiterated the limitations of federalism, but he did promise to send a team of federal mediators when the Community Relations Service came into existence under the Civil Rights Act. According to Dan Warren, the local state attorney, King told him that he refused to leave St. Augustine in defeat although he frankly admitted that he "wanted out." Warren assured King that the state would do its utmost to protect St. Augustine's blacks. Finally, on June 30, Bryant's announcement that he had appointed a four-man "emergency bi-racial committee" gave SCLC the pretext it needed to bring the protests to a close.[73]

SCLC could hardly count the campaign a success. On July 3 DeWolf wrote to King that a key member of the biracial committee "is under heavy pressure to quit." He did, and the committee vanished into thin air, never having met. On August 5 the grand jury appointed its own committee, but this, too, failed to materialize, most of the appointees declining to serve. SCLC also failed to desegregate St. Augustine's public accommodations in advance of the Civil Rights Act; its influence in securing the passage of the act was negligible. SCLC had not only failed to bring about federal intervention, it did not even persuade the government to call into question its grant for the city's quadricentennial. Even the merchants had refused to negotiate.[74]

The campaign also raised a number of questions about SCLC's modus operandi. Its tactics left local whites angry and bitter; indeed, the strategem of inviting Klan attacks seemed geared towards deliberately fomenting a "white backlash." Clearly, SCLC did not expect concessions to come from the white population as a whole; instead, as in Birmingham, it put pressure on the bankers and businessmen who, SCLC believed, pulled the political strings. Even here, however, there was inconsistency. SCLC set great store by voluntary desegregation: when it came about through legal or legislative compulsion, King argued, whites were able to cling to the belief that blacks were social inferiors and that race relations had always been harmonious. "This is morally wrong," he insisted. "We want them to admit that segregation is evil and take it upon themselves to rid this city of it."[75] But was it realistic to expect whites to make such an admission, especially when they were being subjected, like motel owner James Brock, to economic pressure and physical disruption?

Even if nonviolent direct action is considered to be a simple form of coercion—a means of compelling people to do something they do not wish to do—it might still be asked whether SCLC's tactics were either necessary or effective. SCLC wanted the merchants to desegregate before the Civil Rights Act took effect, but it is difficult to see why. What difference did it make if they desegregated under the pressure of direct action or the compulsion of the law? The former was no more "voluntary" than the latter. Moreover, at the same time that SCLC was insisting that the merchants desegregate of their own volition, it was stirring up Klan violence and thereby increasing their exposure to violent retaliation should they choose to do so. In the event, the Civil Rights Act, backed up by legal action from the NAACP Legal Defense Fund, desegregated St. Augustine's public accommodations. The effects of direct action seem to have been largely negative.

In the most recent and thorough analysis of the campaign, David Colburn delivered a severe verdict on SCLC's tactics. By continuing the demonstrations into the second half of June, he implied, SCLC wrecked the chances for a genuine peace. It then quitted the city for a truce which King must have known to be fraudulent. SCLC also failed to build a grass-roots movement, leaving blacks in a "precarious position from which they would be able to extricate themselves only with great difficulty." The black community, he concluded, "paid a heavy price for inviting King into the city."[76]

Clearly, the campaign was hurriedly conceived and poorly planned. SCLC anticipated a quick and easy victory, and miscalculated. But the protests were not wholly futile. SCLC did succeed in publicizing the growing Klan menace; although it failed to move the federal government, by enticing the klansmen out of the woodwork it compelled the state to take note of the problem. Farris Bryant was no George Wallace. The latter's demagogic intransigence, he believed, led only to "the effective assertion of federal power and the creation of racial violence." Unlike Wallace, Bryant counselled obedience to the law and made an honest effort to suppress Klan violence. His "special police force" brooked no nonsense from Davis and Stuart, and cracked down hard on white troublemakers. Confiscating weapons by the score, not hesitating to arrest whites, the special police force made itself hated among the local white citizenry. While less progressive than his predecessor, LeRoy Collins, Bryant's response to the situation eased the transition to desegregation. It was ironic that the emergency powers with which Bryant clamped down on the Klan had been created in 1956, at Collins's request, for the purpose of avoiding school integration.[77]

Judge Bryan Simpson also helped to break the Klan's stranglehold of fear. When the motel and restaurant owners, threatened by "Manucy's Raiders," balked at desegregation, Simpson took vigorous action. He ordered seventeen motels and restaurants to open their doors to black customers. He commanded one of Davis's special deputies to resign his position. And he enjoined threats, intimidation, and coercion on the part of Manucy, the Ancient City Gun Club, "and any other person to whom notice of this order may come." As one historian has written, Simpson "put teeth into the Civil Rights Act and . . . brought an end to the violence." C. T. Vivian praised Simpson as "the finest federal judge that we [ever] found." But he would never have acted so firmly had not SCLC's demonstrations brought the Klan out into the open where it could be identified and dealt with.[78]

Finally, SCLC helped to persuade the city's businessmen of the inevitability of desegregation. The protests had hurt them: 122,000 fewer tourists visited St. Augustine in 1964, an estimated loss to the local economy of about $5 million. On July 1, with only five dissenting voices, the hotel, motel, and restaurant owners affirmed their intention to comply with the Civil Rights Act. This was hardly a great leap forward. Yet it signified a readiness to break with the past that stood in sharp contrast to the attitude in, for example, Albany, Georgia, where the city was still toying with the idea of evading desegregation.[79] It must be admitted, however, that the integration of tourist facilities had little benefit for St. Augustine's black population, which, as Colburn pointed out, remains poor, dependent, and oppressed. By now, SCLC had become more realistic, even hardheaded, about the effects of its campaigns upon local black communities. "There is a hardening of attitudes in cities like this one," King told John Herbers of the *New*

York Times. "But other cities see and say, 'We don't want to be another Albany or another Birmingham,' and they make changes. Some communities, like this one, have to bear the cross."[80] Nevertheless, the campaign had been frustratingly inconclusive; the thing SCLC wanted most, federal intervention, had not occurred. "King was depressed, sad, angry," wrote William Robert Miller. "His ebullient hopes of a few weeks ago had crumbled." If SCLC were to achieve another breakthrough it seemed that it would have to return, as Bevel had contended all along, to Alabama.[81]

Eight

All the Way with LBJ

Bevel had refused to go to St. Augustine, claiming to be exhausted and in need of a rest. In fact, as C. T. Vivian explained, "Bevel just didn't think it was worth fighting for. Bevel had some other things in mind growing out of the Alabama situation."[1] Convinced that Governor Wallace and his cohorts provided SCLC with its most exploitable opponents, Bevel had been searching for an appropriate locale for almost a year. Early in June, he took the Alabama staff to Tuscaloosa, where SCLC's local affiliate had encountered tough opposition when it began demonstrating against segregation in the new courthouse. During one of the protests, the police attacked a group of marchers and lobbed tear gas grenades into a crowded church. Tuscaloosa might, perhaps, have developed into a major campaign had King committed SCLC

in strength. By the time SCLC pulled out of St. Augustine, however, it
was far too late to embark upon another major campaign.[2]

When King met the Alabama staff in Birmingham on July 6, he
disclosed that for the rest of the summer SCLC should concentrate on
the limited goal of monitoring the state's compliance with the Civil
Rights Act, which had become law four days earlier. He promised to
send staff members to both Tuscaloosa and Selma, where reports had
come in of businesses still refusing to serve blacks. If whites continued
to resist integration, King promised, SCLC would take legal action and
perhaps call in the new Community Relations Service; failing that, it
could mount demonstrations to force federal action. But he stressed
that there were no immediate plans to move into either city. That
Selma might be the target of SCLC's next major drive was evident,
nonetheless, from King's decision to send Abernathy and Young there
immediately after the staff meeting.[3] That night, after a SNCC-orga-
nized "Freedom Day" during which only five blacks were allowed to
take the voter registration test, Abernathy assured a mass meeting that
SCLC was "behind you, with you, and even in front of you every step
of the way."[4]

With St. Augustine out of the way and the Alabama campaign
postponed, four other issues consumed most of SCLC's energies during
the rest of 1964. Two of them, the Freedom Summer and the presidential election, already formed part of SCLC's calculations. The other
two, the ghetto riots and the public attack on King by J. Edgar Hoover,
were wholly unexpected.

King told his Alabama staff on July 6 that he regarded the Freedom
Summer as the most important civil rights initiative in 1964. This
massive voter registration and political education campaign, involving
the bulk of SNCC's staff and hundreds of Northern white college students, had already riveted the nation's attention on Mississippi
through the disappearance of three young civil rights workers in
Neshoba County. Meanwhile the SNCC-dominated coalition which
organized the summer project, COFO, was building an integrated Freedom Democratic party, which intended to challenge the seating of the
official, "lily-white" state delegation at the Democratic National Convention in August.

SCLC's material contribution to COFO was negligible. After Bevel
was reassigned to Alabama in the spring of 1963 SCLC lacked a Mississippi field secretary; only the Citizenship Education Program, directed by Annel Ponder and Victoria Adams, gave it an organizational

presence in the state. But King gave strong moral support to COFO both in Mississippi and at the Democratic convention. He also sprang to the project's defense at a meeting of the "Big Six" in June. Roy Wilkins argued that the sending of a thousand white students to Mississippi would only embarrass the administration and help Goldwater; neither he nor Whitney Young favored giving any money to COFO through the Council on United Civil Rights Leadership. But King replied that the Freedom Summer was the most creative thing in the movement, and eminently worthy of financial support.[5] Towards the end of July he made a five-day tour of Mississippi accompanied by Abernathy, Young, Bevel, and four other staff members. His reception ranged from "pounding and shrieking enthusiasm" in Greenwood, a SNCC stronghold, to cool politeness in Jackson, where the NAACP held sway. "The pattern was always the same," recalled Charles Fager, a white SCLC staff member. "First the local minister spoke, then Bevel, and then King." Fager rated Bevel the most rousing speaker: "He was a firebrand and got the audience riled up."[6]

The rioting which erupted in New York as King toured Mississippi cast an ominous shadow over the presidential election and posed a daunting challenge to SCLC and the civil rights movement. The outbreak, which spread to Rochester, Jersey City, Philadelphia, and elsewhere, confirmed the warnings which A. Philip Randolph and others had been giving for months: that the appalling social deprivation of the Northern ghettos, together with the rising militancy of their inhabitants and the weakness of established black leadership, added up to an explosive and dangerous mix. What made the situation all the more perilous, he believed, was the "emergence of an organized Right," which was skilfully exploiting the racial fears and phobias of the white working class. Pollsters and commentators had been analyzing the "white backlash" since the summer of 1963. In the spring of 1964, however, this diffuse sentiment was translated into a dynamic political movement by Governor George Wallace. Entering the presidential primaries in a bid for the Democratic nomination, Wallace took a third of the vote in Wisconsin, 30 percent in Indiana, and 43 percent in Maryland. In some of the Indiana steel districts, his share of the poll soared to 70 percent.[7]

This performance astonished and alarmed white liberals and blacks. In April, Randolph called for a "state of the race" conference to analyze and combat these trends before black extremism and white backlash produced a vicious spiral of violence and reaction. Clarence Jones expressed the same urgency and apprehension when he wrote to King on April 15, warning of the "counter-revolutionary alliance of forces" being forged by Wallace, and bewailing the "total collapse of effective civil rights leadership" since the March on Washington. This leadership vacuum, he added, enabled a handful of unrepresentative activists to bring the entire civil rights movement into disrepute with such gimmicks as the world's fair "stall-in." But "in the absence of any constructive alternative," he predicted, such misguided and divisive tactics would continue to generate adverse publicity, alienate whites, and damage the cause. In April, however, King's eyes were still firmly on the South. He and other black leaders virtually ignored Randolph's proposal for a top-level meeting to consider Northern problems.[8]

But SCLC could hardly ignore the riots, especially when King received a direct invitation from Robert Wagner, the mayor of New York, to attend a crisis meeting of black civic, political, and trade union leaders at Gracie Mansion. King's initial instinct was to say no; if he went to New York, he told Jones, "the Communist groups would do everything they could to discredit me." Nevertheless, he decided to go, and on July 27 and 28 joined Bayard Rustin, Cleveland Robinson, and others in lengthy discussions with Wagner. The blacks pressed for the creation of a civilian review board to investigate complaints about police misconduct; they also asked for the immediate suspension of the officer whose fatal bullet had sparked the riot. Rustin tried to convince Wagner that the root of the problem was unemployment, and that New York should seek emergency funds from the federal government to create jobs in the ghetto. King's participation, although generally welcomed by blacks, aroused a certain amount of criticism, especially as he failed to meet black leaders in Harlem before seeing Wagner. King could not quite escape the feeling that he had unwittingly placed himself in the role of "Uncle Tom." Rustin advised him to stay out of the Harlem "mess." The outcome of the talks underlined their futility: Wagner refused to set up a civilian review board.[9]

The riots also led to SCLC's first attempt to work in a Northern city, when King responded to an invitation from the Rochester, New York, Council of Churches. That city had seen some of the fiercest rioting: Governor Rockefeller had sent in the National Guard; the outbreak caused 1,000 people to be arrested and left 350 injured. King sent a seven-man team led by Young and Bevel. But the SCLC staff members found it hard going: such was the hostility among young blacks to "nonviolence" that the staff found it prudent not to mention the word. In a sermon at Rochester's Central Presbyterian Church, Young confessed that he represented "a group [that] was as unpopular as anybody else. . . . [N]onviolence had been so misinterpreted in the Negro community of the North that to come as a member of a non-violent movement . . . is to put two strikes on you to start with." They stayed in Rochester a few weeks only, whereafter the local ministers turned to Saul Alinsky's more experienced group, the Industrial Areas Foundation.[10]

What did SCLC learn from the riots? Its response was ambivalent. On the one hand, King called for a thorough reappraisal of goals and strategy—a "soul-searching"—on the part of the civil rights movement. But there is little evidence of any "soul-searching" exercise by SCLC's leadership. King still asserted that blacks in the North gained vicarious satisfaction from the progress being made by their Southern cousins, and in an article published in November, drafted by Clarence Jones, blamed a "sensation-seeking press" for blowing up "essentially small events to the level of catastrophes." Others in SCLC also played down the riots. Young denied that police brutality approached the scale of the problem in the South. He did not even see the riots as primarily racial: they were "class disruptions rather than race disruption." Joseph Lowery, chairman of the SCLC board, simply dismissed the rioting as "gang tactics" that had no connection with the civil rights movement.[11] SCLC also made little attempt, apparently, to assimilate and interpret its experience in Rochester. It had always recruited in the churches; it went against SCLC's grain to organize among the people who shunned the churches and frequented bars, pool halls, and street corners.

But King also grasped that the social phenomenon of rioting could not be cured by moral condemnation. Shortly after his visit to New York he described to Robert Penn Warren his immediate reaction to the abuse he had been subjected to in Harlem. His initial feelings had been ones of rejection and resentment—to think of his own sacrifices, and how "your own people don't have an understanding . . . [and are] seeking to destroy your image at every point." But then he had stopped feeling sorry for himself: "I started including them in the orbit of my thinking. . . . [W]hat about the society which made people like this?"[12]

Until now, King had given little consideration either to the economic hardship which afflicted most blacks or to the complex forces which created and perpetuated the ghetto. There was, in fact, a marked duality in King's interpretation of poverty and social pathology. One side of him, as befitted the son of a father who went from rags to riches, viewed economic success or failure in terms of individualism. Thrift, hard work, and self-help made all the difference; these, after all, were the qualities through which his father achieved middle-class status. As King wrote in a graduate essay, his father had "never made more than an ordinary salary, but the secret is that he knows the art of saving and budgeting. . . . He never wastes his money at the expense of his family." In *Stride Toward Freedom*, written a decade later in 1957–58, King used language redolent of Booker T. Washington to scold blacks for too often being criminal, dirty, inebrious, thriftless, and boisterous. The Negro, he added, should "act now to lift himself up by his own bootstraps." Even after the 1964 riots, King was predicting that the most pressing need after desegregation would be "a sort of Operation Boot-Strap" whereby blacks, as individuals, "work desperately to improve their own conditions and their own standards."[13]

King was never, on the other hand, simply a bourgeois individualist. In the same student essay in which he praised his father's frugality he also spoke of seeing the breadlines of the 1930s and "the effect of this early childhood experience on my present anticapitalist feelings." Friends later commented on King's unease over his comfortable upbringing: "One reason he was so determined to be of service," Levison believed, "was to justify the privileged position he'd been born into." His exposure to Marxist thought as a graduate student enabled him to mold these vague feelings into a conscious rejection of unbridled capitalism. Of course, King never considered himself a "Marxist." Echoing the conventional definitions of the day, he associated Marxism with the rejection of religion and spiritual values, a shallow economic determinism, and the absolute supremacy of the state, all of which he emphatically repudiated. Yet Marx had raised "basic questions," he believed, and "in so far as he pointed to the weaknesses of traditional capitalism, contributed to the growth of a definite self-consciousness in the masses, and challenged the social conscience of the Christian churches, I responded with a definite 'yes.'" When he wrote *Stride Toward Freedom*, he resisted his publisher's suggestion that he tone down his criticism of capitalism. "Capitalism can lead to a practical materialism," he insisted, "that is as pernicious as the [theoretical] materialism taught by Communism."[14]

These opposing strands coexisted in King's mind without his being aware of any inherent contradiction. In practice, King had approached the struggle for racial justice in a nonideological way, hoping to overcome bigotry and prejudice through pressure, certainly, but also by appealing to the idealism and Christian principles of the "great decent majority." He looked upon racism as a Southern anachronism which would, in the course of a decade or so, die a natural death. His ultimate vision was the integration of the Negro into the existing structure of society; capitalism was not at issue. King showed little indication of sharing the belief, so common among veterans of the Old Left, that racism was primarily a function of class oppression, a product of the economic system. His radicalism struck many older Socialists as skin-deep, his attraction to Marx more an intellectual affectation than an authentic political commitment. Although Marx "does have an appeal for King," wrote Lawrence Reddick in his 1959 biography, King was nevertheless a bourgeois reformer, not a political radical. "There is not a Marxist bone in his body."[15]

King's older advisers had often tried to persuade him that race and economics could not be kept apart. Even if racism were to magically disappear, blacks could never attain parity with whites through thrift and self-help alone. When inequality had such deep historical roots, equality of opportunity could never lead—to use the fashionable phrase of the time—to "equality of result." With such a highly structured and technologically oriented economy, moreover, poverty tended to be self-perpetuating; the economic boom of the wartime and postwar years had eliminated the mass poverty of the 1930s, but the poverty that remained was more intractable, less susceptible to the eroding influence of economic growth. The economists and sociologists who "rediscovered" poverty in the early 1960s shared a conviction that the eradication of "structural" poverty demanded government intervention. Against the analytical depth of John Kenneth Galbraith and Michael Harrington, King's stress on economic individualism looked superficial and simplistic. Indeed, given the inauguration in 1964 of the government's War on Poverty, it was clearly out-of-date.[16]

In *Why We Can't Wait*, King took a step towards "rediscovering" poverty himself, calling for a "broad-based and massive Bill of Rights for the Disadvantaged." This proposal reflected the thinking of Stanley Levison and Clarence Jones, who wrote this section of the book. The "Bill of Rights" concept attempted to marry, not altogether successfully, two separate but related ideas. It began as a plea for "special compensatory measures" to assist blacks, a suggestion clearly borrowed from Whitney Young's "Marshall Plan for the Negro." Citing the postwar GI Bill as an acceptable precedent for special treatment for a particular group, King's ghostwriters—using legalese that made King's own writing seem graceful—argued that "the robberies inherent in slavery" justified discrimination in favor of blacks; such "compensatory treatment . . . could be regarded as a settlement in accordance with the accepted practice of common law." Later, they tried to find what Jones described as "an intellectual bridge" between the idea of preferential treatment for the Negro and preferential treatment for all poor people.[17]

King's reorientation towards the problem of social and economic equality occurred gradually; it was a painful political education which he did not complete until he had lived among the poor in Chicago. But if King and his Southern colleagues still underestimated the scale of Northern problems and the potential for violence, they were quick to grasp the political implications of the riots. They knew at once that black violence, whatever its source, aided Goldwater. The Goldwater threat so alarmed SCLC that it agreed to suspend direct action until after the election. The NAACP took the initiative in seeking to curtail demonstrations. A month earlier, Roy Wilkins had decried "phony" militancy and unnecessary "screaming for demonstrations." It was no secret, moreover, that Johnson was looking to black leaders for an end to abrasive protests; as vice-presidential aspirant Hubert Humphrey advised the NAACP at its annual convention, the time had come "to stack the banners for a while."[18] On July 22, therefore, after the Harlem riot subsided, Wilkins invited civil rights leaders to confer in New York about a common policy towards the "twin threat" of rioting and Goldwater. The upshot was a moratorium on direct action which received the backing of King, Wilkins, Randolph, and Whitney Young. "The major energy of the civil rights forces," they stated, "should be used to encourage the Negro people, North and South, to register and to vote." John Lewis and James Farmer, representing SNCC and CORE, refused to sign.[19]

SCLC's determination to do nothing that might help Goldwater and hurt Johnson placed King in an awkward political position. He was pledged to support the Mississippi Freedom Democratic party (MFDP). Yet Johnson was bent on seeing that the regular Mississippians remained seated and preventing a divisive and embarrassing fight on the floor of the national convention. How far should King go in his support for the challengers—dare he antagonize President Johnson?

Bayard Rustin advised King that the MFDP challenge represented a political minefield, and that King had to tread very warily indeed. Although Rustin had no formal position in SCLC beyond membership

of the research committee, he had once again become important to
King. King valued him both for his political knowledge and his organizational skills, which had been impressively displayed in connection
with the March on Washington and the New York City school boycott
of February 3, 1963. His addition to the staff, King believed, would give
SCLC a much-needed "shot in the arm."[20] But Rustin was searching
for his own independent base, and now, after a lifetime of moving from
one organization to another, he had found the platform he wanted in
the shape of the A. Philip Randolph Institute, a kind of social democratic "think tank" created specifically for Rustin, to be financed by
the AFL-CIO. But although he turned down King's offer of a job with
SCLC, he undertook to help King on an informal basis and became, in
effect, his leading political adviser.

Rustin's talents also impressed SNCC, which attempted to utilize
them on behalf of the MFDP challenge. SNCC wanted Rustin to
organize demonstrations in Atlantic City during the Democratic National Convention. Rustin was at first agreeable to the idea, assuring
SNCC that he could assemble at least twenty five thousand demonstrators outside the convention hall. By July, however, he had clearly
cooled to the idea of coordinating the convention protes : at an MFDP
strategy meeting in Jackson, which King and James Farmer also attended, he placed so many conditions on the job that he effectively
ruled himself out.[21]

Why did he change his mind? Rustin had two great worries, which
he communicated to King in no uncertain terms. First, he doubted his
ability—or anyone else's—to keep the protests at Atlantic City under
control. Farmer's grip on CORE was weak, he believed, and the people
he characterized as "left youngsters" and "kooks" might get out of
hand. Second, he feared that demonstrations would alienate powerful
allies whom SCLC could ill afford to lose. Walter Reuther had "hit the
roof," he told King, at the mention of possible obstruction at the convention; "we have to be sensible," he added, and do nothing to attack
"our friends." As the convention drew nearer, Rustin forcefully reminded King not to become involved in any demonstrations: Reuther,
Helstein, "and most of the people we know are very distressed over the
way things are opening up"; if any civil disobedience occurred, "there
will be a terrific squabble." King agreed that demonstrations would be
unwise, but told Rustin that he was thinking of staging a protest of his
own, a fast: it "would be a creative thing with spiritual overtones, and
would not place me in the position of doing nothing." Rustin, for the
moment, did not try to talk him out of it.[22]

Lyndon Johnson pulled every string, enlisted every ally, and used all the forces at his command, including the FBI, to defeat the MFDP challenge. Joseph Rauh, the MFDP's chief lawyer, also happened to be the general counsel of the United Auto Workers, Reuther's union. "The heat was on to a terrific degree," he recalled. "There were so many hatchet men that you had to stand with your back to the wall."[23] King felt the pressure himself. He gave up the idea of a fast. He also dropped out, at the last minute, of a meeting between black leaders and President Johnson on August 19, just three days before the convention. Rauh had wanted King to attend the meeting so that he could argue for the seating of both delegations, a possible compromise which the MFDP could accept. Given Johnson's propensity for dominating a conversation, Rauh advised, King "should just grab the ball and run and say, 'you've got to seat them both, Mr. President.'" But Rustin persuaded King not to go, a decision he had no cause to regret. The meeting turned out to be a "fiasco," Rustin told a friend: Johnson talked for fifteen of the twenty minutes, expounding on the threat of the white backlash with the aid of impressive-looking charts. Randolph thought the session a complete waste of time. On August 21, Rustin advised King to leave the convention as soon as he had given his testimony to the Credentials Committee the next day. The fact that King had broken his foot, he added, gave him a plausible reason for limiting his participation. Rustin himself planned to avoid Atlantic City altogether.[24]

King stayed throughout the convention and, with Young and Fauntroy, lobbied hard for the seating of the MFDP; King's hotel suite, in fact, became one of the nerve centers of the challenge. In order to oust the white regulars, the MFDP needed to secure enough support within the Credentials Committee—at least eleven members—to bring the issue before the convention at large; then, with the backing of eight state delegations, it could force a roll call vote. But Johnson exerted sufficient pressure on the committee to block a minority report, and he charged Sen. Hubert Humphrey with the task of working out a specific compromise that kept the regular delegation in place and prevented a floor fight. "Johnson was testing me one more time," Humphrey wrote in his autobiography; unless he succeeded, he believed, Johnson would choose another vice-president. At a meeting in King's suite on the evening of August 23, Humphrey put forward a compromise: the convention could give the MFDP seats for two "at-large" delegates, require all delegations to pledge their loyalty to the national ticket, and devise new rules to make sure that in future all delegations would be selected without regard to race.[25]

During the next two days, Humphrey pleaded with Rauh and the MFDP to accept the compromise. There were angry scenes as he explained why the president insisted on choosing the two "at-large" delegates so as to exclude "that illiterate woman" Fannie Lou Hamer, the sharecropper's wife whose testimony before the Credentials Committee about how she had been arrested and beaten for attempting to register had been televised across the nation to Johnson's embarrassment and fury. Bob Moses of SNCC, the chief architect of the MFDP, exploded in anger, calling Humphrey a racist. Later, when the television falsely reported that the MFDP had accepted the compromise, Moses accused Humphrey of treachery and stormed out of the room. Hamer tried to shame Humphrey. "Here sat this little round-eyed man with his eyes full of tears," she recalled of one meeting, "when . . . Rauh said if we didn't stop pushing like we was pushing them . . . Mr. Humphrey wouldn't be nominated that night for Vice-President."[26]

On Monday, August 24, Reuther flew in from Detroit to help Humphrey "sell" the plan. The UAW's president had strongly opposed Johnson's inclusion on the ticket in 1960; now, however, he was an ardent convert and, like most liberals, regarded party unity and Goldwater's defeat as far more important than a little local difficulty in Mississippi. He did not mince words. Unless he accepted the compromise, he told Rauh, he could forget about his job with the UAW—he would break him, destroy him. He also pointedly reminded King that his union had made a number of sizeable contributions to SCLC. "I've never seen such back-breaking pressure," Rauh said later.[27]

On the fifth day of the convention, August 26, King and Rauh decided to recommend acceptance of the compromise. Speaking to the MFDP delegation, Bayard Rustin, who had come to the convention at King's request, urged the challengers to "think of our friends in organized labor, Walter Reuther and others, who have gone to bat for us. If we reject this compromise, we would be saying to them that we didn't want their help."[28] The election involved more than race, he argued: it involved a choice between war and peace. Blacks should do nothing that might give ammunition to Goldwater. King, too, spoke in favor of acceptance, but he was far less positive about the compromise. "The SNCC people were terrified that [he] would sway the delegation," recalled Edwin King, one of the delegates, but "he did not pressure us strongly to take it. . . . His position, as he told me, was that he wanted to see us take this compromise because it would mean strength for him. . . . '[B]ut if I were a Mississippi Negro, I would vote against it.' " The MFDP did exactly that; Johnson's attempt to pick the two delegates stuck in too many throats. To SNCC, Atlantic City became a symbol of betrayal. For many, the whole sorry episode furnished irrefutable proof of the racism of the Democrats and the perfidy of white liberals. Bob Moses never spoke to Rauh again.[29]

King, on the other hand, had to face political reality. The administration put such pressure on the delegates that by August 25 he and his aides discovered that "people who were previously friendly are getting harder to find." The crack of the White House whip caused support for the MFDP to crumble.[30] The compromise at least represented something; rejection brought nothing. For King himself to have counselled rejection would have been more than futile: Johnson and Reuther would have regarded it as a political slap in the face. SCLC needed the support of both these powerful men if its 1965 Alabama campaign were to succeed; why deliberately alienate them? This, in essence, was Rustin's argument, but King accepted it out of conviction, not because he blindly followed Rustin. By 1964 King was no longer a political novice.

King also shared—up to a point—Rustin's belief in coalition politics. Civil rights could not possibly remedy economically rooted inequalities which resulted in poverty, unemployment, poor housing, and medical neglect, Rustin argued, especially when profound structural changes like automation were reducing the economic opportunities available to the poor still further. Such problems had to be solved at the national level, "through assistance from the federal government—tearing down slums . . . [and] putting everybody back to work." And the necessary measures—radical measures—could only be achieved by means of political action: blacks had to act as part of a larger, majority coalition. They needed white allies. The March on Washington, Rustin contended, had created the germ, at least, of a political alliance between trade unions, church organizations, white liberals, and blacks. At the same time, the growth of the Negro vote in the South, and the probable defection of the most extreme Southern conservatives to the Republican party, promised to not only strengthen the liberal-labor-Negro alliance but also present the opportunity for a basic political realignment. Cleansed of its racists and reactionaries, the Democratic party could become an effective instrument for radical social change. Only as part of such a political coalition could blacks achieve full employment, fair employment, an adequate minimum wage, decent housing, a national health scheme, and so on.[31]

The experience of St. Augustine seemed to indicate a serious weakness in Rustin's argument: it was one thing to broach the possibility of coalition with Northern liberals and trade unions, quite another to see poor and working-class whites as the natural allies of the black proletariat. Indeed, SCLC's experiences in the South had taught it that the business elite was far more amenable to desegregation and racial change than the white working class. Nevertheless, the practical rewards of a coalition strategy had been underlined by the passage of the civil rights bill, the launching of the War on Poverty, and Johnson's commitment to free health care for the aged and the poor. Coalition politics found strong advocates in Young, Fauntroy, Vivian, and others on the executive staff; to the members of the research committee, the necessity for white allies seemed obvious. In a passage which Rustin drafted, King stressed this theme in his speech to the SCLC convention on October 1. "Demonstrations can call attention to evil . . . but are not a program for removing evil itself"; in order to induce Congress to appropriate "billions of dollars" for social uplift, "we must add our political power to that of other groups."[32]

But King's views on coalition politics did not wholly accord with Rustin's. King argued in favor of preferential treatment for blacks; Rustin opposed it. They differed, too, in their attitude to direct action. Rustin had attempted to perpetuate the March on Washington coalition, under the aegis of A. Philip Randolph, with the aim of bringing about a united and coordinated approach to direct action. When this effort failed, however—a failure best exemplified in the divided and ineffective black response to the Birmingham church bombing—Rustin began to doubt whether nonviolent protest could ever have any significant impact on problems like Klan terrorism, police brutality, unemployment, and the growth of de facto segregation.[33] His experience in organizing the first New York school boycott convinced him that direct action was not only ineffective but also intensified black anger and frustration. Mass demonstrations could no longer continue to be the main tactic of the civil rights movement. Blacks now had to make the transition, Rustin believed, "from protest to politics." The day of direct action was virtually over.[34] But King still regarded nonviolent protest as an essential weapon, vote or no vote, North or South. He might de-emphasize or suspend direct action in order to gain a temporary political advantage, but he could never abandon it entirely. If the goals were just, the tactics sound, and the execution dignified and disciplined, demonstrations might bring latent racism and prejudice to the surface, but they could not damage the black cause or alienate true friends and allies.

Towards the end of the summer, SCLC laid plans for a "get-out-the-vote" campaign prior to the November elections. While King stumped the Northern cities, Hosea Williams organized a voter registration drive in the South. With a budget of $50,000 and a staff of twenty-five, Williams concentrated on the areas of easy registration, particularly Virginia, the Carolinas, and Georgia, so as to maximize the results.[35]

In view of the fact that Goldwater trailed Johnson in the opinion polls and, by common consent, stood virtually no chance of being elected, SCLC's efforts against the Republican might seem like a case of overkill. King's own denunciations of Goldwater were quite vehement: there were "dangerous signs of Hitlerism" in the Republican campaign; a Goldwater triumph would bring "violence and riots . . . on a scale we have never seen before." In an interview after the election, King termed Goldwater "the most dangerous man in America. He talked soft and nice, but he gave aid and comfort to the most vicious racists and the most extreme rightists in America." When SCLC assembled for its annual convention at the end of September, any pretense of nonpartisanship was abandoned. "We are going to speak and campaign for the President wherever and whenever necessary," Abernathy promised. The board of directors urged blacks to work for "an overwhelming plurality for the new Administration."[36]

Not long after Johnson's landslide victory, during the second week in November, King and the executive staff met in Birmingham to discuss plans for the Alabama campaign and consider the continuing problem of SCLC's organizational structure.

SCLC was in reasonably good financial health: between September 1963 and August 1964 its receipts totalled $626,000. The New York office, now in the capable hands of Adele Kanter, sent out 390,000 pieces of literature and received nearly 15,000 contributions amounting to about $150,000. This left an overall profit of $117,000. Only slightly down from the previous year, SCLC's income enabled it to maintain its full-time staff of sixty-two.[37]

Internally, however, SCLC still suffered from financial waste and administrative confusion. Two new staff members, Harry Boyte and Randolph Blackwell, tried to remedy this situation by tightening SCLC's financial controls and devising a clearer, more disciplined structure for the organization. Boyte, a white North Carolinian then in his early fifties, joined SCLC in October 1963 as an assistant to King.

Discovering that too many staff members wasted too much of SCLC's time and money, he produced a series of memoranda laying down stricter rules for office procedures and personnel policies. Unauthorized absences of an hour or more, for example, were to be charged against annual leave. In April 1964, as SCLC moved steadily deeper into debt, Boyte recommended rigid budget control for each department and a thorough review of organizational structure. Nothing appeared to change, however: financial records remained slipshod or nonexistent. Jesse Blayton, the highly competent accountant who scrutinized SCLC's books, complained in September that "your resident auditor performed almost no duties ordinarily required of that office" and noted that his own recommendations of the previous year had been "observed for a few days only, then abandoned."[38]

Randolph T. Blackwell, who succeeded Young as program director, came to SCLC from the Voter Education Project, but had spent most of the previous ten years teaching economics and sociology at black colleges in North Carolina and Alabama. Like Boyte, he tried to introduce business management techniques in order to eliminate the tangled lines of authority that seemed to encourage prodigality and disarray. Blackwell proposed dividing SCLC into departments: voter registration (Williams), direct action (Bevel), citizenship education (Cotton), the Washington office (Fauntroy), nonviolent education (Lawson), Operation Breadbasket (Bennette), and Operation Dialogue, a new program to be headed by Harry Boyte. The field staff were to be supervised by C. T. Vivian, the director of affiliates. In theory, each department head was responsible to Blackwell, who, in turn, answered to Young. King retained a personal veto in all SCLC's affairs.[39] In practice, Blackwell's reorganization had little impact. The field staff continued to work under Bevel and Williams, who vied with each other for control over them and resented having to answer to anyone but King. Blackwell's attempt to impose discipline on such men got nowhere. As Young put it, "Each one of these guys is terribly egocentric. . . . They don't like to follow directions from anybody."[40]

Operation Dialogue attempted to realize King's long-held desire for a program to promote interracial understanding and reconciliation. Boyte outlined his ideas to the executive staff on November 12, during the Birmingham retreat. He began by pointing out that blacks and working-class whites were coming into increasingly sharp competition as automation, and now cybernetics, eliminated a growing proportion of unskilled and semiskilled jobs. In order to help counteract the divisive effects of race, Boyte proposed to involve SCLC's white staff members in group discussions with Southern whites. By education and persuasion they would combat racist myths, alert whites to their common economic interests with blacks, and encourage sympathetic communication between the races. They would, above all, endeavor to "reach the many Southerners of good will who fear contact with Negroes because of reprisals by segregationists." Before, during, and after SCLC's direct action campaigns, Operation Dialogue could serve the practical function of facilitating negotiations.[41]

Boyte possessed wide experience in welfare and service agencies, having worked for the National Youth Administration, the Red Cross, and the American Friends Service Committee. In Atlanta, he had been involved in volunteer work with the Urban League and the Council for Human Relations. His proposal for Operation Dialogue had the kind of philosophical tenor that appealed to King, laced as it was with quotations from Martin Buber, Thomas Merton, and other theologians. But the program was never very successful in its own terms. Education might well be antithetical to racism, but the number of whites who were exposed to Operation Dialogue's arguments represented a drop in the ocean. Moreover, the department's activities tended to involve people who were already sympathetic to blacks rather than members of the prejudiced majority; workshops with human relations councils amounted to preaching to the converted. Nevertheless, the Operation Dialogue staff played an important role in the Selma protests—not as the sponsor of polite group discussions, but as SCLC's stalking-horse. During the weeks preceding the campaign, Boyte and other white staff members moved through the city engaging white Selmians in conversation, assessing white attitudes, analyzing the local "power structure," and weighing the potential for violence.[42]

SCLC's plans for a campaign to demand the right to vote had been maturing for some time. The need for such a campaign was obvious: in large areas of the South blacks were still disfranchised through a combination of intimidation, baffling registration procedures, and biased registrars. True, throughout the South as a whole—and even in parts of the Deep South—the black electorate had increased substantially in recent years. Across the Deep South, however, black registration reached only 40 percent of the white level. Apathy, induced by decades of political exclusion, accounted for part of this disparity, but discrimination—subtle in cities like Birmingham and New Orleans, blatant in the rural Black Belt—explained most of it.[43]

Civil rights legislation had conspicuously failed to end the systematic exclusion of blacks from the polling stations. The laws suffered from four major weaknesses. When it came to establishing the existence of discrimination, the burden of proof fell upon the lawyers of the Justice Department. Each voting rights suit required the painstaking accumulation of masses of evidence, many months of legal preparation, and the inevitable delays which attended the judicial process. Second, in the great majority of its suits the Justice Department attacked discrimination in single counties rather than entire states; favorable court decisions left other counties unaffected, for each county had its own registration procedures. The Justice Department could not, moreover, take the sympathy of the courts for granted: even federal judges had segregationist leanings and sometimes actively impeded the implementation of federal civil rights law. As with school desegregation, the obstructionist tactics of Southern lawyers and legislatures, often aided and abetted by the bench, made progress in establishing equal voting rights slow, erratic, and uncertain. Finally, the law did not eliminate complicated application procedures, inconvenient registration hours, or, above all, literacy and "constitutional interpretation" tests. When administered by biased white officials, these continued to prevent black people from voting.[44]

By 1964 these inadequacies had become glaringly obvious. Civil rights legislation, the 1964 act included, proved little use to the COFO workers in Mississippi, whose summer registration drive, to quote Garrow, produced "almost as many acts of violence by local whites as it did new black voters." Over two years of intensive work by SNCC nudged black registration from barely 5 percent to less than seven. The situation was slightly better in Alabama, but still only one black adult in five was a registered voter. In the South as a whole, the Justice Department had filed seventy voting rights suits, but these, according to Garrow's liberal estimate, added fewer than thirty-eight thousand black voters. In 1964 Burke Marshall admitted that the federal government had failed "to make significant advances . . . in making the right to vote real for Negroes in Mississippi, large parts of Alabama and Louisiana, and in scattered counties in other states."[45]

The voting statistics of Selma made it a natural target for a crusade against disfranchisement. Although Dallas County, in which the town was situated, had been singled out for several Justice Department suits, whites in Selma still comprised 99 percent of the electorate although they made up less than half the population. Between May 1962 and August 1964 seven black applicants in eight were rejected by the board of registrars; three-quarters of all the white applicants were accepted. The registration "test," revised in September 1964, included four questions on the Constitution, four on government, a reading test, and a dictation. According to one calculation, the test had at least one hundred permutations. To make the process yet more difficult, registration took place only two days a month, and the application form contained more than fifty questions. In the adjacent counties of Lowndes and Wilcox, where blacks outnumbered whites more than two to one, there were no black voters at all.[46]

   This state of affairs cried out for new legislation, and SCLC decided to use Selma and the Alabama Black Belt as a means of dramatizing the need and creating the demand. In February 1963, Kennedy had proposed that the federal courts should be empowered to appoint federal registrars in areas where fewer than 15 percent of the black population were registered. This provision was omitted, however, from the bill which became the 1964 Civil Rights Act. SCLC wanted a new act to incorporate something similar, but with a much higher threshold for the appointment of federal registrars. At the same time, SCLC wanted any new legislation to circumvent the judicial approach, whereby discrimination had to be proven to the satisfaction of a federal judge before any action could take place. Low black registration per se should be sufficient evidence of discrimination, thereby "triggering" federal registration. SCLC also wanted the complete abolition of literacy and "interpretation" tests.[47]

   As well as being apposite to these demands, Selma had two other vital advantages. First, the city had an active and interested black community which had already organized, with SNCC's help, a campaign for the vote. SNCC had worked in Selma since February 1963 when Bernard and Colia Lafayette began a voter registration drive and encouraged local blacks like Amelia Boynton and Frederick Reese to form the Dallas County Voters League. Local ministers founded another group, the Dallas County Improvement Association, shortly afterwards. In September SNCC began a series of peaceful demonstrations which culminated in a "Freedom Day" on October 7, when more than two hundred blacks lined up outside the Dallas County Courthouse to take the registration test. White resistance, however, was unyielding and effective: the registrars limited new black voters to a trickle; the police arrested marchers and pickets on such charges as parading without a permit, truancy, and incitement to riot. Another "Freedom Day" in July 1964 proved equally unsuccessful, and elicited a draconian injunction from Judge James A. Hare which banned virtually all civil rights activity. Nevertheless, SNCC had stimulated black interest in voting and established, in the words of James Forman, "a firm beachhead in the heart of Alabama's Black Belt."[48]

SNCC's activities had revealed that Selma was to Alabama what Greenwood was to Mississippi: a town where, as one reporter wrote, "almost every element of white resistance is present . . . in magnified form."[49] In 1956 Roy Wilkins called Selma "the seat of things in Alabama"—birthplace of the state's first and, by 1957, strongest citizens council. With about three thousand members, the council united men of wealth and political influence in a campaign to snuff out black insurgency by means of economic pressure and reprisals. Negroes who attempted to register were fired, and their names placed on blacklists which the council circulated among local employers. Any business taking on a blacklisted person faced a boycott by white customers and suppliers.[50] If it rejected the Klan's violence, Selma's social elite shared its crude racism. The editor of the *Selma Times-Journal* explained in 1961 that he opposed the Klan for pragmatic reasons: "I wouldn't mind killing half a dozen niggers if it would do any good. . . . Scratch 'em and you'll find that they're all savages underneath."[51]

The sheriff of Dallas County, James G. Clark, had become a byword in Alabama for strong-arm methods against blacks and civil rights workers. Disdaining to limit his activities to Dallas County itself, Clark and his posse of volunteers had crushed demonstrations in Gadsden and Tuscaloosa; he had also taken his men to Notasulga, near Tuskegee, to assist a force of state troopers under Albert J. Lingo in blocking school integration. Political allies of George Wallace, Clark and Lingo often worked in tandem, acting as a kind of mobile anti–civil rights task force. Clark's temperament made him a natural target for the kind of tactics SCLC had used in Birmingham to discredit "Bull" Connor. Actually, Clark was even more vulnerable: whereas Connor possessed a modicum of political sense, Clark had none. Regarding violence as a first resort, he scorned the policy of peaceful arrests and preferred, with Lingo, to break up demonstrations with clubs, tear gas, and electric cattle-prods. Clark did not care to hide his methods from the press and had few qualms about assaulting reporters and cameramen. Like Connor, only more so, Clark presented SCLC with "the perfect public villain."[52]

By 1964, however, an informal group of influential whites, including the town's leading bankers, had become seriously concerned about Selma's growing reputation for extreme racism. Aware of SCLC's interest in their community, they feared that Clark's antics might give

SCLC a perfect lever for bringing about federal intervention. They were also disturbed by the local recruiting efforts of the National States Rights party, which had virtually supplanted the Klan in and around Selma. "This group is at present nameless and has not come out into the open, but evidently has power," SNCC's project director, John Love, reported in mid-September. In order to ease racial tensions, the whites met Love and local black leaders and committed themselves to further discussions. As a sign of good faith they had the "white" and "colored" signs removed, at Love's request, from the water fountains at the courthouse.[53]

But the main concern of the "moderate" segregationists was to curb Jim Clark. The sheriff had already attracted four Justice Department suits; meanwhile, a voting rights suit, filed as long ago as 1960, was working its way slowly through the courts. If SCLC were subjected to the same treatment as SNCC, it would have a chance to spring the legal trap. To undercut Clark's power, therefore, the "moderates" persuaded the new mayor of Selma, Joseph Smitherman, to create the post of director of public safety so that Wilson Baker, a man who shared their views, controlled the police force. Baker, Clark was told, would deal with any future demonstrations.[54]

Although SCLC had no detailed knowledge of these maneuvers at the time of its November retreat, it already knew better than to stake an entire campaign on Selma itself. As the tactics of the South's white supremacists became more sophisticated, so did SCLC's. Bevel had not specified targets in his original plan for the Alabama campaign, but he had discussed, in some detail, the relative advantages of mounting protests in a single city or in several places at once. Each approach had its advantages, he concluded; for maximum effect they should both be utilized. If Baker responded with Pritchett-like restraint, therefore, SCLC could move into the surrounding counties of Perry, Wilcox, Lowndes, and Hale. It could also organize demonstrations in Montgomery. With sufficient persistence and agility, it ought not be too difficult to precipitate a dramatic confrontation, under circumstances of SCLC's own choosing, somewhere in Alabama's Black Belt.

SCLC's intervention in Selma could be expected to arouse a good deal of grumbling, and perhaps some outright opposition, within SNCC. Organizational rivalry apart—and there was never any shortage of that—many SNCC workers were strongly critical of SCLC's modus operandi. The two organizations had very different methods and styles of working. SNCC believed in organizing communities "from the bottom up," and this entailed the slow, painstaking task of founding and

nurturing indigenous organizations that were representative, democratic, and built to last. SCLC's confrontational approach involved the
engineering of short-lived crises; it paid little heed to building local
organizations, as its almost complete neglect of its own affiliates attested. Even if on rare occasions SCLC evoked some form of federal
intervention, SNCC workers complained, the results were evanescent
and superficial for the great majority of blacks. Black advancement, to
be solid and secure, had to proceed from a strong and secure local base.
SCLC's campaigns actually left local black organizations exposed, ener-
vated, divided, and often disillusioned.

SNCC workers also detested SCLC's style of leadership. SCLC made
no pretense of being a democratic organization; it unashamedly revolved around King. SNCC prided itself on its democratic ethos, and
had acquired a positive aversion to centralized or "charismatic" leadership. In contrast to the blatant authoritarianism of SCLC or the
bureaucratic centralism of the NAACP, SNCC practiced "participatory
democracy," whereby all important decisions were the subject of group
debate and the product of a broad consensus. Only by participating in
genuinely democratic organizations, SNCC workers believed, could
blacks develop the confidence and experience to mold their own future. The simpleminded adoration with which many blacks regarded
King exasperated SNCC. More important, this hero worship often
seemed to discourage action. It was psychologically comforting to believe that a Moses figure could lead them to the promised land, but
this belief, SNCC insisted, bore no relation to political reality. Blacks
had to think and act for themselves.

A growing political rift interlaced these differences. Its work in Mississippi, particularly the failure of the MFDP challenge, brought into
question SNCC's most cherished beliefs. After Atlantic City, a brood-
ing sense of frustration, futility, and defeat hung over the organization.
This feeling manifested itself in different ways. Some SNCC workers
became cynical and apathetic. Others became profoundly alienated
from the federal government and deeply distrustful of white liberals.
SCLC-style demonstrations, with their premise that black suffering
evoked white sympathy, no longer had their former appeal. Skepticism
about the capacity of the body politic to respond to injustice ran deep.
Nor could many SNCC workers any longer subscribe, without qualifi-
cation, to nonviolence; they could not, in good conscience, advise
Mississippi blacks to love their white oppressors and neglect their self-
defense. Finally, for complex reasons, the experience of the Freedom
Summer had left many of SNCC's black staff members hostile and

resentful towards the white volunteers who had become their co-workers.[55]

But these internal tensions, frustrations, and problems did not yet paralyze SNCC or render it incapable of joint action with SCLC. The reminiscences of SNCC veterans sometimes exaggerate the differences between the two organizations at this time, projecting the ideological quarrels of 1966 back to 1964–65. In reality, SNCC's attitude to SCLC was ambivalent. On the one hand it had deep reservations about SCLC, but on the other hand it recognized that SNCC needed SCLC as much as SCLC needed SNCC. Although SNCC might criticize SCLC for exploiting its talent for local organizing, the exploitation was not one-way. SNCC frequently called upon SCLC to bring publicity to its campaigns or give a boost to its fundraising. If it did not unreservedly welcome SCLC's coming to Selma, SNCC recognized that it could utilize King's proven mass appeal to further its own organizing efforts. Some SNCC workers believed that King could be radicalized and pulled in SNCC's direction. In addition, friendship and the camaraderie of struggle still counted for something. The civil rights movement was a small world; one could not spend two or three or four years in the Deep South without forging personal ties which transcended organizational boundaries. Such ties continued to sustain the working relationship between SNCC and SCLC.

The decision to invite SCLC to Selma finally rested with the local black leaders, not with SNCC. In mid-November, shortly after the Birmingham meeting, C. T. Vivian visited Frederick Reese, head of the Dallas County Voters League, to determine whether SCLC could expect such an invitation. Reese welcomed SCLC's help, and preparations for the campaign began in earnest. King wished to start the campaign in the New Year and reach some kind of conclusion by the end of March. By May, he hoped, SCLC could begin preparing for a shift to the North.[56]

The preparations for Selma had barely got underway when J. Edgar Hoover created a sensation by informing a group of women journalists that King was "the most notorious liar in the country," repeating the allegation twice and explicitly encouraging the reporters to quote him. His words were splashed onto headlines the next day as part of what the *New York Times* called "a broadside of uncharacteristic public charges."[57]

The ostensible reason for Hoover's outburst was King's criticism of the FBI's performance in investigating civil rights violations. Two years earlier, King had complained that FBI agents stationed in the South were often native Southerners whose sympathies sometimes lay with the segregationist whites; this made it difficult for them to investigate objectively complaints lodged by Negroes. It also made blacks reluctant to approach the FBI in the first place. King volunteered these comments when asked about a report on Albany, Georgia, written by Howard Zinn and published by the Southern Regional Council, that was highly critical of the bureau. King said he agreed with the report: "Every time I saw an FBI agent in Albany," he added, "they were with the local police."[58]

The controversy touched off by Hoover's attack focused almost entirely on the accuracy of these criticisms. The civil rights movement rallied to King's defense. At the White House on November 19, a delegation of black leaders that included Roy Wilkins, Whitney Young, and A. Philip Randolph told Johnson that they fully endorsed what King had said about the FBI. So did Jack Greenberg of the NAACP Legal Defense Fund and James Farmer of CORE, the latter calling for Hoover's dismissal. The Southern Regional Council expressed "unreserved faith" in King, and one of its officials, Leslie Dunbar, corroborated King's remarks about the FBI agents in Albany, adding that the bureau's inaction there had been the nadir of the Justice Department's performance in the South. Roy Wilkins summed up the black reaction when he affirmed that "99 per cent of Negroes" agreed that "the FBI has not been as diligent as it could have been in the civil rights struggle."[59]

But the public argument over the FBI's efficiency obscured some of the other reasons for Hoover's animus towards King. True, the director was notoriously thin-skinned; as Nicholas Katzenbach, who was the acting attorney general at the time, recalled, "There was no greater crime in Mr. Hoover's eyes than public criticism of the Bureau, and Dr. King's repeated criticisms made him a Bureau enemy." Katzenbach was on shakier ground, however, when he went on to argue that "the only thing unique about Dr. King was the intensity of the feeling and the apparent excesses to which the Bureau went in seeking to destroy the critic." As David Garrow pointed out, it stretches credulity to imagine that King's relatively mild criticisms of 1962 could have prompted Hoover's outburst two years later, or accounted for the vicious FBI campaign to vilify and discredit him.[60]

Hoover's "off-the-record" allegations at the memorable November 18 press conference—that King associated with Communists and was "one of the lowest characters in America"—may well provide more reliable clues as to his underlying motives. The director's right-wing views, together with the wiretap evidence that King had continuing contacts with Stanley Levison, convinced him that the civil rights leader was, in the words of Victor Navasky, "either under Communist control or a conscious fellow traveller." Reports to this effect had been flowing to the White House and Justice Department since 1962 and, as mentioned earlier, became more copious, dogmatic, and explicit after the March on Washington. In January 1964 Hoover repeated the allegation to a group of congressmen during a closed session of the House Appropriations Committee. His charges soon became common knowledge in Washington.[61]

Although Hoover conceded publicly that the civil rights movement "is not, and never has been," controlled by Communists, the FBI was churning out "evidence" of King's "Communist" associations up to the week of his death. That King was a Communist in all but name appears to have been accepted without question by Hoover, his aides, and the great majority of FBI agents. According to Charles Brennan, who worked in Domestic Intelligence and then Internal Security, the wiretaps revealed that "King had once asserted that he was a Marxist and would have liked to have professed it publicly had it not been for the realization that it would have destroyed his capacity to serve as a leader in the civil rights movement."[62] It is highly unlikely that King made any such statement, although he did use the term "socialist" in a similar context, as well as express qualified admiration for Marx. But such distinctions were lost on the FBI. Above all, there was the supposedly damning evidence of King's friendship with Levison. With a relentless logic based on the twin pillars of guilt by association and the reductio ad absurdum, the bureau regarded Levison's mere presence in the circle of King advisers as sufficient to contaminate King with the poison of communism.

There seems little doubt that Hoover also found King's private life repugnant. Indeed, Garrow has argued that the director's abhorrence of King's extramarital sexual liaisons came to overshadow resentment of his criticisms or hostility to his political radicalism. With evidence about King's private life from wiretaps and "bugs" in hotel rooms, Hoover and Assistant Director Sullivan "quickly became obsessed with Dr. King's sexual behavior and the possibilities of recording more of it." Their prudish shock over what they discovered, Garrow contends, accounted for "the transformation of the King case in the winter of 1963–64" into "a new desire to discredit King personally." Only obsessive, puritanical disgust, he believes, could explain why Hoover attacked King, rather than some other more obviously militant black leader, with such single-minded vigor.[63] Yet Hoover had been monitoring the private lives of American citizens for decades; could he have been so easily shocked? It seems that he already perceived King as a dangerous subversive, moreover, before he had acquired extensive knowledge of the man's private behavior. One thing, however, is beyond dispute: the evidence gathered from the bugs and wiretaps gave Hoover a weapon he thought would finally destroy King.

"No holds were barred," Sullivan later admitted. "Microphone surveillance" began in January 1964 and continued intermittently until November 1965. After King's death the bureau admitted to having installed some sixteen different bugs, nearly all of them in hotel rooms. There may have been many more. The first, to the delight of the Domestic Intelligence Division, picked up sounds akin to sexual intercourse during a party in King's suite at the Willard Hotel in Washington. Transcriptions of the recordings were promptly sent to Johnson but withheld, on Hoover's instructions, from Robert Kennedy. But when a bug in Los Angeles recorded King reciting tasteless jokes about the late president, the director made sure that the attorney general received a transcript. The Los Angeles material, an FBI internal memorandum drooled, "is replete with [——] from King and his friends," and "contains further excellent data indicting King as one of the most reprehensible [——] individuals on the American scene today."[64] In February, Burke Marshall informed Robert Kennedy that the bureau had been leaking derogatory information about King to newspapermen, and that he had complained about this to presidential assistant Bill Moyers. In April, the bureau tried to block the award of honorary degrees to King by Marquette University and Springfield College: in each case a senior agent informed one of the college trustees about the evidence of communism and immorality. In August, when the bureau learned that King was seeking an audience with the pope, it "orally briefed" Cardinal Spellman, that scourge of the Left, "so that such information could be passed on to the Pope." To the FBI's dismay, however, Pope Paul agreed to see King.[65]

Why did Hoover wait until November 1964 to attack King publicly? Perhaps the very nature of the material in the FBI's possession inhibited Hoover from fully exploiting it—the last thing he wanted was a public discussion of the bureau's use of bugs and wiretaps. Perhaps the news of King's Nobel Prize so angered him that he threw caution to the winds. It seems fanciful, however, to think that a man of Hoover's character would fly off the handle because King won the Nobel Peace Prize, especially when one considers the fact that his public attack on

King occurred a month after news of the award. Hoover was more calculating than that: as Ed Guthman put it, he "stored his grievances and bided his time." Hoover held back the most potentially damaging material on King, gathered in early 1964, because he awaited "an opportune time," some "propitious point in the future," when it could do maximum damage to King's career and minimal damage to his own.[66]

The time was ripe in mid-November, not before. Hoover dare not attack King publicly before the presidential election; to do so would have infuriated Johnson. The president had little love for King, but he had allied himself to the civil rights cause and would have construed such an attack as an attempt on the part of Hoover to cause him political embarrassment. Thus in February Hoover rejected a proposal to leak personal information about King to congressmen "or anyone else at this time."[67] True, he had talked to a congressional committee about the King material, but he could correctly claim that the information was being given in confidence. It was also true that as the year wore on Hoover became increasingly frustrated by his failure to undermine King's standing. The inability of the Internal Revenue Service to find irregularities in King's tax returns, or those of SCLC and the Gandhi Society, precluded a Capone-style prosecution and heightened his impatience. By the end of 1964, Hoover's campaign against King looked like a failure as his target went from strength to strength: Birmingham, the March on Washington, *Time's* "Man of the Year," and now the Nobel Prize. It was not this last, however, that occasioned Hoover's onslaught; after all, nothing the FBI might do could stop King receiving the award. Was it mere coincidence that Hoover's notorious press conference took place only days after SCLC's Selma planning retreat? Certainly, the Nobel Prize ceremony brought no relaxation of the FBI's efforts to discredit King. These were prosecuted with greater vigor than ever during the early months of 1965: the period of the Selma campaign.

Hoover now gave the signal for the personal material on King— transcripts, photographs, even recordings—to be made available to editors, reporters, politicians, religious leaders, and other King sympathizers. DeLoach, the head of the bureau's Crime Records Division— its public relations department—offered the material, personally or through subordinates, to some of the best-known journalists in the nation, including Ben Bradlee of *Newsweek*, Mike Royko of the *Chicago Daily News*, John Herbers of the *New York Times*, and Ralph McGill, editor of the *Atlanta Constitution*. Many of those contacted refused to look at the material; none used it. Meanwhile, Sullivan ordered an edited tape of the Willard Hotel recording, accompanied by an anonymous letter, to be sent to Coretta King.[68]

Press circles in New York, Washington, and Atlanta were soon buzzing with stories and rumors about the smear campaign, and they did not take long to reach King. How should he respond? When Harry Wachtel first heard Hoover's November 18 comments, his immediate, angry reaction was to draft a blistering counterattack, to be issued in King's name, which concluded by inviting President Johnson to demand Hoover's resignation. Rustin thought the statement too strident and impolitic, and offered some suggestions to tone it down.[69] Before it could be got out, however, King, then in the Bahamas, telegraphed a brief reply of his own in which he declined to "engage in a public debate" with the director, and expressed backhanded sympathy for a man who had "served his country so well" but had "apparently faltered under the awesome burdens, complexities and responsibilities of his office." In a telephone interview, King denied ever having advised blacks not to report complaints to the FBI, and restated his dissatisfaction with the bureau's record. Its poor performance, he added, reflected the FBI's "appeasement of political powers in the South. If this continues, the reign of terror in Mississippi, Alabama and Georgia will increase rather than subside."[70] In a call to his secretary, Dora McDonald, King instructed SCLC's senior staff members to "hit Hoover from all sides."[71]

But with reports of the FBI-inspired leaks reaching SCLC almost daily, King had to confront some unpalatable facts. The response of other black leaders, especially Roy Wilkins, had been heartening. The president, on the other hand, had been conspicuously silent in King's defense.[72] It seemed unrealistic to think that SCLC could force the resignation of a national icon like Hoover. If it tried, moreover, what would Hoover's reaction be? A public scandal—a divorce—could ruin King's career. As Wachtel later put it, "Everything pointed toward the problem of how Hoover would respond if Dr. King said in effect, 'you're a liar, prove your case. If you call me a liar, prove it. . . .' Libel and slander or public debate of famous personalities can easily lead to destruction of an ongoing movement."[73] After a meeting of the research committee at the end of November, King decided to seek a meeting with Hoover in an effort to patch up the quarrel. Wachtel, now advising caution, tried to reassure King that Hoover wanted an accommodation as much as he did.[74]

The afternoon of December 1 saw King in Hoover's office, accompanied by Abernathy, Young, and Fauntroy. According to DeLoach's account of the meeting, Abernathy opened by expressing "the appreciation of the Negro race for the Director's fine work in the field of civil rights." This note of insincerity set the tone for the rest of the meeting. King, who spoke next, did not even criticize, much less confront, Hoover. He denied ever having claimed that the bureau was ineffective, stating that the only time he had criticized the FBI "was because of instances in which Special Agents who had been given complaints in civil rights cases regarding brutality by police officers were seen the following day being friendly with those same police officers." He praised the FBI's work in Mississippi, and commended the director's report on the summer riots. King reassured Hoover that when he found Communists or former Communists on his staff, he dismissed them; as a Christian, he opposed communism as a "crippling totalitarian disease."[75]

The next fifty minutes of the hour-long meeting were Hoover's. For most of the lengthy monologue the director stoutly defended the FBI's civil rights record. He was especially proud of the bureau's success in infiltrating the Klan which, he claimed, he had been fighting ever since the 1920s. In Mississippi, where the FBI had the cooperation of the governor and the highway patrol, the Klan was on its last legs. In Alabama, however, the bureau was having a harder time "because of the psychoneurotic tendencies" of George Wallace. Hoover then fed King a "tidbit": the Chaney-Schwerner-Goodman murders had been solved and the case would soon be brought to trial. He then lectured King on the civil rights problem. Negro leaders should concentrate on voter registration, and on "educat[ing] the Negro in the skills so that they could compete in the open market." The FBI, he explained, was glad to employ Negro agents, but most Negro applicants lacked the required qualifications. Hoover favored the desegregation of eating places and schools, but strongly opposed busing.

Towards the end of the meeting King broke in to mention SCLC's plans for Selma, revealing that his white staff had infiltrated the white community and discovered "a great potential for violence." If violence occurred, could the FBI be on hand to assist? Hoover repeated his determination to crush "backwoods terrorists," and said that the bureau had helped to develop five cases in Selma itself, including one against Sheriff Clark. However, FBI agents could only observe and investigate; they could not protect anyone.

Hoover's performance disarmed the SCLC visitors. "When he was bending over backwards trying to show us that he was doing the job," recalled Young (who did not utter a word during the meeting), "it was kind of hard to bring up another subject when he took up all the time."[76] The encounter ended with King thanking Hoover, and Hoover urging King "to get in touch with us" any time he felt it was necessary. According to Young, Hoover congratulated King on the Nobel Prize, but if he did say this DeLoach thought it diplomatic to omit the fact from his minutes. The meeting had avoided the real cause of contention, but King hoped for the best and flew to London a few days later, the first stop on his Nobel Prize tour. Wachtel and Rustin were guardedly optimistic about the future. King should now play down the issue, Wachtel thought; "Martin has *not* to spell out too much of this Hoover business."[77]

While King was in Europe, Harry Boyte visited Selma to assess the situation and advise on last-minute preparations before the launch of the protests. By now, city and county officials were well aware of SCLC's general plans; indeed, in the best Gandhian tradition Frederick Reese of the Dallas County Voters League had informed Wilson Baker, Selma's director of public safety, of the proposed program of action.

Boyte reported that Sheriff Clark had apparently agreed to let Baker handle the demonstrations. Selma's "power structure," he added, had been meeting during the past few months to discuss the racial situation. The five dominant figures—three bankers, an attorney, and the managing editor of the local newspaper—shared the same outlook, Boyte thought; he planned to meet them in order to make a fuller assessment and open "another channel of communication if we do undertake the direct action program." Boyte warned of a certain amount of tension between SCLC, SNCC, and the local black leaders. SCLC's reputation for "hit-and-run" tactics had clearly preceded it: local blacks were not entirely convinced that SCLC would "stay in Selma and see a program through; they are worried that we will come into town and leave too soon." SCLC ought to give a definite assurance that this would not happen. There was also some friction between Bevel and John Love, SNCC's project leader. A meeting to clear the air, with C. T. Vivian taking part, should be held as soon as possible. On the legal front, Boyte reported, the injunction against public meetings was being attacked in federal court by the "Inc. Fund" and would come before a three-judge panel of the Fifth Circuit Court of Appeals sometime in January. Boyte predicted a two-to-one decision to set aside the injunction.[78]

When King returned from Europe to read Boyte's report, he was feeling mentally and physically exhausted. Not that his reception in the Old World had been anything less than enthusiastic. The high

point of the trip, apart from the Nobel Prize ceremony itself, came on
December 5 when King preached at the Evensong service in St. Paul's
Cathedral. He was the guest of Canon John Collins, an old supporter of
SCLC and an acquaintance of Bayard Rustin from the early days of the
Campaign for Nuclear Disarmament. The *Times* described King's sermon as a "spellbinding performance. . . . Quotations rolled off his
tongue: he was actor, poet and preacher all at the same time." At a
press conference afterwards, flanked by Rustin and Abernathy, King
told reporters that the FBI would have to go all-out to protect the
rights of Negroes, and that he had made this clear to Hoover. He also
warned that Britain's developing racial ghettos were "festering sores"
which stored up trouble for the future.[79]

King's triumphant homecoming included a reception by Mayor
Wagner in New York, a luncheon with Governor Rockefeller, and a
meeting with the president. But the FBI pressed ahead with its surrep-
titious campaign of character assassination. Hoover had already sent
an updated version of the report "Communism and the Negro Movement" to Johnson, leading cabinet members, and top defense officials.
Carl Rowan, the black director of the U.S. Information Agency, also
received a copy.[80] Not content with the existing surveillance material,
Hoover ordered a new batch of transcriptions made. While these were
being prepared, bureau officials continued to "brief" journalists and
assorted public figures. The director clearly had no intention of letting
King off the hook: in a speech on December 12 he made another thinly
veiled reference to "morally corrupt charlatans" in the civil rights
movement. A week later he sent another report on King, describing his
conduct in Europe, to Johnson and other government officials.[81]

Three days after Christmas, King travelled to Montgomery to final-
ize arrangements for the Selma "Freedom Day" set for January 2, 1965.
The pressure of the forthcoming campaign, the fatigue of travel, and
the burden of Hoover's attacks had taken their toll; Coretta King con-
fided to Young that she was concerned about her husband's well-being.
As King prepared for SCLC's greatest challenge since Birmingham, a
package lay in the basement of his home in Atlanta. It contained a
spool of magnetic tape. An accompanying note described King as a
"colossal fraud," a "dissolute, abnormal moral imbecile," and an "evil,
abnormal beast." The final paragraph read as follows: "King, there is
only one thing left for you to do. You know what it is. You have just 34
days in which to do [it] (this exact number has been selected for a
specific reason, it has a definite practical significant [*sic*]). You are
done. There is but one way out for you. You better take it before your

filthy, abnormal fraudulent self is bared to the nation." We can only speculate on King's reaction had he read this note before Christmas; it is not inconceivable that he would have cancelled the forthcoming protests. Thanks to SCLC's inefficiency, however, the package was not opened until January 5. And by then the Selma campaign had already begun.[82]

Nine

Selma

By 1965 SCLC had become accustomed to the charge that it deliberately provoked violence. To those at the receiving end of its protests, SCLC's claim to be "nonviolent" was laughable—the ultimate hypocrisy. "Martin Luther King and the Nazi Party work hand in hand in provoking local people," complained Joe Smitherman, the mayor of Selma. "Everywhere you go you see the two together."[1]

Critics cynically suggested that King sought out the Birminghams and Selmas of the South in order to sustain his high-profile international reputation, which he clearly enjoyed, and to buoy up SCLC's finances, which were never healthier than after a dramatic "spring offensive." After all, there were plenty of "soft" targets in the South—Mobile, Atlanta, Nashville—where easy victories could be had and violence avoided. Indeed, the die-hard white supremacist areas were shrinking enclaves confined, for the most part, to the rural Black Belt. Subjected to persistent pressure from a vo-ciferous minority of extreme racists, Southern politicians still paid lip service to segregation. Economic self-interest, however, dissuaded most businessmen from swimming against the federal tide, and their read-iness to accept desegregation was not lost on the politicians. Fewer and fewer whites, moreover, were prepared to defend the disfranchisement of blacks. Surely it made more sense, as the NAACP constantly ar-gued, to concentrate on the cities where the battle was already half-won, leaving the Selmas and Greenwoods to wither on the vine or be picked off at leisure.

It would be naive to suppose that organizational self-interest never entered SCLC's calculations. But there were sound strategic reasons for concentrating on the die-hard South: SCLC's roots were in those areas; moreover, the quickest route to legislation, SCLC believed, was through crisis and confrontation. SCLC designed its campaigns to stir up feeling outside the South by putting on a show—a dramatic clash between violent whites and nonviolent Negroes that would arouse the press, the pulpit, the politicians, and the president. The desire for such a confrontation determined both the target and the tactics. SCLC's strategy, David Garrow argued in his study of the Selma campaign, "bordered on nonviolent provocation."[2]

Yet the assertion that SCLC "provoked" white violence has to be qualified. In rare moments of candor SCLC admitted that the success of its protests depended upon the extent to which its opponents re-sponded with violence. It denied, however, that the nonviolent pro-tester in any way caused that violence. To blame peaceful demonstrators for the violence of their oppressors was tantamount, in King's view, "to condemning the robbed man because his possession of money precipitated the evil act of robbery."[3] If their nonviolent efforts to secure constitutional rights elicited violence from racist whites, then logic, law, and morality required society to punish the per-petrators of violence, not expect its victims to passively accept in-justice. Violence was part and parcel of white supremacy; by defying an oppressive regime, the nonviolent protester brought that underlying violence to the surface, making it visible to the outside world. In a set of notes he prepared for a press conference, King anticipated the ques-tion "Does your movement depend on violence?" by writing, "When you give witness to an evil you do not cause that evil but you oppose it so it can be cured."[4] The paradox that SCLC invited white violence but denied in any sense provoking it was best explained, perhaps, by An-

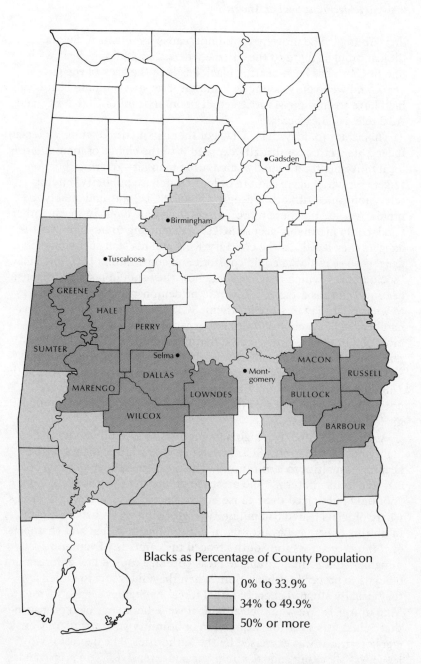

Blacks as Percentage of County Population

☐ 0% to 33.9%

▨ 34% to 49.9%

■ 50% or more

The Black Population of Alabama, 1965

drew Young: "The movement did not 'cause' problems in Selma. . . . [I]t just brought them to the surface where they could be dealt with. Sheriff Clark has been beating black heads in the back of the jail for years, and we're only saying to him that if he still wants to beat heads he'll have to do it on Main Street, at noon, in front of CBS, NBC, and ABC television cameras."[5]

This is not to deny that SCLC consciously incurred white violence; indeed, its tactics continually exposed it to the charge of manipulating local movements in a coldly calculating manner—offering them as targets for white aggression in order to purchase publicity; buying television time with other people's blood. SCLC was undeniably manipulative, and nowhere more so than in Selma. Nobody, on the other hand, could justifiably accuse SCLC of disguising to its followers the dangers they faced; on the contrary, King and his staff spelled out those dangers so that blacks could confront and control their fear. The SCLC "sociodrama," which taught people how they should respond to abuse, beatings, and gas attacks, left would-be demonstrators in no doubt as to what might lay in store for them. SCLC's attitude to violence was hardheaded but realistic: it did not expect to challenge the South's most obdurate racists without suffering casualties. "There can be no remission of sin," King once wrote, "without the shedding of blood."[6] SCLC's claim to leadership rested upon the fact that its staff shared the same risks as the rank and file. King came under the most severe criticism when he appeared to be avoiding the perils that he invited his followers to brave.

At the same time, by staging its protests in carefully contrived, highly public situations, SCLC tried to evoke white violence while keeping casualties to a minimum. The press, therefore, played a crucial role in its strategy. "The presence of reporters," wrote Paul Good, "not only publicized their cause but also acted as a deterrent in places where officials feared bad publicity." Television crews had an especially inhibiting effect; as Bayard Rustin put it, "Businessmen and chambers of commerce across the South dreaded the cameras." Even in Birmingham and Selma, extensive press coverage caused law enforcement officials to proceed with caution. When they did resort to violence, they usually stopped short of lethal force. As Stanley Levison wrote to King in April, "We would be at fault if we believed our own propaganda that Selma was a terrible expression of brutality and terrorism. Considerable restraint was exercised by the authorities. The degree of violence was shocking and startling, but not extensive." The propaganda value of violence depended more on the quality of the confrontation

and the press's ability to report it than on the seriousness of the violence itself. Snarling dogs, gushing fire hoses, and club-wielding troopers had more impact than murders and bombings if reporters and film
crews were present. Nonviolent protest, King wrote, "dramatized the
essential meaning of the conflict and in magnified strokes made clear
who was the evildoer and who was the undeserving victim." SCLC
sought to evoke *dramatic* violence rather than *deadly* violence, and
King, as one commentator pointed out in 1965, constantly retreated
"from situations that might result in the deaths of his followers."[7]

Selma's white leaders were well aware that SCLC hoped to
"provoke" Sheriff Jim Clark. Impressed by the success of Laurie Pritchett's methods in Albany, Wilson Baker decided to avoid making arrests if possible and to prevent violence at all costs: "We were
determined not to give them what they wanted."[8] True, Baker had no
authority over Clark, the elected sheriff of Dallas County, but he could
at least keep Selma's police force on a tight rein. He also persuaded
Clark—or thought he had—to let the city take care of the demonstrations. Smitherman and Baker advised local whites to conform to the
Civil Rights Act. They had even made conciliatory gestures towards
SNCC. By observing the letter of the law and responding with level-
headed restraint, they believed they could avert the confrontation
which SCLC would attempt to engineer.

On the last day of 1964, the rest of the Alabama field staff joined
Bevel in Selma to prepare for SCLC's first mass meeting. On January 2
King addressed seven hundred people at Brown Chapel. Reminding his
audience that only three hundred blacks could vote in the county, he
condemned the registration tests as a "deliberate attempt to freeze
voter registration at their present undemocratic levels." This meeting,
he went on, marked the beginning of a "determined, organized, mobilized campaign to get the right to vote everywhere in Alabama. . . . If
they refuse to register us, we will appeal to Governor Wallace. If he
doesn't listen, we will appeal to the legislature. If the legislature
doesn't listen, we will seek to arouse the Federal Government by
marching by the thousands to the places of registration. We must be
willing to go to jail by the thousands. We are not asking, we are
demanding the ballot."[9] For most of the next two and a half weeks
King was out of Selma, leaving Bevel to prepare for a "Freedom Day"
on January 18. The initial aim, Young informed the *New York Times*
man, John Herbers, was to get large numbers of applicants to the
courthouse on the two voter registration days; "future action will depend on what happens then."[10]

Bevel lost no time in personalizing the campaign: "If we can get out and work Jim Clark will be out picking cotton with my father in about two years." Within a few days he had recruited about one hundred volunteers to be divided between five wards; two staff members, one from SCLC and one from SNCC, worked with each group. The SNCC and SCLC staffs began each day with a joint meeting, an arrangement which, according to Bevel, "cut down on the friction between the two organizations." On January 12 about two hundred students came to watch a film about the sit-in movement, and seventy came back for a second session the next evening. "Most churches will be available for meetings," Bevel reported; "the ministers have gone on record as accepting and adopting the [SCLC] program for Selma and Alabama." During a brief visit on January 14, King disclosed that the "Freedom Day" would involve not only "a massive march on the court house" but also a test of "every restaurant, every theater, every motel" to see if they admitted blacks.[11]

On January 18 King and John Lewis led four hundred prospective applicants to the Dallas County Courthouse. They waited there all day in a vain attempt to register. On the way they had scrupulously obeyed a city parade ordinance, making sure to walk in groups of four or five, ten feet apart, and taking care to stop for traffic lights. SCLC thus hoped to establish that blacks in Selma were making bona fide attempts to register to vote. The city police, under Baker, did not interfere; as Arthur Capell, editor of the *Selma Times-Journal*, put it, "If we can only get the bastards out of town without getting them arrested, we'll have 'em whipped."[12]

The first day was therefore a tactical victory for Baker, for he managed to persuade Clark to keep his posse out of sight and refrain from making any arrests. That night, the SCLC staff members and the leaders of the voters league planned the next move. They decided to try another "stand-in" the following day in the hope that Clark and his men would start to arrest, or at least handle roughly, the waiting blacks. If the day passed without incident, on the other hand, SCLC intended to pick another target: Marion, perhaps, the seat of Perry County where out of five thousand black adults fewer than three hundred could vote; or Camden, the county seat of Wilcox, where no blacks at all were registered. Baker, who learned of these plans from an informant, realized that he could foil SCLC by controlling Clark for one more day.[13]

Clark's patience, however, was already strained to the limit. A vain and weak-willed man, Clark, in Baker's opinion, had less control over his possemen than they had over him. He was also easily influenced by his old friend and ally Judge Hare, an avid exponent of "scientific" racism who regarded blacks, particularly Selma's blacks, as utterly unfit to vote.[14] At the courthouse on January 19 Clark ordered the blacks to line up in an alley and, if and when they were allowed into the building, to go through the side entrance. When the blacks objected he arrested sixty-two people for unlawful assembly and five others for criminal provocation. SCLC was jubilant: Baker's strategy had disintegrated after only one day. King and his staff agreed to step up the protests in Selma so as to further incense Clark and exacerbate the obvious tension between Clark and Baker.[15]

While lawyers from the Inc. Fund prepared to file suit against Clark in federal court, the sheriff arrested another 150 people on January 20 for refusing to line up outside the side entrance. Baker was furious, and the two law enforcement officials stood in front of the courthouse glaring at each other. As Clark continued to thwart Baker's plan, the campaign picked up momentum and local blacks gained in confidence. A march by one hundred teachers on January 22 boosted morale still further. Although they left the courthouse after being pushed away by Clark and his men, the fact that they had joined a public protest at all qualified as some kind of breakthrough. When they arrived back at Brown Chapel they were given a standing, cheering ovation.[16]

The following day, Judge Daniel Thomas of the federal district court in Mobile issued a temporary restraining order naming Clark and four other county officials. Thomas forbade the harassment and intimidation "of those legally attempting to aid others in registering to vote, or encouraging them." Although he accused both sides of bad faith, he instructed the registrars to speed up the processing of applicants. The injunction was a victory of sorts, but its vague terms meant that it had little effect upon the registrars. Nor did it prevent Clark from making arrests, for he enforced the order as if it meant that no more than a hundred people (the figure mentioned by Thomas as an acceptable number of daily applications) could stand outside the courthouse at any one time. By January 30, when the registration office closed for the month, Clark had arrested 56 people for refusing to leave the line.[17]

On January 28 SCLC decided to escalate the protests. On February 1 King violated the parade ordinance by leading 265 people to the courthouse; Baker had them all arrested, including King and Abernathy. In the afternoon 500 schoolchildren joined them in jail. SCLC also began demonstrations in Marion, with Albert Turner, the thirty-seven-year-old head of the Perry County Civic League, leading 300 people to

the courthouse. None were arrested; none were registered. Turner
joined the SCLC staff to work alongside James Orange and other staff
members who were already in Marion.[18]

On February 5, the *New York Times* published a "Letter from Martin Luther King, Jr., from a Selma, Alabama, Jail," dated the day of his
arrest. It pointed out that there were more blacks in jail in Selma than
there were black voters; it also appealed for donations to SCLC. But
King had no time for lengthy prison letters, for he spent most of his
time in jail mapping out the tactics of the campaign and sending detailed instructions for Andrew Young. On February 2, he wrote Young a
list of twelve points outlining how to keep national attention on
Selma. The first three concerned the federal government. "Make personal call to President Johnson urging him to intervene in some way,"
such as involving the Justice Department, sending a personal emissary,
and issuing a public plea to city and county officials. King also told
Young to get in touch with LeRoy Collins, the head of the Community
Relations Service, and to "follow through on suggestion of having a
congressional delegation to come in for personal investigation."[19]

King then suggested ways of maintaining the pressure in Selma
itself: "5. Keep some activity alive every day this week. 6. Consider a
night march to the city jail protesting my arrest (an arrest which must
be considered unjust). Have another night march to court house to let
Clark show true collors [sic]. 7. Stretch every point to get teachers to
march. 8. Immediately post bond for staff members essential for mobilization who are arrested. 9. Seek to get big name celebrities to come
in for moral support. 11. Call C. T. and have him return from Cal. in
case other staff is put out of action." Interestingly, King scratched his
tenth instruction, which told Young to contact Governor Nelson
Rockefeller "and other Republican big names to come out with strong
statements about the arrests, the right to vote and Selma." Perhaps he
thought it impolitic, knowing Lyndon Johnson, to solicit Republican
help at this stage. His last instruction seemed to embody the fear that
SCLC might, in his absence, lose the initiative: "Local Selma editor
sent telegram to President calling for Congressional Committee to
come and study true situation of Selma. We should join in calling for
this. By all means don't let them get the offensive. They are trying to
give the impression that they are an orderly and good community
because they integrated public accommodations. We must insist that
voting is the issue and here Selma has dirty hands. Let me hear from
[you] on all this tomorrow," he concluded.

After talking with Clarence Jones, Young phoned the White House and asked presidential assistant Lee White to pass on King's requests. The following day, Johnson announced that he was determined to see that the right to vote "is secured for all our citizens." He added, however, that the government intended to act under existing legislation. Also in Washington, Walter Fauntroy arranged for a group of House Democrats, including the black congressmen John Conyers and Charles Diggs, to observe voter registration in Selma on Friday, February 5. J. Edgar Hoover followed SCLC's deliberations attentively, sending regular summaries of the wiretapped conversations of King's advisers to Bill Moyers at the White House.[20]

In Selma itself, SCLC stepped up the protests in line with King's instructions, although there were no night marches. On February 2, another 520 people were arrested in two separate incidents. In the first, Hosea Williams led 120 adults to the courthouse, where they asked to see the registrars. Clark stated that the office was closed; when they refused to leave he arrested them. Shortly afterwards, the sheriff rounded up about 400 high school students, led by SCLC staff member Daniel Harrell, when they marched on the courthouse. February 3 saw a record number of arrests: 700 in Marion and 300 in Selma, bringing the total in jail to 2,600.[21]

The next day King sent Young another set of instructions. Clearly heartened that the protest had spread to Perry County, he asked that Young or Williams speak at a mass meeting in Marion that night. He also urged legal action to speed up voter registration in the county and to get those in jail released; "We must let Marion know we are concerned." Anxious to expand the campaign to other Black Belt counties, King asked for two meetings to be arranged for Monday, February 8— one in Hayneville, Lowndes County, the other in Montgomery. "That will give continuity to [the] Alabama drive and demonstrate that we aren't stopping with one community. Send at least three or four staff members into Lyons [Lowndes] by Saturday." He also told Young to ask Sammy Davis, Jr., to give a benefit concert in Atlanta some time in March or April—"I find that all of these fellows respond better when I am in jail."

King planned to leave jail on February 5, and with meticulous attention to detail he briefed Young as to the manner of his departure: "If all goes well get us out at 1:00 P.M. tomorrow. We will go directly to Federal building to see Congressmen. Set press conference for 2:30. Prepare the kind of statement that I should send to press on release from jail. When it is definite that we are coming out let the press know the time so they will be on hand at the jail for our release. Get a local citizen to sign our bond in order to save money. Check this with Baker." His penultimate instruction betrayed King's worry that Young might make a wrong decision and cause the protests to falter: "Insist on seeing me before there is an official call-off of demonstrations here in Selma. Chief Baker will bend if you insist that a settlement cannot be reached without such consultation. Be sure to brief me on all aspects of the pending order from judge Thomas."[22]

Later that day, what King feared came to pass: when Thomas issued another injunction against Clark and the county officials, Young suspended the demonstrations. Thomas's order seemed encouraging; it instructed the board of registrars to accept one hundred applications a day, relax the literary test and cease failing people for trivial mistakes, and process all the applications submitted during the next four months by the end of June. Any rejected applicant could appeal directly to the judge, and he promised to appoint a federal referee if the board failed to speed up registration. Thomas also told Clark to let applicants line up in front of the courthouse and to stop arresting civil rights workers for peacefully encouraging them. Young was caught in a dilemma. To continue the protests might seem like an act of bad faith; to stop them might halt the campaign's momentum. He at first said that the marches were to go ahead as planned, calling Thomas's order "disappointing." He added that "we are so emotionally caught up in the movement that it is hard for us to be objective [about the order]. We feel like we can have very little faith in this unless something is done about Jim Clark." Young later told reporters that King wanted to "think about" the Thomas order overnight, finally announcing that he had sent word for the demonstrations to be suspended.[23]

But King's final note from prison reveals that Young called off the marches on his own initiative. When King discovered what had transpired, he dashed off the following message:

Call Jack [Greenberg] tonight and let him know that we don't feel that they are moving fast enough. Thomas' restraining order is far from clear. Nothing has been done to get Judge Hare's injunction dissolved. Nothing has been done to clear those who were arrested for contempt. They were not picketing the court or disturbing it but picketing the registrars who are housed in the court house. In[sist] that the events here are too important for Jack not to be here in person.

Also please don't be too soft. We have the offensive. It was a mistake not to march today. In a crisis we must have a sense of drama. Don't let Baker control our movement. We may accept the restraining order as a partial victory, but we can't stop.[24]

These prison notes, with their grasp of detail and tactical skill, reveal a resourceful and determined leader. King's coolness and resolve showed that he refused to be intimidated or cowed by Hoover and the FBI. Yet he was laboring under an immense strain. King had received countless hate letters since December 1956. The note which Coretta showed him on January 5, however, had shaken him. King played the accompanying tape in the presence of his wife, Abernathy, Young, and Lowery; they immediately suspected the FBI. This crude ploy failed in its object: Coretta stayed loyal to her husband, and the Selma protests went ahead. But King was angry, worried, and probably a little frightened. After monitoring the telephone conversations of King and his advisers, Charles Brennan informed William Sullivan that King appeared to be "on the verge of a mental breakdown."[25]

King realized that he now had to do what Wachtel had earlier advised him not to: confront Hoover about the smear campaign and demand that it cease forthwith. But the director made himself unavailable, and when Young and Abernathy questioned DeLoach on January 11, Hoover's assistant coolly denied their allegations. "He assured me that the FBI wouldn't do something like that," Young recalled.[26] Nobody in SCLC placed much credence in the denial, but the FBI had, in effect, shot its bolt. Its masterstroke had failed, and its efforts to destroy King's reputation continued to misfire, as evidenced by its futile attempt to dissuade Atlanta notables from attending an interracial banquet to honor the city's Nobel laureate. Three days after this successful event, and two days before King went to jail in Selma, a frustrated Hoover again warned that "self-serving individuals" and "pressure groups" could expect no protection from the FBI. King ignored this veiled threat. Nevertheless, colleagues worried about his health, and urged him to take a break from Selma in order to rest. The momentum of events, however, kept King in the forefront of the campaign. He must have been heartened to receive a comforting letter from Nelson Rockefeller at this time. "We all read with deep concern and sadness," the governor wrote, "reports in the press of the renewal of attacks against you personally." He assured King that he was following his efforts in Selma "with deep interest."[27]

When he left jail on February 5, King promptly announced that the protests were to expand across the Black Belt. As he indicated in his prison notes, he found plenty to criticize in Judge Thomas's order and realized that it would be fatal to demobilize at this stage. The day he and Abernathy posted bond, another five hundred people, mostly children, were arrested in Selma.[28] There was a lull during the weekend,

when King returned to Atlanta, but he told his staff to set up a mass
meeting in Montgomery on Monday, February 8, to be followed by a
march to the courthouse on Tuesday morning.[29] He also asked Young
to see whether a mass meeting could be arranged in Lowndes County
later in the week. No blacks ever voted in Lowndes, although they
made up 80 percent of the population. "I don't know of any Negro
registrations here," explained a local registrar, "but there is a better
relationship between the whites and the niggers here than any place I
know of." The county's fearsome reputation had thus far deterred civil
rights workers, and Roy Reed of the *New York Times* quoted "observers here" as predicting that whites in Lowndes would "react sharply to
the Negro movement."[30]

King also disclosed upon leaving jail that he intended to see President Johnson so that he could press the case for a voting bill. Johnson,
however, took umbrage at King's presumptuousness, and Harry
Wachtel, who was arranging the appointment, had to go through an
elaborate ritual to assuage the president's sense of secrecy and protocol. Johnson *would* see King, Lee White told him, but only on the
strict condition that he keep that fact to himself. For public consump-
tion, Wachtel had to concoct the story that King had an appointment
to see the attorney general only, and was merely "hopeful" of meeting
the president—if, of course, the latter could take time off from more
pressing affairs of state like Vietnam. "Now King knows . . . he is not
dealing with a friend," Wachtel told Clarence Jones, "but with a
Texan."[31]

Nevertheless, the administration seemed to be responding to the
events in Selma. On February 6, the same day that Lee White chided
Wachtel, another presidential assistant—George Reedy, the White
House press secretary—announced that the government intended to
make a "strong recommendation" to Congress regarding voting rights.
This was its first public commitment to new legislation. By the end of
the weekend the ADA had come out for a voting rights law, and on
Tuesday, February 9, Congressman John Lindsay of New York introduced a voting bill in the House. In his meeting with Katzenbach that
same day, King specified the features which a new law needed if it
were to make universal adult suffrage a reality. The president, who had
overcome his pique enough to meet King, stated that the Justice Department was hard at work and that a measure could be expected "very
soon." But neither Johnson nor Katzenbach disclosed any details; nor
did they indicate whether it was a bill or a constitutional
amendment.[32]

Johnson's friendly stance presented a refreshing contrast to the critical neutrality adopted by the Kennedy administration during most of the Birmingham campaign. In Selma the federal government, in the form of the Community Relations Service, was even now trying to arrange biracial talks. But local concessions were not SCLC's primary goal: it needed to rouse Northern public opinion to such a pitch of concern that voting rights legislation became a political imperative. However, the Montgomery drive, launched by King on February 8, turned out to be a damp squib as fewer than two hundred people marched to the courthouse with him the next morning. The press took some delight in pointing out that King, of all people, should have known the relative ease with which blacks in Montgomery could register. The drive in Lowndes County failed to materialize altogether, partly because King's aides considered Lowndes far too dangerous to risk a visit by King himself.33

For the next month the campaign, in the words of Roger Wilkins, "sputtered along and appeared to be going nowhere."34 SCLC's tactical problems were real enough: flagging enthusiasm in Selma; logistical difficulties in extending the protests to surrounding counties; and declining press interest in the absence of a dramatic confrontation. But observers underestimated SCLC's patience and persistence, and were wont to write premature obituaries whenever a few days passed without mass arrests. SCLC did not doubt that the elusive confrontation would soon take place, if not in Selma itself, then in Perry, Wilcox, or Lowndes counties. Until it did, Jim Clark could be relied upon to provide the press with copy. Reporters usually describe the sheriff's brutish behavior with amused irony, but they rarely mentioned the skill with which SCLC goaded Clark. When he went into hospital for exhaustion, for example, SCLC staff members led two thousand children to the courthouse to pray for his "speedy recovery." They even sent flowers to the hospital. A few days later, when C. T. Vivian upbraided Clark in front of the television cameras for making applicants stand in the rain, the sheriff punched him in the face. The film crews not only recorded the incident but also pictured Clark and his men poking their billy clubs at the camera lenses and pushing the newsmen away. In the lexicon of nonviolence this was "moral jujitsu," a way of rattling the opponent and encouraging him to commit discreditable deeds. In the opinion of Wilson Baker, SCLC manipulated Clark "just like an expert playing a violin."35

On February 10, after returning from Washington, King held a strategy meeting at Selma's Torch Motel to consider two pressing questions. The first concerned Judge Thomas's injunction of February 4. In an effort to speed up voter registration, Thomas had ordered all those wishing to register to sign an "appearance book" so that they could be processed in order of application. If the board of registrars failed to process these applications by the end of June, Thomas undertook to appoint a federal registrar. On February 8, however, James Bevel, with the support of many in SNCC, denounced the "appearance book" as a trick and told the press that blacks should refuse to sign it. King, then in Montgomery, was uncertain how to respond; "Martin agonized for two days," Shuttlesworth recalled, before deciding to overrule Bevel.36 At the strategy meeting he argued that the "appearance book" at least represented a step in the right direction, adding that the attorney general had assured him that all who signed the book would be registered—if not by the board then by the federal courts. Although Ivanhoe Donaldson and Diane Bevel remained skeptical, SNCC agreed to stop boycotting the book.37

The second issue concerned the focus of the campaign: should the protests continue to concentrate on Selma, or should they be shifted to the adjacent counties? King and Young advocated the latter course: the black people of Selma were tired, they argued; they had carried the entire weight of the campaign and could not possibly sustain this burden for another three or four months. Instead of allowing the movement in Selma to peter out through sheer exhaustion, it should be stopped so as to leave local blacks with a feeling of victory, albeit partial victory. The thrust of the campaign ought to be redirected, King explained: in order to get a voting rights bill passed "we need to make a dramatic appeal through Lowndes and other counties." Another advantage of moving to Lowndes, Young pointed out, was that the county lay within the jurisdiction of U.S. district judge Frank M. Johnson, who had been far more sympathetic to the civil rights movement than Judge Thomas. The participants of the strategy meeting agreed to extend the protests into the surrounding Black Belt counties "so as to let the Nation and the press know that this movement is not losing momentum." On Monday, February 15, King and Shuttlesworth led marches in Selma, Marion, and Camden involving a total of twenty-eight hundred people. Two days later, King emerged from another strategy meeting promising "a broader focus of civil disobedience," including night marches.38

Marion, in Perry County, now found itself in the eye of the storm. On February 18, the day after the first night march, the police arrested SCLC worker James Orange. "They took me to the jail and was gonna

lynch me," Orange recalled. "But it got to Albert Turner, and he mobilized a mass meeting and a march." Young sent Willie Bolden and two
other staff members to assist Turner. More than four hundred people
met at the Zion Chapel Methodist Church that evening, and at nine-
thirty, after a rousing speech by C. T. Vivian, they began filing out of
the church to march across the street to the courthouse. Chief of
Police T. O. Harris ordered them to disperse.³⁹

Willie Bolden described what happened next: "All of a sudden, out
of nowhere, we heard cameras being broken, newspapermen being hit,
and looked around and saw folk trying to run out of the church. And
what they had done, they had gone through the side and back of the
church, and the troopers were outside along with local police and
sheriff department, beating folk out of there." Bolden and his two co-
workers were arrested. Cager Lee, eighty-two years old, was among
those at the back of the church. "The man with clubs came around
saying 'Nigger go home.' They hauled me off and hit me to the street
and kicked me. It was hard to take for an old man." The police, the
deputies, and the troopers then chased blacks off the streets. "They
turned all the lights out, shot the lights out, and they beat people at
random," Albert Turner remembered. "They didn't have to be marching. All you had to do was be black." A group of blacks took refuge in a
cafe, and several state troopers burst in after them, one of them club-
bing Mrs. Viola Jackson, Cager Lee's daughter. Jimmie, her son, tried to
restrain the offending trooper but was shot in the stomach and crit-
ically injured. Eight days later, Jimmie Lee Jackson died.⁴⁰

The police riot in Marion received far less publicity than the events
in Selma seventeen days later on "Bloody Sunday." In Marion, however,
journalists were themselves attacked, and found it impossible to function. "It was a very hairy situation," Richard Valeriani of NBC related.
"The townspeople were out in force. They harassed anybody trying to
cover it, sprayed black paint on the lenses of the cameras, and generally jostled us and intimidated us. So there was no filming."⁴¹ In addition, the attack took place in the dark, with most of the action behind
the church; few if any reporters got a clear view of what was happening. Largely for these reasons, the first newspaper accounts placed
some credence on the police chief's assertion that "a lot of
Nigras . . . got rocks and bottles and started throwing them." John Herbers of the New York *Times* described the events as a "riot" which the
police and troopers eventually "brought under control." The next day,
however, he corrected this impression, writing that "the state troopers
waded into the Negroes with flailing night-clubs when they did not

disperse immediately." Other reporters also denied that the troopers had been quelling a "riot." Within a few days it became possible to piece together what had taken place: the city and county police, plus fifty state troopers under the ubiquitous Al Lingo, had launched an unprovoked attack. Jim Clark was seen among the troopers, dressed in civilian clothes but wielding a club. The fact that the streetlights darkened when the attack began made it obvious in retrospect that the whole affair had been planned. The mayor of Marion, R. O. Pegues, virtually admitted as much when he told John Herbers that "last night they got outside leadership from Selma and . . . were determined to take over the town. Of course, we can't have that."[42]

By the time the truth had been established, the story was "cold." Nevertheless, the events in Marion had two important consequences. First, by allowing newsmen to be attacked, Lingo and his chief, Governor Wallace, earned the condemnation of both the national and the state press. NBC, UPI, the *Birmingham News*, and the Alabama Press Association all complained to Wallace and demanded that the assailants be brought to justice. The *Alabama Journal* denounced the attack as a "nightmare of State Police stupidity and brutality." Second, Marion gave the campaign a martyr and impelled SCLC to devise an audacious response. SCLC abandoned night marches in light of Jackson's injury. On February 22, however, King announced plans for a "motorcade to Montgomery. We hope to have our forces mobilized to have carloads of people from all over the state to march on the capitol." Two days later, King began a fundraising trip to California; he planned to return on March 1 for a tour of the registration lines in at least four Black Belt counties. Meanwhile, SCLC expanded into Hale County, sending James Orange to Greensboro, and also, at long last, into Lowndes County, where James Bevel began working in Hayneville.[43]

While King was in California, the idea of a motorcade to Montgomery underwent a metamorphosis. On the evening of February 25, Bevel was discussing the plan with Orange when, as the latter recalled, a local woman, Mrs. Lucy Foster, suggested that they *march* to Montgomery instead. Bevel seized upon the idea and became more and more excited by it. The next evening, after Jackson had died from his wounds, Bevel told a mass meeting in Selma that "the death of that man is pushing me kind of hard. The blood of Jackson will be on our hands if we don't march. Be prepared to walk to Montgomery. Be prepared to sleep on the highways." Returning to Selma, King endorsed the idea, and at the memorial service for Jackson on March 3, Bevel announced that King planned to lead the march himself. The fifty-mile walk would begin four days hence.[44]

In his eulogy to Jackson, King denounced the "timidity of a federal government that is willing to spend millions of dollars a day to defend freedom in Vietnam but cannot protect the rights of its citizens at home." King's first public reference to Vietnam could not have pleased the president. With South Vietnam facing collapse, Johnson had already decided to expand America's military involvement in the war. Only the week before, he had ordered continuous bombing of North Vietnam, and intensive preparations were underway for the landing of American troops on a large scale. Vietnam, not Selma, was dominating the headlines. True, SCLC had managed to swell the demand for voting rights legislation, and the administration had pledged to support that demand. Johnson, however, seemed in no hurry to act. Alternative proposals had been sent to him as long ago as December 28, yet he still had to choose between them. The debate between those arguing for a bill and those advocating a constitutional amendment gave him a convenient excuse for delay. King saw the president for one and a half hours on the evening of March 5. He argued in favor of a bill, to be introduced without delay, that should apply to all elections, ban all literacy tests, and allow the appointment of federal registrars if black registration failed to reach a certain level. Beyond saying that legislation was being completed, Johnson was noncommital, giving no details and making no promises.[45]

As SCLC prepared to march to Montgomery in a dramatic bid to arouse public opinion, its relations with SNCC became increasingly problematic. SNCC's Alabama staff vigorously opposed the Selma-to-Montgomery march, terming it a futile, dangerous, and distracting gesture. Some even welcomed the prospect of a split with SCLC. On March 6, SNCC's executive staff met in Atlanta and spent the better part of two days defining SNCC's position in respect of the march and discussing its relationship with SCLC. Most voted against the march. Yet James Forman and others made a strong case for some kind of limited participation by SNCC: the whole thrust of its work in Selma pointed in the direction of marching; SNCC had already made verbal commitments; by boycotting the march, SNCC would stand accused of promoting factionalism and disunity. SNCC's differences with SCLC were not ideological, Forman insisted; they merely derived from "different techniques of working." Courtland Cox thought they were ideological, but agreed with Forman that SNCC should continue to cooperate with SCLC, even if their relationship was "fuzzy." In the end, SNCC told SCLC that although a majority of the executive staff opposed the march, SNCC members could participate as individuals and SNCC would render token support.[46]

While SNCC deliberated in Atlanta, King pondered the question of whether he should lead the march in person. The FBI, to its credit, had diligently alerted King to numerous assassination threats; when King met the research committee in New York on March 5, he had round-the-clock police protection. Many of the threats were real, and Attorney General Katzenbach strongly advised King not to march. The research committee agreed that it would be senseless to expose King to the serious risk of being murdered. Rustin and Wachtel were delegated to prepare a statement explaining King's "limited participation"—a march of fifty miles would take about four days; King would not be leading it on the first day. On March 6, a Saturday, Governor Wallace banned the march and pledged to stop it; few doubted that he meant what he said. On Sunday morning, the day of the march, Clarence Jones sent telegrams to the president and the attorney general calling Wallace's statement "an open invitation for commission of acts of violence against person of Dr. King. . . . Respectfully urge you dispatch federal marshals to location of proposed march." Andrew Young, ever the optimist, predicted to Jones that "they would probably just march out . . . and then turn round and come back."[47]

In Selma, however, people could sense the impending violence. Lingo's state troopers were deployed on the far side of the Edmund Pettus Bridge with clear orders from Wallace to halt the march; Clark and his posse were on hand to assist. Wilson Baker suspected that Wallace and his cohorts were plotting an attack; pressed by Mayor Smitherman to help them stop the demonstration, he refused point-blank and threatened to resign on the spot. Only by arresting the marchers at the outset, he insisted, could violence be avoided. "I knew one spark could set it off," he later recalled, "and that I was not going to have any part of it." As the six hundred marchers assembled with their backpacks and sleeping bags, a doctor from the Medical Committee for Human Rights told them how to react in the event of tear gas: "Don't panic. Don't rub your eyes. Wash them with water if you can. And we'll be on hand to help." When the marchers, led by John Lewis and Hosea Williams, cleared the bridge they were not only teargassed, but also clubbed and trampled as two hundred state troopers charged at them with such force that, as one reporter put it, "the wedge . . . seemed almost to pass over the waiting column instead of through it."[48]

Clark's posse then pursued the marchers as they stumbled and fled back to Brown Chapel. Blacks in the surrounding housing project began to throw bricks and brandish weapons. Young, who had arrived from Atlanta earlier that day, made frantic efforts to calm them. "He played such an important part of saving a bloodbath," Baker recounted a decade later. "He was just running wild up and down to these apartment units: 'Get back into the house with this weapon. . . . We're not going to have any weapons out.'" Baker himself, appalled and furious, ordered Clark and his "cowboys" off the scene. All told, some seventy-eight blacks needed medical attention, of whom seventeen were taken to hospital. John Lewis suffered a brain concussion.[49]

At the mass meeting in Brown Chapel that evening, the mood of anger and outrage made the demand for another march irresistible. SNCC now reversed its position and insisted on one. The SCLC leaders there readily concurred. "There just had to be a march," Young later explained, "some kind of nonviolent demonstration to get the expression out. If there wasn't, you would have had real violence. . . . [A]s we looked around the room at the bandages and bruises, we knew we had to do something." SCLC's Atlanta office announced that King had decided to lead a second march on Tuesday, and invited clergymen and religious leaders from all over the nation to participate. Randolph Blackwell sent out two hundred telegrams in King's name. SCLC's lawyers prepared to attack the Wallace ban in federal court.[50]

The response to King's national call was immediate and impressive. Hundreds of clergymen and other sympathizers converged on Selma. Some had been contacted by SCLC's regional representatives; others by its supporting affiliates in California and Massachusetts. But most offered their help spontaneously: George Lawrence, SCLC's New York representative, received about four hundred sympathetic phone calls in the twenty-four hours after the attack on Pettus Bridge. By the morning of March 9, at least 450 white clergymen had gathered at Brown Chapel, ready and eager to march. They included James Pike, the Episcopal bishop of California, and John Wesley Lord, the Methodist bishop of Washington, D.C. Many of the clergymen were old supporters of the civil rights movement, but most, like the scores of lay people present, had travelled to Selma on impulse after viewing the graphic television film of the attack on Pettus Bridge.[51]

On March 8 SCLC's lawyers asked U.S. district judge Frank M. Johnson to overrule Wallace's ban and prohibit any interference with the planned march to Montgomery. Johnson, however, advised the attorneys to postpone the march until formal court hearings could be held; he scheduled these to begin on Thursday, March 11. Johnson's request took SCLC's leaders by surprise, causing dismay and bitterness. When King and Abernathy arrived in Montgomery they held a long discussion with Andrew Young, Hosea Williams, James Forman, and James Farmer. Williams and Forman argued for holding the march regardless. King, on the other hand, had always obeyed the federal courts and had no desire to defy Johnson, whose record on civil rights was outstanding. If the marchers set out for Montgomery before March 11, moreover, they would not have federal protection; another attack by Wallace's troopers could not be ruled out. After discussing the situation over the phone with Jack Greenberg, Harry Wachtel, and Clarence Jones, King instructed his lawyers to inform Johnson that he agreed to postpone the march.[52]

Emotionally, however, King rebelled against the idea of meekly obeying the court. Not to march would rob the campaign of momentum and drama, deprive SCLC of the initiative, and disappoint the hundreds of sympathizers who had journeyed to Selma. It would also exacerbate the widening rift between SCLC and SNCC. By the time King appeared at Brown Chapel in Selma shortly before midnight, the clamor to march had reached a high pitch of emotional intensity. During the long rally, speaker after speaker had roused the audience with demands for immediate action. None were more impassioned than James Bevel, who denounced the president's use of force in Vietnam when there were "two million white savages here in Alabama." When King at last spoke, he struck reporter Andrew Kopkind as "subdued (for him) and strangely personal," giving the impression "that he was involved in some profound struggle with his conscience." Desperately anxious to atone for his absence on Sunday, he announced that he would be marching: "The only way we can achieve freedom is to conquer the fear of death. Man dies when he refuses to stand up for what is right, for what is just, for what is true."[53]

For three hours after the rally, King stayed up to agonize over his decision in the company of Young, Abernathy, and other members of the executive staff. He went over the arguments for not marching that were being pressed on him by the Justice Department: the government would support SCLC in the court hearings; Judge Johnson would decide against Wallace and for the civil rights movement; if the march took place without federal sanction or protection people might be injured or killed. At four in the morning King finally retired, with most of his colleagues urging him to stand firm. An hour later he received a telephone call from Katzenbach, who urged him to postpone the march until after the hearings. King refused. Later in the morning, SCLC's dilemma became excruciating: Judge Johnson handed down an injunction against the march; at eleven-thirty the president released a statement urging all sides to obey the courts.[54]

Wracked by indecision, King placed a conference call to Rustin and Wachtel in New York; with him in Selma were Young, Clarence Jones, and Jack Greenberg. People in Selma suspected some kind of federal conspiracy to throttle a legitimate protest, King complained; the government seemed to be giving the robber three more days of robbery before it allowed a hearing on whether the original robbery had been wrong. There had to be some kind of confrontation, he insisted, so as to expose the brutality of the police. Greenberg, however, urged caution, arguing that if King took the marchers merely to the point of Sunday's attack he could avoid violating the injunction and give the troopers no excuse for resorting to violence. If they agreed not to march, he added, they would be confirming their decision of the previous day, not binding themselves to the injunction. Wachtel emphatically disagreed. Last night, he pointed out, they had decided not to march of their own volition; the injunction, however, represented an intolerable imposition which made it imperative to march. Equally important, the *New York Times* reported an upsurge of support for SCLC: Roy Wilkins was calling for federal troops; sympathy demonstrations had taken place in various Northern cities. The injunction was unconstitutional, he argued; King should ignore it. Rustin agreed: a failure to march might do incalculable damage to both King and the nonviolent movement.[55]

Soon afterwards, however, King received a visit from LeRoy Collins, the head of the Community Relations Service. Collins had been dispatched to Selma with specific instructions from Lyndon Johnson to prevent a violent confrontation, which, in the president's view, meant stopping the march. But Collins realized upon arriving in Selma that this would be next to impossible. He therefore suggested a compromise to King: if he, Collins, could persuade Lingo and Clark to let the marchers alone, would King agree to stop the march at Pettus Bridge and return to Selma after a symbolic confrontation? President Johnson, he added, was determined to enact voting rights legislation as soon as practicable. King recognized a way out when he saw one, and although he gave no firm commitment—he could not guarantee to control the marchers—he was clearly responsive to the idea. Collins hurried off to convince Lingo and Clark to cooperate.[56]

About fifteen hundred would-be marchers had now assembled at Brown Chapel, most of them ready and willing to defy the injunction. Harangued by SNCC workers throughout the morning, they were becoming impatient; as one minister put it, "We didn't come from all over the country just to stand around." If SCLC refused to march,

SNCC would surely march regardless. At about 2:30 P.M., King and Abernathy finally emerged to announce that the demonstration could begin. "There may be beatings, jailings, tear gas," King warned, "But I would rather die on the highways of Alabama than make a butchery of my conscience." Unknown to the marchers, however, King had tacitly agreed to the "partial march" compromise worked out by Collins, who had extracted a commitment from the Wallace forces that they would refrain from using force as long as the marchers halted and turned back when they reached the far side of the Pettus Bridge. As the column set off, Collins handed King a map depicting the route he should take and the exact spot where he should halt the marchers. The tall Floridian then positioned himself by the state troopers, with the intention of restraining any individuals who might break ranks. King adhered to the agreement, turning the marchers around after a brief pause for prayers. Addressing them afterwards, King looked on the bright side: "When Negroes and whites can stand on Highway 80 and have a mass meeting, things aren't that bad."[57]

But some of the marchers felt confused, disappointed, and angry, particularly when the troopers, in a sly move to discomfit King, had parted ranks and left the road to Montgomery invitingly open. The SNCC workers were disgusted by King's apparent duplicity. King, without doubt, was deeply embarrassed by the episode, and spent the next few hours secluded in Brown Chapel while Young and Bevel tried to placate his angry followers. He then departed for Montgomery, staying away from Selma for four days. When he appeared in Johnson's court on March 11, he conceded that "there was a tacit agreement at the bridge that we would go no further," an admission which saved him from a contempt citation but made him appear less than frank in denying the existence of a prior arrangement with Collins.[58] Nevertheless, it is difficult to fault King's decision to obey the injunction. The march may have been anticlimactic, but in accepting the Collins compromise SCLC emphasized its respect for the federal courts, avoided offending Lyndon Johnson, and refrained from an action that would have been widely criticized as irresponsible, provocative, and dangerous. Had King pressed on with the march, the president told Collins afterwards, "the blood would be running knee-deep in the ditches." It would not have been that bad, Collins thought, "but it would have been bad."[59]

The truncated march also failed to diminish the swelling demand, both in and out of Congress, for a law to end disfranchisement once and for all. Even before Bloody Sunday, a major potential obstacle had been removed when Everett Dirksen, the Republican leader in the Senate, declared himself to be in favor of voting rights legislation. After the attack of March 7, the demand for legislative action increased geometrically, as the deeds of the Alabama authorities summoned forth reproach and condemnation. The *New York Times* editorialized that "the scene in Selma resembled that in a police state," and a few days later urged the president to "find a way for the Negroes of the South to win their inalienable rights." The paper also praised King as the symbol of "mature responsible leadership which always seeks peaceful solutions through legal and political means," adding a warning that "young Negro hotheads" would be encouraged if he did not succeed. More significant, perhaps, was the similar editorial position adopted by the *Birmingham News*, which had criticized King so bitterly two years earlier.[60]

The reaction in Congress was equally pronounced: according to Garrow's tally, forty-three congressmen and seven senators called for voting rights legislation on March 9 alone. Outside Congress, Bloody Sunday triggered a wave of sympathy demonstrations, including a march of ten thousand in Detroit led by the mayor and the governor, one of fifteen thousand in Harlem, and a rally in Washington that attracted a similar number. More striking than the size of these demonstrations was the extent of clerical participation. Two hundred nuns went on the Harlem march. In Washington, 150 clergymen attended a meeting called by SCLC's Walter Fauntroy to protest Johnson's "unbelievable lack of action." Fauntroy and Bishop Paul Moore headed a delegation which obtained an audience with the president. Eugene Carson Blake and John Wesley Lord led another clerical delegation, and complained afterwards that Johnson had given them a "snow job." The clerical presence was nowhere stronger than in Selma itself. As Kopkind pointed out, despite its bathetic ending, the March 9 protest had "added the really stunning force of the white clergy; the spontaneous response in a matter of hours to the appeal for help . . . was the most impressive part of the demonstration." White clergymen continued to pour in, and subsequent marches were largely designed, as one SCLC staff member admitted, "to give . . . the ministers something to do before they go home." Richard Hofstadter's description of progressivism could now be applied with even greater accuracy to the civil rights struggle: "No other major movement in American political history . . . had ever received so much clerical sanction."[61]

The continuing protests in Selma were soon overshadowed by events in Montgomery and Washington. In the Alabama capital, hearings on SCLC's application for an injunction against Wallace and Clark began on March 11; five days later a team of NAACP lawyers headed by Greenberg submitted a detailed plan for a five-day march from Selma to Montgomery. Outside the court, while the hearings were still in progress, SNCC mounted a series of marches and sit-ins. The protests reached a violent climax on March 16, when James Forman tried to lead a march from Jackson Street Baptist Church to the Montgomery County Courthouse. The marchers, six hundred strong, found their way blocked by the police, whereupon they sat down on the sidewalk, "becoming increasingly loud and boisterous." When a group led by Forman attempted to cross the street, ten mounted deputies proceeded to break up the demonstration and pursue the fleeing protesters, many of them Northern white students, back to the church.[62] King hastened to show solidarity with SNCC and returned to Montgomery to have a long discussion with Forman about tactics and SCLC-SNCC relations. At a rally attended by twelve hundred people, Forman angrily called for a campaign of civil disobedience in Washington that would "tie up the buses, the trolley cars, and the taxicabs." King, speaking after him, proposed the less drastic alternative of a peaceful, "all-out" march to the Montgomery courthouse. He also demanded a public apology from Sheriff Mac Davis. By all accounts, King's speech made a strong impact, and Forman reluctantly went along with the plan. In the morning, Forman and King led two thousand marchers to the courthouse and, after a lengthy conference with the sheriff, extracted the apology. In return, the black leaders undertook to apply for parade permits before they marched in future.[63]

Relations between SNCC and SCLC remained tense. Forman and other staff members still smarted over King's "betrayal" at the Pettus Bridge on March 9. The SNCC demonstrations in Montgomery had no clear purpose, however, and seemed to function largely as a release for SNCC's anger and frustration over SCLC's dominance in Selma. The journalist Pat Watters called them "ugly, cop-baiting demonstrations." James Bevel criticized SNCC's tactics as irresponsible; warning demonstrators not to fight with the police, he pointed out that "Wallace would love for you to knock a policeman's eye out. Then he could go on television and talk about a one-eyed policeman for two months." The Montgomery protests aroused misgivings within SNCC as well, and when the executive committee met a few weeks later, Forman was subjected to strong criticism.[64]

SNCC's growing irascibility disturbed King. He was well aware that many in SNCC resented his style of leadership, but, as he told Clarence Jones on February 18, "The movement must have a leader, because any ideology is fostered around . . . a leader around whom supporters can rally." SNCC lacked a sense of political timing, he complained: instead of keeping its bitterness towards SCLC within the inner circle, it made its feelings known to the press. Consulting his advisers on March 18, King expressed the fear that Forman's call for civil disobedience might lead to serious violence. But he rejected Rustin's advice that he break with SNCC; instead, he asked Harry Belafonte to help patch up SNCC-SCLC relations.[65]

When Judge Frank Johnson finally approved SCLC's plans for a Selma-to-Montgomery march, Bevel, Young, and Williams spent the days before March 21 trying to persuade SNCC to take part. As always, John Lewis was eager to cooperate, but Forman and others remained hostile to the project. Their arguments were maddeningly inconsistent: they objected to demonstrations, but had just mounted some of the largest in SNCC's history; they accused SCLC of staging marches for the benefit of Northern whites, but had themselves imported several hundred white students to Montgomery. Factionalism, declining morale, and crumbling internal discipline made it increasingly difficult for SNCC to formulate and adhere to a coherent position. In the end SNCC declined to endorse the march but did, in fact, participate.

By the time the march took place, its original purpose had already been fulfilled. On March 13, after a meeting with Governor Wallace, President Johnson finally unveiled the main features of the administration's voting rights proposal and promised to submit it within days rather than weeks or months. Two days later he addressed a joint session of Congress. Paying tribute to Selma as a "turning-point in man's unending search for freedom," Johnson vowed that with this measure, unlike the 1964 civil rights bill, "there must be no delay, or no hesitation, or no compromise with our purpose." On March 17, the same day that Judge Johnson approved the Selma-to-Montgomery march, the administration bill reached the Senate. It proposed to empower the attorney general to suspend literacy and other voting tests, as well as appoint federal registrars, in any state or county where less than half the voting-age population were registered voters on November 1, 1964, or actually cast ballots in the presidential election. The formula covered Louisiana, Mississippi, Alabama, Georgia, South Carolina, Virginia, and North Carolina, but it left out Texas, Arkansas, Florida, and Tennessee.

The introduction of the voting rights bill did not, however, make the march to Montgomery purposeless or redundant. First and foremost, the march gave Southern blacks the most convincing evidence they had yet seen that the federal government had become their firm ally. Not only had a federal court approved the march, but also the president had federalized the Alabama National Guard and deployed troops, marshals, and the FBI to afford the marchers physical protection. No previous civil rights demonstration, not even the March on Washington, had enjoyed what amounted to federal cosponsorship. The march symbolized the defeat of the die-hard segregationists, imparting pride and confidence to blacks throughout the South. The sheer size of the march, and the galaxy of famous leaders and entertainers who participated in some way, intensified its uplifting effect. From SCLC's office in Atlanta, Randolph Blackwell drummed up support by "wiring and telegramming and cabling people to come. . . . I felt that every force that could be rallied should be rallied at this point." The influx of sympathizers swelled the march to some thirty thousand on the final day. Stanley Levison, who flew down from New York to be present at the climax, thought it significant that so many people had made this pilgrimage. "In the Montgomery airport I was struck by the unfamiliarity of the participants," he wrote King. "They were not long-committed white liberals and Negroes. They were new forces from all faiths and classes."[66] All in all, the march provided a magnificent conclusion to the campaign.

King's direction of the protests had been nothing less than masterful. But was Selma a more successful campaign than Birmingham, as Garrow has argued? Judged by the length of time between demonstration and legislation, the difference between Birmingham and Selma does not seem great. The protests in Birmingham began in early April 1963; the civil rights bill was conceived in mid-May and presented to Congress a month later. The Selma campaign started at the beginning of January 1965, but Johnson did not introduce the voting rights bill until mid-March. Admittedly, the voting rights bill had an easier passage through Congress than the earlier measure, which did not become law until July 1964. Even so, the passage of the voting rights bill, completed on August 6, took considerably longer than anticipated, with swift action by the Senate followed by disappointing delays in the House. Given that the circumstances were far more propitious in 1965—the civil rights forces were stronger, the segregationists weaker, and the political climate more auspicious—it is difficult to conclude with any degree of certainty that Selma represented a greater accomplishment than Birmingham.

It would be equally wrong to assume that by 1965 SCLC was simply pushing against an open door. True, President Johnson had, in late 1964, directed the Justice Department to begin work on voting legislation, but this is hardly firm evidence as to his real intentions. The leaders of the NAACP, Roy Wilkins and Clarence Mitchell, had the distinct impression that Johnson was in no hurry to press for further civil rights legislation.[67] If—and the evidence is far from clear on this point—the president intended to proceed with a voting measure in 1965, it was the public reaction to events in Selma that persuaded him to revise his legislative timetable in order to expedite the legislation. The protests at Selma also ensured that the legislative remedy took the form of a congressional bill rather than a time-consuming and cumbersome constitutional amendment. Finally, without Selma it is unlikely that a measure as strong as the voting rights bill could have reached the statute book. The provisions of the Voting Rights Act were far in advance of what the ADA, for example, had deemed politically feasible.[68]

Contemporary observers, especially on the Left, often asserted that SCLC's strategy had been "carefully worked out in consultation with high Administration Liberals."[69] But this view greatly exaggerated the degree of complicity between SCLC and the Johnson administration. To the president, the Selma protests were far from welcome; he disliked demonstrations and, as Eric Goldman tactfully put it, "was no admirer of Martin Luther King." Certainly, King and his colleagues perceived the government as an ally; certainly, as Pat Watters noted, SCLC "knew what the liberals in Washington wanted" and adapted its tactics accordingly. Yet King consistently turned down administration requests to leave the streets and confine the struggle to the courts and ballot boxes. To be sure, King turned round on Pettus Bridge on March 9. However, it was not political pressure that told him to do so, but his own belief that blacks ought to set a moral example to their opponents by obeying the federal courts no matter how painful the consequences. "It was often very confusing—and frustrating—to his followers," Bayard Rustin admitted. "But that was Martin's faith, and he was always the leader."[70]

SAMPLE BALLOT

BALLO

Ten

The Crisis of Victory

The Voting Rights Act represented the crowning achievement of the civil rights movement. Desegregation in public accommodations was already an accomplished fact. Now, with apparently unshakable resolve, the federal government undertook to make universal suffrage a reality. As blacks across the South flocked to the registration offices, the foundations of white supremacy lay in ruins.

Yet the victory of Selma gave way to crisis, not fulfilment. White domination remained a political reality, white prejudice a persisting fact. And the civil rights movement had no program or plan for translating the notional equality of the law into the social actuality of shared wealth and power. Confused, divided, and weary from battle fatigue, the black movement in the South ground to a halt. Within a year, it had virtually disintegrated.

For blacks in the North, now more than half the nation's black population, the reforms of 1964–65 meant little. They could already vote, eat in restaurants, and attend "integrated" schools, yet segregation still circumscribed their lives. "More Negroes attend *de facto* segregated schools today than when the Supreme Court handed down its famous decision," Bayard Rustin noted. "And behind this is the continuing growth of racial slums, spreading over our central cities and trapping Negro youth in a milieu which . . . sows an unimaginable demoralization."[1] Trapped within the ghetto, victimized by poverty, discrimination, police brutality, and political neglect, life often amounted to little more than a daily struggle for survival. Events in the South merely highlighted the magnitude of this social crisis, underlining black powerlessness and pushing black frustration to the boiling point.

Veterans of the New Deal era were often quicker to perceive the danger and challenge of the situation than younger leaders like King. Addressing the twice-postponed Conference of Negro Leaders in January 1965, A. Philip Randolph reminded his audience of the fate of the labor movement in the late 1930s, when the federal legislation it had struggled so long and hard to secure brought "a sense of relaxation and weakened the will to struggle and resulted in the loss of much of its freedom." The greatest danger of counterrevolution, he warned, came at the moment of apparent victory: the civil rights movement was already in decline, while the "white backlash" seemed to be picking up momentum. In order to stave off social reaction and stem the tide of black racism, the civil rights movement had to involve the Negro masses in a new coalition oriented towards social and economic reform. According to Rustin, that coalition should press for radical and thoroughgoing change, because equality could never be achieved "within the framework of existing political and economic relations."[2]

Stanley Levison also saw a parallel with the 1930s, but reached rather different conclusions. The labor movement of that period, he wrote King, had achieved profound and significant changes, even though these stopped short of revolution. By treading a similar reformist path, the civil rights movement could go far in improving the lot of Northern Negroes. Levison doubted the feasibility of the kind of radical coalition envisaged by Rustin; it could certainly not be fashioned out of the existing civil rights coalition, which, he pointed out, had come together to support moderate, gradual reform. This coalition was broad but shallow, he argued: "It is militant only against shocking violence and gross injustice. It is not for deep radical change." It would be a grave tactical error, he warned, to accept Rustin's assertion that equality could be achieved *only* by means of revolutionary change: this was the mistake the Communist party had made in the early 1930s when it contended that "no deep-going improvements were attainable without socialism." Americans were no more ready to accept the need for revolution now than they had been then, yet the lesson of the 1930s showed that important reforms could be accomplished within the existing system.[3]

Both these prognoses, however, turned out to be mistaken. The radical coalition advocated by Randolph and Rustin failed to materialize, and the civil rights coalition demonstrated its fragility and instability by breaking up under the impact of the white backlash, the war in Vietnam, black nationalism, and urban rioting. By 1966 the political climate had changed beyond recognition. Not only were demands for further reform rejected: existing reforms came under attack from the reconstituted alliance of Southern Democrats and Northern Republicans. Congress blunted the thrust of school desegregation, reduced outlays for the War on Poverty, and defeated a civil rights bill. With the "conservative coalition" stymieing reform, the parallel with the 1930s became all too obvious. Moreover, hopes that the Voting Rights Act might liberalize the South received a sharp blow as the political career of George Wallace went from strength to strength and, fuelled by the Northern "white backlash" acquired even greater national significance.

As SCLC moved north to grapple with the economic problems of the big-city ghetto, it found itself caught in the middle of these abrupt and confusing changes. With bewildering suddenness it stood isolated, bereft of political influence. By 1966 SCLC's impotence had become painfully apparent, and King, recognizing the demise of the civil rights movement, embarked on a radical path that eventually led to the Socialist-oriented Poor People's Campaign.

In the afterglow of Selma, the possibility of decline seemed remote. Financially, SCLC had never been better off: between September 1964 and June 1965 its income exceeded $1.5 million, more than double the total for the preceding year. Some contributions were munificent. The Teamsters Union gave twenty-five thousand dollars; Ann Farnsworth, a wealthy heiress, gave an equal amount. But the bulk of SCLC's income came in the form of small donations—the average was ten dollars— from members of the public. Many gifts were unsolicited, but most arrived in response to the various appeals put out by SCLC's New York office. "Utilizing Selma we went far beyond our objective," Adele Kan-

ter reported. Advertisements in the *New York Times* netted fifty thousand dollars; postal appeals to the seventy-five thousand people on
SCLC's mailing list brought in over ten times that amount. All told,
the New York office raised nearly half a million dollars over and above
its running costs. Relying on its regular contributors, Kanter predicted,
"we can conservatively estimate at least a quarter of a million dollars a
year."[4]

What kind of people gave money to SCLC? It was easy enough to
identify contributors by region: they were heavily concentrated in the
Northeastern states, and in Illinois and California. Beyond this, however, SCLC could only guess at the nature of its supporters. Levison
thought that the typical contributor was probably elderly and upper
middle class; Kanter disagreed, claiming that young middle-class
types—especially academics and professionals—predominated. Identifying them by religion was also problematic. Levison speculated that
SCLC had a smaller proportion of Jewish contributors—perhaps only
10 percent of the total—than the other civil rights organizations, and
he worried that its strong Christian identity might be deterring Jews.
King, it must be remembered, raised half of SCLC's income himself
through countless speeches and appearances before colleges, trade
unions, professional groups, churches, and religious organizations. One
fact was beyond doubt: as its income grew, SCLC became increasingly
dependent upon whites for financial support.[5]

The financial windfall produced by Selma enabled SCLC to grow at
a time when falling receipts were forcing SNCC and CORE to contract. By the summer of 1965 SCLC had taken on 125 new workers,
giving it a full-time staff of about 200 people. SCLC now had field
secretaries in every Southern state except Florida and Tennessee. Most
of the new staff members were black Southerners, but they also included many Northerners as well as a sprinkling of whites. Stoney
Cooks, a black student from Indiana, and Melody Heaps, a young
white woman from Chicago, both travelled to Selma on impulse and
signed on as staff members after the march to Montgomery. A few of
the new recruits, like Frank Surrocco and Shirley Mesher, came from
SNCC and CORE. Although the staff remained overwhelmingly black,
the time had long passed when Harry Boyte could be called SCLC's
"token white."[6]

The most important addition to the staff in terms of his impact on
SCLC was a black South Carolina–born divinity student named Jesse
Jackson. While studying at North Carolina A&T, Jackson had played a
leading role in the strong and effective direct action campaign which

shook the city of Greensboro in 1963. Now at the Chicago Theological Seminary, he arrived in Selma after Bloody Sunday with a group of fellow students. "I remember getting a little annoyed," Andrew Young recalled, "because Jesse was giving orders from the steps of Brown's Chapel and nobody knew who he was."[7]

The executive staff underwent little change in 1965. Robert L. Green, a professor at Michigan State University, became director of the Citizenship Education Program, which had been under the nominal supervision of Young. Junius Griffin took over the post of public relations director after the death of Ed Clayton. One change, however, had the most profound implications for SCLC's future. When the board of directors met in Baltimore in April, King asked that Ralph Abernathy be designated "Vice President-at-large"—his automatic successor if he died or became incapacitated. Dumbfounded, the board gave its approval. King's request had come as a bolt from the blue, and nobody was more astonished than C. K. Steele, SCLC's senior vice-president. "I went to his room afterwards and jumped on him about it," Steele recounted years later. King apologized for not consulting him, "and said some other things that I would not go into." King's advisers were appalled by the choice. Few thought that Abernathy possessed the intelligence, ability, or drive to lead SCLC effectively. During staff meetings he had a habit of falling asleep. People could only speculate as to why King made the decision. According to Abernathy, the initiative for the move was King's alone: "He said . . . if there was any one person who could really keep the team together, then it was me." But others suspected that King had given in to his friend's entreaties.[8]

Stanley Levison emerged from exile after Selma to become closely and openly involved again in SCLC's affairs. He had continued to convey occasional advice to King through Clarence Jones, but had had very little direct contact with King since July 1963. When King spotted him at a fundraising concert in New York on April 4, however, he called him over to ask his opinion about SCLC's proposal for an economic boycott of Alabama. A few days later, Levison sent King the lengthy memorandum cited above. King had always been impressed by Levison's political sagacity and organizational skill, and had accepted his exclusion from SCLC with great reluctance. But the political climate had now changed, King felt, and in May 1965 he invited Levison back into his circle of advisers. Levison soon became immersed in SCLC's fundraising activities. He also joined the research committee and began attending SCLC staff meetings and retreats. According to Levison, when he raised the question of whether it was wise for them to work together again, King replied, "There's nothing to hide. And if anybody wants to make something of it, let them try."[9]

One of Levison's first pieces of advice to King was to drop the Alabama boycott. The boycott idea had originated with Bevel, who envisaged the Selma protests as merely the opening phase of a much larger campaign. Instead of being satisfied with the voting rights bill, Bevel argued, SCLC should insist on the immediate participation of blacks in the government of Alabama; it had to expose Wallace and the legislature as an undemocratic and illegitimate regime, forcing the federal government to supervise new state elections on the basis of a free and universal franchise. Bevel pressed for a direct action campaign in Montgomery of at least a month's duration, accompanied by a nationwide economic boycott of Alabama. If, as he anticipated, the protests culminated in thousands of arrests, SCLC could then appeal to foreign nations to join in the boycott. Explaining his plan to SNCC, he argued that whites in Alabama should be compelled to choose between "eating and fucking around with Negroes." If they responded with further repression, "we want the federal government to come in here, register Negroes, and throw out the present government as un-Constitutional."[10]

Hosea Williams, on the other hand, argued that SCLC ought to concentrate on voter registration and had drawn up a plan for a program, "Summer Community Organization and Political Education" (SCOPE), which called for the recruitment of one thousand Northern students to work in 120 Black Belt counties. Williams's program had much to commend it. SCLC had often been accused of neglecting voter registration. It had wanted to mount such a drive for some time, and finally had the money to finance it. SCOPE appealed to the board of directors; it also received a warm welcome from the affiliates, which often complained about lack of contact and support from Atlanta. Above all, SCOPE was a logical follow-up to the Selma campaign, and had the obvious attraction of taking advantage of the voting rights bill, which SCLC expected to become law shortly.

King hesitated to decide against either plan. He did not relish the prospect of further demonstrations so soon after Selma; that campaign had exhausted the staff, himself included, and he felt that the voting rights bill gave SCLC a valid reason to call "Victory" and pause for a rest. Yet Bevel had proved himself to be a resourceful tactician—he and Diane had, after all, put together the plan which resulted in Selma. King found the boycott idea appealing. He had briefly considered a boycott of Mississippi, in conjunction with SNCC, at the end of 1964.

With Wallace still obdurate after Selma, and with white terrorism on the rise, why not try it in Alabama? SCLC's internal politics, moreover, made King reluctant to reject the boycott idea out of hand: Bevel and Williams were bitter rivals, and he did not wish to side with one against the other. There were, in addition, people on the executive staff who doubted Williams's organizing abilities and strongly opposed entrusting the entire field staff to his control.[11]

Torn between the two proposals, King approved both. After a two-day staff meeting in Selma, he decided to press ahead with a national economic boycott of Alabama, with the aim of free elections and an end to violence. Unveiling the plan on the March 28 edition of "Meet the Press," he disclosed that SCLC would call the boycott for an initial period of ten days, extending and escalating it according to Wallace's response. Two days later, a delegation led by Joseph Lowery met the governor for an hour and a half; they asked him for evening and weekend voter registration hours, the removal of the poll tax, the employment and upgrading of blacks by state agencies, and the curtailment of violence and police brutality. "We didn't attack him in any vicious manner," said Lowery, "but I did try to impress him with the moral responsibility that was his."[12]

On April 2, at the Baltimore board meeting, King elaborated on the proposed "escalated economic withdrawal" from Alabama. The first stage called upon businesses to stop building new plants in the state and halt the expansion of existing ones; SCLC also expected the federal government to enforce Title VI of the 1964 Civil Rights Act by cancelling grants, loans, and contracts if it found racial discrimination in federally assisted programs. If the boycott moved into stage two, SCLC would ask churches, trade unions, corporations, and other private institutions to remove their investments from the state. The third stage involved a consumer boycott of goods produced by companies which, like the Hammerhill Paper Company, persisted in locating new plants in Alabama. The board approved the plan in spite of strong misgivings. The Atlanta office put out, under King's name, a lavishly produced pamphlet explaining the boycott—*An Open Letter to the American People.*[13]

King's Northern advisers regarded the Alabama boycott as impractical and misguided. Rustin thought it "stupid," and warned the SCLC board that it would cause an effusion of white support.[14] Levison argued that SCOPE, not a boycott of Alabama, represented the logical next step after a struggle for voting rights. "The casual manner of proposing the boycott and the impression that this was your central program caused deep disquiet," he told King. And so it did. The *New York Times*, which had backed King so forthrightly during the Selma campaign, called the boycott "wrong in principle and . . . unworkable in practice." Northern governors like Mark Hatfield of Oregon and Edmund Brown of California refused to support it. The NAACP and the Urban League were distinctly cool towards the idea. President Johnson emphatically opposed it. Most damaging of all, the boycott attracted little backing from organized labor and received near universal condemnation from businessmen. Speaking to the Bar Association of New York on April 21, King defended the boycott as a form of civil disobedience, recalling the boycott of British merchants before the Revolution and Jefferson's trade embargo during the Napoleonic Wars. "Is there no parallel here which commends itself to you?" he asked, almost plaintively. In truth, the parallels were farfetched, and the speech won few converts. Two days earlier, during a visit to Selma, King had already indicated that he might cancel the boycott if SCLC decided that "enough progress had been made."[15]

The direct action phase of Bevel's plan also misfired. Some blacks considered the plan too radical; others were simply exhausted and, like Frederick Reese of Selma, wanted to suspend demonstrations. In the event, it proved difficult to spread the protests into surrounding Black Belt counties. Although SCLC had bases in Perry and Wilcox counties, it failed to establish a bridgehead in Lowndes and had trouble expanding into Hale and Greene. In Greensboro, Hale County, it took two weeks to gain access to a meeting place, and no demonstrations occurred until July. In Eutaw, Greene County, SCLC staff members were twice "run out of town" by conservative blacks. Demopolis, in Marengo County, proved more welcoming, and beginning on April 15 SCLC mounted daily marches to the courthouse. Even so, the Black Belt failed to catch fire.[16]

In mid-May, King formally opened "Phase Two" of the Alabama campaign with a call for demonstrations outside the capitol building in Montgomery. But people failed to show up to the mass meetings in any strength, and the turnout for a demonstration on May 25 was embarrassingly small. SCLC received little help from the Montgomery Improvement Association, whose conservative-minded leaders wished to avoid a confrontation with the city administration. Jesse Douglas, the MIA's president, complained to Randolph Blackwell that "the relationship between SCLC workers and the MIA workers is at an all time low." According to Douglas, Bevel's staff treated the MIA office with scandalous disrespect: "Reports are: gambling, stealing, disrespectful conduct, opening of mail, discarding of mail, breaking of locks, entering unlawfully, thievery, etc." Without the MIA behind it, SCLC found it impossible to build a strong local base. By the end of May, "Phase Two" had fizzled out, and the Alabama boycott was quietly dropped. It had been a "verbal threat," Shuttlesworth explained. "We just threw it up in the air to show Alabama officials we could do something more than just march, sing and talk."[17]

In Selma itself, the pullout of SCLC staff and the continuing intransigence of the city council produced a feeling of frustration and disappointment. Biracial discussions began on April 7, but they produced no significant concessions. A boycott of downtown stores collapsed, and the local black leadership dissolved into quarreling factions. Once again, SCLC found itself accused of abandoning a community after using it for its own ends. Even SCLC's friends expressed concern. The Reverend John B. Morris, director of the Episcopal Society for Cultural and Racial Unity, complained to Young that the meetings at Brown Chapel were breaking up "for lack of leadership"; blacks still needed guidance and inspiration from Bevel, Williams, Vivian, or King. When Blackwell visited Selma on May 5 he found blacks confused, divided, and often hostile towards SCLC. The administration of relief supplies, in particular, was causing grave discontent.[18]

King eventually sent Harold Middlebrook, a junior but experienced staff member, to repair some of the damage. And that proved no easy task. By sorting out the relief program and organizing a voter registration drive, Middlebrook helped to rebuild the movement and restore morale. But the Dallas County Voters League still felt impotent in the face of the city council. "The situation is so demoralizing," Reese told King in November, "that our people are fast losing patience." The fact that the DCVL had always been a weak organization—it had been set up by SNCC and enjoyed little support from local ministers—made SCLC's failure to provide adequate leadership after Selma all the more lamentable.[19]

The aftermath in Selma also highlighted a growing division between SCLC and SNCC over political strategy, a disagreement that foreshadowed the later ideological clash over "Black Power." By 1965 SNCC was committed to the development of independent political parties for blacks at the state and local level—"Freedom Democratic" parties. Its first real attempt to implement this strategy came in the Alabama Black Belt, and grew up alongside SCLC's own expansion into Selma and the surrounding countryside. In Dallas County, SNCC supported a splinter party, the Dallas County Freedom Organization, which opposed the DCVL's strategy of supporting Wilson Baker in his bid to oust Jim Clark from the sheriff's office. Andrew Young tried to patch up the quarrel by arguing that Baker represented an acceptable transition between the old order and the new. To SNCC, however, Baker and Clark were interchangeable. Most blacks supported the DCVL's line, and Baker defeated Clark with the help of strong black support in 1966.[20]

Nevertheless, the split in Dallas County raised the larger question of SNCC-SCLC relations, especially with regard to SCOPE. Some SNCC workers strongly opposed SCOPE, and believed that SNCC should refuse to cooperate with it. "It will be the same shit as in Selma," grumbled Silas Norman, SNCC's Alabama project director, "where the SCLC executives are gone and have left the flunkies." A thousand white students meant "a thousand individuals each with their own private program." Annie Pearl Avery, who worked in Hale County, registered SNCC's long-standing complaint that "SCLC will come in after SNCC does the ground work. All SCLC has is King and Reverends."[21] Selma, of course, had brought SNCC's criticisms of SCLC into sharp focus. On March 7, John Lewis and Silas Norman had written King to complain of a "lack of effort, and a serious unwillingness on the part of key SCLC staff . . . to deal honestly with SNCC."[22]

But the desire to cooperate with SCLC outweighed such complaints. When SNCC's executive staff met in Holly Springs, Mississippi, experienced staff members like Marion Barry, Ivanhoe Donaldson, and John Lewis agreed that it would be folly to openly criticize SCLC. "What we have to do is to try to radicalize King," argued Barry. "Those of us who have been around for a while can see the great change in King, and there are members of SCLC who are pushing for the same thing."[23] On April 20, SNCC and SCLC held a joint meeting in Atlanta, with Harry Belafonte acting as umpire, to thrash out their differences. It helped to clear the air. "In terms of overall goals, SCLC is very radical," reported Stokely Carmichael, a tall and articulate veteran of the Mississippi project who was now working in Lowndes County. "King said economic problems were the real issues of the country, but didn't know how to get to them. . . . I think the cats are honest." Carmichael, one of the most forceful advocates of cooperation, argued that SNCC, rather than ignoring SCLC, should turn King's mass appeal to its own advantage by organizing in the same counties. SCLC had gained access to the churches in Hale County, he pointed out, when SNCC had failed. If SNCC established a solid local base, "the students coming down with SCOPE will have to come to the SNCC workers. The same holds true for King. . . . The people will follow King, but he'll still have to go through the SNCC workers." Here lay the germ of the tactic which Carmichael used with such spectacular success during the Meredith March in 1966.[24]

SNCC and SCLC cemented their rapprochement on April 30, at a second joint conference. On one issue, however, they failed to reach agreement. Allegations of Communist influence within SNCC had been receiving considerable publicity, most notably in the widely syndicated newspaper column by Robert Novak and Rowland Evans. SNCC could more easily refute such charges, King argued, if it openly renounced communism and abjured Communist support. The previous year he had urged SNCC to reject help from the National Lawyers Guild. Then as now, however, SNCC insisted on a policy of nonexclusion, and Lewis and Forman refused to issue the kind of disclaimer which King thought politic. The disagreement is interesting in that it provides another illustration of King's persistent concern to defend the civil rights movement from allegations of communism.[25]

SCOPE finally got under way at the end of May. The volunteers were self-selected in that Williams asked Northern colleges to do their own recruiting after "adopting" one of the Black Belt counties on SCLC's list. Bayard Rustin organized the training sessions in Atlanta. In addition to the usual indoctrination into nonviolence, the volunteers received talks on politics and voter registration from Young, Clarence Mitchell, and Norman Hill. Anxious to avoid some of the tensions and problems which had arisen from the influx of white students into Mississippi in 1964, Rustin told the volunteers to dress conservatively, behave modestly, and defer to the local SCLC affiliate. Demonstrations, unless authorized by Williams, were forbidden. SCOPE turned out to be far smaller than originally envisaged. King and Williams claimed that 650 students took part, but the SCLC records show that only about 300 attended the training sessions, and the project covered 51 counties rather than 120.[26]

SCOPE produced only a modest rise in black registration. By mid-August, SCLC claimed to have added 26,000 new voters, but this estimate is a liberal one. The disappointing results stemmed, in part, from the unexpectedly late passage of the voting rights bill, which did not become law until August 6. Before then, most applicants were rejected. In Selma, for example, the drive led by Harold Middlebrook produced only 56 new voters out of 1,470 applications. By the time the Voting Rights Act took effect, SCOPE had less than a month to run, and the departure of the students after Labor Day "brought many voter registration drives to an almost complete halt."[27]

In Georgia, about one hundred SCOPE volunteers worked in fifteen counties. They often encountered tough white opposition. Repression summoned forth demonstrations when Williams lifted the ban on direct action at the end of July. In Crawfordville, Taliaferro County, SCOPE workers were beaten and jailed, and SCLC used marches, picketing, and an economic boycott in an effort to desegregate the town. A high school principal and five teachers were fired by the board of education for their connection with SCOPE. Later, when SCLC pressed for school desegregation, whites in Crawfordville retaliated by firing their maids and domestic workers.[28] SCOPE also moved into the surrounding counties of Lincoln, Warren, and Wilkes. Among the poorest in Georgia, these northeastern counties represented virgin territory for the civil rights movement. "For virtually all of the white people here," the *New York Times* observed, "resistance of one kind or another appears to be the reaction to Negro protests." In terms of new black voters, the results were meager.[29]

Southwest Georgia remained equally hostile. In Americus, where SNCC had been working since 1963, SCOPE volunteers from Washington State University managed to register only forty-five blacks in a month. When four Negroes were arrested on July 20 for standing in the "white" line during a local election, Williams sent Ben Van Clarke and Willie Bolden, his young lieutenants from the Savannah movement, to organize demonstrations. At a press conference on July 26, Williams and John Lewis demanded a new election, the release of those arrested, longer registration hours, the appointment of black registrars, and a biracial committee. A federal court soon freed the prisoners, but SCLC pressed on with demonstrations and began a boycott of white-owned stores. As Bolden put it, "From now on, we're going to live black, sleep black, buy black, walk black, and wear black." City and county officials resisted the demand for a biracial committee, but after semiofficial talks instigated by Sumter County Attorney Warren Fortson—who was later forced to leave Americus when Clarke publicly revealed his role as a mediator—the county agreed to appoint three black polling clerks. In the space of two days, 647 blacks were registered. Within a week there were 1,500. Neither Sumter nor any other county in Georgia, however, received federal registrars in 1965.[30]

In Alabama, about eighty SCOPE workers and a dozen full-time staff members operated in fifteen counties. Outside the urban centers, the events in Selma had done little to soften white opposition to black voting. When SCLC moved into Hale County, for example, where blacks made up two-thirds of the population, local whites reacted "with revulsion and cold fury."[31] Landlords evicted tenants; families fired their servants; two black churches were burned to the ground. When SCLC held marches in Greensboro to protest the use of the literacy test, the police arrested nearly five hundred people and broke up one demonstration with tear gas. Judge Daniel Thomas refused to issue an injunction against the police, and although he voided the literacy test, he allowed the county registrars to devise an "easier" one. Shortly afterwards, Hale became one of six Alabama counties to receive federal examiners, and black registration rose from 236 at the beginning of August to 3,242 by September 25. The increases in the other five counties were also impressive: 295 to 4,257 in Marengo, 320 to 6,789 in Dallas, 289 to 2,466 in Perry, 0 to 1,496 in Lowndes, and 0 to 6,085 in Wilcox.[32]

But elsewhere in Alabama and the South the increase in registration was far less spectacular, partly because the Justice Department sent federal examiners into only twenty-four counties between August 6 and late October. In counties without federal examiners, restrictive and discriminatory practices continued to disfranchise blacks. In Alabama, for example, most counties allowed voter registration during the business hours of the first and third Mondays of each month. Thus on August 16, 600 blacks stood in line outside the Barbour County Courthouse in Eufaula, but only 265 managed to fill out application forms. In Butler County, 568 waited; 107 registered. The pattern repeated itself throughout much of Alabama, Georgia, and the Carolinas. In all but eleven counties of North Carolina, the registration offices stayed shut until October. Results were particularly dire in Georgia, where black registration increased by only sixteen thousand between August 6, 1965, and January 14, 1966. The corresponding figures for Alabama and Mississippi were one hundred thousand and seventy-six thousand. This disparity is explained by the fact that the Justice Department sent no federal registrars to Georgia until the spring of 1967.[33]

King soon became strongly critical of the manner in which the Voting Rights Act was being enforced. On August 5, he had urged the president to appoint federal registrars in all the counties covered by the legislation. But during the twelve months following the passage of the bill, the government appointed registrars in only forty-two counties—fewer than one-fifth of the number eligible. The attorney general, Nicholas Katzenbach, defended this policy of selective enforcement by stressing the extent of voluntary compliance and by arguing that "the most important generating factor [in black voter registration] is local organization." Without local registration drives, he claimed, "even the presence of [federal] examiners has been of limited gain." But King poured scorn on these arguments. In a report to SCLC's administrative committee on November 12, he complained that the Voting Rights Act had not received adequate federal support. Armed with statistics from the Civil Rights Commission, he pointed out that counties with federal registrars in Alabama experienced double the increase in black registration of counties without federal registrars. The level of registration in Barbour County, for example, was only about one-third that of Wilcox. "To expect a Black Belt Negro to face up to the hometown court house of George Corley Wallace is asking just a little bit too much."[34]

King also worried that the growth of black registration was being stunted by white violence and intimidation, which showed no sign of abating. Indeed, 1965 saw an alarming rise in the number of civil rights–related murders: twenty people were killed that year, compared to fourteen in 1964 and thirteen in 1963. Eleven of the 1965 murders took place in Alabama and Mississippi, and no convictions had been obtained in any of these cases. Murder represented the crest of a swelling wave of white aggression. The Southern Regional Council compiled a list of 122 acts of intimidation, reprisal, and violence that took place between September 1965 and February 1966, and the list was by no means exhaustive. The bigotry of Southern courts encouraged white violence by conferring immunity on the known murderers of civil rights activists. In September a Lowndes County jury acquitted Deputy Sheriff Tom Coleman of the murder of Jonathan Daniels, a young white seminarian who was working with Stokely Carmichael. The fatal shooting had taken place in broad daylight and in sight of numerous witnesses. A month later the alleged killer of Viola Liuzzo, a Northern volunteer who had been murdered while driving between Selma and Montgomery on March 25, was acquitted by another Alabama jury. When he learned of this verdict on October 23, King vowed to seek new legislation to reform the system of jury selection and make homicide a federal crime. A week later, after a two-day conference in Selma, SCLC announced a "campaign for equal justice" to force action from the government. SNCC and the American Civil Liberties Union pledged their support. "Katzenbach may dread the thought," King told the administrative committee, "but a second Reconstruction may be necessary, . . . a reconstruction of the courts, the juries, the registration and election procedures, and control of the Klan."[35]

On November 6, SCLC decided to concentrate its staff in Alabama, so that the "campaign for equal justice" could run in tandem with an intensive voter registration drive. It had become obvious that SCLC was spread far too thinly in the South. By focusing on Alabama, which had more federal registrars than any other state, SCLC hoped to facilitate the election of Negroes in the Black Belt and help defeat George Wallace—to be more accurate, his wife, Lurleen—in the 1966 state elections. Hosea Williams's preelection strategy called for a two-pronged drive: one in the Black Belt; the other in the cities of Birmingham, Montgomery, Mobile, Dothan, and Tuscaloosa.[36]

Confusion of purpose, however, dogged the new Alabama campaign: was it a direct action movement or a voter registration drive? Despite a morale-boosting visit by King in early December, the "campaign for equal justice" turned out to be a damp squib. Reporting to the SCLC board, Williams attributed its failure to black apathy and white repression, but poor tactics also played a part. The marches failed to elicit white violence, and in Greenville marchers actually hurled stones at the police. In Greene County, Sheriff Lee simply allowed the marches to proceed without let or hindrance, and they soon became, in the words of the *Richmond Afro-American*, "an almost uneventful series of strolls." The *Southern Courier*, a movement paper, complained that the demonstrations were badly planned and poorly directed: "The SCLC leaders have not been very careful about explaining the aims of the marches to the people." SNCC gave the protests little active support. They might have attracted greater publicity had they been staged in Lowndes County, scene of the Liuzzo and Daniels murders, but now a SNCC enclave.[37]

In Birmingham, SCLC's strongest urban base, the campaign failed to get off the ground. Ben Mack, an assistant to Hosea Williams, met the board of the ACMHR on November 11 to explain SCLC's plans for demonstrations. However, as a police surveillance report noted, "It seems that they are very confused about the strategy." SCLC proposed a forty-five-day drive to register some of the eighty thousand unregistered blacks—two-thirds of the adult black population of Jefferson County—while at the same time staging marches around the "equal justice" theme. But the ACMHR showed little enthusiasm for demonstrating on behalf of "equal justice." If marches were to be held at all, Calvin Wood argued, they should deal with the issue of employment, for there were still no black firemen or policemen. Joseph Lowery, on the other hand, thought that demonstrations would be futile because, in his opinion, the personnel board was to blame rather than the mayor or city council. The ACMHR finally agreed that voter registration, coupled with a demand for federal examiners, should provide the focus of the campaign. The drive began shortly before Christmas.[38]

The Birmingham drive soon exposed divisions within the local black leadership as well as friction between the ACMHR and SCLC. A. G. Gaston, the black millionaire who had backed the 1963 campaign, now embarrassed SCLC by criticizing the marches that began in early January. Gaston's opposition was all the more irritating in view of his frequent contact with Mayor Boutwell, who virtually ignored the ACMHR. At a mass meeting on January 11, Shuttlesworth and Williams told Gaston to "keep his mouth shut," and Williams urged blacks to boycott Gaston's numerous businesses. Shuttlesworth's own leadership, however, had come under increasing criticism. Since 1962 Shuttlesworth had resided in Cincinnati, and his refusal to relinquish the ACMHR presidency struck many as selfish and unreasonable. He was also embroiled in a dispute with his own congregation, a section of which had called for his resignation. By 1966, others in the ACMHR, notably Ed Gardner, aspired to the leadership. Joseph Lowery was another potential contender. Lowery, like Shuttlesworth a found-ing member of SCLC and now chairman of the SCLC board, moved to a pastorate in Birmingham in early 1965. Modest, moderate, but also intelligent and assertive, he soon gravitated to a position of influence. He was critical of both Shuttlesworth and Williams. A conference with Andrew Young and several visits by King helped to quiet the infighting and swing the quarreling clerics into line.[39]

In spite of the dissension, the campaign had a successful outcome. On January 20 the Justice Department appointed more than twenty federal registrars in Jefferson County. Boutwell attacked the decision on television, pointing out that the board of registrars had already extended its working week from three days to five, including Satur-days, and that Jefferson had "the best record . . . of any county in any state in the Southeast." But John Doar, the assistant attorney general, insisted that racial discrimination still persisted: the registrars "re-jected as 'illiterate' Negroes who were as literate as many accepted white applicants," used the application form "as a strict test for Negroes but not for white persons," and rejected blacks on the basis of personal questions that were not asked of whites. One thousand blacks registered on the first day of federal registration. During the next month, some thirteen thousand more were added to the voter rolls.[40]

By the end of 1965, however, SCLC's field staff was seething with discontent. Part of their frustration stemmed from SCLC's hit-and-run tactics; when they put down roots in a local community, staff mem-bers often resented being suddenly redeployed elsewhere. King some-times warned his staff not to become too attached to their communities. "He made a speech," James Orange recalled, "saying that we were shacking with the community . . . [and] we weren't gonna marry the community. Our job was to get stuff started and then move on and get stuff started in other areas." But many staff members found it demoralizing to be continually shifted from place to place, often not knowing where they were going to be from one week to the next. The arrogance and aloofness of the executive staff also caused profound dissatisfaction. Members of the field staff persistently complained of being ignored or, at best, fobbed off with white lies and promises that were never fulfilled. Placing the field staff under the insensitive and overbearing Williams merely exacerbated the situation. "You don't realize the strength of your own personality," Young wrote Williams. "I am sure that you don't mean to abuse people, but quite often you do."[41]

Williams's administration of SCLC's voter registration program provoked a string of complaints from the student volunteers, the affiliates, the research committee, and the executive staff. The most frequent criticism was that promised funds and help failed to materialize. The president of the Petersburg Improvement Association protested that a colleague had to journey to Atlanta and confront Williams in person in order to have SCOPE workers sent to Virginia.[42] The field staff, one volunteer wrote Williams, "in many cases feel that assistance from HQ is hardly worth the time and effort required to obtain it. A case in point: some supplies long promised the Monroe project, all available at HQ, never arrived, despite repeated personal and telephone requests and promises."[43] Randolph Blackwell was appalled by SCOPE's waste, inefficiency, and indiscipline. At an executive staff meeting he accused Williams of "empire-building," and in an angry letter to King he urged an immediate end to the project: "It has cost freedom contributors ten times what it should have. . . . The operation has raised suspicion of financial dishonesty. And, there has been the most dangerous kind of irresponsible quest for publicity." SCLC's auditor was shocked by Williams's extravagance; unless it were curbed, he warned King, "the job you are paying me to do will be impossible." The Reverend F. R. Rowe of Fitzgerald, Georgia, called SCOPE "the worst run program I have ever seen." Observing Williams's efforts from the distance of New York, Bayard Rustin and Stanley Levison came to a similar verdict.[44]

SCOPE in many ways exemplified SCLC's organizational weaknesses and highlighted the differing conceptions held by the preachers and the intellectuals of the kind of organization SCLC ought to be. Intellectuals like Blackwell and Levison abhorred SCLC's waste, inefficiency, and maladministration; they constantly pressed upon King their own ideas for giving SCLC organizational strength and stability.

SCLC needed to professionalize its fundraising, they argued, forge closer links with the affiliates, strengthen its administration, and develop sound financial practices. Blackwell told King that "the conflict between myself and Mr. Williams . . . goes to the bottom of the philosophy of the organization. It raises in a very serious way the question of whether we can at this point develop the structural discipline needed."[45] SCLC's preachers, on the other hand—and Williams, despite his lay background, could be counted among them—prized spontaneity and religious inspiration above bureaucratic notions of professionalism and efficiency. Whereas Levison complained about the amateurishness of SCLC's fundraising efforts, Abernathy prided himself on the fact that "this is a faith operation, and somehow, when we need the money, it's always there."[46] The preachers were oriented towards action, not administration; towards protest rather than programs. They often broke the organization's rules with reckless abandon. Writing about SNCC's view of leadership, James Forman noted that "what had been born as an affirmation became a simplistic negation." This was sometimes equally true of SCLC's attitude towards efficiency.[47]

King, of course, was both a preacher and an intellectual, and he possessed a critical awareness of the need for both structure and spontaneity. He wanted SCLC to acquire a mass membership, develop a sounder administration, and devise a more professional system of fundraising. In order to strengthen its organizational structure, however, SCLC required programmatic continuity; it needed to lay down roots. And this went against its very grain—as King told Orange, SCLC should be agitating in one place after another. Confrontation and challenge were part of King's makeup, and Williams, Bevel, and Young each shared these qualities to some degree. The "call of battle," as Wachtel put it, always came before organizational self-interest.[48] The battle in the South appeared to be won; as Bevel told the SCLC convention in August, the civil rights movement had ceased to exist from the moment Lyndon Johnson signed the Voting Rights Act.[49] In fact, the battle in the South was far from over, but, having mortally wounded the dragon of Southern segregation, SCLC instinctively turned to face the Goliath of Northern discrimination. "It is time to start thinking about where we are going after we are through with the Alabama Black Belt," Bevel argued. "We will go to Harlem, and do something about housing and income. . . . Then we will go to South Africa and start a movement there. After that we want to find a way to use nonviolence instead of war and armaments."[50]

War and armaments were very much in the news by the summer of 1965, as the American military buildup in South Vietnam continued apace. In July the number of U.S. troops in that embattled country surpassed seventy-five thousand, and President Johnson, claiming that his own search for peace had been stymied by Hanoi, declared that no ceiling existed as far as troop levels were concerned. By October, America's army in Vietnam had doubled and was still growing.[51]

This turn of events appalled King. From the very beginning of the 1965 escalation, he regarded the administration's policy as thoroughly misguided. Pacifism, of course, had become deeply rooted in King's philosophical outlook. His opposition to the war, however, also rested upon a political base. King appraised the Vietcong insurgency as a nationalist revolt against a corrupt and oppressive regime; the United States, in seeking to extirpate that revolt, had adopted a policy tantamount to neocolonialism. King took care not to reveal his sympathy for the insurgents, but on May 11, during a tour of the Alabama Black Belt, he urged the administration to negotiate with the Vietcong. A month later, speaking in Petersburg, he raised the possibility of an organized campaign against the war: "There is no reason why there can't be peace rallies like we have freedom rallies."[52]

There was a certain irony in the fact that King's advisers were urging King to be cautious about moving north while at the same time encouraging him to speak out on Vietnam. On July 22, at a meeting called by King, the research committee agreed that a resolution should be presented to the SCLC convention supporting King's position and calling upon the delegates to work for peace. It was also ironic that the president himself inadvertently encouraged King to launch a peace initiative by assuring him of the administration's eagerness to negotiate. At the suggestion of Rustin and Wachtel, therefore, King decided to use SCLC's annual convention as a public platform from which to launch a dramatic peace initiative. Addressing the convention on August 12, he asked Johnson to make an "unconditional and unambiguous statement" declaring his willingness to negotiate with the National Liberation Front, the political arm of the Vietcong. As a demonstration of good faith, the United States should stop its bombing campaign, while North Vietnam should drop its insistence upon the immediate, unilateral withdrawal of American forces. Both sides should be prepared to accept mediation by the UN. To break the present deadlock, King proposed to write to Ho Chi Minh, U Thant, and other involved leaders.[53]

But King had walked into a political mine field. Neither he nor his advisers anticipated the hostile reaction that ensued. The enormity of their miscalculation could be seen in the fact that SCLC's board of directors, that most docile of bodies, refused for once to act as a rubber stamp. When Andrew Young apprised the board of King's plan, there were immediate objections from C. K. Steele, Joseph Lowery, and other senior members. "I don't think SCLC is structured to go into this kind of complex, difficult and confusing area," stated Lowery. At the instance of L. D. Reddick, the board voted to refer the matter to its resolutions committee. By the time King spoke to the full convention, Rustin and Young, who had to draft an acceptable resolution, clearly sensed the deep unease among the delegates. In his own speech on August 11, Young advocated caution. "We are as much against the war in Vietnam as anyone," he affirmed, "but let us not abandon our tried and trusted methods of producing social change to get on a band-wagon that's playing a 'square' tune." The only sure road to peace, he argued, was "the long haul of building . . . an enlightened electorate." On August 13, Young and Rustin concocted a resolution which, in effect, disassociated SCLC from King's initiative.[54]

King soon found himself out on a limb. According to one opinion poll, only about a quarter of the public thought that "the United States had made a mistake sending troops to fight in Vietnam."[55] Johnson was at the peak of his popularity, and he enjoyed the support of conservatives and liberals alike in his firm stand against what Vice-President Humphrey called "militant, aggressive Asian Communism, with its headquarters in Peking, China." Many liberals, including Humphrey, had decided to swallow their doubts about the war in order to retain the president's favor. Instead of eliciting praise, therefore, King's proposal evoked scornful and often condescending derision. One of the few organs to support him, the well-meaning but little-read *Nation* magazine, complained that King was "deluged by threatening editorials and cartoons." *Time*, which did not turn against the war until the end of 1967, scolded King for "confusing the cause."[56]

The rest of the civil rights movement cold-shouldered King. Civil rights groups regarded themselves as single-issue organizations, and this was as true of SNCC and CORE as it was of the NAACP and the Urban League. James Farmer fought successfully to defeat an anti-war resolution at CORE's own annual convention. To have opposed the war would have been "too easy a cop-out," he later explained; "it would simply confuse the issue." Not even SNCC had yet taken a formal stand against the administration's actions in Vietnam. The peace movement had no grassroots work going on, James Forman argued;

SNCC would make a tactical mistake if it shifted its focus to the war issue. The venerable Socialist A. Philip Randolph doubted that civil rights leaders had any "mandate from the Negro masses" to oppose the administration over Vietnam. Broadly speaking, he was probably correct. According to a poll commissioned by *Newsweek*, only 18 percent of blacks favored U.S. withdrawal. Bayard Rustin was astonished by the negative response to King's initiative which he encountered in Harlem. Blacks did not consider the war their problem, he told Wachtel. They wanted King to stop talking about Vietnam and concentrate on racial discrimination.[57]

Lyndon Johnson was incensed by King's naive attempt at peacemaking. His professed desire for a negotiated settlement, however, made it difficult for the president to openly attack King. He therefore employed a subtle combination of flattery, duplicity, and pressure in order to induce King to drop his initiative. He spoke to King personally, telling him that secret negotiations hung in the balance; Arthur Goldberg, the liberal Supreme Court judge who had recently become U.S. ambassador to the UN, would be glad to brief him on the diplomatic background. Meeting King on September 10, Goldberg confirmed that peace was, indeed, close at hand, but warned King not to say anything which might encourage Ho Chi Minh to stiffen his position. To make the message quite plain, Senator Thomas Dodd of Connecticut stated that King possessed "absolutely no competence" in foreign affairs and had "alienated much of the support he previously enjoyed in Congress."[58]

King knew very well that the senator was a confidant of the president: "I'm convinced that Lyndon Johnson got Dodd to say this," he told his advisers during a telephone conference. The administration seemed intent on cutting him down, he noted, and the press was stacked up against him. Rustin and Wachtel had already discussed King's dilemma and concluded that he should drop his Vietnam initiative; if he continued to involve himself in foreign policy, Rustin warned, his opponents "are going to come down on him like a house on fire." Levison agreed, arguing that King ought to keep quiet about Vietnam and remain a civil rights leader rather than become a peace leader. King, by now, needed little persuading. "I really don't have the strength to fight this issue and keep my civil rights fight going," he conceded. He already felt "overloaded . . . and emotionally fatigued," and could not afford a battle with the administration. "I think we have to admit that I am going too far." On September 28, after another conference call, he decided to withdraw his plan to write to Ho Chi Minh. Levison became somewhat exasperated, however, when King suggested that his statement of retraction should condemn the war as immoral. "Martin," he told him, "we've just gone over this and decided that you're not the person to do this." On October 5 King issued his recantation. As he admitted to his staff in 1967, "My name then wouldn't have been written in any book called *Profiles of Courage*."[59]

By the time of King's climb down, preparations for a Northern campaign had become SCLC's top priority. Before August, its plans had proceeded at a leisurely pace. In April the board gave its reluctant approval for a Northern "pilot project." Immediately afterwards, King conferred with twenty black leaders in New York and won their blessing for SCLC's working in the North on a "consultative" basis. After visiting Boston and several other cities, King called an SCLC retreat in Warrenton, Virginia—the first since the Black Mountain meeting of January 1964—to discuss the move north. For three days in mid-June the executive staff and King's Northern advisers sketched out goals, pondered tactics, and considered possible targets. The alternatives included a direct action campaign in Chicago, of perhaps two months' duration, in support of the school desegregation drive being conducted by the Coordinating Council of Community Organizations (CCCO), Chicago's civil rights coalition.[60]

The leading members of the research committee all expressed reservations about going north. They feared that Northern support for the civil rights movement would fall away if the movement came to the North. They also worried about abandoning the South at precisely the time that the Voting Rights Act presented SCLC with a golden opportunity to transform Southern politics. If SCLC did move north, Clarence Jones argued, it should choose a more important issue than school desegregation. Among the executive staff members, Williams and Blackwell found themselves agreeing for once when they advocated a continuing focus on the South. But Young and Bevel shared King's enthusiasm for striking out in a new direction. In the teeming cities of the North, Young told the SCLC convention, the sheer power of numbers was "awesome"; it needed to be "organized and disciplined in the interest of positive social change." If the team that had organized Selma were turned loose on Chicago, he speculated, SCLC could recruit enough people—perhaps one hundred thousand—to enable it to bring the city to a grinding halt. The potential for nonviolent direct action seemed almost limitless.[61]

Even as Young spoke, however, the bloodiest riot since the Detroit outbreak of 1943 was unfolding in Los Angeles. The riot in the Watts district of that city lasted six days and left thirty-five people dead; in its duration and destructiveness it dwarfed the Harlem riot of 1964. On August 15, when the scale of the eruption had become horribly apparent, King cut short a stay in Puerto Rico to visit Watts. Rustin tried to dissuade him from going, but ended up agreeing to accompany him. "King's pilgrimage," *Newsweek* commented, confirmed "a single shattering fact of the Los Angeles riot—the orthodox civil rights movement of the South has not reached the black masses in the wildernesses of the urban North."[62]

King took a more positive view. *Time* and *Newsweek* had concentrated on the hecklers in Watts, he told Levison on August 25. Yet "the greatest response I got . . . was when I told them that we can't hate all white people; that some of our greatest allies, people who had died for our freedom, were white people. And they just went wild over that." He had to decide now whether SCLC should concentrate on the South or the North: "Since the riots we just feel that there is a need to kind of reevaulate our whole programmatic thrust for the next few months, particularly re our work in the North. Because Chicago has been pleading with us to come on in." Levison tried to restrain King. SCLC had to be very cautious about going north, he warned: would the achievements outweigh the disadvantages, especially in terms of fundraising? Watts had undoubtedly hurt SCLC's direct-mail program; a Northern campaign could well damage it further.[63] King would not be held back, however. At an emergency meeting of the executive staff he argued that SCLC should move north without delay. "Chicago is on fire with a nonviolent movement. They want us to come in September. We must not ignore their call." Bevel, as eager to go north as King, emphasized the need for preparation and training: "Time, money and energy must go into workshops just to reach people, so that as they begin to move they communicate love to white people who will be watching. . . . We must concentrate on bringing white people along." But King insisted on the need for haste: "The present mood dictates that we cannot wait." Meetings with the Chicago movement leaders were arranged for early September, to be followed by special retreats for the SCLC staff. King gave Bevel a dozen staff members to begin advance work in Chicago itself. Appearing on "Face the Nation" at the end of August, King somberly warned that "other Los Angeles situations" could develop, "and in even more serious proportions," unless the federal government embarked upon "a massive action program . . . to improve the lot of the Negro masses."[64]

The choice of Chicago was not a difficult one; indeed, it was more a case of Chicago choosing SCLC than SCLC choosing Chicago. King's desire to work in a city of major importance narrowed the alternatives to a handful, and of these only Chicago gave SCLC a warm and unambiguous invitation. There, civil rights groups were united—so it appeared—and eager for SCLC's help. The CCCO comprised about forty groups which had formed a loose coalition in a drive to improve and desegregate the city's public schools. After two years of ineffectual protests, the CCCO implored King to assist its campaign. "Come to Chicago," wrote Kyle Haseldon, editor of *Christian Century.* "We need what you have to offer." During a three-day visit in July, King spoke before about thirty-five thousand people and led a march of ten thousand to the city hall—the largest civil rights demonstration in Chicago's history. At the concluding rally on July 26, King talked in terms of repaying a debt. SCLC was exhausted from Selma and busy with voter registration, "but the telegrams kept coming. Persons who had come to aid us in Albany, Birmingham and in the early days of the Freedom Rides . . . urged that we 'come over to Macedonia' and stand by our brethren in their hour of trial." Chicago had also been an important source of financial support for SCLC ever since the organization's inception in 1957.[65]

Knowledgeable Chicagoans warned King that marches and demonstrations would carry little weight with Richard J. Daley, one of the ablest and strongest big-city mayors in the country. Daley, a political animal through and through, had one overriding interest: to perpetuate the rule of the Cook County Democratic organization, the last of the old-style urban political machines. As long as the machine controlled the black vote—and most black voters still dutifully backed machine-endorsed candidates—Daley could afford to ignore the civil rights movement. "Dr. King may be reluctant to believe this," one commentator told him, "but the Negro voter perpetuates the system that appalls Dr. King." With the black vote in his pocket, Daley could increase his appeal to the white voters by treating the CCCO with contempt. Independent aldermen like Leon Despres contended that Daley would refuse significant concessions until he saw either his black support or his white support seriously threatened. The civil rights movement had to beat the machine at its own game: the winning of elections.[66]

But SCLC never seriously contemplated a political campaign. For one thing, the various groups which made up the CCCO could not agree upon a political strategy. Some argued that Daley had done an excellent job in many respects, and doubted that a change in the mayor's office would represent a change for the better. In a battle against the machine, moreover, outstanding liberals like Senator Paul H.

Douglas could well be among the casualties. As a nonpartisan coalition, the CCCO could not take political sides without dividing itself. Its Committee on Independent Political Action turned down a plan to create a "Freedom Democratic" party but could not decide on an alternative strategy. Objectors to the third-party idea argued that any anti-machine effort, even if ostensibly independent, would in fact benefit the Republicans. The very strength of Daley's machine discouraged a political challenge. Dick Gregory, the black comedian-turned-social-activist, planned to run as an independent candidate for mayor in 1967, but few took his candidacy seriously. "The Democratic party is for all practical purposes the only party in the city," said John McDermott of the Catholic Interracial Council.[67]

Daley's power did not deter King. On the contrary, he preferred to deal with a clearly defined "power structure," whether it be a Southern chamber of commerce or a Northern political boss, which had the authority to negotiate and the ability to deliver. He considered Chicago unique, one black leader remembered, "in that there was one man, one source of power, who you had to deal with. He knew this wasn't the case in New York or any other city. He thought if Daley could be persuaded of the rightness of open housing and integrated schools that things would be done."[68] Moral suasion accompanied by nonviolent pressure had worked in the South; it could surely be made to work in Chicago.

On January 26, 1966, King moved into a tenement apartment in Lawndale, part of Chicago's West Side ghetto. A week later, in a buoyant mood, he phoned Levison and Rustin and extended an invitation to visit. "You have to live in the slums though," he told Levison. "You can't live in a bourgeois hotel. You'll be in the midst of the slums and you'll get dope addicts and gang leaders coming in on you." Rustin sensed a disaster in the making. Even if SCLC declined to challenge Daley politically, he warned, the Democrats and their allies would still perceive King's efforts as a threat: "If Dick Gregory really runs there will be some real problems. You add to the Negro protest the peace movement—all of which I am in favor of, and don't misunderstand me—you will, however, run into a vicious attack . . . on the part of the labor movement and other elements which have a vested interest in getting the Democrats in." But King could not be discouraged. Once Daley began to feel threatened, he believed, he would come to him offering concessions. "Well," he told his advisers, "we have some exciting days ahead."[69]

Eleven

Defeat in Chicago

As an exemplar of Northern racism, Chicago could hardly be bettered. Intense and often violent hostility to blacks has long been a hallmark of the nation's second city. In the early years of the century the Great Migration of blacks from the Southern countryside intensified white antagonism and led to the riot of 1919, a four-day spasm which left thirty-eight people dead. Blacks were already concentrated in the South Side of Chicago and largely excluded from the rest of the city. The riot reinforced this pattern and, in the words of historian Allan Spear, "destroyed whatever hope remained for a peacefully integrated city." Segregation did not have the force of statute—it did not need to. The Chicago Real Estate Board (CREB), which excluded blacks, fostered and perpetuated a dual housing market that made segrega-

tion a social and economic reality. In 1921 the CREB adopted the
"restrictive covenant," a model sales contract which prohibited the
buyer from selling or renting to blacks. By the 1940s such covenants
applied to four-fifths of all white-owned residential property.[1]

During the postwar decades, segregation increased rather than diminished. Despite a 1948 ruling by the Supreme Court which outlawed the restrictive covenant, the city's real estate brokers, lending
institutions, and white property owners found ways of continuing to
exclude blacks from white areas. Outright violence provided a final
sanction against unwanted black neighbors. Attempts by blacks to live
outside clearly defined black areas triggered arson, bombings, and at
least a dozen riots between 1945 and 1964. The laxity of the authorities in quelling these outbursts confirmed the prevalent belief
that Chicago's "color line" had the tacit support of city hall. As the
black population swelled from 250,000 in 1940 to almost a million
twenty years later, the South Side ghetto expanded and a second black
enclave came into being on the West Side, adjacent to the downtown
Loop. White out-migration—between 1932 and 1960 Chicago experienced a net decline in its white population of 424,000—exacerbated
the pattern of residential segregation. With the exception of a few
neighborhoods, white and black lived in separate and exclusive zones,
the one out of choice, the other from necessity. True, about 10 percent
of Cook County's blacks lived outside Chicago proper, but the vast
majority of them resided "in the ghettos of . . . satellite cities, such as
Evanston, or in all-Negro suburbs." Yet the Democratic administration
of Mayor Daley, which had governed Chicago since 1955, insisted that
blacks lived in separate areas "because of cultural, social and other
ties," not because of discrimination. There were no "ghettos" in Chicago, Daley claimed.[2]

The Urban League, usually the most cautious and conservative civil
rights organization, had taken the lead in attempting to puncture this
official complacency. Edwin C. Berry reconstructed the Chicago Urban
League after a disastrous schism in 1955. Dissatisfied with its traditional role as a "glorified employment agency," Berry set out to expose
and document the reality of racial discrimination. In 1956 he called
Chicago the most segregated city in the United States and, gathering
together a talented research staff, proceeded to supply chapter and
verse. The South, he contended, was less a geographic region than a
"state of mind, much of which has moved to Chicago." More than any
other individual, "Bill" Berry paved the way for the black protest

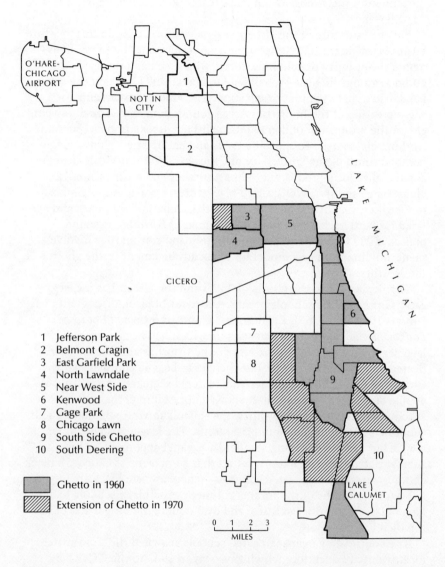

1 Jefferson Park
2 Belmont Cragin
3 East Garfield Park
4 North Lawndale
5 Near West Side
6 Kenwood
7 Gage Park
8 Chicago Lawn
9 South Side Ghetto
10 South Deering

Ghetto in 1960

Extension of Ghetto in 1970

The City of Chicago

movement of the 1960s. When SCLC came to Chicago, he became a
key adviser.[3]

But the structure of the Urban League, with its organic ties to white
business, made it impossible for Berry to undertake the kind of "dynamic community organizing efforts" which he had promised. Neighborhood groups like the Woodlawn Organization (TWO), on the other
hand, had a more popular orientation. The Woodlawn Organization
was a creation of the Industrial Areas Foundation, Saul Alinsky's vehicle for the promotion of democratic self-help associations in poor and
working-class areas. Founded in 1961, and embracing a ghetto neighborhood south of the University of Chicago, TWO was a federation of
about eighty local groups, including churches and businessmen's
clubs. Once set up, TWO spurred black voter registration, organized
rent strikes, fought the university's "urban renewal" schemes, and agi-
tated for better schools. Charles Silberman of *Fortune* magazine
praised TWO for its emphasis on self-help and community involvement, holding it up as a model for black advancement in the ghettos of
the North.[4]

Thanks largely to the efforts of TWO and the Urban League, segregation in the public schools became the focus of black discontent. The
famous 1954 decision of the Supreme Court in *Brown* v. *Board of
Education* had applied only to schools which had been segregated by
law; segregated schools in the North, the Court assumed, merely reflected patterns of residence. But the Urban League claimed that the
Chicago Board of Education actively fostered segregation, creating a
double standard of education. It showed, for example, that while ghetto
schools operated on double shifts, the schools in white neighborhoods
contained hundreds of empty classrooms. The league also documented
a wide disparity in teaching standards. A panel appointed by the city
substantiated these charges: it found that 84 percent of Chicago's black
children attended segregated schools—schools where blacks made up
at least nine-tenths of the total enrollment. And black schools had
larger classes, inferior facilities, and over double the proportion of un-
certified teachers.[5]

The controversy over segregated schools spawned the Committee
for Integrated Education, which gave way in 1963 to the CCCO, a
coalition of about forty organizations, both black and white. The
CCCO organized two, one-day school boycotts, which enjoyed wide
support from black parents. The city refused, however, to accede to the
CCCO's main demand: the dismissal of Benjamin C. Willis, the super-
intendant of schools. Willis denied the charge of segregation and ada-

mantly refused to transfer black children from overcrowded ghetto schools to underused "white" schools. The issue came to a head in 1965, when the board of education renewed Willis's contract. On June 10 the CCCO began to stage protest marches; during the following month the police arrested about seven hundred demonstrators, most of whom had been picketing the home of Mayor Daley. The American Civil Liberties Union challenged the arrests on the grounds of the First Amendment. Nevertheless, the protests soon declined from an initial peak of six hundred marchers a day to fewer than one hundred. The CCCO wanted SCLC to put fire into the campaign.[6]

By the time King arrived in January, however, the CCCO had suffered a humiliating defeat. On July 4 it had played its trump card, requesting the federal government to suspend the payment of $34 million earmarked for aid to Chicago's schools. The CCCO charged the board of education with doing nothing to redress inequalities between black and white schools, and acting in collusion with the real estate board to confine blacks to segregated areas. By gerrymandering school boundaries to follow patterns of racial change, the board had violated Title 6 of the 1964 Civil Rights Act, which outlawed discrimination in federally assisted programs. Later in July, the House Committee on Education and Labor, chaired by Adam Clayton Powell, heard testimony in support of the complaint. Professor Philip Hauser of the University of Chicago called Chicago's black schools "unequal and inferior," and likened Willis to George Wallace as a "symbol of segregation."[7] On October 1, after its own investigation, the Department of Health, Education, and Welfare "froze" the funds in question—the first time the government had invoked Title 6. But this victory proved transient: five days later, after an irate Daley had voiced his opinion of HEW's decision to President Johnson, the federal aid was "unfrozen." Assessing the impact of this turnabout, the Urban League concluded that "any administrator invoking [Title 6] sanctions can expect to be pilloried." There was a real danger, it warned, that the Civil Rights Acts, like the Reconstruction legislation of the previous century, might atrophy and die through lack of enforcement. Indeed, three years passed before the government again applied financial sanctions against a Northern school system. At a retreat in Williams Bay, Wisconsin, the CCCO and SCLC revised their goals to include housing and employment.[8]

King hoped that James Bevel could devise an effective strategy for the campaign. During the last three months of 1965, Bevel and his team of fourteen established themselves on the West Side and surveyed

their surroundings. What they found appalled them: rents of $90 a
month for dingy, unsanitary apartments; a median family income of
less than two-thirds the white average; an unemployment rate double
that of the city as a whole; one family in three on public assistance.
Such conditions bred poor health, crime, alcohol and drug addiction,
and family breakdown. This blight, Bevel reasoned, was not simply a
by-product of inadvertent neglect, lingering prejudice, and mass migration. The ghetto persisted because powerful outside interests had an
economic stake in it. By confining blacks to limited areas, the real
estate interests boosted prices and interest rates within the ghetto and
enabled absentee landlords to levy extortionate rents for crumbling
slums. Merchants made minimal investments, charged premium
prices, and then carried off their profits to the suburbs. The building
unions excluded blacks so as to increase the wages and job security of
their white members. The Democratic machine condoned and buttressed these parasitic arrangements. Bevel likened the system to the
colonialist exploitation of Africa: "Outsiders take things out and don't
put anything back in."9

As he evolved this analysis, his ideas on how to approach the problem underwent a transformation. When he arrived in Chicago, Bevel
had been anxious to reach out to the white population, enlisting the
support of students, businessmen, suburban housewives, and all people
of goodwill. He had wanted to indoctrinate blacks in nonviolence so
that they could "communicate love to white people." As they began
their work, however, Bevel and his staff were forced to de-emphasize
interracialism and nonviolence as a *philosophy*. Apart from deep racism in the white population, the reciprocal antiwhite sentiments of
many ghetto blacks, particularly the young, made a movement of
"black and white together" problematic. Some SCLC workers found
themselves pandering to antiwhite feelings in order to get a hearing.
After listening to a speech by Al Sampson, one clergyman complained
to King of "the revenge motivation which underlay his entire
presentation."10

By the end of 1965 Bevel was thinking in terms of a "grassroots
movement" of the black poor that could act independently of, and even
in opposition to, the white majority. To raise the political consciousness of the masses and wean them away from Daley's machine,
he proposed to organize slum-dwellers into self-governing associations.
These could awaken the poor to their collective power, enabling them
to bargain with landlords, merchants, employers, and the city government. In a report to SCLC's administrative committee, he argued that

tenant unions could provide a starting point for this type of organization. Yet the name "tenant union," he added, "may not convey the
breadth and depth we seek to organize around. . . . Perhaps UNION TO
END SLUMS could more fully convey what we are planning to create."
To this end, Bevel began organizing in the East Garfield Park district of
the West Side, starting with an area of seven thousand people.[11]

As Bevel's team labored on the West Side, Jesse Jackson was laying
the groundwork for Operation Breadbasket. Jackson actually wore two
hats. Recruited during the Selma campaign, he returned to Chicago to
liaise between the CCCO and SCLC. In October he received a Ford
Foundation grant to work as a community organizer in Kenwood-
Oakland, a South Side neighborhood which had been "annexed" by the
ghetto after the Second World War. Conditions there, as reported by
Jackson, were as bad as anything to be found on the West Side. Working
through churches, parent-teacher associations, and other local groups,
Jackson tried to involve residents in the Kenwood-Oakland Community Organization, which he founded and led himself. Jackson's second, more important task was to enlist the support of Chicago's black
ministers. SCLC needed churches for meeting places and organizing
centers. It also wanted to establish Operation Breadbasket so that ministers could instigate consumer boycotts—or use the threat of such
boycotts—to force white employers to hire more blacks. Jackson, not
yet ordained himself, won the backing of Clay Evans, pastor of the
Fellowship Baptist Church and president of the Baptist Ministers Conference. When King outlined the Operation Breadbasket concept to a
meeting at Jubilee Temple on February 11, more than three hundred
preachers heard him. Under Jackson's direction, Operation Breadbasket
began to take root.[12]

It was a mark of his swift rise in SCLC's hierarchy that Jackson met
King at Chicago O'Hare International Airport when the latter arrived
on January 5 to attend a two-day conference with the CCCO leadership. The agenda of this conclave showed that SCLC still had to find
living quarters for King, Andrew Young, and Bernard Lee, and that a
structure for the SCLC-CCCO alliance had yet to be devised. King
decided to rent an apartment in the heart of the West Side ghetto. A
precise resolution of the second question had to wait, but it was agreed
that King and Albert Raby, the convener of the CCCO, should act as
co-chairmen of a Chicago Freedom Movement. King undertook to increase SCLC's Chicago staff from fourteen to fifty and to spend at least
two days a week in the city.[13]

At a press conference on January 7, King defined the campaign as a "multi-faceted assault" on the evils of the city slum. Acknowledging his debt to Bevel, he argued that the problem was "simply a matter of economic exploitation." He promised a three-stage campaign. The first was to be an effort to combat the "somnolence of despair" in the ghettos by uniting the poor in "Unions to End Slums." In stage two, beginning on March 1, the movement would employ probing demonstrations to "reveal the agents of exploitation" and mold "community consensus . . . around specific targets." By May, the movement's "nonviolent army" should be ready to launch "massive action," with the help and support of "the major religious groups, the trade union movement and various elements of the liberal community." The campaign demanded a positive response from city, state, and federal governments. SCLC had always used local situations to dramatize the need for national solutions. "Our work will be aimed at Washington," King stated. SCLC expected, at the very least, a significant expansion of the War on Poverty and the passage by Congress of "open-housing" legislation.[14]

The resources with which SCLC could mount this ambitious campaign were pitifully small. The money which came in response to Selma had been eaten up by SCOPE; by late 1965 SCLC found itself going into debt as contributions declined. To make matters worse, SCLC discovered in November that it had $190,000 less than it thought it had. Dumbfounded, King flew to New York with Abernathy and Young to discuss SCLC's finances with Levison and Wachtel. One promising source of income was the Gandhi Society, which, having at last gained tax-exempt status, had been reconstituted as the American Foundation on Nonviolence. AFON had no other function than to act as a channel for tax-exempt contributions, although it could only finance SCLC projects which fell within the category of education or voter registration. By early 1966, however, SCLC's financial plight had worsened. AFON produced far less than Wachtel had anticipated, and general contributions failed to pick up. By February, SCLC's income had fallen to between $200 and $300 a day, and it owed $50,000— SCLC had still not cleared its debts from SCOPE, and plans for a second summer project had to be scrapped. "I just can't have this hanging over my head," King told Levison. "We have to have a more sound way of operating."[15]

In April, Adele Kanter presented a guardedly optimistic report on SCLC's fundraising from the New York end. Advertisements and direct-mail appeals had netted $215,000 between September 1965 and

February 1966, and Kanter expected another $175,000 by May. "If we have lost some [contributors] on the Vietnam situation," she specu- lated, "we revived others which have been dormant." But Levison was far less sanguine. While the direct-mail program seemed to be holding up, the overall context was one of falling contributions and diminish- ing interest in civil rights. Many white liberals had erroneously con- cluded that the struggle for equality had been won and that the problem of poverty was being taken care of by various government programs. Above all, the war in Vietnam had displaced civil rights as the most important public issue and was diverting money away from civil rights organizations and towards the growing peace movement. It was a sign of the times that King's literary agent advised her client not to write another article on nonviolence because she doubted that any of the major magazines would buy it. In a letter to King in May, Levison warned of a $450,000 deficit if the present trend continued: "Please consider this a 'firebell in the night.'" For the first time, Levison complained to Clarence Jones, "Martin . . . is not being real- istic about finances and is trying to turn his back on it."16

But King never neglected fundraising for long. Towards the end of March he embarked on a European tour, raising $100,000 in Sweden alone, where Harry Belafonte performed a benefit in Stockholm. Typ- ically, King worried that if the presentation of the check at the Swed- ish consulate received too much publicity, people might conclude that SCLC's financial problems had been solved. Fundraising in Chicago became an integral part of the campaign, and King became convinced that the city contained vast resources which had yet to be fully ex- ploited. "The money is here in Chicago," he told Levison. "It's a mat- ter of organizing it." In addition to several thousand churches, there were social clubs, fraternities, and wealthy business people such as barbers and beauticians: "These are middle-class Negroes who will not demonstrate but will give money. . . . We believe firmly that there is $50,000 here waiting for you if you organize. . . . There is a lot of money in the white community that we haven't tapped. . . . They will give if you can just get to them. Guilt makes you give in many in- stances. I think we have it here, a gold mine, but we haven't tapped it." Jesse Jackson became a key figure in exploiting this potential. With access to hundreds of black churches through Operation Breadbasket, he also developed numerous contacts with black businessmen, profes- sionals, and entertainers. A talented and handsome preacher, Jackson's lively meetings pulled in people and dollars. The combined efforts of its fundraisers, however, failed to pull SCLC out of the red. By July, after an unplanned and expensive march through Mississippi, its debts had mounted to $402,000.[17]

With no prospect of taking on additional workers, SCLC found its staffing levels hopelessly inadequate. With never more than fifty staff members in the city, Chicago overwhelmed SCLC's resources. The West Side contained three hundred thousand blacks and Puerto Ricans; the black population of the entire city stood at approximately a million. Bevel complained that the CCCO furnished little help; most of its members "had little contact with the slums," he told SCLC's board, and were "not really prepared to aid in the task of grassroots community organizing." SCLC's own efforts, on the other hand, also came in for criticism. SCLC "is such a loose, unstructured organization," one observer complained, "that it is difficult to catch hold of it when you want to."[18] Contacting people on a building-by-building, block-by-block basis resembled voter registration work, which had never been SCLC's métier. SCLC workers thrived on spontaneity and dramatic confrontations; with their fondness for oratory and action, many found community organizing tedious and unrewarding. They discovered that the black preacher lacked the singular prestige he enjoyed in the South, and that the church was an inadequate organizing tool. Some became dispirited by the apathy, hostility, and cynicism they encountered. Lack of discipline and direction—what SNCC called "floating"—began to infect the staff.

The recruitment of black youths, who had provided much of SCLC's demonstration manpower in the South, posed an especially difficult challenge. The ghettos were plagued by teenage gangs which indulged in petty and serious crime, fought among themselves, and displayed hostility towards all established authority. The gangs were disdainful of the church, antagonistic towards whites, and contemptuous of the word "nonviolence." Young, Bevel, and Orange had experienced something of their cynicism and alienation when they worked briefly in Rochester in the summer of 1964. In Chicago the gangs were larger, stronger, and more violent. Orange recalled that the first time he tried to interrupt a gang fight, the combatants turned on him. "I guess what surprised them was I didn't fight back. I went to the doctor and just had a busted nose, busted lip." But Orange soon learned to speak the language of the group. One awestruck observer watched this giant of a man handle a meeting between two rival gangs: "Listen you goddam [expletive], I've whipped more white men and more niggers than any man in this room. Now you can kill me if you want to, but before you do I'm going to kill one from the Blackstone Rangers and one from the Cobras. Two of you at least are going to die before you kill me." The two groups then sat down and began to listen.[19]

SCLC claimed a large measure of success for its work with the Chicago gangs. In an early report from the West Side, Bevel wrote that "a real transformation seemed to be taking place in the lives of some of the boys." In May, he claimed that three thousand gang members were being trained in nonviolence and would soon be ready to "close down Chicago." A month later, SCLC organized a gang "convention" at the palatial Palmer House, where King urged the youths to stop fighting among themselves and start working with the Chicago Freedom Movement. "From that period on," Orange remembered, "we worked with these guys." Some became King's unofficial bodyguards; others served as marshals on demonstrations. "We saw some of the most violent individuals accepting nonviolent discipline," King related in 1967. "I remember walking with the Blackstone Rangers [the most notorious of Chicago's gangs] while bottles were flying from the side-lines, and I saw their noses being broken and blood flowing from their wounds; and I saw them continue and not retaliate, not one of them, with violence." But others were skeptical about these claims. "King's aides have failed in their stated attempt to make movement workers out of the Blackstone Rangers," wrote Judy Coburn in *New Republic*. To be sure, a few gang members joined SCLC's crusade, but most remained cynically aloof and continued their own internecine vendettas. Even those attracted to King found it difficult to accept SCLC's emphasis on interracialism and nonviolence. "As he preached non-violence to them" Coretta King recalled, "many of them still said, 'We believe in violence.' "[20]

Progress in organizing the poor was thus slow and uncertain, and SCLC compounded its difficulties by spreading itself too thinly. Bevel envisaged a confederation of tenant unions, embracing every area of the West Side. It was another version of the "Freedom Army" idea, and equally impractical. If he had spent more than a year in Alabama and failed to drum up the equivalent of a regiment, what chance did he have of recruiting a division, let alone an army, in Chicago? By March, an embryonic "Union to End Slums" had been formed in East Garfield Park, but it had yet to attract active mass support. The effectiveness of tenant unions remained to be demonstrated. One reporter sat in on a staff meeting in which Bevel led a discussion of tactics. " 'What kind of pressure do we put where?' he would ask, but no-one seemed able to answer him." The campaign had bogged down. "We haven't gotten things under control," Young admitted. "The strategy hasn't emerged yet."[21]

King's attempts to dramatize slum conditions were imaginative but unproductive. On January 26, under the glare of popping flashbulbs, he moved into a squalid Lawndale apartment. But as local journalist Mike Royko cynically and accurately commented, "Chicagoans already knew about slums. Whites were indifferent and Negroes didn't have to be reminded where they lived." A month later, SCLC occupied a dilapidated apartment building with the aim of collecting the rent money itself and spending it on necessary repairs. King termed the takeover a "supralegal trusteeship." In carrying out this gambit, however, SCLC ignored two of the basic steps which it normally insisted upon before any direct action: collection of the facts and negotiation. To SCLC's embarrassment, the landlord turned out to be "very old, very sick, and almost as poor as his tenants." Three months later, after much adverse criticism, the courts ordered SCLC to restore the property to its owner, who shortly afterwards died. Levison complained to Young that by attacking private property, SCLC made itself look like "a gang of anarchists." During the brief "trusteeship" SCLC spent $2,000 on repairs but collected only $200 in rent. The episode did little to make the "internal colonialism" analogy seem plausible.[22]

King genuinely believed that by drawing attention to slum conditions SCLC might instill a greater sensitivity in the city government towards the problems of Chicago's black poor. But Mayor Daley's politicking, although shrewd, betrayed a lack of concern which he found exasperating and depressing. The machine's first reaction to SCLC's interest in Chicago had been transparently hollow. In September 1965 it sponsored the Chicago Conference to Fulfill These Rights, Inc.—the name being taken from the title of President Johnson's proposed Washington conference on civil rights. It then packed this body with aldermen, state legislators, judges, and other machine stalwarts. "We have adequate leadership here," intoned Ralph Metcalfe, a black alderman from the South Side; King's interest in Chicago stemmed from "ulterior motives."[23] Faced with the inescapable fact of King's presence, Daley assured him of the city's cooperation in tackling the evil of slum housing. Copious press releases from city hall detailed current progress in spraying apartments against vermin, prosecuting building violations, and securing federal loans for the rehabilitation of old structures. When he met King on March 26, the mayor defended his urban programs and challenged critics to put forward practical and realistic suggestions. They could, he pointed out, do something about slums themselves by forming nonprofit corporations that could attract federal grants and loans. Daley's primary concern became evident the next day, when the *Chicago Tribune* reported that "City Hall was buzzing . . . with joyous relief" after King stated, "I'm not leading any campaign against Mayor Daley. I'm leading a campaign against slums."[24]

Social justice, King had come to believe, demanded nothing less than a drastic redistribution of wealth in favor of the poor, yet Daley's shallow responses reminded him that there was still no disposition on the part of government to even consider such a policy. Writing in *Nation*, he attributed the stiffening of white resistance to the civil rights movement to the fact that blacks were now attacking "financial privilege." During his visit to Europe in late March, King praised America's "amazing capacity to accept changes," but blamed "powerful forces . . . who make high profits at the Negro's expense" for the persistence of the ghetto. His brief stay in Sweden, which again impressed him with its absence of poverty, accentuated King's growing doubts about the American economic order and increased his attraction to Scandinavian-style democratic socialism.[25]

Although Bevel still argued in favor of a long organizing drive to be crowned with a massive rent strike, by May SCLC was girding itself for demonstrations. Accustomed to operating in campaigning seasons of two or three months, SCLC wanted to end the sparring match with city hall and engineer some form of dramatic confrontation. Community organizing gradually faded into the background. Plans went ahead for a mammoth open-air rally and march on city hall to mark the beginning of the direct action phase. Advised by Bill Berry that June 12 left too little time to achieve a respectable turnout at the Soldier Field stadium, SCLC settled on June 26.[26]

At the end of May, the SCLC-CCCO steering committee discussed goals and tactics. The issue of housing dominated the agenda. As long as blacks found themselves confined to segregated ghettos, then rents and house prices would stay high, overcrowding would continue, and equality would be chimerical. Discrimination by real estate brokers had been prohibited by city ordinance since 1963, but the law went unenforced and unobserved. In 1965 the American Friends Service Committee mounted a campaign to promote "open occupancy" in the northern suburbs, collecting twelve thousand signatures in favor of nondiscrimination in an effort to exert moral pressure on the real estate industry. Yet only thirteen hundred whites expressed a readiness to accept black neighbors, and there were not enough blacks prepared to seek homes in white areas to make open housing anything more than the pet project of a few white liberals. Now, in conjunction with the Friends, SCLC proposed direct action against the realtors in the form of pickets, all-night vigils, and sit-ins. Targets were to be selected on the basis of tests by "dummy" homeseekers, with blacks and whites applying for the same accommodation and then comparing results for evidence of discrimination. Such evidence would not be difficult to find. Marches through Chicago's "lily-white" neighborhoods, certain to evoke vehement local reactions, would put the ball squarely in city hall's court. Within the CCCO some were fearful of a massive white backlash; others relished the prospect of an "eyeball to eyeball encounter" with the bigoted white suburbanites. In his submission to the strategy meeting, Jesse Jackson endorsed the need for an "Exodus to the West" in florid biblical imagery: "Our battle plans call for us to march around the southwest side of Chicago until the walls of opposition come tumbling down. Our line of march leads us to the northside of Chicago until the walls of the segregating slum are destroyed. We'll march in the suburbs until Caesar lets our people go wherever there are houses and apartments available."[27]

On June 8, the Chicago Freedom Movement revealed its demands. They came under the headings of housing and education, with specific demands addressed to federal, state, and local government. The education demands included more, better, and integrated schools; learning centers for adults and high school dropouts; the teaching of Negro history. The most important demands dealt with housing. The CFM wanted Congress to pass the civil rights bill. It also asked for the integration of public housing and the construction of ten thousand new units each year, to be scattered throughout the city. To further break up the ghettos and create an "open city," it proposed the creation of ten "demonstration cities," each with a population of one hundred thousand of whom no more than a third should be black. The remaining demands included the allocation of municipal services according to density of population, the replacement of the state property tax by a personal income tax, and the building of a "gigantic recreation and cultural center" alongside the Taylor Homes public housing project. According to one of King's biographers, these demands were "carefully devised so that they would be impossible to accept or execute," thereby giving SCLC an excuse to begin demonstrations. But the June 8 document was a basis for discussion, not an ultimatum, and during the following month the demands were watered down considerably.[28]

If King hoped for sympathetic and sweeping action from the federal

government on the problems of the urban ghetto, the White House
Conference on Civil Rights, which took place during the first two days
of June, came as a bitter disappointment. Postponed from 1965, the
original purpose of the conference had become entangled in the divisive, acrimonious, and distracting controversy over the Moynihan
report on the Negro family. During the intervening months, moreover,
the civil rights movement had become—or was perceived to have become—a political liability, as black nationalism, rioting, and demands
for open housing fuelled the growing "white backlash." A discernible
policy of downgrading the race issue had emerged by the end of 1965,
most evident, perhaps, in the administration's lenient, gradualist—
critics said delinquent—enforcement of the Civil Rights and Voting
Rights acts. The White House conference itself indicated that further
black demands would receive short shrift. "Action was discouraged,"
wrote Andrew Kopkind, "if not exactly paralyzed, by a tightly-struc-
tured program, CIA-worthy controls, and a huge 'consensus' guest
list." Civil rights leaders were swamped by corporate executives, bankers, union officials, and Democratic party faithfuls. Floyd McKissick,
the new leader of CORE, tried to introduce a resolution on Vietnam
but was quickly ruled out of order. Resolutions from the floor were not
allowed and no votes were taken. King was not asked to speak, and
Johnson virtually ignored the conference report. Andrew Young tried to
be charitable: "It's a nice tea-party . . . but it's not much more than
that. The President got himself into a corner last year promising things
he couldn't deliver. Vietnam got in the way."[29]

Vietnam had become an obsession with the president. Adverse comment and criticism drove him to a fury which, in the opinion of his
chief aide, Bill Moyers, "bordered on paranoia." Opponents became
enemies, and behind every enemy Johnson detected the hand of communism. The FBI assiduously encouraged this fantasy, responding with
alacrity and diligence to presidential requests for "namechecks" on
political opponents and for evidence of the Communist party "line" in
the speeches of Senate doves. King, too, had been marked as an enemy;
his circumspection in opposing the war helped him not one whit. The
Meredith March, a three-week trek through Mississippi which SCLC
undertook with SNCC and CORE in June, graphically illustrated both
Johnson's lack of interest in the civil rights movement and his personal
antipathy to King.[30]

After the disaster of the Meredith March, King was pleased by the
turnout of sixty thousand at the Soldier Field rally which finally took
place on July 10. But others were not so impressed. "Anything less

than a spectacular success in turning people out for the rally," Bill Berry had warned, "will be a severe blow to the entire movement and its leaders." By "spectacular success" he was thinking in terms of one hundred thousand or more. The absence of Archbishop James P. Cody, the Catholic prelate of Chicago, may have robbed the event of as many as fifteen thousand people.[31]

It is doubtful that King expected anything new from Daley when he led a delegation to see the mayor on July 11. Two days before, he had complained that the mayor's response so far had been to "play tricks with us—to say he's going to end slums but not doing any concrete things." Predictably, Daley repeated his assertion that the city already had "massive" antislum programs and was doing all that could practicably be done. The criticisms of the civil rights delegation made him uncomfortable and angry; when he spoke to the press afterwards, the *New York Times* described him as "scarlet faced, as his words tumbled over each other in indignation." King, for his part, called for a "direct confrontation with the forces of power," promising demonstrations and mass arrests. He also repeated his oblique threat of the previous day that the black vote might be mobilized against the machine. This was pure bluff, however. The CFM had done nothing to prepare a political challenge. The overwhelming victory of black congressman William Dawson in the June primary demonstrated that the machine could still count on the loyalty of the South Side.[32]

The attendance at Sunday's rally could well have been affected by the searing heat wave that hung over the Midwest. With temperatures hovering around one hundred degrees, black children turned on fire hydrants so that they could dance in the spray to cool off. It had long been a common practice in the city's poorer neighborhoods, but on Tuesday, July 12, Fire Commissioner Robert Quinn ordered the hydrants turned off lest the water pressure fall too low. Almost at once, altercations broke out between the police and local residents. On the West Side, youths turned the hydrants back on again, claiming that the police had let them stay open in an Italian neighborhood close by. When the police began making arrests, members of the crowd started to throw missiles and break into nearby stores. Before long, more than one hundred policemen found themselves attempting to quell a riot. Martin and Coretta King dined with Mahalia Jackson that evening, and as they drove to a West Side church afterwards they saw "gangs of young men milling around and heard the sharp sound of guns." By the time they reached the church, dozens of youths had been arrested, and some were badly beaten. With young blacks threatening to "tear up the city," King, Raby, Young, and Lee hurried to the police station to post bond for the prisoners. But the youths at the church refused to be mollified and stormed out of the meeting when somebody accused them of vandalism. For one of the few times in his life King lost control of an audience, which melted away in fear, anger, confusion, and recrimination. Outside, the crowds were getting larger and more volatile. Lee and Young bundled King into a car for his own safety, assuring him that the staff could "take care of things."[33]

As had been the pattern in Watts a year earlier, and in Harlem in 1964, morning brought a respite, but rioting erupted with increasing intensity over the next few nights. Significantly, the South Side stayed relatively calm, but on the West Side King and his staff worked round the clock for three days to no apparent effect. "The people we're work-ing with are so much a part of the problem," Young told Levison, "that we have as much fight to keep them from encouraging the riots." At one intersection, crowds of about a thousand people battled 150 po-licemen. Two miles away, the police were fired at from the windows of a housing project. By July 14 the riot area covered six hundred blocks. That night, rioting came to within a stone's throw of King's Lawndale apartment. Coretta King later recalled this "nightmare" experience:

> When we were driven back to the apartment, the riot was going full swing. . . . I went upstairs and found a British reporter and an AP reporter waiting. I asked them to be seated while I started getting ready for bed. The first thing the children did was to run to the window to see where the shots were coming from. I really shouted at them: "Get away from that window or you'll get your heads shot off!" . . . [The] reporters were pretty nervous, and I tried to reassure them, though I could understand that because they were white and in that neighborhood that night, any-thing could happen. . . . I remember after getting the three younger chil-dren to bed, Yolanda and I were looking out of the back window at a grocery store a few yards away. Young rioters were looting the store.

The next day, Governor Otto Kerner ordered the National Guard into the West Side. Two people had already died.[34]

After the first night of violence, Young and Lee insisted that King stay off the streets, both for his own safety and because the crowds were so obviously impervious to reason. But King asked his staff to bring young blacks back to his apartment, where they could talk in private. Roger Wilkins of the Community Relations Service recalled arriving at King's flat to find him sitting on the floor surrounded by "semiarticulate gang kids": King "was having a seminar on nonviolence, trying to convince these kids that rioting was destructive; that the way to change a society was to approach it with love of yourself and mankind and dignity in your own heart. For hours this went on; and there were no photographers there, no newsmen. . . . He kept two assistant attorney generals of the United States waiting for hour while he did this. And when we did talk to him, it was four in the morning."[35] Yet in a press conference on Friday morning, Daley asserted that SCLC had deliberately encouraged rioting. "I think you cannot charge it directly to Martin Luther King," he conceded, "but surely some of the people came in here and have been . . . instructing people in how to conduct violence. . . . There isn't any doubt that the disorders were not [sic] organized." It transpired that Bevel's staff had shown films of the Watts riot to ghetto youths—but the object had been to illustrate the futility of rioting and the efficacy of nonviolent direct action. Daley was understandably anxious to avoid a meeting with King, but he found himself confronted in his office that afternoon by a dozen representatives of the Chicago Freedom Movement, including Berry, Raby, and King. Thus cornered, Berry later related, the mayor adopted a conciliatory tone, assuring King that "we know you did nothing to cause the disorders and that you are a man of peace." He agreed to have the fire hydrants fitted with sprinklers and turned on again. The larger questions of segregation, slums, and police brutality were glossed over in the urgency of the moment: as Berry put it, "We were worried about now, right now, so we didn't go back to the big problems."[36]

Few in SCLC believed the rioting to be anything other than a disaster. Speaking to Young over the telephone during the height of the violence, Levison urged SCLC to lay the blame for the outbreak squarely upon Daley, suggesting that the riot might shake the mayor's political grip on Chicago. But Young disagreed, pointing out that Daley's control over the South Side appeared as secure as ever. When Levison argued that the rioting probably evoked a widespread feeling that Daley was getting what he deserved, Young again demurred. "Daley is in a very good position, even with us, because we have to say that [Orlando W.] Wilson is a damn good police commissioner."[37]

A small ray of encouragement came not from city hall or Washington, but from the state capitol in Springfield. The Illinois legislature had consistently defeated fair housing legislation, but on July 13, Governor Kerner promulgated an executive order authorizing the state to refuse licenses to any real estate brokers found guilty of racial, ethnic, or religious discrimination. At every level of government, however, the real estate industry was fighting a tenacious and effective campaign against open housing. The Illinois Association of Real Estate Boards immediately obtained an injunction against the Kerner order. On the national level, the industry was mobilizing for a determined lobbying drive against the civil rights bill, which had yet to pass the House of Representatives. And at the city level, the Chicago Real Estate Board kept up its legal opposition to the 1963 fair housing ordinance.[38]

Faced with intransigence from the realtors and malign neglect from city hall, SCLC went ahead with demonstrations in Chicago's white neighborhoods. On July 27 the CFM adopted an "Open City Action Report," which proposed to test racial toleration in ten areas. The first test consisted of an all-night vigil outside a real estate office in Gage Park, in the southwestern part of the city. The protest came to a premature end when two hundred jeering whites drove the pickets away. The next day, July 30, the first march proper took place, when an integrated group of 250 returned to Gage Park. Local whites shouted abuse and hurled bottles. When a seventy-car convoy disgorged the marchers again the next day, a furious white crowd wrecked two dozen vehicles and injured sixty people. Al Raby and Jesse Jackson were both struck by missiles.[39]

King and Raby criticized the police for being "either unwilling or unable to disperse the riotous mobs." Thereafter the police were present in larger numbers, and they made a determined effort to keep the white crowds at bay. The sight of the white policemen protecting the marchers, however, drove the local populace to a higher pitch of fury. On August 2, 140 policemen battled a thousand whites in Belmont-Cragin, an area northwest of Lawndale. When Bevel led 350 marchers back there the following day, the size of the white crowd had doubled. The police line held. On August 5, King led a march through Gage Park in person. At first he seemed nonchalant about the white onlookers, who numbered between four and five thousand. The presence of 1,000 policemen did not, however, prevent the 800 marchers from being pelted with "rocks, bottles, cherry bombs and eggs—some dropped by residents perched in trees." The violence disturbed King and frightened him, although he did not show it at the time. After a rock struck his head, causing him to fall to his knees, he joked, "It hurts, but it's not an injury."[40]

No sooner had the marches got underway than King began to receive peace feelers from city hall. In a remarkable volte-face, the South Side's five Democratic aldermen sought a meeting with the leadership of the CFM, complaining that they had been "excluded" from the civil rights movement. After three hours of talks on August 4, the black politicians assured King and Raby that they supported their goals. Significantly, however, they could not agree to the demand that no more high-rise public housing should be built in the ghetto. The CFM, moreover, wanted to deal with the head of the machine, the "Boss," not his underlings. A few days later, King received a written communication from the mayor's office. It dangled the promise of an extra $50 million for urban renewal—which blacks cynically dubbed "Negro removal"—three hundred additional jobs for black security guards in the housing projects, and the employment of the first black journeyman glazier by the Chicago Housing Authority. King, in Jackson, Mississippi, had no hesitation in rejecting this package. The forays into Chicago's white neighborhoods continued for three more weeks. On August 7, Bevel and Raby took fifteen hundred protesters—the largest demonstration so far—back to Belmont-Cragin. Rain and a thousand policemen kept the white crowd fairly subdued.[41]

On August 8, Jesse Jackson dropped a bombshell: the CFM had scheduled simultaneous marches for two days hence, one in Bogan, the other in Cicero. Bogan was an area of Irish, Italian, and East European immigrants and their descendants; like all such Chicago neighborhoods, it wanted to remain "white." Cicero's reputation was more sinister. A suburb of seventy thousand people, it had become notorious in the 1920s and 1930s as the Mafia's main base in Cook County. It also had the dubious distinction of having stopped any blacks from living there. In 1952, Gov. Adlai Stevenson called out the National Guard in order to quell a riot against Negro "intruders." According to Don Rose, the CFM's publicity director, Jackson "seriously overstepped his authority" in announcing the Cicero march. King, in Mississippi at the time, apparently had no intention of marching through Cicero so soon, if at all. "We were batting the threat around for leverage, never saying anything definite about it," Rose later explained.[42]

Sanctioned by King or not, Jackson's announcement sent shock waves through city and county halls. The sheriff of Cook County, Richard B. Ogilvie, warned that the white reaction in Cicero could "make Gage Park look like a tea-party"; he promised to use "every possible legal means" to prevent the march. The prospect of a Cicero bloodbath also horrified many of the CFM's white sympathizers, evoking anxious demands that the marches should stop. The weightiest voice belonged to Archbishop Cody, who warned on August 10 that further demonstrations "will very likely [result in] serious injury to many persons and perhaps even loss of life." The leaders of the CFM, he added, had a "serious moral obligation" to consider a halt to the marches; "with a heavy heart," he urged them so to do. Another key CFM supporter, Robert Johnson of the United Auto Workers, also changed his mind. In March, he had vowed that "the UAW is in this thing all the way." But on August 11, Johnson joined other labor leaders in meeting Daley and then endorsing Cody's plea.[43]

This sudden hemorrhage of white support caused agonized debate within the CFM, but it failed to stop the marches. The Joint Action Board affirmed that "those who would express their convictions through nonviolent demonstrations must be protected." From Mississippi, Young wired Cody that a pause would be considered; in Chicago, however, Bevel and Raby rejected Cody's appeal. "We ask the Archbishop . . . not to abandon us now," Raby urged. Bevel publicly castigated Cody for deserting the movement: "When there's trouble, Daley sticks up his liberal bishop to say, 'You've gone far enough.' Well, we've got news for the man. If the bishop doesn't have the courage to speak up for Christ, let him join the devil." The day the archbishop made his statement, Bevel led five hundred marchers through the Loop, stopping outside the office of the Chicago Real Estate Board. Two days later, Bevel, Jackson, and Raby took seven hundred marchers, half of them white, into Bogan. When local reaction was milder than expected, they decided to hold simultaneous marches in Bogan, Gage Park, and Jefferson Park on August 14. No date had been fixed for the Cicero march, but the tactic of multiple marches, which stretched the police to the limit, served equally well. About one thousand people took part in Sunday's triple protest. Although they walked into the usual barrage of bricks and bottles, the most serious violence occurred away from the marches, in Marquette Park, where Nazi and Klan orators encouraged a crowd of three thousand whites to go on the rampage.[44]

The *Chicago Tribune* fulminated against the CFM's tactics. "Causing violence to achieve political ends is criminal syndicalism," it asserted. "If the marchers keep up their sabotage it will be time to indict the whole lot of them." The *Tribune*'s angry editorials provided one yardstick of the marches' effectiveness. Provocative or not, they placed Daley in a quandary. With the police attempting to protect the marchers, his administration was receiving the blame for what most whites perceived as a black invasion. And with the autumn elections approaching, the Republicans stood to benefit from the "backlash." "Every time we march," Bevel exulted, "Daley loses 10,000 votes—

from the whites." Moreover, with the CFM staging multiple marches, and with a Cicero march in the offing, there was a real possibility that the white crowds might swamp the police and inflict serious casualties. Andy Young hinted that SCLC was prepared to bring about martial law. As Mike Royko later put it, "King had Daley reeling. . . . Another 1919 was getting closer all the time."[45]

Desperate to stop the marches, Daley agreed to a "summit conference" with the CFM and other interested parties, to be held on August 17 at St. James's Episcopal Church. The CFM fielded a fourteen-man negotiating team, headed by King, Raby, Young, Bevel, Berry, and Jackson. The "other side" included Daley, Alderman Thomas Keane, and representatives from industry, the banks, and the real estate board. Ben W. Heineman, president of the Chicago and Northwestern Railway, chaired the meeting. Heineman had a genuine interest in civil rights—he had chaired the recent White House conference—but was nevertheless recognized to be one of Daley's men. The presence of several distinguished clerics, on the other hand, helped SCLC. An eleven-point plan offered by the Chicago Commission on Human Relations provided a basis for the discussion; its main points consisted of promises by CREB, the mortgage bankers, and the savings and loan associations to urge their members to practice nondiscrimination. But the CFM had no intention of stopping the demonstrations for such flaccid, unenforceable promises.[46]

One thing became clear immediately after the talking began: Daley would agree to virtually anything in order to secure a cancellation of the marches. The CFM realized, however, that commitments by Daley had little value in the absence of hard-and-fast commitments from CREB: CREB was the main obstacle to open housing and bore the brunt of the CFM's arguments. Yet CREB appeared immoveable. Its spokesmen, Ross Beatty and Arthur Mohl, denied any responsibility for housing discrimination and disclaimed any duty to fight it. Real estate agents merely represented their clients, they argued; they had no power to change social attitudes or solve social problems. CREB could not bargain away something that lay outside their power to give. It would be ruinous for realtors to defy the expressed wishes of their clients.

King would have none of this. Restaurant and hotel owners across the South had used these arguments to hold out against desegregation. Yet when the Civil Rights Act came into being, they adapted to the change and suffered no loss of clientele. King dismissed the claim that realtors merely reflected the attitudes of their clients as a sophistry. He

pointed out that the industry had spent $5 million to kill California's
fair housing law, and was presently lobbying Congress to defeat the
civil rights bill. The real estate industry was hardly neutral: it had
helped to *create* discriminatory attitudes. Realtors had to confront the
immorality of discrimination, insisted King, and recognize the danger
of having Negro cities ringed by exclusive white suburbs. Bevel pointed
out that Negroes felt insulted and humiliated by the realtors' refusal to
serve them; it was now safer for blacks in Birmingham, he added, than
for blacks in Chicago. A remark by Young to the effect that ghettos
bred neurosis and violence caused Daley to angrily object to what he
took to be a prediction of further riots. Young politely refuted Daley's
erroneous allegation.

Early on in the talks, the chairman, Heineman, showed his true
colors when he attempted to limit the negotiating time—a classic
device of employers—by refusing any adjournment until some kind of
agreement had been reached. But the CFM would not allow itself to be
stampeded or pressured into a premature cancellation of the marches.
Shortly after midday, when the meeting recessed, King talked in private with Heineman, Cody, and Bishop Montgomery, chairman of the
Conference on Race and Religion. They agreed to the formation of a
subcommittee in order to continue the negotiations and work out the
substance of a settlement. Meanwhile Beatty and Mohl of CREB, prodded by Daley, drafted a statement that moved in the direction of the
CFM's demands.

When the meeting reconvened later in the afternoon, however, nobody on the CFM side found CREB's statement satisfactory. Raby,
Bevel, Young, and others tried to pin Beatty down as to its precise
meaning: Was CREB now undertaking to withdraw its opposition to
Chicago's fair housing ordinance? The answer, despite Beatty's ob-
fuscations, was in the negative. Daley pleaded for an end to the
marches, asking the CFM to trust in the good faith of the city. His
request for a moratorium, however, infuriated Raby, who berated the
mayor for the city's failure to act against white violence. Only an end
to discrimination, he insisted, could bring an end to the marches. King
intervened to break the tension, making a long, calm, and cogent statement in defense of the marches. The meeting represented progress, he
added, and he wanted the negotiations to continue, but the CFM was
not yet ready to surrender its most precious right and only real means
of pressure. The session ended with both sides accepting Heineman's
proposal for the appointment of a subcommittee, and agreeing to meet
again on August 26 to consider the committee's draft.

Two days later, on August 19, the city obtained an injunction against the CFM restricting the marches to one a day, with a maximum of five hundred people. The CFM responded by staging marches beyond the city limits, in Chicago Heights and Evergreen Park. On the same day, King led a march in South Deering; the police had to club white hecklers in order to clear a path for him. While continuing the marches in accordance with the injunction, the CFM finally settled on a date for the Cicero excursion: Sunday, August 27. At a rally of fifteen hundred people at the New Liberty Baptist Church, King declared that "no one is going to turn me around at this point. We can walk in outer space, but we cannot walk in the streets of Cicero without the National Guard." On August 25, Al Raby and Alvin Pitcher met the town attorney of Cicero to discuss the route of the march. Governor Kerner readied the National Guard.[47]

When the negotiators met again on August 26, both sides accepted the ten-point agreement drafted by Bishop Montgomery's subcommittee. King and Raby complained about the injunction; they also expressed concern about the implementation of the pact. Nevertheless, they undertook to end the marches. Speaking to reporters afterwards, King hailed the agreement as "far-reaching and creative." *Newsweek* described it as "a solid vindication of Southern-style protest in a Northern city."[48]

But the "Summit Agreement" was riddled with loopholes. The *Chicago Tribune*, which had recently described King, Bevel, and Raby as "paid professional agitators," immediately detected the two most obvious weaknesses. First, there was no timetable for implementation; second, CREB still refused to drop its legal action against Chicago's fair housing ordinance. Nicholas Von Hoffman of the *Washington Post*, a seasoned Chicago-watcher, detailed the other loopholes in a devastating critique. For example: the real estate board agreed to withdraw its opposition to the "philosophy" of fair housing legislation, but insisted that any law should apply to owners as well as brokers. There was virtually no prospect, however, of the state legislature passing such a sweeping law, and Congress had recently watered down the civil rights bill to exempt owner-occupiers—60 percent of the housing market—from the proposed ban on discrimination. Indeed, on August 25 Ross Beatty stated on the radio that if realtors were forced to sell or rent to Negroes, they would go out of business. When King questioned him on this during the final negotiation, Beatty's response had been confused and pathetic. CREB, in fact, had yielded nothing of substance since August 17.[49]

The rest of the agreement hinged on the enforcement of the city's ordinance and the promotion of integration by the Chicago Housing Authority. In respect of the first, the Commission on Human Relations promised a "significantly higher level of effective enforcement activity." But the vagueness of this pledge, and the commission's past laxity in investigating complaints of discrimination, did little to inspire confidence. The promises of the Chicago Housing Authority appeared, at first sight, to be a little more precise. The CHA agreed to "seek scattered sites for public housing and will limit the height of new public housing structures in high density areas to eight stories." The integration of public housing, however, depended upon the Department of Welfare, which undertook to find "the best housing for recipients . . . regardless of location." This was far from a commitment to actively relocate blacks into white areas. The other features of the ten-point agreement were even less substantial. The mortgage and lending associations simply reiterated their statement of August 17 in which they "affirmed" that nondiscrimination was already their policy. As for the demand that the Federal Deposit Insurance Corporation suspend members found guilty of racial discrimination, the best the CFM could get was a promise by Roger Wilkins, head of the Community Relations Service, to "inquire into the questions raised, under existing law."[50]

All in all, the Summit Agreement amounted to little more than various pledges of nondiscrimination. The burden of translating these promises into reality fell to the Chicago Conference on Race and Religion, which accepted the "responsibility for the education and social action programs necessary to achieve open housing." But the CCRR, although well-meaning, had no statutory authority and little political weight. Its promise to set up a separate, permanent committee to implement the agreement evoked a dismissive and sarcastic comment from Nicholas Von Hoffman: "Chicago is already overstocked with 'blue-ribbon' committees which don't meet and arouse themselves only . . . when somebody asks what they've been doing." As Bevel admitted, "The problem is the follow-up." The CFM appointed its own committee to monitor the agreement, setting a target of 1 percent black occupancy in seventy-five white areas by May 1967. Towards the end of October the committee accused the city of having ignored the August 27 pact. It also reported that in tests of real estate offices in Bogan, Gage Park, Belmont-Cragin, and other areas, "in every case, the white family was served and the Negro family discriminated against." Yet the CCHR had failed to suspend the license of a single broker. A second follow-up report in January claimed that only one out of twenty-three all-black public housing projects had been integrated, and that this had been more than offset by the creation of two new segregated ones. Visiting Chicago on October 28, King demanded "something tangible." The march into Cicero had not been cancelled, he warned; "we simply postponed it."[51]

In a report to SCLC's administrative committee, King optimistically detected "some evidence that the pact's good faith will be upheld." He nevertheless gave his approval to a crash program of voter registration in Chicago so that "slum dwellers can begin to break the grip of machine politics."[52] Hosea Williams arrived in mid-December, with fifteen members of his Southern staff, brimming with confidence that he could "change things politically" in the city. But the drive failed miserably. After two months SCLC had contacted an infinitesimal fraction of the 150,000 unregistered blacks in Chicago. How many it actually persuaded to register is unclear: Williams claimed 32,000; the city, which refused to open neighborhood registration centers, put the figure at 320. This poor showing was partly the result of inadequate funding, but it also reflected the reluctance of the CCCO to mount an all-out attack on the Democratic machine.[53]

Explaining his failure, Williams pointed to a lack of political awareness on the part of Chicago's blacks. While Negroes in the South were flexing their political muscles, he complained, "here, the Negro has been so plantationized that he feels there's no hope of ever breaking the stranglehold."[54] As Bevel's staff had discovered earlier in the year, slum-dwellers responded to SCLC's moral entreaties with apathy, cynicism, and sometimes hostility. "A lot of people here won't even talk to us," Lester Hankerson lamented. Without doubt, many welfare recipients, public housing tenants, and city employees felt dependent on the machine, a feeling skilfully and assiduously cultivated by the Democratic precinct captains. Even so, SCLC's failure owed much to simple incompetence. Williams sent his team to Chicago virtually "blind"; he had done little research into local conditions—not even the weather. "I don't have the right kind of clothes," complained Hankerson, at an acrimonious staff meeting on December 14. "I cannot afford to expose my body to this kind of weather. . . . I'm full of cold right now and need a shot." Sam Wells, from Albany, Georgia, thought he had been "thrown into hell." Leon Hall summed up the anger of the staff when he argued that "they shouldn't have brought us up here with so little preparation and organization." Williams, however, heard none of this. "No one will say anything when Hosea is here," Dana

Swan complained. "And if you do, he'll bullshit you out of it or ignore you."[55]

In April 1967 Daley was reelected to a fourth four-year term. He received a 73 percent plurality, winning more than four-fifths of the black vote. SCLC had not only failed to defeat Daley, it had not even come close. With his political base more secure than ever, Daley ignored King and the CCCO and forgot about the Summit Agreement. The campaign for open housing had failed as completely as the drive for integrated schools. As the CCCO fell apart, Raby resigned as its convener and chief spokesman. "When the next riots hit," he warned, "the whites had better not look to me to cool things. That was what the Chicago Freedom Movement was trying to do, but the Mayor wasn't listening."[56]

If the city could renege on the housing agreement with such ease, why did King assent to such an insubstantial pact, especially when it seemed that the CFM—notwithstanding the city's injunction—had the momentum on its side? Some argued that King, betraying his ineptitude as a negotiator, threw away a winning hand. "The movement scared the you-know-what out of Daley and he was telling them, 'Okay, okay, whatever you want but you tell me how to get it,'" related Eugene Callahan of the CCHR. "I think the movement could have gotten control of the whole poverty program, for instance. But when you talk specifics, when you talk multiple real estate listings to Martin Luther King, he gets that glazed look in his eyes. One friend of mine . . . came out of the meeting ashen-faced at what they got."[57] The disappointing terms also reflected King's reluctance to press the threat of a march into Cicero: his anxiety to avert bloodshed undermined his capacity for hard bargaining. "He gave away that Cicero march," one of the white negotiators told a reporter. "They would have given him almost anything not to make it, and he gave it away at the beginning of the meeting."[58] Andy Young summed up the alternatives facing SCLC: "It was a choice of going into Cicero and having all-out war, which I don't think we were prepared for, or taking this agreement." In fact, there was a third alternative: to break the injunction. But as Young later explained, "We weren't prepared at that point to pay $5,000 a day for violating an injunction. We didn't have the tens of thousands of people that would have been necessary to fill up the Chicago jails."[59]

Disunity within the CCCO spurred King's eagerness to reach a settlement. Arguments over the wisdom of the Cicero march reflected wider disagreement over the efficacy of SCLC's confrontation strategy. To the critics, white exclusiveness was an unshakeable reality; to confront it head-on, from a position of political isolation, was self-defeating. They feared that the open-housing marches, far from increasing support for the CFM's objectives, only intensified white resistance to integration. Even if the law could guarantee freedom of choice in housing—and there was little evidence that it could—how many blacks would risk life and limb by moving to Bogan, Gage Park, or Cicero? Exploiting white animosity might be a useful lever against city hall, but any gains at the conference table could well be outweighed by the resulting white blacklash. White liberals who had supported King in the South now questioned the viability of nonviolent tactics in the North. The planned chaos which had seemed so inspiring in Birmingham and Selma, when viewed from afar, became frightening when it occurred in Chicago.

SCLC had lived with talk of a "white backlash" for three years and had always dismissed the notion that direct action did anything more than expose prejudice that was already there. To the white trade union and religious leaders who backed the CCCO, however, the hostility and anger which the open-housing marches evoked were dangerous new forces. After the riots in Gage Park and elsewhere, they began to ask whether the marches might not be reinforcing white prejudices. If King had turned down the Summit Agreement and persisted with the marches, his white support, already eroding, would have crumbled. Young later castigated Cody and the other religious leaders for their "insipid moral neutrality," which, he believed, caused them to betray the movement:

> They were really trying to be neutral and serve as arbitrators in what was a moral issue that they had to take sides on. They tried to be a mediator between the movement and the Mayor, as though there were wrongs on both sides. And they were just really naive. . . . When we tried to raise the issue of the injunction with the Mayor, it was the Federation of Churches representative who got up and interceded and tried to block it. He . . . suggested that the court should decide on it. He never realized that to take an injunction case on up to the Supreme Court would cost from $25,000–50,000. And, of course, they never suggested that they should contribute towards that.[60]

After Chicago, Young had little faith in the church as a vehicle for social reform.

There was another, quite straightforward, reason why King accepted the pact: he trusted the other signatories to keep their part of the bargain. In doing so, he made two crucial errors. First, promises by the mayor and the religious leaders cut little ice with the real estate interests: King went against his own dictum that the political power structure follows the economic power structure, not vice versa. As C. T. Vivian argued, SCLC confronted Daley rather than the real estate board; the Summit Agreement was a "deal with everybody but those who made the decisions." Second, King badly underestimated the mendacity and duplicity of his opponents. Vivian thought SCLC let Daley off the hook by stopping the marches too soon: "We should have *forced* that thing into Cicero . . . even if it meant some of our skulls being cracked, because that's our line." Later, analyzing the city's failure to live up to the agreement, King arrived at the same conclusion. "I look back over," he told his staff, "and wish we'd gone to Cicero."[61]

SCLC discovered in Chicago that discrimination was a far more insidious and tenacious enemy than segregation. It also found itself progressively more isolated as the administration turned its back, as too many blacks stayed cynically aloof, and as white liberals joined the anti-war movement or swelled the conservative chorus in calling for an end to demonstrations. Now, as the Chicago campaign sputtered to its dispiriting conclusion, SCLC found itself confronting a new, altogether different, and in some ways more dangerous, challenge—one that came from within the civil rights movement itself. In June 1966 the ideological tensions which had already stretched black unity almost to the breaking point finally split the movement asunder. In addition to fighting white racism, SCLC had to fend off an attack upon its fundamental principles. That attack came in the form of a deceptively simple slogan consisting of two words and an exclamation mark: "Black Power!"

Twelve

"Black Power!"

King was attending the White House Conference on Civil Rights, with Andy Young and Harold Middlebrook, when James Meredith announced his intention to march through Mississippi in order to "tear down the fear that grips the Negroes" and encourage black voter registration. They greeted his plan with skepticism, Middlebrook recalled, "because we were asking the question, 'Now is he really concerned about doing the job or is he concerned about just gaining something for himself?' "[1] The man who integrated the University of Mississippi in 1962 had become a symbol of black courage and achievement. But his moody individualism, coupled with an arrogant sense of self-importance, set Meredith apart from the civil rights movement and aroused doubts about his motives and judgement. On the face of it, his protest seemed little more than a self-seeking attempt to prove that history had not passed him by. It also seemed suicidal: probably the most hated black man in Mississippi, his chances of completing the walk were deemed to be slight.

Yet when two shotgun blasts felled Meredith on June 6, the second day of his trek, SCLC's instinctive reaction was to take up the march. News of the shooting reached the executive staff during a meeting in Atlanta. "There was a momentary hush of anger and dismay throughout the room," King later wrote. "Soon the silence was broken, and from each corner of the room came expressions of outrage." The discovery that he had been wounded, not killed, "did not alter our feeling that the civil rights movement had a moral obligation to continue along the path that Meredith had begun." Plans for Chicago were pushed to one side, and the following morning King flew to Memphis, accompanied by Abernathy, Lee, Williams, and Charles Morgan of the ACLU. Floyd McKissick of CORE, also intent on continuing Meredith's project, boarded their plane after flying from New York. Upon arriving in Memphis, King and McKissick went directly to Bowld Hospital, where Meredith endorsed their proposal. With the arrival of Stokely Carmichael, the "Meredith March" became a joint venture between SCLC, SNCC, and CORE.[2]

As Williams drove down Highway 51 to locate possible campsites, others tried to reach sympathizers across the country and persuade them to come to Mississippi. King himself was constantly on the phone, Morgan remembered, "for no matter how tired or sick or overwhelmed with work he was, many white liberals would not respond to his aides."[3] Keen to "strike while the iron is hot," King did not want logistical problems to delay action: when somebody pointed out that the marchers needed tents, mobile canteens, and toilets, he replied that they should "get started and talk about that while we're walking."[4] In the afternoon the marchers piled into four cars and motored to Hernando, Mississippi, the scene of the shooting. The small band walked for about three hours, with King, Carmichael, McKissick. and Cleveland Sellers in the vanguard. The Mississippi Highway Patrol provided an escort, but insisted that the marchers walk on the grass shoulder—at one point shoving the four leaders off the pavement. James Lawson teased Carmichael for his refusal to fight back: "You see, Stokely, the difference between you and the military is that a soldier has singleness of purpose. When you get shoved you get confused. If you're really not nonviolent, you ought to get a gun and be a guerilla."[5] But the mood of some marchers seemed bitter. "If one of these damn Mississippi crackers touches me," King remembered one saying, "I'm gonna knock the hell out of him."[6]

Lacking camping equipment, the marchers returned to Memphis at dusk. In King's room at the black-owned Lorraine Motel, the leaders discussed the conduct of the march. Among their number were several members of the "Deacons for Defense," a group from Bogalusa, Louisiana, that had gained recent notoriety by providing armed protection for civil rights workers. The Deacons wanted to carry guns on the march, and both McKissick and Carmichael supported them. King did not object to the Deacons' participation, nor did he oppose the principle of self-defense. He insisted, however, that guns and self-defense had no place in an organized protest or demonstration. Unless all those taking part adhered to nonviolence and left behind their weapons, he warned, SCLC could not support the march. "I believe in nonviolence not only as a religious and moral matter," King told them, "but also as a matter of tactics. If you want a violent march, go have one, . . . but don't expect me to join in your march. Don't try to bring me into your violence. We'll watch. We'll pray for you as you head off into Mississippi." According to Morgan, King's statement had the desired effect: "We'll take your way, Doctor," one of the Deacons replied, "till we know it doesn't work." On the question of white participation, another bone of contention, King also got his way, although he agreed that white marchers ought not to outnumber the black ones.[7]

Unknown to King, however, SNCC was bent on fomenting these disagreements in order to wrest the march from his leadership. King, preoccupied with Chicago, had lost touch with SNCC, and did not appreciate the significance of recent changes in that organization. SCLC's Southern staff, on the other hand, knew about and deplored SNCC's sharp turn towards black nationalism. The issue had come to the fore in Alabama, where the SNCC staff, led by Carmichael, had formed a separate political party in overwhelmingly black Lowndes County. Carmichael regarded the Democratic party as irretrievably racist; he intended the Lowndes County Freedom Organization to serve as a model for independent political action by Negroes through-out the Black Belt. The LCFO was not a separatist organization in the sense of excluding whites; yet, as SNCC's historian noted, "The emblem chosen for the new organization—a snarling black panther—was unmistakably significant."[8] Hosea Williams and Albert Turner, SCLC's Alabama field secretary, regarded SNCC's Black Panther party as a misguided and dangerous expression of black nationalism. They also criticized SNCC for continually attacking black organizations like the Alabama Democratic Conference (ADC), which operated within the official Democratic party. SCLC had its own differences with the NAACP-dominated ADC, and had recently formed a political grouping of its own, the Confederation of Alabama Political Organizations. Nevertheless, COAPO, too, worked within the Democratic party structure, and cooperated with the ADC in urban centers like Birmingham.[9]

On January 23, 1966, the Alabama staffs of SNCC and SCLC had attempted without success to thrash out their differences. Carmichael argued for the rejection of coalitions with whites, dismissing the ADC as a "bourgeois" group that worked against the interests of the black masses. Randolph Blackwell, who journeyed from Atlanta to mediate the dispute, replied that SCLC worked with all groups and classes in the black community, and had not yet concluded that the Negro had no political future within the existing party system. He strongly objected to the "Uncle Tom" label which SNCC was trying to pin on the ADC and the NAACP. Williams condemned the Black Panther party less elegantly but no less forcefully: "Will Negroes treat white folks like white folks treated them? We may mess around here and create a monster in Alabama. . . . We can't go pitting race against race." SNCC and SCLC agreed upon a fragile truce, although it amounted to little more than an undertaking not to attack each other in public. Blackwell delivered a stiff warning that SCLC would frown upon any attempt by SNCC to control, dominate, or disrupt the meetings of other organizations. Reporting to Young, he advised that "it might be desirable for our staff to avoid discussion of the SNCC program wherever possible."[10]

The results of the Alabama primaries, however, were a poor advertisement for coalition politics. With the easy victory of Lurleen Wallace—George Wallace could not succeed himself—hopes for a political realignment based on black votes received a massive blow. All told, about 180,000 blacks cast ballots, almost all of them for Richmond Flowers, the former attorney general who had investigated the Klan, prosecuted the killer of Jonathan Daniels, and made reconciliation between the races the theme of his campaign. The black vote, however, was swamped by the ballots of 750,000 whites—a record turnout—of whom only 3 percent voted for Flowers. "It would be a mistake to suppose that segregationist sentiment in Alabama is the last gasp of a dying and archaic system," wrote William Brink and Louis Harris; "actually, it is showing more strength than ever." Taken with the results in Mississippi and Georgia, where John Bell Williams and Lester

Maddox coasted to victory as unashamed segregationists, the spring primaries seemed to demonstrate that the kind of class-based inter-racial alliance which King envisaged in his celebrated Montgomery speech was a utopian fantasy. The morale of SCLC's Southern staff, already poor, sank to a new low.[11]

To many in SNCC, the Alabama elections underlined Carmichael's contention that the existing political parties had nothing to offer blacks. When SNCC's staff met at Kingston Springs, near Nashville, in mid-May, Carmichael ousted John Lewis as the organization's chair-man, a change that marked a decisive shift towards black separatism. Blacks could only enter coalitions with whites, Carmichael argued, on terms of equality and mutual respect; as such conditions did not yet exist, blacks were compelled to organize independently. In order to build racial cohesion and strength, moreover, SNCC placed a fresh emphasis on "black consciousness"—an appeal to black culture, soli-darity, and racial pride. SNCC's tradition of interracialism, as ex-pressed in the goal of integration and the practice of black and white staff members working alongside each other, was now perceived as an impediment to black consciousness. The job of organizing blacks, SNCC concluded, could only be effectively undertaken by other blacks. Although SNCC had not yet adopted the position that whites should be excluded from its ranks, as some black staff members were advocating, it seemed obvious that whites could play little part in an organization dedicated to independent black action. To affirm its new orientation, SNCC rejected an invitation to the White House Con-ference on Civil Rights, and urged "all black Americans to begin build-ing independent political, economic, and cultural institutions."[12]

SNCC's repudiation of nonviolence was less well-publicized but equally significant. The advisability of self-defense—which in the Deep South meant, in effect, carrying guns—had long divided SNCC. Their experiences in Mississippi persuaded many staff members of the futility of attempting to dissuade local blacks from defending them-selves against white aggression. SNCC had to accept the fact that many ordinary blacks possessed weapons and were prepared—quite rightly, in the view of some SNCC field workers—to use them in self-defense. During a debate on nonviolence in June 1964, the executive committee agreed to stand by any SNCC worker "caught in the home of another person who is armed." But it stopped short of approving the carrying of arms by SNCC workers themselves. By 1965, however, many staff members did possess guns. When Marion Barry criticized the practice, Carmichael retorted that "we are not King or SCLC. They don't do the kind of work we do, nor do they live in the areas we live in. They don't ride the highways at night. To King and SCLC non-violence is everything. To us, we see it as a form of tactic, and in demonstrations we are nonviolent." By the time of the Meredith March, Carmichael was prepared to extend the right of self-defense to demonstrations as well.[13]

Carmichael viewed the Meredith incident as a golden opportunity to publicize SNCC's new emphasis on independent black action, or "black power." He had already used King's prestige as a means of furthering SNCC's work in Alabama, and he had no qualms about exploiting it in Mississippi. In order to prevent King quitting the march after the first day, Carmichael gave way to his insistence on non-violence and white participation, but later, when SCLC had become too involved in the march to pull out, he intended to challenge these principles once more—this time on grounds of SNCC's own choosing. In order to successfully manipulate King's prestige, however, Carmichael had to ensure that SNCC did not become absorbed in a broad coalition that watered down its more radical aims. He therefore deliberately sought to exclude Roy Wilkins and Whitney Young, who arrived in Memphis on the evening of June 7. More than a decade later, Carmichael explained his intentions in the following words: "King's role was dangerous to us. Not only did he occupy the center stage in terms of public popularity. He had the strongest personality. King could take a middle position among us and appear to be the real arbitrator. We wanted to pull him to the left. We knew that if we got rid of Young and Wilkins, the march is ours."[14]

When the civil rights leaders met in the conference room of the Lorraine Motel, the gulf between Carmichael and Wilkins immediately became evident. The leader of the NAACP proposed that the purpose of the march should be to rally support for the civil rights bill currently before Congress. In addition to outlawing discrimination in housing, this measure proposed rules for the selection of juries and stiff federal penalties for attacks on, or intimidation of, civil rights workers. The Meredith shooting had spurred congressional interest in the bill, then languishing in committee. Carmichael, on the other hand, was interested in neither the civil rights bill nor civil rights unity, and, as he later admitted, deliberately baited Wilkins into leaving. He insisted upon a strident "manifesto" that Wilkins viewed as an attack on the president. According to Charles Morgan, who witnessed the ensuing confrontation, Carmichael slammed his hand on the table and shouted, "That cat the President's a bigot!" As Wilkins remembered the incident, "Stokely accused me of selling out the people, and his SNCC claque backed him up. . . . Finally, in disgust, I left the meeting to catch a 1:10 A.M. plane home." Whitney Young left with him.15

Carmichael believes that King played into his hands by failing to come to Wilkins's defense. "Dr. King might have been shocked too, but he didn't say a word. King was just beautiful." According to Morgan's account, King simply "sighed, shook his head, smiled wearily and adjourned the meeting." Perhaps King allowed his dislike of Wilkins to influence his judgement. Perhaps he believed that he could dominate SNCC, as he had done in Albany and Selma, and calculated that by breaking with the NAACP he was validating his "militancy" in SNCC's eyes. Whatever his thinking, King was clearly ignorant of SNCC's intention to utilize the march as a platform for racial separatism.16

Despite their differences, a feeling of comradeship soon grew up between the leaders of the march. Cleveland Sellers of SNCC later recalled his surprise when he discovered that King was "easygoing, with a delightful sense of humor," as well as "much less conservative than we initially believed." King felt uplifted by the enthusiastic crowds that lined the roadside. "From the very beginning of the march," wrote Sellers, "poor blacks . . . were awestruck by Dr. King's presence. . . . The same incredible scene would occur several times each day. The blacks along the way would line the side of the road, waiting in the broiling sun to see him. As we moved closer, they would edge out onto the pavement, peering under the brims of their starched bonnets and tattered straw hats. As we drew abreast someone would say, 'There he is! Martin Luther King!' This would precipitate a rush of 2,000, sometimes as many as 3,000 people. We would have to join arms and form a cordon in order to keep him from being crushed." When King preached at a little rural church in Cleveland, hundreds of blacks surrounded the packed hall, trying to catch his words through the open windows. Such reactions were all the more exhilarating in view of the fact that SCLC had hardly worked in Mississippi at all. "Oh man, yes!" Young enthused. "We can break this state open."17

On June 12, while King visited Chicago, Carmichael and McKissick discussed the route of the march with Bob Greene of SCLC. They wanted to leave Highway 51, the direct route to Jackson, in order to make a westward swing into the Delta. When he rejoined the march, King agreed. As the column left Grenada, King recalled later, "Stokely did not conceal his growing eagerness to reach Greenwood. This was

SNCC territory." Questioned by a reporter about his excitement, Carmichael observed enigmatically, "We've got all the cards." Visiting Chicago again—unwisely perhaps—as the marchers entered Greenwood, King allowed SNCC to set the stage for its carefully contrived publicity coup. After a brief arrest for pitching tents in a schoolyard, Carmichael escalated the rhetoric of violence at an evening rally on June 16: "This is the 27th time I've been arrested. I ain't gonna be arrested no more. . . . [Police chief] Buff Hammond has to go. I'm gonna tell you, baby, that the only way we're gonna get justice is when we have a black sheriff. . . . Every court house in Mississippi should be burnt down tomorrow so we can get rid of the dirt." The following night, after more speeches in a similar vein, Willie Ricks shouted the question, "What do you want?" prompting the response, "Black Power!" Carmichael repeated the slogan, which the crowd was soon echoing enthusiastically. A discomfited King tried to define black power in terms of conventional political power, but the slogan struck reporter Nicholas Von Hoffman as "totalitarian sounding," especially when black nationalism and violence were "the constant topics when the marchers pitch camp."[18]

SNCC seemed bent upon ridiculing nonviolence. Freedom songs were given new words: "I'm gonna bomb when the spirit say bomb . . . cut when the spirit say cut . . . shoot when the spirit say shoot." After Greenwood, the arguments between the SNCC and SCLC staffs became open and acrimonious. In Belzoni, reporter Von Hoffman witnessed an extraordinary three-cornered dispute between Willie Ricks, Bob Greene, and Chief of Police M. L. Nichols. When one of the policemen unbuttoned his holster, Greene ordered Leon Hall to fetch John Doar, the assistant attorney general, who represented the only real federal authority on the march. Ricks, however, threatened to burn down the courthouse if any of the marchers came to harm. When the chief laconically observed that the courthouse was fireproof, Ricks went one better: "Then we'll bomb it." Greene eventually separated the two, warning the chief that both he and Ricks agreed that "we're not going to take any more of that crap" from the police. The Mississippi authorities, however, were well aware of the friction between SNCC and SCLC. An informant working for the State Sovereignty Commission reported that Greene condemned Ricks's violent language at a heated staff meeting that night, warning him that King might withdraw SCLC from the march. "The consensus drawn," the informant observed, "[was] that if it were not for all of the nationwide publicity and financial support, a large percentage of those groups participating in this 'March' would like to call a halt to it. However, they are committed and cannot do anything about it." From Atlanta, King urged the marchers to drop the talk of black power on the grounds that it "tends to give the impression of black nationalism."[19]

King was now desperate for support. The march looked thin and ragged, and, as Young complained, many of the participants appeared to be "irresponsible and erratic characters." King toyed with the idea of pulling out but decided to soldier on; as he told Levison, Rustin, and Fauntroy in a telephone conference, "We're in it for good or ill and we have to make the best of the opportunity." But King found it difficult to arouse enthusiasm for the march among his colleagues and advisers. Rustin refused to take part, complaining that the march was degenerating into a black nationalist protest. If he joined the march himself, Carmichael and McKissick would be sure to attack him: "It will be Atlantic City all over again." He agreed to drum up support in New York, but made little effort to do so. Even Levison and Wachtel found excuses for not taking part. As the march entered its third week, King felt that he had made a terrible mistake getting involved: the sooner it ended the better.[20]

In their eagerness to embarrass King, the federal and state authorities also undermined his efforts to counteract SNCC's angry rhetoric. On June 16 Governor Paul Johnson reduced the highway patrol escort from twenty to four, explaining that "we are not going to wet-nurse a bunch of showmen from all over the country." Five days later, when King led 250 marchers to Philadelphia, scene of the Schwerner-Chaney-Goodman murders, the state authorities proved utterly delinquent. At the Neshoba County Courthouse King came face-to-face with Deputy Sheriff Cecil Price, who barred him from ascending the steps. Turning his back to Price to address the marchers, King told them that "I believe in my heart that the murderers of the three young men are around me at this moment." When one of the white hecklers shouted, "They're right behind you," Price smirked and passed a whispered command to a man beside him. Responding to an arranged signal, the whites lobbed bottles and firecrackers at the marchers, who were spat at, shoved, and pummelled. Wendell Hoffman, a CBS cameraman, and Paul Good, a freelance reporter, considered this attack more frightening than anything they had previously witnessed in the South. King and the marchers beat a retreat to Indianola. Asked if they intended to return, King replied, "We've got to. We've got to. I've never seen such a terrible town in my life."[21]

In a Catholic parish house in Yazoo City, King pleaded with Carmichael and McKissick that night to abandon the black power slogan. "I mentioned the implications of violence that the press had already attached to the phrase. And I went on to say that some of the rash statements on the part of a few of the marchers only reinforced the impression." But he failed to persuade them. "Martin," Carmichael admitted, "I deliberately decided to raise this issue on the march in order to give it a national forum." King, according to his later account, simply laughed: "I have been used before. One more time won't hurt."[22] The events in Philadelphia had raised the debate between nonviolence and self-defense beyond the level of theory: even as the leaders disputed, SNCC workers in the Philadelphia "Freedom House" were trading shots with Klan attackers. Meeting in Canton the next day, the Deacons for Defense vowed to go armed to Philaldephia when King led a return visit there on June 24.[23]

It was difficult to argue against self-defense when the White House left the marchers to the mercy of the state authorities. Sending a telegram to the president, King asked for federal protection on the second Philadelphia march. The only reply he received, however, consisted of a bland statement from an assistant White House press secretary assuring the marchers that they could trust in Governor Johnson. As if to underline the president's contempt, one hundred state troopers attacked the marchers as they tried to pitch their tents in a Canton schoolyard that evening. The patrolmen fired tear gas canisters, then kicked and hit those who had failed to clear the site. "I thought I was really going to die," Young remembered. "It was my first experience with tear gas. . . . I completely lost my cool. I didn't say it, but I thought to myself, 'If I had a machine gun, I'd *show* those mother-fuckers!'" The gas had a similar effect on Carmichael, who had to be physically restrained by McKissick and King. Paul Good spoke to King after the attack and remembered it as the only instance, "from a memory encompassing dozens of times I saw him hard-pressed, that he seemed physically and emotionally shaken." Another request for federal protection drew another negative response, and the attorney general, Nicholas Katzenbach, chided the marchers for trespassing.[24]

The Meredith March ended in Jackson on June 26 with an unconvincing display of unity. The march had given hope and encouragement to thousands of black Mississippians; it took the civil rights movement to towns like Grenada and Belzoni for the first time; it gave SCLC a foothold in Mississippi. But these gains had to be weighed against the impact of black power. The white elite was overwhelmingly hostile to the slogan. *Time* labelled it "the new racism,"

and likened it to the "wild-eyed doctrines of the Black Muslims."
Similar strictures could be found throughout the press. The administration, too, denounced the slogan, with President Johnson urging the
nation to think in terms of "democratic power" rather than "black
power" or "white power." Two days later, on July 6, Vice-President
Humphrey echoed these sentiments at the NAACP convention. "Racism is racism," he declared, "and there is no room in America for
racism of any color. We must reject calls for racism, whether they
come from a throat that is white or one that is black." A cartoon by
Herblock, which appeared in the *Washington Post* the following day,
expressed the misgivings of many white liberals. It depicted a huge,
menacing genie emanating from a bottle labelled "Black Power," with a
lone Negro looking up in terror. It was captioned "Dangerous
Genie."[25]

Irony abounded in the furor over black power. SNCC's argument
that white hostility compelled blacks to organize separately was
hardly new, having long been tacitly accepted by other civil rights
organizations. The NAACP, despite its commitment to interracialism,
had long been overwhelmingly black. In the South, its local branches
made little attempt to recruit white members and sometimes actively
discouraged them. At a meeting of civil rights leaders in June 1965,
Roy Wilkins had argued that blacks ought to combat the attitude that
"anything that is all black is all bad, anything that has some white is
good."[26] Within the trade unions, blacks had organized separately in
the Negro American Labor Council, a body promoted and supported by
A. Philip Randolph, Bayard Rustin, and Cleveland Robinson. Belying
its emphasis on integration, SCLC itself had always been almost exclusively black; indeed, when SCLC was founded, Virginia Durr, la-
menting its failure to include whites, described it as "racist." Only in
1966, when its all-black board threatened to become an embarrassment, did King appoint whites to SCLC's governing body.[27] Taken
literally, the concept of black power was neither novel nor exceptiona-
ble. But Carmichael did not wish the slogan to be taken literally, and
his vague and ambiguous rhetoric encouraged biased and exaggerated
interpretations. As SCLC staff member Leon Hall put it, "Stokely
didn't get a chance to give any meaning to black power. He threw the
words out, and before he could explain it the press had taken it and
used it as a bludgeon."[28]

SNCC's new slogan also ended the gentleman's agreement according
to which civil rights organizations did not feud in public. At the
NAACP convention Roy Wilkins denounced black power in vehement

terms. He noted that CORE had adopted a resolution calling for armed self-defense, and warned that "such a publicized posture" could lead to an "indiscriminate crackdown by law officers under the ready-made excuse of restoring law and order . . . [and] is as likely to encourage counter-violence as it is to discourage violent persecution." But he directed his main attack against the black power slogan:

> No matter how endlessly they try to explain it, the term "black power" means anti-white power. . . . It is a reverse Mississippi, a reverse Hitler, a reverse Ku Klux Klan. . . . We of the NAACP will have none of this. We have fought it too long. It is the ranging of race against race on the irrelevant basis of skin color. It is the father of hatred and the mother of violence. It is the wicked fanaticism which has swelled our tears, broken our bodies, squeezed our hearts, and taken the blood of our black and white loved ones. It shall not poison our forward march.[29]

Wilkins's verbal onslaught dismayed King. Interviewed on July 8, he voiced the suspicion that the NAACP had been waiting for an opportunity to repudiate and isolate SNCC: "They think they are the only civil rights organization." Randolph, too, looked on with alarm. He implored the quarreling black leaders to reject an invitation to appear on "Meet the Press" lest a televised debate "further stimulate confusion and disunity." But the debate went ahead and did nothing to paper over the cracks.[30]

Some of his advisers urged King to join Wilkins in denouncing SNCC and black power. Carmichael was reaping political havoc, Clarence Jones complained; he had to be isolated. "There comes a time when you have to call a spade a spade, and you have to fight for the supremacy of your theory." Rustin took a similar view and advised King to come down firmly against SNCC: "You can't continuously put yourself in the middle. . . . It's bad with a large segment of white liberals, and it's also bad with the Negro middle classes." But King resisted this advice. When Rustin drafted a statement which condemned strategies of "violence, reprisal or vigilantism," King refused to add his signature to those of Wilkins, Randolph, and Whitney Young. "I must be in a position," he insisted, "where I won't be lumped in with Roy and Whitney."[31]

Why was he so indulgent towards SNCC and black power? He immediately identified the slogan—and, more important, its surrounding rhetoric—as a profound threat to the civil rights movement. Violence and separatism had to be rooted out, he believed, if black advances were to be secured and protected. King had always stressed, moreover, that blacks should act on a higher moral plane than their oppressors. Yet he also recognized the emotional appeal of the slogan. The words expressed a "cry of disappointment," he wrote; they encapsulated the pain and despair produced by unrelenting poverty, brutality, discrimination, and broken promises. King knew from his experiences in Chicago how deep was the despair, how intense the anger. Such emotions could not be exorcized simply by attacking black power and castigating SNCC. On the contrary, an all-out attack along the lines of Wilkins's diatribe would probably strengthen the slogan's appeal and diminish his own standing among young blacks. King was always acutely conscious of the need to avoid taking positions that might lend credence to the charge of "Uncle Tomism."[32]

Despite its connotations of violence and separatism, moreover, King did not find black power wholly repugnant. The slogan struck a responsive chord among blacks because it expressed "a psychological call to manhood." Its stress on the word "black" stirred powerful emotions which, King believed, reflected residual feelings of inferiority and submissiveness. Inasmuch as it dispelled these negative feelings and evoked racial pride, he had no quarrel with the slogan. Nor did he object to the concept of black power in the sense of group solidarity, collective effort, and the pooling of political and economic resources: "No one can deny that the Negro is in dire need of this kind of legitimate power." King made plain his opposition to black power as a slogan. Instead of defining it solely in terms of violence and separatism, however, he tried to emphasize its constructive elements.[33]

Finally, King believed that he could better combat doctrines of violence and separatism by debating with the black nationalists than by anathematizing them. He had too much respect for SNCC to simply turn his back on it. It also went against his instincts to publicly attack other black organizations. Dialogue and debate were in his blood, and he rebelled against the idea of lumping together all advocates of black power and treating them as untouchables. Some had to be isolated as dangerous extremists. But most, he believed, were merely confused and misguided; they could be persuaded of the futility of violence and separatism through rational argument. King looked forward to a time when the controversy over black power had abated, when SCLC could once again function as the keystone of a united black coalition.[34]

But the black power controversy refused to die. Sometimes Carmichael defined black power in the kind of moderate terms which King emphasized—when, for example, he likened the concept to the American tradition of ethnic-group politics. But the slogan was less a coherent ideology or strategy than an emotional expression of anger, frustration, and bitterness. As Clayborne Carson has argued, instead of seeking to dispel the charge that black power meant antiwhite violence, Carmichael contributed to this misconception "through his vague implications of future racial retribution." Although he denied the allegation of reverse racism, the tone and style of his rhetoric implied a general hostility towards whites. Before long, such hostility became overt as Carmichael began referring to "honkies" and SNCC expelled its remaining white staff members. Like King, but in a different way, SNCC learned to manipulate the news media's fascination with violence. As Ella Baker put it, "With their own need for recognition, [SNCC] began to respond to the press."[35]

SCLC found itself unable to blunt the appeal of black power, and King's efforts to restore civil rights unity came to nothing. The only way to neutralize the doctrine, Andrew Young believed, was through a clear demonstration of the efficacy of nonviolent direct action: "We have got to deliver results—nonviolent results in a Northern city."[36] Yet this is what SCLC conspicuously failed to do in Chicago. Indeed, SCLC's campaign exposed a deep vein of racism which seemed to undermine the rationale of nonviolent protest. "Where housing is concerned," wrote the social psychologist Thomas Pettigrew, "much of the subtlety which clothes racial prejudice in the North is lost," an assertion which numerous opinion polls amply documented. Most whites wished to live away from blacks; they regarded even "token" integration with dismay and alarm.[37] Even more than the campaign for school integration, the demand for fair housing mobilized the forces of racism and conservatism in a counterattack on the civil rights movement. By 1966 a string of populous states had thrown out fair housing legislation. Such defeats confirmed the evidence of opinion polls, real estate practices, and the growth of ghettos. King was surely correct in arguing that SCLC's open-housing marches, far from provoking a "backlash," actually identified a social cancer.[38]

As the ruling party nationally and the dominant party in the Northern cities, the Democrats felt profoundly threatened by black demands for open housing: the issue was already splitting the Democratic coalition of blacks and working-class "ethnics." Democratic leaders were terrified by the prospect of a mass defection of white voters in the cities and suburbs of the North. The housing provisions of the civil rights bill hung like an albatross around the party's neck. Alarmed congressmen reported that their mail was running one hundred to one against open housing. Northern Democrats attempted to fend off what

they saw as certain disaster in the midterm elections by voting 150 to
33 to exempt owner-occupiers. Some wanted to scrap the fair housing
section altogether in order to salvage the sections on jury reform and
federal protection of civil rights workers. On September 14, however,
the entire bill was lost when the Senate rejected cloture. In contrast to
1964 and 1965, administration pressure for the bill's passage had been
feeble. As Lyndon Johnson wrote in his memoirs, "Open housing had
become a Democratic liability."[39]

Writing in the *New York Times* after the bill's failure, Gene Roberts
noted the obvious: rioting, the war in Vietnam, and the controversy
over black power were sapping the strength of the civil rights movement at precisely the time that white opposition was becoming stronger, more coherent, and more aggressive. King recognized the tragic
irony of the situation: the cry for black power came when blacks were
at their most powerless for many years. SNCC and CORE were both
dying, Levison gloomily observed, "and as they die they're going to be
noisier and noisier and more militant in their expression." Would
SCLC suffer the same fate?[40]

During the later months of 1966, SCLC's staff, both leaders and led,
became increasingly demoralized. The recurrence of black rioting, the
fragmentation of the movement, and the growth of white opposition
far outweighed the ephemeral victory of the Summit Agreement. The
staff was floundering in confusion, King lamented; Young was so depressed that he felt like resigning. James Bevel became absorbed with
the anti-war movement, taking a year-long leave of absence starting in
the New Year. The departure of several other senior staff members
reflected and reinforced this sense of creeping pessimism. By the end
of 1966 Vivian, Blackwell, Boyte, and Greene had all tendered their
resignations, leaving SCLC woefully short of executive manpower, especially in the field of administration.[41]

The morale of the field staff also suffered. Bevel's preoccupation
with Vietnam left the Chicago staff virtually unsupervised, and their
discipline quickly eroded. When he came to Chicago in December,
Hosea Williams claimed, "many of SCLC's regular staff members were
doing little more than laying around their rooms all day, playing cards,
drinking and smoking pot (dope)." Williams blamed the Chicago staff
for the failure of his voter registration drive: their indiscipline affected
the Southerners, making them lazy and rebellious. When he required
all staff members to start work at 8:30 A.M., "only the staff members
from the South showed up. After a week or so the staff members from
the South began not showing up." He then lost control of the staff, he

admitted, and neither Abernathy nor Young proved capable of restoring discipline. "Our staff problems are unbelievable," Williams wrote King.[42]

King's advisers recommended a long strategy meeting, perhaps a retreat, to analyze the state of the movement and its relationship to the changing political climate. "We need to sit down," Levison insisted, "talk, discuss, raise questions, examine some theory, and stop letting action send us on, kind of mindlessly, from day to day." During the second week of October King held several lengthy meetings with the research committee to define SCLC's position in respect of black power. In mid-November, SCLC held a three-day staff retreat in Frogmore, South Carolina, to consider the wider question of where blacks now stood after a decade of struggle.[43]

King's speech to the SCLC staff on November 14, 1966, should be included among his most significant statements, for it staked out the radical position which guided him for the remainder of his life. SCLC's experiences in Chicago had clearly shaken King's optimism: the white mobs in Bogan and Gage Park dramatically contradicted the notion that racism was a Southern anachronism. For all its achievements, he admitted, the civil rights movement "did not defeat the monster of racism. We have got to see that racism is still alive in our country. And we have got to see that the roots of racism are very deep in America." True, whites had adapted with relative ease to the desegregation of public accommodations and the enforcement of equal voting rights. But they had done so only because those changes were superficial: they cost whites virtually nothing; they did not greatly alter the lopsided and inequitable distribution of wealth and power in America. Indeed, the economic position of the Negro poor had deteriorated. Outside the South, moreover, schools and housing were becoming more segregated rather than less. The gains of the previous decade had led blacks to underestimate the forces arrayed against them; only a minority of whites, King reluctantly concluded, were genuinely committed to racial equality.

This had become evident the moment blacks began to threaten the economic basis of their subordination. When SCLC tried to eradicate the ghetto, for example, it had inadvertently challenged one of the foundations of the capitalist economy. "You can't talk about ending slums without first seeing that profit must be taken out of slums. You're really . . . getting on dangerous ground because you are messing with folk then. You are messing with Wall Street. You are messing with the captains of industry." This, he insisted, was the real source of the "white backlash." To be sure, rioting and inflammatory rhetoric hurt the black cause, but underlying the stiffening white resistance was a "reaction to questions being raised by the civil rights movement which demand a restructuring of the architecture of American society."[44] As he told the SCLC convention in August, the struggle was no longer a fight for civil rights: it had evolved into a confrontation against "the giants of vested interest."[45]

King offered no blueprint for the future. "I am still searching myself," he admitted. "I don't have all the answers, and . . . certainly have no pretense to omniscience." Nevertheless, of one thing he felt certain: gross inequalities demanded radical solutions. It was not enough for the state to guarantee legal and political equality while leaving the eradication of poverty to private enterprise—especially if, as King was convinced, private enterprise constituted a large part of the problem. Automation and cybernation were eliminating millions of jobs in the private sector, and such losses could only be made good by the state. Work should be redefined so that people could be paid for making art, furthering their education, or assisting those in need. The government ought to underwrite the economic security of its citizens by guaranteeing a decent income for all. Sweden had already moved in this direction, King pointed out: here was a country without slums, without poverty or unemployment, and where every citizen had free access to quality education and an excellent health service. Sweden had achieved this by distributing its wealth more equitably.

This brought King to the heart of his message: perhaps the United States should be moving towards a similar kind of democratic socialism. Lest he shock his staff by mere mention of the word "socialism" King carefully explained the difference between Scandinavian-style social democracy and communism or Marxism. Yet even Marxism, he went on, should not be dismissed out of hand. "I always look at Marx with a yes and a no. And there were some things that Karl Marx did that were very good. . . . [T]his man had a great passion for social justice." Although he found aspects of Marxism abhorrent, Marx had laid bare the exploitative and unjust nature of capitalism. And this, King insisted—"Now Hosea, I want you to hear this, because you are a capitalist"—remained as true in the 1960s as it had been in the 1860s. "Now this is where I leave Brother Marx and move on toward the Kingdom. . . . I am simply saying that God never intended for some of his children to live in inordinate superfluous wealth while others live in abject, deadening poverty."

King warned his staff against the growing clamor for black power. While the concept of black power was acceptable, the slogan was being bandied about in a misguided and destructive manner. It had become a clarion call for black separatism; worse, "it sounds like you are trying to say black domination." Worst of all, the rhetoric of black power encouraged the idea that violence was a practical alternative when, in fact, violence was utterly self-defeating. In Watts, he reminded his staff, all but one of the thirty-five dead had been black, and the rioters had ended up destroying their own neighborhoods. Violence could never be an effective strategy, only a nihilistic expression of rage, "disruption for disruption's sake." SCLC had to convince blacks that it was suicidal. Most advocates of violence knew this, King went on, and were guilty of dishonesty and hypocrisy. He had little respect for "the people who stand on street corners and preach about violence [but] always go home at night." By way of example, he told of an incident during the Meredith March concerning Charles Evers, who had become the NAACP's Mississippi field secretary upon the murder of his brother, Medgar. At one of the evening rallies, King related, Evers had orated on the need for blacks to fight back with guns, evoking an excited response from the audience. But King had interrupted him, pointing out that Medgar's killer had been acquitted by a white jury and was living close by: "If you're that violent, why don't you go up the highway to Greenwood and kill the man who killed your brother?" This incident held a special significance for King, for he often referred to it when arguing against violence.[46]

The certitude of King's analysis of the political background highlighted the doubt and hesitancy of his views on goals and tactics. Excluding separatism and violence, three broad strategies needed to be considered: political action, community organization, and nonviolent direct action. The limitation of political action could be simply stated: as a despised minority, blacks received a disporportionately small share of the rewards and benefits of political participation. By joining coalitions, it is true, they could form part of a governing majority. As in Chicago, however, segregation was the tacit sine qua non for political horse trading. As one cynic put it, "one man, one vote" proved a limited instrument of change when "there are two other men, also voting, whose economic and social interests are served by keeping the first man subjugated."[47]

Bayard Rustin still contended that the Johnson landslide had paved the way for a progressive coalition. As the white backlash became more pronounced, however, the argument looked increasingly threadbare. Far from promoting working-class unity, the civil rights movement seemed to be splitting the working class along racial lines, threatening the very existence of the old New Deal coalition. By 1966, wrote Brink and Harris, "the defections from the Democratic party of the late-arriving Catholic minorities" had become "crystal clear in state after state." As the political scientist James Q. Wilson noted, the prospect of forging a stable liberal—let alone radical—coalition was remote. Not only had the political realignment envisaged by Rustin and King failed to materialize, but 1966 also witnessed the re-emergence of the conservative coalition in Congress—that informal alliance of Southern Democrats and Northern Republicans which had stymied so many proposals for social reform between 1938 and 1964. Black demands for economic security—the Urban League's "Marshall Plan for the Negro," Rustin's "Freedom Budget," King's guaranteed annual income—fell on deaf ears. Even the minuscule War on Poverty was being whittled away. Although he continued to sound the coalition theme occasionally, King on the whole shared Levison's view that the civil rights coalition was dead. After Chicago, he regarded most white liberals with barely concealed disdain. He also found it impossible to share Rustin's enthusiasm for organized labor—only the United Packinghouse Workers had stuck with SCLC during the open-housing marches. "Something tragic" had happened to the labor movement, he complained. "So often it's the most conservative. I have found in many instances businessmen [are] more progressive."[48]

Given the immense power of Richard J. Daley, King was curiously dismissive of local politics. Demographic trends meant that many of the nation's largest cities would soon contain black majorities—Washington, which still lacked home rule, already did. But the prospect of black mayors did not greatly excite King. His lack of enthusiasm stemmed, in part, from a belief that the scale of urban reconstruction needed to make Chicago a decent place for blacks to live in required billions of dollars from the federal government. It also reflected the fact that black mayors were a mixed blessing if they owed their election to the existence of black ghettos and exclusive white suburbs. His mixed feelings about black mayors came out most clearly in a speech he made in Louisville, in 1967: "We're hemmed in. We can't get out. They won't pass the fair housing bill right here. And that's true in every city in this country. . . . Since our white brothers and sisters don't want to live by us, other than those dedicated few, what we're going to have to do is just control the inner city. . . . We're going to have to get the mayor. And the minute we get elected mayor, we've got to begin taxing everybody who works in the city who lives out in the suburbs. I know that sounds mean, but I just want to be realistic."[49]

In statements like this, King implied a retreat to the ghetto, albeit a temporary retreat. The rate of integration was so infinitesimal that it did virtually nothing to relieve the poverty, congestion, and physical deterioration of the black inner-city areas. "Let's face the fact," he told a Chicago audience. "Most of us are going to be living in the ghetto five, ten years from now. But we've got to get some things straightened out straight away."[50] Discussing his forthcoming appearance before the Ribicoff committee, a Senate investigation of the "urban crisis," King told Levison that he wanted to present a fresh approach to the problem, one that placed less emphasis on integration: "[We] need to make the ghetto more liveable, because no matter how much open housing you have, you'll not get all the poor people out of the ghetto immediately. You have to make life liveable for those who will be in the ghetto. . . . Bayard and Phil are taking the approach that . . . the job is as much to improve the cities and rural areas of the South so you won't have the problem of [blacks] running away [to the North] to improve conditions."[51] As things stood, however, there seemed little likelihood of a concerted and committed effort by either the government or the private sector to revitalize these areas.

"Community organization" had long been advocated by SNCC as a sounder basis for bringing about political and social change than either conventional party politics or nonviolent direct action. Much of the conflict between SCLC and SNCC in the South had involved the question of "mobilizing versus organizing." SCLC's crisis-confrontation tactics, SNCC complained, had too often left blacks disorganized, exhausted, demoralized, and vulnerable to white retaliation. In Chicago SCLC had tried to avoid this by taking a leaf from SNCC's book: Bevel's "Union to End Slums" represented an attempt to give the black poor an organizational framework for political and direct action, and to create an indigenous leadership capable of carrying on after SCLC departed. "We've got to do more in terms of organizing people into permanent units," King admitted, "rather than on a temporary basis just for demonstrations."[52]

Community organization, however, turned out to be something of a cul-de-sac. The immense practical difficulties of reaching and involving the urban poor have already been described. Even when community organizations had been formed, it was far from clear exactly how they were supposed to effect change. The rent strike, for example, was a tactic of limited usefulness. True, SCLC-organized tenant unions won more than a dozen housing contracts, which committed landlords and managers to maintaining their buildings to specified standards. But these tenant unions embraced a mere ten thousand people—a far cry from Bevel's original goal of three hundred thousand. In addition, it transpired that the much-hated "slumlord" was not always a rapacious exploiter who reaped excessive profits. In areas like Lawndale, vandalism and rent arrears made rental property a hazardous investment. "The only way I can make a profit," one property manager explained, "is because I buy buildings from landlords who are desperate to get out." Many buildings were simply abandoned. At the end of 1966 the tenant unions in East Garfield Park reported that landlords "have expressed strong desires to get rid of their property." Unless money became available for rehabilitation, they predicted, "the tenant union movement is at a dead end."53

For a time, King shared Bevel's enthusiasm for tenant unions. In the summer of 1966 he was thinking in terms of a five-year drive to organize slum-dwellers in all the major cities. By the end of the year, however, he recognized this plan to be unrealistic. SCLC could not possibly undertake such a gargantuan task in light of the difficulties it had experienced in Chicago. "In all frankness," King confessed, "we found the job greater than even we imagined."54 More fundamentally, community organization suffered from the same weakness as the separatist strategy of black power: it amounted to little more than self-help. Like the War on Poverty, it fostered the fallacy that the poor could somehow organize themselves out of their poverty. King knew better: an OEO grant here, an FHA loan there could have but a marginal impact on ghetto conditions. The economic problems confronting blacks, he wrote, "will only be solved by federal programs involving billions of dollars." Community organization offered the illusion of power without the substance.55

This left nonviolent direct action. SCLC had yet to show that its tactics could work in the North: the outcome of the Chicago campaign spoke for itself. The evidence of opinion polls, moreover, confirmed the fact that demonstrations no longer evoked white sympathy for the plight of blacks. Contrary to King's belief, most whites had always disapproved of direct action. White opinion had been malleable, however, as long as demonstrations were largely a Southern phenomenon and when strict adherence to nonviolence enabled the news media to portray blacks as the blameless victims of racist aggression. In addition, the fear of potential black violence and the belief that King's leadership could prevent it had given many whites a pragmatic reason for acquiescing in the nonviolent crusades of the Southern civil rights movement. King himself, moreover, had repeatedly reassured whites that through timely civil rights legislation violence could be averted.

The urban riots changed all this. As Godfrey Hodgson noted, television coverage of the rioting conveyed the distorted impression that blacks were engaging in vicious and indiscriminate violence against whites. The fact that "the killing had been done by white men, and by white men in uniform at that," was lost amid the dramatic pictures of looting and burning buildings, the wild rumors of black snipers, the interviews with white businessmen whose stores had been attacked, and the hysterical reactions of newspaper editors and politicians.[56] Whites were understandably alarmed by the outbreaks, but their responses often bordered on the irrational and the paranoid. Almost half of those polled by the Harris organization blamed the riots on Communists, subversives, and outside agitators; most seemed "unaware or unbelieving of . . . the conditions the Negro himself considers most responsible." Even President Johnson suspected that Russian or Cuban money lay behind the violence. The riots also made it increasingly difficult for whites to distinguish between riots and demonstrations. The West Side riot in Chicago, coming in the middle of SCLC's campaign, did nothing to dispel this confusion. By late 1966, Brink and Harris reported, "85 per cent of all whites had come to the conclusion that demonstrations were hurting the Negro cause."[57]

King refused to concede that nonviolent direct action had exhausted its usefulness, but several of his colleagues left SCLC to pursue different strategies. Blackwell founded Southern Rural Action, Inc., a new Atlanta-based organization designed to promote economic cooperatives. Vivian departed to undertake community organizing in Chicago, heading a training center for black ministers financed by the Ford Foundation. Bevel was leaving to organize the Spring Mobilization, a massive demonstration against the war in Vietnam to be held in New York on April 15, 1967. As the Summit Agreement became a dead letter, King threatened to renew the open-housing marches, but neither he nor his staff felt any eagerness to stage another direct action campaign in Chicago. "We wanted to return South," Young recalled, "to familiar terrain."[58] Williams argued for more voter registration in Alabama and Mississippi, a view shared by Harry Wachtel. Rustin, too, advocated a political thrust, and he made it known through the press that the Summit Agreement, in his view, merely vindicated his warning to King that SCLC ought to steer clear of Chicago.[59]

In December 1966, King attempted to distil his thinking on the state of the black movement in a new book, aptly entitled *Where Do We Go from Here?* Bogged down in fundraising, he made little progress. On January 14, therefore, he flew to Jamaica so that he could enjoy an uninterrupted three or four weeks. Bernard Lee remembered an incident at the airport during the outward journey. King bought a copy of *Ramparts* magazine, and came across an article by William Pepper, entitled "The Children of Vietnam," which described and illustrated the horrifying effects of napalm, a chemical weapon employed by the United States forces. The photograph of a dead baby stared out from the page. King was sickened and conscience stricken. The lifeless child testified to the moral bankruptcy of American policy and to the cowardice of his own silence over the war. The time had come to break with the administration and campaign for peace.[60]

Thirteen

The Politics of Peace

Throughout 1966 King had tried to avoid the war issue. He shunned the mushrooming peace rallies and eschewed public discussions of Vietnam. When Linus Pauling asked him to sponsor a fund for anti-war political candidates, he politely refused. "I have to think about fundraising for SCLC," he told Rustin and Levison, both of whom approved of his caution. When he referred to Vietnam on public platforms, he restricted himself to the observation that rising military expenditure had led to reduced funding for the War on Poverty. "I shouldn't get into the Vietnam thing too much," he told Levison in December. "In an indirect way I should be lashing out on this question of cutting back on domestic programs."[1]

Yet King had never completely stifled his opposition to the

war, as the Bond affair showed. In January 1966, SNCC attacked the administration for pursuing "an aggressive policy in violation of international law." As a consequence, the Georgia legislature refused to seat Julian Bond, a newly elected black representative, who had endorsed SNCC's statement. King actively backed SNCC's campaign to have Bond, an ex-SNCC staff member, seated. But he did not confine his comments on the affair to the obvious constitutional issues of free speech and democracy. Preaching to his congregation on January 16, he insisted that "our hands are dirty in the war in Vietnam. . . . I'm tired of the press and others trying to brainwash people and let us feel that there are no issues to be discussed in this war."[2] In March, King again underlined his abhorrence of American policy when he wrote in a newspaper column that "a war in which children are incinerated, in which American soldiers die in mounting numbers . . . is a war that mutilates the conscience." And in an interview for WNDT television, a public station in New York, he repeated his call for negotiations with the Vietcong. The United States, he complained, was in the position of opposing a people who were seeking self-determination. A few weeks later, King let Clarence Jones draft a telegram of support for an anti-war rally in Washington.[3]

It would be naive, therefore, to interpret King's decision to join the anti-war movement as a road-to-Damascus conversion occasioned by his emotional reaction to a magazine article. King operated in the real world of politics: like other civil rights leaders, he was continually forced to seek compromises, on a pragmatic basis, in the light of changing circumstances. He had spoken out against the war in 1965, only to back down when convinced of the damage he might inflict on SCLC, the civil rights movement, and his own reputation. But the situation had changed since then; the political arguments for avoiding the war issue no longer seemed so compelling. By the end of 1966 the president had already lost interest in civil rights, the Congress had taken a sharp lurch to the right, and the civil rights movement had disintegrated. There could be little to lose in breaking with the administration. With military outlays spiraling out of control when the War on Poverty—insignificant by comparison—was being curtailed, King reasoned that the war itself had become the greatest single stumbling block to further social progress.

King was well aware of SCLC's internal divisions over Vietnam. During 1966, however, opinion within the upper echelons of the organization hardened against the war. In 1965 James Lawson had travelled to Vietnam as part of a peace-seeking mission sponsored by the Fellowship of Reconciliation. In February 1966, he and three other senior staff members—Harry Boyte, John Barber, and Robert Greene—helped to organize anti-war rallies in Atlanta and other Southern cities. Two months later, the SCLC board was finally persuaded to approve a resolution sharply critical of American policy: the administration, it stated, should "seriously examine the wisdom of prompt withdrawal." According to the FBI wiretap summaries, Levison, Wachtel, and Bevel lobbied for the resolution, while Rustin attempted to have it toned down. As the war dragged on, however, Rustin became increasingly isolated in his reluctance to criticize the administration. Abernathy attacked the war in a little-publicized speech at Brandeis University in November. Bevel left SCLC at the end of the year to devote himself exclusively to anti-war activities. Outside SCLC, too, opposition to the war was mounting fast. The question facing King was no longer whether to join the peace movement but when to join it.[4]

Even in Jamaica, King could not escape the war issue. No sooner had he arrived in his secluded villa than Bevel turned up, unannounced and uninvited, in an effort to recruit him for the Spring Mobilization on April 15. His obsession with the war, his wild preaching, and his fantastic suggestions disturbed King. "Bevel sounds like he's off his rocker and needs a psychiatrist," he told Young over the phone. Nevertheless, Bevel's visit reinforced King's doubts about the wisdom of remaining silent. Soon afterwards he accepted an invitation from *Nation* magazine to participate in a conference on American foreign policy. He intended to deliver a strong attack on the war.[5]

When he flew back to the United States on February 18, King paused in Miami to place a conference call to Young, Levison, and Cleveland Robinson. He had to do more to oppose the war, he informed his advisers; he could no longer stand on the sidelines. But he had to decide how far to go and what form his opposition should take. He could make a series of speeches on Vietnam, urging young men to become conscientious objectors, "but it would be way over on page 30." In order to be effective, he felt, the peace movement needed to have the strength of numbers:

> You must have mobilization behind you. . . . You have to have the masses behind you before you can go to the President. . . . Students are against the war in Vietnam. The more you keep it alive the more you turn other people against it, and Lyndon . . . can't stand this constant

bombardment. I think there is a need for this development. I see it as tying the peace movement to the civil rights movement, or vice versa. I don't see getting out of civil rights, but we could be much more successful if we could get the peace people to do it—to cooperate, to have a march on Washington around the cut-backs in the poverty programs.

The crucial question which demanded his immediate attention was whether or not to accept Bevel's invitation to march to the United Nations on April 15. Young and Robinson felt that he should: SCLC ought to be in the forefront of the peace movement. "You have to have the ghettos mobilized," Young argued. "That's where the masses of people have to be mobilized."

Levison disagreed. Whatever the soundness of his views on the war, King would not succeed in bringing large numbers of Negroes into the peace movement. On the contrary, he stood to lose black support and weaken his status as a civil rights leader. He might even find himself isolated, and ineffective in both movements. Levison doubted that administration policy could be changed through marches and demonstrations. Instead of becoming a "small-time peace leader," King ought to use his influence politically, in alliance with figures like Robert Kennedy and Walter Reuther. "I think you will move ten times as many Negroes if you are associated with the Kennedys, the Reuthers and the Fulbrights than you will if you are associated with Norman Thomas and Spock. Most Negroes don't really know who they are." King should stay away from the Spring Mobilization, especially when there were serious doubts as to the mental stability of its organizer.[6]

King agreed to delay making a firm decision until he consulted the research committee on March 6. Meanwhile, at the *Nation* conference in Los Angeles, he delivered his first public speech against the war. American foreign policy, he asserted, was "supporting a new form of colonialism. . . . We are presently moving down a dead-end road that can only lead to national disaster."[7]

The research committee failed to dissuade King from joining the Spring Mobilization, even though Rustin, Levison, Wachtel, Fauntroy, Reddick, and Greene all advised him not to march. The protest was "non-exclusionary," they warned: King would be rubbing shoulders with Communists and Vietcong supporters. It would be folly to become identified with such a motley and unrepresentative collection of pacifists, hippies, and left-wing extremists. In view of its ecumenical nature and anti-Establishment tone, the Spring Mobilization would probably do more harm than good. King stood to alienate his natural supporters—white liberals and blacks—if he took part in this kind of fringe movement; the financial consequences for SCLC would be disastrous. Was it wise, moreover, to speak from the same platform as Stokely Carmichael, whose incendiary language could only embarrass King? Bevel, who attended the meeting at King's request, made light of these objections. The issue was simple, he insisted: Americans had to choose between mass murder and peace. This was simplistic nonsense, Levison retorted. But King sided with Bevel. He did not wish to be considered a coward; he intended to march. He agreed to mull over the decision for a few more days, however, before finally committing himself.[8]

His advisers continued to press King to change his mind. By the end of March, however, the die had been cast, and King looked forward to the march with a sense of excitement and relief. "At times you do things to satisfy your conscience," he explained,

> and they may be altogether unrealistic and wrong tactically, but you feel better. I just know, on the war in Vietnam, that I will get a lot of criticism, and I know it can hurt SCLC. But I feel better, and I think this is the most important thing. Because if I lose the fight then SCLC will die anyway. But if I have the feeling that I am right, I can make enough contacts to raise the money. And I feel that we are so wrong in the [Vietnam] situation that I can no longer be conscious about this matter. I feel so deep in my heart that we are so wrong in this country, and the time has come for a real prophecy. And I'm willing to go that road.[9]

The Spring Mobilization would probably be the largest march for peace in the history of the United States, he predicted; its significance could not be gainsaid.[10] On March 25 King led an anti-war demonstration in Chicago, walking beside Benjamin Spock, the eminent pediatrician now gaining fame and notoriety as an outspoken critic of the war. A few days later, in Louisville, SCLC's board of directors committed the organization to "do everything in our power to end that war." The board was far from happy, however, with King's decision to take part in the Spring Mobilization.[11]

It was ironic that the speech King delivered at the Riverside Church in New York on April 4, "Beyond Vietnam," had been designed, in his own words, "to neutralize the 15th." But instead of softening the criticism he anticipated after the Spring Mobilization, this speech precipitated such a deluge of hostile comment that it backfired utterly.[12]

Drafted in large part by Vincent Harding, then teaching at Spelman
College in Atlanta, "Beyond Vietnam" shocked many of King's supporters by expressing an underlying sympathy for the Vietcong insurgents and for revolutionary movements throughout the Third World.
The United States, King asserted, failed to understand that communism was primarily a revolt against the failures and injustices of capitalism. In Latin America, Africa, and Asia, colonialism had left a
legacy of revolutionary nationalism, and it was the duty of the West to
support these revolutions. In Vietnam, the United States should "admit that we have been wrong from the beginning," and "atone for our
sins and errors" by withdrawing all military forces, recognizing the
National Liberation Front, and making reparations "for the damage we
have done." Under the cloak of anticommunism, he charged, the
United States had become "the greatest purveyor of violence in the
world today."[13]

King had already discounted some of the ensuing criticism. He was
hardly surprised, therefore, when the NAACP and the Urban League
swiftly disassociated themselves from his position. The hostility of the
Luce press was also to be expected—*Life* accused King of advocating
"abject surrender in Vietnam" in a "demagogic slander that sounded
like a script for Radio Hanoi." King had also anticipated an immediate
and sharp decline in SCLC's income.[14]

But King was taken aback by the strength of criticism from people
he had expected to be sympathetic. The *Washington Post* dismissed his
speech as "sheer inventions of unsupported fantasy," disputing many
of King's facts and figures. People who had respected King in the past,
it added, would "never again accord him the same confidence." Even
that paragon of liberalism, the *New York Times,* failed to support King.
The criticism which distressed King most came from Ralph Bunche,
the black United Nations diplomat and fellow Nobel Peace Prize laureate. Bunche endorsed the NAACP's statement that King had committed a "serious tactical mistake" in his effort to "merge" civil rights and
peace. A variation of the "merger" theme was provided by Thurgood
Marshall, who acknowledged King's right to dissent from administration foreign policy, but not "as a civil rights leader."[15]

Most surprising, perhaps, was the attitude of Bayard Rustin. In a
newspaper column in March he defended King's "right to debate" the
war, but welcomed any criticisms that might "encourage Dr. King to
embark upon a re-examination of his position." Rustin advised blacks
to shun the peace movement because their immediate problems were

"so vast and crushing that they have little time or energy to focus upon international crises." In another article he urged blacks to seize the opportunity provided by the armed forces "to learn a trade, earn a salary, and be in a position to enter the job market on their return." This was strange advice coming from a former conscientious objector and veteran of the Fellowship of Reconciliation and the War Resisters League. As Godfrey Hodgson put it, Rustin "found himself in the tragic posture, for a lifelong pacifist, of justifying the war in the name of a radical coalition that never materialized."[16]

Rustin explained his stance by arguing that blacks could gain nothing without the support of President Johnson: how could they denounce him one day and ask him the next for help over schools, housing, and jobs?[17] His position disgusted Levison and Wachtel. Rustin had become "a very tired radical," Levison believed, and was seeking respectability, status, and financial security by acting as a mouthpiece of the AFL-CIO and the administration. His failure to help SCLC, his increasing friendliness towards Roy Wilkins and the NAACP, his leaks to the press, and his position on the war convinced Levison that he was not to be trusted. "You are going to have to rethink this business of treating Bayard as one of your advisers," Levison told King, "and rather treat him like John Morsell or Roy [Wilkins], where you are on your guard."[18] Even Wachtel, who had enormous admiration for Rustin, found his attitude to the war question "nauseating."[19] Yet King refused to treat Rustin as an enemy. On the contrary, he continued to seek his advice, critical though it might be.

The force of the liberal repudiation of King provided indirect but strong evidence of the fact that support for the war—or, at least, silence on the issue—represented the administration's loyalty test. According to Carl Rowan, black journalist and recent director of the U.S. Information Agency, Lyndon Johnson "flushed with anger" when he read the wire service summaries of "Beyond Vietnam."[20] White House aide John P. Roche advised the president that "King—in desperate search of a constituency—has thrown in with the commies." King was "inordinately ambitious," he added, "and quite stupid."[21] Documentary "evidence" came from the FBI, which assiduously reported the "influence" over King of "communist" Stanley Levison and "communist sympathizers" Harry Wachtel and Clarence Jones. True to form, the bureau portrayed King as a weak character whom the wily Levison manipulated at will. Lyndon Johnson, it seems, was very much in tune with Hoover's perception of reality. According to Bill Moyers, Johnson considered King "a naive black preacher [who] was being duped by a Communist."[22] Carl Rowan's journalistic attack on King, which appeared in *Reader's Digest*, the most widely read magazine in the United States, looked uncannily like an administration-inspired attempt to damage his reputation. Rowan referred to "talk of communists influencing . . . the young minister." King had developed "an exaggerated appraisal" of himself, he added, and "no longer seemed to be the selfless leader of the 1950s." And in attacking the war he had "alienated many of the Negro's friends and armed the Negro's foes . . . by creating the impression that the Negro is disloyal."[23]

If the strength of the liberal onslaught came as a shock to King, it did not surprise Levison. King had invited this kind of response, Levison told him, by being too radical, too frank, too moralistic, and too naive. Levison criticized "Beyond Vietnam" for its attack on imperialism and its implied attack on American capitalism. It had also been a mistake to speak from the viewpoint of a Vietcong peasant. King's likening of napalm to the medical experiments of the Nazi concentration camps had needlessly offended many sympathizers, especially Jews. Participating in the Spring Mobilization would only increase King's isolation, Levison warned: "I am afraid that you will become identified as a leader of a fringe movement, when you are much more." Speaking to his friend Alice Loewi, Levison referred to King's naivete in suggesting to him that if a thousand Americans went to Hanoi and stood on the bridges and the steel plants, America would be compelled to halt the bombing. "King should realize that he is dealing with the State Department and the Pentagon," Levison told Wachtel, "and not some stupid sheriff in the South."[24]

King occasionally hinted that he might bend to the pressure, especially after the Bunche statement. As the Spring Mobilization neared, he wondered how to "pull away" from the war issue after April 15. But these crises of confidence passed, and the march to the United Nations proved a memorable success. Instead of the 75,000 predicted by Levison or the 100,000 predicted by King, about 250,000 people turned out for the protest. The opponents of the war might well be in a minority, but their numbers were growing fast. If Levison and Rustin remained skeptical about the anti-war movement, King received encouragement and support from Harry Belafonte, Cleveland Robinson, Harry Wachtel, James Lawson, and many other friends and colleagues.[25]

Andrew Young played an important role in helping to define SCLC's relationship to the predominantly white anti-war movement. Belying his reputation as SCLC's most prominent conservative, Young attacked the war as a catastrophe and applauded King's decision to break with the administration. When asked to comment on Carl Rowan's article, he castigated the black journalist as a "sophisticated Uncle Tom."[26] With his close and varied contacts among Northern white liberals, Young sensed the depth of anti-war feeling and rejected the argument that King might become isolated. Levison, frustrated in his attempt to restrain SCLC's leader, complained to Wachtel that Young was "pulling King to the left" on the war issue.[27]

King had no intention, therefore, of backing down a second time. In the wake of the Spring Mobilization he stepped up his opposition to the war and hit back at the critics. Appearing on NBC's "Meet the Press" on April 16, Secretary of State Dean Rusk asserted that the "Communist apparatus" had been "working very hard" to support the anti-war demonstrations. On CBS's "Face the Nation" that same day, however, King ridiculed such charges and chided America for its "paranoid fear of Communism." Completely unrepentant about "Beyond Vietnam," he urged "young men who feel that this is an abominable and unjust war to apply for their status as conscientious objectors."[28] He also criticized the board of the NAACP for its statement, timed to coincide with the Spring Mobilization, that King was mistakenly trying to merge the peace movement and the civil rights movement. The charge was absurd, he retorted; nevertheless, the issues of peace and racial progress "are tied together, and I'm going to keep them together."[29] He even telephoned Ralph Bunche to complain about his criticism. According to King, Bunche said that he agreed with his position on Vietnam completely. "He just felt so guilty that I felt sorry for him. He wasn't telling the truth and all, so I just got off of him."[30] On April 27, at a meeting of civil rights leaders in Suffern, New York, Rustin, Wilkins, and Whitney Young again attempted to convince King that his position on Vietnam was tactically unsound. King would not be persuaded. In a speech to the SCLC staff, he emphasized the depth of his commitment in very personal terms:

> I thought people were mean when we stood up in civil rights. But they threaten me a little more now when we go into a city. The security is greater now, because the threats have increased. I thought about all of that. So I was prepared for everything that came. . . . The cross may mean the death of your popularity. It may mean the death of your bridge to the White House. It may mean the death of a foundation grant. It may cut

your budget down a little, but take up your cross and just bear it. . . . I backed up a little when I came out in 1965. My name then wouldn't have been written in any book called *Profiles of Courage* [sic]. But now I have decided. I will not be intimidated. I will not be harassed. I will not be silent. And I will be heard.[31]

King nevertheless deemed it prudent to distance himself from the New Left. On April 23 he travelled to Cambridge for the launch of "Vietnam Summer," a project organized by the Clergy and Laymen group. Modelled on the lines of a Southern voter registration drive, Vietnam Summer enlisted thousands of student volunteers to hand out leaflets and knock on doors. The following day King joined Joe Rauh of ADA in a new peace group called "Negotiation Now." Preaching at Ebenezer at the end of the month he reiterated his call for young men to register as conscientious objectors and praised Muhammed Ali's refusal to be inducted. The end of May saw King and Young in Geneva, where they attended the peace conference "Pacem in Terris II." A memorable photograph shows King shaking hands with Fran Van Do, the foreign minister of South Vietnam.[32]

Behind all this activity lay a fundamental problem: how could opposition to the war be chanelled into effective political pressure? One strategy, advocated by Norman Thomas and Benjamin Spock, was to run a third-party "peace" candidate in the forthcoming presidential election. King, they believed, would be the ideal standard-bearer. "I suggest that he be nominated with the idea of withdrawing," Thomas wrote, "if, by some miracle, one of the majority parties would nominate a candidate who came out clearly for peace." King might attract five to ten million votes, he predicted, if he stayed in the race.[33] King found the idea intriguing and gave it serious thought. Towards the end of April, however, he made a firm decision not to run. The danger of fatally weakening his support among blacks seems to have swayed King most. Many blacks failed to understand his motives, Young complained, and suspected SCLC's leader of inordinate ambition. According to a Harris poll, only a quarter of all blacks supported King's position on the war.[34]

King found the idea of another "March on Washington" far more attractive. Opinion within the anti-war movement, however, was divided over what form such a protest should take. Some wanted a mass rally along the lines of the 1963 event; others argued for a more militant protest employing mass civil disobedience. King and Young were among the first group, and had grave reservations about the kind of confrontational tactics being advocated by sections of the New Left. When coupled with insurrectionary rhetoric, they feared, such tactics could only alienate potential sympathizers and encourage government repression. After several meetings with representatives of SANE, ADA, Clergy and Laymen, and various other moderate anti-war groups, the prospects for mounting a peaceful and dignified mass rally towards the end of the summer seemed good. There was such a ground swell of opposition to the war, Young thought, that even the New Left would end up supporting this kind of event.[35]

But SCLC's plans for another "March on Washington" were overtaken by contingent and unforeseen events. June ushered in the brief but bloody Arab-Israeli war, which pushed Vietnam from the headlines and robbed the peace movement of publicity and momentum. "Half of the peace movement is Jewish," Levison cynically noted, "and the Jews have all become 'hawks.'" Certainly, Israel's decisive use of military power strengthened, albeit temporarily, the administration's claim that victory in Vietnam was both possible and near. Then came the ghetto riots of July and August, a violent spasm of unprecedented scale. By then King had shelved the "March on Washington" idea, at least as far as 1967 was concerned. SCLC refused to take part in October's "March on the Pentagon," which King regarded as foolish in the extreme.[36]

The alternative that remained was the "dump Johnson" strategy proposed by Allard Lowenstein. Lowenstein contended that "the great bulk of the antiwar movement was conventional, moderate, . . . reformist, mainstream"—people who had little in common with the alienated radicals of the New Left.[37] They would be reluctant to break with Johnson, but doubly reluctant to repudiate the Democrats. Working within the Democratic party in order to nominate a "peace" candidate was more realistic than either a third party or a resort to the streets. Lowenstein hoped that King could help rally the anti-war forces behind this political thrust. As his ally in the ADA, Curtis Gans, told Andrew Young, "Dr. King is probably the only person who could bridge the gap between the left and right wings of the movement."[38]

Lowenstein evoked sharply contrasting reactions in people. Some believed that his apparent sincerity and enthusiasm masked deviousness and political opportunism.[39] But King found his arguments convincing and his demeanor appealing. Lowenstein also had solid liberal credentials behind him: he had helped to organize the MFDP;

he was also a friend of Frank Graham, the former senator from North Carolina who had supported SCLC, in a modest way, since its inception. King invited both men to serve on the board of AFON, SCLC's tax-exempt foundation, and he asked Lowenstein to join the board of SCLC itself. At SCLC's convention in August, King stated that he would "very, very definitely oppose" Johnson's renomination.[40]

But the hope that King might act as a unifying force in the peace movement was rudely shattered at the National Convention for a New Politics, which began in Chicago on the last day of August. The conference had been conceived a year earlier as a means of promoting a common anti-war strategy for the 1968 elections. It turned out to be a fiasco. No sooner had the thirty-five hundred delegates arrived at the Palmer House than a black caucus, consisting of about four hundred people, demanded half the committee seats and half the conference votes. The black caucus also demanded that the conference support "black self-determination" and condemn "imperialist Zionist war." King made the opening speech, but it went badly. "The black nationalists gave me trouble," he told Levison. "I just barely was able to finish. They are trying to take the Convention over. They are trying to run the white people out." The ensuing wrangle lasted four days and left bitter feelings all round. The black caucus won their demands, but at the cost of alienating many whites, diverting attention from the war issue, and destroying any hope of overall unity. The black nationalists resorted to outright intimidation in order to push through their demands: when James Bevel proposed to speak against the Middle East resolution, some of them threatened to kill him. "You don't have to do Mickey mouse things to prove your identity," Bevel complained. "What is really needed is to get rid of the fascist mentality in this country."[41]

Levison breathed a sigh of relief over the outcome of the convention. Its organizer, Dr. Martin Perez, was married to Ann Farnsworth, the wealthy heiress who had given about $100,000 to SCLC since 1965. Levison feared that King might be lured into the New Left again. But there was no danger of that now. King left the convention after the first night; Bevel, Young, and Williams stayed on but were appalled by the air of unreality that surrounded the speeches and debates. Words like "revolution" and "bringing down the system" were bandied about with such thoughtlessness that language become debased and meaningless. As Young put it, "These cats don't seem to know the country has taken a swing to the right." Writing to Martin and Ann Perez,

Young called the black nationalists "too sick to build anything," and complained that the white radicals of SDS had taken "such a romantic view of the riots, it gives a totally distorted impression of ghetto leadership."[42]

By the summer of 1967 the anti-war movement appeared to have run out of steam. The Spring Mobilization had had no discernible effect on government policy and, as the Palmer House debacle illustrated, the opponents of the war were incapable of agreeing upon a common political strategy. It became increasingly evident that ending the war might take years rather than months. Meanwhile the problems of the black poor could not be ignored. If rioting and repression continued in the same vicious spiral, King feared, the outcome could well be a right-wing administration of fascist hue. SCLC could not afford to make Vietnam its overriding concern; as Young explained to Ann Farnsworth, "We felt a certain urgency to work among the Negro ghettos as both the source of our power and the point of our responsibility."[43]

In the spring of 1967, however, SCLC found itself virtually immobilized by organizational problems. In March, the auditor reported that SCLC had drawn upon loans and reserves to the tune of $137,000: "We are experiencing difficulty in operating the Conference from day-to-day receipts." Sixteen staff members had to be dropped in March, another seven in April. Contributions fell so sharply in April and May that SCLC drew up a list of forty-eight more names to be dropped. Some were eventually reprieved, but by the end of May SCLC had shed more than a third of its staff, reducing the total to eighty-five, fewer than half of whom were in the field.[44]

Political developments abroad also hampered SCLC's fundraising. One fundraising idea, a pilgrimage to the Holy Land led by King, with SCLC making a profit of $50 from each of the anticipated two thousand pilgrims, had to be dropped because of the volatile situation in the Middle East. "I just think this would be a big mistake," King told his advisers when he decided to cancel. "I don't think I could come out unscathed."[45] The political tension in Nigeria meant that plans for a month-long visit to Africa, to take place after a fundraising tour of Europe, had to be scrapped. Mrs. Freddye Henderson, who ran the Atlanta travel agency which tried to arrange these tours, complained that "it is so frustrating when working with ministers and church people who are confident that 'the Lord will make a way.'" One foreign engagement, however, King did keep. In May he agreed to accept an honorary degree from the University of Newcastle upon Tyne, and in mid-November he collected the degree from the duke of Northumberland at a ceremony that had been built around his visit. Andrew Young was appalled by England's open racism. "They even have a shoe polish called 'Nigger,'" he complained. "They have no sensitivity on this question."[46]

By the summer of 1967 the downward trend in SCLC's income appeared to have halted. The direct-mail fundraising program held up remarkably well, and SCLC picked up numerous contributors from SNCC, whose violent rhetoric, hostility to whites, and condemnation of Zionism had alienated virtually all its white support.[47] Even so, it became increasingly unrealistic to wage a two-front war, and the staff reductions drastically eroded SCLC's Southern base. By May it had only fourteen field staff in the South, scattered over six states. SCLC's links with its local affiliates became tenuous indeed: "They often complain about the fact that they don't hear from us," Herbert Coulton reported. The paucity of SCLC workers, together with the collapse of SNCC and the decline of CORE, contributed to a dramatic decrease in Southern civil rights activity. By early 1967 observers were pronouncing the civil rights movement dead or, in the words of *New York Times* reporter Gene Roberts, fighting "a last-ditch battle for survival in its few remaining spheres of influence."[48]

SCLC was not merely shrinking: it sometimes appeared to be dissolving into anarchy as morale and internal discipline deteriorated. The departure of several senior staff members weakened SCLC's administration—never its strongest point—and left the field staff all but unsupervised. No replacement had been found for Randolph Blackwell; Bevel was still on leave of absence; and Young spent so much time travelling with King that SCLC was, in effect, without a full-time executive director. This left Hosea Williams in charge of the field staff, and his record did not inspire confidence—SCOPE had been a shambles; the Chicago voter registration drive a complete failure. Levison was so enraged by Williams's public comments about the "apathy" of Chicago Negroes that he urged King to fire him. But this King refused to do. "Hosea is so damned sensitive," Young explained, "that he really cries and pleads, and Martin comes to his defense."[49]

Meanwhile, the field staff languished. SCLC's project in Grenada, Mississippi, for example, had been practically forgotten by the executive staff since September 1966, when King, Young, and Williams had escorted a group of black children to a newly desegregated school. In

April 1967 a visiting white minister complained to Young that SCLC had effectively abandoned Grenada. Staff members had been pulled out without explanation or warning, and the current project director, Robert Johnson, was "indolent, unimaginative, and possesses neither the capacity for, nor the interest in, being a community leader." No action was taken, however, and in July Young received a second, more urgent missive, this time from a local black resident. "We need direct action quick," he wrote, "either the Negroes policemen in Grenada will ruin this project along with the staff. The police force as it seem send the Negroes cop to intimidate the staff and everyone in the movement. There has been numerous quarrel among the staff." In August Young finally sent Leon Hall to investigate the problem. Hall reported that the Grenada project was "in a state of confusion."[50]

Alternately neglected and berated, the field staff became dejected, resentful, and apathetic. "I just do not believe you have been appraised of the psychological, moral and physical status of your staff," Williams wrote King in March.

> Our Field Staff is tired. . . . [W]e have constantly pushed them since the St. Augustine campaign. I know, I know, you and the Executive Staff (most of them) have pushed just as hard; but, there is a difference. The many different responsibilities we have as leaders make our work so diverse that they are an automatic safety valve for low morale and exhaustion. A rest (the right kind) would eliminate many of the faults of our staff. If you remember, we talked about a two month "rest and study" retreat for the staff. This retreat was to include daily lectures (some by you), discussions, daily meditation periods, daily study or reading, recreation and rest periods and plenty of good food. I strongly urge this retreat if SCLC intends to maintain an effective, representative Field Staff.[51]

Williams also complained about King's remoteness from the executive staff. Only a chosen few—Ralph Abernathy, Andy Young, Dorothy Cotton—could approach him freely: "Personally, I have been at a loss to communicate my feelings to you. I am not sure it is my job, nor am I sure you would listen to me."

At a five-day retreat in Frogmore, South Carolina, in late May, the field staff were given the opportunity to air their grievances. All agreed that their treatment by the executive staff left much to be desired. Time and again, they complained, their superiors gave them new postings without any preparation or consultation. "There is a real problem," said one, "about being sent into a project with no prior

orientation about the local set-up." Grenada was an obvious example.
SCLC "should be in there fully," another staff member argued, "or she
should not be there in the first place." The field staff resented their low
status within the organization; even the typists, they complained,
treated them as inferiors.[52]

As always, King replied to such criticisms patiently, sym-
pathetically, and philosophically. Many of the problems they referred
to arose not out of personal failings or organizational deficiencies, but
from "the existential situation in which we find ourselves, day in and
day out." The executive staff shared their sense of frustration, he explained: "So often, things are just wrong, and we don't know why."
Stress and anxiety were inevitable. "It is impossible for people to live
with as much tension as we live with every day." Fear and tension
could only be controlled through a commitment to nonviolence, a
willingness to suffer, and a belief in the Resurrection. "I may die in
this movement, [but] I don't mind," he reminded the staff. "I settled
that long ago. . . . I don't think anybody can be free until you solve
this problem." SCLC had its problems, but it was not lost. "You may
be no further than Meridian, Mississippi," King said, "but you are on
the right road. Being lost is being on Highway 78 trying to get to Los
Angeles."[53]

But inspirational speeches could not, as King well knew, cure
SCLC's internal problems. As he pondered the lessons of Chicago and
considered the enormity of the task ahead, the need for a stronger and
more disciplined organizational structure became evident. "King has
finally reached a point," Levison told Adele Kanter, "where he realizes
that the organization needs organization."[54]

King outlined his thoughts on SCLC's future shape in a paper which
he presented to the executive staff on March 21. SCLC need not concern itself, he argued, with the formulation of detailed programs: there
already existed a plethora of blueprints for alleviating poverty and
combatting discrimination. It was therefore naive to suggest, as some
liberals did, that the failure of the civil rights movement to suggest
realistic programs accounted for government inaction, especially when
the government was failing to enforce those civil rights laws already
on the statute book. Black demands were being ignored because blacks
lacked power: "We have got to put the horse (power) before the cart
(programs). Our nettlesome task is to discover how to organize our
strength into compelling power so that government cannot elude our
demands." Until now, he admitted, SCLC had specialized in mobilization rather than organization; it had attracted support for its short-

lived confrontations, but "did not assemble the support for new stages of the struggle." Now, however, SCLC had to grapple with the task of "organizing tenants, organizing welfare recipients, organizing the unemployed and the underemployed." But this would prove impossible unless SCLC developed a "sound, solid, and stable organizational structure."[55]

Instilling bureaucratic discipline and efficiency was no easy task, as the efforts of Baker, Walker, Boyte, and Blackwell had shown. King wanted to strengthen the executive staff by recruiting Lowery, and re-recruiting Blackwell and Greene. He even toyed with the idea of placing Wyatt Walker in charge of the Chicago project. Once having left the staff, however, people rarely came back, and the search for administrative talent was slow to yield results. The initiative for hiring William Rutherford as executive director came from Young, whom King wished to promote to some new, higher post so that he could continue to travel with him and represent SCLC at high-level meetings with other organizations. Rutherford had no background in civil rights, having lived in Europe for the past seventeen years. Since 1958 he had run a management consultancy and public relations firm based in Geneva. Young had long wanted to hire an efficiency expert to sort out SCLC's convoluted structure, and Rutherford, whom he had met in Geneva in May, appeared to have the right kind of expertise. After attending the SCLC convention in August, Rutherford agreed to take on the job. "I would certainly like to apply management rationalization technics to SCLC," he informed Young.[56]

King looked to Jesse Jackson and Operation Breadbasket to strengthen SCLC's Northern base, currently centered on Chicago. Under the direction of Fred Bennette, Operation Breadbasket had focused on Atlanta, but the branch that Jackson developed in Chicago dwarfed the Atlanta operation. With the help of a young white minister whom he had met at Chicago Theological Seminary, David Wallace, Jackson enlisted the support of enough black clergymen to make a city-wide economic boycott of carefully selected businesses feasible and effective. The object of such boycotts, or "selective buying campaigns," was simple: if a business enjoyed Negro custom, it ought to employ a commensurate proportion of black workers. A significant disparity between the two ratios was regarded as evidence of discrimination, and if the business in question would not be persuaded to close the gap, then Operation Breadbasket organized a consumer boycott to exert economic pressure. Clearly, the effectiveness of such boycotts depended upon a number of variables: the size and significance of the black market, the solidarity of the boycott, and the nature of the product being boycotted.[57]

After its inception in February 1966, Chicago's Operation Breadbasket went from strength to strength. In April it picketed forty stores owned by Certified Grocers, whose subsidiary, the Country Delight Dairy Company, employed no black drivers or salesmen. The parent company lost an estimated $500,000 during four days at Easter. It soon agreed to take on more black employees and to include blacks in its better-paying jobs. In June and July Operation Breadbasket negotiated agreements with four other dairy products companies. It then prized employment concessions from soft drinks firms such as Pepsi, Coca-Cola, and Seven-Up. In November it picketed High-Low supermarkets, and in May 1967 it took on the retail giant A&P, winning a detailed written agreement promising 770 additional jobs for blacks, as well as 1,200 summer jobs for black teenagers. In October 1966 Jackson and Wallace broadened the goals of Operation Breadbasket to include the strengthening of black-owned businesses, and the A&P contract specified a commitment to stock the products of black-owned companies, bank with black-owned financial institutions, and utilize black-owned garbage disposal and other services. Jackson and Wallace also appointed a "follow-up" committee to monitor implementation of these agreements. By the summer of 1967, Operation Breadbasket claimed to have won 2,200 new jobs for blacks. Jackson's performance had been "sensational," Levison told Clarence Jones.[58]

King was equally impressed. In November 1966 he promoted Jackson to the post of director of economic development. As conceived by C. T. Vivian, this new department should work with SCLC's local affiliates to make use of government grants and loans to rehabilitate slums, build low-income housing, train the unemployed, and finance other "anti-poverty" schemes. Vivian left SCLC, however, before the department could get off the ground, and when Jackson took over it was little more than a name. In practice, economic development meant Operation Breadbasket, and King expected Jackson to repeat his Chicago success throughout the country. In July, at a conference of more than 150 black ministers at Chicago Theological Seminary, Operation Breadbasket was launched as a national program covering twenty cities. Jackson replaced Fred Bennette as the overall head of the operation and joined SCLC's executive staff.[59]

The prominence accorded to Operation Breadbasket, and King's call at the SCLC convention for black political power, led some observers to detect a fundamental shift in SCLC's strategy away from integration and towards a moderate, reformist version of black power. In a limited sense, this was true. SCLC's experience in Louisville, Kentucky, during the spring and summer of 1967 seemed to underline the lesson of Chicago: that in housing—the bedrock of segregation in schools and jobs—the strength of white racism made integration, in the short term at least, a practical impossibility.

SCLC had threatened demonstrations in Louisville since January, and King held SCLC's spring board meeting there to underline that threat. On April 11, however, the city's board of aldermen rejected a fair housing ordinance, whereupon the local civil rights coalition, the ad hoc Committee on Open Housing, began a campaign of direct action. For the next seven weeks blacks marched through Louisville's white neighborhoods. As in Chicago, the police fended off angry whites. Unlike Chicago, the police also arrested hundreds of blacks under a court injunction. King's brother and six other leaders were indicted for contempt; when the court jailed them for thirty days, negotiations with the city broke down. King visited Louisville on May 3 and held a fruitless discussion with Mayor Schmied. He also found the Committee on Open Housing sharply divided over tactics. One faction proposed to physically disrupt the Kentucky Derby, the city's world-famous sporting and tourist event; the other faction, led by the NAACP, advocated an economic boycott with no physical disruption. The tactic of holding marches through white neighborhoods also provoked disagreement. King took a middle position, arguing in favor of the marches but against disruption of the derby. After an all-night strategy session his views prevailed. On May 6, Derby Day, the committee organized a march through Louisville's deserted downtown, while twenty-five hundred police and National Guardsmen patrolled the racetrack.[60]

A week later, King paid another visit to the city, with Ralph Abernathy and Hosea Williams. When they addressed a rally at Mount Zion Baptist Church, the *Louisville Defender* reported, it was "a wonder the very stones of the edifice didn't come out of the walls to join the march." Each time King and the SCLC "big guns" departed, however, the marchers dwindled. In June, after a month of intermittent protests, the campaign fizzled out. As the fall elections drew nearer, both the NAACP and SCLC's local affiliate turned to voter registration. The *Defender*, Louisville's black newspaper, argued that the marches had had "virtually no effect" and that, as in Milwaukee, blacks were sim-

ply "saddled with a negative City Council." The *Defender's* publisher,
Frank Stanley, had been skeptical about direct action from the start,
calling demonstrations "old hat." When King returned to the city on
August 2, in the wake of the riots in Newark and Detroit, his mood
seemed pessimistic, his faith in nonviolent direct action at a low ebb.
"Our country is still a racist country," he told a voter registration rally.
"I am sorry to have to say to you that the vast majority of white
Americans are racist, either consciously or unconsciously." If whites
refused to accept integration, blacks had to use their bloc vote to gain
political control of the cities.[61]

When he committed SCLC to Cleveland in June, this is precisely
what King set out to do. He sent half a dozen staff members to the city
and spent at least two days a week there himself, for the clear but
unstated purpose of electing Carl Stokes, who was running for mayor
against Ralph Locher, the white incumbent. Jesse Jackson set up a
branch of Operation Breadbasket, James Orange and Al Sampson organized tenant unions, but the main thrust of the campaign was voter
registration.[62]

King saw a number of clear advantages in Cleveland. Smaller than
Chicago, it had one, relatively compact, black ghetto. The city lacked a
strong political machine, and the mayor appeared to have alienated the
bulk of the black vote. Cleveland had an attractive black candidate in
Carl Stokes. Above all, the mushrooming of exclusive white suburbs
had given the city a black population of about 38 percent. "In Chicago
we made the mistake of trying to do everything ourselves," King admitted; in Cleveland SCLC would attempt to "organize the
organizers."[63]

In this case the organizers were the United Pastors, a loose association of black ministers formed after the previous year's riot. But SCLC
also wanted to involve—or failing that, to neutralize—the local black
nationalists, especially Ahmed Evans and his followers. King was delighted that Evans agreed to cooperate with the drive, and in the weeks
before the election they pounded the streets together, stopping in bars,
pool rooms, and everywhere Evans could find people. Through his own
personal influence, King believed, he managed to win Evans to nonviolence, even if only tactical nonviolence:

> The interesting thing is that he was not agreeing with me philosophi-
> cally, but a certain communication spiritually and psychologically [took
> place], and the fact that I took time out with him. You see, Ahmed had

never been registered to vote and he registered in this campaign. We told
him . . . that the local mayor wants us to burn the city down because
that would assure his reelection. . . . When the boys would get out of line
then Ahmed would call them in and tell them that was not the way. . . .
[T]hey were as happy as they could be . . . [that] they had seen one or two
victories. . . . [M]y presence kinda pulled it together and gave the Negro
hope.

King was struck by the argot he heard: "They say everything in slang,"
he told a white friend, "like you are a 'mellow dude.' "[64]

Stokes beat Locher in the Democratic primary, and went on to narrowly defeat his Republican opponent, Ralph J. Perks, to become the
first black mayor of a major city. He won over 90 percent of the vote in
the predominantly black wards and about 20 percent in the mainly
white ones. Stokes, however, later belittled SCLC's contribution,
claiming that "we already had the black community organized, mobilized and energized." Fearful of alienating white supporters, he had
urged King to stay away. King's presence, Stokes thought, probably
hurt more than it helped.[65]

But King never abandoned SCLC's commitment to integration.
Rather, as Godfrey Hodgson observed from the vantage point of the
mid-1970s, "King, at the end of his life, came to understand the need
for a degree of black separatism as a means" to that end. This was true,
moreover, only in the negative sense that the outlook for sympathetic
government action seemed so bleak that blacks had to fall back upon
self-help and bloc voting. Jobs from Operation Breadbasket and black
mayors were minimalist goals—palliatives, not solutions. Even the
best mayors, who understood the awful dimensions of current urban
and racial problems, lacked the resources to solve them. In the structure of national politics, mayors had relatively little power. Only the
federal government could reconstruct the central cities on the scale
required. Only the federal government could guarantee a universal living wage.[66]

By 1967 King was clearly thinking in terms of socialism, although
he deliberately refrained from using the term "socialism" in public—
"People have so many hangups to it, and respond so emotionally and
irrationally."[67] Here, however, he met resistance from his colleagues,
especially from Jesse Jackson. King criticized Jackson for being too
absorbed in the "externality" of Operation Breadbasket and failing to
understand the need for a radical reform of the entire economy. "He

was quite rough on Jesse," Young recalled, "because he said
that . . . Breadbasket will not solve the problem, . . . that jobs would
finally have to be provided by the public sector rather than the private
sector, and that Breadbasket was essentially a private sector program."
At the SCLC convention in August, King urged his audience to think
about fundamental reform: "Why are there 40 million poor people in
America?"

> When you begin to ask that question, you are raising questions about the
> economic system, about a broader distribution of wealth. When you ask
> that question, you begin to question the capitalistic economy. And I'm
> simply saying that more and more, we've got to begin to ask questions
> about the whole society. We are called upon to help the discouraged
> beggars in life's market place. But one day we must come to see that an
> edifice which produces beggars needs restructuring. . . . You see, my
> friends, when you deal with this, you begin to ask the question, "Who
> owns the oil?" You begin to ask the question, "Who owns the iron
> ore?"[68]

But how could capitalism be challenged and transformed? How
could America's "privileged groups" be induced to "give up some of
their billions?" Some white radicals, including Stanley Levison, argued
that the riots might produce some good by shocking or frightening the
government into making concessions. But King and Young saw little
evidence of this. For the second year running, Congress rejected a civil
rights bill and cut back the War on Poverty. It even voted down a $40
million appropriation earmarked for rodent-control programs. In the
aftermath of the Newark and Detroit riots, the House Un-American
Activities Committee enjoyed a new lease on life searching for the
"Communists" and "agitators" supposedly organizing the violence. A
bill making it illegal to incite or encourage rioting sailed through the
House 377 to 23. President Johnson's only response to the worst rioting in the nation's history was to appoint a national advisory commission to study the disorders. "At best," King told the SCLC convention,
"the riots have produced a little additional anti-poverty money . . . and
a few water-sprinklers to cool the children of the ghetto."[69]

Some suggested more radical forms of direct action. In the Northern
ghettos, Levison argued, nonviolent protest ought to be escalated to
the level of civil disobedience: "For the cities we have to go higher."
Again, King and Young were skeptical. "It won't work," Young contended, "because when you do it on a big scale it isn't recognized as
such."[70] After the Newark and Detroit riots, King's pessimism deep-

ened. War, poverty, and racism were tied together, he thought, in an inseparable and destructive triplet. With its influence abroad crumbling, its cities convulsed by rioting poor, and its civilization being corrupted by excessive materialism, the United States seemed to be "headed the way of the Roman Empire." People expected him to have answers, he told his wife, but he had none.[71]

Fourteen

Mobilizing the Poor

On October 23, 1967, King testified before the National Advisory Commission on Civil Disorders. Afterwards, King told reporters that the causes of the riots were obvious; what was lacking was the political will to tackle them. Since the government refused to act, therefore, SCLC intended to stage protests in Washington itself—not merely one-day demonstrations, but prolonged and massive civil disobedience. Poor people would "camp right here in Washington . . . by the thousands and thousands until the Congress of our nation and the federal government will do something to deal with the problem." If necessary, he added, SCLC was prepared to disrupt the functioning of the city.[1]

King was initially skeptical about the possibility of escalating nonviolent direct action to the level of massive civil disobedience. True, he had suggested the idea at the SCLC convention on August 15, in a speech drafted by Levison, but he had spoken in the most general terms and without a great deal of conviction.[2] During the following month, however, encouraged by Levison and Young, King persuaded himself that more radical tactics could indeed be success-fully employed in a "Poor People's Campaign." On August 21, *Newsweek* published a Harris opinion poll which claimed that whites "are ready and willing to pay the price for a massive, Federal onslaught on the root problems of the ghetto." Discussing the poll with Levison, King argued that the time was ripe for a dramatization of poverty in a place like Mississippi, coupled with a national appeal for legislative action. They agreed that the best place to dramatize urban poverty would be Washington itself. A few weeks later, King and Young had lunch with the editors of *Time,* and were pleasantly suprised by the depth of their concern over the decline of the inner cities and the problem of poverty. King became more convinced than ever that the reactionary behavior of Congress did not reflect public opinion: all it showed was that the Southern racists had combined with the Northern reactionaries to stymie the will of the majority. Their unholy alliance had been broken in 1964–65. It could be broken again.[3]

The idea of bringing poor people *to* Washington originated with Marian Wright, a lawyer working for the NAACP Legal Defense Fund in Mississippi. In June 1967, the NAACP conducted a survey of pov-erty in twelve Mississippi counties. "The condition of the Negro in Mississippi defies adequate description," the survey reported: blacks were suffering from hunger, malnutrition, even starvation; the sick often received no medical attention; the food stamp program was ut-terly inadequate. Wright suggested to King that a group of poor people from Mississippi ought to go to Washington and stage a sit-in at the national headquarters of HEW—perhaps in the office of Secretary Wirtz—to draw attention to the government's lamentable failure to eradicate such appalling conditions. Bringing two or three thousand poor people to Washington from across the nation was a logical exten-sion of Wright's idea. Levison, remembering the Bonus March of 1932, suggested erecting a tent city in the heart of the capital to house this army of the poor.[4]

In mid-September, at a retreat in Warrenton, Virginia, SCLC's key board members, senior staff members, and Northern advisers debated the pros and cons of a campaign along these lines. James Bevel argued long and hard that the plan was misguided: ending the war in Vietnam should be SCLC's primary objective. Indeed, Bevel thought the issue of peace so critical that it outweighed every other consideration. King disagreed. If logic pointed towards an all-out campaign for peace, practical considerations weighed against such a course. It was far easier to campaign for jobs than against the war: Bevel's proposal for a "stop the draft" movement was impractical; the majority of the press was still behind the administration over the war. On the other hand, there was growing support in the country for a stepped-up attack on poverty. King assured Bevel and other doubters that in dramatizing poverty SCLC could compel the government to reassess its priorities and thereby weaken support for the war. After a solid week of discussion, SCLC committed itself to the proposed "Poor People's Campaign."5

The Poor People's Campaign differed from all SCLC's previous efforts. For the first time, SCLC set out to build a movement from scratch. And this movement would not be a black affair: King envisaged an interracial alliance of the poor embracing Indians, Puerto Ricans, Mexican-Americans, and Appalachian whites. The circumstances in which it proposed to do this, moreover, could hardly have been more inauspicious. The president was still obsessed with Vietnam. Congress was dominated by reaction. Black separatism made interracial cooperation increasingly difficult. The ghetto riots showed no sign of abating and, if they recurred, would nullify the impact of nonviolent protests.

How could SCLC induce black militants to support such a movement? When he spoke to blacks, King hammered away at the theme that rioting and violence were futile. Riots not only made their "white brothers sicker," they were utterly self-defeating as well. Blacks were killed in the riots, not whites; black neighborhoods were being destroyed, not white ones. People who advocated violence merely invited repression and defeat. Armed insurrection could only succeed when, as in Cuba and Vietnam, the insurgents commanded the support of the people and the government could not count on the loyalty of its armed forces. Neither condition obtained in the United States: talk of revolution was sheer fantasy.6

More to the point, nonviolent protest could work, King insisted. About the time of the Warrenton retreat, he and Bernard Lee met a group of young black militants in New York. It soon became apparent that nonviolence had been so misrepresented in the North that these youths equated it with conservatism and passivity. When King explained what massive, disruptive civil disobedience entailed, their attitude became more sympathetic. Young blacks could be won to nonviolence, King believed, if they had the chance to join a movement of sufficient militancy and power. Nonviolence had only failed in the North, he argued, because "it just hasn't been tried hard enough. . . . Now I know nonviolence will work. I know it will work."[7]

SCLC also had to contend with the conservatism of the black clergy. It had been difficult enough to involve black preachers in the civil rights movement; how would they respond to a campaign which had overtones of socialism and which directly challenged the federal government? King's solution was simple: the black church must be radicalized. In November 1967 SCLC received a grant of $230,000 from the Ford Foundation for a "Ministers Leadership Training Program" (MLTP). Organized by T. Y. Rogers, SCLC's new director of affiliates, the program aimed to educate and coordinate 150 black ministers from fifteen cities. Because they lacked formal education, Young told the planning committee, "the complexities of the urban situation has left them paralyzed. They have been peddlers of influence . . . rather than instruments of real power." If ten preachers in a given city could be politically educated, they could become a political force to be reckoned with. The chosen preachers, King explained, had to be "oriented to the values that control SCLC. . . . We must develop their psyche. Something is wrong with capitalism as it now stands in the United States. We are not interested in being integrated into *this* value structure. Power must be relocated: a radical redistribution of power must take place. We must do something to these men to change them." The first MLTP workshops took place in Miami during the week of February 18–24, 1968. They became, in effect, orientation sessions for the Poor People's Campaign.[8]

In his speeches to the MLTP, and to other black gatherings in the South, King tried to dispel the bourgeois individualism that still pervaded the black clergy and middle class. The campaign was not a quest for special privileges or "something for nothing." Those who urged the Negro to "lift himself up by his own bootstraps" were perpetuating a historical myth: no other ethnic group had achieved economic security entirely through self-help. Whites had received all manner of government assistance, the most obvious example being free land. Blacks were not only denied land, but also suffered a unique discrimination based on color. In demanding jobs and income, therefore, "we are going to demand what is ours." Lest anyone object that this amounted to "welfare," or even "socialism," King pointed to the enormous sums which the government pumped into agriculture and industry. "When it's given to white people it's called subsidy. Everybody in this country is on welfare. Suburbia was built by federally-subsidized credits. And the highways were built by federally-subsidized firms to the tune of ninety per cent." America already had "socialism for the rich," he insisted; only the poor had to endure "rugged, free enterprise capitalism."[9]

To gird SCLC for this most ambitious of campaigns, King promised the new executive director, Bill Rutherford, a free hand in matters of administration and staff discipline. Young was promoted to the new post of executive vice-president. Assisting Rutherford in the task of administering SCLC was another newcomer, Bernard Lafayette, twenty-eight years old, a veteran of the Nashville sit-ins and the Freedom Rides. After working in Selma as a SNCC field secretary, Lafayette had engaged in community organizing for the American Friends Service Committee, working in Chicago and Boston. His link with the Quakers was important, for the AFSC agreed to back the Poor People's Campaign with staff and money. Lafayette and Rutherford joined King, Abernathy, and Young in a new "last say" steering committee, created to strictly monitor the organization's expenditure. SCLC had recovered from the financial backlash following King's entry into the peace movement, but its finances were still shaky. Harry Belafonte performed a series of concerts for SCLC in October, but these brought in far less money than King had anticipated. The direct-mail program continued to generate income, but Levison noted a worrying trend: "The amount of money stays the same but the contributors are fewer. And that's not a healthy situation."[10]

When Rutherford took up his post in December he could hardly believe the waste and indiscipline he found. Going through SCLC's accounts he noted "an alarming state of affairs": many of the field staff claimed for unauthorized trips, stays in motels, long-distance phone calls, and other unnecessary items. He also discovered an almost complete lack of contact between the scattered field projects and the Atlanta office. Cleveland was a particularly bad case. After visiting the project on December 16 he transferred three staff members and warned the remaining two that they would be swiftly replaced "if they are unable to carry out their assignments in a responsible manner." Rutherford also found that the behavior of some senior staff members left much to be desired. On December 11 he reprimanded Jesse Jackson for failing to attend an executive staff meeting; in future, he warned, absence would entail a $50 fine, tardiness a $25 fine. Hosea Williams so resented Rutherford's orders that he threatened to resign. But King was thrilled by this new broom. Rutherford had "really got things moving around here," he told Levison. "I see for the first time real administration developing. He's done in a week what hasn't been done in two or three years. . . . I do see us really pulling out in a way I've always longed for."[11]

King was dismayed, however, by the continuing opposition to the campaign from Jesse Jackson and James Bevel. At a meeting of the executive staff on December 27, they again pressed their objections. "There is a problem with the staff not being clear on this project," Jackson complained. If people received government jobs, he added, they would develop a feeling of dependence on the government; could SCLC then get their support over future issues? Bevel restated his belief that peace in Vietnam should be SCLC's priority. "We must have an issue that speaks to young people," he argued; the young were more concerned about the war than about poverty. Then he raised a tactical objection: if SCLC staged demonstrations in Washington, would President Johnson "give enough opposition for us to build up steam and momentum"?—he was not likely to react like "Bull" Connor or Jim Clark. "Where do you ultimately put pressure on the man?" Bevel argued for a movement "that is so structured as to put the American power structure leaders looking like clowns. To get the war machine to attack us rather than us attacking the war machine." King himself had many times asserted that the war in Vietnam represented the main stumbling block to social progress. But now he argued that the war was not susceptible to nonviolent protest: "The thing you are talking about is much harder to mobilize around and takes much longer. You have a lot of people agreeing with you but they are not willing to spend five years in jail over it. In addition, you have the national press against you. I see levels of struggle in this campaign with this one being the second level." People would respond to the campaign, he insisted: "What is more basic an issue than jobs and incomes?"[12]

But the field staff, charged with recruiting three thousand poor people from ten cities and five rural areas, found their task daunting and perplexing. All previous SCLC campaigns had been based upon local protest movements; some kind of organizational structure already existed. Now, the staff were told to drum up support, organize local committees, and raise funds for an as yet nonexistent national campaign. Many found themselves assigned, moreover, to cities with which they had little or no acquaintance. The vagueness of the campaign's goals added to their difficulties: what exactly was a "Bill of Economic and Social Rights," and how could they explain it to the poor? "We were sort of hung up staff-wise on what the demands would be," recalled Al Sampson, who had been assigned to Newark. "When you talk about mobilizing people from Mississippi, they're going to

leave the plantation; what are they going to be able to come back
with? People are going to be leaving their rat-infested apartments that
the slum landlords are going to be filling up with somebody else; what
are they going to come back with?" James Orange, assigned to Philadelphia, found his task overwhelming: "I didn't know what to do!"
The director of Philadelphia's Freedom House, SCLC's base, complained to King that Orange's talks were "unbelievably confusing," and
advised SCLC to postpone its activity in the city until the staff were
better prepared.13

With so much confusion and discontent, SCLC held a three-day
staff meeting in mid-January. Lecturing the staff at Ebenezer's education building, King patiently explained the goals, the strategy, and the
tactics of the campaign. After stressing the impractical and self-defeating nature of violence, he elucidated the theory and practice of civil
disobedience. In the South, he explained, SCLC had broken laws that
were patently racist; in the North, on the other hand, they might have
to violate laws that had no direct bearing on the problem of discrimination. "Conditions become so bad that you have to break a law,
which on its face is just and sound, in order to call attention to an
unjust condition." To allay any doubts about the morality of civil
disobedience, King cited the examples of Socrates, the early Christians,
the Boston Tea Party, and Chief Albert Luthuli of South Africa.14

King's exegesis of civil disobedience failed to convince all the field
staff, many of whom continued to complain about the lack of clear
demands. Addressing them two days later, on January 17, King admitted that the discussions had been "rather stormy," and that "the winds
of anger were blowing mighty hard." King tried to reassure them that
much of their anxiety was groundless: the act of planning itself tended
to exaggerate people's fears and uncertainties. "If, in 1955 . . . we had
called a meeting and said, 'We're going to take two months to plan the
Montgomery bus boycott,' we would never have had the Montgomery
bus boycott." Now, however, SCLC had to operate on a different basis,
"planning a little more, and a little longer in advance." Other confu-
sions stemmed from living in a confused society. "We live in a sick,
neurotic nation," King pointed out. "And I'm convinced that makes for
our schizophrenia. And I don't want to analyze anybody but myself.
But I know that I have it."

On the matter of demands, King discounted the importance of having comprehensive and detailed proposals. Poor people were not going
to be "fired up" by a long list of demands, and proposals like a negative
income tax were too complex for them to understand. If SCLC dramatized the basic problems, the rest would follow: when it launched its

campaigns in Birmingham and Selma "we didn't have one thing on paper—nothing." Poverty was such a clear-cut and compelling issue that detailed demands were superfluous. The goal of jobs and income was "so possible, so achievable, so pure, so simple that even the backlash can't do much to deny it, . . . so non-token and so basic that even the black nationalists can't do much to deny it." He, for one, did not care if the demands remained unspecific: "Let's just go to Washington." SCLC could no longer wait, he insisted; the nation needed a movement. Demonstrations would give the poor a sense of dignity and destiny. They would unite existing allies and create new ones. "Out there on the line," moreover, "black folk and white folk get together in a strange way." Above all, SCLC had to keep alive a feeling of hope. Hope was the kingdom of God, "an inner power within you," driving people to strive for their ideals. Hope was "the courage to be"; it was a refusal to be stopped or to give up.[15]

If King's arguments persuaded the field staff, many friends, advisers, and supporters remained skeptical about the campaign. Indeed, some were gravely disturbed by SCLC's talk of massive civil disobedience. Harold DeWolf, his old theology tutor, warned King that "anything which looks like an attempt to coerce the action of Congress would be not only illegal, but would probably result in . . . the election of an even more reactionary Congress." In addition, prolonged disruption might degenerate into aimless disorder: "Have you considered the danger of provoking a Fascist-type revolution . . . which might put the country under the direct rule of the military-industrial complex, ending civil liberties and civil rights and precipitating World War III?"[16]

Bayard Rustin had similar fears. At a meeting of the research committee on January 29, he strongly opposed any form of civil disobedience. In the prevailing climate of political reaction, he argued, disruptive tactics would make matters worse, leading to further backlash and repression. They would also, he predicted, attract to the protest "the most irresponsible and uncontrollable elements." SCLC had lost control of the Meredith March at a time when "the splintering and confusion were quite simple as compared with the present mood." Even if SCLC stayed within the letter of the law, Rustin doubted whether it would be able to maintain nonviolent discipline. Michael Harrington, who attended the same meeting, echoed some of these doubts. "The current Congress was a miserable one," he later explained. "We felt that another demonstration would make a strong moral point, but we were afraid it wouldn't register as a victory in the public eye."[17]

Responding to these fears and doubts, King and Young began to play down the threat of massive disruption. "We aren't going to close down the Pentagon," he told the conference of black ministers in Miami. "Anybody talking about closing down the Pentagon is just talking foolishness. We can't close down Capitol Hill." It was absurd to suppose that three thousand poor people could coerce Congress or the president: the success of the campaign ultimately depended "on the response of the people of the nation." Direct action should generate public sympathy, not create disruption for its own sake. King stressed that SCLC's demands were moderate, sensible proposals capable of winning broad public support. He wanted to promote consensus, not conflict.[18]

Behind SCLC's radical rhetoric, therefore, the strategy and tactics of the Poor People's Campaign closely resembled the pattern of Birmingham and Selma. Far from raising a "nonviolent army" to "close down Washington," SCLC planned to bring only three thousand demonstrators. True, King described this as merely the "first wave," but long experience had taught that tactics, not numbers, were the most critical factor. Any acts of civil disobedience, therefore, would be symbolic, not coercive. The campaign's focus was to be a shantytown of the poor built, without official permission, on government property. Any attempt by the authorities to evict the occupants would evoke memories of the army's attack on the Bonus Marchers in 1932. According to the plan drawn up by Young, during the first two weeks of the campaign delegations of poor people would lobby congressional committees, individual congressmen, and government agencies. The campaign would then move to the level of protest: HEW and the Department of Agriculture would be the targets of sit-ins; sick people could jam hospital waiting rooms; thousands of schoolchildren might boycott their classes to picket the board of education. SCLC might even organize a ceremonial dumping of ghetto garbage on the steps of the Capitol. "By the end of June," Young predicted, "we will have gotten some response or all of us will be in jail."[19]

During the first week of February, King spent several days in Washington to explain the campaign to a special meeting of SCLC's board and to canvass local support. The board approved his plans, but with a distinct lack of enthusiasm. When he met SNCC's new chairman, moreover, King encountered outright opposition. Bill Rutherford was appalled by SNCC's pseudo-revolutionary antics. "Rap Brown and his commandos [occupied] the place with walkie-talkies and bodyguards," he told Levison. "They . . . disrupted our meeting and literally kept SCLC board members out of the meeting." King was far too indulgent towards the black nationalists, Rutherford complained; only Hosea

Williams stood up to them and "put things like this on the table." Afterwards, when Rutherford pointed out how damaging it would be if SNCC denounced the campaign, King had lost his temper and berated him. "He said to me, 'the enemy is violence, violence begets violence,' and he went into one of those preaching things. I didn't react at all." King could draw some comfort from the attitude of Stokely Carmichael, by now a firm friend. No longer in SNCC, Carmichael had moved to Washington and organized a group called the Black United Front. While skeptical about the campaign's chances of success, he promised King the BUF's support.[20]

King was accustomed to opposition and criticism. More discouraging to him was the slowness of SCLC's progress in recruiting poor people. At a meeting of the executive staff in Atlanta on February 11, he raised the possibility of calling off the campaign unless the staff did better:

> We are not doing our homework. We have not gotten off the ground as far as engaging in the enormous job ahead. We are dealing with a national confrontation like we are working in St. Augustine. We have not recruited twenty folks that are people who will go and stay with us. I am disturbed about the fact that our staff has not gotten to the people we are talking about—not young people, middle-class people etc., but the hardcore poor people. . . . If we cannot do it, I would rather pull out now—the embarrassment and criticism would be much less than if we went to Washington with about 300 people. . . .
>
> I find, generally, an enthusiasm about this project mainly because something needs to be done now. I find a skepticism on the part of most black militants. My feeling is that we are doing much more on getting the support on the top than we are on getting the support on the grassroots level. We can get a lot of people there; that is no problem. But the much greater thing is for us to get the *poor people* who will be demanding something because they have been deprived.

His colleagues pledged to redouble their efforts, and the target date for the opening of the campaign, originally April 1, was put back three weeks. King himself embarked on a series of "people-to-people" tours, driving himself to the point of physical exhaustion. Early in March, after being ordered to rest by his doctor, he took a brief vacation in Mexico. According to Abernathy, however, he found it impossible to rest or relax. To his friend, who had returned from a month-long overseas trip, King seemed worried, depressed, and "very, very jittery." During the ministers workshop in Miami, the police had told him to stay in his hotel room for two consecutive nights because of threats against his life. In Philadelphia, on the other hand, he had refused police protection. Rutherford became increasingly worried about King's safety.[21]

The FBI viewed SCLC's efforts with hostility and alarm. King's opposition to the Vietnam War, his advocacy of civil disobedience, and his increasingly open criticisms of capitalism all served to reinforce the bureau's perception of King as a threat to national security, a Communist, and a traitor. However, as David Garrow notes, after the failure of its blackmail attempt and "smear campaign" of 1964–65, the FBI seemed more concerned with weakening SCLC as an organization than discrediting King as an individual. Hoover became more circumspect in leaking information about King's private life. Instead, the FBI concentrated on hampering SCLC's fundraising efforts and on influencing the press through its Crime Records Division. Some of the FBI's activities seemed relatively innocuous. Through the Crime Records Division it disseminated unfriendly newspaper articles, passed on bureau-inspired editorials to cooperative editors and publishers, and furnished friendly reporters with "embarrassing questions" to ask King about his stance on Vietnam. Occasionally, however, the bureau pulled off a coup. In November 1966, for example, it had alerted reporters to a proposed meeting between King and James Hoffa, the unsavory boss of the Teamsters Union, which King wanted to keep quiet. The leak caused consternation among King and his advisers, and the meeting was cancelled. Apparently, it did not occur to them that the source of the leak might be an FBI wiretap, even though they often joked about FBI eavesdroppers causing interference.[22]

The success of the FBI's efforts to starve SCLC of funds is difficult to gauge, but many of them clearly failed. In November 1967, for example, learning that SCLC had been awarded $230,000 from the Ford Foundation, bureau agents contacted John Bugas, vice-president of the Ford Motor Company, to apprise him "as to the subversive backgrounds of King's principal advisers." This ploy failed to stop the grant. The FBI had similar lack of success, it seems, in preventing SCLC from receiving federal grants. In 1966–67, SCLC was awarded $109,000 from the Department of Education; $61,000 from the Department of Labor; and more than $500,000 from the Office of Economic Opportunity. When bureau officials learned about the second grant, they sent a copy of the King "monograph," entitled "Communist Influence in Racial Affairs," to the secretary of labor.[23]

With the announcement of the Poor People's Campaign, the FBI's attempts to destroy SCLC's effectiveness took on a fresh urgency. Through James Harrison, a paid informant on the executive staff, it received a steady flow of information about goings on inside King's organization; it also gleaned a wealth of intelligence from the Levison wiretap. When he discovered that SCLC had held a Poor People's Campaign planning retreat in late 1967, the head of the new Racial Intelligence Section, George C. Moore, requested permission to reinstall the wiretap on SCLC's Atlanta office. On January 2, Hoover put the request to Attorney General Ramsey Clark, who promptly rejected it on the grounds that "there has not been an adequate demonstration of a direct threat to national security." Stymied over the wiretap, the FBI proceeded with a campaign to sabotage SCLC's efforts. Early in March, the Racial Intelligence Section held a conference in Washington to discuss methods of disrupting "black nationalist hate groups," which had been included in the bureau's "counter-intelligence program," CO-INTELPRO, the previous August. In a directive to all its field offices on March 4, FBI headquarters ordered a concerted offensive against "the most violent and radical groups," including action to "prevent the rise of a 'messiah' who could unify, and electrify, the militant black nationalist movement." King, the directive pointed out, "could be a very real contender for this position."[24]

The FBI paid particular attention to the Poor People's Campaign. Section chief Moore instructed field offices to begin a "rumor campaign" in order to undermine SCLC's recruiting drive. They could spread stories about disorganization and lack of funds within SCLC; circulate threats of "violence and bodily harm" to participants; encourage a belief that demonstrators would have their names taken "and welfare checks from the Government discontinued"; and stress the opposition to the campaign from Washington's black community. "We would point out also that the Project is strictly for Martin Luther King's benefit, which is actually the case." The response from the field was lackluster. The Baltimore office proposed making and circulating a leaflet picturing King with Elijah Muhammed. The idea fell through, however, when the Chicago office pointed out that "contact between King and the [Nation of Islam] is not a heretofore unknown happening," and that this kind of publicity would not damage King's standing among blacks. The Jackson office had the idea of advertising fictitious meetings featuring King as the main speaker. Detroit suggested disrupting SCLC's transportation arrangements by promising to supply buses that it had no intention of delivering.[25]

After four summers of rioting, the fear that SCLC's campaign would spark serious violence extended far beyond the FBI. The attorney general, Ramsey Clark, later described the feeling of alarm and apprehension in government circles as "a paranoia, literally." Congress anxiously sought ways of banning the protests. Many blacks, too, including SCLC supporters, predicted that violence might erupt if the Poor People's Campaign went ahead. On March 8, in a memorandum which she circulated to every member of the SCLC board, Marion Logan, the board's assistant secretary, told King that "I doubt very seriously that the April Demonstrations will, as you say, 'succeed in moving the conscience of the Congress.'" If, as she feared, SCLC proved unable to control its volunteers, the protests could well ignite another summer of rioting. Washington already resembled an armed camp, she noted, making the potential for violence "explosive." Two weeks earlier, Bayard Rustin publicly declared his opposition to the campaign, calling upon King to cancel it. This might involve a loss of face, he conceded, but "he'll lose a lot more face if he conducts the demonstrations and fails."26

By March, however, SCLC was at last making headway in its preparations for the campaign. The quota of two hundred volunteers from each city or area had been not only filled but exceeded. "Philadelphia already has 600," Young exulted. "Mississippi has 5 or six hundred. Every place is running over." Contributions had also picked up: donations from the direct-mail program were running "way ahead of last year," Levison reported; a single day, February 23, saw the arrival of $15,000. The campaign was also beginning to attract the support of trade unions and religious organizations. And an interracial coalition of the poor finally seemed to be taking shape when more than fifty nonblack organizations met in Atlanta to endorse SCLC's plans. Myles Horton, who worked among the poor whites of Appalachia, left the meeting full of enthusiasm. "I believe we caught a glimpse of the future," he wrote Young. "We had there in Atlanta . . . the making of a bottom up coalition." The Poor People's Campaign was picking up momentum.27

It was to the considerable annoyance of his staff, therefore, that King decided to address a rally of striking sanitation workers in Memphis, especially when it involved delaying a tour of Mississippi and changing the venue of a March 18 staff meeting. He had been made aware of this dispute by Billy Kyles, a Memphis pastor, during the ministers workshop in Miami. On February 23 the police attacked a group of marchers with night-sticks and "mace," a new chemical antipersonnel spray. Kyles jokingly suggested that King might need to visit Memphis to "help us out."28

Kyles had swung the Memphis branch of the NAACP behind the

thirteen hundred sanitation workers on February 14, two days after the start of the strike. The union, the American Federation of State, County, and Municipal Employees, was reluctant at first to accept this support, lest the strike be labelled a "racial" issue. Kyles, like other black ministers, was interested in the men rather than the union; as the workers were fighting for union recognition, however, this distinction soon became academic. Any misgivings the black ministers may have harbored about backing the strikers were dispelled by the police, who sprayed several prominent clergymen with mace on February 23. The following day about 150 black citizens, half of them ministers, formed an organization to coordinate support for the strike which they called Community on the Move for Equality (COME). The COME strategy committee, headed by James Lawson, set about organizing daily marches to city hall and nightly mass meetings. COME also called upon blacks to boycott all stores in the downtown area, the restaurant and dry-cleaning businesses of Mayor Henry Loeb, and the two local dailies, the *Commercial-Appeal* and the *Press Scimitar,* which had both denounced the strike. By early March, blacks in Memphis had closed ranks behind the strikers. It became apparent, however, that the struggle would probably be bitter and long. Jerry Wurf, AFSCME's president, regarded it as a crucial test of his union's strength. "I am not going to leave Memphis," he told Loeb; "the union is not going to leave Memphis. . . . I'm bringing in everything that I have." But Loeb was determined not to recognize the union: "Even if garbage piles up over an apartment roof, I'm not going to budge."[29]

When Wurf and other union officials were enjoined by the chancery court—an action that prompted Loeb to break off negotiations with the union—the role of COME became all the more important. But although the mayor listened to the ministers, he refused to relent on the issues of a dues checkoff and union recognition. Faced with a stalemate that could lead only to eventual defeat for the strikers, COME decided to have national black leaders address the rallies so as to bolster morale and attract publicity. By then, recalled COME's chairman, the Reverend Ralph Jackson, "some of us had decided that if Loeb succeeded at this the black community would no longer be an entity. . . .[W]e had to bring sufficient pressure." Roy Wilkins came on March 14, speaking to nine thousand people at the enormous Mason Temple. "Don't give an inch," he urged. "I don't come here to make threats. But anybody who runs around picking on peaceful people is building for trouble." Bayard Rustin, who appeared on the same platform, emphasized his favorite theme of black-labor solidarity.[30]

COME above all wanted a visit by King. King's support would imply a major escalation of the struggle which, they reasoned, might weaken Loeb's support in the city council. If not, then there was always a chance that King might adopt the fight as his own. The ministers did not admit to wanting to embroil SCLC in the strike; it would be a question of one visit, they insisted. But as Ralph Jackson later confessed, they calculated that King would be reluctant to stay out of the fight once his own prestige had become involved. Their invitation went out at the end of February, but King, exhausted by the Poor People's Campaign, was loathe to accept. Inundated by pleas from friends in Memphis, he soon relented. As described by James Lawson, who did most of the persuading, the strike had all the classic features of the supposedly moribund civil rights movement: packed mass meetings, church-based leadership, and a spirit of nonviolence. The issue in dispute, moreover, was one of the questions that King sought to dramatize in the Poor People's Campaign. "Most of our poor are working every day," he emphasized in his speeches, and they stayed poor, in part, because they were unorganized. All labor had dignity: the only thing that made a job "menial," King argued, was its derisory wage.[31]

On March 18, after a last-minute telephone briefing from Lawson, King flew into Memphis with Andrew Young. Abernathy, Bevel, and other staff members were already in the city. Collecting King from the airport, Lawson and Jesse Epps, one of the union leaders, revealed that there would not, after all, be ten thousand people at the Mason Temple. King's face dropped. "Yes," Epps went on, "you're going to be speaking . . . before 15,000 people. No one else can get in the house." King was delighted, and the reception he received lifted his spirits. "They were whooping up everything he'd say," remembered Kyles, "hanging on to his every word." Sensing the mood of the audience and responding to it, King suggested a day-long general strike if Loeb refused to budge. "And you let that day come, and not a Negro in this city will go to any job downtown. When no Negro in domestic service will go to anybody's house or anybody's kitchen. When black students will not go to anybody's school." The crowd roared its approval, drowning out his closing words. When he sat down, Lawson suggested that he lead a march the following morning. King was immediately receptive to the idea, but he wished to complete his Mississippi tour first. They quickly decided on another date, March 22. Returning to the lectern, King announced the march and urged everyone to stop work or stay out of school that day. The fight in Memphis, he affirmed, marked the beginning of the Poor People's Campaign.[32]

Afterwards, at the Lorraine Motel, King talked and joked with his friends in the COME leadership. The mass meeting had moved and impressed him. Rustin had been telling him that nonviolent protest was a spent force, and that the volatile mood of the ghettos made marches and demonstrations too dangerous. Yet COME was staging daily marches with no hint of violence, and holding nightly rallies which often drew more than ten thousand people. "I've never seen a community as together as Memphis," he told Levison a few days later. "And it hasn't received that much coverage." Some of his colleagues, however, were angry that King should allow himself to become side-tracked. "We were trying to organize the Poor People's March," Young later stated. "We felt he didn't have any business going to Memphis."[33]

Because of snow, the march had to be rescheduled for March 28. Meanwhile, King worked feverishly to build up support for the Washington protests. After leaving Memphis on March 19, he visited Mississippi, Alabama, and Georgia before flying to New York. There, in addition to preaching at Wyatt Walker's church, he discussed the demands of the campaign with the research committee. He also visited Marian Logan, staying up most of one night in an effort to make her abandon her opposition to the campaign. His cajoling and pleading, however, failed to change her mind. On March 27 he toured New Jersey and, encouraged by the large and friendly crowds, decided to travel to Memphis the following morning rather than that night. If he caught an early flight, he could arrive in time for the march.[34]

It turned out to be a fateful decision. King's plane was late, and the march, scheduled to start at ten o'clock, had to be kept waiting. As the crowd became impatient and restless, Kyles argued that they should begin without King. But Lawson, the chief organizer, insisted that they wait. As the minutes dragged by, onlookers and bystanders milled along the route of the march, clogging the sidewalks and spilling onto the pavements. Some of these spectators, it transpired, were criminals who had come to thieve rather than cheer. At the assembly point for the marchers, Clayborne Temple, several hundred teenagers were being harangued by a group of self-styled "militants" who called themselves the Black Organizing Project, or the "Invaders." Unknown to King and SCLC, the Invaders felt that they had been ignored by COME, and were intent on embarrassing Lawson and his fellow preachers. As the inexperienced parade marshals congregated at the head of the column, trying to clear the route, in the rear, John Smith, Charles Cabbage, and other Invaders denounced nonviolence, exhorting their listeners to take more extreme measures.[35]

If marchers wanted to act on the Invaders' inflammatory words, they had ready-made weapons to hand: the union had made up hundreds of placards attached to two-by-two sticks. Marrell McCullough, an undercover police officer, reported that these were being distributed among the teenagers, many of whom tore off the cards to bare the sticks. The Memphis Police Department conveyed this information to Special Agent William Lawrence of the FBI. Neither the FBI nor the MPD, however, warned the march organizers. Harold Middlebrook and others nevertheless recognized the danger, and attempted to confiscate as many of the sticks as they could find. But they did not have time to round up all of them.[36]

By the time King arrived from the airport at about eleven o'clock, the scene around Clayborne Temple was chaotic. People surged about his car, preventing it from reaching the church. King and Abernathy struggled out, disturbed by the milling crowds and obvious lack of discipline. They nonetheless acceded to Lawson's suggestion that they dispense with the usual briefing and begin the march forthwith. As they pushed their way to the head of the column, Lawson strode ahead trying to clear a path: "We had just hundreds of people from Linden to Beale Street, in the street, on the sidewalk, everywhere." At the back of the march, which the marshals had neglected, bottles of wine were being passed around in brown bags. At the front, a group of teenagers ignored the marshals and ensconced themselves directly behind Abernathy and King.[37]

The marchers turned left into Beale Street and then right into Main, which led north to city hall. Before the head of the column reached the second corner, however, the sound of breaking glass could be heard to the rear. Lieutenant Arkin of the MPD saw sticks being thrown through store windows: "Almost as if spontaneously, Negroes who had been in the march began looting these stores . . . and running in all directions." According to Lawson, on the other hand, the main culprits were thieves and shoplifters who had mingled with the crowds; certainly, as the marchers turned into Main Street, windows were also being broken ahead of them. At that point, Lawson decided to bring the demonstration to an end; borrowing a megaphone from a police officer, he ordered the marchers to return to Clayborne Temple. Billy Kyles, at the tail end of the column, rushed up Linden Street to stop any more marchers turning into Beale. When he reached the corner and looked down Beale, he saw window after window being caved in: "Kids were throwing things and running." The police, with permission to break up the march, then "waded into the crowd and started beating people who were coming back." Then, Kyles related, "they started shooting this tear gas." The marchers stumbled back to Clayborne Temple. They were still not safe from the gas, however: when the police saw some stone-throwing youths take refuge in the church, they fired several canisters into the vestibule. By the day's end, sixty-two people had been injured, four of them with gunshot wounds. A sixteen-year-old boy, Larry Payne, had been shot dead. Thirty-eight hundred National Guardsmen patrolled the streets, helping to enforce a 7:00 P.M. curfew.[38]

When Lawson stopped the march, a group of parade marshals hustled King down a side street. Bernard Lee flagged down a private car and, explaining to its driver, a black woman, that King was in danger, commandeered the vehicle. With Lee at the wheel, and escorted by two police motorcycles, they sped away from the melee. When the police refused to take them to King's hotel, the Peabody, on the grounds that it was too close to the disorder, they checked into a suite at the Rivermont. King, although shaken and upset, had regained his composure when the local leaders began arriving at the hotel in the early afternoon. Questioning Lawson, Kyles, and Ralph Jackson, King learned of COME's difficulties with the Invaders. Although King remained outwardly calm, Abernathy and Lee berated the COME leaders for their ineptitude: their planning and organization had been totally deficient; and if they had been experiencing problems with the Invaders, why had they failed to inform SCLC? All agreed, however, on the absolute necessity for continuing the daily marches, and for King to return to Memphis to lead another, successful, demonstration.[39]

On the morning of March 29, King received some unexpected visitors: Charles Cabbage, Calvin Taylor, and Charles Harrington of the Invaders. The purpose of their visit was clearly self-serving. Although they disclaimed any responsibility for the previous day's violence—they had ostentatiously shunned the march itself—they calculated that if they were receiving the blame for the disruption SCLC would have to take them seriously. Abernathy was hostile to them, believing that they had wrecked the march and endangered King, but King, typically, decided to seek their cooperation. He listened patiently as Cabbage offered his analysis of the violence. The ministers in COME had misjudged the mood of the people, he explained; the Invaders were much more in tune with black youth, but Lawson had denied them any say in the campaign. The ministers had even ordered their telephone cut off, refusing to give them twenty dollars. By ignoring the young they had magnified the possibility of violence. When King asked about their organization, Cabbage soon raised the question of money: could SCLC help to finance their "cultural unification program?" King was noncommittal: his organization might be able to help the Invaders, but only if they promised to cooperate fully in preventing any repetition of Thursday's violence. He sharply dismissed Cabbage's reply that the Invaders could not be expected to control "the people." If they had no influence over "the people," King insisted, then they should not pretend to speak on their behalf. SCLC could only work with their group if they renounced violence and used their influence constructively. If they accepted this condition, he would meet them on his return to Memphis.[40]

Afterwards, facing the press, King did his best to disassociate SCLC from the debacle of March 28. "We had no part in the planning of the march," he stressed; "our intelligence was absolutely nil." Nor would the violence "in any way affect" SCLC's plans for Washington. Moreover, to offset this setback, he intended to return to Memphis shortly to lead a "massive, nonviolent demonstration" in support of the striking sanitation workers. This time his own staff would prepare the ground, making a special effort to involve the young militants, perhaps by training them as parade marshals, a tactic which had averted trouble in Chicago and elsewhere. Later that day, in Washington, Young confirmed that the Poor People's Campaign was still on, although SCLC's return to Memphis might necessitate another delay in beginning the protests.[41]

The violence in Memphis was a godsend to the FBI. In an "urgent" cable to William Sullivan, local agent Robert Jensen reported that King had been obviously frightened during the march, saying, "I've got to get out of here." Clearly, Jensen argued, King had been "primarily interested in preservation of himself and made no effort to quiet [the] group that was following his leadership." In Washington, COINTELPRO sprang into action. On March 28 it put together a "news story" to be fed, through the Crime Records Division, to friendly press contacts. "Memphis may only be a prelude to civil strife in our Nation's Capitol [sic]," it stated in part. Another "blind memorandum," drafted the next day, drew attention to King's "hypocrisy" in staying at the white-owned Rivermont Hotel when Memphis had a "first-class Negro hotel." Hoover approved both these efforts. Ever hopeful, he also made another request to the attorney general for a wiretap on SCLC's Atlanta office. "Despite this violence in Memphis," he pointed out, "Levison and King are continuing their plans for this massive civil disobedience . . . in Washington." Ramsey Clark ignored the request.[42]

In fact, King had almost persuaded himself that the Poor People's Campaign ought to be called off. He recognized only too well that the violence of March 28 represented a disaster of the first order. It had dealt a damaging blow to his own leadership. Equally serious, it made the future of nonviolence seem bleak. The question was no longer whether nonviolent protest could be effective, but whether it was still

possible to hold a nonviolent march at all. Perhaps, he told his colleagues, he should step aside and let groups like the Invaders indulge
their fantasies of violence. His message that violence was suicidal was
not getting through; if his words did not convince, then bitter experience might. Young tried to argue that in a sick, violent society no one
man, no single organization, could possibly guarantee complete nonviolence. But King would not be assuaged: this violence had erupted
within their own ranks, and in a march he had been leading. He proposed to go on a fast, and through this fast to appeal to the leadership
of Memphis, as well as those who participated in the violence, to come
to him in a united front firmly pledged to nonviolence. "I think that
this kind of powerful spiritual move . . . would be a way of unifying
the movement."[43]

Shortly before King left Memphis on the afternoon of March 29,
Levison phoned him from New York and attempted to dissuade him
from cancelling the Poor People's Campaign. Levison had long been
worried that SCLC was painting itself into a corner by undertaking to
prevent violence and rioting. If it made this its criterion of success, he
told King, it was certain to fail. King seemed to be saying "that you
must have 100 percent adherence to nonviolence even by those who
are not your followers. How can you ever get that?" Levison drew an
analogy with the labor movement. In the 1930s strikes had also been
equated with violence; indeed, they had often been accompanied by
bombings and dynamiting. But the workers had disclaimed responsibility for the violence and persisted in their struggles. To have abandoned
strikes because of violence would have played into the employers'
hands: "The other side can always find a few provocateurs no matter
what you do." If SCLC called off its protests because of the violence of
a tiny minority, it would be falling into the same trap. "I'm just very
bothered by the idea that you would be accepting the logic of the press,
which is that if you can't control 100 per cent but only 99 per cent,
you are a failure. This kind of arithmetic makes no sense. . . . What
you can say is that you can control your followers. You are not undertaking to control everybody else. . . . I just can't see you getting into a
position where you are undertaking to eradicate all violence, because
you are destined to fail." The way to proceed was not to embark on a
fast, which he doubted would sway the violent elements, but to persist
in nonviolent struggle.

But King disputed this logic. This had been no ordinary riot, he
pointed out: "Let's face it, this was a riot that broke out right in the
ranks of our march. These fellows would be in line and they would
jump out, do something, and come back to hide within the group."

How could SCLC press ahead with the Washington protests when it had shown itself to be incapable of controlling its own marchers? The fact that the violent elements had been a small minority was little comfort: the press would play up the violence and write him off as an ineffective leader. King also rejected Levison's comparison with the labor movement of the 1930s:

> You did not have a labor leader . . . who rose up as a symbol of non-violence. It didn't matter about violence. It mattered tactically but not philosophically and in terms of the leadership of the man. He had not become the symbol of rallying people around a philosophy and method of nonviolence. What we are faced with is that the press . . . will put many Negroes in doubts. It will put many Negroes in the position of saying, "Well, that's true: Martin Luther King is at the end of his rope. . . . [Y]ou watch your newspapers. Watch the *New York Times* editorials. I think it will be the most negative thing about Martin Luther King that you have ever seen.

The Poor People's Campaign was doomed, King believed. It would be more difficult to recruit people now, and those who had already volunteered might drop out through fear of violence. He intended to discuss the situation with the executive staff the next day, and invited Levison to attend the meeting.[44]

The disturbance in Memphis hardly merited the term "riot." The FBI noted that the window breaking and looting had been confined to three blocks. It also knew from informants that fewer than one hundred people had been involved, and that these were petty criminals rather than politically motivated militants. As King predicted, however, the press seized upon the violence to cast doubt on the Poor People's Campaign. Some papers, like the *St. Louis Globe-Democrat*, quoted almost verbatim from the FBI handouts. After four years of rioting, however, the press needed little prompting. "Dr. King's pose as a leader of a non-violent movement has been shattered," gloated the *Memphis Commercial-Appeal*. "He now has the entire nation doubting his word when he insists that his April project . . . can be peaceful." For good measure, the paper carried a cartoon showing a frightened King fleeing the riot; it was captioned, "Chicken à la King." None of King's precautions, warned the *New York Times*, could prevent the Poor People's Campaign from turning into "another eruption of the kind that rocked Memphis." *Newsweek*, too, thought Memphis a "portent of what could happen in Washington." Without mentioning King by name, the president himself fired an unmistakable warning shot. The events in Memphis, he stated, "remind us of the grave peril rioting imposes." Despite the fact that the MPD and the National Guard had the situation well in hand, Johnson offered Tennessee federal assistance to maintain order. The alacrity with which he made this offer contrasted sharply with his foot-dragging during the far more serious Detroit riot.[45]

When the executive staff met at Ebenezer Baptist Church on the morning of March 30, King, in somber mood, dwelled on the serious implications of the Memphis debacle. Despite his earlier statement to the press, he said, he might well cancel the Poor People's Campaign. He also stated his grave doubts about the wisdom of going back to Memphis. Jesse Epps, the sole representative of the Memphis movement, argued that SCLC could not afford to pull out of the second march. The press had depicted King as having run away from the March 28 demonstration: that impression, however false, had to be challenged and dispelled. SCLC could hardly go to Washington, moreover, until it had given a clear demonstration of its ability to stage a peaceful march in Memphis; otherwise, its assurances of nonviolence would ring hollow and the press would continue to predict a repetition of March 28. But Young and others opposed returning to Memphis: SCLC should cut its losses and concentrate on the Poor People's Campaign, a massive enough task in itself. Bevel and Jackson, however, began to restate their old objections to the very concept of the Poor People's Campaign. This angered King, and he did something most unusual: he singled out three staff members, including Bevel and Jackson, for scathing criticism. He then left the meeting, complaining that his staff had failed to demonstrate both their commitment to the campaign and their ability to organize it.

The discussions continued, without King, throughout the afternoon. Gradually, as the debate proceeded, those present arrived at a consensus. King had been wrong, they agreed: the issue in Memphis was not the future of nonviolence, but poverty and racism. SCLC had not caused the violence of March 28, and it should not abandon its most effective weapon, the ability to march in the streets, because of it. It was not SCLC's task to stop rioting; rather, it had to attack the conditions that breed violence through demonstrations and other forms of nonviolent protest. Better planning, better organization, and better training would ensure the success of a second march in Memphis. The struggle of the sanitation workers, moreover, raised exactly those issues that SCLC intended to dramatize in Washington. A return to Memphis would provide a logical and fitting prelude to the Poor People's Campaign. Then, as Levison related the next day, we began to realize that we had dealt with everything we could deal with. . . . And there was a complete unanimity. At this point Joe Lowery . . . said very quietly, "The Lord has been in this room this afternoon. I know He's been here because we could not have deliberated the way we did without the Holy Spirit being here. And the Holy Spirit is going to be with us in Memphis and Washington." And then, because he was a little embarrassed at giving a little sermon, he ends up giving a kind of Indian war whoop. At which point Andy got up and started to do a little dance. And then somehow all of us were standing up, shaking hands with each other. Then we called [Dr. King] and told him he had to come down because he had just missed something great . . . and we went over it and he was completely convinced.

It was perhaps the most inspiring meeting he had ever experienced with SCLC, Levison thought. It lasted ten hours.[46]

King ordered Jackson, Bevel, and Williams to be in Memphis by April 1, leaving ample time to prepare for the second big march, scheduled for April 5. Cooperation with the Invaders was seen as crucial to its success, and the COME leadership welcomed SCLC's help in dealing with them. "It was just too difficult to try to plan strategy and argue ideology with them," Billy Kyles remembered; SCLC "had guys who were full time to do nothing but work with militants."

Chief among these experts was James Orange, who arrived in Memphis on March 31. Discussions with the Invaders began forthwith, and they hinged on two related issues: SCLC's insistence that the Invaders commit themselves to nonviolence; and the Invaders' demand for a greater share in "the action." Orange, in effect, had to mediate between the Invaders and COME. His task was rendered more difficult by the Invaders' hostility to Lawson, as well as by their extravagant financial demands. On the evening of April 2, Ralph Jackson of COME met Cabbage and several other Invaders at the Lorraine Motel. He quickly squashed any suggestion that Lawson should be replaced; he did, however, offer the young blacks two seats on the COME strategy committee. The question of financial support from SCLC had to wait until King's arrival on April 3.[47]

King flew into Memphis amidst a welter of rumors that he might never leave the city alive. King was taking a risk, city attorney Frank Gianotti warned; "in the turmoil of the moment" he might even be killed. Two days earlier, a reservations clerk at American Airlines received an anonymous message that a bomb would be aboard King's flight. She immediately notified the FBI, who in turn alerted the MPD,

Military Intelligence, the Secret Service, and the Federal Aviation Administration. The first King knew about the threat was when his plane was delayed for an hour at the Atlanta airport. Dr. King was on the plane, the pilot told the passengers, and all of the bags had to be checked. King laughed, but the incident stayed in his mind.[48]

Upon their arrival in Memphis, King, Abernathy, and Lee went to a meeting with the COME leadership at James Lawson's church. They then checked into the Lorraine Motel, where they met the Invaders. King opened the discussion by asking Cabbage and his colleagues whether they could work with an organization dedicated to nonviolence; if not, then SCLC could have nothing to do with them. The Invaders assured King that they were not a violent group, but demurred when pressed for an undertaking to prevent violence on the second march. Given the mood of Memphis blacks, they contended, neither they nor SCLC could guarantee a nonviolent march. Their response angered Abernathy and Lee, who sensed that the Invaders were less interested in supporting the strike than in securing funds for themselves. Young helped to break the deadlock, and the Invaders eventually agreed to serve as parade marshals. On the question of money, King was sympathetic. He promised to back the Invaders if they decided to approach other organizations for funding, and he did not rule out some financial assistance from SCLC.[49]

In the evening King delivered his last, and many consider his best, speech. Addressing a relatively small audience at the Mason Temple, he gave an oration of such impassioned intensity that it left his listeners moved and stunned. As he neared the end of the speech, King astonished his colleagues by dwelling on the time he had been stabbed, almost fatally, in 1958—he rarely referred to this incident, and had never talked about it at such length in public. Sitting behind him on the platform, Harold Middlebrook wondered how the speech would end, for King had already used several of his standard perorations. When the climax came, it electrified the audience. He didn't care what happened to him now, he said. Only that morning his plane had been delayed by a bomb scare.

> And then I got into Memphis. And some began to . . . talk about the
> threats that were out—what would happen to me from some of our sick
> white brothers. Well I don't know what will happen now. We've got some
> difficult days ahead. But it really doesn't matter with me now, because
> I've been to the mountaintop. And I don't mind. Like anybody, I would
> like to live a long life; longevity has its place. But I'm not concerned
> about that now. I just want to do God's will. And he's allowed me to go
> up to the mountain. And I've looked over. And I've seen the Promised

Land. So I'm happy tonight, I'm not worried about *anything*, I'm not fearing *any* man. "Mine eyes have seen the glory of the coming of the Lord."

The microphone failed to catch "His truth is marching on." The audience rose to its feet, applauding wildly. Many had tears streaming down their faces; some were openly weeping. As his fellow preachers gathered round him, King sat impassively, as if dazed. His colleagues knew that he was still disturbed about the recent violence, and that he had not quieted his doubts about the Poor People's Campaign. "Martin depressed everyone and talked about pulling out," Rutherford told Levison. "We all bucked him up and kept him in the fight."[50]

On April 4 SCLC's lawyers, together with Lawson and Young, appeared in federal court to argue that Judge Bailey Brown should dissolve the injunction against the march that he had issued the previous day. King spent most of the afternoon presiding over a staff meeting which discussed SCLC's relations with the Invaders. Most of his colleagues were suspicious of the young militants; as John Smith recalled, "They felt that we were trying to rip them off and that they wanted no part of us." King had taken a friendlier line, but now felt annoyed by the group's absurd demands and shilly-shallying over nonviolence. When Hosea Williams suggested placing three or four of the Invaders on SCLC's staff, King emphatically rejected the idea. Nobody could work for SCLC, he insisted, if they were attracted to violence. Williams attempted to defend "tactical violence," but King would have none of it. He did not expect people to embrace nonviolence as a philosophy or way of life, but he could not appreciate any man who had not at least learned to accept nonviolence as a necessary tactic. Refusing to let the matter drop, King paced the room, "preaching" to his staff, something he normally did only during retreats. The meeting broke up at about one o'clock. Later, an irate Williams discovered that the Invaders had been billing their two motel rooms, as well as their meals, to SCLC's account. He made them leave the motel forthwith.[51]

Later in the afternoon, Young reported that Judge Brown had decided to reject the city's request for an injunction: the second march could go ahead, albeit with restrictions. This news elated King. Shortly after six, after dressing for dinner, King emerged from room 306 to linger on the balcony while Abernathy finished shaving. In the courtyard below his aides stood about chatting, waiting to go with King to the Kyles home. A few minutes later, James Earl Ray fired a single shot from a rear bathroom window in a rooming house opposite the motel. As Marrell McCullough, an undercover policeman posing as one of the

Invaders, tried to staunch King's wound, Young began to weep. "Oh my God, my God, it's all over."[52]

James Lawson believed that the strike would have succeeded of its own accord. Nevertheless, King's death assisted the strikers' cause. After the murder, one councilman recalled, "Henry Loeb looked like a man who had just been hit in the face by a bomb." On April 5, three hundred ministers, both blacks and whites, marched to city hall to call for recognition of the union. Businessmen, too, began to press for a quick settlement. With additional prodding from the Justice Department and the Department of Labor, Loeb agreed to resume direct negotiations with Wurf and other officials of AFSCME. April 8 witnessed a memorial march and rally organized by COME and SCLC. King's widow led the twenty-thousand-strong procession and addressed the rally. The other speakers included Abernathy, Lawson, Bayard Rustin, and Walter Reuther. On April 16 the city finally consented to a "Memorandum of Understanding" with AFSCME. When they ratified the agreement, the thirteen hundred strikers "broke into thunderous cheering."[53]

King's death also facilitated the passage of the 1968 Civil Rights Act, which incorporated the fair housing proposals of the failed 1966 civil rights bill. The resurrected measure had been stalled in the House Rules Committee since March 19. On the day King was buried in Atlanta, however, the committee voted to accept the Senate's version of the bill without delay, and on April 10 the House approved this recommendation by 229 votes to 195. A spokesman for the National Association of Real Estate Boards, the most vigorous opponent of the bill, reckoned that King's assassination caused nearly thirty congressmen to change their votes.[54]

But King's death also had more destructive consequences. Riots in Chicago, Baltimore, Washington, and elsewhere left thirty-nine people dead. While far less sanguinary than the riots of 1967, these outbreaks were equally effective in fuelling the "white backlash" and increasing the political isolation of black Americans. The belief that the FBI, the CIA, or even the White House had ordered the assassination gained widespread currency among blacks, including some in SCLC. For many blacks, King's murder proved beyond doubt the futility of nonviolence and the irredeemable evil of white society. The demise of King strengthened black separatism, whose expressions became increasingly nihilistic and self-defeating.

During the last two years of his life, King had been torn between his old faith in the capacity of liberal democracy for enlightened self-reform, and a Marxian view of the state as an engine of capitalist exploitation. That he became more radical is certain: the need for a thoroughgoing redistribution of wealth and power was a consistent and insistent theme of his public and private statements. Occasionally, in his most pessimistic moods, he feared that the United States was drifting toward fascism. Yet King could never forget that the federal government had once been his ally; he had dealt with two presidents on a personal basis. Experience had taught him that the state, far from being a monolithic "power elite," was actually a tangle of competing forces and institutions, its workings subject to the complex and unpredictable influence of personality, faction, localism, and bureaucratic self-interest. He wanted to believe that the current reactionary trend was a passing phase, the irrational spin-off of rioting and war. Although shaken by Chicago and alienated from the president, he convinced himself that public opinion was malleable and the government still susceptible to the right kind of pressure.

What if King had lived? Would his efforts to nudge America in the direction of democratic socialism have succeeded? Did SCLC truly have the potential to become the "radical middle" of a new interracial coalition based on economic justice for the poor? At first glance, it seems unlikely. The essential conditions for SCLC's victories—peace, black unity, and presidential favor—no longer obtained, and King's attempts to repeat those victories during a period of civil disorder and political turmoil produced opposition even within SCLC. King admitted that "we're riding on the forces of history and not totally shaping things," but those forces now seemed to be working against SCLC. "Martin had done about all that he could," thought Young.[55]

Yet King had bounced back from defeat time and again, to the astonishment of his friends and the dismay of his enemies. The political situation in 1968 was volatile and fluid: the election of Richard Nixon and the years of "benign neglect" were not a foregone conclusion. With the withdrawal of Lyndon Johnson from the presidential race, perhaps King would have cancelled the Poor People's Campaign, as Levison advocated, to campaign for Robert Kennedy. In terms of influence and accomplishment, King outstripped all other black leaders and would-be leaders; his effectiveness, his ability to deliver, put him in a class of his own. His capacity to adapt to changing circumstances would surely have been tested to the limit, but a healthy and astute pragmatism had always informed his outlook. "I am still searching myself," he admitted to his staff. "I don't have all the answers, and I certainly have no claim to omniscience." He knew that there was no magic formula for social progress. The right combination of pressure and persuasion could only be discovered in struggle, in resistance, even in defeat.[56]

Fifteen

The Abernathy Years

Ralph Abernathy's first important decision as president of SCLC was to press ahead with the Poor People's Campaign. King's murder created a wave of support for the campaign. Blacks rallied round the protest or muted their criticism. Contributions poured in on an unprecedented scale: the direct-mail program raised almost half a million dollars in a month; a single advertisement in the *New York Times*, signed by Harry Belafonte, brought in $320,000. Volunteers came forward in such numbers that SCLC easily exceeded its target of three thousand demonstrators. "The people are responding," Levison marvelled. "The poor, for the first time almost in this century, are really assembling to go to Washington." Buses full of poor people began arriving in the federal capital on May 11, and the campaign kicked off the following day with a rally addressed by Coretta King and Robert Kennedy. Washington was about to witness "the greatest nonviolent demonstration since Gandhi's salt march," predicted Young. "We may be here two or three years," Bevel warned.[1]

Resurrection City, a plywood and canvas town erected near the Washington Monument, was intended to dramatize to the press, Congress, and the nation the desperate plight of America's poor. Instead, it became a massive liability to SCLC. Rain soon turned the ground into mud; the city became crowded, disorganized, and squalid. Discipline began to deteriorate: "We got a lot of untrained, undisciplined people caught up in the emotion of the situation," Young admitted. Fights became common and petty crime rife. Teenagers from the street gangs of Memphis and Chicago were a constant source of trouble; some even brought guns into the camp. By May 22, some two hundred residents had been expelled. "They went around and beat up on our white people," explained Young. "We had to get them out." Even then, fights and thefts continued to plague the camp.[2]

SCLC had given virtually no thought to the question of how Resurrection City ought to be organized and administered. Once it had been built and occupied, it devoured SCLC's time, energy, and resources. As Bill Rutherford complained on June 2, "We've been spending more time trying to run the City, trying to cope with its problems, than dealing with actions." And administering a town of three thousand people was a task for which SCLC was singularly ill-suited. James Bevel appointed himself "mayor" of Resurrection City and proceeded to run the camp "with an almost studied arrogance." Jesse Jackson, who was accorded the more modest title of "city manager," soon replaced him. The modesty of his title, however, did not inhibit Jackson from seeking to dominate the protests. His quest for personal publicity so outraged the rest of the staff that Abernathy demoted him and placed Williams in charge of the camp. "That's when all the confusion started," James Orange claimed. "He would . . . yell at people, and that didn't work." SCLC talked about democracy, but failed to practice it. "They do not consult us," complained Reyes Tijerina, the leader of the Mexican-American contingent.[3]

By the end of May, Resurrection City had become a positive embarrassment to SCLC. With the press focusing on the mud, the disorganization, and the bickering among the staff, the basic issues which SCLC hoped to dramatize became thoroughly obscured. SCLC's leaders became an unpopular establishment against which the city's inhabitants directed their anger and frustration. When board member Marian

Logan visited the camp in early June, she was disgusted by SCLC's leadership. "The staff of SCLC is living at the Pitts Motel," she complained, "while the poor people are up to their ass in mud." Unless the situation improved, she warned, she would advise her friends not to contribute any more money.[4]

As the campaign floundered, Abernathy asked Bayard Rustin to coordinate the mammoth demonstration on June 19 with which SCLC hoped to climax their protests. Rustin agreed on condition that there be no civil disobedience or disruption, that he enjoy full authority over the planning and organization of the event, and that the campaign put forward a set of realistic demands.[5]

But Rustin's appointment only compounded SCLC's problems. His previous opposition to the campaign was well known and had angered many of King's colleagues. Now he further aroused their suspicion and hostility by attempting to narrow SCLC's demands. After he joined the campaign, newspapers began to report that SCLC's "real strategy" was to seek some kind of face-saving exit from Washington, "even if it is only a dressed-up collection of what Federal agencies are already prepared to do." On June 2 Rustin issued "A Call to Americans of Goodwill," which embodied his own list of demands; Congress "felt trapped," he explained, "by Mr. Abernathy's nameless demands for an instant millenium." But only Young, it transpired, had approved the document; others in SCLC were infuriated by it. It made no reference to Vietnam; it failed to mention the demands of the other racial minorities; it did not even include the recent proposals of the Kerner commission. Hosea Williams called the document "a bunch of jazz and nonsense," telling the press that Rustin had no authority to speak for SCLC.[6]

Caught in the middle of this public row, Abernathy dithered. On June 3 he phoned Levison and pleaded with him to help remedy the confusion. But Levison, treating King's successor with unconcealed disdain, declined to help. The situation was beyond repair, he stated. "It is incredible to me that Bayard was brought in, and if Andy suggested it he should have his head examined." The next day, speaking to Young, Levison voiced his suspicion that Rustin was making a deliberate effort to sabotage the campaign. Rustin, however, claimed that Abernathy, as well as Young, had approved the "Call." A few days later, having failed to obtain Abernathy's clear and unambiguous support, Rustin resigned. Sterling Tucker, director of the Washington bureau of the Urban League, took over his job. But "Solidarity Day" on June 19 attracted only fifty thousand people. Five days later, Resurrection City came to an ignominious end when the police cleared the site and confiscated SCLC's mule train. The National Parks Service presented SCLC with a bill for $71,000. "Whoever cleared us out," Young confessed, "may have done us a favor." The Poor People's Campaign secured a handful of minor concessions from federal agencies, but it could hardly be counted a success. President Johnson all but ignored it. And Congress, for the third year running, reduced federal expenditure on social programs.[7]

SCLC had violated the basic canons of nonviolent protest. Instead of leading the press it found itself responding to press criticism; it lost the initiative. Instead of gradually escalating the protests to create a sense of drama and momentum, it let the campaign drift aimlessly. The demonstrations and sit-ins did not get underway until late May, and they were badly planned and poorly led. They allowed the camp dwellers to let off steam but did not form part of any coherent strategy. In Birmingham and Selma, King went to jail during the early days of the campaign in order to set an example and inspire his supporters. When Abernathy went to jail in Washington, the campaign was over, bar the shouting. Blacks in Washington virtually shunned the protests. In New York, Levison watched in amazement as SCLC made one false move after another. "They came to Washington with a million dollars; they had support no other organization ever had. It takes genius to dissipate it, but they did it."[8]

Despite the flattening of Resurrection City, SCLC was reluctant to admit defeat and leave Washington. On July 16, however, after a series of ragged marches to Capitol Hill, Abernathy advised the remaining protesters to go home. At its eleventh annual convention, held in Memphis in August, SCLC undertook to continue the campaign by setting up a "poor people's embassy" in Washington, by lobbying the national party conventions, and by working to unseat reactionary congressmen. Although it reaffirmed its commitment to nonviolence, the convention endorsed the principle of black power. It also vowed to assist the working poor in their struggle for higher wages and union recognition. Henceforth, Young predicted, SCLC would move "from the realm of symbol to the realm of power." Behind the fervor of SCLC's return to Memphis, however, an absence of unity and confidence afflicted the organization. The ostentatious applause for Abernathy could not conceal the doubts about his leadership that were eating away at SCLC's morale and support. "Like a great religious revival," one newspaper noted, the convention needed "the eloquence, insight and magnetism of a great leader." It did not need to spell out the obvious.[9]

Nobody could gainsay Abernathy's loyalty, dedication or personal courage. Since December 1955 he had shared King's danger by travelling with him, marching beside him, and sharing his prison cells. In nominating Abernathy as his successor, King had stated that no man was closer to him or better acquainted with his philosophy and ideals. The evening before his death, King referred to him as "the best friend that I have."

Abernathy's misfortune was that he served King so selflessly for so long that he developed few of the qualities necessary for effective leadership of an organization like SCLC. Whereas Bevel and Williams had argued with King, whereas Walker and Young showed administrative talent and political sagacity, whereas Jackson displayed independence and ambition, Abernathy had remained doggedly self-effacing, quite willing, as one staff member put it, "to stay in the basement of SCLC for thirteen years." Humility was the quality most often ascribed to him. "I never tried to duplicate [King] or steal the show," he remembered. "In press conferences, he'd take all the questions without referring any to me." When asked to assess his role in SCLC, Wyatt Walker called it "tangential." Abernathy had been King's "spiritual brother . . . and indispensable in that sense." Perhaps understandably, neither man did anything to prepare for the eventuality of Abernathy's succession. Without King, Abernathy seemed uncertain and insecure. Instead of developing his own individual style—his speeches had always been earthy and funny—he tried to imitate King. Whereas King had a "dream," he had a "vision." King had written "Letter from Birmingham City Jail"; Abernathy wrote a letter from the jail in Charleston. By attempting to emulate King's intellectual style, he often sounded dull and pompous. People felt "he was trying to put on the airs of Dr. King," Septima Clark complained in 1971. "I just wish he would be himself."[10]

In November 1968, at Young's suggestion, the executive staff secluded themselves in an Atlanta motel for two days, with two psychiatrists present, in an effort to reduce the bickering and tension which had been so much in evidence during the Poor People's Campaign. "People went all the way back to Albany, Georgia," Young related, "and dug up all kinds of various grudges they have been holding." Young considered it the most constructive staff meeting since King's death. Colleagues criticized Abernathy for laziness, egotism, and lack of intellect. Abernathy himself confessed to the envy he used to feel when King received honors and awards. Others frankly admitted that they had found King remote and unapproachable. At the end of the session, most felt that the air had been cleared and Abernathy's position strengthened. But one of their main conclusions, that they had yet to "bury" King, seemed to represent an evasion of the problem. As Lawrence Reddick told Abernathy with some acerbity during a research committee meeting shortly afterwards, King could no more be "buried" than Gandhi. It was not SCLC's task to "bury" King, but to realize his ideals.[11]

No amount of group analysis could confer upon Abernathy the respect and authority that had been King's. "That was another aspect of the problem his death left us," Young admitted: King's lieutenants were used to sharing authority as equals; they had refused to take orders from anyone but King. While King lived, their egotism and ambition had been restrained; personal antagonisms had been kept in check. But these restraints had now disappeared: antipathies which had simmered for years now boiled over and became increasingly destructive; the discipline which King had imposed through the force of his personality crumbled. Men like Bevel and Jackson became arrogantly assertive, even insubordinate. Rutherford, whom King had employed to bring order and discipline to the organization, soon lost his authority and became a spent force. "Every member of that staff is a little feudal lord that has been given a principality," Levison told Rustin, "and with Martin as the king it actually worked. But with anyone else it needs a total reorganization." Rustin, who had designed SCLC with Levison's help, agreed on the need for a complete overhaul. "As long as Martin was there you had pretty much of a rubber-stamp board, but it didn't matter because he had the genius to pull victory out of the jaws of defeat. But without a strong disciplined staff, and without a board now which is going to help keep that staff disciplined, that thing is bound to fall apart."[12]

Levison and others wanted to see some form of collective leadership emerge within SCLC, as well as a greater degree of democracy and shared decision making. King had the unique ability to appeal to a variety of groups and audiences: he could communicate with students, clergymen, intellectuals, white liberals, and blacks of all classes. In order to sustain this broad appeal, SCLC now needed to project a number of personalities. Abernathy was strikingly popular with Southern blacks, especially the rural poor; Young appealed to Northern white liberals; Jackson had created an impressive following among blacks in Chicago. Jackson, in particular, had the kind of mass appeal that SCLC sorely needed. "Jackson has a charisma of his own," Coretta King noted, not long after her husband's death. "And if he isn't corraled and used in our organization he's going to do it outside." Coretta King thought that she herself had a role to play in some kind of collective leadership. Intelligent, strong-willed, and devoted to nonviolence, she wanted nothing more than to dedicate her life to furthering her husband's ideals. True, she had hitherto played virtually no part in SCLC—an all but exclusively, almost aggresively, male-dominated organization. But after King's death she suddenly became a public figure in her own right, and her quiet dignity commanded widespread sympathy and respect. Her popularity, moreover, extended to white as well as black.[13]

But SCLC obstinately remained a leader-oriented organization, projecting Abernathy as the "Joshua" who, by divine sanction, was following in the footsteps of King-Moses. Talk of collective leadership became tantamount to disloyalty. Indeed, many of the board and lower-echelon staff members became so angered by the continual sniping at Abernathy that they began to support his leadership as a way of thumbing their noses at SCLC's critics. The leadership circle which had revolved round King soon disintegrated.

Bevel was the first to go. His ideas had always blended the brilliant and the bizarre. After King's death, however, they became merely bizarre. At a staff retreat in January 1969 to discuss possible actions on the anniversary of the assassination, Bevel proposed an international mobilization focusing on disarmament: Abernathy and Coretta King ought to embark upon a world tour in an effort to induce governments to cut their military expenditures by 10 percent. This saving should then be dedicated to peaceful purposes. But his plan came to nothing; Coretta King and others found his compulsive talking and obsessive enthusiasm disturbing. They were even more disturbed by his next idea: SCLC should undertake to defend King's alleged assassin, James Earl Ray, who was about to stand trial in a Tennessee court. Even if Ray were found guilty, Bevel argued, SCLC would be preventing him from becoming a scapegoat for America's racism. "We've got to stop people from running around saying Dr. King is dead. . . . He lives, man! We've got to flush out all the lying people hiding behind the coattails of James Earl Ray." Rebuked by Abernathy for floating this idea in public, and increasingly alienated from his colleagues, Bevel resigned a few months later and drifted into obscurity.[14]

Young had been widely touted in the press as King's natural successor. The fact of his popularity among white liberals, however, caused other staff members to question his loyalty, as did his friendship with Coretta King and Stanley Levison. In fact, Young had no desire to fight for SCLC's presidency, and he doggedly supported Abernathy's leadership. But he had little inclination to remain with SCLC. King's death, the fiasco of the Poor People's Campaign, and the interminable staff conflicts had sapped his morale and strength. "We're not healthy," he admitted in 1969. "We're an exhausted organization right now. . . .[T]he toll of some ten years of constant pressure is beginning to tell on all of us." In 1970 he resigned from SCLC to seek a new career in politics.[15]

Failing to find a niche in SCLC's leadership, Coretta King also decided to go her own way. Although she initially hoped for a place on the executive staff, she soon turned her formidable energies towards the construction of the Martin Luther King, Jr., Center for Nonviolent Social Change. In addition to memorializing her husband, she wanted this edifice to incorporate a library and archive, as well as an educational center where nonviolence could be studied and taught. Her plans for the center soon brought her into conflict with SCLC, for she insisted on claiming the sole use of her husband's name in matters of fundraising. The ensuing legal wrangle soured relations between King's widow and King's organization. Despite their reservations about the grandiose nature of Coretta King's plans, many of King's friends and advisers, disillusioned with Abernathy's leadership, agreed to support her endeavor. After Young left the staff, Levison's role in SCLC came to an end. Wachtel found himself dropped from the board of directors after he attempted, at the Detroit meeting of December 1971, to bring an issue to the vote.[16]

The same board meeting precipitated the resignation of Jesse Jackson, easily the most damaging loss of all. As early as 1969, Jackson was being described in the press as SCLC's next president. In the years after King's death, when SCLC was starved of victories, the apparent success of Operation Breadbasket in Chicago was all the more conspicuous. According to one analysis, many of the jobs for which it claimed credit failed to materialize. But specific results were less important in the eyes of the press than Jackson's personal dynamism, which he displayed to good effect each Saturday morning at the lively and entertaining Operation Breadbasket mass meetings. Writing in *Harper's* in March 1969, Richard Levine assessed Jackson as "probably the most powerful Negro in Chicago," and speculated that he might be the "heir to Dr. King." A month later, in *Look*, George Goodman was even more lavish in his praise. Inside SCLC, he wrote, "there is no man better equipped to match wits and the arguments of ultra-militant blacks. . . . Jackson has the size and the brains and the power to marshal human force behind him." A *Time* special edition devoted to "Black America" made Jackson its leading story; Abernathy was barely mentioned.[17]

Such plaudits must be judged in the context of the current white enthusiasm for "black capitalism." As his biographer, Barbara Reynolds, points out, Jackson seemed far less threatening to whites than either King or Abernathy. King had questioned the very basis of American capitalism; Jackson eschewed talk of socialism and made the promotion of black businesses his major concern. Blacks had to develop their own "private economy," he maintained; they needed a "capital base in the black community." For obvious reasons, white politicians and businessmen found this message far more palatable than King's demand for massive federal subventions to the poor. "Black capitalism" posed no threat to existing institutions; it did not burden the government or the taxpayer. It could even be endorsed by the Nixon administration. Whites also found much that was acceptable in what Jackson said about integration. When King had talked of "little black boys and black girls joining hands with little white boys and white girls," he meant these words to be taken literally as well as metaphorically. For King, integration had to embrace social integration: living and working with people of other races and cultures was an enriching experience. Jackson, by contrast, deemphasized integration, calling it "imitation and forced assimilation." Blacks were already separate, he told *Time.* "The question becomes whether we remain separate and dependent or become separate and independent—obviously, that's the way we've got to go." Whites who abhorred the prospect of black neighbors could only applaud such sentiments.[18]

While beaming its approval on Jackson, the press belittled or ignored Abernathy. Was such treatment a reflection of Abernathy's dull ineptitude? Or did it reflect the fear that Abernathy, like King, represented a radical threat to American institutions? Abernathy certainly remained closer to King's views than did Jackson. He continued King's campaign against the Vietnam War and his crusade on behalf of the poor. He attempted to make poverty a public liability requiring drastic government action. He looked for solutions at the national rather than the local level. "I don't believe in black capitalism," he affirmed, "but black socialism." No wonder *Time* and the Nixon administration preferred "the new black localism" of Jackson and others—"figures who are learning to create black self-help groups . . . and to work among the black poor to give them hope and the techniques to improve their living conditions."[19] In many ways, Jackson's emphasis on black capitalism and self-help was more in tune with political realities in the America of the 1970s than Abernathy's economic radicalism. Jackson, in addition, had many of the leadership qualities that Abernathy lacked.

Yet Jackson's driving ambition offended many SCLC veterans. No sooner had King died than Jackson began propagating the myth that he had cradled the dying leader in his arms; newspapers were soon repeating the erroneous claim that King's last words had been uttered to Jackson. During the Poor People's Campaign, Jackson, in the words of one colleague, "went wild for the headlines." Others in SCLC suspected Jackson of converting Operation Breadbasket into his own personal power base. King himself, shortly before his death, had challenged Jackson to leave his "personal kingdom" in Chicago to build Operation Breadbasket in other cities. "When we put Jesse in charge of the boycott operation," Young explained, "it was . . . so we could hit thirty or forty cities simultaneously. . . . But Jesse could never get out of Chicago to do it." His reluctance to leave that city, even for regular SCLC staff meetings, soon bordered on open insubordination. "Jesse just kept chipping away at Abernathy's authority," Hosea Williams stated, "breaking every rule in the book."[20]

In December 1971, when evidence of financial improprieties in Operation Breadbasket caused Abernathy to discipline him, Jackson quit SCLC. He took the Chicago branch of Operation Breadbasket with him. With the launching of Operation PUSH, Jackson proclaimed himself to be an independent civil rights leader of national stature. His defection deprived SCLC of its most popular officer and most effective fundraiser. It also robbed SCLC of its principal base in the North.

By the time of the Abernathy-Jackson schism, observers had already pronounced the civil rights movement dead. "Very little direct action . . . activity is to be found anywhere in the South today," the *New York Times* reported in 1970. Nevertheless, SCLC proved that it could still utilize nonviolent protest to effect on occasion, and the period 1968–71 saw a minor revival of its work in the South. School desegregation schemes which perpetuated segregation by other means, and which led to the closure of black schools and the dismissal of black teachers, provided the focus of several campaigns. In 1970, for example, Hosea Williams led school integration demonstrations in Perry County, Georgia, which involved 430 arrests. In Butler, Alabama, the firing of three black teachers prompted fifteen weeks of SCLC-led demonstrations during the summer of 1971. After more than 300 arrests, including those of Williams and Abernathy, the authorities of Butler and Choctaw County agreed to reinstate the teachers, form a biracial committee, and hire black policemen.[21]

SCLC also carried out effective voter registration campaigns. In the summer of 1969, four years after it had first initiated demonstrations in Greene County, Alabama, SCLC conducted a voter registration drive and in an election carried out under strict federal supervision, blacks won control of the county commission and the board of education. This was the first time that blacks took political control of a black-majority county as a direct consequence of the Voting Rights Act. A similar metamorphosis occurred in Sandersville, Georgia, where the first demonstrations did not take place until October 1969. After a bitter two-year struggle marked by mass arrests, shootings, and attempted bombings, Washington County saw the election of three blacks to the Sandersville City Council.[22]

SCLC's most impressive achievement was in helping to win the Charleston, South Carolina, hospital workers strike. In March 1969, the Charleston Medical College Hospital fired a dozen employees who happened to be active members of the Retail, Wholesale, and Department Store Workers Union, whereupon the hospital's mostly black, mostly female work force struck. A week later, their fellow workers at the Charleston County Hospital did likewise. The strikers' demands were simple: union recognition, an increased wage, and an end to discriminatory employment practices. Within days, more than one hundred strikers had been arrested for violating an injunction against picketing.

When Ralph Abernathy and a team of SCLC organizers arrived in Charleston in early April, they utilized the many contacts which they had established over the years through the Citizenship Education Program to mobilize support for the strike. The repressive àctions of the city and state authorities, which imposed an early evening curfew and brought in two battalions of the National Guard, played into SCLC's hands by solidifying the black community in support of the strike. Young was at first pessimistic about the chances of success: SCLC had no leverage with the federal government. But Levison advised him that victory was possible: "You'll have to settle in for a siege. . . . If it keeps going on, it will assume the character of Montgomery." It was an astute assessment: the campaign picked up momentum, and more than one thousand people went to jail between April and July. Through the efforts of Young and Fauntroy, an impressive array of groups and individuals were enlisted in support of the strikers. Additional labor support came from the UAW and the Drug and Hospital Workers Union. In July the strikers were able to return to work with union recognition, a thirty-cents-an-hour wage increase, and the reinstatement of their dismissed colleagues.[23]

But there were no new national victories. At a time when the Nixon administration sought to slow the pace of school desegregation, weaken the Voting Rights Act, encourage the suppression of demonstrations, and ignore black demands through a policy of "benign neglect," SCLC's national campaigns were defensive ones. The 1969 Hunger Marches, the largest of which Jesse Jackson led in Springfield, Illinois, succeeded only in preventing proposed reductions in welfare benefits, but, as Walter Fauntroy noted, "to 'hold the line' against the forces of reaction . . . is indeed a victory in times like these." Black vulnerability was underlined in a shocking manner the following year: at Jackson State College in Mississippi a student dormitory was riddled by police bullets, causing two deaths; in Augusta, Georgia, a disorderly demonstration ended with the killing of six blacks, all of them shot in the back by policemen, often several times. State officials were arrogantly unrepentant about the slayings. Governor Williams of Mississippi had nothing but praise for the police, while Maddox of Georgia, ignoring the fact that the Augusta demonstrators were unarmed, warned, "If they shoot at our guardsmen and firemen, they had better be prepared to meet their maker." Attorney General John Mitchell responded to the killings by blandly condemning "violent demonstrations" and "unrestrained reactions." For five days the spirit of Selma seemed to revive, as SCLC organized a 110-mile march through Georgia to protest against the growing repression.[24]

SCLC could not, however, disguise its inability to bring about further social progress for blacks and poor people, and its attempts to mount ambitious national projects became increasingly futile. Critics complained that it engaged in an endless round of marches and rallies that produced little except bombastic rhetoric. Its involvement with the anti-war movement, its alliance with the National Welfare Rights Organization, and its support for such causes as the California grape workers overextended its declining resources and diluted their impact. SCLC neglected its Southern base and appeared to become swallowed up among other national movements. In 1972 SCLC experienced a long-predicted financial collapse: after the Poor People's Campaign its staff had dwindled from 125 to 61; now the decline in contributions was so severe that another 21 staff members had to be dropped. By 1973 only 17 people remained on the payroll, and in August Abernathy renounced the presidency, blasting those blacks who "now occupy high positions made possible through our struggle . . .but will not support the SCLC financially." Persuaded to withdraw his resignation, he soldiered on for another four years. SCLC's financial problems, in reality, were more a symptom of SCLC's decline than a basic cause of it. After all, at the time of the Birmingham campaign, perhaps its greatest achievement, SCLC had a staff no larger than the one Abernathy commanded in 1973. As Young admitted after the Poor People's Campaign, "I think sometimes that we do better when we are poor and scuffling."25

The civil rights movement had been fuelled by black optimism and a favorable political climate. Neither condition obtained under the Nixon administration. In contrast to the faith they had placed in the federal government during the Johnson years, most blacks, according to a 1970 Harris poll, felt "profound cynicism about the American political system," a disillusionment which had "almost totally alienated blacks from government, both federal and local." Their pessimism was not misplaced. Surveying white attitudes across the nation, *Time* uncovered little but hostility towards black demands: "universal opposition to busing children to once-black schools, [and] annoyance at what strikes whites as special treatment for blacks seeking education and jobs." Exploiting these sentiments, the Nixon administration succeeded in uniting blacks against it, but that unity merely underlined their lack of political influence. After King's death, black militancy became more shrill and extreme, but the base of black activism shrank. The repression of revolutionary groups like the Black Panthers ushered in a period of quietism and apathy. Veterans of SCLC and SNCC often found this a disorienting, disillusioning time. The words of Leon Hall, a junior SCLC staff member, spoke for many of them:

I spent a couple of years in limbo, going between deep bitterness and anger and not being very creative or productive. . . . We started out in the Movement with youth and zeal and the expectation that we could change the society, in essence, overnight. That did not happen, nor did years and years of challenging meet the early expectations. Some have become embittered and angry and cannot relate at all anymore.

For others there is no place to go. The society has become a closed society for them. The days of the big marches are gone. There's no place in the country where many of the Movement people can work with the

same drive, the same motivation, that they had in the Movement. . . .
They are boat-rockers. . . . They become bitter too because they worked
hard to open doors for others, and now those others pass them by. . . .
Not only is society closed for them, but the organizations from which
they came, to which they belonged, no longer exist. . . . The organization
was like a family. So when the organization was lost, the family for many
of these people was too.[26]

The inauguration of King's birthday as a national holiday in 1986
prompts the obvious question: what did King and SCLC achieve? Their
outstanding victory, the Voting Rights Act, has wrought a remarkable
change in the South's political landscape. Between 1964 and 1975, the
black electorate increased from 2 million to 3.8 million. In Alabama,
black registration increased from 19.3 to 58.1 percent; in Georgia, from
27.4 to 56.3 percent; and in Mississippi, from 6.7 to 67.4 percent. By
1976, black registration across the South stood at 63.1 percent, only
five percentage points below the white level. The number of black
elected officials had climbed to 1,913, a larger total than the rest of the
nation put together. In the cities and in parts of the Black Belt, some
striking political changes have occurred: the election of a black sheriff
in Lowndes County and a black mayor in Birmingham testify to the
success of the civil rights movement.[27]

But that success is a limited one. Blacks are still grossly underrepresented in the halls of government. By 1980, the number of black
elected officials had risen to 2,458, yet blacks still held a mere 3
percent of the South's elective offices while constituting one-fifth of
the South's population. The Voting Rights Act survived the Nixon
administration's attempt to weaken its scope; indeed, in several
important respects it has been strengthened. In 1975, moreover, a
majority of Southern congressmen voted to renew the act for a further
seven years. Nevertheless, there is convincing evidence that whites
have persevered in their attempts to minimize the impact of the black
vote. Although the barriers to black registration have all but disappeared, new obstacles to fair representation crop up in the guise of "at-
large" city and county elections, multimember legislative districts,
gerrymandered political boundaries, and a host of other more or less
sophisticated methods of nullifying or diluting the black vote. Only
section 5 of the Voting Rights Act, enforced by a vigilant federal
judiciary, inhibits the widespread adoption of such discriminatory
devices. Legislation cannot, however, eliminate individual prejudice.
There is ample reason to believe that white racism continues to

restrict black representation, by and large, to areas with black majorities or near majorities. This appears to be equally true, moreover, in
the North. Taking the United States as a whole, the 5,606 blacks who
held elective office in 1983 comprised a little over one percent of all
elected officials. Yet blacks make up fully 12 percent of the total
population.[28]

The relatively small number of black elected officials, however, un-
derstates the influence of the emergent black vote in the South. Even
when they lack the numbers to elect a member of their own race, black
voters can frequently defeat white candidates or, conversely, supply
their margin of victory. Had the racial polarization of the 1960s become the dominant characteristic of Southern politics, then blacks
would be an impotent and isolated minority. Indeed, the "lily-white"
strategy pursued by nascent Republican organizations in Georgia,
South Carolina, and elsewhere seemed to presage a partisan realignment in which whites deserted the Democratic party en masse in
order to reestablish their racial and political dominance. Should such a
party switch occur, political scientist Numan V. Bartley predicted in
1970, "the Second Reconstruction would be followed by the rule of
Bourbon Democrats, this time calling themselves Republicans."[29]

The vigor of party competition, however, has prevented this kind of
clear-cut realignment, giving blacks more room for political maneuver.
The resilience of the Democratic party did not, it is true, necessarily
benefit blacks. White Democrats often responded to the Republican
challenge by stressing their segregationist credentials and pointedly
ignoring black voters. Thus many contests witnessed two candidates,
both equally conservative, attempting to outflank each other on the
race issue. In Alabama, the Wallace organization proved so successful
in beating off challenges from the Right that, as Alexander P. Lamis
noted, it could control the Democratic nominations and steamroller
the Republican opposition without any black support.[30]

By the early 1970s it was nevertheless apparent that the kind of one-
party domination that characterized Alabama was becoming excep-
tional. Elsewhere, party competition made the black vote too pivotal to
be discounted or deliberately alienated. The lessening of overt racial
tensions, moreover, slowed the white exodus from the Democratic
party and paved the way for tacit but effective black-white electoral
alliances. As Lamis has written, "skilful Democratic party leaders" in
South Carolina and elsewhere "were quick to make a quiet accommodation with blacks," while retaining enough white support to give
them winning majorities. Governors elected by this type of coalition—

Jimmy Carter of Georgia, Reuben Askew of Florida, John West of South Carolina, Cliff Finch of Mississippi, Edwin Edwards of Louisiana, and many others—eschewed appeals to white prejudice, openly courted black voters, and accepted desegregation as a fait accompli. Even George Wallace, finding himself dependent on black support in his effort to recapture the governorship in 1982, played down his segregationist past and actively sought black allies. As Andrew Young put it, "It used to be Southern politics was just 'nigger' politics—a question of which candidate could 'outnigger' the other. . . . [But] now that we've got 50, 60, 70 percent of the black votes registered, everybody's proud to be associated with their black brothers and sisters." The Voting Rights Act has brought about a striking transformation in the climate, at least, of political debate.[31]

But the kind of political realignment envisaged by SCLC's strategists has thus far failed to materialize. Although the racist demagogy that polluted political discourse during the era of the civil rights movement has largely vanished, the egalitarian rhetoric which succeeded it did not imply any commitment to radical, or even mildly redistributionist, economic policies. The nonsegregationist Democrats who assembled biracial coalitions rarely campaigned as liberals, sometimes made coded gestures to racist sentiment, and usually avoided the kind of policies that might be offensive to their conservative white supporters. The black-white coalitions of the contemporary South are therefore unstable alliances between two groups whose political views and objectives are in many respects fundamentally opposed. While blacks have consistently favored social and economic liberalism, whites of all classes have become increasingly disenchanted with federal programs which, in their eyes, benefit blacks at the expense of white taxpayers. "The low status whites are . . . Georgia's most politically conservative people," wrote Numan V. Bartley in 1970; the idea that blacks and whites would unite across class lines behind economic and social reform was "ludicrous." In 1975 Bartley and his collaborater, Hugh D. Graham, extended this conclusion to the entire South after a comprehensive survey of political trends. Whites might have conceded defeat on the segregation issue, they argued, "but . . . underlying the region's newly found racial moderation was a continuing commitment to social conservatism."[32]

Neither the expansion of the black electorate nor the emergence of a two-party system have made the South markedly more receptive to the kind of economic radicalism espoused by SCLC. Despite—or perhaps because of—the dynamic economic growth of the "Sun Belt," the

South remains the region where local taxation is most regressive, where trade unions are most feeble (every state has an anti-union "right-to-work" law), and where a disproportionate share of the nation's poor reside. The South's two-party system, Lamis concluded in 1984, had not yet provided blacks with a political structure appropriate to the "sustained promotion of their interests."[33]

The relative political isolation of blacks becomes more apparent in the context of presidential voting. In every election since 1964, blacks found themselves allied with a minority of the white voters. With the exception of 1976, moreover, the solid Democratic vote delivered by blacks failed to offset the decline in Democratic support among whites.[34] Blacks are thus yoked to a minority political party, and a declining minority party to boot. Far from strengthening and radicalizing the Democrats, the civil rights movement hastened the disintegration of the New Deal coalition, as both Southern whites and Northern "ethnics" abandoned their traditional allegiance to embrace the social and economic conservatism of the Republican party.

The electoral success of the Reagan-led "New Right," and the subsequent dismantling of many Great Society programs, highlight the failure of SCLC's efforts to put democratic socialism on the political agenda. The decline of organized labor—trade union membership plummeted between 1970 and 1980—effectively undermined Bayard Rustin's strategy of constructing a political majority on the basis of a Negro-labor-liberal alliance. And the likelihood of an assertive movement of the poor, of the kind King tried to initiate in 1967–68, seems remote in light of the political apathy that became increasingly characteristic of the poor during the 1970s. Voter turnouts, even in presidential elections, slumped, and "disproportionate numbers of minority, low-wage, young and female voters [have] become permanent abstentionists."[35] In the Carter-Ford race, the national turnout dipped to 54 percent; four years later, barely 53 percent of the electorate bothered to cast ballots. Although voter turnout in the South has risen to approach the national average, there is evidence that in the South, too, an increasing number of blacks are ceasing to participate in the electoral process. From a peak of 63 percent of those eligible in 1976, black voter registration declined to 57 percent in 1980. White registration, on the other hand, continued to rise, reaching 72 percent at the time of the Carter-Reagan contest. Black political influence appears to have reached a plateau, and might even be on the wane. King's lament that "our political leaders are bereft of influence in the councils of political power" needs to be qualified, but it is still broadly accurate.[36]

Black advances in the economic sphere have been limited and precarious. True, nonwhite workers in stable, full-time employment increased their median income from 66 percent of the white average in 1960 to 79 percent in 1978. But the high rate of irregular and part-time employment among nonwhites meant that the overall income of nonwhite male workers remained, on average, only 64 percent of the white level. Black unemployment, 15 percent in 1985, remains more than twice the rate among whites. In 1985 the median income of black families stood at only 56 percent of the white level—little improvement over the rate obtained twenty years earlier. Over a third of all black families are still classified as "poor" according to the restrictive federal definition. Dependent upon low-wage jobs and federal income-support programs, most blacks remain on the margins of the economy.[37]

Concentrated in the declining central cities, blacks are peculiarly ill-placed to take advantage of new employment opportunities. In the suburbs of Chicago, for example, the number of jobs increased by 71 percent during the 1960s; in Chicago itself, on the other hand, total employment fell by 12 percent, although the city's population diminished by only 5 percent. With the acceleration of "white flight" and the extension of the ghetto, the quality of housing enjoyed by Chicago's blacks has markedly improved. But the racism that SCLC dramatized in 1966 still segregates the population, excluding even affluent blacks from the suburbs. The high-sounding promises of the Chicago Summit Agreement turned out to be worthless. Faced with a 1969 court order requiring it to locate new public housing outside the ghetto, the Chicago Housing Authority refused to build any accommodation at all until another court order, in 1973, compelled it to do so. Black marches through Marquette Park in 1976 evoked the same kind of white hostility that greeted SCLC ten years earlier. In Chicago, as in other cities, the impact of the 1968 Civil Rights Act has been negligible. Housing segregation "persists on a massive scale," writes one authority, "virtually unaffected by racial changes in other realms."[38]

In the sphere of foreign policy, SCLC's influence has been equally evanescent. The view that SCLC helped to end the war in Vietnam is hard to sustain. America's withdrawal from Vietnam, moreover, disproved the notion that resources previously devoted to war and defense would be transferred to nonmilitary use. Military spending and rearmament has carried on apace; the money "saved" on Vietnam did not help blacks and poor people. As Bayard Rustin put it, "The peace

windfall never materialized." The Carter administration promised a
new approach to world affairs, stressing the value of nonintervention,
human rights, and disarmament. Within two years, however, it re-
verted to traditional Cold War policies. With the election of Ronald
Reagan, defense spending escalated sharply and foreign policy re-
gressed to the dogmatic antiradicalism of the Truman-Eisenhower
years.[39]

It might be argued that blacks in the South destroyed segregation
only to discover what blacks in the North already knew: that laws
against discrimination represented an unfulfilled promise, not a representation of fact. A dispassionate analysis might also conclude that in
abolishing segregated public accommodations, the civil rights movement, to quote Bayard Rustin, "affected institutions which are relatively peripheral to the American socio-economic order and to the
fundamental conditions of life of the Negro people." Indeed, Rustin
contended that the halfhearted white resistance to desegregation reflected the fact that Jim Crow was anachronistic and economically
redundant: the structure of segregation was "imposing but hollow."[40]

There is a danger, however, of slighting SCLC's achievement by un-
derestimating the depth and duration of the white opposition to desegregation. It is true that many of SCLC's battles concerned issues that
were mainly symbolic: the humiliation involved in being confined to
the back of the bus, being addressed by one's given name, continually
seeing signs stating "white only." Yet the tenacity with which whites
defended these symbols of domination suggest that in attacking segregation, the civil rights movement struck at the heart of the Southern
caste system. Desegregation and universal suffrage did not end discrimination or eliminate poverty, but they did knock away the two
main props of white supremacy—and the destruction of institu-
tionalized white supremacy was the essential precondition for black
advancement.

Blacks achieved dignity as a people not only in removing the South's
racist totems, but also in the means whereby they attained that goal.
Although few shared King's total commitment to nonviolence, the
examples of Lebanon and Northern Ireland point to the logic and validity of his philosophy. It would be facile to suppose that nonviolence
can be utilized at will, in any given situation. The violence of a Northern Ireland stems from deeply rooted nationalisms, and it was precisely the *absence* of a strong nationalist tradition among Southern
blacks that made nonviolence a feasible strategy. SCLC did not impose
an alien philosophy upon a puzzled and skeptical people, but skilfully

attuned its methods and its message to the idealism of the black church. Its articulation of the Exodus myth drew upon a folk tradition that went back to slavery days. SCLC worked with the grain of Southern black history and culture, not against it.

No one understood that history and culture, nor expressed the aspirations of black Southerners, better than Martin Luther King, Jr. SCLC itself was far more than King, but his death revealed how completely he dominated it through intellect, personality, moral example, and organizational skill. King raised at least half of SCLC's funds virtually single-handed. Only he could move and influence such a variety and number of Americans. None of his colleagues matched the depth of his commitment to nonviolence. King's courage, dedication, and idealism have often been noted. But he also possessed more subtle qualities of leadership. He had the ability to use people—not in a manipulative or exploitative manner, but in the sense of utilizing their talents to further an ideal. Unrelentingly self-critical himself, he tolerated weakness, frailty, and error in his colleagues for the sake of harnessing their strengths. He was also willing to let other people use him if he thought it served a constructive purpose. Young and others thought King irritatingly indecisive, but his fondness for consultation and debate strengthened his decision making. Aware that people were constantly seeking to influence and manipulate him, he sought out different opinions. He took few steps without being advised of the possible consequences. He therefore blamed no one for his mistakes but himself.

Why did SCLC fail to acquire the solidity and stability of the NAACP? Ella Baker thought that it started out on the wrong footing with its King-centered structure. Levison believed that SCLC should have recruited a dues-paying mass membership, thus freeing it from its precarious dependence upon white contributors. According to Wachtel, SCLC ought to have stayed in the South, to consolidate and fully exploit its victories there. Rustin blamed SCLC's decline on, among other things, the absence of a democratic framework within the organization. King's advisers all agreed that the decision to go to Chicago was a costly and avoidable error.

Yet the people who designed and built SCLC had been less interested in constructing an organization than in structuring a nascent movement. Rustin, Levison, and Baker viewed organization as a means to an end, not an end in itself. During their long careers as political activists they had worked with or through a variety of organizations and movements, including labor unions, pacifist groups, the NAACP—

and, yes, the Communist party—in their quest for radical change. King viewed SCLC in the same pragmatic light. If SCLC ceased to serve as a vehicle for reform, he believed, it would lose its purpose. Time after time, he placed organizational self-interest and self-preservation after the pursuit of his ideals; "If I lose the fight," he once said, "then SCLC will die anyway." SCLC did not fail: it may have lost the struggle for economic justice, but it won its original battle against white supremacy. Indeed, by opening up avenues of political advancement it became, to some extent, a victim of its own success. Nothing was more natural than SCLC's decline, for it derived its strength from an insurgency which it shaped and guided but did not create. Without the power of marching feet behind it, SCLC lost its dynamism. "We are a movement," said one of its staff, "not an organization."[41]

Notes

Abbreviations

AC	City Archives, Albany, Ga.
ADA	Papers of Americans for Democratic Action, Wisconsin State Historical Society, Madison (microfilm).
BM	Burke Marshall Papers, John F. Kennedy Presidential Library, Boston, Mass.
BP	Governor Farris Bryant Papers, Florida State Archives, R. A. Gray Building, Tallahassee, Fla.
BPL	City Archives, Birmingham Public Library
BUC	King Papers, Mugar Library, Boston University
FOF	Facts on Film (Nashville, Southern Education Reporting Service)
FOR	Papers of Fellowship of Reconciliation, Peace Collection, Swarthmore College, Swarthmore, Pa.
House	House Select Committee on Assassinations, *Hearings on the Assassination of Martin Luther King, Jr.*, 95th Cong. 2d sess., 1978.
HUC	Ralph J. Bunche Oral History Collection, Moorland-Spingarn Library, Howard University, Washington, D.C.
JFK	John F. Kennedy Presidential Library, Boston, Mass.
KP	King Papers, Martin Luther King, Jr., Center, Atlanta, Ga.
MLK	Library and Archive, Martin Luther King, Jr., Center for Nonviolent Social Change, Atlanta, Ga.
MSU	Sanitation Strike Archival Project, Mississippi Valley Collection, John Willard Brister Library, Memphis State University
NAACP	NAACP Papers, Library of Congress, Washington, D.C.
SCLC	SCLC Papers, Martin Luther King, Jr., Center, Atlanta, Ga.
Senate	Senate Select Committee to Study Governmental Operations with

Respect to Intelligence Activities, *Hearings*, vol. 6, *The FBI*, 94th Cong., 1st sess., 1975.

A note on FBI sources. The FBI wiretap material falls into two categories. The "raw" transcripts of the wiretaps on King's telephones and on the telephones of the SCLC office are closed to the public until 2027. Summaries and excerpts from these transcripts, however, are included in the "King file," which has been released under congressional order and under the Freedom of Information Act. These summaries must be treated with caution, for words, phrases, and sentences are frequently wrenched out of their context to portray King and SCLC in the worst possible light. Nevertheless, they yield valuable information, particularly with regard to the conversations by and between King, Bayard Rustin, Clarence Jones, and Harry Wachtel. (Wachtel's own telephone was not tapped; those of Rustin and Jones were. The "King file" also contains information from the Rustin and Jones wiretaps.) The transcripts of the wiretaps on Stanley Levison's telephones, on the other hand, have been released in their "raw" form, and with relatively few deletions. The transcriptions are of varying quality: some are summaries and paraphrases, others word-for-word transcriptions. When quoting from this material, I have felt free to alter faulty punctuation and correct obvious errors.

Introduction

1. Morgan quoted in *New York Times*, January 7, 1972; Abernathy quoted in Pat Watters, *Down to Now: Reflections on the Southern Civil Rights Movement* (New York, 1971), p. 175.
2. Paul Good, " 'No Man Can Fill Dr. King's Shoes'—But Abernathy Tries," in *Black Protest in the Sixties*, ed. August Meier and Elliott Rudwick (Chicago, 1970), p. 287.
3. Bayard Rustin, *Strategies for Freedom: The Changing Patterns of Black Protest* (New York, 1976), pp. 38–39.
4. Herbert Butterfield, *History and Human Relations* (London, 1951), pp. 72–73.
5. David J. Garrow, *Protest at Selma: Martin Luther King, Jr., and the Voting Rights Act of 1965* (New Haven, 1978); Charles Fager, *Uncertain Resurrection: The Poor People's Washington Campaign* (Grand Rapids, 1969), pp. 25–26.
6. Good, " 'No Man Can Fill Dr. King's Shoes'—But Abernathy Tries," p. 287.
7. Herbert Gans, *Deciding What's News: A Study of CBS Evening News, NBC Nightly News, Newsweek, and Time* (New York, 1979), p. 136; Eugene D. Genovese, *In Red and Black: Marxian Explorations in Southern and Afro-American History* (New York, 1972), pp. 155–56.
8. Blackwell quoted in Howell Raines, *My Soul Is Rested: Movement Days in the Deep South Remembered* (New York, 1977), p. 499.

9. Merton cited in David H. Fischer, *Historians' Fallacies: Toward a Logic of Historical Thought* (New York, 1970), pp. 240–41.

10. F. M. Barnard, "Accounting for Actions: Causality and Teleology," *History and Theory* 20 (1981): 301.

11. King, *Stride Toward Freedom* (London, 1959), pp. 127–29; Coretta Scott King, *My Life with Martin Luther King, Jr.* (New York, 1969); Harry H. Wachtel, interview by Adam Fairclough, July 11, 1985; Morgan quoted in Raines, *My Soul Is Rested,* p. 197.

Chapter 1

1. Virginia Durr to Clark Foreman, December 7, 1955, Virginia Durr Papers, Radcliffe College.

2. *New York Times,* June 16 and 21, 1953; August Meier and Elliott Rudwick, "The Origins of Nonviolent Direct Action in Afro-American Protest," in *Along the Color Line: Explorations in the Black Experience* (Urbana, 1976), pp. 365–66; Everett H. Buell, "The Politics of Frustration: An Analysis of Negro Leadership in East Baton Rouge Parish, 1953–1966," Master's thesis, Louisiana State University, 1967, pp. 116–23; T. J. Jemison and Johnnie Jones, interview by Judy Barton, April 12, 1972, Library and Archive, Martin Luther King, Jr., Center for Nonviolent Social Change, Atlanta (library hereafter cited as MLK). The Baton Rouge boycott began when bus drivers went on strike rather than implement a new ordinance which embodied the "first come, first served" principle, and when the state attorney general ruled the law illegal. The protest ended when the city reenacted the ordinance in a form acceptable to the drivers and the state.

3. J. Mills Thornton III, "Challenge and Response in the Montgomery Bus Boycott of 1955–56," *Alabama Review,* July 1980, pp. 181–204.

4. King to Bayard Rustin, September 20, 1956, file drawer 8, folder 34, King Papers, Mugar Library, Boston University (collection hereafter cited as BUC).

5. *Tallahassee Democrat,* June 1, 1956; Malcolm Johnson, interview by Jackson Lee Ice, pp. 7–12, part of "An Oral History of the Civil Rights Movement in Tallahassee, Florida, 1956–1966," transcripts in Special Collections, Strozier Library, Florida State University.

6. Numan V. Bartley, *The Rise of Massive Resistance: Race and Politics in the South During the 1950s* (Baton Rouge, 1969), pp. 217–33.

7. Everett C. Ladd, *Negro Political Leadership in the South* (New York, 1966), pp. 222–54; Doug McAdam, *Political Process and the Development of Black Insurgency, 1930–1970* (Chicago, 1982), p. 135. Of the six preboycott leaders in Tallahassee, "three were employed in the state supported school system; none of the five new leaders was a state employee";

see Lewis Killian and Charles Grigg, *Racial Crisis in America: Leadership in Conflict* (Englewood Cliffs, N.J., 1964), p. 86.

8. Gunnar Myrdal, *An American Dilemma: The Negro Problem and American Democracy* (New York, 1944), pp. 867–78; David M. Tucker, *Black Pastors and Leaders: Memphis, 1819–1972* (Memphis, 1975), pp. 101–2. For the conservatism of the black church between the wars, see also Benjamin E. Mays and Joseph W. Nicholson, *The Negro's Church* (New York, 1933), pp. 58–59, 249, 279; Charles S. Johnson, *Growing Up in the Black Belt: Negro Youth in the Rural South* (Washington, D.C., 1941), p. 169.

9. Wartime racial tensions in the South are described in Howard W. Odum, *Race and Rumors of Race* (Chapel Hill, 1943); and James A. Burran, "Urban Racial Violence in the South During World War II," in *From the Old South to the New*, ed. W. B. Fraser and W. B. Moore (Westport, Conn., 1981), pp. 167–77.

10. *Smith* v. *Allwright*, 321 U.S. 649 (1944).

11. Bartley, *Rise of Massive Resistance*, pp. 7–9; Ladd, *Negro Political Leadership*, pp. 59–60; William H. Chafe, *Civilities and Civil Rights: Greensboro, North Carolina, and the Black Struggle for Freedom* (New York, 1980), pp. 32–35.

12. Thornton, "Montgomery Bus Boycott," pp. 171–93; A. W. West, interview by Judy Barton, January 26, 1972, p. 4, MLK; Virginia Durr to Clark Foreman, April 14, September 16, 1953, April 25, 1955, Durr Papers.

13. Rosa Parks, interview by Cynthia S. Brown, *Southern Exposure*, Spring 1981, pp. 16–17; Frank Adams, *Unearthing Seeds of Fire: The Idea of Highlander* (Winston-Salem, 1975), p. 122.

14. Thornton, "Montgomery Bus Boycott," pp. 187–90; Virginia Durr to Clark, Palmer, and Corliss, February 24, 1956, Durr Papers.

15. Thornton, "Montgomery Bus Boycott," pp. 196–200; Harris Wofford, *Of Kennedys and Kings: Making Sense of the Sixties* (New York, 1980), p. 112.

16. West, interview by Barton, p. 21.

17. L. D. Reddick, "The Bus Boycott in Montgomery," *Dissent*, Spring 1956, p. 111; Rufus Lewis, interview by Judy Barton, January 24, 1972, pp. 3–4, MLK; Virginia Durr to Clark, Palmer, and Corliss, February 24, 1956, Durr Papers.

18. Reddick, "Bus Boycott in Montgomery," p. 111.

19. John Dollard, *Caste and Class in a Southern Town* (Garden City, 1937; reprint, 1957), p. 242; S. S. Seay, interview by Judy Barton, January 25, 1972, p. 11, MLK.

20. Martin Luther King, Jr., *Stride Toward Freedom: The Montgomery Story* (London, 1959), p. 50; Thornton, "Montgomery Bus Boycott," p. 198. King later wrote that "we almost resolved to end the protest" on the afternoon of December 5, (*Stride Toward Freedom*, p. 56).

21. Reddick, "Bus Boycott in Montgomery," p. 109; *New York Times*, February

23 and 24, 1956; Virginia Durr to Clark, Palmer, and Corliss, February 24, 1956, Durr Papers; *Montgomery Advertiser,* February 24, 1956.

22. Gregory B. Padgett, "C. K. Steele and the Tallahassee Bus Boycott," Master's thesis, Florida State University, 1977, pp. 25–27.

23. Padgett, "Tallahassee Bus Boycott," pp. 29–30; James Hudson, interview by Jackson Lee Ice, August 2, 1978, pp. 10–20; C. K. Steele, interview by Ice, January 26, 1978, pp. 2–3; Russell L. Anderson, p. 51; Edward Norwood, pp. 12–18, all interviewed by Ice in 1978; Bartley, *Rise of Massive Resistance,* p. 233.

24. Statement by Mayor Winterle, June 2, 1956; Inter-Civic Council to city commission and Cities Transit Inc., June 4, 1956, minutes of city commission, City Hall, Tallahassee; *Tallahassee Democrat,* June 2 and 7, 1956; Padgett, "Tallahassee Bus Boycott," pp. 32–39; Steele, interview by Ice, p. 5.

25. Steele, interview by Ice, p. 7; Norwood, interview by Ice, p. 21.

26. King Solomon Dupont, interview by Ice, p. 27.

27. Meier and Rudwick, "Origins of Nonviolent Direct Action," pp. 366–67, 380–86.

28. King, "Our Struggle," *Liberation,* April 1956, pp. 4–5; *New York Times,* April 27, 1956.

29. Thornton, "Montgomery Bus Boycott," p. 229; *Tallahassee Democrat,* July 9, 1956.

30. Bartley, *Rise of Massive Resistance,* p. 81; Virginia Durr to Clark Foreman, February 15, 1954, Durr Papers; *New York Times,* February 25 and March 14, 1956; Thornton, "Montgomery Bus Boycott," pp. 182–84, 211–15.

31. Bartley, *Rise of Massive Resistance,* pp. 184–89; Aldon D. Morris, *The Origins of the Civil Rights Movement* (New York, 1984), p. 75. "Being president of the NAACP I would have preferred the NAACP having [control of the boycott], but I did not try to exert any pressure to get them to give it to the NAACP" (Steele, interview by Ice, p. 2).

32. Cooke quoted in L. D. Reddick, *Crusader Without Violence: A Biography of Martin Luther King, Jr.* (New York, 1959), p. 152; statement by Gov. LeRoy Collins, July 2, 1956, Collins Papers, Florida State Archives.

33. Morris, *Origins of the Civil Rights Movement,* pp. 68–69. For the repression of the NAACP, see Bartley, *Rise of Massive Resistance,* pp. 212–24.

34. Profile of Rustin from Milton Viorst, *Fire in the Streets: America in the 1960s* (New York, 1979), pp. 200–11; August Meier and Elliott Rudwick, *CORE: A Study in the Civil Rights Movement, 1942–1968* (New York, 1973), pp. 9–38.

35. James Farmer, *Lay Bare the Heart: An Autobiography of the Civil Rights Movement* (New York, 1985), pp. 186–87; Howell Raines, *My Soul Is Rested: Movement Days in the Deep South Remembered* (New York, 1977), pp. 46–48; John M. Swomley to Wilson Riles, February 21, 1956, FOR Papers, Swarthmore College.

36. Farmer, *Lay Bare the Heart*, p. 187; John M. Swomley to Glenn Smiley, February 29, 1956, FOR Papers.

37. Glenn Smiley to Muriel Lester, February 28, 1956; Smiley to John Swomley and Alfred Hassler, February 29, 1956, both in FOR Papers.

38. Glenn Smiley to William Stuart Nelson, July 11, 1958, FOR Papers; Glenn Smiley, interview by Katherine Shannon, September 12, 1967, pp. 36–37, Ralph Bunche Oral History Collection, Howard University (collection hereafter cited as HUC).

39. King, "Our Struggle," p. 6; minutes of MIA special committee, September 25, 1956, file drawer 4, folder 16, BUC; Robert L. Cannon to Alfred Hassler and Glenn Smiley, October 3, 1956, FOR Papers; King, *Stride Toward Freedom*, p. 207; Morris, *Origins of the Civil Rights Movement*, pp. 159–62.

40. E. D. Nixon, pp. 28–30, 38–39; Moses Jones, p. 11; S. S. Seay, pp. 24–26, all interviewed by Judy Barton in January 1972, MLK; Meier and Rudwick, "Origins of Nonviolent Direct Action," pp. 387–89; Smiley to Nelson, July 11, 1958, FOR Papers.

41. Virginia Durr to Clark Foreman, February 15, 1957, Durr Papers.

42. Stanley D. Levison, interview by James Mosby, February 14, 1970, p. 9, HUC.

43. Wyatt T. Walker, quoted in Earl and Miriam Selby, *Odyssey: Journey through Black America* (New York, 1971), p. 284.

44. Viorst, *Fire in the Streets*, pp. 32–33; Thornton, "Montgomery Bus Boycott," pp. 198–200; Rufus Lewis, interview by Barton, p. 16.

45. Paul Good, *The Trouble I've Seen: White Journalist/Black Movement* (Washington, D.C., 1975), p. 20.

46. Rufus Lewis, interview by Barton, p. 19; Raines, *My Soul Is Rested*, p. 56.

47. King, speech to MIA mass meeting, December 5, 1955, from sound track of the film, *King: A Filmed Record, Montgomery to Memphis*, dir. Eli Landau, 1970.

48. Dollard, *Caste and Class in a Southern Town*, p. 243.

49. Stephen B. Oates, *Let the Trumpet Sound: The Life of Martin Luther King, Jr.* (New York, 1982), pp. 85–95; Raines, *My Soul Is Rested*, pp. 60–61.

50. King, *Stride Toward Freedom*, pp. 137–40.

51. King, *Stride Toward Freedom*, p. 69; Jemison, interview by Barton, p. 32; Moses Jones, interview by Barton, pp. 3–4; Robert E. Johnson, interview by John H. Britton, September 6, 1967, pp. 22–25, HUC; Durr to Clark Foreman, February 15, 1957, Durr Papers.

52. Minutes of the Atlanta conference, May 12, 1956; invitations to conference on "Nonviolence and the South," January 8–10, 1957; Glenn Smiley to Bill Miller, January 14, 1957, all in FOR Papers; Douglas Moore to King, October 3, 1956, file drawer 8, folder 10, BUC; Smiley, interview by Shannon, pp. 58–59.

53. Rustin to King, March 8, 1956, file drawer 1, folder 29, BUC; King to

Rustin, July 10, 1956; King to Rustin, September 20, 1956, file drawer 8, folders 22 and 34, BUC.

54. Morris, *Origins of the Civil Rights Movement*, pp. 102–3; Ella J. Baker, interview by John H. Britton, June 19, 1968, p. 12, HUC.

55. *New York Times*, September 14, 1979; David J. Garrow, *The FBI and Martin Luther King, Jr.: From "Solo" to Memphis* (New York, 1981), p. 42.

56. *Washington Post*, December 15, 1975.

57. Robert Terrell, "Discarding the Dream," *Evergreen Review*, May 1970, p. 72; Baker, interview by Britton, p. 8; Levison, interview by Mosby, p. 17.

58. Meier and Rudwick, *CORE*, pp. 10, 60–70; Morris, *Origins of the Civil Rights Movement*, pp. 128–32; Smiley, interview by Shannon, pp. 59–60; Virginia Durr to Clark Foreman, May 29, 1956, Durr Papers.

59. National Council of Churches, meeting on relief, placement, and relocation, February 17, 1956, transcript, pp. 28–29, series 5, box 42, ADA Papers; *New York Times*, March 1, 1956; "In Friendship," minutes of Executive Committee, July 19, 1956, box 23, A. Philip Randolph Papers, Library of Congress; Mrs. Ralph J. Bunche and Mrs. Roy Wilkins to John W. Swomley, November 26, 1956, FOR Papers.

60. Randolph to Ella Baker, March 7, 1956, box 23, Randolph Papers; John W. Swomley to Glenn Smiley, February 29, 1956, FOR Papers; Randolph to George D. Cannon, June 21, 1956, box 2, Randolph Papers.

61. Steele, interview by Ice, pp. 34–35; Reddick, *Crusader Without Violence*, pp. 184–85.

62. Raines, *My Soul Is Rested*, pp. 62–63; Morris, *Origins of the Civil Rights Movement*, pp. 82–83.

63. Baker, interview by Britton, pp. 22–23; Terrell, "Discarding the Dream," p. 72.

64. Levison, interview by Mosby, p. 15; SCLC constitution and by-laws, 1958, box 32, folder 4, SCLC Papers (collection hereafter cited as SCLC), MLK; plans for SCLC structure, file drawer 1, folder 17, BUC.

65. List of affiliates, n.d., box 50, folder 3, SCLC.

66. Board of directors, box 36, folder 14, SCLC; list of officers and board members on SCLC stationery, 1958; Seay, interview by Barton, p. 5; Louis Lomax, *The Negro Revolt* (New York, 1962), p. 104. The graduates of Morehouse and/or Alabama State were King, Ralph Abernathy, C. K. Steele, T. J. Jemison, Kelly Miller Smith, L. D. Reddick, Fred Shuttlesworth, and Samuel W. Williams.

67. Daniel C. Thompson, *The Negro Leadership Class* (Englewood Cliffs, 1963), p. 35.

68. Wyatt Walker's estimate, cited in William Brink and Louis Harris, *The Negro Revolution in America* (New York, 1963), p. 108.

69. Myrdal, *American Dilemma*, pp. 873–76; King, as quoted by Levison, interview by Mosby, p. 9. Morris's description of SCLC as the "decentralized political arm of the black church" contains a kernel of truth,

but it underestimates the conservatism of the church and exaggerates SCLC's influence; see Morris, *Origins of the Civil Rights Movement*, pp. 77–91.

Chapter 2

1. Morris, *Origins of the Civil Rights Movement*, p. 93.
2. Rustin to King, May 19, 1960, file drawer 6, folder 134, BUC; Rustin to Maude Ballou, March 4, 1960, file drawer 7, folder 54, BUC; Levison to King, July 14, 1958, file drawer 16, folder 24, BUC.
3. Wofford, *Of Kennedys and Kings*, p. 115; Rustin and Levison, telephone conversation, July 21, 1968, transcript of telephone conversation recorded by FBI wiretap on Levison's telephone, Levison file, copy in MLK.
4. King to Wilkins, telegram, February 10, 1957, group 3, series B, container 204, NAACP Papers, Library of Congress; Randolph to Eisenhower, June 10, 1957, box 31, Randolph Papers.
5. Viorst, *Fire in the Streets*, pp. 211–12; memo regarding Prayer Pilgrimage, n.d.; memorandum on opening remarks by A. Philip Randolph, April 18, 1957, both in Randolph Papers.
6. Rustin to King, May 10, 1957, file drawer 4, folder 35, BUC.
7. Oates, *Let the Trumpet Sound*, p. 120; King, Prayer Pilgrimage speech, May 17, 1957, file drawer 2, folder 11, BUC. David L. Lewis, *King: A Critical Biography* (Baltimore, 1970), pp. 91–93.
8. Rustin and Levison to King, n.d., file drawer 1, folder 29, BUC; Reddick, "Martin Luther King and the Republican White House," in *Martin Luther King, Jr.: A Profile*, ed. C. Eric Lincoln (New York, 1970), p. 76.
9. Herbert S. Parmet, *Jack: The Struggles of John F. Kennedy* (New York, 1980), p. 370.
10. Merle Miller, *Lyndon: An Oral Biography* (New York, 1980), pp. 249–58; Virginia Durr to Clark Foreman, October 14, 1957, Durr Papers.
11. Virginia Durr to Clark Foreman, February 15 and October 14, 1957, March 17, 1958, Durr Papers.
12. *Time*, February 18, 1957, pp. 13–16.
13. Reddick, in *Martin Luther King, Jr.: A Profile*, ed. Lincoln, pp. 79–89; Randolph to King, Wilkins, and Granger, June 23, 1958; Randolph to King, July 9 and August 19, 1958; King to Randolph, July 18, 1958, all in box 31, Randolph Papers; Levison to King, June 10, 1958, file drawer 1, folder 29, BUC; for Powell's intrigues, see Herbert S. Parmet, *Eisenhower and the American Crusades* (New York, 1972), pp. 505–8.
14. Levison interview by Mosby, pp. 13–14. A number of cities, notably Richmond, Little Rock, and Dallas, abandoned bus segregation before *Browder* v. *Gayle*. In Albany, Georgia, on the other hand, segregation was still being enforced in 1962.
15. Paul D. Bolster, "Civil Rights Movement in Twentieth-Century Georgia,"

Ph.D. diss., University of Georgia, 1972, p. 171; Martin Luther King, Sr., with Clayton Riley, *Daddy King: An Autobiography* (New York, 1980), pp. 153–55.

16. *New York Times,* June 9, 1956; Meier and Rudwick, "Origins of Nonviolent Direct Action," p. 368; Catherine A. Barnes, *Journey from Jim Crow: The Desegregation of Southern Transit* (New York, 1983), pp. 124–28; Glenn Smiley, "Birmingham and the Recent Protest," November 18, 1958, FOR Papers; Smiley, interview by Shannon, p. 37. Barnes points out that in 1960 only a handful of cities in the Deep South had desegregated their buses. She also notes that a number of bus boycotts occurred in the early 1960s.

17. King to Roy Wilkins, December 16, 1957, group 3, series B, container 204, NAACP.

18. Rustin to King, June 19, 1957, file drawer 3, folder 54, BUC; untitled plans for Crusade for Citizenship, n.d., file drawer 1, folder 18, BUC.

19. Crusade for Citizenship plans; King to Wilkins, December 16, 1957; Wilkins to King, January 20, 1958, both in group 3, series B, container 204, NAACP; Wilkins to King, January 14, 1958, file drawer 4, folder 23, BUC.

20. Morris, *Origins of the Civil Rights Movement,* pp. 120–23; Farmer, *Lay Bare the Heart,* pp. 189–90; John M. Brooks, report of SCLC meeting, May 27–28, 1958; Wilkins to Medgar Evers, April 2, 1957, group 3, series B, container 204, NAACP.

21. Brooks to Wilkins, June 2, 1958, box 4, Wilkins Papers, Library of Congress.

22. *Montgomery Advertiser,* January 19, 1956; King to Wilkins, March 3, 1956; Wilkins to King, April 12, 1956, both in file drawer 8, folder 12, BUC.

23. Morris, *Origins of the Civil Rights Movement,* p. 122; Robert E. Johnson, interview by John H. Britton, September 6, 1967, p. 22, HUC. The Reverend Matthew McCollum advised King not to invite Daisy Bates, the NAACP leader from Little Rock, to an SCLC meeting in Columbia, South Carolina, because "her appearance would make it impossible for very many of our supporters to continue their cooperation" (McCollum to King, August 14, 1959, file drawer 4, folder 153, BUC).

24. King, "Recommendations to Committee on Future Program," October 27, 1959, file drawer 4, folder 153, BUC.

25. Morris, *Origins of the Civil Rights Movement,* p. 128; Farmer, *Lay Bare the Heart,* p. 190.

26. Morris, *Origins of the Civil Rights Movement,* pp. 126–28; minutes of the Atlanta conference, May 12, 1956, FOR Papers.

27. Letters from contributors, box 1, folder 1, SCLC; Baker, interview by Britton, pp. 32–33; Morris, *Origins of the Civil Rights Movement,* pp. 117–18.

28. Baker, interview by Britton, pp. 18–19; minutes of SCLC executive board, October 18, 1957, file drawer 4, folder 153, BUC.

29. King to Abernathy, June 16, 1958, file drawer 6, folder 134, BUC; Levison to King, November 28, 1958, file drawer 1, folder 29, BUC; Lewis, *King*, p. 118.

30. Baker to King, November 15, 1958, file drawer 6, folder 134, BUC; King to Tilley, April 3, 1959, file drawer 9, folder 10, BUC; Baker, interview by Britton, p. 36.

31. Ella Baker, report of the director to the executive board, May 15, 1959, file drawer 4, folder 153, BUC; Baker, interview by Britton, pp. 24–25.

32. Baker, interview by Britton, p. 37; Morris, *Origins of the Civil Rights Movement*, pp. 112–13.

33. Baker, interview by Britton, pp. 34–37; Oates, *Let the Trumpet Sound*, p. 514, note 124; Septima P. Clark, interview by Judy Barton, November 9, 1971, pp. 39–40, MLK; Raines, *My Soul Is Rested*, pp. 481–82; King, "Advice for Living," *Ebony*, n.d., clipping among FOR Papers.

34. Baker, interview by Britton, pp. 16, 37–40.

35. Garrow, *FBI*, p. 27; Virginia Durr to Clark and Marie Foreman, [1958], Durr Papers; Reddick, *Crusader Without Violence*, pp. 179 and 211.

36. Ella Baker, report of the executive director, May 16–September 29, 1959; "Recommendations Adopted by the Executive Committee and Delegates," October 1, 1959, file drawer 6, folder 153, BUC.

37. "Recommendations," October 1, 1959, file drawer 4, folder 153, BUC.

38. King, "Recommendations to the Committee on Future Program," October 27, 1959; Ella Baker, memo to the administrative committee: "SCLC as a Crusade," October 23, 1959, file drawer 6, folder 153, BUC; King to Levison, November 19, 1959, file drawer 1, folder 29, BUC; Rustin was taking part in a protest against French nuclear testing in the Sahara.

39. David J. Garrow, *Protest At Selma*, pp. 2–4, 220–27; Elliott M. Zashin, *Civil Disobedience and Democracy* (London, 1972), pp. 160–78.

40. King, *Stride Toward Freedom*, p. 205; *New York Times*, March 21, 1956.

41. King, *Stride Toward Freedom*, p. 96.

42. Ibid., pp. 208–9. It is perhaps significant that critics like Virginia Durr, who thought King's emphasis on love and nonviolence naive and unrealistic, came to recognize his political sagacity after talking with him in private. See Durr to Clark Foreman, two undated letters of 1959, Durr Papers.

43. Lomax, *Negro Revolt*, pp. 97–98.

44. King to Smiley, October 24, 1957, FOR Papers.

45. It was not until 1964 that the Supreme Court made a definitive ruling that places of public accommodation could *not* deny access on grounds of race or color. Even then, three justices dissented, arguing that "the Fourteenth Amendment . . . does not compel either a black man or a white man running his own private business to trade with anyone against his will." Prior to this decision (*Bell* v. *Maryland*, 378 U.S. 226), the federal government maintained the same position.

46. Ralph H. Hines and James E. Pierce, "Negro Leadership After the Social Crisis: An Analysis of Leadership Changes in Montgomery, Alabama," *Phylon*, Spring 1965, pp. 169–72.
47. Steele, interview by Ice, pp. 30 and 49.
48. James W. Vander Zanden, *Race Relations in Transition: The Segregation Crisis in the South* (New York, 1965), p. 57; Levison to King, November 3, 1958, file drawer 1, folder 29, BUC.
49. Steele, interview by Ice, p. 26.
50. Levison, interview by Mosby, pp. 19–20. It is significant, perhaps, that Levison misplaced this conversation by more than three years: it actually took place in 1963. Like many others who looked back over the period, Levison exaggerated both the speed with which direct action caught on and the extent to which it eclipsed other strategies. See King and Levison, telephone conversation, May 23, 1963, FBI Levison file, MLK.

Chapter 3

1. Miles Wolff, *Lunch at the Five and Ten: The Greensboro Sit-Ins* (New York, 1970), pp. 11–56; Chafe, *Civilities and Civil Rights*, pp. 112–19; *Time*, May 2, 1960, p. 14; Southern Regional Council, *The Student Protest Movement: A Recapitulation* (Atlanta, 1961), p. 3.
2. Biography of Lawson: Viorst, *Fire in the Streets*, p. 117; Tucker, *Black Pastors and Leaders*, pp. 119–21.
3. James Lawson, interview by David Yellin and Bill Thomas, July 1, 1968, p. 6, Sanitation Strike Archival Project, Mississippi Valley Collection, John Willard Brister Library, Memphis State University (collection hereafter cited as MSU); Viorst, *Fire in the Streets*, pp. 103–4; Watters, *Down To Now*, pp. 50–52.
4. Viorst, *Fire in the Streets*, p. 117.
5. Ibid., pp. 107–11; James Lawson, interview by Joan Beifuss and Bill Thomas, July 21, 1969, pp. 13–15, MSU; *New York Times*, March 4 and June 14, 1960; J. Robert Nelson, "Vanderbilt's Time of Testing," *Christian Century*, August 10, 1960.
6. *New York Times*, April 7 and 20, 1960; Wallace Westfeldt, *Settling a Sit-In* (Nashville, 1960), pp. 1–6.
7. *New York Times*, March 2, 3, 7, 9–12, 1960; L. D. Reddick, "The State vs. the Student," *Dissent*, Summer 1960, pp. 220–28; Dan Wakefield, *Revolt in the South* (New York, 1960), p. 121.
8. *New York Times*, March 20 and 21, 1960; Viorst, *Fire in the Streets*, p. 117; *Time*, February 10, 1961, p. 14.
9. Virginia Durr to Clark Foreman, [1960], Durr Papers; *New York Times*, April 1 and 12, June 8, 1960; LeRoy Collins, interview by author, August 8, 1985; Helen Fuller, "We Are All So Very Happy," *New Republic*, April 25, 1960, pp. 15–16; Meier and Rudwick, *CORE*, pp. 106–7.

10. Baker, interview by Britton, pp. 40–41.
11. For the founding of SNCC, see Howard Zinn, *SNCC: The New Abolition-ists* (Boston, 1964), pp. 17–34; Clayborne Carson, *In Struggle: SNCC and the Black Awakening of the 1960s* (Cambridge, Mass., 1981), pp. 19–24.
12. Baker, interview by Britton, pp. 41–46; Baker, "Bigger than a Hamburger," speech to Raleigh conference, reprinted in *Southern Patriot,* June 1960; Oates, *Let the Trumpet Sound,* p. 517, note 155; Morris, *Origins of the Civil Rights Movement,* pp. 215–17; James Lawson, interview by Beifuss and Thomas, p. 16.
13. Martin Oppenheimer, "The Genesis of the Southern Negro Student Move-ment," Ph.D. diss., University of Pennsylvania, 1963, pp. 70–72, 97; Raines, *My Soul Is Rested,* p. 106; *New York Times,* April 17, 1960; Helen Fuller, "Southern Students Take Over," *New Republic,* May 2, 1960, p. 16; James Lawson, "Non-violent Way," *Southern Patriot,* April 1960. The "statement of purpose" was formally adopted at a second conference in May, held in Atlanta. It was at this meeting that SNCC elected its first chairman, Marion Barry of Nashville. At a third conference in October, also held in Atlanta, Barry was succeeded by Charles McDew. King and Lawson spoke at all three meetings.
14. James Lawson, "Eve of Nonviolent Revolution," *Southern Patriot,* November 1961; Vincent Harding, "Martin Luther King, Jr., and the Sec-ond Coming of America," in *Have We Overcome? Race Relations since Brown,* ed. Michael V. Namorato (Jackson, 1970), p. 60.
15. Wilkins to King, [April 1960], group 3, series B, container 204, NAACP; Jackie Robinson to King, May 5, 1960, file drawer 9, folder 1, BUC.
16. King to Robinson, June 19, 1960, file drawer 9, folder 1, BUC; Benjamin Mays to Roy Wilkins, May 18, 1960, box 5, Wilkins Papers.
17. James Farmer to Wilkins, report on Oscar Lee conference and meeting with Ella Baker and Co., June 10, 1960, box 5, Wilkins Papers.
18. Levison to King, [March 1960], file drawer 1, folder 29, BUC.
19. Committee to Defend Martin Luther King and the Southern Freedom Struggle, minutes, March 7, 21, 28 and April 4, 1960; statement of income and expenditure, for period ended July 31, 1960, box 23, Randolph Papers.
20. Levison to Randolph, January 10, 1961, box 23, Randolph Papers; Levison and O'Dell, report on New York office, October 15, 1960 to August 31, 1961, box 57, folder 11, SCLC; FBI surveillance report, May 10, 1960, New York office, FBI Levison file.
21. Conference on general organization, May 10–11, 1960, file drawer 1, folder 31, BUC.
22. Wyatt T. Walker, interview by John H. Britton, October 11, 1967, pp. 1–12, HUC.
23. Ibid., pp. 12, 45, 50–51.
24. Adams, *Unearthing Seeds of Fire,* pp. 118–41; Maxwell Hahn to Charles Jones, April 28, 1961; Myles Horton to King, May 2, 1961; Maxwell Hahn

to Wesley Hotchkiss, July 13, 1961, all in file drawer 7, folder 11, BUC; Andrew J. Young, "Proposed Budget: CEP," n.d., file drawer 7, folder 44, BUC. The Dorchester Academy had been founded by the AMA in 1870. McIntosh County was also notable for its high proportion of black landowners.

25. *New York Times*, February 23, 1961; Adams, *Unearthing Seeds of Fire*, pp. 84–100; Irwin Klibaner, "The Southern Conference Educational Fund: A History," Ph.D. diss., University of Wisconsin, 1971, pp. 136–83; Alan Stang, *It's Very Simple* (Belmont, Mass., 1965), p. 104. For the ADA's efforts to undermine SCEF, see correspondence between James Loeb and Aubrey Williams, January 1947; Kenneth Douty to E. D. Hollander, May 3, 1955; Sidney Hollander to E. D. Hollander, May 5, 1955; Sidney Hollander to James Dombrowski, May 14, 1955, all in series 2, box 263, ADA Papers. Dombrowski had also helped to create the Highlander Folk School back in the 1930s.

26. Garrow, *FBI*, pp. 24–25; Anne Braden, "A View from the Fringes," *Southern Exposure*, Spring 1981, pp. 69–73; Klibaner, "Southern Conference Educational Fund," pp. 323–59; Young to James and Diane Bevel, February 18, 1963, box 141, folder 5, SCLC; Roy Wilkins to Maxwell E. Foster, Jr., March 27, 1957, group 3, series B, container 204, NAACP.

27. For example, Virginia Durr to Clark Foreman, March 21, 1960, Durr Papers.

28. Walker, interview by Britton, p. 21; *Southern Patriot*, March 1963.

29. Clark, interview by Barton; Adams, *Unearthing Seeds of Fire*, pp. 110–18; Walker, interview by Britton, p. 84.

30. Walker, interview by Britton, pp. 22 and 50; "Fundraising program," n.d., box 36, folder 3, SCLC; Walker, "General Program for 1960–61," box 37, folder 4, SCLC.

31. Ralph Abernathy, treasurer's report, September 1, 1960–August 31, 1961; auditor's report: fiscal year ended August 31, 1961, box 57, folders 10 and 13, SCLC; McAdam, *Political Process and the Development of Black Insurgency*, pp. 123–25.

32. *Southern Patriot*, November 1960; Milton Reid to King, January 10, 1961; King to Reid, January 12, 1961; Reid to Walker, January 25, August 4 and 8, 1961, all in file drawer 7, folder 46, BUC.

33. Wachtel, interview by author; minutes of SCLC board meetings, September 27, 1961; May 16, 1962; April 16–17, 1964, box 29, folder 1, KP.

34. Samuel Lubell, *White and Black: Test of a Nation* (New York, 1964), pp. 53–70; Numan V. Bartley and Hugh D. Graham, *Southern Politics and the Second Reconstruction* (London, 1975), p. 186; Virginia Durr to Clark Foreman, [1959 or 1960], Durr Papers.

35. Oppenheimer, "Genesis of the Southern Negro Student Movement," pp. 85–87; Rustin to King, February 6, 1961, file drawer 7, folder 39, BUC; King and Levison, telephone conversation, January 4, 1967; Levison and

Moe Foner, telephone conversation, January 16, 1968, both in FBI Levison file, MLK.

36. Rustin to King, June 15, 1960, file drawer 1, folder 29, BUC; King to Chester Bowles, June 24, 1960, file drawer 3, folder 10, BUC; Wofford, *Of Kennedys and Kings*, pp. 51–52; Joseph L. Rauh to Roy Wilkins, July 28, 1960, series 5, box 47, ADA Papers.

37. Oates, *Let the Trumpet Sound*, pp. 158–60; Ora Spaid, "Promised Land," *Christian Century*, September 21, 1960; Wofford, *Of Kennedys and Kings*, pp. 12–13.

38. Raines, *My Soul Is Rested*, pp. 89–92, 473; Walker, interview by Britton, p. 97.

39. Harold Middlebrook, interview by Joan Beifuss and Bill Thomas, July 18, 1968, p. 5, MSU; King, fundraising appeal, October 20, 1960, Randolph Papers.

40. Wofford, *Of Kennedys and Kings*, pp. 13–15; Jean Stein and George Plimpton, *American Journey: The Times of Robert Kennedy* (New York, 1970), pp. 10–11.

41. Raines, *My Soul Is Rested*, pp. 97–99.

42. King to Coretta King, October 26, 1960, KP.

43. Wofford, *Of Kennedys and Kings*, pp. 16–22; Coretta King, *My Life with Martin Luther King, Jr.*, pp. 202–4.

44. Wofford, *Of Kennedys and Kings*, pp. 23–25; Theodore H. White, *The Making of the President, 1960* (New York, 1961), p. 387; Walker, interview by Britton, p. 97.

45. Roy Wilkins to Harris Wofford, April 5, 1961, Wofford Papers, John F. Kennedy Presidential Library (library hereafter referred to as JFK).

46. King, "Equality Now," *Nation*, February 4, 1961, pp. 91–95.

47. Administrative committee, minutes, March 8–9, 1961, box 36, folder 11, SCLC; James Wood to Stephen Currier, January 13, 1961; King to Currier, May 3, 1961; Currier to King, July 20, August 18, 1961, all in file drawer 7, folder 46, BUC; Carl M. Brauer, *John F. Kennedy and the Second Reconstruction* (New York, 1977), pp. 114–15.

48. Marvin Rich to Page Wilson, information re proposed Freedom Ride, April 27, 1961; CORE press release, May 2, 1961, series 2, box 39, ADA Papers; Walker, interview by Britton, p. 38; Farmer, *Lay Bare the Heart*, p. 200.

49. Raines, *My Soul Is Rested*, p. 121; Fred L. Shuttlesworth, interview by James Mosby, September 1968, pp. 39–40, HUC; Robert Kennedy and George Cruit, transcript of telephone conversation, May 15, 1961, copy in Alabama State Archives, Montgomery.

50. In 1946 the Supreme Court ruled that a Virginia statute requiring bus segregation constituted an undue burden on interstate travel (*Morgan* v. *Virginia*, 328 U.S. 373, 378–79); in 1950 it declared that dining service aboard trains should not be denied to "passengers holding tickets entitling them to use it" (*Henderson* v. *United States*, 339 U.S. 816, 824); in 1960 it

applied this ruling to restaurants connected with interstate bus services (*Boynton* v. *Virginia,* 364 U.S. 454).

51. Watters, *Down To Now,* p. 102, Jayne Lahey to Robert Kennedy, summaries of telephone calls from Floyd Mann and Fred Shuttlesworth, May 17, 1961, Robert Kennedy Papers, General Correspondence, 9, JFK.

52. Robert Kennedy, summary of telephone conversation with John Patterson, May 20, 1961, Robert Kennedy Papers, JFK; Wofford, *Of Kennedys and Kings,* pp. 153–54.

53. Virginia Durr to Robins, July 25, 1961, Durr Papers, Alabama State Archives; Edwin Guthman, *We Band of Brothers: A Memoir of Robert Kennedy* (New York, 1971), pp. 168–72.

54. Viorst, *Fire in the Streets,* pp. 154–55; Raines, *My Soul Is Rested,* pp. 127–29; Walker, interview by Britton, pp. 19–20; Burke Marshall, interview by Louis Oberdorfer, May 29, 1964, pp. 19, 28–30, JFK; Guthman, *We Band of Brothers,* pp. 172–78.

55. Viorst, *Fire in the Streets,* p. 156; Raines, *My Soul Is Rested,* pp. 13–31; Farmer, *Lay Bare the Heart,* pp. 206–7; Baker, interview by Britton, pp. 92–94.

56. Robert Kennedy and Ross Barnett, transcript of telephone conversation, May 23, 1961, Robert Kennedy Papers, JFK; Arthur M. Schlesinger, Jr., *Robert Kennedy and His Times* (London, 1978), p. 299.

57. Stein and Plimpton, *American Journey,* pp. 96–102; Guthman, *We Band of Brothers,* pp. 154–55.

58. Freedom Rides Coordinating Committee (FRCC), minutes, May 26, 1961, box 35, folder 2, SCLC; *New York Times,* May 28, 1961.

59. Walker, interview by Britton, pp. 35–38; FRCC, minutes, August 3, 1961, box 35, folder 2, SCLC; Walker and Henry Schwarzchild to Robert F. Kennedy, July 3, 1961, box 35, folder 1, SCLC; Walker, statement to Interstate Commerce Commission, August 15, 1961, box 35, folder 3, SCLC.

60. William Goldsmith, "The Cost of the Freedom Rides," *Dissent,* Fall 1961, pp. 501–2; Meier and Rudwick, *CORE,* pp. 139–44; Reddick to King and Walker, September 18, 1961, file drawer 7, folder 39, BUC. CORE had spent $138,000 by the end of June; SCLC about $40,000.

61. Lewis, *King,* pp. 136–37. "Given what is now known about CIA penetration of institutions within the United States," Godfrey Hodgson has speculated, "the intriguing possibility that Jenkins was working for the government cannot be dismissed out of hand" (*In Our Time: America from World War II to Nixon* [London, 1976], p. 190).

62. *New York Times,* August 30, 1961; James Forman, *The Making of Black Revolutionaries* (New York, 1970), pp. 158–221; Walker, interview by Britton, pp. 13–16. SCLC's involvement also stemmed from the fact that Walker had authorized one of the Nashville Freedom Riders, Paul Brooks, to observe the Monroe situation on behalf of SCLC.

Chapter 4

1. Walker, report of the director, October 1961–September 1962, box 36, folder 12, SCLC.
2. Good accounts of the Albany protests can be found in Bolster, "Civil Rights Movements in Twentieth-Century Georgia," pp. 255–84; Lewis, *King*, pp. 140–70; Howard Zinn, *The Southern Mystique* (New York, 1964), pp. 149–211.
3. The groups represented were the NAACP, the NAACP Youth Council, the Ministerial Alliance, the Criterion Club, the Negro Voters League, and the Federation of Women's Clubs.
4. Asa D. Kelley to W. G. Anderson, September 23, 1961; Kelley to William H. Dennis, September 13, 1961; list of members of Citizens' Advisory Committee on Urban Renewal, City Archives, Albany, Georgia (collection hereafter cited as AC).
5. Bolster, "Civil Rights Movements in Twentieth-Century Georgia," pp. 48, 256.
6. E. D. Hamilton et al. to mayor and city commissioners, December 15, 1960, AC; C. B. King, interview by Judy Barton, March 15, 1972, pp. 6–7, MLK; S. A. Roos (city manager) to Kelley, October 24, 1961, AC. The Criterion Club comprised, for the most part, middle-class professionals and businessmen.
7. Bolster, "Civil Rights Movements in Twentieth-Century Georgia," pp. 258–59; Vernon Jordan, field report, October 13, 1961, group 3, series B, container 408, NAACP.
8. Vernon Jordan and Gloster Current, summary of telephone conversation, December 14, 1961, group 3, series B, container 408, NAACP; Slater King, interview by Stanley Smith, p. 6, HUC.
9. Albany Movement, minutes, November 17, 1961, AC.
10. City commission, minutes of special meeting, October 30, 1961, AC.
11. Laurie G. Pritchett, "Albany Movement," October 19, 1962, AC; SNCC press releases, December 12 and 14, 1961. Pritchett was careful to ensure that the arrests took place *outside* the station so as to avoid charges that they violated ICC regulations.
12. *New York Times*, December 16 and 18, 1961.
13. Vernon Jordan, Ruby Hurley, and Gloster Current, summary of telephone report, December 18, 1961, group 3, series B, container 408, NAACP; *Atlanta Constitution*, December 18, 1961; statement by city commission, December 18, 1961, AC.
14. Lewis, *King*, p. 154; James Forman, *The Making of Black Revolutionaries*, (New York, 1972), p. 254; *New York Times*, December 15, 1961; handwritten chronology of negotiations, December 10–16; Solomon Walker to mayor and commissioners, December 15; Kelley to M. S. Page (two drafts),

December 15, 1961; Kelley to Anderson and Page, December 16, 1961, all in AC.

15. Walker, interview by Britton, pp. 32–33; Bolster, "Civil Rights Movements in Twentieth-Century Georgia," pp. 32–33; statement by city commission, December 18, 1961, AC; Marion Page, interview by Stanley Smith, August 1968, p. 6, HUC; Lewis, *King*, pp. 153–54.

16. Lewis, *King*, p. 153; Walker, interview by Britton, pp. 33–34.

17. SCLC board-staff consultation, minutes, January 4–5, 1962, box 36, folder 15, SCLC; Walker, report of the director, October 1961–September 1962, p. 3, box 36, folder 12, SCLC.

18. *Southern Patriot*, November 1961; *SCLC Newsletter*, July 1963.

19. Forman, *Making of Black Revolutionaries*, p. 160; Lester McKinnie to Wyatt Walker, October 8, 1962, box 36, folder 20, SCLC. The three other students were Marion Barry, Lester McKinnie, and Charles Sherrod.

20. Aaron Henry to Walker, August 4, 1962, box 35, folder 3, SCLC. Henry was a pharmacist and NAACP activist in Clarksdale. He also served on SCLC's board.

21. *SCLC Newsletter*, April 1962; Andrew Young to Jack Minnis, February 26, 1963, box 138, folder 2, SCLC.

22. Jim Bishop, *The Days of Martin Luther King* (New York, 1971), p. 175; *SCLC Newsletter*, April 1962.

23. Bernard Lee to Andrew Young, January 18 and 22, 1963, box 139, folder 6, SCLC.

24. Herbert V. Coulton, "September through December in the Fourth Congressional District," n.d., box 143, folder 11, SCLC. These registration figures are taken from Southern Regional Council, "Negro Voter Registration in Southern States," Atlanta, June 7, 1957.

25. Coulton, "January through March," n.d., box 142, folder 17, SCLC.

26. Middlebrook, interview by Beifuss and Thomas, pp. 7–9; Bolster, "Civil Rights Movements in Twentieth-Century Georgia," pp. 178–82, 275–77; J. H. Calhoun, report of the Georgia voter registration director, May 9, 1962, box 140, folder 5, SCLC. The Statewide Registration Committee was set up in 1957 by the Georgia Voters League. Calhoun made his run for Congress in 1946.

27. Bolster, "Civil Rights Movements in Twentieth-Century Georgia," pp. 233–43; Hosea L. Williams, "History and Philosophy of the Southeastern Georgia Crusade for Voters," n.d., box 140, folder 7, SCLC; Andrew Young, report to the president and administrative committee, December 1962, box 138, folder 21, SCLC.

28. Bolster, "Civil Rights Movements in Twentieth-Century Georgia," pp. 205–6.

29. Jack Minnis to Wiley Branton, February 28, 1963, box 138, folder 2, SCLC.

30. Garrow, *FBI*, pp. 53–54; Young to Minnis, February 26, 1963; Branton to

King, February 28, 1963, both in box 138, folder 2, SCLC; SCLC field secretaries meeting, minutes, December 19–21, 1962, box 138, folder 11, SCLC; Southern Regional Council, *First Annual Report of the Voter Education Project, April 1, 1962–March 31, 1963* (Atlanta, February 26, 1965), pp. 15–18.

31. Walker, interview by Britton, p. 22; report on civil rights leadership meeting, March 20–21, 1962, in minutes of SNCC regional meeting, Atlanta, March 24, 1962, box 7, SNCC Papers, MLK.

32. By 1961 the Alabama courts had awarded $500,000 in damages against the ministers, with $2.5 million pending. The commissioners also sued the *New York Times* for publishing the advertisement.

33. *New York Times*, May 31, 1961.

34. Wachtel, interview by author. Large contributors usually made their donations to specified churches, which then passed on the money to SCLC. Wachtel thought the practice unsound and possibly illegal.

35. King and Levison, telephone conversation, April 10, 1962, FBI Levison file, New York office file; Clarence Jones to King, April 18, 1962, King Papers, Martin Luther King, Jr., Center (collection hereafter cited as KP).

36. William Kunstler, *Deep In My Heart* (New York, 1966), pp. 89–93; correspondence by Clarence Jones concerning formation of the Gandhi Society, April–June 1962, box 11, KP.

37. Garrow, *FBI*, pp. 44–45.

38. Ibid., pp. 47–49; Levison and O'Dell, telephone conversation, May 1, 1962, FBI Levison file, MLK.

39. Levison and O'Dell, telephone conversation, June 20, 1962, FBI Levison file; Senate Select Committee to Study Governmental Operation with Respect to Intelligence Activities, *Final Report*, book 3 (Washington, D.C., 1976), p. 95; director to Atlanta and New York, July 20, 1962; director to Atlanta, October 23, 1962; Fred J. Baumgardner to William C. Sullivan, October 22, 1962, all in House Select Committee on Assassinations, *Hearings on the Assassination of Martin Luther King, Jr.*, 95th Cong., 2d sess., 1978, 6:133–38 (hereafter referred to as House).

40. Stephen A. Roos, former city manager, interview by David J. Garrow and Louise Cook, May 14, 1982, MLK; statement of the Albany Movement, January 23, 1962, AC; Vernon Jordan, monthly report, January 31, 1962, group 3, series B, container 408, NAACP; minutes of special meeting of city commission, January 27, 1962; statement of city commission, "To the Leaders of the Albany Movement," January 30, 1962, both in AC.

41. Minutes of special meetings of city commission, January 27, 29, 31, 1962; Albany Movement, statement of demands to bus company, January 29, 1962; C. L. Carter, president of Cities Transit, Inc., to mayor and city commissioners, January 30, 1962; report of police committee, January 31, 1962, all in AC. The city maintained that it did not interfere with the

running of the buses; the Albany Movement asserted that Pritchett was perpetuating segregation by means of threats and selective arrests.

42. C. B. King, interview by Barton, pp. 22–23.

43. Leonard Gilbey to Pritchett, July 23, 1962; J. E. Lloyd to Pritchett, July 25, 1962; W. G. Anderson and M. S. Page to Pritchett, January 14, 1962, all in AC. The impact of the boycott was diminished by the fact that the downtown retailing area was already in decline due to the opening of new shopping malls on the city's outskirts.

44. Raines, *My Soul Is Rested*, pp. 398–99; Pritchett, summary report, 1961–62 fiscal year; Pritchett to Kelley, "Albany Movement," October 19, 1962, both in AC.

45. William W. Hansen, field report, July 7–22, 1962, Hansen Papers, MLK; Peggy Dammond to James Forman, field report, August 1962, p. 4, box 19, SNCC Papers, MLK; Kunstler, *Deep in My Heart*, pp. 98–101.

46. Hansen, field report, July 7–22, 1962, Hansen Papers, MLK; Pritchett to Kelley, "Albany Movement," October 19, 1962, p. 2, AC; Walker, interview by Britton, p. 41.

47. Andrew Young, "Church and Citizenship," text of sermon, July 17, 1962, pp. 10–11, box 135, folder 15, SCLC.

48. *Christian Science Monitor*, July 14, 1962. In a paper drafted by King, dated July 17, the Albany Movement asked for the right of peaceful protest, speedy trials and the return of cash bonds, desegregation of the buses (if and when service was resumed), and a timetable for the desegregation of parks, libraries, lunch counters, swimming pools, and schools.

49. Kunstler, *Deep in My Heart*, p. 102; Hansen, field report, July 23–August 8, 1962 Hansen Papers, MLK.

50. C. B. King, interview by Barton, pp. 29–30; Slater King, interview by Smith, pp. 12–13. This meeting is also described in Kunstler, *Deep in My Heart*, pp. 106–7; Penny Patch, field report, August 1962, box 19, SNCC.

51. Kunstler, *Deep in My Heart*, pp. 102–3; Vernon Jordan, monthly report, August 27, 1962, group 3, series B, container 408, NAACP.

52. Pritchett et al., "Activities of the Albany Movement," July 24, 25, 1962, surveillance reports; proclamation by mayor and city commission, July 14, 1962; list of pistol permits, July 1960–July 1962, all in AC.

53. Pritchett et. al., "Activities of Dr. Martin Luther King, Jr., and the Albany Movement," July 27, 1962, AC; King, prison diary, file drawer 16, folder 9, BUC.

54. Levison and unknown male, telephone conversation, August 3, 1962, FBI Levison file, MLK; Brauer, *John F. Kennedy and the Second Reconstruction*, pp. 172–76; Kunstler, *Deep in My Heart*, pp. 118–19; Burke Marshall, interview by Oberdorfer, p. 70; William L. Taylor to Lee White, August 15, 1962, Lee White Papers, 21, JFK.

55. Levison and unknown male, telephone conversation, August 3, 1962, FBI

Levison file, MLK. Levison stated that King had sent him a letter from jail suggesting that Robert Kennedy arrest the city commission for violation of civil rights.

56. *Atlanta Constitution,* July 18, 1962; *Washington Post,* July 30, 1962; *Norfolk Virginian-Pilot,* August 1, 1962; S. A. Roos, memorandum, August 4, 1962, AC; Coretta King, *My Life with Martin Luther King, Jr.,* p. 212.

57. Anderson and Elza Jackson to Kelley, telegram, August 10, 1962; E. Freeman Leverett to Kelley, August 6, 1962; H. H. Perry et al. to Hilliard P. Burt, n.d., all in AC.

58. Anderson, Page, et. al., statement to city commission, August 15, 1962; statement by city commission, August 16, 1962; "Albany Manifesto," August 16, 1962, all in AC; Raines, *My Soul Is Rested,* p. 401; Bolster, "Civil Rights Movements in Twentieth-Century Georgia," p. 280; Reese Cleghorn, "Epilogue in Albany," *New Republic,* July 20, 1964, pp. 16–18; Slater King, "The Bloody Battleground of Albany," *Freedomways,* Winter 1964, p. 96.

59. Walker, interview by Britton, p. 27.

60. Ibid., pp. 26–27; Andrew Young, "Albany: An End or a Beginning?" *Southern Patriot,* October 1962.

61. King, *Why We Can't Wait* (New York, 1964), p. 44; minutes of staff conference held at Dorchester, September 5–7, 1963, box 153, folder 21, SCLC; Shuttlesworth, interview by Mosby, pp. 48 and 61.

62. Bayard Rustin, *Strategies for Freedom,* pp. 23–24; Wyatt Walker, "The American Dilemma in Miniature: Albany, Georgia," text of speech, March 26, 1963, box 37, folder 8, SCLC; Meier and Rudwick, *CORE,* pp. 112, 165–68.

63. Levison, interview by Mosby, p. 19; C. T. Vivian, interview by Vincent J. Browne, February 20, 1968, p. 42, HUC.

Chapter 5

1. Carl T. Rowan, *South Of Freedom* (New York, 1952), p. 156; Robert G. Corley, "The Quest for Racial Harmony: Race Relations in Birmingham, Alabama, 1947–1963," Ph.D. diss., University of Virginia, 1979, pp. 115–16; Dave Hyatt to regional directors, "Answers to Questions re the National Conference of Christians and Jews and the Situation in the South," June 15, 1956, series 5, box 42, ADA Papers; Bartley, *The Rise of Massive Resistance,* pp. 87 and 105.

2. Corley, "The Quest for Racial Harmony," pp. 166–67.

3. *New York Times,* April 12, 1960; U.S. Commission on Civil Rights, *1961 Report: Justice* (Washington, D.C., 1961), pp. 29–36.

4. Fred Shuttlesworth, interview by Joyce Ladner, November 19, 1969, cassette, MLK. Glenn Smiley described Shuttlesworth as a "courageous leader, but devoid of organizational knowledge, headstrong and wild for

publicity, almost to the point of neurosis, undemocratic and willing to do almost anything to keep the spotlight on himself"; see Smiley, report from Birmingham, November 10, 1958; and Shuttlesworth's reply to Smiley of December 23, 1958, written after "Bull" Connor stole the report and made it public, both in FOR Papers.

5. Corley, "The Quest for Racial Harmony," p. 130; Glenn Smiley, "Birmingham and the Recent Protest," November 18, 1958, FOR Papers; U.S. Commission on Civil Rights, *Justice*, p. 35. Shuttlesworth launched the bus boycott against the wishes of the ACMHR board.

6. Shuttlesworth to city commissioners, June 25, 1958; Shuttlesworth to Mayor James Morgan, August 11, 1958, both in Albert C. Boutwell Papers, City Archives, Birmingham Public Library (library hereafter cited as BPL).

7. Corley, "The Quest for Racial Harmony," pp. 130–45.

8. Ibid., pp. 233–34; George R. Osborne, "Boycott in Birmingham," *Nation*, May 5, 1962, pp. 397–401; Richard L. Warren, "Birmingham: Brinkmanship in Race Relations," *Christian Century*, May 30, 1962, pp. 689–90; *Time*, May 4, 1962, p. 16.

9. Letters to Connor protesting closure of parks, "Bull" Connor Papers, box 8, folder 12, BPL; Smyer quoted in Joe David Brown, "Birmingham, Alabama: A City in Fear," *Saturday Evening Post*, March 2, 1963, pp. 15–18; Corley, "The Quest for Racial Harmony," pp. 226–29; E. E. Holland to Burke Marshall, April 30, 1962; David J. Vann to Marshall, January 19 and 22, 1963, both in Burke Marshall Papers, JFK. Robert Kennedy cancelled a planned visit to Birmingham on Vann's advice.

10. Corley, "The Quest for Racial Harmony," pp. 235–37; Shuttlesworth, interview by Mosby, p. 57.

11. Walker, interview by Britton, p. 53; Raines, *My Soul Is Rested*, p. 167.

12. Walker, interview by Britton, pp. 52–53.

13. Levison quoted in Stein and Plimpton, *American Journey*, pp. 114–15.

14. Minutes of executive staff meeting, January 23, 1963, box 36, folder 15, SCLC.

15. Shuttlesworth, interview by Mosby, pp. 47–48; Shuttlesworth, interview by Ladner; W. E. Chilcoat and C. C. Ray to J. Moore, re: ACMHR meeting, February 4, written February 7, 1963, Connor Papers, box 13, folder 2, BPL.

16. Walker, interview by Britton, pp. 54–55.

17. King and Levison, telephone conversation, March 10, 1963, FBI Levison file, MLK.

18. Shuttlesworth to King and Walker, March 15, 1963, KP.

19. C. R. Jones to Jamie Moore, "Re: March 11 Meeting in Abyssinia Baptist Church," March 12, 1963; Chilcoat and Jones to Moore, re: March 18 meeting at Seventeenth Street Church of God, written March 20, 1963, both in box 13, folder 2, Connor Papers.

20. Walker, interview by Britton, pp. 27–35, 52–59; draft timetable for "Project X," [January or early February 1963], KP.

21. King, "Bold Design for a New South," *Nation*, March 30, 1963, pp. 259–62; King and Levison, telephone conversation, March 6, 10, 1963, FBI Levison file, MLK.

22. Alan F. Westin and Barry Mahoney, *The Trial of Martin Luther King* (New York, 1974), p. 51; Walker, interview by Britton, p. 56; Walker, draft timetable for "Project X," KP.

23. King, *Why We Can't Wait*, pp. 56–58; Kunstler, *Deep in My Heart*, p. 174.

24. Westin and Mahoney, *Trial of Martin Luther King*, pp. 54–62; King, *Why We Can't Wait*, pp. 70–71; Clarence Jones and Levison, telephone conversation, April 1, 1963, FBI Levison file, MLK.

25. *Chicago Defender*, April 4, 1963, May 11–17, national edition; *Birmingham World*, editorials of April 10, 13, 17, 20, 1963. The *World* was part of the chain of newspapers owned by C. A. Scott of Atlanta, a longtime conservative and a strong critic of King, Walker, and SCLC.

26. R. E. Whitehouse and R. A. Watkins to Moore, "April 3 Meeting at St. James Baptist Church," April 5, 1963, Connor Papers; King, *Why We Can't Wait*, pp. 65–68; William R. Miller, *Martin Luther King, Jr.* (New York, 1968), p. 135; Rev. John Cross, interview by Judy Barton, March 23, 1972, pp. 13–14, MLK; Brink and Harris, *The Negro Revolution*, p. 108.

27. Kunstler, *Deep in My Heart*, pp. 183–84. King and Shuttlesworth met the businessmen on April 8; they spoke to the ministers the following day.

28. This description of the mass meetings is based on the police surveillance reports in box 13, folder 2, Connor Papers; the recording of the May 6 mass meeting at New Pilgrim Baptist Church on *Lest We Forget*, vol. 2, Folkways Records, FD 5487; King, *Why We Can't Wait*, pp. 60–63.

29. Whitehouse and Watkins to Moore, "April 5 Meeting at Thurgood Baptist Church," April 10, 1963, Connor Papers.

30. David J. Edwards to Paul W. McGann, "Additional Data on Economic Impact of Racial Disturbance: Department Store Sales," June 23, 1963, box 21, Lee White Papers, JFK.

31. Walker to King and Abernathy, progress report, April 20, 1963, KP.

32. King, *Why We Can't Wait*, pp. 68–69; *New York Times*, April 7, 1963; Walker, interview by Britton, pp. 59–60.

33. Walker, interview by Britton, pp. 59–60; Walker, in Robert Penn Warren, *Who Speaks for the Negro?* (New York, 1966), pp. 226–27; *New York Times*, April 8, 1963.

34. Whitehouse and Watkins to Moore, "April 8 Meeting at First Baptist Church," April 10, 1963; "April 10 Meeting at St. James Baptist Church," April 12, 1963, both in Connor Papers.

35. Westin and Mahoney, *Trial of Martin Luther King*, pp. 68–71; Raines, *My Soul Is Rested*, p. 155.

36. Walker, interview by Britton, p. 61; King, *Why We Can't Wait*, pp. 71–73.

37. Corley, "The Quest for Racial Harmony," p. 254; Charles Morgan, *A Time to Speak* (New York, 1964), pp. 151–53; Raines, *My Soul Is Rested*, pp.

196–97. The talks were arranged through the Reverend Norman Jimerson, a friend of Morgan and a white official of the Alabama Council on Human Relations. The black negotiators included Shuttlesworth, Nelson Smith, Andrew Young, and Vincent Harding. The Boutwell administration officially commenced on April 15, but the outgoing commissioners refused to hand over power. This confused situation persisted until May 23, when the Alabama Supreme Court confirmed Boutwell and the new council.

38. Statement by the Justice Department, April 13, 1963, box 17, Burke Marshall Papers, JFK; *Chicago Defender*, April 15, 1963.

39. Levison and Jones, telephone conversation, April 13, 1963; Joan Daves and Levison, telephone conversation, April 19, 1963, both in FBI Levison file, MLK; Coretta King, *My Life with Martin Luther King, Jr.*, pp. 229–33; King and Coretta King, April 15, 1963, transcript of telephone conversation, box 13, folder 2, Connor Papers.

40. Walker to Marshall, April 16, 1963; Marshall to Robert Kennedy, April 23, 1963, both in Burke Marshall Papers; Walker to King and Abernathy, progress report, April 20, 1963, KP.

41. See, for example, King, "Love, Law, and Civil Disobedience," *New South*, December 1961, pp. 4–11; King, "A Message From Jail," August 1962, box 27, folder 10, SCLC; [Ed Clayton], *This Is SCLC* (Atlanta, April 12, 1963); Walker, "The American Dilemma in Miniature: Albany, Georgia," March 26, 1963, pp. 6–8, box 37, folder 8, SCLC.

42. Walker, interview by Britton, p. 73. King's "Letter" is reprinted in *Why We Can't Wait*, pp. 76–95. The earlier version published by the AFSC had a slightly different text and the longer title, "Letter From Birmingham City Jail." King was provoked to write the "Letter" by a statement in which eight prominent Alabama clergymen condemned the demonstrations, praised the police, and appealed for "law and order."

43. Westin and Mahoney, *Trial of Martin Luther King*, pp. 90–141. SCLC's legal defense was headed by the NAACP Legal Defense Fund, which fielded its two senior lawyers, Jack Greenberg and Constance Baker Motley.

44. Kunstler, *Deep in My Heart*, p. 189; Walker, interview by Britton, pp. 62 and 67; police memo, May 1, 1963; M. N. House, memo, April 30, 1963; Allison to Moore, "April 30 Meeting at Metropolitan Church," May 1, 1963, all in Connor Papers. In 1970, Kunstler stated that "Martin was about the most indecisive man I've ever seen. . . . Martin wouldn't make up his mind about using the school kids and Bevel just went out and organized the kids into a demonstration"; see Robert Terrell, "Discarding the Dream," p. 75.

45. Whitehouse, Watkins, and T. H. Cook to Moore, "May 2 Meeting at Sixth Avenue Baptist Church," May 3, Connor Papers.

46. James Orange, "With the People," *Southern Exposure*, Spring 1981, pp. 110–11; Walker, interview by Britton, pp. 58–63; *Christian Science*

Monitor, May 4, 1963; *Washington Post*, May 4–8, 1963; *Chicago Defender*, May 6–8, 1963; *Nashville Tennessean*, May 7, 1963.

47. Raines, *My Soul Is Rested*, p. 154; Walker, interview by Britton, pp. 62–63; Forman, *The Making of Black Revolutionaries*, p. 312. The main incidents of rock throwing occurred on May 3 and 7. The tension was heightened by the arrival of several hundred state troopers, who were directly responsible to Gov. George Wallace.

48. *Washington Post*, May 4, 1963.

49. Recording of May 6 meeting (see note 28).

50. Levison and O'Dell, telephone conversation, May 14, 1963, FBI Levison file, MLK; Donald Wilson to Robert Kennedy, "Reaction to Racial Tension in Birmingham, Alabama," May 9, 10, 14, 1963, Robert Kennedy Papers, JFK.

51. Marshall, in Stein and Plimpton, *American Journey*, pp. 115–17; *Washington Post*, May 11, 1963; Corley, "The Quest for Racial Harmony," pp. 262–64.

52. Vincent Harding, "A Beginning in Birmingham," *Reporter*, June 6, 1963, p. 16; Corley, "The Quest for Racial Harmony," pp. 265–69; Michael Dorman, *We Shall Overcome* (New York, 1964), pp. 180–83; Burke Marshall, interview by Anthony Lewis, June 20, 1964, p. 101, JFK; *Washington Post*, May 11, 1963.

53. Corley, "The Quest for Racial Harmony," pp. 269–70; Dorman, *We Shall Overcome*, pp. 183–84; King, *Why We Can't Wait*, pp. 104–5; King, typed note, [May 8, 1963], box 139, folder 7, SCLC.

54. *Washington Post*, May 11, 1963; Shuttlesworth, interview by Ladner, MLK; Raines, *My Soul Is Rested*, pp. 170–74.

55. Jones and Levison, telephone conversation, May 10, 1963, FBI Levison file, MLK; Walker, interview by Britton, pp. 81–82.

56. Shuttlesworth, interview by Ladner; Corley, "The Quest for Racial Harmony," p. 270; *New York Times*, August 3, 1963. When the black negotiators met the business leaders on the morning of May 10, haggling over the precise wording of the agreement delayed the announcement until 2:00 P.M. On May 9, reporters were told that a biracial committee, to be set up under the agreement, would set a timetable for the desegregation of schools and the reopening of parks. According to Andrew Young's notes, the blacks also thought that the timetable included the desegregation of motels and movie theaters, and the hiring of black policemen (box 49, folder 29, SCLC). But the whites refused to allow such a timetable to be included.

57. *New York Times*, May 12, 1963; *Time*, May 24, 1963, p. 22; Joanne Grant quoted in John A. Williams, *The King God Didn't Save* (London, 1971), p. 191; Forman, *The Making of Black Revolutionaries*, p. 315; Bishop, *The Days of Martin Luther King*, p. 310; August Meier and Elliott Rudwick, *From Plantation to Ghetto* (London, 1970), p. 268.

58. Dorman, *We Shall Overcome*, pp. 195–215.

59. King and Levison, telephone conversation, May 21, 1963, FBI Levison file, MLK. Shuttlesworth and Bevel both pressed for more demonstrations and a school boycott.

60. Text of agreement in King, *Why We Can't Wait*, pp. 105–6. Compare with SCLC's original demands, "Points for Progress," May 6, 1963, KP.

61. Richard Sikes, speech of May 13, in *Congressional Record*, 88th Cong., 1st sess., 109:8364; Cross, interview by Barton, p. 25.

62. *Washington Post*, May 11, 1963.

63. Woods quoted in Raines, *My Soul Is Rested*, p. 163.

64. *Chicago Defender*, May 18–24, 1963, national edition.

65. Corley, "The Quest for Racial Harmony," p. 288.

66. Dorman, *We Shall Overcome*, pp. 211–12; King, Shuttlesworth, and Abernathy to Smyer et al., May 17, 1963, box 139, folder 7, SCLC; Ed Holland to Marshall, June 19, 1963; Marshall to Pierre Salinger, October 9, 1963, both in box 17, Marshall Papers, JFK.

67. *New York Times*, June 21, 1963; *Wall Street Journal*, July 16, 1963.

68. King, *Why We Can't Wait*, p. 113; James O. Haley to Jerome Cooper, July 9, 1963, box 29, Marshall Papers; Emory O. Jackson, interview by Stanley Smith, February 1968, p. 29, HUC; Corley, "The Quest for Racial Harmony," p. 280.

69. Shuttlesworth, "The National Civil Rights Crisis," June 5, 1964, address to ACMHR, copy in Connor Papers; Walker, interview by Britton, p. 28.

70. Garrow, *Protest At Selma*, pp. 135–49.

71. Ibid., p. 145.

72. Guthman, *We Band of Brothers*, p. 213; transcript of press conference, in *Kennedy and the Press: The News Conferences*, ed. Harold W. Chase and Allen H. Lerman, (New York, 1965), pp. 449–50; Theodore C. Sorenson, *Kennedy*, (London, 1966), p. 548. According to Brauer, Kennedy began to contemplate major legislation as early as May 7.

73. Roy Wilkins, interview by Berl Bernhard, August 13, 1964, p. 23, JFK; Burke Marshall, interview by Lewis, p. 61.

74. George Bailey, "From Birmingham," *Reporter*, May 23, 1963, p. 12; James Farmer, "The New Jacobins and Full Emancipation," in *Black Protest*, ed. Joanne Grant (Westport, Conn., 1968), p. 377; NAACP press release, July 13, 1963, in FOF; Meier and Rudwick, *CORE*, p. 214. Roy Wilkins was himself arrested on a picket line in Jackson, Mississippi, prompting King to privately joke, "We've baptized Brother Wilkins"; Levison and Jones, telephone conversation, June 2, 1963, FBI Levison file, MLK.

75. Transcripts of press conferences of May 22, July 17, August 1, 1963, in Chase and Lerman, *Kennedy and the Press*, pp. 449–50, 464, 470; Sorenson, *Kennedy*, pp. 547–49; Brauer, *John F. Kennedy and the Second Reconstruction*, pp. 238–50. Brauer argues that the emphasis on getting blacks "off the streets and into the courts" was a strategem to win Republican

and conservative support for the bill. But it also, he admits, "reflected the administration's underlying concern."

76. Victor S. Navasky, *Kennedy Justice* (New York, 1977), p. 218.

77. King, *Why We Can't Wait*, p. 87. For warnings about the growth of black extremism, see, for example, Louis Martin to Theodore Sorenson, May 10, 1961; G. Mennen Williams to John F. Kennedy, June 15, 1963, both in Robert Kennedy Papers, JFK.

78. Levison and Jones, telephone conversation, May 26, 1963, FBI Levison file, MLK; Schlesinger, *Robert Kennedy*, p. 348.

79. Marshall, interview by Lewis, pp. 98–99.

80. King, Levison, and Jones, June 1, 1963; Levison and Jones, June 2, 1963; Levison and Alice Loewi, June 3, 1963, all telephone conversations in FBI Levison file, MLK; King, "See You in Washington," talk to SCLC staff, Atlanta, January 16, 1968, transcript, pp. 5–6, KP.

81. Joseph L. Rauh, interview by Katherine Shannon, August 28, 1967, p. 51, HUC; *Congressional Record*, 88th Cong., 1st sess., 109:7778–8784; *Life*, May 17, 1963, pp. 30–31.

82. Watters, *Down To Now*, pp. 124–25; Shuttlesworth, interview by Mosby, p. 69; John F. Kennedy, speech of June 11, 1963, draft, General Correspondence, box 9, Robert Kennedy Papers, JFK; *Life*, May 24, 1963.

83. *Washington Post*, May 5, 1963; Whitehouse and Watkins to Moore, "May 6 Meeting at Sixteenth Street Baptist Church," May 7, 1963, Connor Papers; Young interviewed in *Martin Luther King, Jr.: A Documentary*, ed. Flip Schulke (New York, 1976), p. 66; Cross, interview by Barton, p. 42.

84. Recording of May 6 meeting (see note 28); Young in Stein and Plimpton, *American Journey*, pp. 117–18.

85. Allison and Watkins to Moore, "April 15 Meeting at St. James Baptist Church," April 17, 1963; Young quoted in Navasky, *Kennedy Justice*, p. 150; Shuttlesworth speech in Watters, *Down to Now*, p. 234; Shuttlesworth, interview by Mosby, pp. 61–62.

Chapter 6

1. *Winston-Salem Journal*, June 17, November 15, 1963; *New York Times*, June 22, 1963.

2. August Meier, "New Currents in the Civil Rights Movement," *New Politics*, Summer 1963, p. 14.

3. Financial secretary-treasurer's report, September 1, 1962–August 31, 1963, box 57, folder 17, SCLC.

4. Clarence Jones to King, June 24, 1964, box 13, folder 21, KP; *New York Times*, July 2, 1963; Jesse B. Blayton, supplementary report on the financial affairs of the Southern Christian Leadership Conference, September 1, 1962, to August 31, 1963, box 57, folder 20, SCLC; minutes of executive

staff meeting, May 4, 1964, 32, 7, KP. King raised a good half of SCLC's total income through public appearances.

5. See, for example, Andrew Young, in Raines, *My Soul Is Rested*, p. 475.
6. King, "Power for the Powerless," text of speech to executive staff, March 1967, p. 6, box 144, folder 30, SCLC.
7. Adam Roberts, "Martin Luther King and Nonviolent Resistance," *World Today*, June 1968, p. 234.
8. Bolster, "Civil Rights Movements in Twentieth-Century Georgia," pp. 244–48; *Savannah Morning News*, June 4–18, 1963; *New York Times*, June 13, 1963.
9. Bolster, "Civil Rights Movements in Twentieth-Century Georgia," pp. 250–52; *Savannah Morning News*, June 15, 18–21, 25, July 3, 1963; *New York Times*, June 18–22, 1963; Ben Van Clarke, "Siege at Savannah," *Freedomways*, Winter 1964, pp. 131–34.
10. Bolster, "Civil Rights Movements in Twentieth-Century Georgia," pp. 252–53; *Savannah Morning News*, July 11–14, 1963; *New York Times*, July 13, 1963.
11. *Savannah Morning News*, July 17, 1963; *New York Times*, August 2–4, September 2, 1963; Raines, *My Soul Is Rested*, pp. 493–95; Jerome K. Heilbron to Burke Marshall, July 24, 1963; Burke Marshall to Mayor Malcolm MacLean, July 26, 1963, both in Marshall Papers.
12. James W. Ely, Jr., "Negro Demonstrations and the Law: Danville as a Test Case," *Vanderbilt Law Review*, October 1974, pp. 931–32.
13. Bolster, "Civil Rights Movements in Twentieth-Century Georgia," pp. 225–44.
14. *Richmond News-Leader*, June 6, 1963; "Re: Danville," June 12, 1963; Benjamin Muse, "Danville, Virginia," October 8, 1963, both in box 31, Marshall Papers.
15. Ely, "Negro Demonstrations and the Law," pp. 935–43; *Richmond News-Leader*, June 15, 1963; *Washington Post*, June 22, 1963.
16. *Richmond News-Leader* quoted in Ely, "Negro Demonstrations and the Law," pp. 934–37; Peggy Thompson, "A Visit to Danville," *Progressive*, November 1963, p. 28; Sally Belfrage, "Danville on Trial," *New Republic*, November 2, 1963; Kunstler, *Deep In My Heart*, pp. 216–18; call from Alan Marer regarding Danville legal proceedings, June 19, 1963, box 31, Marshall Papers.
17. *Roanoke Times*, June 30, 1963; *Richmond News-Leader*, July 2, 1963; *Washington Post*, July 12 and 13, 1963; *Norfolk Journal and Guide*, July 20, 1963.
18. *Baltimore Sun*, July 29, 1963; Milton Reid to King, July 30, 1963, box 20, folder 11, KP; Kunstler, *Deep in My Heart*, p. 330.
19. Herbert V. Coulton, "Voter Registration in Danville," n.d., box 142, folder 11, SCLC.

20. Major Johns, reports to Andrew Young, April, May 10, June 14, late June, 1963, box 140, folders 13–15, SCLC.

21. Daniel Harrell, report from Louisiana, n.d.; Lavert H. Taylor to Young, August 29, 1963, both in box 140, folder 15, SCLC; Meier and Rudwick, *CORE*, pp. 221–23.

22. Jack Brady [Jack O'Dell?], report from Lake Charles, October 18, 1963; report from Lake Charles and Calcasieu Parish, October 20, 1963; Juanita Daniels, voter registration report, October 1963; Young to Harrell, October 2, 1963; Harrell to Young, November 8, 1963; Jack Brady, "Analysis of Voter Registration Program in Calcasieu Parish," November 17, 1963, all in boxes 140 and 141, SCLC.

23. *New York Times*, June 13–16, 19–22, 24, 28, August 4, 1963; Meier and Rudwick, *CORE*, pp. 215–16.

24. Ely, "Negro Demonstrations and the Law," p. 968.

25. Howard Zinn, "The Limits of Nonviolence," in Grant, *Black Protest*, p. 313; Meier and Rudwick, *CORE*, p. 265.

26. King, *Why We Can't Wait*, pp. 116–19; Lubell, *White and Black*, p. 113; Earl Black, *Southern Governors and Civil Rights* (London, 1976), p. 322.

27. Lee White to John F. Kennedy, notes for meeting with businessmen, June 4, 1963, box 21, Lee White Papers, JFK.

28. *Wall Street Journal*, May 10, 1963.

29. Viorst, *Fire In The Streets*, pp. 216–23; Clarence Jones to Randolph, May 6, 1963, box 11, folder 15, KP.

30. King and Levison et al., telephone conversation, June 10, 1963, FBI Levison file, MLK.

31. Ibid.; King and Levison, telephone conversation, June 12, 1963, FBI Levison file, MLK.

32. Garrow, *FBI*, pp. 60 and 94.

33. Ibid., p. 61; Schlesinger, *Robert Kennedy*, pp. 355–58; Wofford, *Of Kennedys and Kings*, pp. 215–17; Navasky, *Kennedy Justice*, pp. 141–43.

34. Garrow, *FBI*, pp. 62–63; Burke Marshall to Sen. Peter H. Dominick, July 31, 1963, box 8, Marshall Papers; Kennedy press conference, July 17, 1963, in Chase and Lerman, *Kennedy and the Press*, p. 464.

35. Joseph Dolan to Robert Kennedy, "Civil Rights Legislation," July 17, 1963, Robert Kennedy Papers, JFK.

36. *New York Times*, June 12 and 13; Jones and Levison, telephone conversation, June 17, 1963, FBI Levison file, MLK.

37. Alfred Hassler to Herman Hill, September 20, 1963, FOR Papers; Earl Caldwell to Burke Marshall, July 11, 1963, Marshall Papers; Jack Conway, interview by Larry Hackman, April 10, 1972, p. 80, JFK. The original plan drafted by Norman Hill, Tom Kahn, and Bayard Rustin included suggestions for direct action, but these were omitted when the plan was presented to the "Big Six" on July 2; see Norman Hill, interview by James Mosby, March 12, 1970, pp. 15–16, HUC.

38. *New York Times,* July 3, 1963; Forman, *The Making of Black Revolution-aries,* p. 332; David Cohen to John P. Roche, July 3, 1963, series 5, box 47, ADA Papers.

39. *New York Times,* November 15, 1963; Rauh quoted in Hodgson, *In Our Time,* p. 160; *Wall Street Journal,* August 28, 1963; *New Republic,* November 2, 1963, pp. 3–4.

40. James L. Adams, *The Growing Church Lobby in Washington* (Grand Rapids, 1970), p. 9; Rauh, interview by Shannon, pp. 53–54; Hill, interview by Hackman, p. 24.

41. *Wall Street Journal,* August 30, 1963; *New York Times,* September 1, 1963, sec. 4; draft of executive order, August 27, 1963, Robert Kennedy Papers, Personal Correspondence, box 11, JFK.

42. *Wall Street Journal,* May 24, 1963; *Time,* July 26, 1963, p. 10. For opinion poll evidence on opposition to direct action, and on the "white backlash," see *Newsweek,* August 12, October 21; *Saturday Evening Post,* September 7, 1963, pp. 19–21; Gallup poll of July 17, in George Gallup, *The Gallup Poll,* vol. 3, 1959–1971 (New York, 1972).

43. *SCLC Newsletter,* September 1963. For the debate within the civil rights movement over whether to intensify or move away from direct action, see Art Sears and Larry Still, "Should Negro Civil Rights Groups Merge?" *Jet,* July 18, 1963, p. 16; *Wall Street Journal,* August 27, 1963; Vincent Harding, "So Much History, So Much Future: Martin Luther King, Jr., and the Second Coming of America," in *Have We Overcome?* ed. M. V. Namorato (Jackson, 1979), p. 60.

44. Erik Barnouw, *Tube of Plenty: The Evolution of American Television* (New York, 1975), pp. 324–26.

45. Fred J. Baumgardner to William C. Sullivan, August 23, 1963, reproduced in House, 6:140–42.

46. William C. Sullivan to A. H. Belmont, August 30, 1963; Baumgardner to Sullivan, September 16, 1963; Sullivan to Belmont, September 25, December 24, 1963, all in House 6:143–66.

47. Navasky, *Kennedy Justice,* pp. 121–23; Wyatt Walker, keynote address delivered at the seventh annual convention, September 25, 1963, text, pp. 9–10, box 129, folder 34, SCLC.

48. *New York Times,* September 16, 1963.

49. Shuttlesworth, interview by Ladner; Diane Nash to King, report from Birmingham, September 17–20, 1963, box 141, folder 8, SCLC; "SNCC Plan of Action," Burke Marshall to Robert Kennedy, September 30, 1963, Marshall Papers (summary of plan by Thelton Henderson from copy shown him by Shuttlesworth).

50. *New York Times,* September 25, 1963; Walker, keynote address, pp. 10–11, box 129, folder 34, SCLC.

51. *New York Times,* September 20 and 28, October 5, 1963; Blaik and Royall to Robert Kennedy, March 12, 1964, box 18, Marshall Papers.

52. Shuttlesworth to Blaik and Royall, October 2, 1963, BPL; *New York Times,* September 25 and October 10, 1963; Allison and Watkins to Moore, reports of mass meetings on September 30 and October 1, 1963, police files, BPL.

53. Allison and Watkins, report of October 7 mass meeting, police files, BPL; *New York Times,* October 9, 1963.

54. King, "Direct Action in Birmingham, Danville and Montgomery," October 1963, box 32, KP.

55. *New York Times,* October 19 and 23, November 17, 1963; Burke Marshall to Pierre Salinger, October 9, 1963, Marshall Papers.

56. Shuttlesworth to King, November 7, 1963, box 22, folder 11, KP.

57. Rustin to King, memo on strategy of the integration movement, November 5, 1963, box 20, folder 39, KP.

58. *Richmond News-Leader,* September 27, 1963.

59. Young to King, "Voter Registration in the North," October 21, 1963, box 135, folder 15, SCLC.

60. *New York Times,* July 22, 1963.

61. The idea for the book was suggested by Levison, who also supplied the title. When King had difficulty finishing it, Levison discussed possible editors and ghostwriters with Joan Daves, King's literary agent, and himself worked on the introduction and final chapter of the book. Aware of the need to avoid direct contact with King, he used Clarence Jones as a go-between, although he did meet King once in order to discuss the book. As he explained to his friend Alice Loewi, "I don't want to maintain contact and yet this was an obligation I took . . . and you can't just let it go"; Loewi and Levison, telephone conversation, October 8, 1963, FBI Levison file, MLK.

62. King, "Direct Action in Birmingham, Danville and Montgomery," October 1963, box 32, KP.

63. St. John Barrett to Burke Marshall, "Danville, Virginia," August 31, 1963; Heslip W. Lee, confidential report on Danville, September 16–17; Benjamin Muse, "Danville, Virginia," October 8, 1963, all in Marshall Papers.

64. *New York Times,* October 18 and 20, November 10, 13, 17, 1963; *Washington Post,* October 7, 13, 16, 1963; *Baltimore Afro-American,* November 30, 1963; Young to King et al., "Danville, Virginia: Weekend Activities," November 18, 1963, KP.

Chapter 7

1. Walker, interview by Britton, pp. 85–93.

2. Ibid., pp. 89–94; Walker to King, re: staff discipline, n.d.; Walker to King, letter of resignation, October 3, 1963, both in box 36, folder 1, KP.

3. Dora McDonald to King, [1962], file drawer 16, folder 27, BUC; Levison and O'Dell, June 20, 1963; Haskell and Levison, May 20, 1966; Levison

and Jones, March 11, 1964, all telephone conversations in FBI Levison file, MLK; Walker, interview by Britton, p. 93.

4. Kunstler, *Deep in My Heart*, p. 286; Walker, interview by Britton, pp. 83–84; Steele, interview by Ice, p. 23.

5. Steele, interview by Ice, pp. 23–24; Raines, *My Soul Is Rested*, p. 500.

6. Braden, "A View from the Fringes," pp. 73–74; Klibaner, "Southern Conference Educational Fund," pp. 332–57; Young to James and Diane Bevel, February 18, 1963, box 141, folder 5, SCLC.

7. *Southern Patriot*, November 1961.

8. *Newsweek*, February 13, 1967, p. 17.

9. Steele, interview by Ice, pp. 23–24.

10. Kunstler, *Deep in My Heart*, p. 49; biographical sketch, box 125, folder 18, SCLC; Selby, *Journey through Black America*, pp. 353–56; *New York Times*, February 9, 1964.

11. Raines, *My Soul Is Rested*, pp. 499–500. See also the remarks by Young in George Goodman, "He Lives, Man!" *Look*, April 15, 1969, p. 31; and Williams in Barbara A. Reynolds, *Jesse Jackson* (Chicago, 1975), p. 321.

12. Raines, *My Soul Is Rested*, p. 474; Andrew Young, interview by Katherine Shannon, July 16, 1968, pp. 18–19, HUC.

13. Raines, *My Soul Is Rested*, p. 499.

14. Miller, *Martin Luther King, Jr.*, pp. 98–99; "An Interview with Andrew Young," *Playboy*, July 1977, p. 74; Bishop, *Days of Martin Luther King*, p. 49; King remarks in transcript of staff discussion, May 24, 1967, box 49, folder 13, SCLC.

15. Jones and Wachtel, telephone conversation, May 21, 1964; Rustin and Robinson, telephone conversation, June 11, 1964, both in FBI King file, MLK; Wachtel to King, May 20, 1964, box 25, folder 24, KP.

16. Reddick to King, June 19, 1964, box 20, folder 5, KP; Levison and Coretta King, telephone conversation, July 21, 1968, FBI Levison file, MLK.

17. Wachtel, interview by author.

18. DeLoach testimony, House 7:49.

19. *New York Times*, February 16, 1978.

20. Oates, *Let the Trumpet Sound*, p. 292.

21. Ibid., pp. 379–80; unidentified male and Levison, telephone conversation March 6, 1967, FBI Levison file, MLK.

22. As Levison complained in Levison and Joan Daves, telephone conversation, December 6, 1966; Levison and Bill Stein, telephone conversation, November 16, 1967, both in FBI Levison file, MLK.

23. King wrote virtually all of *Stride Toward Freedom* (1958), over half of *Why We Can't Wait* (1964), and about two-thirds of *Where Do We Go From Here?* (1967). Only *The Trumpet of Conscience* (1968), a series of broadcast lectures published in book form, was entirely ghosted.

24. Sorenson, *Kennedy*, p. 588; Schlesinger, *Robert Kennedy*, pp. 360–61; Senate 6:208.

25. Garrow, *FBI,* pp. 78–96; Simeon Booker, "RFK Retreats on Rights Bill," *Jet,* October 31, 1963; Wofford, *Of Kennedys and Kings,* p. 128; Bishop, *Days of Martin Luther King,* pp. 279, 318–19. Navasky (*Kennedy Justice,* p. 150) argues that the main reason why Kennedy approved the wiretaps was "to avoid problems with the FBI." Yet one can infer from the Sorenson biography of John Kennedy that the administration accepted much of what the FBI told them about Levison at face value. Note also Edwin Guthman's comment to the Church committee (Senate, *Final Report,* book 3, p. 92) that "the question of whether [Levison] was influencing King . . . was not fully decided, but in those days we accepted pretty much of what the FBI reported as being accurate."

26. Virginia Durr to Clark Foreman, [1959], Durr Papers; Levison and Joan Daves, telephone conversation, November 26, 1963, FBI Levison file, MLK; King, *Why We Can't Wait,* pp. 145–46; "Our New President," *Amsterdam News,* February 1, 1964.

27. King, "The Negro Revolution in 1964," *SCLC Newsletter,* January 1964; "Of the Civil Rights Bill," *SCLC Newsletter,* March 1964; Lewis, *King,* p. 237.

28. *Wall Street Journal,* August 27, 1963; Larry Still, "Should Negroes Stop Demonstrating?" *Jet,* October 24, 1963.

29. Lewis, *King,* pp. 233–35; King, address at the "Pilgrimage for Democracy," December 15, 1963, box 27, folder 30, SCLC, Harry Boyte, "Atlanta's False Image," *SCLC Newsletter,* January 1964; *Student Voice,* December 16, 1963.

30. John H. Britton, "City Has No Rallying Point," *Jet,* February 6, 1964; Pat Watters, "Atlanta: Fruits of Tokenism," *Nation,* February 17, 1964. SCLC had now withdrawn from Danville, claiming victory, when the city council became the first in the South to adopt a fair employment ordinance. With staff to spare, it agreed to support SNCC's campaign.

31. SNCC press releases, January 11 and 16, 1964, FOF.

32. *New York Times,* January 12, 19–20, 26–31, February 1–2, 1964; Good, *Trouble I've Seen,* pp. 25–46; Walker, interview by Britton, pp. 75–76.

33. Bishop, *Days of Martin Luther King,* p. 31.

34. Reynolds, *Jesse Jackson,* pp. 106–12.

35. Bevel to King, "Non-violence v. Brinkmanship," n.d., box 3, folder 14, SCLC.

36. Clayton to King, November 13, 1963; Jones to King, January 31, 1964, both in box 33, folder 21, KP; Levison and Jones, telephone conversation, March 11, 1964, FBI Levison file, MLK; Levison and Jones, telephone conversation, February 5, 1964, FBI King file, MLK. SCLC failed to put out a "mailing-shot" at the time of the Birmingham campaign.

37. Jones and Levison, telephone conversation, June 15, 1963, FBI Levison file, MLK; Jones and Wachtel, December 8, 1963; Jones and King, December 13, 1963; Jones and Wachtel, February 2, 1964; Greenberg and Jones,

March 24, 1964, all telephone conversations in FBI King file, MLK; Jones to King, March 6 and June 24, 1964; Kunstler to King et al., [November 1963], both in box 13, KP.

38. King and Jones, telephone conversation, March 31, 1964, FBI King file, MLK; minutes of executive staff meeting, May 4, 1964, box 32, folder 7, KP.

39. Walker, interview by Britton, p. 78; minutes of SCLC board meeting, April 16–17, 1964, box 29, folder 1, KP.

40. Discussion of CUCRL (Council on United Civil Rights Leadership) meeting, May 15, 1964, box 7, SNCC Papers, MLK.

41. Bevel, "Program for Action in Alabama," [January–February 1964], box 28, folder 6, KP; *New York Times,* March 5, 1964; *SCLC Newsletter,* March 1964; SCLC, *Handbook for Freedom Army Recruits,* n.d., copy in police files, BPL; *Montgomery Advertiser,* May 8, 1964.

42. Minutes of executive staff meeting, May 4, 1964, box 32, folder 7, KP; Bevel, "Program for Action in Alabama," p. 4, box 28, folder 6, KP.

43. King, transcript of interview, May 10, 1964, in *Face the Nation,* vol. 7 (New York, 1972), p. 206; *St. Petersburg Times,* May 19, 1964.

44. Virginia Durr to Clark and Marie Foreman, November 5, 1963, box 1, folder 33, Durr Papers; *Nashville Tennesseean,* December 9, 1963; *Montgomery Advertiser,* March 5, 1964; Young to Jack Minnis, February 26, 1963, box 138, folder 2, SCLC.

45. Good, *Trouble I've Seen,* p. 88.

46. Student Christian Movement and SCLC, "Florida Spring Project," March 11, 1964, copy in Florida Legislative Investigation Committee, *Racial and Civil Disorders in St. Augustine* (Tallahassee, February 1965), pp. 72–77 (report hereafter cited as FLIC). The Massachusetts Christian Leadership Conference had been organized in late 1963. Under its auspices, a group of clergymen and theology students had participated in SCLC demonstrations in Williamston, North Carolina, in November.

47. Kunstler, *Deep in My Heart,* pp. 272–83; *Florida Times-Union,* April 1, 1964; *Miami Herald,* April 2, 1964; *New York Times,* March 29–31, April 1, 1964.

48. File of letters on Peabody arrest; Jeffrey D. Beeson to Bryant, April 6, 1964, both in Farris Bryant Papers, Florida State Archives, Tallahassee (hereafter cited as BP).

49. *New York Times,* April 2–4, 1964. SCLC's main demands were the release of arrested demonstrators and the dropping of charges; desegregation of schools and public accommodations; an end to police brutality; the hiring of five more Negro policemen; fair employment practices; no reprisals against civil rights activists; and the establishment of a biracial committee.

50. John Gibson, reports from St. Augustine, May 2 and 4, 1964, box 20, folder 41, KP; John Gibson, interview by John H. Britton, April 26, 1968, pp. 42–

43, HUC; David R. Colburn, *Racial Change and Community Crisis: St. Augustine, Florida, 1877–1980* (New York, 1985), pp. 79–81. Gibson recalled in 1968 that King called in Walker, Abernathy, and Lee to discuss the plan with him. On Gibson's May 4 report, however, King wrote, "Important. Discuss with Andy."

51. Walker to King, "Suggested Approach and Chronology for St. Augustine," [May 26/27, 1964], box 20, folder 44, KP. The "stall-in" plan created an acrimonious controversy within the civil rights movement: CORE proposed to block access to the world's fair by stalling cars on all the access routes. King criticized the plan as tactically unsound, but refused to condemn it outright. The "stall-in" never actually materialized. See also Vivian, interview by Browne, p. 45.

52. The "Old Slave Market" was an open-sided pavilion in the center of town that was actually a WPA structure of the 1930s which replaced an earlier building and was now used by elderly whites to sit out and play cards and checkers.

53. Robert W. Hartley, "A Long, Hot Summer: The St. Augustine Racial Disorders of 1964," Master's thesis, Stetson University, 1972, pp. 58–62; *New York Times*, May 30 and 31, 1964; Good, *Trouble I've Seen*, pp. 75–78; King to Johnson, May 29, 1964, box 27, folder 37, SCLC.

54. Kunstler, *Deep in My Heart*, pp. 289–96; Leon Friedman, "The Federal Courts of the South: Judge Bryan Simpson and His Reluctant Brethren," in *Southern Justice*, ed. Friedman (New York, 1965), pp. 197–201; Hartley, "Long, Hot Summer," 65–69; E. F. Emrich to Bryant, "Racial Situation, St. Augustine," June 5, 1964, BP. Simpson asked for a suspension of demonstrations on June 3 pending his decision; Young, for SCLC, agreed.

55. Virgil Stuart, brief comments on the racial situation in St. Augustine, FLIC, pp. 144–45.

56. Rev. Irvin Cheney, "St. Augustine Ku Klux Klan Meeting," n.d., BP; Robert B. Hayling, interview by John H. Britton, August 16, 1967, p. 41, HUC; Hartley, "Long, Hot Summer," pp. 18–37. The St. Augustine (St. Johns County) Klan was set up by Connie Lynch, an organizer for the Atlanta-based National States Rights Party. With a hard core of about two dozen, the Klan could number its supporters and sympathizers in the hundreds.

57. Hartley, "Long, Hot Summer," pp. 38–39; transcript of telephone conversation between Robert Hayling and Jimmy Kynes, Florida attorney general, October 28, 1963; E. F. Emrich to Kynes, "Racial Matter: Fatal Shooting, St. Augustine," October 28, 1963, BP.

58. Mal Ogden to Bryant, "St. Augustine Racial Problem," February 10, 1964, BP. On January 14 the NAACP had again asked for negotiations, pointing out that the two people whom the city had called "non-acceptable," Hayling and Eubanks, had resigned. But the city rejected this request as it had all others.

59. Vivian, interview by Browne, p. 48.

60. *Young v. Davis*, No. 64-133-Civ-J (M.D. Fla. 1964), preliminary injunction,

June 9, 1964, BP; *Johnson* v. *Davis*, No. 64-141-Civ-J, summarized in Friedman, "Federal Courts of the South," pp. 199–201.

61. Good, *Trouble I've Seen*, pp. 88–89; Michael Waldron, "After Dark in St. Augustine," *Nation*, June 29, 1964, p. 648; *St. Petersburg Times*, June 10, 1964; *Miami Herald*, June 11, 1964; report of highway patrol/Special Police Force, June 10, 1964, BP.

62. *New York Times*, June 12, 1964; Colburn, *Racial Change and Community Crisis*, p. 93; Clarence Jones and Wyatt Walker, telephone conversation, June 8 and 9, 1964, FBI King file, MLK; Lee White to King, June 11, 1964, quoted in Hartley, "Long, Hot Summer," p. 75; report of King transportation detail, June 12, 1964, BP.

63. John Herbers, "Crucial Test for Nonviolent Way," *New York Times Magazine*, July 5, 1964, sec. 6, pp. 5 and 30.

64. Highway patrol/Special Police Force reports, June 11–13, 1964, BP. The highway patrolmen noted that the Klan marches included a number of gun-bearing special deputies, whose only identification consisted of armbands.

65. *Miami Herald*, June 15, 1964.

66. Hartley, "Long, Hot Summer," pp. 81–82.

67. Ibid., pp. 82–83; Bryant, Executive Order 1, June 15, 1964; Special Police Force reports, June 15–18, 1964, both in BP; *New York Times*, June 17, 1964.

68. *Washington Post*, June 20, 1964; presentment of St. Johns County grand jury, June 18, 1964; King and Hayling, answer to presentment of grand jury, June 19, 1964, both in BP; handwritten original in KP.

69. *New York Times*, June 18 and 19; reports of Cpl. C. L. Marrs, June 18, 1964; Lt. W. B. Norris, June 19, 1964; Lt. Henry Randall, June 19, 1964, all in BP. Randall reported that an off-duty policeman had dived into the pool to apprehend the swimmers, and that as he led one of the arrested demonstrators away, one of the deputy sheriffs "caught hold of the subject's arm and started twisting it and taking an occasional punch."

70. *New York Times*, June 19, 1964.

71. Special Police Force reports, June 17–21, 1964, BP; FLIC, pp. 117–18; Hartley, "Long, Hot Summer," pp. 98–100.

72. *St. Petersburg Times*, June 26, 1964. On June 20 Bryant issued an executive order banning night marches. Simpson overruled him two days later.

73. Wachtel, interview by author; Oates, *Let the Trumpet Sound*, p. 297; Colburn, *Racial Change and Community Crisis*, pp. 107–110; *New York Times*, July 1, 1964.

74. Harold DeWolf to King, July 3, 1964, box 8, folder 24, KP; David R. Colburn, "The St. Augustine Business Community: Desegregation, 1963–1964," in *Southern Businessmen and Desegregation*, ed. D. R. Colburn and E. Jacoway (Baton Rouge, 1982), pp. 228–30.

75. Good, *Trouble I've Seen*, p. 100.

76. Colburn, *Racial Change and Community Crisis*, pp. 100–110, 210. Col-

burn's implied judgement that King's rejection of the June 18 offer of the grand jury wrecked the chances for a genuine truce seems a little harsh. In view of the city's adamant opposition to a biracial committee ever since 1960, when Governor Collins urged all Florida communities to set them up, it seems rather fanciful to suggest that the committee proposed by the grand jury would have been any less fraudulent than the one ostensibly created by Bryant twelve days later.

77. Bryant to Clarke Mason, September 11, 1963, BP; Hartley, "Long, Hot Summer," pp. 85–87; FLIC, pp. 18, 108–12, 145–46; Mary Brooks Gober to Bryant, June 18, 1964, BP. State attorney Dan Warren consistently urged Bryant to crack down on "Manucy's Raiders."

78. Hartley, "Long, Hot Summer," pp. 108–9; Vivian, interview by Browne, p. 52.

79. FLIC, p. iii; Colburn, *Racial Change and Community Crisis*, pp. 145–48; *New York Times*, July 2 and 3, 1964.

80. John Herbers, *The Black Dilemma* (New York, 1973), pp. 26–27.

81. Miller, *Martin Luther King, Jr.*, pp. 194–95.

Chapter 8

1. Vivian, interview by Browne, p. 53.

2. *Montgomery Advertiser*, April 23, 1964; *Birmingham News*, June 5 and 9; *New York Times*, June 13, 1964. Tuscaloosa was the home of Robert Shelton, head of the United Klans of America, which had, according to an FBI estimate, about ten thousand members.

3. Report on SCLC leadership meeting, July 6, 1964, police files, BPL. This detailed surveillance report was probably the result of an electronic "bug."

4. Jerry DeMuth, "Black Belt, Alabama," *Commonweal*, August 7, 1964, p. 537.

5. Minutes of SNCC staff meeting, June 9–11, 1964, box 7, SNCC Papers, MLK. COFO included SNCC, CORE, SCLC, and the Mississippi state (not the national) NAACP.

6. Miller, *Martin Luther King, Jr.*, p. 195; *New York Times*, July 23, 1964; Good, *Trouble I've Seen*, pp. 124–28; Sally Belfrage, *Freedom Summer* (New York, 1965), pp. 172–77; Terrell, "Discarding the Dream," p. 76.

7. Randolph to King et al., April 7, 1964, Randolph Papers; William Brink and Louis Harris, *Black and White: A Study of U.S. Racial Attitudes Today* (New York, 1967), p. 105.

8. Jones to King, April 15, 1964, box 13, folder 20, KP.

9. King and Jones, telephone conversation, July 25, 1964, FBI King file, MLK; *New York Times*, July 28–30, 1964; Rustin and unidentified person, telephone conversation, July 28, 1964, FBI King file, MLK.

10. James Ridgeway, "Alinsky in 'Smugtown,'" *New Republic*, June 26, 1965,

pp. 15–17; *SCLC Newsletter*, July–August 1964; Andrew Young, sermon, August 9, 1964, p. 6, box 135, folder 25, SCLC.

11. King, statement on the New York riots, July 27, 1964, box 27, folder 38, SCLC; "President's Annual Report," in *Summary of Eighth Annual Convention* (Atlanta, 1964), pp. 5–6; Joseph E. Lowery, "Keynote Address," in *Summary of Eighth Annual Convention*, p. 9; King, "Negroes are *Not* Moving Too Fast," *Saturday Evening Post*, November 7, 1964, pp. 8–9; Young, sermon, August 9, 1964, p. 6, box 135, folder 25, SCLC.

12. Warren, *Who Speaks for the Negro?* p. 220.

13. King, "An Autobiography of Religious Development," ca. 1948, file drawer 14, folder 22, BUC; *Stride Toward Freedom*, pp. 212–13; Warren, *Who Speaks for the Negro?* pp. 209–10.

14. Levison interview, in Stein and Plimpton, *American Journey*, pp. 108–9; King, *Stride Toward Freedom*, pp. 86–93; "How Should A Christian View Communism?" in King, *Strength To Love* (New York, 1963), pp. 114–23; Oates, *Let the Trumpet Sound*, p. 131. See also Melvin C. Watson to King, August 14, 1952, file drawer 15, folder 50, BUC, for the reaction of an orthodox Marxist to King's sermon on Christianity and communism.

15. Reddick, *Crusader Without Violence*, p. 233.

16. James T. Patterson, *The Welfare State in America, 1930–1980* (Durham, England, 1981), pp. 21–23.

17. King, *Why We Can't Wait*, pp. 134–40; Jones and King, telephone conversation, February 1, 1964, FBI King file, MLK; King to Hermine Popper, February 3, 1964, Popper Papers, Schlesinger Library, Radcliffe College. Levison became involved in the "ghosting" of *Why We Can't Wait* partly because he felt that Nat Lamar was doing a poor job, partly out of a feeling of obligation to King—he had originally suggested a book on Birmingham—and also, one suspects, because he wished to maintain a link with King through Clarence Jones.

18. *New York Times*, June 22, 1964; Peter de Lissovoy, "Legalists, Publicists, Activists," *Nation*, July 13, 1964.

19. NAACP press releases, July 25 and 31, 1964, FOF; *New York Times*, July 30, 1964.

20. Wachtel and Jones, telephone conversation, February 12, 1964, FBI King file, MLK. King wanted Rustin to act as SCLC's Northern representative, and Rustin initially accepted this offer. By mid-March, however, he had apparently lost interest in the job.

21. Minutes of the executive committee, December 27–31, 1963, and May 10, 1964, box 6, folder 1, SNCC Papers, MLK; Len Holt, *The Summer That Didn't End* (London, 1966), pp. 163–64.

22. King and Rustin, telephone conversation, July 26, August 5, 1964, FBI King file, MLK. Rustin's own personal influence within CORE had suffered as a result of the resignation from CORE of Norman Hill, a friend and political ally. In his autobiography, James Farmer explained that Hill

had been part of a cabal to oust him from CORE's leadership and replace him with Rustin. He therefore demanded Hill's resignation.

23. Joseph Rauh, in Ann C. Romaine, "The Mississippi Freedom Democratic Party through August 1964," Master's thesis, University of Virginia, 1969, pp. 311–18. This work is a collection of transcribed and edited interviews with MFDP participants, and a brief summary of the party's origins and the events of the convention challenge.

24. Rustin and Rauh; Rustin and Cleveland Robinson, August 18, 1964; Rustin and Helstein, August 19, 1964; Rustin, King, and Young, August 21, 1964, all telephone conversations in FBI King file, MLK.

25. Viorst, *Fire in the Streets*, pp. 261–64; Hubert H. Humphrey, *The Education of a Public Man* (New York, 1976), p. 299.

26. Romaine, "Mississippi Freedom Democratic Party," pp. 266–71, 214.

27. Ibid., pp. 201–3, 272–73, 336–43.

28. Forman, *The Making of Black Revolutionaries*, p. 392.

29. Romaine, "Mississippi Freedom Democratic Party," p. 279; Rauh, interview by Shannon, p. 74; James Farmer, interview by Page Mulhollan, July 20, 1971, p. 6, JFK.

30. Cartha DeLoach to Walter Jenkins, morning summary of activities, August 25, 1964, in Senate 6:715.

31. Warren, *Who Speaks for the Negro?* p. 240. For Rustin's growing commitment to coalition politics, see his speech to the SNCC conference at Howard University, quoted in Nat Hentoff, *The New Equality* (New York, 1964), pp. 225–27; his comments on direct action at the time of the riots, in *New York Times*, August 3, 1964; and his influential article, "From Protest to Politics: The Future of the Civil Rights Movement," first published in *Commentary*, February 1965, pp. 25–31, and reprinted in *The New Radicals*, ed. Paul Jacobs and Saul Landau (New York, 1966), pp. 293–308. For a critical evaluation of Rustin's evolution, see Sam Bottone, "The Push Beyond Liberalism," *New Politics*, Summer 1964, pp. 37–38.

32. *New York Times*, October 2, 1964; Rustin and Rachelle Horowitz, telephone conversation, October 2, 1964, FBI King file, MLK.

33. For Rustin's attempt to continue the March on Washington structure, see Rachelle Horowitz to John Lewis, September 5, 1963; Rustin, memo to local committees and contacts of the March on Washington, September 16, 1963, both in box 16, SNCC. Rustin told King on December 5 that Randolph decided to close the March on Washington office at the insistence of Roy Wilkins, who viewed it as a rival to the NAACP-dominated Leadership Conference on Civil Rights.

34. Rustin, "From Protest to Politics," pp. 303–8; *Strategies for Freedom*, pp. 41–42.

35. Hosea Williams to Andrew Young, "Southwide Get-Out-the-Vote Campaign," September 4, 1964, box 140, folder 1, SCLC.

36. *New York Times*, September 13 and 30, 1964; King, *Playboy* interview, January 1965, p. 77; *Summary of Eighth Annual Convention*, p. 17.

37. Abernathy, annual financial report, 1963–64, box 57, folder 19, SCLC; Adele Kanter to Young, annual report on the New York office, box 49, folder 1, SCLC.

38. Harry Boyte, memos on office procedures and personnel policies, December 1963; proposed review of organizational structure and budget control, April 22, 1964, both in box 29, folder 7, KP; Jesse B. Blayton, supplementary report on the fiscal affairs of the Southern Christian Leadership home office, September 1, 1963, to August 31, 1964, box 57, folder 20, SCLC.

39. Randolph T. Blackwell, "Why Should SCLC Be Departmentalized?" n.d., box 145, folder 16, SCLC; "Executive Staff Retreat," November 1964, box 36, folder 15, SCLC.

40. Goodman, "He Lives, Man!" p. 31.

41. Blackwell to King, "New Department in SCLC," n.d., box 145, folder 15, SCLC; Harry G. Boyte, "Dialogue: An Interpretation," in "Executive Staff Retreat," part 3, November 12, 1964, box 36, folder 15, SCLC.

42. [Ed Clayton], "The Men Behind Martin Luther King," *Ebony*, June 1965, p. 170; biographical sketch of Harry George Boyte, box 123, folder 47, SCLC. Joining Boyte's staff in late 1964 were Charles Allen Lingo (the white staff member who had participated in the famous Monson Motor Lodge "dive-in") and Mew-Soong Li, a Hawaiian trained in social administration. Rachel DuBois, whose experience in community relations work went back to the 1930s, joined in January 1965.

43. Pat Watters and Reese Cleghorn, *Climbing Jacob's Ladder: The Arrival of Negroes in Southern Politics* (New York, 1967), pp. 376–77; Black, *Southern Governors and Civil Rights*, pp. 327–30; Southern Regional Council, "Negro Voter Registration in Southern States," Atlanta, June 7, 1957, with addenda for 1960 and 1965. For the more subtle types of discrimination practiced in Birmingham and New Orleans, see John Doar to Walter Boudin and Crawford Johnson, March 30, 1966, Boutwell Papers, BPL; and the inappropriately titled article by Charles McCord, "Anatomy of a Registration Drive: A Success Story from New Orleans," *Interracial Review*, May 1962, pp. 1–11.

44. Watters and Cleghorn, *Climbing Jacob's Ladder*, pp. 212–19; Navasky, *Kennedy Justice*, pp. 98–118, 194–95, 244–48; *Report of the United States Commission on Civil Rights, 1963* (Washington, D.C.), pp. 13–25; Harold Fleming, "The Federal Executive and Civil Rights," *Daedalus*, Fall 1965, pp. 938–39; Garrow, *Protest at Selma*, pp. 8–30.

45. Garrow, *Protest at Selma*, p. 21; Watters and Cleghorn, *Climbing Jacob's Ladder*, p. 213. According to Aaron Henry, president of the Mississippi state conference of the NAACP, "The Civil Rights Act of 1964 has not

helped to get one Negro registered in the State of Mississippi"; U.S. Commission on Civil Rights, *Hearings Held in Jackson, Mississippi, February 16–20, 1965* (Washington, D.C.), 1:158–59.

46. Southern Regional Council, *Second Annual Report of the Voter Education Project* (Atlanta, February 26, 1965), pp. 3–4; SNCC, *Special Report: Selma, Alabama* (Atlanta, September 26, 1963), p. 1; *Congressional Quarterly*, March 19, 1965, p. 2; *New York Times*, January 16, 1965.

47. Fleming, "The Federal Executive and Civil Rights," pp. 738–39; King, *Playboy* interview, January 1965, p. 70; *New York Times*, February 10, 1965; King, "Civil Right No. 1—The Right to Vote," *New York Times Magazine*, March 14, 1965, sec. 4, pp. 94–95.

48. SNCC, *Selma*, pp. 2–5; *Southern Patriot*, October 1964; DeMuth, "Black Belt, Alabama," pp. 536–38; Forman, *The Making of Black Revolutionaries*, pp. 347–53.

49. *New York Times*, October 13, 1963.

50. National Council of Churches, meeting on relief, placement, and relocation, February 17, 1956, minutes, p. 26, series 5, box 42, ADA; Bartley, *Rise of Massive Resistance*, pp. 87–89; Mark Suckle, research notes on Selma based on personal interviews, February 21–23, 1965, SNCC Papers, MLK.

51. Benjamin Muse, "Alabama," October 18, 1961, box 31, BM.

52. Charles Fager, *Selma, 1965: The March that Changed a Nation* (New York, 1974), pp. 4–5; DeMuth, "Black Belt, Alabama," p. 537; Good, *Trouble I've Seen*, pp. 52–56; *Time*, March 19, 1965, p. 15.

53. Mark Suckle, research notes, SNCC Papers, MLK; J. A. Love, "Selma, Alabama: Local Organizations," September 14, 1964, box 47, SNCC Papers, MLK.

54. Harry G. Boyte to Randolph Blackwell, report on Selma visit last week, December 6–13, written on December 14, 1964, box 146, folder 8, SCLC.

55. For black-white tensions arising out of the Freedom Summer, see Romaine, "Mississippi Freedom Democratic Party," pp. 59 and 132.

56. Staff assignments, [mid-November 1964], box 32, folder 8, KP.

57. *New York Times*, November 19, 1964.

58. Garrow, *FBI*, pp. 54–56.

59. *New York Times*, November 20, 22, 30, 1964.

60. Katzenbach testimony, Senate 6:209; Garrow, *FBI*, pp. 79–84.

61. Navasky, *Kennedy Justice*, p. 146; Garrow, *FBI*, pp. 110–11.

62. Brennan testimony, House 4:346.

63. Garrow, *FBI*, pp. 151–59.

64. Mark Lane and Dick Gregory, *Code Name Zorro: The Murder of Martin Luther King, Jr.* (Englewood Cliffs, 1977), pp. 79–80; Garrow, *FBI*, pp. 54–56; Sullivan to Belmont, January 6 and 13, 1964; Baumgardner to Sullivan, March 6, 1964, both in House 6:192–205; Garrow, *FBI*, pp. 106–110.

65. Baumgardner to Sullivan, April 4 and 7, 1964; DeLoach to Mohr, April 8, 1964; Baumgardner to Sullivan, August 8 and 17, all in House 6:256–74; Burke Marshall to Robert Kennedy, February 20, 1964, box 31, BM.

66. Guthman, *We Band of Brothers*, p. 262; Sullivan to Belmont, January 8, 1964, in House 6:164–66; Garrow, *FBI*, pp. 114–15.

67. Garrow, *FBI*, p. 111.

68. Garrow, *FBI*, pp. 125–31; *Washington Post*, May 18, 1976. According to Navasky (*Kennedy Justice*, p. 138), Congressman Robert Sikes of Florida was also shown transcripts.

69. Wachtel, interview by author; Rustin and Wachtel, telephone conversation, November 19, 1964, FBI King file, MLK.

70. *New York Times*, November 20, 1964.

71. King and McDonald, telephone conversation, November 19, 1964, FBI King file, MLK.

72. *New York Times*, November 20, 1964. Johnson "simply listened and gave no comment and no opinion," stated Wilkins, after he saw the president on November 19. According to the conversation between Rustin and Wachtel cited in note 69, Wilkins told both Johnson and Hoover that "whether or not they had anything [on King], he didn't give a damn."

73. Senate, *Final Report*, book 3, pp. 163–64.

74. Wachtel, interview by author.

75. DeLoach to Mohr, "Martin Luther King Appointment with Director," minutes of meeting, December 2, 1964, House 6:167–76.

76. Raines, *My Soul Is Rested*, pp. 477–78; Young, *Playboy* interview, p. 75.

77. Rustin and Wachtel, telephone conversation, December 2, 1964, FBI King file, MLK.

78. Boyte to Blackwell, December 14, 1964, box 146, folder 8, SCLC.

79. *London Times*, December 6, 1964.

80. Garrow, *FBI*, pp. 131–33.

81. DeLoach to Mohr, December 10, 1964, House 6:177. DeLoach wrote Hoover that there was no need for more transcriptions "inasmuch as the controversy has quieted down considerably." Hoover insisted otherwise: "I think it should be done *now* while it is fresh in the minds of the specially trained agents." The result was another 321 pages of material. See Hoover's speech, *New York Times*, December 13, 1964.

82. New York *Times*, December 29, 1964; Coretta King, *My Life with Martin Luther King, Jr.*, p. 29; Garrow, pp. 125–33; Senate, *Final Report*, book 3, pp. 158–60. The original note has not survived, but a copy or early draft was found among Sullivan's files. Sullivan stated in 1975 that the object of the exercise was "to blackmail King into silence, . . . to stop him from criticizing Hoover . . . [and] to diminish his stature. In other words, if it caused a break between Coretta and Martin Luther King, that would diminish his stature." The tape was mailed on November 21.

Chapter 9

1. *New York Times*, January 22, 1965.
2. Garrow, *Protest At Selma*, p. 4.
3. King, "Letter from Birmingham City Jail," pp. 8–9.
4. King, handwritten notes, [March 1965], KP.
5. James H. Laue, "Power, Conflict, and Social Change," in *Riots and Rebellions*, ed. Don R. Bowen and Louis H. Masotti (Beverly Hills, 1968), p. 90.
6. King, handwritten notes, KP.
7. Good, *Trouble I've Seen*, p. 53; Rustin, *Strategies for Freedom*, p. 45; Levison to King, April 7, 1965, KP; King, *Why We Can't Wait*, pp. 39–40; August Meier, "On the Role of Martin Luther King," in *Black History: A Reappraisal*, ed. Melvin Drimmer (Garden City, N.Y., 1968), p. 445.
8. Raines, *My Soul Is Rested*, pp. 215–16.
9. *New York Times*, January 3, 1965.
10. *New York Times*, January 4, 1965.
11. James Bevel, report to R. T. Blackwell, January 12, 1965, box 146, folder 10, SCLC; *New York Times*, January 15, 1965.
12. Fager, *Selma, 1965*, pp. 29–30; *New York Times*, January 19, 1965; Paul Good, "Beyond the Bridge," *Reporter*, April 8, 1965, p. 24. King was assaulted by a local white when he registered—the first black to do so—at Selma's Albert Hotel.
13. Raines, *My Soul Is Rested*, pp. 215–18; Fager, *Selma, 1965*, pp. 33–35.
14. Lewis, *King*, p. 264. Hare believed that "most of your Selma Negroes are descended from the Ibo and Angola tribes," who were particularly untrustworthy. "Even today I can spot their tribal characteristics. They have protruding heels, for instance."
15. *New York Times*, January 20, 1965.
16. *New York Times*, January 21 and 22, 1965; Fager, *Selma, 1965*, pp. 36–40.
17. *New York Times*, January 24, 26–28, 1965.
18. *New York Times*, February 1–4, 1965.
19. King, prison notes, February 2–3, 1965, KP.
20. Young and Jones, telephone conversation, February 3, 1965; J. Edgar Hoover to Bill Moyers, February 3 and 4, 1965, both in FBI King file, MLK; Garrow, *Protest at Selma*, pp. 49–51; *New York Times*, February 5, 1965.
21. *New York Times*, February 4, 1965.
22. King, prison notes, February 3–4, 1965, KP.
23. *New York Times*, February 5, 1965.
24. King, prison notes, February 4, 1965, KP.
25. Garrow, *FBI*, pp. 133–34; Raines, *My Soul Is Rested*, pp. 476–77; Brennan testimony, House 6:344.
26. Garrow, *FBI*, pp. 134–36; Raines, *My Soul Is Rested*, pp. 478–79; DeLoach to Mohr, January 11, 1965, in Senate, *Final Report*, book 3, pp. 169–70.

27. *New York Times*, January 31, 1965; King and Wachtel, telephone conversation, January 27; Rustin and Abernathy, telephone conversation, February 17, 1965, both in FBI King file, MLK. Rockefeller to King, January 27, 1965, box 20, folder 26, KP. On February 14, King's doctor ordered him to rest.

28. *New York Times*, February 6, 1965. This brought the total number of arrests to thirty-three hundred.

29. *New York Times*, February 7, 1965; King, statement and notes dictated to Dora McDonald, February 7, 1965, KP.

30. *New York Times*, February 7, 1965. Young, Bevel, and Vivian visited Lowndes County on February 6.

31. Rustin and Wachtel, telephone conversation, February 6; Wachtel and Jones, telephone conversation, February 7, both in FBI King file, MLK; *New York Times*, February 5 and 6, 1965.

32. *New York Times*, February 6–10, 1965; Oates, *Let the Trumpet Sound*, pp. 343–44; Garrow, *Protest at Selma*, pp. 49–58.

33. *New York Times*, February 10, 1965; *Time*, February 19, 1965, p. 17.

34. Miller, *Lyndon*, p. 429. Wilkins, the nephew of Roy, was then working in the Community Relations Service.

35. *Newsweek*, February 1, pp. 19–20, February 22, 1965, p. 20; *New York Times*, February 13, 1965; *Time*, February 26, 1965; p. 19; Raines, *My Soul Is Rested*, p. 218. As James Vander Zanden noted in 1963, nonviolent demonstrators often engaged in "subtle provocations. They offer their 'cheek' with the prospect of receiving a slap"; see "The Non-Violent Resistance Movement Against Segregation," *American Journal of Sociology*, March 1963, pp. 548–49.

36. Shuttlesworth, interview by Mosby, pp. 81–82.

37. "Wednesday Night at the Torch Motel," minutes of strategy meeting, February 10, 1965, box 94, SNCC Papers, MLK. Bevel was not present at the meeting, having been jailed two days earlier.

38. Ibid.; *New York Times*, February 16 and 18, 1965. SCLC secured parade permits for these marches and there were no arrests.

39. Fager, *Selma, 1965*, pp. 72–74; Orange, "With the People," p. 112; chronology of Selma campaign, box 146, folder 9, SCLC.

40. Raines, *My Soul Is Rested*, pp. 206–11; *New York Times*, February 22, 1965.

41. Raines, *My Soul Is Rested*, pp. 410–11.

42. *New York Times*, February 19, 20, 22, 1965.

43. *New York Times*, February 20, 23–25, 27, 1965.

44. Orange, "With the People," p. 112; Raines, *My Soul Is Rested*, pp. 212–13; Fager, *Selma, 1965*, p. 81; *New York Times*, February 27 and March 4, 1965.

45. Fager, *Selma, 1965*, p. 85; Garrow, *Protest at Selma*, pp. 36–37, 68–70; *New York Times*, February 24 and 26, March 2 and 6, 1965.

46. Minutes of executive committee, March 6–7, box 3, SNCC.

47. Baumgardner to Sullivan, March 3, 1965; Jones and King; Jones and Young, telephone conversations, March 6, 1965; Jones to Johnson and Katzenbach, telegrams, March 7, 1965, all in FBI King file, MLK.

48. Fager, *Selma, 1965*, p. 92; Raines, *My Soul Is Rested*, p. 220; *New York Times*, March 8, 1965.

49. Raines, *My Soul Is Rested*, pp. 221–22. Williams, it seems, led the marchers over the bridge against King's wishes; see W. R. Witherspoon, *Martin Luther King, Jr.* (Garden City, 1985), pp. 172–77.

50. Westin and Mahoney, *Trial of Martin Luther King*, p. 170; *New York Times*, March 8, 1965; Raines, *My Soul Is Rested*, p. 501.

51. *Time*, March 19, 1965, pp. 15–16; *New York Times*, March 9, 1965; Dean Peerman and Martin E. Marty, "Selma: Sustaining the Momentum," *Christian Century*, March 24, 1965, pp. 358–59; Max L. Stackhouse, "The Ethics of Selma," *Commonweal*, April 9, 1965, p. 75.

52. Westin and Mahoney, *Trial of Martin Luther King*, pp. 169–70; Garrow, *Protest at Selma*, pp. 83–84.

53. Andrew Kopkind, "Selma: Ain't Gonna Let Nobody Turn Me 'Round," *New Republic*, March 20, 1965, p. 7.

54. Garrow, *Protest at Selma*, p. 85; Bishop, *Days of Martin Luther King*, p. 386; Westin and Mahoney, *Trial of Martin Luther King*, p. 172; *New York Times*, March 10, 1965.

55. King and Rustin, et al., telephone conversation, March 9, 1965, FBI King file, MLK; Westin and Mahoney, *Trial of Martin Luther King*, p. 173.

56. Thomas R. Wagy, "Governor LeRoy Collins of Florida and the Selma Crisis of 1965," *Florida Historical Quarterly*, April 1979, pp. 403–20.

57. Kopkind, "Selma," pp. 7–8; Wofford, *Of Kennedys and Kings*, pp. 181–82; Good, "Beyond the Bridge," p. 26; Bishop, *Days of Martin Luther King*, pp. 386–88; Lewis, *King*, pp. 278–82; Collins, interview by author.

58. *New York Times*, March 12, 1965. Lewis described King's account of the march in "Behind the Selma March" (*Saturday Review*, April 3, 1965, pp. 16–17, 57) as a "transparent misrepresentation of the facts," as indeed it was.

59. Collins, interview by author.

60. *New York Times*, March 3, 9, 11, 14 (sec. 4, p. 10), 1965.

61. Garrow, *Protest at Selma*, pp. 87–103; Fager, *Selma, 1965*, pp. 106–21; John Cogley, "The Clergy Heeds a New Call," *New York Times Magazine*, May 2, 1965, sec. 4, pp. 42–54; *New York Times*, March 12, 13, 18, 1965; Kopkind, "Ain't Gonna Let Nobody Turn Me 'Round," p. 7; *Time*, March 26, 1965, pp. 13–14; Richard Hofstadter, *The Age of Reform* (New York, 1955), p. 152.

62. *New York Times*, March 17, 1965.

63. *New York Times*, March 17 and 18, 1965.

64. Watters, *Down to Now*, p. 324; *New York Times*, March 18, 1965; minutes of executive committee, April 12–14, 1965, box 3, SNCC Papers, MLK.

65. King and Jones, telephone conversation, February 14, 18, 20, 1965; King and Wachtel et al., telephone conversation, March 18, 1965, both in FBI King file, MLK.

66. Raines, *My Soul Is Rested*, pp. 502–3; Levison to King, April 7, 1965, box 14, folder 40, KP.

67. Garrow, pp. 36–41; Clarence Mitchell to Roy Wilkins, February 1, 1965, box 7, Wilkins Papers; Roy Wilkins, *Standing Fast: The Autobiography of Roy Wilkins* (New York, 1982), p. 306.

68. Steven F. Lawson, *Black Ballots: Voting Rights in the South, 1966–1969* (New York, 1976), pp. 307–9; "Joe [Rauh] suggested that the automatic feature could go into effect when the registration of Negroes was less than 15 per cent of the potential voter population. If this is applied on a state wide basis, Mississippi would be about the only state affected" (Mitchell to Wilkins, February 1, 1965, Wilkins Papers.)

69. James Weinstein et al., "Reply to 'Up From Irrelevance,'" in *The New Radicals*, ed. Jacobs and Landau, p. 276. See also Meier, "On the Role of Martin Luther King," pp. 443–48.

70. Eric Goldman, *The Tragedy of Lyndon Johnson* (New York, 1968), pp. 376–77; Watters, *Down to Now*, pp. 124–25; Westin and Mahoney, *Trial of Martin Luther King*, p. 62.

Chapter 10

1. Rustin, "From Protest to Politics," in *The New Radicals*, ed. Jacobs and Landau, p. 296.

2. A. Philip Randolph, "The Crisis of Victory," January 30, 1965, box 17, Randolph Papers; Rustin, "From Protest to Politics," pp. 301–2.

3. Levison to King, April 9, 1965, box 14, folder 40, KP.

4. Financial report, September 1, 1964 through June 30, 1965, box 57, folder 23, SCLC; Adele Kanter, "National Direct Mail Fundraising Program," [April 1964 to July 1965], box 49, folder 1, SCLC.

5. Kanter, "National Direct Mail Fundraising Program," box 49, folder 1, SCLC; Kanter and Levison, telephone conversation, December 21, 1966; Young and Levison, telephone conversation, June 6, 1967, both in FBI Levison file, MLK.

6. King, annual report, in *Summary of Ninth Annual Convention* (Atlanta, October 1965), pp. 1–4, box 150, folder 28, SCLC; Raines, *My Soul Is Rested*, p. 233; Renata Adler, "Letter from Selma," *New Yorker*, April 10, 1965, p. 145.

7. Chafe, *Civilities and Civil Rights*, pp. 176–200; Reynolds, *Jesse Jackson*, pp. 54–55.

8. Oates, *Let the Trumpet Sound*, pp. 366–67; Steele, interview by Ice, pp. 36–37; Raines, *My Soul Is Rested*, p. 517; Coretta King and Levison, telephone conversation, May 15, 1968; Rustin and Levison, telephone conversation, July 21, 1968, both in FBI Levison file, MLK.

9. Levison and Jones, telephone conversation, April 6, 1965; King and Jones, telephone conversation, May 21, 1965, both in FBI King file, MLK; Navasky, *Kennedy Justice*, p. 146.

10. Fager, *Selma, 1965*, pp. 166–67; "Alabama Staff Workshop," April 21–23, minutes, box 94, SNCC Papers, MLK.

11. Fager, *Selma 1965*, p. 167; Raines, *My Soul Is Rested*, p. 485; plans for Mississippi boycott, box 146, folders 25–28, SCLC.

12. *New York Times*, March 29–31, 1965.

13. *Baltimore Afro-American*, April 10, 1965; "Statement by Martin Luther King, Jr.," SCLC news release, April 2, 1965, box 121, folder 9, SCLC; King, *An Open Letter to the American People* (Atlanta, n.d.), box 121, folder 14, SCLC.

14. Rustin and Tommy Smith, telephone conversation, March 31, 1965, FBI King file, MLK; minutes of SCLC board meeting, April 1, 1965, box 29, folder 5, KP.

15. Levison to King, April 9, 1965, KP; *New York Times*, March 30, 1965; Mark O. Hatfield to King, March 31, 1965; Edmund G. Brown to King, April 12, 1965, box 1, folder 7, KP; Andrew Kopkind, "Boycotting Alabama," *New Republic*, April 17, 1965, pp. 11–13; King, "The Civil Rights Struggle in the United States Today," April 21, 1965, pp. 14–15, box 28, folder 2, SCLC; *New York Times*, April 20, 1965.

16. Fager, *Selma, 1965*, p. 168; chronology of Selma campaign, box 146, folder 9, SCLC; *Birmingham News*, April 21, 1965; *New York Times*, April 29, 1965.

17. *New York Times*, May 25, 1965; Fager, *Selma, 1965*, p. 169; Ralph H. Hines and James E. Pierce, "Negro Leadership after the Social Crisis: An Analysis of Leadership Changes in Montgomery, Alabama," *Phylon*, Spring 1965, pp. 169–70; Jesse L. Douglas to Randolph T. Blackwell, April 7, 1965, box 142, folder 18, SCLC.

18. Fager, *Selma, 1965*, pp. 170–97; *New York Times*, May 17, 1965; Morris to Young, April 2, 1965, box 44, folder 12, SCLC; Blackwell, report on a visit to Selma, May 10, 1965, box 28, folder 21, KP.

19. Reese to King, November 8, 1965, box 21, folder 14, KP.

20. "Selma, Alabama," March 8, 1965, box 25, SNCC Papers, MLK; notes from Dallas County, n.d., boxes 25 and 47, SNCC Papers, MLK.

21. Minutes of executive committee, April 12–14, 1965, box 6, SNCC; "Alabama Staff Workshop," April 21–23, 1965, minutes, box 94, SNCC Papers, MLK.

22. John Lewis and Silas Norman to King, March 7, 1965, box 23, folder 17, KP.

23. Minutes of executive committee, April 12–14, 1965.

24. "Alabama Staff Workshop," April 21–23, 1965, minutes.

25. Joint statement by King and Lewis, SCLC news release, April 30, 1965, box 27, folder 55, SCLC; King, Rustin and Wachtel, telephone conversa-

tion, May 2, 1965, FBI King file, MLK; Forman, *The Making of Black Revolutionaries*, pp. 367, 380–83.

26. *Newsweek*, June 28, 1965, p. 22; Watters, *Down To Now*, pp. 333–34; King, president's annual report, August 11, 1965, p. 3, box 130, folder 28, SCLC; Junius Griffin to Randolph Blackwell, memo, June 28, 1965, box 145, folder 15, SCLC; SCLC-SCOPE public relations, memo, n.d., box 170, folder 10, SCLC.

27. King, president's report, p. 3; Garrow, *Protest At Selma*, p. 130; U.S. Commission on Civil Rights, *The Voting Rights Act: The First Months* (Washington, D.C., 1965), p. 35.

28. SCLC press release, June 1, 1965, box 121, folder 9, SCLC; *Macon Telegraph*, May 28, 1965; *Atlanta Constitution*, May 29 and 30; *Atlanta Daily World*, June 6, 1965; *Chicago Defender* (national edition), October 16–22, 1965; press release by Dr. Martin Luther King, Jr., October 14, 1965, KP.

29. *New York Times*, November 1, 1965.

30. Bolster, "Civil Rights Movements in Twentieth-Century Georgia," pp. 301–15; *Americus Times-Recorder*, July 27–August 10, 1965; *New York Times*, August 4, 5, 7, 1965.

31. *Charlotte Observer*, June 5, 1967.

32. *Birmingham World*, July 21, August 4, 11, 1965; *New York Times*, August 2–4, 1965; U.S. Commission on Civil Rights, *The Voting Rights Act*, p. 37.

33. U.S. Commission on Civil Rights, *The Voting Rights Act*, pp. 14–37; Watters and Cleghorn, *Climbing Jacob's Ladder*, pp. 260–61; King, "Voter Registration in the South Since the Voting Rights Act," report to the administrative committee, November 12, 1965, box 28, folder 2, SCLC.

34. Nicholas Katzenbach, "A Lesson in Responsible Leadership," *New South*, Spring 1966, pp. 55–60; King, report to the administrative committee, SCLC.

35. *New York Times*, January 31, 1966; Southern Regional Council, *The Continuing Crisis: An Assessment of New Racial Tensions in the South* (Atlanta, May 1966); Charles Morgan, *One Man, One Voice* (New York, 1979), pp. 45–46; *New York Times*, October 24 and November 11, 1965; King, report to the administrative committee, SCLC.

36. Hosea Williams, bimonthly progress report, December 7, 1965, box 170, folder 10, SCLC; "Alabama Project," n.d., box 165, folder 15, SCLC.

37. Hosea Williams, report to the board of directors, April 12 and 13, 1966, box 131, folder 9, SCLC; *Richmond Afro-American*, November 27, 1965; *Southern Courier*, November 20 and 21, 1965.

38. Unsigned memos, November 2, 11, 12, December 13, 1965, police files, BPL; Paul Good, "Birmingham: Two Years Later," *Reporter*, December 2, 1965, pp. 21–24; *Southern Courier*, January 1–6, 1966; William C. Hamilton, memo to Albert Boutwell, January 18, 1966, Boutwell Papers, BPL.

39. Unsigned memo, November 8, 1965; report of talk with [Rev. Ed] Gardner, February 16, 1966; reports of mass meeting on January 16, 1966, all in police files, BPL; Shuttlesworth to King, October 14, 1965, box 22, folder 14, KP; *Southern Courier*, January 1–6, 22–23, 1966.

40. *Southern Courier*, January 29–30, 1966; *New York Times*, January 25, 1966; transcript of ABC television and radio interview with Albert Boutwell, January 21, 1966; John Doar to Walter Boudin and Crawford Johnson, March 30, 1966, both in Boutwell Papers, BPL; Watters and Cleghorn, *Climbing Jacob's Ladder*, p. 262.

41. Orange, "With the People," pp. 112–15; Andrew Young to Hosea Williams, December 31, 1965, box 167, folder 1, SCLC. For the complaints of the field staff, see "Discussion of Application of Non-Violence and the Application of the Basic Precepts to Field and Staff Relations," n.d., box 32, folder 9, KP; Mark Harrington to King, "Christmas Project in Birmingham," December 20, 1965, box 28, folder 6, KP; Shirley Mesher to King, February 21, 1966, box 165, folder 13, SCLC.

42. David E. Gunter to Andrew Young, September 9, 1965, box 52, folder 20, SCLC.

43. Pierce Barker to Hosea Williams, September 4, 1965, box 35, folder 1, KP.

44. Minutes of executive staff meeting, August 26–28, 1965, box 46, folder 8, SCLC; Blackwell to King, August 25, 1965, box 28, folder 23, KP; Marc Saddler to King, March 20, 1966, box 28, folder 14, KP; Bolster, "Civil Rights Movements in Twentieth-Century Georgia," p. 224.

45. Levison to King, June 27, 1965, box 14, folder 40, KP; Blackwell to King, "A General Overview of SCLC," February 14, 1966, box 28, folder 23, KP.

46. *Baltimore Afro-American*, April 10, 1965.

47. Forman, *The Making of Black Revolutionaries*, p. 410.

48. Wachtel, interview by Fairclough.

49. *Atlanta Constitution*, August 13, 1965.

50. *New York Times*, March 28, 1965, sec. 4, p. 6.

51. Stephen Ambrose, *Rise to Globalism: American Foreign Policy, 1938–1980* (London, 1980), p. 242; Marvin Kalb and Elie Abel, *Roots of Involvement: The United States in Asia, 1784–1971* (London, 1971), p. 192.

52. Bishop, *Days of Martin Luther King*, p. 402; *Norfolk Journal and Guide*, July 10, 1965.

53. Jones and Levison, telephone conversation, July 14, FBI King file, MLK; Wachtel to King, July 26, 1965, box 25, folder 31, KP; Rustin and Wachtel, date unspecified, in memo of August 5, 1965; King and Rustin et al., August 8, 1965, both in FBI King file, MLK; King, speech to SCLC Convention, August 12, 1965, box 28, folder 7, SCLC.

54. Minutes of SCLC board meeting, August 9, 1965, box 29, folder 5, KP; Young, "An Experiment in Power," August 11, 1965, box 131, folder 1, SCLC; *Summary of Ninth Annual Convention* (Atlanta, 1965), p. 20, box 130, folder 28, SCLC.

55. Leslie H. Gelb, with Richard K. Betts, *The Irony of Vietnam: The System Worked* (Washington, D.C., 1979), pp. 205–18.

56. Humphrey quoted in Harry Ashmore and William C. Baggs, *Mission to Hanoi* (New York, 1968), p. 340; Humphrey, *The Education of a Public Man*, pp. 318–39; *Nation*, October 11, 1965, pp. 205–6; *Time*, July 20, 1965, p. 20.

57. Farmer, interview by Mulhollan, p. 9; handwritten minutes of SNCC staff meeting, November 29, 1965, box 3, SNCC; A. Philip Randolph to Dr. Jerome Davis, September 14, 1966, box 2, Randolph Papers; Brink and Harris, *Black and White*, p. 274; Wachtel and Rustin, telephone conversation, September 13, 1965, FBI King file, MLK. SNCC finally decided to oppose the war in November 1965, but did not publicly state this position until 1966.

58. Lewis, *King*, pp. 302–5; Bishop, *Days of Martin Luther King*, p. 415; *Norfolk Journal and Guide*, September 18, 1965.

59. King and Levison et al., telephone conversation, September 1965, FBI Levison file, MLK; Wachtel and Rustin, telephone conversation, September 13, FBI King file, MLK; King and Rustin, et al., telephone conversation, September 28, 1965, FBI Levison file, MLK; King, "Statement on Vietnam," October 5, 1965, KP; speech at staff retreat, Frogmore, South Carolina, [March 1967], p. 34, KP. King was referring, of course, to *Profiles in Courage*, John F. Kennedy's Pulitzer Prize–winning study of unpopular but principled stands taken by U.S. senators.

60. *New York Times*, April 3 and 4, 1965; Airlie House retreat, June 7–10, 1965, list of invitees, box 34, folder 15, KP; [Walter Fauntroy?], "Programmatic Action Proposed for Chicago," n.d., box 5, folder 26, KP.

61. Clarence Jones and unknown male, telephone conversation, June 12, 1965, FBI King file, MLK; Wachtel, interview by author; Oates, *Let the Trumpet Sound*, p. 379; Andrew Young, "An Experiment in Power," August 11, 1965, box 131, folder 1, SCLC.

62. *Newsweek* quoted in Jerry Cohen and William S. Murphy, *Burn, Baby, Burn! The Los Angeles Riot, August 1965* (New York, 1966), p. 278; King and Rustin, August 14, 1965; Rustin and Roy Wilkins, Rustin and Wachtel, August 15, 1965, all telephone conversations in FBI King file, MLK.

63. King and Levison, telephone conversation, August 25, 1965, FBI Levison file, MLK.

64. Minutes of executive staff meeting, Hilton Inn, Atlanta, August 26–28, 1965, SCLC, box 46, folder 8; King, transcript of interview, August 29, 1965, in CBS News, *Face the Nation*, vol. 8 (New York, 1972), p. 210.

65. Kyle Haseldon to King, April 12, 1965, box 1, folder 25, SCLC; *New York Times*, July 8 and 27, August 1, 1965; King, "March on Chicago" speech, July 26, 1965, box 28, folder 4, SCLC. SCLC ruled out New York on account of the factionalism of the black leadership there and the opposi-

tion of Adam Clayton Powell. In Philadelphia there was bitter rivalry between CORE and the NAACP, whose leader, Cecil Moore, expressed open contempt for King and plainly stated that he wanted SCLC to stay away. Boston and Los Angeles were also unsuitable.

66. Len O'Connor paper, January 7, 1966, box 5, folder 28, KP; David Halberstam, "Daley of Chicago," *Harper's*, August 1968, pp. 32–33.

67. Arnold Schuchter, *White Power/Black Freedom* (Boston, 1968), p. 65; Lawrence Landry, working paper to the organizing conference of the Committee for Independent Political Action, n.d., SCLC Papers; Lewis, *King*, pp. 314 and 331; Lois Wille, "Mayor Daley Meets the Movement," *Nation*, August 30, 1965, p. 95.

68. Mike Royko, *Boss: Mayor Richard J. Daley of Chicago* (London, 1972), pp. 127–31.

69. King, Levison, and Rustin, telephone conversation, February 1, 1966, FBI Levison file, MLK.

Chapter 11

1. Allan H. Spear, *Black Chicago: The Making of a Negro Ghetto* (Chicago, 1967), p. 221; Schuchter, *White Power/Black Freedom*, pp. 79–85.

2. Mayer Weinberg and Faith Rich, "A Report of Official Segregation in Chicago Public Schools," July 27, 1965, box 149, folder 11, SCLC; Thomas M. Landye and James J. Vanecko, "The Politics of Open Housing Legislation in Chicago and Illinois," in *The Politics of Fair Housing Legislation*, ed. Lynn W. Eley and Thomas W. Casstevens (San Francisco, 1968), pp. 69–72; U.S. Commission on Civil Rights, *1961 Report, Book Five: Justice* (Washington, D.C., 1961), pp. 40–41; James Q. Wilson, *Negro Politics* (Glencoe, Ill., 1960), pp. 101–2; Royko, *Daley of Chicago*, pp. 127–31.

3. Wilson, *Negro Politics*, pp. 139–42; Lerone Bennett, Jr., "North's Hottest Fight for Integration," *Ebony*, March 1962, pp. 31–38; Lerone Bennett, Jr., *Confrontation: Black and White* (Baltimore, 1966), pp. 205–8.

4. Royko, *Daley of Chicago*, pp. 134–35; James Ridgeway, "Poor Chicago," *New Republic*, May 15, 1965, p. 19; Charles E. Silberman, *Crisis in Black and White* (New York, 1964), pp. 207–8, 318–48.

5. Bennett, "North's Hottest Fight," pp. 31–35; Wille, "Mayor Daley Meets the Movement," p. 92; *U.S. News*, August 2, 1965, pp. 54–55; *New York Times*, July 12, 1965; Chicago Urban League, *Public School Segregation: City of Chicago, 1963–64 and 1964–65* (Chicago, May 2, 1965), box 149, folder 26, SCLC.

6. Wille, "Mayor Daley Meets the Movement," pp. 92–94; Kevin P. Buckley and Richard Cotton, "The Marchers and the Machine," *Reporter*, November 4, 1965, pp. 30–31; *New York Times*, July 12, August 1, 1965.

7. CCCO to Francis Keppel, July 4, 1965, box 149, folder 13, SCLC; CCCO, "Gerrymandering Chicago Schools," December 7, 1965, box 149, folder

12, SCLC; John Herbers, *The Lost Priority: What Happened to the Civil Rights Movement in America?* (New York, 1970), pp. 139–40.

8. Herbers, *The Lost Priority,* pp. 141–42; Lois Wille, "The Payoff in Chicago," *New Republic,* October 23, 1966, p. 11; Harold M. Brown to Edwin C. Berry, November 5, 1965, pp. 3–6, box 150, folder 26, SCLC; *New York Times,* October 11, 1965.

9. "The Near West Side," n.d.; "Portrait of a Slum, Lawndale-Slumdale," n.d.; "North Kenwood," n.d., all in box 150, SCLC; James Bevel, "Chicago Project," December 9, 1965, box 150, folder 25, SCLC; Bevel quoted in *New York Times,* March 24, 1965. The concept of internal colonialism did not originate with Bevel, of course. The Communist party had used it in the 1930s when it advocated independence for the Southern Black Belt. More recently, figures as diametrically opposed as Malcolm X and Kenneth B. Clark had likened the ghettos to internal colonies.

10. Minutes of executive staff meeting, August 26–28, 1965; James Bevel, "Chicago Report," November 8, 1965, box 150, folder 22, SCLC; *New Republic,* July 30, 1966, p. 6; Kenneth R. Young to King, March 6, 1966, box 38, folder 9, SCLC.

11. Rowland Evans and Robert Novak, "Dr. King's Man," *Nashville Tennesseean,* December 17, 1965; Bevel, "Chicago Project," box 150, folder 25, SCLC.

12. Reynolds, *Jesse Jackson,* pp. 55–56; *Chicago Defender* (national edition), February 5–11, 1966; Jesse L. Jackson and David M. Wallace, annual report to the board of directors, March 1967, FOF; Jackson, report to Rev. Andrew Young: from October to May, May 20, 1966, SCLC.

13. Reynolds, *Jesse Jackson,* p. 56; *Chicago Defender,* January 6, 1966; agenda for SCLC-CCCO Conference, January 5–6, 1966, box 149, folder 8, SCLC; *New York Times,* January 8, 1966. Young, Bevel, Vivian, C. K. Steele, and Bernard Lee also attended the conference.

14. King, "The Chicago Plan," SCLC news release, January 7, 1966; *Chicago Tribune,* January 8, 1966; *Newsweek,* January 31, 1966, p. 17.

15. King and Jones, telephone conversation, September 30, November 15, 1965, FBI King file, MLK; Levison and King, telephone conversation, November 5, 1965; Levison and Jones, telephone conversation, November 6, 1965, both in FBI Levison file, MLK; Marc Saddler to King, March 29, 1966, box 28, folder 14, KP; Levison and King, telephone conversation February 8, 1966, FBI Levison file, MLK.

16. Adele Kanter, "National Direct Mail Fundraising Program," in report to the board of directors, April 12–13, 1966, box 131, folder 9, SCLC; King to Rev. Leon Davis, June 1, 1966, box 5, folder 30, KP; King and Levison, telephone conversation, July 1, 1966, FBI Levison file, MLK; Levison to King, May 20, 1966, box 14, folder 40, KP; Levison and Jones, telephone conversation, June 1, 1966, FBl Levison file, MLK.

17. Swedish Information Service news release, June 30, 1966, box 122, folder

4, SCLC; King and Levison, telephone conversations, July 1 and 12, 1966, FBI Levison file, MLK; Jesse Jackson to King, "Fund Raising in the Context of Economic Development in the North," November 2, 1966, box 32, folder 1, KP; audit report of the SCLC, August 30, 1965 to June 30, 1966, box 58, folder 2, SCLC.

18. Bevel, "Direct Action Report, Chicago," in report to the board of directors, April 12–13, 1966, box 131, folder 10, SCLC; Bruce Cook, "King in Chicago," *Commonweal*, April 29, 1966, pp. 175–77.

19. Orange, "With the People," p. 112; Levison and Roy Bennett, telephone conversation, May 13, 1966, FBI Levison file, MLK.

20. Bevel, "Chicago Project," November 8, 1965, box 150, folder 22, SCLC; *Chicago Defender*, May 11 and June 13, 1966; Orange, "With the People," pp. 113–14; King, *The Trumpet of Conscience* (New York, 1968), p. 58; Judy Coburn, "Open City," *New Republic*, September 17, 1966, p. 10; Coretta King, *My Life with Martin Luther King, Jr.*, pp. 282–83.

21. Bevel, "Direct Action Report, Chicago," in report to the board of directors, April 12–13, 1966, box 131, folder 10, SCLC; *Southern Courier*, March 5 and 6, 1966; *New York Times*, March 24, 1966.

22. Mike Royko, *Daley of Chicago*, p. 143; Lewis, *King*, pp. 317–18; David A. Satter, "West Side Story," *New Republic*, July 2, 1966, p. 17; Levison and Roy Bennett, telephone conversation, March 1, 1966, FBI Levison file, MLK.

23. *New York Times*, September 8, 1965; *Chicago Defender*, September 9, 1965.

24. Royko, *Daley of Chicago*, pp. 142–43; *New York Times*, March 24 and 25, 1966; *Chicago Defender*, March 28, 1966; *Chicago Tribune*, March 25 and 26, 1966.

25. King (first draft by Levison), "The Last Steep Ascent," *Nation*, March 14, 1966, pp. 288–92; King, European tour speech, March 1966, box 28, folder 23, SCLC.

26. Outline for discussion of proposed freedom march, n.d., box 47, folder 6, SCLC; Edwin C. Berry to King, May 23, 1966, box 47, folder 3, SCLC.

27. North Shore Summer Project: survey report, n.d., box 150, folder 8, SCLC; Sally Olds, "The White Liberal Takes a Stand," *Community*, December 1965, pp. 9–11; Landye and Vanecko, "The Politics of Open Housing Legislation in Chicago and Illinois," pp. 82–100; Bevel, "Direct Action Report, Chicago," box 131, folder 10, SCLC; W. Werner Gentz to King, October 14, 1965, box 1, folder 32, SCLC; Jesse Jackson, "A Strategy to End Slums," report to CCCO-SCLC strategy session, May 31, 1966, box 149, folder 53, SCLC.

28. Satter, "West Side Story," pp. 18–19; "Survey of Attainable Goals of the Chicago Freedom Movement," n.d., box 47, folder 6, SCLC; *Chicago Defender*, June 11–17 (national edition); Bishop, *Days of Martin Luther King*, p. 437.

29. Lee Rainwater and William L. Yancey, *The Moynihan Report and the Politics of Controversy* (Cambridge, Mass., 1967), passim; Andrew Kopkind, "No Fire This Time," *New Republic*, June 18, 1966, pp. 15–16; *Charlotte Observer*, June 2, 1966.

30. Bill Moyers testimony, in Senate, *Final Report*, book 3 (Washington, D.C., April 14, 1976), pp. 92–93; *Final Report*, book 2 (April 26, 1976), pp. 8 and 17.

31. Berry to King, May 23, 1966, box 47, folder 3, SCLC; *Chicago Defender*, July 11, 1966; Junius Griffin, "Progress Report: Chicago Freedom Rally and March," June 28, 1966, box 149, folder 30, SCLC. The *Chicago Defender* estimated the turnout at thirty thousand.

32. *New York Times*, July 9 and 12, 1966; *Chicago Defender*, July 12, 1966; Richard Cotton, "Negro Politics: Old Style and New," *Reporter*, August 11, 1966, p. 21.

33. *Washington Post*, July 13 and 24, 1966; *Chicago Tribune*, July 13, 1966; Bruce Cook, "The Chicago Riots," *Commonweal*, August 5, 1966, pp. 492–93; Coretta King, *My Life with Martin Luther King, Jr.*, pp. 285–87.

34. *New York Times*, July 14, 1966; *Washington Post*, July 14 and 15, 1966; Royko, *Daley of Chicago*, p. 145; Coretta King, *My Life with Martin Luther King, Jr.*, p. 289.

35. Merle Miller, *Lyndon*, pp. 436–37.

36. *Chicago Tribune*, July 16, 1966; *Washington Post*, July 16, 1966; *Chicago Defender*, July 18, 1966; Royko, *Daley of Chicago*, pp. 145–46.

37. Levison and Young, telephone conversation, July 12, 1966, FBI Levison file, MLK.

38. Landye and Vanecko, "Politics of Open Housing Legislation in Chicago and Illinois," pp. 99–100; *Chicago Tribune*, July 14, 1966; *New York Times*, July 22, 1966; Congressional Quarterly Service, *Revolution in Civil Rights* (Washington, D.C., 1968), pp. 76–77.

39. *Chicago Defender*, July 28, 1966; *New York Times*, July 30 and 31, August 1, 1966; *Washington Post*, August 1, 1966.

40. *New York Times*, August 2–4, 1966; Reynolds, *Jesse Jackson*, p. 61; *Washington Post*, August 6, 1966.

41. *Chicago Defender*, August 6–12, 1966 (national edition); *Washington Post*, August 5, 1966; Paul Good, "Bossism, Racism, and Dr. King," *Nation*, September 19, 1966, p. 241.

42. *Washington Post*, August 8, 1966; *New York Times*, August 9, 1966; Reynolds, *Jesse Jackson*, p. 65.

43. *New York Times*, August 10 and 11, 1966; Michael E. Schmiltz, "Catholics and the Chicago Riots," *Commonweal*, November 11, 1966, p. 160; *Chicago Defender*, March 12–18, 1966 (national edition); *New York Times*, August 11 and 12, 1966.

44. *New York Times*, August 12 and 13, 1966; *Chicago Defender*, August 11, 1966; *Chicago Tribune*, August 13, 1966; *Washington Post*, August 11–15, 1966.

45. *Chicago Tribune*, August 18, 1966; Coburn, "Open City," p. 10; *New York Times*, August 16, 1966; Royko, *Daley of Chicago*, p. 148.

46. The following account of the negotiations is based upon the minutes taken by John L. McKnight in "The Summit Negotiations," August 17–August 26, 1966, box 5, folder 31, KP.

47. *Chicago Tribune*, August 20, 1966; *New York Times*, August 21, 1966; *Washington Post*, August 22, 23, 26, 1966; *Chicago Tribune*, August 26, 1966.

48. McKnight, "The Summit Negotiations," box 5, folder 31, KP; *New York Times*, August 27, 1966; *Newsweek*, September 5, 1966, pp. 18–19.

49. *Chicago Tribune*, August 9 and 27, 1966; *Washington Post*, August 29, 1966; McKnight, "The Summit Negotiations," box 5, folder 31, KP.

50. *Chicago Tribune*, August 27, 1966; *Washington Post*, August 29, 1966; Good, "Bossism, Racism, and Dr. King," pp. 238–39; Schuchter, *White Power/Black Freedom*, pp. 60–61.

51. *New York Times*, August 28 and October 29, 1966; Bishop, *Days of Martin Luther King*, p. 448; Ben Van Clarke, "The Summit Follow-Up," n.d., SCLC; *Chicago Tribune*, October 29, 1966.

52. King, "One Year Later in Chicago," n.d., box 28, folder 31, SCLC.

53. *Newsweek*, February 13, 1967, pp. 17–18; *New York Times*, January 16, 1966; Schuchter, *White Power/Black Freedom*, pp. 64–65. The drive had a budget of only $23,000.

54. *Newsweek*, February 13, 1967, pp. 17–18.

55. Minutes of staff meeting, December 14, 1966, transcript, box 171, folder 20, SCLC.

56. Schuchter, *White Power/Black Freedom*, pp. 60–61; Royko, *Daley of Chicago*, pp. 149–54; Reynolds, *Jesse Jackson*, pp. 73–74.

57. *Washington Post*, August 28, 1966.

58. Halberstam, "Daley of Chicago," p. 33.

59. *Washington Post*, August 28, 1966; James R. McGraw, "An Interview with Andrew J. Young," *Christianity and Crisis*, January 22, 1968, p. 326.

60. McGraw, "An Interview with Andrew J. Young," pp. 325–26.

61. Vivian, interview by Browne, pp. 43–44; King, "See You in Washington," January 17, 1968, transcript, p. 13, KP.

Chapter 12

1. Middlebrook, interview by Beifuss and Thomas, p. 6.

2. King, *Where Do We Go from Here?* (Boston, 1968), pp. 22–23; *Newsweek*, June 20, 1966, pp. 15–16.

3. Morgan, *One Man, One Voice*, pp. 72–73.

4. Informatieceived by telephone, June 7, 1966, informant report, Mississippi State Sovereignty Commission, reproduced in *Southern Exposure*, Fall 1981, p. 83.

5. *Washington Post*, June 8, 1966; James Lawson, interview by Beifuss and

Thomas, August 21, 1969, pp. 47–48, MSU. As Lawson remembered the incident, Carmichael had to be restrained from striking back at the troopers: "We were convinced that Stokely was planning to tackle those guys. Which was, . . . we told him afterwards, sheer stupidity . . . this was a main argument throughout the march."

6. King, *Where Do We Go from Here?*, p. 25.

7. Ibid., pp. 26–29; Morgan, *One Man, One Voice*, pp. 73–74; Jones and Levison, telephone conversation, June 10, 1966, FBI Levison file, MLK.

8. Carson, *In Struggle*, p. 166. On Carmichael and the LCFO, see Stokely Carmichael, "Who Is Qualified?" *New Republic*, January 8, 1966, p. 22; Andrew Kopkind, "New Radicals in Dixie," *New Republic*, April 20, 1965.

9. August Meier, "Dilemmas of Negro Protest Strategy," *New South*, Spring 1966, pp. 1–5.

10. *Newsweek*, February 7, 1966, pp. 18–19; Blackwell to Young, re: SNCC-SCLC staff meeting, January 23, 1966, box 47, folder 11, SCLC.

11. Pat Watters, "Wallace-ism Is What Alabama (White) Wants," *New Republic*, May 14, 1966, p. 7; *Newsweek*, May 16, 1966, pp. 13–15; Brink and Harris, *Black and White*, p. 102. For SCLC's postmortem on the Alabama primaries, see "SCLC Field Staff Retreat," May 9, 1966, box 145, folder 4, SCLC.

12. Carson, *In Struggle*, pp. 191–206; minutes of central committee, May 17, 1966, box 6, SNCC; *Newsweek*, May 30, 1966, pp. 23–24; *Southern Patriot*, May 1966; Forman, *The Making of Black Revolutionaries*, pp. 448–56.

13. Minutes of executive committee, June 10–11, 1964, p. 15; minutes of executive committee, April 12–14, 1965, both in box 3, SNCC.

14. Viorst, *Fire in the Streets*, pp. 371–72.

15. Morgan, *One Man, One Voice*, pp. 74–75; Wilkins, *Standing Fast*, pp. 315–16.

16. Viorst, *Fire in the Streets*, pp. 371–72; Morgan, *One Man, One Voice*, p. 75. King made no mention of this stormy meeting in *Where Do We Go from Here.*

17. Cleveland Sellers and Robert Terrell, *River of No Return* (New York, 1973), pp. 160–61; *Washington Post*, June 15, 1966.

18. *Washington Post*, June 13, 1966; report of Mississippi State Sovereignty Commission, June 14, 1966, reproduced in *Southern Exposure*, Fall 1981, p. 84; King, *Where Do We Go from Here*, p. 29; *Washington Post*, June 17 and 18, 1966.

19. *Washington Post*, June 21, 1966; report of Mississippi State Sovereignty Commission, June 20, 1966, in *Southern Exposure*, Fall 1981, p. 84.

20. Young and Levison, June 18, 1966; King and Levison, Rustin, and Fauntroy, June 12, 1966; Blackwell and Levison, June 22, 1966; Wachtel and Levison, June 24, 1966; King and Levison, Jones, and Wachtel, June 22, 1966; all telephone conversations in FBI Levison file, MLK.

21. *Washington Post*, June 17 and 22, 1966; Paul Good, "The Meredith

March," *New South*, Summer 1966, pp. 12–13; Paul Good, "A White Look at Black Power," *Nation*, August 8, 1966, p. 116.

22. King, *Where Do We Go from Here*, pp. 30–31.

23. *Washington Post*, June 23, 1966; report of Mississippi State Sovereignty Commission, in *Southern Exposure*, Fall 1981, p. 83.

24. *Washington Post*, June 24, 1966; Good, "Meredith March," pp. 11–13; Andrew Kopkind, "The Birth of Black Power," *Ramparts*, October 1966, p. 6; "An Interview with Andrew Young," *Playboy*, July 1977, p. 74; Good, *Trouble I've Seen*, p. 261.

25. *Time*, July 8, 1966, p. 23; *Washington Post*, July 6 and 7, 1966.

26. Minutes of the Council on United Civil Rights Leadership (CUCRL), June 17, 1965, box 111, SNCC Papers, MLK.

27. Virginia Durr to Clark Foreman, March 17, 1958, Durr Papers; James R. McGraw, "An Interview with Andrew J. Young," *Christianity and Crisis*, January 22, 1968, p. 326.

28. William R. Beardslee, *The Way Out Must Lead In: Life Histories in the Civil Rights Movement* (Westport, Conn., 1983), p. 77.

29. Roy Wilkins, "Steady As She Goes," reprinted in *Black Viewpoints*, ed. A. C. Littleton and M. W. Burger (New York, 1971), pp. 295–96.

30. *New York Times*, July 9, 1966; Randolph to Wilkins, King et al., August 1, 1966, box 2, Randolph Papers; NBC's "Meet the Press," August 21, 1966, transcript, FOF.

31. King and Levison, September 9, 1966; Jones and Levison, October 1, 1966; Rustin and Levison, October 15, 1966, all telephone conversations in FBI Levison file, MLK. The statement that Rustin wanted King to sign was issued as an NAACP press release, "Crisis and Commitment," on October 13, and reprinted in the *New York Times* on October 15. King was upset that the *Times* reported that he endorsed the statement, and, with Levison and Young, suspected Rustin's hand. "When I make these tactical errors," he told Levison, "it's usually when I'm trying to deal with Bayard. . . . It now looks like I'm playing a game of duplicity." For his explanation of why he refused to sign, see *New York Times*, October 17, 1966.

32. King, *Where Do We Go from Here*, pp. 33–36; "Uncle Tomism": for example, see King and Levison et al., September 9, 1966, FBI Levison file, MLK.

33. King, *Where Do We Go from Here*, pp. 36–44.

34. Coretta King, *My Life with Martin Luther King, Jr.*, p. 276.

35. Carson, *In Struggle*, pp. 216–19; Baker, interview by Britton, p. 66.

36. Lewis, *King*, p. 331.

37. Thomas F. Pettigrew, *Racially Separate or Together?* (New York, 1970), p. 223. For opinion poll evidence, see Brink and Harris, *The Negro Revolution*, pp. 138–53; Brink and Harris, *Black and White*, pp. 107–10, 131–32; Stewart Alsop and Oliver Quayle, "What Northerners Really Think of Negroes," *Saturday Evening Post*, September 7, 1963, pp. 19–21. In 1961 the political scientist James Q. Wilson had argued with prescience that demonstrations against housing discrimination would be ineffective be-

cause "anti-Negro practices in real estate do not violate clear community norms . . . [and] no moral stigma attaches to the man who refuses to sell his house to a Negro"; see "The Strategy of Protest," *Journal of Conflict Resolution,* October 1961, p. 295.

38. For the successful opposition to fair housing legislation in California, see Theodore H. White, "Backlash," *Life,* October 16, 1964, p. 102; Donovan Bess, "The Racist Proposition," *Nation,* October 5, 1964, p. 179; Philip Wogaman, "The Fair Housing Controversy in California," *Christianity and Crisis,* August 3, 1964, p. 161; Albert J. Lima, "Why Proposition 14 Won," *Political Affairs,* December 1964, pp. 22–23.

39. *Washington Post,* June 12, 1966; editorial, *Washington Post,* August 2, 1966; *New York Times,* September 20 and 21, 1966; Lyndon B. Johnson, *The Vantage Point: Perspectives of the Presidency, 1963–1969* (New York, 1971), p. 178.

40. *New York Times,* September 16, 1966; Levison and King, telephone conversation, September 29, 1966; King and Levison, telephone conversation, July 1, 1966, both in FBI Levison file, MLK.

41. Levison and King, telephone conversation, September 29, 1966; Jones and Levison, telephone conversation, October 1, 1966; both in FBI Levison file, MLK; Harry Boyte to King, August 3, 1966, box 34, folder 8, KP.

42. Williams to King, March 8, 1967, box 35, folder 18, KP.

43. King and Levison, telephone conversation, July 21, 1966; Jones and Levison, telephone conversation, October 1, 1966, both in FBI Levison file, MLK. For the result of the research committee's discussions on "Black Power," see "Statement by Dr. Martin Luther King, Jr.," SCLC press release, October 11, 1966, FOF.

44. Dr. King's speech: Frogmore, November 14, 1966, transcript, box 28, folder 26, SCLC.

45. King, president's annual report, August 10, 1966, KP.

46. King, Frogmore speech, November 14, 1966, box 28, folder 26, SCLC.

47. Frank Millspaugh, "Should Students Go South?" *Commonweal,* June 18, 1965, pp. 406–9.

48. Bayard Rustin, " 'Black Power' and Coalition Politics," *Commentary,* September 1966, reprinted in Rustin, *Down the Line* (Chicago, 1971), pp. 154–65; Brink and Harris, *Black and White,* pp. 108–12, 182; James Q. Wilson, "The Negro in Politics," *Daedalus,* Fall 1965, p. 50; King, speech to voter registration rally, Louisville, August 2, 1967, pp. 11–12, KP.

49. King, Louisville speech, p. 11, KP.

50. Paul Good, "Bossism, Racism and Dr. King," p. 239.

51. Levison and King, telephone conversation, December 6, 1966, FBI Levison file, MLK. For King's Senate testimony, see "Statement of the Reverend Martin Luther King, Jr.," December 15, 1966, in U.S. Senate, 89th Cong., 2d sess., *Hearings Before the Subcommittee on Executive Reorganization of the Committee on Government Operation: The Federal Role in Urban Affairs* (Washington, D.C.), pp. 2967–85.

52. *Southern Courier,* March 5–6, 1966, p. 4.
53. *Washington Post,* August 1, 1966; *Chicago Tribune,* October 29, 1966; King, "One Year Later in Chicago," pp. 2–4, box 28, folder 31, SCLC; Satter, "West Side Story," pp. 15–18; tenant unions of the Unions to End Slums in East Garfield Park and Lawndale, memo to CFM steering committee, December 30, 1966, box 150, folder 2, SCLC. The CFM succeeded in winning $4 million in federally guaranteed, low-interest loans for the rehabilitation of five hundred slum apartments. Bayard Rustin, however, was highly critical of SCLC's slum rehabilitation program, claiming that the real winners were the slumlords who had attached themselves to the CFM. "Martin is surrounded with a bunch of real estate Negroes in Chicago and doesn't know what he is getting into"; see Levison and Rustin, telephone conversation, January 1, 1967, FBI Levison file, MLK.
54. Brink and Harris, *Black and White,* pp. 68–69, 183; King, "One Year Later in Chicago," p. 8, box 28, folder 31, SCLC.
55. King, *Where Do We Go from Here,* p. 49.
56. Hodgson, *In Our Time,* pp. 266–67.
57. Brink and Harris, *Black and White,* pp. 120–24. See also Richard T. Morris and Vincent Jeffries, "The White Reaction Study," in *The Los Angeles Riots,* ed. Nathan Cohen (London, 1970), pp. 484–512.
58. *New York Times,* January 28, 1967; Reynolds, *Jesse Jackson,* p. 79.
59. Rowland Evans and Robert Novak, "King's Chicago Pillar," *Washington Post,* August 29, 1966.
60. Dick Gregory and Mark Lane, *Code Name "Zorro": The Murder of Martin Luther King, Jr.* (Englewood Cliffs, N.J., 1977), pp. 53–54.

Chapter 13

1. King, Levison, and Rustin, telephone conversation, February 1, 1966; Levison-King, telephone conversation, December 6, 1966, both in FBI Levison file, MLK.
2. King, "Transformed Nonconformist," sermon, January 16, 1966, box 28, folder 20, SCLC.
3. King, "Our Jewish Brother," *Chicago Defender* (national edition), March 5–11, 1966, p. 10; FBI memo, March 9, 1966, FBI King file, MLK; Jones and Young, May 13, 1966, quoted in FBI memo of May 16, FBI King file, MLK.
4. *New York Times,* February 11, and April 14, 1966; FBI memo, April 19, 1966, FBI King file, MLK; Ralph D. Abernathy, "Vietnam and the Negro Revolution," November 1, 1966, box 59, folder 19, SCLC.
5. King, Levison, Young, and Abernathy, telephone conversation, January 19, 1967; Dora McDonald and Levison, telephone conversation, February 8, 1967, both in FBI Levison file, MLK.
6. King, Levison, Young, and Robinson, telephone conversation, February 18, 1967, FBI Levison file, MLK.

7. King, "The Casualties of the War in Vietnam," February 25, 1967, KP; *New York Times*, February 26, 1967. Also speaking at the conference were senators McCarthy, McGovern, and Gruening, and Gov. Mark Hatfield of Oregon.

8. Levison and Rachel DuBois, March 1, 1967; unknown male and Levison, March 6, 1967; Chauncey Eskridge and Levison, March 7, 1967, all telephone conversations in FBI Levison file, MLK; Wachtel, interview by author.

9. Levison and King, telephone conversation, March 25, 1967, FBI Levison file, MLK.

10. King and Levison et al., telephone conversation, April 12, 1967, FBI Levison file, MLK.

11. King, address to peace parade and rally, March 25, 1967, KP; *New York Times*, March 26 and 31, 1967; Morgan, *One Man, One Voice*, pp. 162–63. Charles Morgan drafted the Vietnam resolution.

12. King, Levison, and Joan Daves, telephone conversation, March 27, 1967, FBI Levison file, MLK.

13. King, "Beyond Vietnam," April 4, 1967, SCLC recording, text in KP.

14. NAACP press release, April 15, 1967, FOF; statement by Whitney Young, reprinted in *Current*, May 1967, p. 40; *Life*, April 21, 1967, p. 4.

15. *Washington Post*, April 6, 1967; King and Levison, telephone conversation, April 12, 1967, FBI Levison file, MLK; *New York Times*, May 2, 1967.

16. Bayard Rustin, "Dr. King's Painful Dilemma," *Amsterdam News*, March 3, 1967; "Guns, Bread, and Butter," *War/Peace Report*, March 1967, both reprinted in *Down the Line*, pp. 167–70; Hodgson, *In Our Time*, p. 284.

17. *Newsweek*, May 15, 1967, p. 23; *New York Times*, June 15, 1967.

18. Wachtel and Levison, June 11, 1967; Randolph Blackwell and Levison, June 22, 1966; Levison and King, October 15, 1966, all telephone conversations in FBI Levison file, MLK.

19. Wachtel and Levison, telephone conversation, June 15, 1967, FBI Levison file, MLK.

20. Carl T. Rowan, "Martin Luther King's Tragic Decision," *Reader's Digest*, September 1967, reprinted in *Martin Luther King, Jr.: A Profile*, ed. C. Eric Lincoln (New York, 1970), p. 213.

21. John P. Roche, memo of April 5, 1967, quoted in Garrow, *FBI*, p. 180.

22. Garrow, *FBI*, pp. 181–82; Moyers quoted in Wofford, *Of Kennedys and Kings*, pp. 218–20.

23. Rowan, "King's Tragic Decision, pp. 212–18.

24. King and Levison, April 8, 1967; Levison and Alice Loewi, April 5, 1967; Wachtel and Levison, April 6, 1967, all telephone conversations in FBI Levison file, MLK.

25. King and Levison, telephone conversation, April 12, 1967, FBI Levison file, MLK; *New York Times*, April 16, 1967.

26. Andrew Young, "The Death of God and the Civil Rights Movement,"

notes for speech to the Hungry Club, Atlanta YMCA, February 11, 1967, 49, 27, SCLC; *New York Times*, August 28, 1967.

27. Wachtel and Levison, telephone conversation, April 15, 1967, FBI Levison file, MLK.

28. Nancy Zaroulis and Gerald Sullivan, *Who Spoke Up: Protest Against the War in Vietnam, 1963–1975* (Garden City, N.Y., 1984), p. 111; King, transcript of interview, April 16, 1967, in CBS News, *Face the Nation*, vol. 10, pp. 113–18.

29. SCLC press release, April 12, 1967, FOF; *New York Times*, May 11, 1967.

30. King and Levison, telephone conversation, April 13, 1967, FBI Levison file, MLK.

31. *Newsweek*, May 15, 1967, p. 23; King, speech at staff retreat, Frogmore, South Carolina, May 1967, pp. 28–34, KP.

32. King, Young, and Levison, telephone conversation, May 12, 1967, FBI Levison file, MLK; *New York Times*, April 23 and 24, 1967; King, "Why I Am Opposed to the War in Vietnam," April 30, 1967, transcript of sermon, KP. Stokely Carmichael was in the congregation when King delivered this sermon.

33. King and Levison, telephone conversation January 1, 1967, FBI Levison file, MLK; Norman Thomas to Charles Bloomstein et al., March 30, 1967, Randolph Papers.

34. Levison and King, telephone conversation, April 22, 1967, FBI Levison file, MLK; *New York Times*, May 23, 1967.

35. Levison and Young, telephone conversation, May 7, 1967, FBI Levison file, MLK.

36. Roy Bennett and Levison, May 31, 1967; Levison and King, June 6, 1967; Wachtel and Levison, June 11 and 15, 1967, all telephone conversations in FBI Levison file, MLK.

37. David Halberstam, "The Man Who Ran against Lyndon Johnson," *Harper's*, December 1968, pp. 47–48.

38. Curtis Gans to Young, July 13, 1967, box 39, folder 5, SCLC.

39. Wachtel and Levison, telephone conversation, June 15, 1967, FBI Levison file, MLK.

40. *New York Times*, August 18, 1967.

41. *New York Times*, September 1–4, 1967; King and Levison, telephone conversation, September 1, 1967; James Ridgeway, "Freak-Out in Chicago," *New Republic*, September 16, 1967, pp. 9–12. For a historian's assessment of the convention, see Irwin Unger, *The Movement: A History of the American New Left* (New York, 1974), pp. 137–38.

42. Levison, King, and Young, telephone conversation, July 9; Levison and Wachtel, telephone conversation, July 10, 1967, FBI Levison file, MLK. Renata Adler, "Letter from the Palmer House," in *The Radical Left: The Abuse of Discontent*, ed. W. P. Gerberding and D. E. Smith (Boston, 1970), pp. 32–29; Young to Dr. and Mrs. Martin Perez, September 6, 1967, box 39, folder 10, SCLC.

43. Young to Ann Farnsworth, May 18, 1967, box 39, folder 1, SCLC.

44. Financial report for July 1, 1966 to February 28, 1967, box 58, folder 7, SCLC; Hosea Williams, annual report to the board of directors, March 26, 1967, p. 3, box 133, folder 16, SCLC; Williams to Mew Soong-Li, April 22, 1967, box 47, folder 11, SCLC; letters of dismissal, April 1967, box 64, folder 17, SCLC; Levison and Kanter, telephone conversation, May 31, 1967, FBI Levison file, MLK.

45. King, Levison, Wachtel, and Young, telephone conversation, July 24, 1967, FBI Levison file, MLK.

46. Correspondence concerning African tour, box 28, folder 48, SCLC; Freddye Henderson to William Rutherford, May 3, 1967, box 38, folder 21, SCLC; Levison, King, and Young, telephone conversation, November 19, 1967, FBI Levison file, MLK.

47. "National Direct Mail Fundraising Program," March 28, 1967, box 133, folder 1, SCLC; Adele Kanter and Levison, telephone conversation, June 22, 1967, FBI Levison file, MLK; SNCC fundraising file, April 1967, box 3, SNCC Papers, MLK.

48. Herbert V. Coulton, report for 1967, box 50, folder 23, SCLC; *New York Times*, February 7, 1967.

49. *New York Times*, January 16, 1967; Young and Levison, telephone conversation, January 17, 1967, FBI Levison file, MLK.

50. Paul Brest to Young, April 27, 1967, box 38, folder 20, SCLC; Oscar Mohead to Young, July 4, 1967, box 39, folder 4, SCLC; Leon Hall to executive committee, August 21, 1967, box 47, folder 15, SCLC.

51. Williams to King, March 8, 1967, box 35, folder 18, KP.

52. Wednesday evaluation session: Ralph Abernathy presiding, May 23, 1967, transcript, box 49, folder 13, SCLC.

53. King's reply to criticisms of executive staff, in Wednesday evaluation session, box 49, folder 13, SCLC.

54. Levison and Kanter, telephone conversation, March 7, 1967, FBI Levison file, MLK.

55. King, "Power for the Powerless: SCLC's Basic Dilemma," paper presented to executive staff on March 21, 1967, box 144, folder 30, SCLC.

56. Levison and King, telephone conversation, March 25, 1967, FBI Levison file, MLK; biography of Rutherford, SCLC press release, December 13, 1967, box 122, folder 8, SCLC; Rutherford to Young, May 19, September 1, 1967, box 39, folder 10, SCLC; Rutherford to Young, October 24, 1967, box 39, folder 13, SCLC.

57. Reynolds, *Jesse Jackson*, pp. 106–12.

58. Ibid., pp. 113–22; Jesse L. Jackson and David M. Wallace, annual report on (1) Chicago's Operation Breadbasket and (2) Department of Special Projects and Economic Development, March 1967, FOF; Jones and Levison, telephone conversation, July 13, 1967, FBI Levison file, MLK.

59. Middlebrook, interview by Beifuss and Thomas, pp. 26–27; SCLC press release, July 12, 1967, SCLC.

60. *Louisville Defender*, January 5, 12, 26, February 2, 16, 23, March 2, 16, 30, April 6, 13, 27, May 4, 1967; *New York Times*, April 12, 14, 15, 17, 26, 28–30, May 2, 4–7, 1967.

61. *Louisville Defender*, May 18, 1967, editorial, *Louisville Defender*, September 21, 1967; King, speech to voter registration rally, August 2, 1967, pp. 1–3, KP. See also William Drummond, "Dr. Martin Luther King at the Crossroads," *Louisville Courier-Journal*, August 20, 1967.

62. *Cleveland Call and Post*, May 20 and June 17, 1967.

63. David Halberstam, "The Second Coming of Martin Luther King," *Harper's*, August 1967, p. 41; King and Levison, telephone conversation, June 24, 1967, FBI Levison file, MLK.

64. Halberstam, "The Second Coming," pp. 45–46; King and Levison, telephone conversation, October 9, 1967, FBI Levison file, MLK.

65. Carl B. Stokes, *Promises of Power* (New York, 1973), pp. 100–102. Evans was later convicted of homicide after a 1968 shoot-out that left three policemen and seven blacks dead.

66. Hodgson, *In Our Time*, p. 201; King, speech to Operation Breadbasket meeting, Chicago Theological Seminary, March 25, 1967, pp. 5–6, KP; Halberstam, "The Second Coming," p. 42.

67. Levison and King, telephone conversation, February 27, 1967, FBI Levison file, MLK.

68. Young, interview by Shannon, p. 8; King, president's address, August 16, 1967, reprinted in *The Rhetoric of Black Power*, ed. Wayne L. Brockriede and Robert L. Scott (New York, 1971), pp. 161–62.

69. King and Young et al., August 12, 1967, FBI Levison file, MLK; King, president's address, in *Rhetoric of Black Power*, p. 159.

70. King and Young et al., August 12, 1967, FBI Levison file, MLK.

71. Levison, King, Young, and Wachtel, July 25, 1967, FBI Levison file, MLK; Coretta King, *My Life with Martin Luther King, Jr.*, p. 298.

Chapter 14

1. King, transcript of press conference, October 23, 1967, KP; *Washington Post*, October 24, 1967.

2. King, "The Crisis in America's Cities," draft by Levison, August 15, 1967, KP; *Atlanta Constitution*, August 16, 1967; Levison and Bea Levison, telephone conversation, August 16, 1967, FBI Levison file, MLK.

3. "The Racial Crisis: A Consensus," *Newsweek*, August 21, 1967, pp. 15–18; King and Levison, telephone conversation, August 22, 1967; King, Young, Levison, and Wachtel, telephone conversation, September 21, 1967, both in FBI Levison file, MLK; Young, interview by Shannon, pp. 3–4. King cited the *Newsweek* poll in virtually every speech he made.

4. Young, interview by Shannon, pp. 1–2; Alex Waites and Rollie Eubanks, "Mississippi: Poverty, Despair—A Way of Life," report for 58th annual convention, July 13, 1967, group 3, series B, container 375, NAACP; Schlesinger, *Robert Kennedy*, pp. 872–83; Coretta King, *My Life with Mar-*

tin Luther King, Jr., pp. 298–99; William Rutherford and Levison, telephone conversation, June 2, 1968, FBI Levison file, MLK.

5. Offenburger, interview by Shannon, pp. 9–10.
6. For example, King's speech to Ministerial Leadership Training Program, February 18, 1968, transcript, p. 17, box 28, folder 51, SCLC.
7. Young, interview by Shannon, p. 6; McGraw, "An Interview with Andrew J. Young," p. 327; King, "Why We Must Go to Washington," January 15, 1968, transcript, pp. 19–20, KP.
8. SCLC ministers training program, minutes of national advisory committee, November 27, 1967, pp. 2–6, box 48, folder 11, SCLC.
9. King, "In Search of a Sense of Direction," speech to SCLC board, February 7, 1968, pp. 3–6; speech to Mississippi leaders, February 15, 1968, pp. 5–6; speech to Ministers Leadership Training Program, February 23, 1968, p. 4, all in KP.
10. Press release, December 13, 1967, 122, 8, SCLC; "North and South: Staff News," December 1967, pp. 10–16, SCLC; Levison and Dora McDonald, telephone conversation, October 23, 1967; Young and Levison, telephone conversation, December 15, 1967, FBI Levison file, MLK.
11. Rutherford to James A. Harrison, December 14, 1967; Rutherford to steering committee, December 8 and 11, 1967; "Cleveland Project," December 19, 1967, all in box 48, SCLC; Rutherford to Jackson, December 11, 1967, box 39, folder 15, SCLC; King and Levison, telephone conversation, December 13, 1967, FBI Levison file, MLK.
12. Executive staff meeting, December 27, 1967, transcript, box 49, folder 11, SCLC.
13. Al Sampson, interview by Joan Beifuss, Bill Thomas, and Tom Beckner, August 15, 1968, p. 4, MSU; Orange, "With the People," p. 114; Marjorie Penney to King, December 19, 1967, box 36, folder 16, SCLC.
14. King, "Why We Must Go to Washington," January 15, 1968, KP.
15. King, "See You in Washington," January 17, 1968, KP.
16. Harold DeWolf to King, December 11, 1967, box 8, folder 24, KP.
17. Rustin to King, re: strategy and tactics, January 1968, in Rustin, *Down the Line,* pp. 202–5; Rutherford and Levison, telephone conversation, January 31, 1968, FBI Levison file, MLK; Harrington quoted in Goodman, "He Lives, Man!" p. 25.
18. King, speech to Ministers Leadership Training Program, February 23, 1968, pp. 11–12, KP; *Washington Afro-American,* February 10, 1968.
19. McGraw, "An Interview with Andrew J. Young," pp. 328–29; Rutherford and Levison, telephone conversation, January 31, 1968, FBI Levison file, MLK; Young, interview by Shannon, p. 21; Young quoted in Jose Yglesias, "Dr. King's March on Washington, Part 2," *New York Times Magazine,* March 31, 1968, reprinted in Meier and Rudwick, *Black Protest in the Sixties,* p. 269.
20. Rutherford and Levison, telephone conversation, February 8, 1968, FBI Levison file, MLK; *Washington Afro-American,* February 10, 1968; Yglesias, "Dr. King's March," p. 278.

21. Offenburger, interview by Shannon, p. 32; action committee meeting, February 11, 1968, transcript, p. 1, SCLC; Abernathy testimony, House, *King Hearings* 1:25–26; Billy Kyles, interview by Joan Beifuss and Bill Thomas, July 30, 1968, p. 6, MSU; Rutherford and Levison, telephone conversation, February 8, 1968, FBI Levison file, MLK.

22. Garrow, *FBI* pp. 206–8; Charles D. Brennan to William C. Sullivan, March 3, 1967; Fred J. Baumgardner to Sullivan, October 28, November 3, 1966; R. E. Wick to Cartha D. DeLoach, November 9, 1966, all in House, *King Hearings*, vol. 6, pp. 289–90, 247–51; Levison and Jones; Jones and Levison; Levison and Young; King, Levison, Jones, and Young, November 8, 1966, all telephone conversations in FBI Levison file, MLK.

23. Brennan to Sullivan, October 30, 1967; George C. Moore to Sullivan, November 29, 1967, both in House, *King Hearings*, vol. 6, pp. 283–84, 287–88.

24. Moore to Sullivan, December 13, 1967; director to SAC, Atlanta, December 14, 1967; SAC, Atlanta, to director, December 20, 1967; Moore to Sullivan, December 29, 1967; memorandum for the attorney general, January 2, 1968; Ramsey Clark to Hoover, January 3, 1968, all in House, *King Hearings*, vol. 6, pp. 213–21; director to SAC, Albany (and forty-three other field offices), "Counterintelligence Program, Black Nationalist Hate Groups," March 4, 1968, in Senate, 6:388–91.

25. Moore to SAC, Jackson, March 11, 1968; SAC, Baltimore, to director, March 8, 1968; SAC, Chicago, to director, March 21, 1968; Blakey narration; all in House, *King Hearings*, vol. 6, pp. 369, 316–17, 322–24, 75–79.

26. Testimony of George C. Moore; testimony of Ramsey Clark, both in House, *King Hearings* 6:140 and 366; Marian Logan to King, March 8, 1968, box 40, folder 3, SCLC; *Los Angeles Times*, February 26, 1968. On March 5 another old ally, Joseph Rauh, stated that he would not support the campaign because he felt it would damage Eugene McCarthy's fight for the Democratic presidential nomination.

27. Levison and Young, telephone conversation, March 4, 1968; Jones and Levison, telephone conversation, February 24, 1968, both in FBI Levison file, MLK; *Washington Post*, March 12–14, 16; *New York Times*, March 15, 1968; Horton quoted in Adams, *Unearthing Seeds of Fire*, p. 165.

28. Kyles, interview by Beifuss and Thomas, pp. 9–10; Bishop, *Days of Martin Luther King*, p. 491.

29. Kyles, interview by Beifuss and Thomas, pp. 6–13; Ralph H. Jackson, interview by Ann Trotter and David Yellin, May 24, 1968, pp. 1–22, MSU; Robert E. Bailey, "The 1968 Memphis Sanitation Strike," Master's thesis, Memphis State University, 1974, pp. 48–65; *Memphis Commercial-Appeal*, February 24, March 10, 1968.

30. Bailey, "The 1968 Memphis Sanitation Strike," pp. 66–81; Jackson, interview by Trotter and Yellin, pp. 24–27; *Memphis Commercial-Appeal*, March 15, 1968.

31. Jackson, interview by Trotter and Yellin, pp. 25–30; Lawson, interview by Yellin and Thomas, pp. 3–6; King, "The Other America," speech to Drug and Hospital Workers Union, March 10, 1968, SCLC recording.

32. Lawson, interview by Yellin and Thomas, pp. 6–10; Kyles, interview by Beifuss and Thomas, p. 6; King, Mason Temple speech, Memphis, March 18, 1968, p. 8, transcript, MSU.

33. Kyles, interview by Beifuss and Thomas, pp. 20–24; Levison and King, telephone conversation, March 26, 1968, FBI Levison file, MLK; Young quoted in Reynolds, *Jesse Jackson*, p. 85.

34. Lawson, interview by Yellin and Thomas, p. 10; Bishop, *Days of Martin Luther King, Jr.*, pp. 493–95; Abernathy testimony, in House 1:14–15.

35. Gerald Frank, *An American Death* (London, 1972), pp. 29–30; Kyles, interview by Beifuss and Thomas, p. 27; Lawson, interview by Yellin and Thomas, second tape of July 1, 1968, pp. 1–12; SAC, Memphis, to director, "Sanitation Workers Strike," March 29, 1968, in House 6:472–73.

36. Lawson, interview by Joan Beifuss and David Yellin, July 8, 1970, p. 2, MSU; testimony of Marrell McCullough, House 6:411–32.

37. Kyles, interview by Beifuss and Thomas, pp. 29–30; Lawson, interview by Beifuss and Yellin, pp. 8–12; testimony of Calvin Taylor, House 6:449; J. Edwin Stanfield, *In Memphis: Tragedy Unaverted* (Atlanta, April 3, 1968), pp. 2–4; Frank, *An American Death*, pp. 30–31.

38. Jackson, interview by Trotter and Yellin, second tape of May 24, 1968, pp. 1–17; Kyles, interview by Beifuss and Thomas, pp. 27–39; Lawson, interview by Beifuss and Yellin, pp. 12–31; SAC, Memphis, to director, March 29, 1968, in House 6:473–77; Stanfield, *In Memphis*, pp. 2–4; *Memphis Commercial-Appeal*, March 29, 1968; Bailey, "The 1968 Memphis Sanitation Strike," pp. 92–96.

39. Lawson, interview by Beifuss and Yellin, pp. 15, 39–41; Kyles, interview by Beifuss and Thomas, pp. 42–43; Jackson, interview by Trotter and Yellin, pp. 20–23.

40. Testimony of Calvin Taylor, John B. Smith, and Charles L. Cabbage, in House 6:445–520; Frank, *An American Death*, pp. 35–38; Garrow, *FBI*, pp. 194–95.

41. *Memphis Commercial-Appeal*, March 30, 1968.

42. SAC, Memphis, to Sullivan, March 29, 1968; George C. Moore to Sullivan, March 29; Hoover to Ramsey Clark, April 2, 1968, all in House 6:222–24, 592–94; Garrow, *FBI*, pp. 196–97.

43. Frank, *An American Death*, pp. 32–34; Abernathy testimony, House 1:16–17; Raines, *My Soul Is Rested*, pp. 518–19; Coretta King, *My Life with Martin Luther King, Jr.*, p. 311; Levison and King, telephone conversation, March 29, 1968, FBI Levison file, MLK.

44. Levison and King, telephone conversation, March 29, 1968, FBI Levison file, MLK.

45. SAC, Memphis, to director, March 29, 30, 1968, House 6:483–84, 567–76;

House, *Findings and Recommendations* (Washington, March 29, 1978), pp. 438–39; *New York Times,* March 31, 1968, sec. 4, p. 2; *Newsweek,* April 8, 1968, pp. 15–16; Lyndon B. Johnson, "Statement . . . on the Disorders in Memphis," March 29, 1968, in *Public Papers of the Presidents of the United States: Lyndon B. Johnson, 1968–1969* (Washington, 1970), 1:458.

46. Jesse Epps quoted in Selby, *Odyssey,* pp. 146–47; Frank, *An American Death,* pp. 81–82; Raines, *My Soul Is Rested,* pp. 520–21; Coretta King, *My Life with Martin Luther King, Jr.,* pp. 313–14; Tom Offenburger to SCLC staff, re: the Memphis situation and the Poor People's Campaign, April 1, 1968, SCLC; Alice Loewi and Levison, telephone conversation, March 31, 1968; Adele Kanter, Maya Angelou, and Levison, telephone conversation, April 1, 1968, both in FBI Levison file, MLK.

47. Kyles, interview by Beifuss and Thomas, p. 28; Garrow, *FBI,* p. 198; E. H. Arkin to Frank Holloman, "Civil Disorders in Memphis, February 12 through April 16, 1968," MPD report, in House 4:251.

48. *Memphis Commercial-Appeal,* April 4, 1968; SAC, Memphis, to Atlanta, re: bomb threat to Martin Luther King, April 2, 1968, in House 6:547–48; Frank, *An American Death,* p. 49.

49. Testimony of Marrell McCullough, John B. Smith, and Charles Cabbage, House 6:419, 489, 512; Garrow, *FBI,* pp. 198–99.

50. King, "I've Been to the Mountaintop," speech at Mason Temple, April 3, 1968, edited SCLC recording, full transcript in KP; Lawson, interview by Beifuss and Yellin, pp. 58–59; Harold Middlebrook, interview by Joan Beifuss and Bill Thomas, July 21, 1968, pp. 12–15, MSU; Levison and Rutherford, telephone conversation, April 3, 1968, FBI Levison file, MLK.

51. Garrow, *FBI,* p. 200; Smith testimony, in House 6:466–67; House, *Findings and Recommendations,* pp. 282–85; Middlebrook, interview by Beifuss and Thomas, pp. 17–39.

52. House, *Findings and Recommendations,* pp. 282–85; Raines, *My Soul Is Rested,* p. 525. When King received Young's news he decided to postpone the march until Monday, April 8.

53. Bailey, "The 1968 Memphis Sanitation Strike," pp. 113–24; J. Edwin Stanfield, *In Memphis: Mirror to America?* (Atlanta, April 28, 1968); *Memphis Commercial-Appeal,* April 9 and 17, 1968.

54. Congressional Quarterly Service, *Revolution in Civil Rights* (Washington, 1968), pp. 84–91.

55. "An Interview with Andrew Young," *Playboy,* July 1977, p. 74.

56. King, Frogmore speech, November 14, 1966, p. 1, KP.

Chapter 15

1. *Wall Street Journal,* May 9, 1968; Rutherford and Levison; Andrew Levison and Levison, May 10, 1968; Bea Levison and Levison, May 24,

1968, all telephone conversations in FBI Levison file, MLK; *Washington Post*, April 26 and May 15, 1968.

2. Young, interview by Shannon, p. 28; *Washington Post*, May 22, 1968; *New York Times*, May 23, 1968.

3. Young, interview by Shannon, pp. 30–31; Rutherford and Levison, telephone conversation, June 2, 1968, FBI Levison file, MLK; Charles Conconi and Woody West, "Someone Had to Carry On for King," *New Republic*, July 13, 1968, pp. 13–14; *New York Times*, June 1, 1968; James Orange, interview by Katherine Shannon, July 17, 1968, pp. 34–35, HUC; *New York Times*, May 26, 1968.

4. Marian Logan and Levison, telephone conversation, June 6, 1968, FBI Levison file, MLK.

5. *Washington Post*, May 22, 1968; Tom Kahn, "Why the Poor People's Campaign Failed," *Commentary*, September 1968, pp. 52–54.

6. *Wall Street Journal*, May 29, 1968; *New York Times*, June 3, 1968; *Congressional Quarterly Weekly Report*, June 14, 1968, p. 1467. Rustin's list of demands included the creation of one million new public service jobs; the building of six million new public housing units over ten years; repeal of the 1967 social security restrictions; the extension of the National Labor Relations Act to agricultural workers; and the restoration of recent budget cuts relating to welfare programs.

7. Abernathy and Levison, telephone conversation, June 3, 1968; Young and Levison, telephone conversation, June 4, 1968; both in FBI Levison file, MLK; Kahn, "Why the Poor People's Campaign Failed," p. 53; *Washington Post*, June 25, 1968; *Southern Courier*, July 6–7, 1968; *New York Times*, June 30, 1968.

8. Unidentified person and Levison, telephone conversation, June 11, 1968, FBI Levison file, MLK.

9. *Washington Post*, July 17 and 22, 1968; *National Observer*, August 24, 1968; *Memphis Commercial-Appeal*, August 18, 1968.

10. Reynolds, *Jesse Jackson*, pp. 319–24; Paul Good, "No Man Can Fill Dr. King's Shoes'—But Abernathy Tries," pp. 284–91; Walker, interview by Britton, pp. 80–81; Septima P. Clark, interview by Barton, pp. 63–64. Abernathy was referring to his role during the Montgomery bus boycott, but his words apply equally to his subsequent years as King's deputy.

11. *Newsweek*, December 9, 1968, p. 34; Peter Goldman, *Report from Black America* (New York, 1971), pp. 55–57; Young and Levison, telephone conversation, November 24, 1968; Wachtel and Levison, telephone conversation, November 28, 1968, both in FBI Levison file, MLK.

12. Young quoted in Goodman, "He Lives, Man!" pp. 30–31; Rustin and Levison, telephone conversation, July 21, 1968, FBI Levison file, MLK.

13. Coretta King and Levison, telephone conversation, May 15, 1968, FBI Levison file, MLK.

14. Goodman, "He Lives, Man!" pp. 30–31; Coretta King and Levison, tele-

phone conversation, January 13, 1969; Young and Levison, telephone conversation, January 14, 1969, both in FBI Levison file, MLK; *Nashville Tennessean*, August 9, 1968.

15. Young and Levison, telephone conversation, May 6, 1969, FBI Levison file, MLK; *New York Times*, December 25, 1969.

16. Reynolds, *Jesse Jackson*, pp. 361–62; Wachtel, correspondence with author.

17. Reynolds, *Jesse Jackson*, pp. 347–52; Richard Levine, "Jesse Jackson: Heir to Dr. King?" *Harper's*, March 1969, p. 58; Goodman, "He Lives, Man!" p. 30; *Time*, April 6, 1970, pp. 11–14.

18. Jesse L. Jackson, "Black Power and White Churches," in *Black Viewpoints*, ed. Littleton and Burger, pp. 356–58.

19. *Atlanta Constitution*, January 8, 1969.

20. Reynolds, *Jesse Jackson*, pp. 82–91, 138–40, 314–15.

21. *Atlanta Constitution*, May 12, 1970; *New York Times*, September 12–18, 1971; *Soul Force*, September 1971, p. 4.

22. *New York Times*, August 2 and 3, 1969, February 14, 1970; SCLC, *Soul Force*, August 1969, pp. 3–5; November and December 1971, pp. 4 and 10; David F. Ross, "Black Power," *New Republic*, September 27, 1969, pp. 14–15.

23. Young and Levison, telephone conversation, May 2, 1969, FBI Levison file, MLK; *New York Times*, April 5, 1969; *Soul Force*, August 1969; J. H. O'Dell, "Charleston's Legacy to the Poor People's Campaign," *Freedomways*, Summer 1969, pp. 201–8.

24. Walter Fauntroy, "Poor People's Campaign," *Soul Force*, August 1969, p. 3; William Winn and D. L. Inman, *Augusta, Georgia, and Jackson State University* (Atlanta, June 1970), pp. vi, 22–28; *Newsweek*, May 25, 1970, pp. 36–41; *Time*, June 1, 1970, p. 12; *New York Times*, May 18, 20, 21, 24, 25, 1970.

25. *Los Angeles Times*, October 15, 1972; *Washington Post*, July 10, 1973; Young, interview by Shannon, p. 27.

26. *Time*, April 6, 1970, pp. 18–28; Beardslee, *The Way Out Must Lead In*, pp. 78–80.

27. U.S. Commission on Civil Rights, *The Voting Rights Act: Ten Years After* (Washington, D.C., 1975); *Time*, September 27, 1976, pp. 40–41; Joint Center for Political Studies, *National Roster of Black Elected Officials* (Washington, D.C., 1975), pp. xiv–xv; John Corry, "A Visit to Lowndes County, Alabama," *New South*, Winter 1972, p. 31.

28. U.S. Commission on Civil Rights, *The Voting Rights Act: Unfulfilled Goals* (Washington, D.C., 1981), pp. 15–17; U.S. Commission on Civil Rights, *The Voting Rights Act: Ten Years After*, pp. 21–100; Jack Bass and Walter De Vries, *The Transformation of Southern Politics* (New York, 1976), p. 377; Barbara Taylor, Cliff Kuhn, and Marc Miller, "After Twenty-five Years," *Southern Exposure*, Spring 1981, p. 124; *The Times*, London, August 26, 1983.

29. Numan V. Bartley, *From Thurmond to Wallace: Political Tendencies in Georgia, 1948–1968* (Baltimore, 1970), p. 109.

30. Alexander P. Lamis, *The Two-Party South* (New York, 1984), p. 87.

31. Ibid., pp. 63, 88–90; Earl Black, *Southern Governors and Civil Rights* (London, 1976), pp. 309–26; Young quoted in *Time*, September 27, 1976, p. 40.

32. Lamis, *Two-Party South*, pp. 5, 33, 74, 224–25; Bass and De Vries, *Transformation of Southern Politics*, p. 12; Bartley, *From Thurmond to Wallace*, pp. 103–5; Bartley and Graham, *Southern Politics and the Second Reconstruction* (Baltimore, 1975), pp. 138–41, 167.

33. Samuel Lubell, *The Hidden Crisis in American Politics* (New York, 1970), p. 142; Eva Galambos, *State and Local Sales Taxes in the South, 1973* (Atlanta, Southern Regional Council, 1973); Gretchen Machlachlan, *The Other Twenty Percent: A Statistical Analysis of Poverty in the South* (Atlanta, Southern Regional Council, 1974); Lamis, *Two-Party South*, p. 232.

34. For the racial split in presidential voting, see Lamis, *Two-Party South*, pp. 29, 38, 214. In 1976 Carter won only 46 percent of the Southern white vote; his black support was twice as strong, running as high as 98 percent in Houston and Atlanta. Four years later, Carter's support among whites fell to 35 percent, while his black vote declined only slightly to 93 percent.

35. Mike Davis, "The New Right's Road to Power," *New Left Review*, July–August 1981, pp. 45–46; "The Political Economy of Late-Imperial America," *New Left Review*, January–February 1984, pp. 20–36. Trade union membership in the private-sector workforce declined during the 1970s from 26 percent to 16 percent.

36. Taylor, Kuhn, and Miller, "After Twenty-five Years," p. 124. Voter turnout in the 1984 presidential election, 52.9 percent, was almost identical to the turnout in 1980. Black representation in Congress declined from twenty to nineteen. King quotation: *Where Do We Go from Here?* p. 147.

37. Taylor, Kuhn, and Miller, "After Twenty-five Years," pp. 120–23. A convincing case can be made for the argument that official government statistics greatly understate the extent of poverty. See, for example, Michael Harrington, *Decade of Decision: The Crisis of the American System* (New York, 1980), pp. 225–39; Davis, "The Political Economy of Late-Imperial America," pp. 18–19; *The Times*, London, March 25, 1985; *Financial Times*, London, January 21, 1986.

38. Association of American Geographers, *Contemporary Metropolitan America*, ed. John S. Adams (Cambridge, 1976), 3:212–44; *New York Times*, July 18, 1976; Wade C. Roof, "Race and Residence," *Annals of the American Academy of Political and Social Science*, January 1979, p. 4. According to the analysis in *Contemporary Metropolitan America*, only 15 percent of the blacks in Chicago who earn fifty thousand dollars per annum or more live in the suburbs. In a hypothetical "color-blind" hous-

ing market, two-thirds of Chicago's blacks could afford to move out of the ghetto, and the proportion of blacks working in the suburbs would increase from 21 percent to 44 percent. In 1976 only half of all black families possessed cars, whereas 80 percent of white families did.

39. Rustin, *Strategies for Freedom*, p. 75.
40. Rustin, "From Protest to Politics," in Littleton and Burger, p. 367.
41. Levison and King, telephone conversation, March 25, 1967, FBI Levison file, MLK; Charlayne Hunter, "On the Case in Resurrection City," in *The Transformation of Activism*, ed. August Meier (New York, 1970), p. 11.

Chronology

1953

March 5. Soviet Union announces death of Stalin.
May 7. French capitulation at Dien Bien Phu.
June 18–25. Blacks conduct bus boycott in Baton Rouge, Louisiana.
June 26. Korean armistice signed.
August 20. Soviet Union announces explosion of H-bomb.

1954

May 17. Supreme Court rules, in *Brown* v. *Board of Education,* that racial
  segregation in public schools is unconstitutional.
June 29. CIA-backed coup in Guatemala.
July. "Citizens Council" organized in Indianola, Mississippi, to mobilize white
  opposition to desegregation.
July 21. United States refuses to sign Geneva Accord on Indochina.
August 24. Communist Control Act becomes law.
October. Citizens Council organized in Selma, Alabama.
December 2. Senate condemns, but does not censure, Senator Joseph P.
  McCarthy.

1955

May 31. Supreme Court orders states with segregated public schools to make a
  "prompt and reasonable start" toward desegregation.
July 18–23. Geneva summit conference.

July 22. Alabama enacts "pupil placement law" designed to circumvent desegregation. Other Southern states soon pass similar measures.

August 1. Georgia's Board of Education orders teachers to resign from the
NAACP on pain of dismissal.

October 10. Supreme Court orders University of Alabama to admit Autherine
Lucy, a black applicant.

December 1. Rosa Parks is arrested in Montgomery, Alabama, when she refuses
to surrender her bus seat to a white passenger.

December 5. First day of Montgomery bus boycott. Martin Luther King, Jr.,
elected president of Montgomery Improvement Association.

1956

January 30. King's Montgomery home is bombed.

February 1. MIA institutes law suit against Montgomery's bus segregation
laws.

February 21. Grand jury indicts 115 boycott leaders. Bayard Rustin arrives in
Montgomery to help and advise King.

February 28. "In Friendship," organized by Bayard Rustin, Stanley D. Levison,
and Ella J. Baker, is formally launched in New York.

February 29. University of Alabama expels Autherine Lucy.

March 11. Nineteen Senators and eighty-one Representatives sign the "Southern Manifesto," pledging to use "all lawful means" to reverse *Brown* v. *Board
of Education.*

March 22. King is convicted of leading illegal boycott.

April. Students at South Carolina State College in Orangeburg boycott classes
to protest against official harrassment of NAACP.

April 23. Supreme Court overturns South Carolina bus segregation law.

May 27. Students at Florida A&M University in Tallahassee begin boycott of
segregated buses.

May 29. C. K. Steele elected president of Inter-Civic Council, which coordi-
nates Tallahassee bus boycott.

June 1. State of Alabama outlaws NAACP.

June 5. Fred Shuttlesworth and others organize Alabama Christian Movement
for Human Rights in Birmingham.

June 5. Federal district court, comprising three judges, rules in *Browder* v.
Gayle that Montgomery's bus segregation laws are unconstitutional.

June 30. Bus services in Tallahassee are suspended.

October 23. Start of Hungarian uprising.

October 29. Israel invades Egypt.

October 31. Anglo-French forces invade Egypt.

November 4. Soviet troops attack Budapest and crush Hungarian revolt.

November 6. President Eisenhower is reelected, defeating Adlai Stevenson by

35 million to 26 million in the popular vote, 457 to 73 in the Electoral College.

November 13. Supreme Court affirms illegality of Montgomery's bus segregation laws.

December 20. MIA ends Montgomery bus boycott; buses are desegregated the following day.

December 23. ICC ends Tallahassee bus boycott, but city commission continues to enforce segregation.

December 25. Bomb explodes at Birmingham home of Fred Shuttlesworth.

December 26. Shuttlesworth and twenty others are arrested when they defy Birmingham's bus segregation law.

1957

January 10–11. Sixty blacks meet at Ebenezer Baptist Church in Atlanta to establish "Southern Leadership Conference on Transportation and Non-Violent Integration." King is elected chairman.

February 14. King is elected president of "Southern Negro Leadership Conference" at meeting in New Orleans.

March. King visits Ghana to attend independence ceremonies.

March 25. King meets Roy Wilkins and A. Philip Randolph to plan "Prayer Pilgrimage."

May 17. King addresses Prayer Pilgrimage in Washington, D.C.

June 13. King meets Vice President Richard M. Nixon.

August. Southern Christian Leadership Conference holds its first annual convention, in Montgomery, Alabama.

September 9. The 1957 Civil Rights Act becomes law.

September 24. President Eisenhower sends paratroopers to enforce school desegregation in Little Rock, Arkansas.

October 4. Soviet Union launches *Sputnik* artificial satellite.

1958

January. Ella Baker sets up SCLC office in Atlanta.

January 31. U.S. launches *Explorer* artificial satellite.

February 12. SCLC begins "Crusade for Citizenship."

May. John L. Tilley becomes executive director of SCLC.

June 23. King, Roy Wilkins, A. Philip Randolph, and Lester Granger meet President Eisenhower.

July 15. President Eisenhower sends U.S. marines to Lebanon.

September 3. King arrested in Montgomery.

September 17. Publication of *Stride Toward Freedom*, King's account of the Montgomery bus boycott.

September 20. King narrowly escapes death when a deranged woman stabs him in New York.

1959

February–March. King visits India with his wife, Coretta, and professor L. D. Reddick.

April 15. Tilley resigns as SCLC's executive director; Ella Baker replaces him on a temporary basis.

October. King, Ella Baker and the SCLC board consider ways of making SCLC more effective. King agrees to move to Atlanta.

November. Bayard Rustin formally joins SCLC as part-time public relations director.

December. Revolutionaries led by Fidel Castro overthrow Batista regime in Cuba.

December 28. King meets national officers of the NAACP in an effort to reduce organizational rivalry.

1960

January 1. Castro and his supporters assume undisputed control of Cuba.

February 1. The first "sit-in" is staged by four black students at a Woolworth's lunch counter in Greensboro, North Carolina.

February 17. An Alabama grand jury indicts King for income tax evasion.

February–March. Bayard Rustin and Stanley Levison organize the "Committee to Defend Martin Luther King and the Struggle for Freedom in the South."

March. National Liberation Front intensifies its guerilla war against U.S.-backed Diem regime in South Vietnam.

March 3. James Lawson is expelled from Vanderbilt University for his participation in the Nashville sit-in protests.

March 19. San Antonio becomes first Southern city to desegregate its lunch counters.

March 20. Governor LeRoy Collins of Florida describes lunch counter segregation as "unfair and morally wrong."

April 15–17. The Student Nonviolent Coordinating Committee (SNCC) is organized at a conference, addressed by King and James Lawson, at Shaw University, Raleigh, North Carolina.

April 21. The 1960 Civil Rights Act becomes law.

May 5. Nikita Kruschev reveals that the Soviet Union has shot down a U.S. U-2 spy-plane. The ensuing row wrecks the Geneva summit conference.

May 10–11. King discusses SCLC's future at meeting in New York with Rustin, Levison and Wyatt Walker, SCLC's incoming executive director.

May 28. King is acquitted of the Alabama tax charges by an all-white jury.

June 9. King and Rustin announce plans to picket the Democratic and Republican national conventions.

June 24. King meets Senator John F. Kennedy.

June 28. Rustin resigns from SCLC, having been publicly denounced by Congressman Adam Clayton Powell, Jr.

August. Wyatt Walker replaces Ella Baker as SCLC's executive director.

September. North Vietnam formally backs the National Liberation Front in its campaign to overthrow the Diem regime and end U.S. involvement in Vietnam.

October 19. King and fifty others are arrested during a sit-in at an Atlanta department store.

October 26. King is transferred to Reidsville state prison, after being sentenced to four months' hard labor for violation of parole.

October 28. King is freed on bond after the intervention of Robert F. Kennedy.

November 8. John F. Kennedy wins presidential election, winning 119,000 more votes than Richard Nixon out of 68,800,000 cast.

1961

January 18. In his farewell address, President Eisenhower warns against the "acquisition of unwarranted influence . . . by the military-industrial complex."

January 20. Inauguration of John F. Kennedy.

January 27. Levison and Jack O'Dell organize Carnegie Hall benefit featuring Harry Belafonte and Sammy Davis, Jr.

March 13. President Kennedy launches the Alliance for Progress.

April 17. Cuban exiles, trained and supported by the CIA, land at Cuba's Bay of Pigs. The attempted invasion swiftly collapses.

May. Vice President Lyndon B. Johnson visits South Vietnam.

May 4. Congress of Racial Equality (CORE) begins "Freedom Ride" from Washington to New Orleans.

May 14. Freedom Riders are attacked by white mobs in Anniston and Birmingham, Alabama.

May 17. Students from Nashville launch second Freedom Ride.

May 20. Nashville group assaulted by whites in Montgomery, Alabama.

May 21–22. Freedom Riders and their supporters besieged in Montgomery church as King and Ralph Abernathy conduct mass meeting. Attorney General Robert Kennedy sends federal marshals to Montgomery.

May 26. King becomes chairman of Freedom Rides Coordinating Committee.

June–August. SCLC and other civil rights organizations discuss formation of Voter Education Project with Justice Department and philanthropic foundations.

June 3–4. President Kennedy meets Kruschev in Vienna.

June–August. Tension over Berlin eases with building of Berlin Wall.

July. SCLC begins citizenship classes at Dorchester Center in McIntosh, Georgia. Andrew J. Young is hired to supervise the program.

August 30. Soviet Union resumes nuclear testing, ending three-year moratorium.

September 22. Interstate Commerce Commission prescribes new rules prohibiting racial discrimination in interstate travel. The rules came into effect on December 1.

November 17. Formation of Albany Movement in Albany, Georgia.

December 1. "Freedom Riders" arrested in Albany.

December 11–15. Demonstrations in Albany lead to over five hundred arrests.

December 16. King is arrested in Albany.

December 18. King leaves Albany after local leaders conclude truce with City.

1962

January–February. SCLC begins participation in Voter Education Project, hiring field secretaries to work on voter registration in six states.

March 20. FBI installs wiretap on Levison's office telephone.

March 20–21. Civil rights leaders meet in Greenwich, Connecticut, in attempt to achieve closer cooperation.

April 25. President Kennedy orders resumption of nuclear testing in atmosphere.

May 17. SCLC launches Gandhi Society; SCLC presents President Kennedy with proposals for "Second Emancipation Proclamation."

June. Secretary of Defense Robert McNamara visits South Vietnam and reports that "we're winning this war."

July 10–August 28. SCLC renews protests in Albany, Georgia. King in jail July 10–12 and July 27–August 10.

September 13–15. SCLC executive staff analyzes Albany defeat.

October 1. James Meredith enrolls as the first black student at the University of Mississippi, after federal marshals escorting him are attacked by white rioters.

October 23. FBI begins COMINFIL (Communist infiltration) investigation of SCLC.

October 14–28. Cuban missile crisis.

November 20. Robert Kennedy authorizes FBI wiretap on Levison's home telephone.

1963

January 9–10. SCLC leadership meets at Dorchester Center, Georgia, to plan forthcoming campaign in Birmingham, Alabama.

January 14. General De Gaulle announces that France will quit NATO.

February 6. King and Walker confer with ACMHR board in Birmingham.

March 5. Indecisive result of mayoral election causes SCLC to postpone Birmingham campaign until after the run-off.
April 2. Albert C. Boutwell defeats Eugene "Bull" Connor in run-off of Birmingham mayoral election.
April 3. SCLC and ACMHR begin campaign of nonviolent direct action in Birmingham.
April 12–20. King in jail; writes "Letter from Birmingham City Jail."
April 19. Fred Shuttlesworth explains campaign to Assistant Attorney General Burke Marshall in Washington.
May. Beginning of Buddhist revolt against Diem regime in South Vietnam.
May 2–7. SCLC organizes children's demonstrations in Birmingham.
May 8. SCLC suspends demonstrations.
May 10. SCLC and ACMHR sign desegregation agreement with Senior Citizens Committee.
May 31. Demonstrations begin in Danville, Virginia.
June 11. Governor George C. Wallace fails to prevent admission of three black students to University of Alabama, after President Kennedy federalizes Alabama National Guard. In a nationally-televised address, President Kennedy proposes additional civil rights legislation.
June 12. NAACP field secretary Medgar Evers is assassinated in Jackson, Mississippi.
June 12. SCLC suspends demonstrations in Savannah, Georgia, after a march the previous night ends in rioting.
July 22. King and other civil rights leaders meet President Kennedy to discuss March on Washington. Kennedy tells King to end his relationship with Stanley Levison and Jack O'Dell.
July 22. FBI requests wiretaps on home and office telephones of Clarence Jones. Robert Kennedy approves the request.
July 28. Danville protests peter out.
August. King begins work on *Why We Can't Wait,* an account of the Birmingham campaign.
August 2. Desegregation agreement reached in Savannah.
August 28. Over two hundred thousand people attend March on Washington, where King delivers "I Have A Dream" oration.
September 15. Bomb at Birmingham's Sixteenth Street Baptist Church kills four girls.
October. SCLC leadership meets in Atlanta to discuss possible direct action in Birmingham, Danville, and Montgomery.
October 21. Robert Kennedy approves FBI request for wiretaps on telephones at King's home and SCLC's Atlanta and New York offices.
October 22. King and Shuttlesworth withdraw threat to resume demonstrations in Birmingham.
November 2. U.S.-sanctioned coup in South Vietnam leads to Diem's overthrow and murder.
November 22. John F. Kennedy assassinated in Dallas.

December 3. King meets President Lyndon B. Johnson.

December 23. FBI holds conference in Washington to consider ways of discrediting King.

1964

January 5–7. FBI conducts microphone surveillance of King's suite at Willard Hotel in Washington. At least fourteen other "bugs" are planted in rooms used by King between January 1964 and November 1965.

January–February. James Bevel and Diane Nash draft plans for demonstrations in Alabama centered on the right to vote.

March 28–April 4. SCLC stages demonstrations in St. Augustine, Florida.

Spring. Governor George C. Wallace enters Democratic presidential primaries in Maryland, Wisconsin and Indiana.

May. Harry Wachtel and Clarence Jones organize a "Research Committee" to advise and assist King.

May 1–4. John Gibson assesses prospects for further direct action in St. Augustine.

May 26–June 30. SCLC resumes protests in St. Augustine.

June 11–13. King in jail.

June. Gandhi Society is wound up. NAACP Legal Defense Fund takes over SCLC's important litigation.

July 2. Civil Rights Act becomes law.

June–August. SNCC and CORE conduct voter registration and political education project in Mississippi, the "Freedom Summer."

July 18–26. Rioting breaks out in Harlem and Brooklyn.

July 22–27. King lobbies on behalf of the Mississippi Freedom Democratic Party at the Democratic National Convention.

July 27–28. King takes part in talks with Mayor Robert F. Wagner of New York.

July 29. SCLC, the NAACP and the Urban League agree to moratorium on direct action until after the presidential election. SNCC and CORE reject the moratorium.

July. Wyatt Walker leaves SCLC staff. Andrew Young becomes executive director.

July–August. SCLC team led by Young and Bevel visit Rochester, New York, in wake of riot there.

August 2–3. North Vietnamese boats allegedly attack U.S. ships in Gulf of Tonkin. President Johnson orders retaliatory bombing attack on North Vietnam.

August 7. "Gulf of Tonkin Resolution" passes House (416–0) and Senate (88–2).

September 25. President Johnson declares, "We don't want our American boys to do the fighting for Asian boys. We don't want to . . . get tied down in a land war in Asia."

September 28–30. SCLC convention endorses President Johnson.

October. Kruschev falls from power in Soviet Union.

November 3. Lyndon B. Johnson defeats Barry Goldwater in presidential election, winning 61 percent of popular vote.

November 10–12. Executive staff meet in Birmingham to plan Selma campaign and consider SCLC's restructuring.

November 18. J. Edgar Hoover publicly denounces King as "the most notorious liar in America."

December 2. King meets Hoover in attempt to end quarrel. FBI steps up its efforts to discredit King.

December 10. King receives Nobel Peace Prize in Oslo.

1965

January 2. SCLC begins campaign in Selma in conjunction with SNCC.

January 5. King discovers blackmail letter and tape, sent anonymously by FBI.

January 11. Young and Abernathy meet Hoover assistant Cartha DeLoach.

February. Bayard Rustin urges civil rights movement to shift from direct action to political action in *Commentary* article.

February 1–5. King in Selma jail.

February 6. Viet Cong attack U.S. base at Pleiku. President Johnson orders retaliatory bombing of North Vietnam.

February 9. King discusses need for voting rights legislation with Attorney General Katzenbach, Vice President Humphrey and President Johnson.

February 18. Police and state troopers attack marchers in Marion, Alabama, mortally wounding Jimmie Lee Jackson.

February 26. James Bevel proposes march from Selma to Montgomery.

March 2. President Johnson orders continuous bombing of North Vietnam.

March 5. King meets President Johnson.

March 6–8. SNCC meets in Atlanta to discuss proposed march and consider SNCC's worsening relations with SCLC.

March 7. Police and state troopers attack marchers on outskirts of Selma.

March 8. Thirty-five hundred U.S. marines land at Da Nang.

March 9. King leads marchers to point of March 7 attack.

March 15. President Johnson proposes voting rights legislation in address to joint session of Congress.

March 16. SNCC march in Montgomery attacked by mounted police.

March 22–25. Selma-to-Montgomery march.

March 28. King proposes economic boycott of Alabama.

April 20 and 30. SNCC and SCLC meet to improve cooperation.

April 28. President Johnson sends U.S. marines to Dominican Republic.

May. Stanley Levison joins Research Committee. King drops Alabama boycott.

June–September. SCLC mounts SCOPE program, a voter registration drive in fifty-one Southern counties.

June 8. President Johnson announces that U.S. forces in South Vietnam will seek out and engage the enemy.

June 9–11. SCLC retreat at Warrenton, Virginia, considers possible Northern campaign.

July 28. President Johnson announces that 50,000 additional troops will be sent to Vietnam, bringing U.S. total there to 125,000.

August 6. Voting Rights Act becomes law.

August 12. King calls for negotiations to end war in Vietnam and offers to act as mediator.

August 11–16. Riot in Watts district of Los Angeles leaves thirty-five dead. King and Bayard Rustin visit Watts on August 15.

August 26–28. King tells SCLC executive staff that SCLC will mount campaign in Chicago.

September 10. Arthur Goldberg, U.S. ambassador to the UN, asks King to drop his Vietnam peace initiative. King formally retracts his proposal on October 5.

October–December. James Bevel establishes SCLC presence in Chicago's West Side ghetto.

December 22. SCLC begins voter registration drive in Birmingham, Alabama.

1966

January 6. SNCC condemns U.S. policy in Vietnam as neocolonialist aggression.

January 7. King announces formation of Chicago Freedom Movement.

January 10. Georgia legislation refuses to seat Julian Bond, a former SNCC staff member.

January 23. Alabama staffs of SNCC and SCLC fail to agree on political strategy.

January 24. Federal registrars begin to enroll voters in Birmingham.

March 24. King meets Mayor Richard J. Daley.

April. President Ky of South Vietnam crushes anti-government riots by Buddhists.

April 11–13. SCLC board calls on Johnson administration to consider U.S. withdrawal from Vietnam.

May. SCLC voter registration drive fails to prevent victory of Lurleen Wallace in Alabama Democratic primary. Wallace goes on to succeed her husband as governor.

May. Stokely Carmichael replaces John Lewis as chairman of SNCC.

May 18. President Johnson denounces his Vietnam critics as "nervous Nellies."

June 1–2. White House Conference on Civil Rights.

June 6. James Meredith is shot on second day of march through Mississippi.

June 6–26. SCLC, SNCC, and CORE complete Meredith March. King fails to stop use of "Black Power!" slogan, introduced by SNCC on June 17.

July 4. CORE endorses black power.

July 5. President Johnson criticizes black power. Roy Wilkins denounces it at NAACP convention as a "reverse Ku Klux Klan."

July 12–15. Riot in Chicago's West Side ghetto.

July 18–23. Riot in Cleveland's Hough ghetto.

July 30–August 25. Chicago Freedom Movement stages demonstrations.

August 26. "Summit Agreement" on open housing ends Chicago demonstrations.

September 19. Senate rejects 1966 Civil Rights Bill.

October 14. King refuses to sign statement condemning black power.

November. Democratic losses in Congressional elections. Ronald Reagan elected governor of California.

November 14–16. At staff retreat in Frogmore, South Carolina, King advocates shift toward socialism.

December 5. Supreme Court rules that Julian Bond should be allowed to take his seat in the Georgia legislature.

1967

January. James Bevel takes leave of absence from SCLC to work in the anti-war movement.

January–February. King writes *Where Do We Go From Here?*

February 25. King delivers first public speech attacking U.S. policy in Vietnam.

March 7. Research Committee advises King not to participate in Spring Mobilization.

March 25. King and Benjamin Spock lead anti-war march in Chicago.

April 4. King reads "Beyond Vietnam" at Riverside Church in New York.

April 15. Two hundred thousand people attend Spring Mobilization, which King addresses.

April–May. SCLC stages open housing demonstrations in Louisville, Kentucky.

May 11. National Guard fire on black students at Jackson State College, Mississippi, killing one.

June 5–10. Israel attacks and defeats Egypt, Jordan, and Syria in Six Day War.

June 23. President Johnson meets Soviet leader Aleksei Kosygin at Glassboro, New Jersey.

June. Defense Secretary McNamara orders confidential study of U.S. involvement in Vietnam (later published as *Pentagon Papers*).

June–November. SCLC conducts voter registration drive in Cleveland, Ohio.

July. President Johnson authorizes increase in U.S. Vietnam forces from 480,000 to 525,000.

July 10–11. SCLC launches Operation Breadbasket as national program.

July 12–15. Riot in Newark, New Jersey, leaves twenty-six dead.

July 23–27. Riot in Detroit, Michigan, leaves thirty-five dead. Federal troops are used to restore order.

July 27. President Johnson appoints National Advisory Commission on Civil Disorders.

August 25. FBI extends COINTELPRO to "Black Nationalist Hate Groups," including SCLC.

August 31–September 4. SCLC participates in National Convention for a New Politics, in Chicago.

September 3. Whitney Young and others observe South Vietnamese elections at request of President Johnson.

September 12–17. SCLC retreat at Warrenton, Virginia, discusses King's proposal for a "Poor People's Campaign" in Washington, D.C.

October 1–3. King in Birmingham jail, after Supreme Court upholds 1963 conviction for criminal contempt.

October. Defense Secretary McNamara urges President Johnson to place ceiling on U.S. forces in South Vietnam and stop bombing of North by end of 1967. Johnson rejects these proposals.

November 27–December 2. SCLC staff retreat at Frogmore, South Carolina, to prepare for Poor People's Campaign.

November 30. Senator Eugene McCarthy announces his candidacy for the Democratic presidential nomination.

December 27. James Bevel and Jesse Jackson argue against Poor People's Campaign at executive staff meeting.

1968

January 15–16. SCLC staff meeting in Atlanta to prepare for Poor People's Campaign.

January 21. North Vietnamese troops attack U.S. base at Khe Sanh. Siege continues until March 31.

January 23. North Korea seizes USS *Pueblo.*

January 29. At meeting of Research Committee, Bayard Rustin argues against Poor People's Campaign.

January 30. Robert Kennedy insists he will not run for president.

January 31. Viet Cong guerillas and North Vietnamese regulars launch Tet offensive.

February. Generals Wheeler and Westmoreland request 205,000 additional troops.

February 12. Memphis sanitation workers strike for better pay and union recognition.

February 23. Memphis police break up march in support of sanitation workers.

February 28. President Johnson asks incoming Defense Secretary Clark Clifford to review Vietnam policies.

March 4. FBI plans campaign to disrupt Poor People's Campaign and diminish King's influence.

March 12. Senator Eugene McCarthy wins 42 percent of the vote in the New Hampshire primary.

March 16. Robert Kennedy announces his candidacy for the Democratic presidential nomination.

March 18. King addresses mass meeting in Memphis and promises to lead march in support of sanitation workers.

March 22. President Johnson decides to send only 13,500 additional troops to Vietnam.

March 25–26. The "Wise Men" advise President Johnson to begin gradual disengagement from Vietnam.

March 28. March led by King in Memphis turns into riot and is forcibly dispersed by police. Governor of Tennessee sends National Guard to city; President Johnson offers federal troops.

March 30. SCLC executive staff persuades King to press ahead with Poor People's Campaign and also return to Memphis to lead second march.

March 31. President Johnson announces in televised address that he will not stand for reelection. He also proposes to limit the bombing of North Vietnam and enter negotiations to end the war.

April 4. King assassinated in Memphis. Ralph D. Abernathy succeeds him as president of SCLC.

April 5–9. Widespread rioting leads to thirty-nine deaths and fourteen thousand arrests. The most serious outbreaks occur in Washington, Baltimore, Chicago, and Kansas City. In Chicago, Mayor Daley instructs police to "shoot to kill" looters.

April 8. Twenty thousand attend march and rally in Memphis.

April 9. King buried in Atlanta.

April 10. Congress passes Civil Rights Act which includes partial ban on housing discrimination.

April 16. Memphis sanitation workers call off strike when they win union recognition and a wage increase.

May 12. Poor People's Campaign opens in Washington, D.C.

June 5. Robert Kennedy is shot in Los Angeles and dies the following day.

June 8. James Earl Ray, King's assassin, is arrested at Heathrow (London) airport.

June 19. Fifty thousand attend rally in Washington in support of Poor People's Campaign.

June 24. Police close down "Resurrection City."

July 16. Poor People's Campaign ends.

Illustration Credits

Chapter Eleven: Photograph © with permission of Chicago Sun-Times, Inc., 1987.

Chapter Twelve: Photograph by Bob Fitch, Black Star Photo Agency.

Chapter Thirteen: Photograph from the State Historical Society of Wisconsin.

Chapter Fourteen: Photograph from UPI/Bettmann Newsphotos.

Chapter Fifteen: Photograph by Ronald S. Comedy, from the *Southern Patriot.* Carl and Ann Braden Collection, the State Historical Society of Wisconsin.

Index